A History of Modern

MW00610964

This book is the first major study in several decades to consider Uganda as a nation, from its precolonial roots to the present day. Here, Richard J. Reid examines the political, economic and social history of Uganda, providing a unique and wide-ranging examination of its turbulent and dynamic past for all those studying Uganda's place in African history and African politics.

Reid identifies and examines key points of rupture and transition in Uganda's history, emphasising dramatic political and social change in the precolonial era, especially the nineteenth century, and the continuing repercussions of these developments in the colonial and postcolonial periods. By considering the ways in which historical culture and consciousness has been ever present – in political discourse, art and literature and social relationships – Reid defines the true extent of Uganda's viable national history.

RICHARD J. REID is Professor of the History of Africa at the School of Oriental and African Studies, University of London. He is the author of several books, including *Frontiers of Violence in Northeast Africa* and *Warfare in African History*.

A History of Modern Uganda

RICHARD J. REID
SOAS, University of London

CAMBRIDGE
UNIVERSITY PRESS

CAMBRIDGE
UNIVERSITY PRESS

University Printing House, Cambridge CB2 8BS, United Kingdom

One Liberty Plaza, 20th Floor, New York, NY 10006, USA

477 Williamstown Road, Port Melbourne, VIC 3207, Australia

314-321, 3rd Floor, Plot 3, Splendor Forum, Jasola District Centre, New Delhi - 110025, India

79 Anson Road, #06-04/06, Singapore 079906

Cambridge University Press is part of the University of Cambridge.

It furthers the University's mission by disseminating knowledge in the pursuit of education, learning and research at the highest international levels of excellence.

www.cambridge.org
Information on this title: www.cambridge.org/9781107671126

© Richard Reid 2017

This publication is in copyright. Subject to statutory exception and to the provisions of relevant collective licensing agreements, no reproduction of any part may take place without the written permission of Cambridge University Press.

First published 2017

A catalogue record for this publication is available from the British Library

ISBN 978-1-107-06720-2 Hardback
ISBN 978-1-107-67112-6 Paperback

Cambridge University Press has no responsibility for the persistence or accuracy of URLs for external or third-party internet websites referred to in this publication, and does not guarantee that any content on such websites is, or will remain, accurate or appropriate.

Contents

Explanations, Apologies and Acknowledgements

When I first approached Cambridge with the idea for this book, several years ago, it seemed a relatively simple proposal. This book has proven anything but simple. I have chopped, and changed, and chopped again; I have lost count of the versions of the text and the structure that I have torn up, and of the times I have had to rethink how to incorporate *this*, at least include a mention of *that*, how best to bring out core themes. I am only too aware that this book falls short of its original pretensions. My first *mea culpa* is that while I have aspired to 'decentre' the history of Uganda, I have not really achieved this to my own satisfaction; there is even a dash of hypocrisy in someone who was originally (and who has long been) a historian of Buganda now calling for the need to rebalance and decentre the nation's past. The fact is that the big southern polities *do* dominate the historical record, and it is certainly difficult to prevent them from doing so in a national context. Secondly, I have interpreted 'modern history' loosely in dealing with Uganda over the *longue durée*, and while the focus is on the nineteenth and twentieth centuries, at times I have ranged rather earlier than that. Some will disagree with this periodisation, but I hope it serves, at least, to accentuate the central themes of Uganda's past. Thirdly, the separation by theme here is in many ways artificial; but I have striven for a 'layered approach' rather than a strictly linear one. Moreover, what is left out is just as important as what I've elected to include. In that sense, the book is not designed to completely supplant earlier historiography which in some respects may be deemed 'outdated' but which in others holds up remarkably well, and provides rather more detailed narrative than this book does. I am also profoundly aware that histories of nations in Africa are somewhat unfashionable things, and in many ways unedifying, too; and yet my 'defence' – if one were needed – is that no-one I've spoken to over the last few years about this project has questioned the validity of attempting to write one. The problem, rather, is that they are extremely difficult to do 'well'. My final apology relates to the fact that the bulk of the book was written before the 2016 elections, and something dramatic may have transpired by the time it comes out. But I hope this is largely immaterial to the overall thrust of the narrative, and the conclusions reached.

It is not enough to merely rehash political narratives, which are often in any case well-known, and reiterate the political crises and transitions which invariably pepper the lives of nations. Readers, of course, expect some of that, and their absence would fatally compromise the book itself. Histories of nations are not the same as national histories – although clearly the former can be, and often are, co-opted into the service of the latter. While I certainly have not consciously sought to produce a 'national history', it is nonetheless the case – and in some ways this has only become clear to me as the research and writing have progressed over several years – that I *have* sought to discern the nation as a larger concept; and that with this aim in mind, one must imagine a place – and *imagine* is no doubt the key verb – that is in fact larger than the sum of its parts.[1] E.P. Thompson once observed in relation to class:

If we stop history at a given point then there are no classes but simply a multitude of individuals with a multitude of experiences. But if we watch these men over an adequate period of social change, we observe patterns in their relationships, their ideas and their institutions.[2]

If we substitute 'nations' for 'classes', and broaden 'social change' to include ongoing variations in all other spheres of human life, then we can see that something very similar holds true of national communities, and this seems to me especially apposite in the African context. What is certainly true – at least from my own perspective – is that in order for the writing of a history of Uganda to be an intellectually and politically worthwhile exercise, there must be more than simply a string of smaller narratives which eventually, tributary-like, run into one larger narrative which is the politics of colonial rule and postcolonial sovereignty. Such a book would be better presented as an annotated bibliography.

[1] I have drawn inspiration from beyond Africa, including Robert Colls, *Identity of England* (Oxford, 2002), and Christopher Duggan, *The Force of Destiny: a history of Italy since 1796* (London, 2007).
[2] E.P. Thompson, *The Making of the English Working Class* (London, 1991), 10.

Instead, I have tried to search for *Uganda* as an entity and an idea which is larger than just the politics of what goes on inside the place by that name; a one-dimensional story which might give a reasonable background to a current news story, but which otherwise tells us next to nothing about what Uganda is, or why, or what it is becoming, or what it might become. I am not sure I have succeeded, but it has certainly been an interesting journey – thrilling, joyous, stressful, at times depressing and never anything other than overwhelming. Above all, Uganda is the work of Africans – people who now call themselves Ugandans – and it has deeper roots than the signing of agreements in 1900, or the designing of signs and symbols in the years that followed, important in their way though these were. I finish with another doffing of the cap to E.P. Thompson, who famously wrote of the English working class that '[i]t was present at its own making'.[3] Ugandans were certainly present at theirs, and they continue to be.

Thanks are owed to a larger number of people (and institutions) than can realistically be named here, so a selection must suffice. From the outset, I must record my profound gratitude to the Leverhulme Trust whose award of research project grant in 2012 to explore historical consciousness in Uganda facilitated much of the research underpinning this book. I would also like to thank my own institution, SOAS, and in particular a former faculty dean, Professor Ian Brown, who took a punt on the project at an early stage and provided seed-corn funding. Makerere Institute of Social Research (MISR) provided institutional support in Kampala. The research team at Makerere University have been a joy to work with, and the significance of their input is ineffable: thanks go to Christopher Muhoozi, Pamela Khanakwa, Godfrey Asiimwe and Dixon Kamukama. Charles Twesigye, the energetic force behind the Uganda Society, has been a gracious, interested and supportive host. I must also mention Deo Katono, formerly head of the History Department at Makerere; Remigius Kigongo at the Uganda Museum for giving up his time at a crucial moment; and Ramadhan Bukenya, ever-ready at the Speke Hotel, for the 'logistical' support. In addition, I am deeply grateful to Jon Earle, Neil Kodesh, Derek Peterson, Andrew Reid, Rhiannon Stephens and Justin Willis. It would be remiss of me not to mention Professor Andrew Roberts, who originally

---

[3] Ibid., 8.

supervised my first fumblings in Ugandan history more than twenty years ago. Finally, thank you, Anna: without you, none of it would matter.

I wish to dedicate this book to my girls, May and Thea, who have derived considerable pleasure from a drum I once hurriedly grabbed at Entebbe Airport on the way home, and who made sure that the book didn't get written too quickly.

Maps

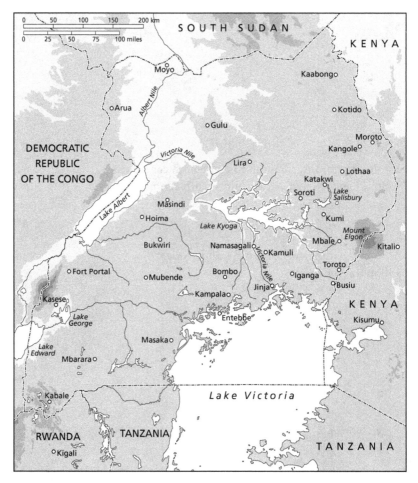

Map 1 Physical Uganda

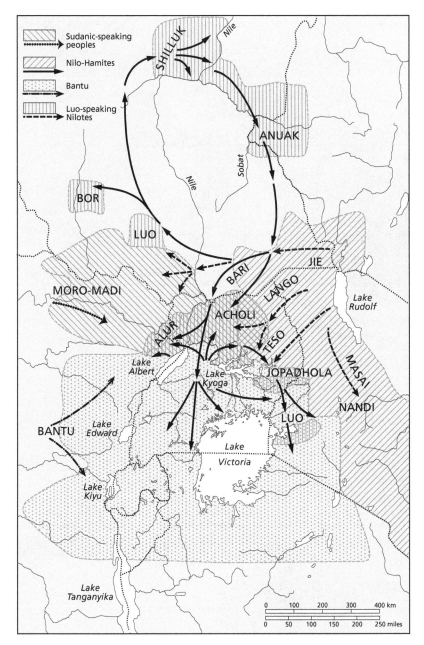

Map 2 Luo migrations, fifteenth to eighteenth centuries

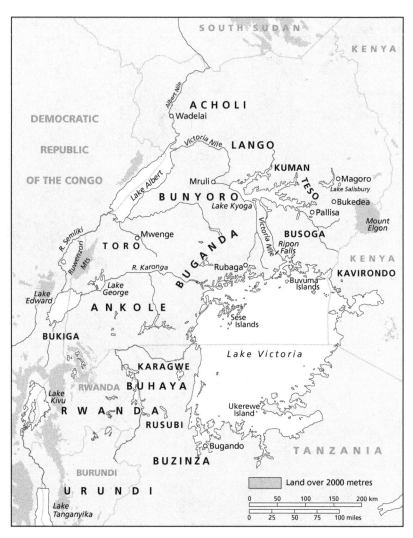

Map 3 States and societies in the nineteenth century

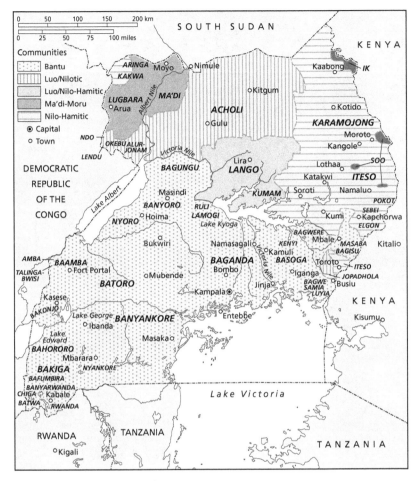

Map 4 Ethnicities in Uganda

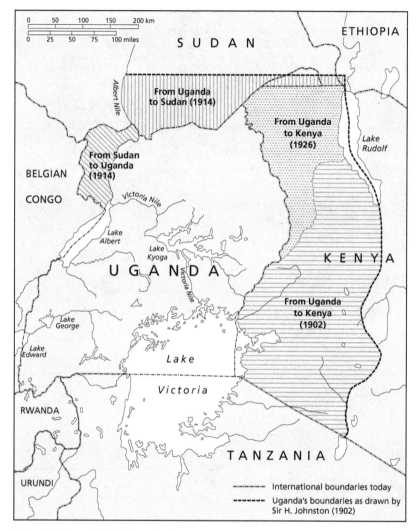

Map 5 Early colonial boundaries

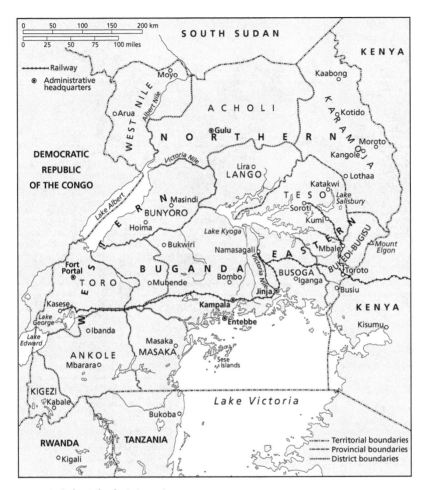

Map 6 Colonial administration

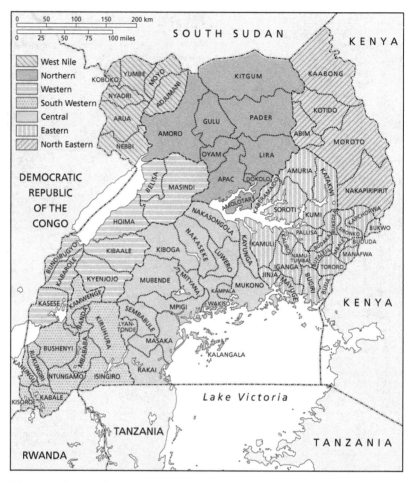

Map 7 Political administration in Uganda today

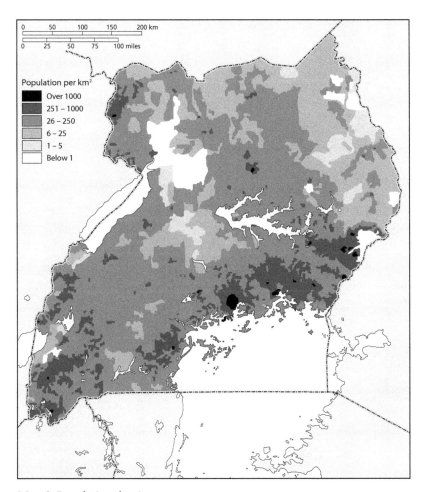

Map 8 Population density

Prologue

A View from the Museum

The Uganda Museum still feels like a haven. You leave the increasingly crushed and chaotic centre of Kampala, cross the sprawling junction at Wandegeya and head north along Kira Road. Within moments, the noise of the city recedes a little, and the road carves its way through a somewhat more suburban, even countrified, scene. For sure, the city has advanced up the road in the last few years, and construction is eating up the land: there are some embassies set off the dual carriageway, a clinic or two, and a university – Victoria University, one of the many new institutions of higher learning spreading across Kampala and indeed across Uganda. There are office blocks in the near and middle distance, apparently largely unoccupied as yet, signifying the Ugandan government's commercial ambitions for Kampala and the nation. But between the buildings, a fairly typical Ugandan scene greets the observer: rolling hills, blanketed in lush green vegetation, separated by deep well-watered gullies. In a few hundred yards, you may be tempted to muse, there are several scenes of 'Uganda': the clamorous rush of Wandegeya; the smart office blocks and business management-focused Victoria University with its blue tinted glass façade; the green hills, offering glimpses of the 'rural' Uganda beloved of generations of travel writers. At this point the reader might expect the usual remarks about an African struggle with modernity, and the contrasts – always the contrasts! – between the romanticised rural and the dysfunctional urban. And lurking beneath it all, perhaps, a longing for *authenticity*. Yet postmodernity has dispossessed us of any belief in 'authenticity', except perhaps in our deepest recesses.

Which brings us to the Museum, located off a quiet-ish bend in the road, far enough out of the city centre to feel like something of a sanctuary. A stolid, uninspiring building, the Museum was moved here in 1954, although a collection of relics dates to 1908 and the earliest days of the British Protectorate. Within as well as without, little has changed since the 1950s. There is much of interest, to be sure: exhibited behind glass are three-dimensional scenes of typical village life, and cross-sections of archaeological excavations; the first Luganda-language Bible; musical instruments, spears and bows, and cooking utensils – part of an extended display of 'tribal artefacts'. A bust of Ham Mukasa – scholar, diarist, local administrator under British colonial rule – confronts the visitor near the entrance, bearing a vague resemblance to Winston Churchill, who also visited Uganda, in 1908, and famously described the place as a tropical paradise.[1] But this is not an exhibition which has undergone much redesign since independence in 1962. Culture is presented in stasis; decades of new research has failed to have much impact on the archaeological cross-sections, gazed on by countless cohorts of local schoolchildren. Even the vibrant though violent nineteenth century is largely skimmed over in favour of the arrival of missionaries, and then the Imperial British East Africa Company, at the end of it; hence the prominence of the bust of Mukasa, who represents the solidly Protestant elite which led the country out of its supposed precolonial savagery into Christian modernity and respectability – though he is, of course, very decidedly a Muganda, a denizen of the kingdom of Buganda, which was (so the Ganda say) the natural centre of ancient civilisation in the region, the partner of the British in the new civilising mission of the twentieth century, and of course the place after which Uganda was actually named.

The Uganda Museum is thus a wonderfully rich place, if understatedly. Frozen in a late colonial moment, the scent of its well-meaning white curators still lingers in the slightly stale air, and the neglect which haunts it is not untypical of many such institutions across the continent; yet this 'house of fetishes' – *Enyumba ya Mayembe*, as the Ganda called it in the 1900s – encapsulates the complex history, and the staggering diversity, of this young yet old nation. And the very fact of its neglect – the powerful sense of what the Museum is *not*, namely a vibrant, updated celebration of Uganda's cultures and histories – tells a story in itself. For while history is everywhere in Uganda, there is fear and mistrust of it, not least on the part of a government which is responsible – or so the official narrative has it – for the country's 'recovery' since the 1980s. And that government has recently had designs on the Uganda Museum. In early 2011, the Ugandan government announced its decision to close down the Museum and to

---

[1] Winston S. Churchill, *My African Journey* (London, 1908).

mothball its contents. In its place, the government proposed to build a multi-storey business complex, the 'East African Trade Centre', which would, among other things, showcase Uganda's arrival as a regional commercial hub.[2] Once built, a floor of the Trade Centre would be set aside for the Museum's artefacts. In the months that followed, the outcry[3] was largely dismissed by officials of the ruling National Resistance Movement (NRM), who made clear their conviction that the Museum is a luxury which attracted no revenue and produced little of any tangible value, yet which occupied prime 'real estate' on the outskirts of Kampala. It was pointed out by keener observers, of course, that the inability of the Museum to do more was undermined by the government's own meagre subsidy – 50 million Ugandan shillings (less than £12,000) in 2011–12, for example.[4] Nonetheless, several civil society organisations took the government to court in an attempt to halt the project.[5] It is by no means certain how the story will end, but at the time of writing, the uproar has subsided somewhat and the project (if there ever actually was one) appears to have been quietly shelved. Yet the issue encapsulates one of the core ideological strands of the NRM, which has ruled Uganda since 1986. Uganda under Museveni is the exemplar of the aggressive developmentalism – the product, at least partly, of liberal economic orthodoxy within the Western donor community – which now dominates political thinking across sub-Saharan Africa. Simply put, the notion of economic 'development' is hegemonic, and success is measured in terms of GDP growth rates. The economic patriotism of the 'new Uganda' regards history with, at best, deep suspicion, and at worst as actively inimical and antagonistic to 'development', associating it with sectarianism and 'tribalism'.

Ideas about modern development versus putatively atavistic sectarianism, the defenders of the 'old' versus the champions of the 'new': these are conflicts that reach back some way in Uganda, and in many ways lie in the very foundations of the nation itself. The NRM's apparent hostility towards the Museum is, on one level, purely a matter

---

[2] *The East African Trade Centre Project*, Ministry of Tourism, Trade and Industry Project Proposal, n.d., Kampala.

[3] See, for example, Ephraim Kamuhangire, 'Don't Destroy the Museum', *New Vision* (Kampala), 10 March 2011.

[4] 'War over Uganda Museum Rages on', *The Observer* (Kampala), 17 July 2012.

[5] The organisations included the Historical Resources Conservation Initiative, the Cross Cultural Foundation of Uganda, the Historical Buildings Conservations Trust and Jenga Afrika.

of development economics, reflective of an antipathy towards non–profit-making activities and institutions. On another level, however, it is emblematic of a mistrust of the past and all that Uganda's troubled history supposedly represents, namely violent disunity. Nothing embodies that position more clearly than the relationship between the NRM and the kingdom of Buganda, with its centre on a hill on the other side of town from the Museum, at Mengo. Buganda's dominance of Ugandan politics – and, to an extent, economics and culture – is of considerable antiquity: it can be traced to the rise of the state to regional hegemony in the late eighteenth century. The kingdom, as many Ganda are keen to emphasise, was never conquered by the British; it *invited* the British in, and offered them partnership in pursuit of the imperial project. However the arrangement is interpreted, it formed the bedrock of the colonial state. In the decades that followed the signing of the Uganda Agreement of 1900 – the legislation which underwired the colonial order and regulated British-African relationships – the Ganda were pre-eminent, as political leaders, as economic entrepreneurs and indeed as the hosts of Uganda's physical administrative and commercial centres. They had the best schools, the best infrastructure, the bulk of economic output and the most political influence; they were also the most numerous single group in the Protectorate, by quite some way.

By the beginning of the 1950s, when ostensibly nationalist parties had begun to coalesce and as decolonisation became an ever more realistic prospect, Buganda was a problem. It was a problem for the British, as *Kabaka* (King) Edward Mutesa led the resurgence of Ganda ethnic nationalism and sought a guarantee that the kingdom's autonomous (and privileged) status would be preserved in any future independent Ugandan state. The *Kabaka* was briefly exiled to London for his troubles, between 1953 and 1955, for the British could not acquiesce to Ganda demands. When he was allowed to return, a compromise was struck. But a distinctively Ganda nationalism had now been unleashed in the ferment of late colonial rule, and this was a problem, too, for non-Ganda political leaders who wished to see a unitary state in which Buganda was brought firmly to heel. In particular, politicians from the north – where there was little of the monarchical and hierarchical tradition associated with Buganda – joined with others to found the Uganda People's Congress (UPC), bitterly opposed to both Ganda hegemony and autonomy. But Ganda ethno-nationalism, defined as it was by a strident royalism and ferocious attachment to the person (and the institution) of the *Kabaka*, was even a problem for other Ganda – particularly Roman Catholic Ganda – who did not see the kingdom's best interests served by such a political programme. A group of them, under the leadership of Benedicto Kiwanuka, formed the Democratic Party – and the DP performed well enough in 1961 elections to form the first internal self-government. In one of the great ironies of modern Ugandan history, however, the UPC made a pact with the Ganda royalist party – the *Kabaka Yekka* (King Alone) movement – in order to marginalise their common enemy the DP, and together UPC leader Milton Obote and the *Kabaka* of Buganda took Uganda to full independence in October 1962.

Whatever mutual advantage there had been swiftly dissipated: in 1966 Obote sent soldiers to occupy the royal palace at Mengo, and Edward Mutesa just about managed to escape into exile – eventually to London, once again, where he died in what some say were suspicious circumstances in 1969. Meanwhile in 1967 Obote abnegated the constitution and proclaimed a new one, in which the 'traditional kingdoms' – Buganda and the other big southern polities, Bunyoro, Toro, Ankole and Busoga – were formally abolished. It was, Obote argued, a blow for unity against anachronistic tribalism and sectarianism. And so it remained until 1993, when the NRM government restored them – all, that is, except Ankole where the old monarchy was a rather more problematic issue (and from whence most of the NRM leadership hailed).[6] It was an extremely popular move among the supporters of kings, not least in Buganda, whose backing Museveni needed in building the new Uganda. He certainly had it, for a while. But the constitutional amendment under which the kingdoms had been restored contained an important caveat, namely that kings (or 'cultural leaders', as they were constitutionally designated) were to stay out of politics and would be responsible for keeping politics out of culture. In time, many Ganda came to see this as unjust and oppressive, and soon came to the conclusion that Museveni was actively seeking to undermine the *Kabaka?* and the kingdom – just as Obote had done, and Idi Amin

---

[6] See Martin R. Doornbos, *The Ankole Kingship Controversy: regalia galore revisited* (Kampala, 2001). The name of the kingdom which formed the basis of 'Ankole' was known as 'Nkore' in the precolonial era; 'Ankole' was the territorially expanded version under British rule, and it has been known by that name subsequently. In the account that follows, I will use 'Nkore' when referring explicitly to the precolonial state, and 'Ankole' when discussing its twentieth-century manifestation.

after him. And so it continues: tensions periodically run high between State House and Mengo, then ease, then heighten again. The kingdom remains a simmering issue at the centre of national politics – the living embodiment of a glorious past to most Ganda, and the most meaningful and relevant political entity in their lives, an incurable headache to many others.

The prolonged jostling between the government and Buganda is of course a matter of competition over precious political resources; but it is also, again, a question of history and the nation. Uganda is small – you could fit it many times into its huge westerly neighbour, the Democratic Republic of Congo – but it encompasses enormous diversity, giving rise to what I describe later in the book as political claustrophobia. And while that diversity is relatively easily celebrated before an audience of tourists – one informative publication, now in its fourth edition, presents Uganda as a kind of 'zoo nation', a stunning panoply of 'tribes' and cultures and idiosyncratic dances[7] – it is rather more difficult to do so when it comes to governance. For diversity has been a problem for successive Ugandan regimes, particularly considering that each distinctive grouping represented locally rooted identities and histories which unless carefully managed could become actively inimical to the nation's well-being. Buganda is perhaps the most visible and largest-scale case of this; but there are a host of others.

One of the central themes threaded through this book is a concern for the past. An odd thing to say, perhaps, given that it is a 'modern history'. But I am not only interested in presenting a version, or versions, of events and processes; I also wish to explore how history has been used to mobilise and marginalise, how the past is continually evoked and reinterpreted, in the forging of political and cultural communities – up to and including the modern nation. And so the Uganda Museum not only occupies prime real estate; it also reflects some important ways of thinking about Uganda's past, in its spatial arrangements, in the nervous twitches it provokes in development-hungry government, and in the understated (and long unchanged) displays of (equally unchanging) 'tribal cultures' positioned just beyond Ham Mukasa's bust. It is a good place to start – and it is still a wonderfully quiet place to rest for a while.

---

[7] *Peoples and Cultures of Uganda* (Kampala, 2011).

1 | *Refractions*

Beholding Uganda

Does Uganda Have a History?

This question is not supposed to be a deliberate insult to nearly forty million Ugandans, or to the decades of work undertaken by their historians and producers of culture; nor is it a throwback to an older idea that Africans possessed no such thing as 'history' until Europeans showed up to inject some purpose into their lives. Rather, the issue is whether, and to what extent, *Uganda*, as a national entity, has a history, and whether it is remotely possible to aim for an integrated view of the nation's past. In that sense, the question is a little more complicated than might first appear, and it very much depends on how we interpret it. Critically, for example, who exactly is part of that history? Even defining Ugandan history in the putatively straightforward terms of territorially delineated entity is problematic, given that the precise boundaries of the British Protectorate were not finally settled until 1926, when the administrative sector then known as Rudolf Province, in the far northeast, was transferred to Kenya. Similarly, West Nile district, in the northwest, was initially part of Belgian Congo, was then briefly administered as part of Sudan, and was only transferred to Uganda in 1912. Earlier still, a swathe of what would become western Kenya was originally considered part of the Uganda Protectorate, when the partition of the region was in motion, and only became part of Kenya in 1902.[1] Even after 1926, the question of where 'Uganda' ends and somewhere else begins has been raised periodically: by Idi Amin in the late 1970s, for example, when the President – himself from a transnational group, the Kakwa, straddling the Ugandan-Congolese border in the northwest – laid claim to a chunk of territory south of the Kagera River in Tanzania. Indeed a few years earlier Amin had also demanded the return of western Kenya to Uganda, considering this swathe of the

---

[1] H.B. Thomas & R. Scott, *Uganda* (London, 1935), 41.

Kenyan Highlands an intrinsic part of his domain. In recent years, President Yoweri Museveni has questioned whether certain groups hovering nervously on the territorial peripheries of the nation are *really Ugandan* – symptomatic of one of the recurrent themes in the country's past, namely anxieties around claims to land, citizenship and belonging. And so questions of territorial delimitation do not necessarily lead to neat answers. Such is the problem with histories of nations – and to be sure, *all* nations have similar tales of peripheral ambiguity. To borrow the famous refrain of immigrant Mexicans to the United States: 'We didn't cross the border; the border crossed us'.

Then there is the very name of the place itself. *Uganda* is essentially a mispronunciation of *Buganda* – the state with which most visitors in the late nineteenth century engaged. Swahili traders, dropping the 'b' from most African place names in the interior, rendered Buganda thus, and the British followed suit. It meant (as did Buganda in the Luganda language) 'the place of the Ganda'. The irony is clear enough: the entire country which was placed under British rule, of which the Buganda kingdom was but one part – albeit an important one – was named after that kingdom, even though the territory encompassed dozens of groups which were distinct in language, culture, economy, political process. This is, to an extent, an accident of history, or more aptly of historical geography.

Nonetheless, leaving such ambiguities aside for the moment, the existence of Uganda's history as a sovereign entity since 9 October 1962, the date on which it achieved independence from Britain, seems undeniable. This was driven home in a very public fashion by the celebration and reflection that attended the nation's fiftieth birthday in 2012 – a noteworthy landmark, and one awarded the appropriate significance by the government, media, business and civil society alike.[2] Several important narratives emerged in the course of the year – in speeches made, in essays written in the mainstream press, in public discussions printed and broadcast – which combined to apparently demonstrate *the history of Uganda*: an integrated, singular history; a *national history*, albeit one largely envisioned and articulated by a metropolitan

---

[2] A number of glossy publications appeared to mark the occasion, and are a mine of 'local knowledge': see, for example, Fountain Publishers' *Independent Uganda: the first 50 years* (Kampala, 2012), and the *Daily Monitor*'s collection of features and articles, *Understand Uganda: 50 years of independence, 9 October 1962 – 9 October 2012* (Kampala, 2012).

middle class. That history dwelt on anticolonial struggle against the British, and the heroes of that struggle; the monstrous darkness that enveloped Uganda during the 1970s under Idi Amin, and the violent aftermath; the resilience of Ugandans in overcoming war, dictatorship, poverty and the AIDS epidemic to build a national community of growing strength and confidence.

Yet what does it mean to write the history of an African nation in the early twenty-first century? The histories of nations are problematic affairs at the best of times – that is, even when there is a degree of received wisdom surrounding the existence of the nation itself, and a critical mass of literature pointing to the fact. There may be disagreement over the antiquity of the concept, and rival interpretations around the provenance and evolution of the accoutrements, the signs and symbols, of the nation.[3] But the histories of African nations can be especially contorted and difficult projects, certainly if the aim of the latter is to demonstrate that nations themselves add up to rather more than the sum of their parts. What, after all, *are* nations in Africa, and how should one go about thinking about their historical trajectory and composition?[4] It has been some time since histories of African nations were mainstream within the professional academy. But in the 1960s and 1970s, much pioneering Africanist historiography was framed in national – indeed sometimes *nationalist* – terms.[5] Newly sovereign African nations were implicitly or otherwise awarded the gravity and ballast of antiquity, most notably by those scholars associated with or inspired by the 'Dar es Salaam school' in Tanzania.[6] National history-writing arguably reached a highpoint with John Iliffe's *Modern History of Tanganyika*, widely regarded as one of the finest examples of the genre and one to which aspirant authors must routinely pay homage

---

[3] For example, M. Guibernau & J. Hutchinson (eds.), *History and National Destiny: ethnosymbolism and its critics* (Oxford, 2004).

[4] See also R.J. Reid, 'States of Anxiety: history and nation in modern Africa', *Past and Present*, 229:1 (2015).

[5] J. Lonsdale, 'The emergence of African nations', in T.O. Ranger (ed.), *Emerging Themes of African History* (Nairobi, 1968).

[6] Ranger (ed.), *Emerging Themes*; A.D. Roberts (ed.), *Tanzania Before 1900* (Nairobi, 1968); I.N. Kimambo & A.J. Temu (eds.), *A History of Tanzania* (Nairobi, 1969); B.A. Ogot (ed.), *Kenya Before 1900* (Nairobi, 1976); A.D. Roberts, *A History of Zambia* (New York, 1976). For a critique, see D. Denoon & A. Kuper, 'Nationalist Historians in Search of a Nation: the "new historiography" in Dar es Salaam', *African Affairs*, 69:277 (1970).

in their own endeavours.[7] Yet by the 1980s few folk were writing the histories of nations, which had been displaced by transnational or regional history,[8] or micro studies of specific bits of nations – the latter increasingly seen as obscuring more than they illuminated in terms of African agency and experience. The revolution which elevated 'history from below' to the mainstream likewise sidelined the nation as a unit of study. And after all, the crisis of legitimacy for the nation itself in Africa, by the 1980s, had depleted the confidence of an earlier generation, and accordingly delegitimised the defining of one's research in strictly national terms.[9] More recently, the nation has been critically deconstructed in terms of claims on citizenship, and questions have been asked about whether they were, after all, the inevitable outcome of decolonisation.[10] A subfield has recently begun to emerge around the study of national days and independence jubilees in modern Africa.[11]

It is true that much of the earlier 'national' work took for granted, very largely, that the nation itself existed; or at least the *place* existed and therefore it was assumed – quite rightly, up to a point – to be a legitimate exercise to tell the story of what had happened *inside* that place. These were, after all, sovereign entities and therefore they had histories. And so it is in more recent years, too, for the handful of scholars who have attempted similar projects. In Dan Branch's outstanding history of independent Kenya, for example, there is no existential crisis, no wrestling with whether or not a history of Kenya is

---

[7] J. Iliffe, *A Modern History of Tanganyika* (Cambridge, 1979).

[8] A. Zimmerman, 'Africa in Imperial and Transnational History: multi-sited historiography and the necessity of theory', *Journal of African History*, 54:3 (2013).

[9] In arguably the most extreme case, Somalia, a change of title was required: in its first incarnation, I.M. Lewis's classic text was published as *The Modern History of Somaliland* (London, 1965), but in its final edition it had become *A Modern History of the Somali* (Oxford, 2002), owing to the effective disappearance of the nation-state.

[10] S. Dorman, D. Hammett & P. Nugent (eds.), *Making Nations, Creating Strangers: states and citizenship in Africa* (Leiden, 2007); F. Cooper, 'Possibility and Constraint: African independence in historical perspective', *Journal of African History*, 49:2 (2008), and more recently his *Africa in the World: capitalism, empire, nation-state* (Cambridge MA, 2014); P. Geschiere, *The Perils of Belonging: autochthony, citizenship and exclusion in Africa and Europe* (Chicago, 2009).

[11] See, for example, a recent special issue of *Nations and Nationalism*, 19:2 (2013), comprising especially pertinent essays by Carola Lentz, Christine Fricke, Konstanze N'Guessan and Izabela Orlowska.

even a worthwhile and valid exercise.[12] Kenya simply *is*, albeit in complicated ways. Perhaps this is a reflection of the self-confidence of the Kenyanist academy. But likewise in John McCracken's long-awaited and empirically robust study of Malawi, there is no time wasted on pondering the conceptualisation of Malawi as a unit of historical study; for McCracken, one of the world's leading experts on the place, the genealogies of Malawi are clear, and indisputable, and straightforwardly demarcated.[13] This is striking, given the broader context of a postmodern turn *against* the nation as a unit of study in the Africanist academy; but then McCracken is a scion of the Dar es Salaam school, as he himself would cheerily admit. Gewald, Hinfelaar and Macola's critically reflective approach to Zambia is something of an exception, as is Alexander Johnston's study of South Africa, the latter part of a Bloomsbury series on the 'invention' of the nation;[14] but a number of recent histories of nations have been fairly linear narratives which are generally unconcerned with deeper existential or ontological issues.[15] More generally, Africa is seen as comprising a peculiar set of cases: arguably with the exception of Ethiopia, and certainly at one time Somalia – singled out for particular attention, for example, by Ernest Gellner[16] – African nations are more often the exotic receptacles of a host of often distinctively potent *subnational* identities, which normatively threaten to rip apart the artificial national entity itself, or at least to claim it for themselves and use it for the advancement of their own agendas.

So, what about the entity itself, the *place* called Uganda? Does the nation itself have a history, or do we only tell the histories of the peoples who happen to live within those boundaries? Yoweri Museveni was in no doubt that Uganda did indeed have a history, if a short and troubled one, when in 2012, during the celebrations marking fifty years of independence, he publicly repented on behalf of all Ugandans for their manifold sins.[17] Presumably, too, did George Wilberforce Kakoma,

---

[12] D. Branch, *Kenya: between hope and despair, 1963–2011* (New Haven, 2011).

[13] J. McCracken, *A History of Malawi 1855–1966* (Woodbridge, 2012).

[14] J.-B. Gewald, Marja Hinfelaar & Giacomo Macola (eds.), *One Zambia, Many Histories: towards a history of postcolonial Zambia* (Leiden, 2008); A. Johnston, *South Africa: inventing the nation* (London, 2014).

[15] Bahru Zewde, *A History of Modern Ethiopia 1855–1991* (Oxford, revised 2nd ed., 2001); T. Falola & M. Heaton, *A History of Nigeria* (Cambridge, 2008).

[16] E. Gellner, *Nations and Nationalism* (Oxford, 1983), 84–5.

[17] 'For the sins of Uganda I repent – Museveni', *New Vision* (Kampala), 18 October 2012.

composer of Uganda's national anthem in the early 1960s, as well as the others involved in the design of Uganda's national signs and symbols. Certainly, for a generation of late colonial activists who later formed postcolonial Uganda's first governing elite, the nation was real enough. Grace Ibingira, notably, wrote of the 'forging', and the 'evolution', of the Ugandan nation from the 1890s onwards in a full-length work of scholarly history in the early 1970s – though his vision was, not untypically, an increasingly disaffected one, reflected in his later novel about the travails of a 'fictional' African country.[18] Judging from his letter to the UN Secretary-General in 1966, *Kabaka* Edward Mutesa II was less sure of the viability of 'Uganda': traditional 'tribal' authority, it seemed, was more important than any chimeric visions of nationhood.[19] The further back we go into the colonial period, the more difficult the question becomes. At any rate, these unitary visions tended to be conceptualised as the products of a colonial modernity rather than rooted in the deeper past which was seen in more disconnected, fragmentary terms. Is it impossible, even undesirable, to think of Uganda as anything other than an empty receptacle into which are poured various ingredients, only to be emptied and refilled at regular intervals? Is Uganda merely – as one Ugandan informant once put it – the hardware, only lacking the appropriate software?[20]

Uganda is not *quite* as artificial as might be supposed – and certainly no more artificial than many others, whether in Africa, Europe or elsewhere.[21] It seems an apposite moment – following several decades of tumult and often rapid change across Africa in general, and certainly in Uganda in particular, and with a number of nations having now passed noteworthy jubilees – to consider the ways in which we might

[18] Grace Ibingira, *The Forging of an African Nation: the political and constitutional evolution of Uganda from colonial rule to independence, 1894–1962* (New York, 1973); and see his later *Bitter Harvest: a political novel* (Nairobi, 1980). Ibingira – involved in the design of Uganda's flag – was a leading figure in the UPC and served in Obote's government until his arrest in 1966. Released in 1971, he later went into self-imposed exile.

[19] 'Annexure to the Appeal by Kabaka Mutesa II to the Secretary-General of the United Nations, 11 March 1966', in D.A. Low (ed.), *The Mind of Buganda: documents of the modern history of an African kingdom* (London, 1971).

[20] Author's field notes and informal interviews, 6 August 2010.

[21] See, for example, A.D. Smith, *Myths and Memories of the Nation* (Oxford, 1999), 163; first published as 'Gastronomy or Geology? The role of nationalism in the reconstruction of nations', *Nations and Nationalism*, 1:1 (1995).

approach the history of an African nation. The foremost publisher in Uganda today, Fountain, was responsible for a brilliantly illustrated pictorial history of Uganda published in 2007.[22] One of the fascinating aspects of this book is that it was published to commemorate '150 years' of Uganda – and yet the selection of '1857' as a starting point is difficult to explain. It is not the accession of Mutesa I of Buganda, which took place around that time. However, it *does* appear to be rooted in the idea that Europeans first came to Uganda around this time, although it is a rather imprecise temporal hook on which to hang the argument: a man named Debono, a Maltese trader, was operating among the Acholi in the course of the 1850s, but Speke and Grant did not tread on 'Ugandan' soil until 1862, and Baker the following year. Whatever the case, the more important issue relates to the very legitimising presence of Europeans in the area – i.e., that 'Uganda begins' only when *bazungu* turn up to give it purpose, form and ultimately legality. This interpretation – privileging as it does the role of the exogenous – supposes that these are disparate peoples only brought together by the much more dynamic, historically meaningful, external forces that bring Africans into the world. In the process, these forces forge the place called 'Uganda', into which various peoples must squeeze themselves. It certainly raises an interesting question: *when* is Uganda? In one sense, perhaps, this is mere frippery: who cares when the place now called 'Uganda' comes into being, or that ultimately it appears to be foreigners who were responsible for it? On the other hand, it is vitally important, because it goes to the very heart of what an African 'nation' is – an externally created, artificial project which hapless natives must try in some way to make function, like a form of arranged marriage; or something rather more organic than that, with deeper historical roots, and linkages, and shared experiences, into which external influences become refracted, and co-opted. In truth, of course, 'foreigners' are usually involved in the making of nations, wherever we find them; and equally there is a level at which the national community only makes sense in contrast to others, to outsiders, to a line of vision which is by definition exogenous.

In wrestling with the question of when does one 'begin' a history of Uganda, I echo Karugire's argument that this is about 'shared historical experience' in the deeper past, not just since the late nineteenth

---

[22] *Uganda: a picture history, 1857–2007* (Kampala, 2007).

century.[23] It is not obvious why *la longue durée* should be any more
problematic in Uganda than elsewhere in the world.[24] Uganda can
be interpreted as an economic, political and cultural 'community', or
'zone', which in fact has a degree of cohesion and interconnection in the
deeper past. In other words, there is a precolonial crucible that becomes
Uganda, a zone of interconnectedness in which the seeds of 'Uganda'
are sown. The notion of a supposedly debilitating 'artificiality' arose
around the time of decolonisation and its immediate aftermath, when
it seemed that the borders of Uganda – and many other 'new' African
nations – now encompassed a range of groups with apparently little
or nothing in common and no experience of working together in the
name of a larger national entity which bore little resemblance to political realities on the ground.[25] It swiftly became clear that competition
at the centre (and indeed at the edges) was over who would control this
newly and externally defined space, inherited from colonial administrations. No doubt, enclosure potentially limited flexibility and placed
restrictions on the earlier options of either violent confrontation or
migration (although the story of Uganda contains plenty of both, in
fact). Rather than having their conflicts played out through a multitude of channels and within a range of spaces, the newly anointed sub-
jects/citizens of Uganda now had just one arena: that of the unitary
state. Yet much was carried forward from the precolonial era within
and around that 'artificial' space. Certainly, it should come as little
surprise that enclosure brought about heightened levels of violence in
postcolonial Uganda. This was the result, essentially, of what might be
termed political claustrophobia. A political culture built around the
notion that 'winner takes all' quickly developed within the confined
space that was the nation-state, and panic – manifest in extraordinary brutality towards, and between, citizens – became part of that
political culture. The regime of Idi Amin perhaps best demonstrates

---

[23] S. Karugire, *A Political History of Uganda* (Nairobi, 1980), 1–2.

[24] See Jeremy Black, *Contesting History: narratives of public history* (London,
2014).

[25] Contemporary analysis is provided in Thomas Hodgkin's classic *Nationalism
in Colonial Africa* (London, 1956), and the core themes were subsequently
developed in the work of, among many others, James Smoot Coleman – see
Nationalism and Development in Africa: selected essays (Berkeley CA, 1994) –
and Basil Davidson, whose thinking culminated in *The Black Man's Burden:
Africa and the curse of the nation-state* (London, 1992).

this. Yet while in some respects precolonial mechanisms for conflict resolution were undermined, much of the violence itself was actually precolonial in origin – most obviously that involving the hegemonic southern kingdoms, especially Buganda. Cultures of violence and militarism long pre-dated the formal creation of 'Uganda', and the fault lines which opened up in the years following Uganda's independence in 1962 were in fact of considerable antiquity. And so, too, were the histories of cultural interchange and reciprocal inspiration, and the economic networks which bound together diverse communities to mutual advantage. If war was old, then socio-economic connectivity was just as deep-rooted.

Terrain has *longue durée*, too, as Braudel argued,[26] and it is perhaps the easier of the tasks before us to define Uganda in terms of its physical geography. Broadly, the territory itself is plateau land, enclosed by a rim of mountains on its western and eastern flanks, and its general elevation rendering it relatively more temperate in climate than much of the surrounding region, despite the fact that it straddles the equator.[27] Uganda lies almost completely within the Nile basin, and around 16 per cent of its total area is open water and swampland, including the major lakes Victoria, Albert, Edward and Kyoga which ring the relatively better-watered southern half of the territory. The White Nile, indeed, in many ways defines and cuts across the territory, flowing out of Lake Victoria at Jinja, intersecting with the western end of Lake Kyoga before moving into Lake Albert, from whence it flows northward out of Uganda and into South Sudan. The southern half of Uganda experiences heavier rainfall, with two main rainy seasons between March and June and between September and November, and this – combined with the prevalence of lakes and waterways – means that southern Uganda has the heavier vegetation, including savannah grasslands and some equatorial forest, and much richer soils. Thus the south has historically been able to support extensive farming and sizeable population densities. In the north, by contrast, rainfall is much lower, and certainly less bimodal: the hot, arid northeast, notably,

---

[26] Fernand Braudel, *The Mediterranean and the Mediterranean World in the Age of Philip II* (Berkeley & Los Angeles, 1994; 1st pub., 1949).

[27] For more detailed overviews of Uganda's physicality, see Thomas & Scott, *Uganda*, Chapters 2 & 3; and in a regional context, S.J.K. Baker, 'The East African environment', in R. Oliver & G. Mathew (eds.), *History of East Africa* vol. I (Oxford, 1963).

experiences only one annual rainy season (March–April). Northern Uganda has much thinner vegetation, and in the dry plains in the north-central and northeast zones, pastoralism is predominant. Of course even within these broad areas, there is considerable – even dramatic – variation, meaning that despite Uganda's relatively compact size it encompasses extraordinary environmental and climatic diversity: the highland regions of the Ruwenzori mountains of the southwest, a polit-ical and cultural frontier land of historical significance, on the upper reaches of which there is a permanent layer of snow, and high rain-fall and lower temperatures on the lower hills; the remarkable sub-snowline landscapes of Mt. Elgon in the east; the dry grasslands of Ankole and the Masaka area, characterised by undulating hills and relatively low rainfall; the moist northern and western strip around Lake Victoria with forest (including the Mabira belt) stretching from Jinja to the Kagera River; the hot and dry Karamoja area in the north-east. The general pattern for the rest of Uganda, however, is plateau land covered by tree savannah, enjoying sufficient rainfall for settled agriculture. Again farming – and, of course, fishing, one of the old-est economic activities in the area – has been greatly assisted by the omnipresence of lakes and rivers. With the exception of the Nile itself, and the clear streams found in the mountainous areas and on the slopes of the western rift valley, rivers are mostly sluggish swamps, such as the Kafu, Katonga, Sezibwa and Mpologoma.

Communities moved into and adapted their economies to particular environments, often nestling alongside rivers and streams or hugging lake shores. At this point, it is important to emphasise the complex-ity of Uganda's human environment, no less than its physical com-position. Defining and enumerating 'ethnic groups' in a rigid sense is dangerous and misleading,[28] but there are more than two dozen reasonably clearly defined and numerically significant ethnic groups in Uganda today, some of which spill over into the neighbouring

[28] There is a substantial literature on the supposed modern 'invention', and the 'reimagining', of ethnic identity, in Uganda as elsewhere: see, for example, Crawford Young, *The African Colonial State in Comparative Perspective* (New Haven & London, 1994), 232–4; and Iliffe, *Modern History*, 323. Some, however, have argued for a more *longue durée* approach: notably J.-P. Chretien & G. Prunier (eds.), *Les ethnies ont une histoire* (Paris, 1989), P. Chabal and J.-P. Daloz, *Africa Works: disorder as political instrument* (Oxford, 1999), 57, T. Spear, 'Neo-traditionalism and the limits of invention in British colonial Africa', *Journal of African History*, 44:1 (2003).

territories of Congo, South Sudan, Kenya, Tanzania and Rwanda. Lake Kyoga and the arc of the Nile between Kyoga and Lake Albert marks, in a necessarily approximate sense, the division between the Nilotic- and Sudanic-speaking north and the Bantu-speaking south. In the latter zone, Bantu-speakers – entering Uganda over the course of the first millennium BCE and the first millennium CE[29] – have been the most numerous of Uganda's language and culture groups, not least because of their settlement in the wetter, more fertile parts of the territory, often close to the rivers and lakes described earlier. These now include the relatively numerous Ganda, Soga, Nyankole (including the Iru and Hima groupings), Nyoro, Kiga, Gwere, and a number of smaller groups. The Sudanic groups in northwest Uganda include the Lugbara and the Madi, and represent the remnants of what was probably a much more widely dispersed language and culture bloc which at one time occupied much of northern Uganda. They were, however, either absorbed or displaced by the Nilotic populations now inhabiting much of the country north of lakes Kyoga and Albert. These are divided into so-called 'Western Nilotes' – notably Acholi, Kumam, Padhola, Langi, Alur – and the 'Eastern Nilotes', including Karamojong, Teso, Pokot, Kakwa and Sebei, who are now included under the generic name 'Ateker'. Even these terms do not always describe fixed or cohesive ethnicities, but rather are umbrella terms – 'Karamojong' is perhaps the best example[30] – denoting several autonomous and distinct subgroups. Several Nilotic groups are geographic outliers – that is to say, they are now located some way from the main linguistic and cultural clusters – owing to economic or political migration over the last 200 years or so.

Conceptualisations and definitions of Uganda have long been dominated by the southern monarchical states, whose histories cast a mightily long shadow across the history of the nation as a whole. To what extent can we take the analysis *and* the narrative away from the south and its territorial, centralised monarchies, and back towards the putative peripheries – especially the north, beyond Lake Kyoga? These have

---

[29] David Schoenbrun, *A Green Place, A Good Place: agrarian change, gender, and social identity in the Great Lakes region to the 15th century* (Portsmouth, NH, 1998), 41–5.

[30] Ben Knighton, 'Globalizing trends or identities through time? The *longue durée* in Karamojong ethnography', *Journal of Eastern African Studies*, 1:3 (2007), 478 fn. 1.

certainly been overlooked by most archivally minded historians, and only a little less so by anthropologists; and yet those areas comprise an enormous chunk of Uganda's total area – at least half, if not a little more. There is an abiding fascination with the structure and political cultures of the monarchical states of the interlacustrine forest zone, and with the archival access associated with such states. In essence, this is about how knowledge is ordered. At the same time, however, it is not purely about the imposition of European visions of worthy and unworthy Africans. The respective social structures in the south and in the north were differently equipped to deal with the various challenges and opportunities encroaching from the outside world. The Acholi, like the Ganda, were heavily involved in the slave trade, for example; but *unlike* the Ganda, the Acholi did not inhabit an adequately arable zone, one in which commercial agriculture could flourish, and therefore were not able to respond positively to the economic directives of the colonial era. Instead, the district became an exporter of labour and a source of militarisation through recruitment into the colonial army. This was a classic case of internal underdevelopment. Even more stark is the case of the Karamojong, who suffered the vagaries of, and state-level hostility to, pastoralist economics. This underdevelopment was undergirded by a scholarly apparatus from the 1950s onwards, and a colonial political mindset before that, which was fixated with particular forms of governance, economic 'growth' and the minutiae of Ganda politics and political intrigue, and with the finest nuances of political opinion, activism and access to the 'native mind', especially with a view to understanding indigenous conceptions of 'modernity'.[31]

Northern groups have at least an equal claim on the making of modern Uganda as do those in the south – through the absolutely critical role northern migrations have played in Uganda's deeper past, not least as the fount of much political innovation; in the provision of labour underpinning the modern Ugandan economy; in the modern dominance of the north in military terms, in colonial and (until the late 1980s) postcolonial armies. Ultimately, the Anglo-Ganda alliance at

---

[31] It is a preoccupation which underpinned early scholarship: see, for example, the very different approaches in K. Ingham, *The Making of Modern Uganda* (London, 1958), D. Apter, *The Political Kingdom in Uganda: a study in bureaucratic nationalism* (Princeton, 1961), L.A. Fallers (ed.), *The King's Men: leadership and status in Buganda on the eve of independence* (New York, 1964) and D.A. Low, *Buganda in Modern History* (London, 1971).

the start of the twentieth century imagined the north as the internal 'other', and this has been perpetuated by the current government – assisted considerably by the war against Kony and the LRA. In sum, to borrow a phrase from an influential economic history paper of some years ago,[32] this is a question of 'reversal of fortune', from north to south. Uganda in origin owes an enormous amount to the north in terms of politics, culture, religion; but the south has latterly come to dominate in political and economic terms, in part the curse of geopolitics and nature, but largely the result of particular hegemonic visions of political and economic modernity. And so in some ways it is no coincidence that the first twenty years of Uganda's independence were dominated by northern governments with self-consciously modernist, unitary and patriotic visions of Uganda.

In Uganda – and elsewhere in Africa – there has been much patriotism, and self-styled patriots have particular ideas about the spatial territory that is the nation. But approaches to a putative national past have been rather more diffident.[33] Uganda is cut across by tensions and conflicts – ethnic, socio-economic, regional, spiritual – but is also characterised by shifting coalitions and alliances, by lines of cooperation and productive contact. What does all this mean, not simply for the daunted author seeking interpretative synthesis, but for conceptualisation of the historical nation itself? Should African nations even *have* or *want* histories? *So what* if they don't have national histories stretching back to the precolonial era? Perhaps this really is a question of developing the history they *need*, and that serves its purpose. Yet of course the peoples living within the nation *do* have precolonial histories, and they *do matter*; their separation from that of the larger political space – the nation – seems a dangerous and unhealthy thing. Above all, there is the question of organic plurality, and the argument that it is only when the deeper past is explored and perhaps even celebrated that the modern nation can ultimately achieve plurality, inclusivity, rootedness, stability. These are not uniquely African questions – comparing the situation in Uganda with the various national history wars since the 1990s around the world, at a time when in Europe, for example, national history had

---

[32] D. Acemoglu, S. Johnson & J. Robinson, 'Reversal of Fortune: geography and institutions in the making of the modern world income distribution', *The Quarterly Journal of Economics*, 117:4 (2002).
[33] Reid, 'States of Anxiety'.

supposedly had its day.[34] And 'national histories' do have enormous implications: for self-identification, plurality, inclusivity, ideas about development, participation, contribution and immigration/migration. An integrated, holistic national history that makes everyone happy is undoubtedly pure fantasy: like unicorns. But in a sense that is not really the point. The exercise itself is the thing, and it is an exercise in temporal demography: who and what populates the past?

It is also worth reiterating the point that all nations have violent roots and are characterised by violence; this is not – despite some popular and enduring misconceptions – something that is a peculiarly 'African' condition, nor is the so-called 'tribalism' that threatened to consume Uganda between the 1960s and the 1980s, and in some ways still does. There are plenty of fissures and fractures and conflicts, of course. Like all nations, Uganda is the product of violence and inequity; like all nations, too, Uganda is the product of a complex network of frontiers and rough edges, which act as buffers against neighbours but which are also places of creativity and loci of control. The state can control troublesome people there, but those troublesome people also contribute ineffably to the nation's sense of itself, and its power, and very often in very practical terms; those populations paradoxically not only act as the necessary 'other' but often contribute the manpower to the economic projects and the military and security apparatus necessary to the nation's own development and self-management. At the same time, however, successive regimes have struggled to realise and articulate the nation, with the result that history wars have very much defined modern Ugandan politics and culture. Historical culture, historical consciousness, has so often been mobilised not at the national level but a range of sub-national levels: the past has had many uses for the component groups of the nation. But ultimately, as an interconnected, discrete field of reciprocal engagement – both violent and otherwise – yes, Uganda has a history.

Uganda Studied

The story of Uganda's birth and growth can be usefully encapsulated in a series of generational snapshots, beginning in around 1900, when

---

[34] See, again, Black, *Contesting History*.

administrator Harry Johnston was not only able to write of the problems but also of the possibilities of the newly-formed Uganda Protectorate. At the heart of his optimistic assessment – born, naturally,
of a confidence in the British imperial mission – was an emphasis on
the positive role of Christianity, which had been introduced barely a
generation earlier, and on the civilising potential of the kingdom of
Buganda.[35] The latter, whose political sophistication had so impressed
European visitors, sat at the privileged centre of the colonial order.
Much progress could be claimed even since Frederick, later Lord,
Lugard's description of Britain's role in the region just a decade before –
Lugard who had made no small contribution to Ugandan history himself as the man who had maintained the Imperial British East Africa
Company's precarious presence in the area, and who had ultimately
ensured early Anglo-Ganda collaboration in the state-building project
underway in the course of the 1890s.[36] By the 1930s, Uganda's rapid
development was captured in a comprehensive survey by Thomas and
Scott, still a rich historical resource, in which they were able to describe
a territory of wondrous diversity but one in which wild terrain was
being traversed by railways and macadam roads, and in which commercial agriculture was conquering the African bush; and of course
they found time to include information on the best places to view
wildlife or – if one preferred – to shoot it.[37]

A generation later, Uganda was on the cusp of independence, and
while the historian Kenneth Ingham could write assuredly in 1958 of
the 'making' of Uganda in what was one of the first modern histories of the country,[38] others focused on what seemed to be intractable
problems for the fledgling nation. The journalist Harold Ingrams
wrote of nationhood as an 'elixir', but in his 1960 book that potion
remained elusive, and it was the 'crisis' of nationhood that seemed set
to dominate Uganda's political horizon for the foreseeable future.[39]
To Ingrams, as to many other observers of Africa in the late colonial period, diversity was a problem. To Scott and Thomas, it was
something marvellous, and their Uganda had been an exotic colonial menagerie; now, however, on the cusp of nationhood, multiplicity

[35] Sir H.H. Johnston, *The Uganda Protectorate*, 2 vols (London, 1902).
[36] F.D. Lugard, *The Rise of our East African Empire*, 2 vols (Edinburgh &
London, 1893).
[37] Thomas & Scott, *Uganda*.   [38] Ingham, *Making of Modern Uganda*.
[39] H. Ingrams, *Uganda: a crisis of nationhood* (London, 1960).

threatened to tear the nation apart even at the point of its creation. Ingrams was writing at the close of a tumultuous decade, in which Buganda had demanded ever greater autonomy from Uganda, and the *Kabaka?* (king) had been exiled to London for two years for the trouble he had caused the British. And that was the problem: Buganda was, in effect – and certainly many Ganda saw the kingdom as – a nation within a nation, and the political scientist David Apter explored the issue of 'neo-traditionalism' in his study of the kingdom in the same period.[40] Of particular interest was the ethno-nationalist organisation *Kabaka Yekka* ('The King Alone'), which agitated for autonomy within and even secession from Uganda. Buganda certainly drew much of the scholarly gaze in the early 1960s, as it seemed the ancient state held the key to the larger nation's success or failure.[41] More broadly, the concern in this period was the supposed antagonism between nation and tribe: would 'tribalism', of which Buganda was the aggressive exemplar, undo the nation?[42]

Fast forward another quarter-century, and the answer was no, but it had come pretty close. If the 'moment' in the late 1950s and early 1960s had seen the nation as, at best, a work in progress, then the late 1980s and early 1990s found Uganda battered and barely afloat. The nation had been used and abused in the interim, wracked by violence and a succession of catastrophic leaders; little wonder, then, that the literature in our snapshot for the period was all about reconstruction, moving beyond trauma, rebuilding lives and institutions. Thus a terrific freeze-frame is provided by Paul Wiebe and Cole Dodge in an edited collection surveying the devastation and contemplating possible solutions.[43] Pioneering collections of essays assembled by Michael Twaddle and Holger Bernt Hansen likewise considered a range of social, economic and political challenges and prospects.[44] Phares Mutibwa's history of Uganda since independence, written at a critical moment in that very history, was unsurprisingly boisterous,

---

[40] Apter, *Political Kingdom.*   [41] For example, Fallers (ed.), *The King's Men.*

[42] P.H. Gulliver (ed.), *Tradition and Transition in East Africa: studies of the tribal element in the modern era* (London, 1969).

[43] P.D. Wiebe & C.P. Dodge (eds.), *Beyond Crisis: development issues in Uganda* (Kampala, 1987).

[44] Notably, for this period, M. Twaddle & H.B. Hansen (eds.), *Uganda Now: between decay and development* (London, 1988) and M. Twaddle & H.B. Hansen (eds.), *Changing Uganda: the dilemmas of structural adjustment and revolutionary change* (London, 1991).

dramatic, but also markedly reflective, characterised by a sense, almost, of bemusement that Uganda had somehow survived.[45] It also concluded on an optimistic note, rooted in a sense that Yoweri Museveni and the NRM might just have discovered the elixir of which Ingrams had written thirty years earlier. But their solution was a combination of careful political management – restoration of the kingdoms, no-party elections – and economic liberalism: the nation was to be restored by the smelling salts of the free market, and Uganda under Museveni was poised to become the poster-child of structural adjustment and beloved of international financial institutions and the donor community. This brings us to our own 'moment'. Assessments of Museveni's Uganda are at best ambivalent, and mostly hinge on the problem that it is, still, Museveni's Uganda: the complexity and hybridity of the President's creeping authoritarianism; simmering internal (and external) conflicts and the potential for their escalation, as well as for their containment; the looming challenges for an oil-producing nation.[46] Underlying these analyses, again, is a sense – even if not explicitly articulated – that Uganda has come some way and achieved a great deal, but once more the country is on the approach to a critical moment, potentially more significant than anything the NRM has yet faced. Our own era is characterised, then, by mounting anxieties. A Whiggish reading of this literary romp might suggest a nation increasingly at ease with itself, and certainly ever more resilient: at each stage, naturally enough, its historical ballast has grown weightier, and while experience can and has been divisive, it has also forged an ever-stronger national community. Yet the diverse human experiences encompassed within the relatively compact space that is Uganda have inspired several generations of writers, autochthonous and foreign, scholarly and otherwise; and that vast body of literature is suggestive not of an integrated national past, but of a rather more atomised, fragmented set of histories.

---

[45] P. Mutibwa, *Uganda since Independence: a story of unfulfilled hopes* (London, 1992).
[46] A.M. Tripp, *Museveni's Uganda: paradoxes of power in a hybrid regime* (Boulder CO, 2010); S. Lindemann, 'Just another change of guard? Broad-based politics and civil war in Museveni's Uganda', *African Affairs*, 110/440 (2011); International Crisis Group, *Uganda: no resolution to growing tensions* (Africa Report No. 187, Nairobi/Brussels, 5 April 2012); B. Shepherd, *Oil in Uganda: international lessons for success* (Chatham House, London, February 2013).

We can trace that body of literature to the middle decades of the nineteenth century. It has become something of a shibboleth that late nineteenth-century Europeans routinely declared Africa to have 'no history' worth speaking of – a judgement based largely on the lack of written documentation in the vast majority of African societies, sub-Saharan at any rate.[47] The reality is a little more complex. In fact a great many Europeans were deeply interested in Africa's history between the 1870s and the 1900s, and it was only with the consolidation of colonial rule in the 1910s and 1920s – and the increasing supremacy of economic agendas – that the continent's past became severed from its supposedly stunted present. During the era of the partition itself, the past mattered a great deal – and in particular, the histories of *states*, for it was this political form which was the mark of relative civilisation, and with which Europeans could most readily empathise and ultimately establish functioning relations. Historical enquiry was part of a process by which Europeans sought legitimate and stable partners in the civilising mission. As such, explorers, missionaries and sundry adventurers frequently looked for the centres and symbols of power and sovereignty, and embarked on quests for ancient lineages and genealogies; these were aspects of social structure which also, of course, denoted nobility and aristocracy, and which were deemed critical if the imperial mission was to have any chance of success. Some kind of historical evolution was at least implicit in the discovery of hierarchy, of rank and status, for this was the *sine qua non* of the semi-civilised state, even if a culturally and geographically beleaguered one. Europeans were thus especially fixated with emperors, kings, 'big men' and princely heredity; their gaze was drawn inexorably towards indications of despotism, absolutism, savage omnipotence – the peculiar product of Africa's turbulent historical trajectory. In their turn, African historians themselves both informed European visions of the past, and would enter this dynamic epistemological marketplace on their own account.

In terms of written commentary, Ugandan historiography dates to the mid-nineteenth century. On their joint expedition across present-day Tanzania in the late 1850s, Richard Burton and John Hanning Speke were both told of powerful kingdoms north of Lake Victoria,

---

[47] For example, J. Vansina, *Paths in the Rainforests: toward a history of political tradition in Equatorial Africa* (London, 1990), xi.

and in particular of the dominant kingdom of Buganda; and although neither travelled there on this occasion, each provided sketchy surveys of Buganda's recent history and current state in their respective accounts of the expedition.[48] These are, in effect, the first contemporary recordings of 'Ugandan' history, albeit second-hand. But it was Speke, on his follow-up expedition to the region to prove that the Nile did indeed flow out of Lake Victoria, who was the first European to visit both Buganda and neighbouring Bunyoro, in 1862, and who in many respects laid the foundations of regional historiography.[49] This time he travelled around the western side of Lake Victoria, through Buddu *ssaza* ('county') and into Buganda, where he stayed for six months; thereafter, he headed north, through Bunyoro and thence homeward towards Egypt. His account of this journey contained extensive historical data and speculation, of variable quality and utility. Speke provided the first king-list for Buganda, for example – it comprised eight names – and an account of state-formation in the area, a process which he famously ascribed to the arrival from the north of lighter-skinned, and therefore more intelligent and culturally advanced, invaders at some point in the distant past. This would become known as the 'Hamitic myth', and would distort comprehension of the region's history for many decades.[50] The idea of Buganda's comparatively advanced civilised state, *vis-à-vis* the surrounding states and societies, would prove remarkably durable, and indeed Speke's writings were representative of a general European fascination with the kingdom at the expense of others in the area.

Thus began a relationship conducted not only in the 'unknown' centre of the continent but carried out, too, along the darkest borderlands between fact and fiction. The European connection was by no means Ugandans' oldest external relationship, but it was of escalating and eventually enormous significance. Drawing on 'oral information', Burton's 'northern races' – as he described the inhabitants of Buganda, Bunyoro and Karagwe – were

---

[48] R. F. Burton, *The Lake Regions of Central Africa* (first published in 2 vols, London, 1860; republished in one volume, New York, 1995); J. H. Speke, *What Led to the Discovery of the Source of the Nile* (Edinburgh & London, 1864).

[49] J. H. Speke, *Journal of the Discovery of the Source of the Nile* (Edinburgh & London, 1863).

[50] C.G. Seligman, *Races of Africa* (London, 1939), perpetuating the fundamental idea, was republished several times, and achieved a fourth edition in 1966.

superior in civilisation and social constitution to the other tribes of Eastern and Central Africa.... [T]hey have built extensive and regular settlements, and they reverence even to worship a single despot, who rules
with a rigor which in Europe would be called barbarity. Having thrown
off the rude equality of their neighbours, they recognise ranks in society;
there is order among men, and some idea of honour in women; they add
to commerce credit, without which commerce can hardly exist; and they
hospitably entertain strangers and guests...Their heads are of a superior
cast; the regions where the reflective faculties and the moral sentiments, especially benevolence, are placed, rise high; the nose is more of the Caucasian
type...and the expression of the countenance is soft, kindly, and not defi-
cient in intelligence.[51]

In other words, their heads were the right shape, they had a strong
king and their women were chaste. A few years later, Speke entered the
kingdom of Buganda. Somewhere in southern Buddu, he fell in love:

I felt inclined to stop here a month, everything was so very pleasant. The
temperature was perfect. The roads, as indeed they were everywhere, were
as broad as our coach-roads, cut through the long grasses, straight over the
hills and down through the woods in the dells – a strange contrast to the
wretched tracks in all the adjacent countries.... Wherever I strolled I saw
nothing but richness, and what ought to be wealth. The whole land was a
picture of quiescent beauty, with a boundless sea in the background.[52]

And so Speke felt able to imagine a history in which the region had
been populated by a conquering superior race, Caucasian in provenance, who had fashioned a crude but markedly superior culture out
of the lush landscape, and imposed order on their little corner of the
world. It was a particular European interpretation of Uganda's immigrant past which proved remarkably enduring.[53] It was a myth – one
that sat well with nineteenth-century British historical thought, with
an emphasis on the inexorable sweep of civilised conquering foreigners; it was a gross, if not wilful, miscomprehension of the dynamics
of the region's deeper past, which was altogether more complicated.
Meanwhile, Speke's roads were profoundly important, and loaded with
meaning; they appealed powerfully to the Victorian mind, and spoke to
a supremacy in intellect and outlook. For Britain, an especially potent
and enduring vision of the Ugandan nation was thus created on the

---

[51] Burton, *Lake Regions*, 391–2.   [52] Speke, *Journal*, 274.
[53] Ibid., Chapter IX, 'History of the Wahuma'.

well-travelled highway running west of Lake Victoria; an idea formed
of the natural political and moral order of things between Speke taking
leave of the king of Karagwe, Rumanika (who he also rather liked), in
December 1861, and his arrival at the Ganda royal capital in January
1862. Uganda's modern reordering lay here, in terms of the external
legitimacy which was to prove vital in consolidating a particular vision
of the territory.

Farther north, meanwhile, Baker's descriptions of his experiences
focus on apparently ceaseless internecine conflict among the Acholi,
and the childish, pathetic behaviour of Kamurasi of Bunyoro. At one
point, having supposedly protected the kingdom from slave-raiders,
Baker finds himself elucidating to a quivering Kamurasi the power of
the British flag: 'I explained that the flag was well known, and might be
seen in every part of the world . . . Seizing the opportunity, he demanded
it, saying, "What shall I do when you leave my country and take that
with you? . . . Give me the flag, and they will be afraid to attack me!"'
Baker refused. Kamurasi, '[t]rue to his uncontrollable instinct of beg-
ging . . . replied, "If you cannot give me the flag, give me at least that
little double-barrelled rifle that you do not require as you are going
home . . . ."'[54] His description of Bunyoro as a land of violent primitives
hostile to the outside world stuck, and proved influential into the late
nineteenth century and beyond. And in Speke's account, too, Kamurasi
is oddly childlike, insecure, always unfavourably compared to his great
rival Mutesa in Buganda. Of course, no one is spared the racialised
characterisations which indicate the savage immaturity evident in *all*
Africans; Mutesa, for example, is frequently depicted by Speke as a
brutally unstable young man, the product of a society which is nau-
seatingly cruel, its members seemingly impervious to the suffering of
others.[55] But in the British mind there is a great gulf between Buganda
and everyone else, and it is the receptiveness of the former, their willingness to become something else, to *improve*, which is of cardinal
importance. It is captured in the journalist and explorer Henry Mor-
ton Stanley's account. In 1875, Stanley purportedly, and singlehandedly, converts a now-matured Mutesa to Christianity; and the *kabaka*
declares to the explorer, 'Stamlee . . . say to the white people, when you

[54] S. Baker, *The Albert N'yanza: Great basin of the Nile and explorations of the
Nile sources*, 2 vols (London, 1866) II, 435.

[55] Speke, *Journal*, 356, 412; A. Kagwa (tr. & ed. M.S.M. Kiwanuka), *The Kings of
Buganda* (Nairobi, 1971), 140–41.

write to them, that I am like a man sitting in darkness, or born blind, and that all I ask is that I may be taught how to see, and I shall continue a Christian while I live'. Stanley, famously, did just that.[56]

The Church Missionary Society responded to Stanley's missive, as did – much to the annoyance of the Anglicans – the French Catholic order based in Algiers, the White Fathers, who arrived two years after the CMS, in 1879.[57] The souls that each would win in the decade that followed were, in political terms, critical to the balance of colonial interests and the very nature of the territory itself. Stanley would later return to Uganda to rescue Emin Pasha, the beleaguered 'administrator' of the ill-fated Equatoria Province who was trapped north of Lake Albert. Again, what would become northern Uganda was depicted as unstable, brutally chaotic, and now – more ominously – under the shadow of the sinister Mahdist state.[58] Such miscomprehensions proved critical in shaping British perceptions of particular groups, later to become marginalised within the colonial order, while at the same time the Ganda proved themselves much more adept at co-option. The era of European exploration, then, was also that of the British imagination,[59] and in the years that preceded the appearance of Lugard's IBEAC force in 1890, land was racialised, associated with hierarchies of political and economic order, and centres and peripheries crystallised accordingly. Buganda was indubitably one of the key actors in the region – although the kingdom's dominant position was waning, and Bunyoro was resurgent – and therefore it was understandable that foreigners were drawn to it. Yet this was also a matter of geographical serendipity. Most outsiders, whether Europeans or coastal Arab merchants, arrived in the region from south of Lake Victoria; they either

---

[56] H.M. Stanley, *Through the Dark Continent*, 2 vols (London, 1899; 1st ed., 1878) I, 255; and see Stanley's letter to the *Daily Telegraph*, 15 November 1875, quoted in Ingrams, *Uganda*, 7–10.

[57] R. Oliver, *The Missionary Factor in East Africa* (London, 1965), Chapter 1, provides a handy narrative overview.

[58] The key sources for – and by – Emin Pasha and his relief expedition include: G. Schweinfurth *et al.* (eds.), *Emin Pasha in Central Africa* (London, 1888), G. Schweitzer (ed.), *Emin Pasha: his life and work*, 2 vols (London, 1898), H.M. Stanley, *In Darkest Africa*, 2 vols (London, 1890), A.J. Mounteney-Jephson, *Emin Pasha and the Rebellion at the Equator* (London, 1890).

[59] For an entertaining and informative overview, T.C. McCaskie, 'Cultural Encounters: Britain and Africa in the nineteenth century', in A. Porter (ed.), *The Oxford History of the British Empire, Vol. III: the nineteenth century* (Oxford & New York, 1999).

marched around the lake on its western side or travelled across it by canoe. Comparatively fewer attempted the more arduous trek from the north, although long-distance trade was also developing in this direction, too, in the course of the nineteenth century. It meant that the Ganda were the region's main gatekeepers, and they generally did very well at both welcoming foreigners – although there were stresses and strains along the way – and imposing themselves on them. From Speke onwards, Europeans were intrigued by this ordered, hierarchical society, with its well-dressed and articulate population, its martial prowess and its broad, straight roads; it was a prosperous, agricultural hub of civilisation – savage, in its way, of course, but everything is relative – in a land of darkness and barbarity, inhabited by bellicose natives living under rudimentary despotisms and, worse, half-naked cattle-keepers.[60]

Thirteen years later after Speke, Stanley came to Buganda and recorded more detail on the kingdom's history, and with rather more panache: the relevant chapter in his book is organised into subsections with such headings as 'Kibaga, the flying warrior', 'Wakinguru, the champion', 'Kamanaya, the conqueror of the Wakedi', 'Suna, the cruel', 'Namujurilwa, the Achilles of Uganda' and so on.[61] Most interestingly, Stanley's king-list extended to thirty-five names – rather more than Speke had gathered. A fair amount of ink has been spilt on this issue, and indeed on the fact that subsequent king-lists varied in length and order of names;[62] in sum, this represented a dramatic opening up of the 'historical space', and was driven by the energy with which African informants entered that space. The late nineteenth century was a period of turmoil and fierce political and religious competition – which frequently exploded into open violence, as Buganda and Bunyoro clashed on their increasingly volatile borders, Buganda fought

---

[60] The complaint, reflecting a slight exaggeration, that when foreigners came to write about Uganda they invariably wrote about Buganda is not as true as it perhaps once was, but more has probably been written on the history and culture of Buganda than on all the other states and societies in Uganda combined. This was expressed to the author on his first visit to Uganda in 1995, while undertaking doctoral research on, alas, Buganda.

[61] Stanley, *Dark Continent*, I, Chapter 14.

[62] For example D. Henige, '"The Disease of Writing": Ganda and Nyoro kinglists in a newly literate world', in J.C. Miller (ed.), *The African Past Speaks* (Folkestone & Hamden, 1980); B. Ray, *Myth, Ritual and Kingship in Buganda* (New York, 1991), 207–9; C.C. Wrigley, *Kingship and State: the Buganda dynasty* (Cambridge, 1996), 26–7 & *passim*.

a civil war, and then a small group of British army officers arrived, heralding the encroachment of the imperial frontier. These events drove interest in the deep past among both Ugandans and Europeans.

Where Speke and Stanley led, others followed in their historical enquiries, and many of the missionary accounts in particular contained historical information of varying quality and credibility. In the early 1880s, Robert Felkin and Charles Wilson of the CMS wrote on aspects of Buganda's past in their book-length account of ministry and travel in the region;[63] but it was in the late 1880s and early 1890s that there was especially intense scrutiny of Buganda's history in print, against a backdrop of political crisis in the kingdom, and no doubt as part of a missionary-led interventionist lobby. Alexander Mackay and Robert Ashe were foremost in that lobby, and offered insights into the region's history with a view to explaining both its degraded state but also its enormous potential for development, given British civilising intervention.[64] Meanwhile, official or semi-official representatives of foreign interests published their own accounts of Buganda's historical development – even if, as in the case of Captain J. R. L. Macdonald, these were sometimes cobbled together using Stanley and a handful of other recent European sources.[65] The German adventurer Karl Peters, who was briefly in Buganda at the beginning of the 1890s in an abortive attempt to secure the area for Bismarck, sought in a rather fantastical thesis to make connections between the Ganda and ancient Egypt.[66] The British emissary Gerald Portal produced a somewhat more prosaic survey, and was more concerned with the political evolution of the kingdom, depicting an impossibly intricate and hierarchical system which was largely at the mercy ('as in England during the Middle Ages') of particularly charismatic and brutal monarchs.[67] By the time the missionary John Roscoe, a prolific author and amateur anthropologist, was compiling his own encyclopaedic interpretation of

---

[63] C.T. Wilson & R.W. Felkin, *Uganda and the Egyptian Soudan*, 2 vols (London, 1882); see also R.W. Felkin, 'Notes on the Waganda tribe of Central Africa', *Proceedings of the Royal Society of Edinburgh*, 13 (1885–6).

[64] A.M. Mackay (ed. J.W. Harrison), *A.M. Mackay, Pioneer Missionary of the Church Missionary Society to Uganda* (London, 1890); R.P. Ashe, *Chronicles of Uganda* (London, 1894).

[65] J.R.L. Macdonald, *Soldiering and Surveying in British East Africa* (London, 1897).

[66] K. Peters (tr. H.W. Dulcken), *New Light on Dark Africa* (London, 1891).

[67] G. Portal, *The British Mission to Uganda in 1893* (London, 1894).

the precolonial kingdom in the early 1900s, he was very clear about the possibilities offered by oral history:

[T]aking into consideration the remarkably accurate memories of the people, their graphic power to recount the details of events long past, and their conservatism in religious ceremonies and social customs, the reader will recognise that it is possible to obtain from them a fairly accurate account of past ages.[68]

Built into this expression of wonderment at the 'accuracy' of native history-telling, of course, is the notion that the past (substitutable with 'tradition') was somehow unchanging – which in turn gives it its adhesive social power. Roscoe, who supplied 'raw data' to the Cambridge anthropologist Sir James Frazier, represented the beginnings of semi-professional ethnographic history, and he replicated his approach to Buganda – focusing on the power of ritual and symbolism in the kingdom's political and cultural development – in later studies of Bunyoro and Ankole.[69] Meanwhile, this was by no means a monopoly of the Anglican mission, as the wealth of historical detail in Father Julien Gorju's regional survey demonstrates.[70] Gorju was a leading figure in the White Fathers mission. Some years later, the prolific Italian missionary Father Joseph Pasquale Crazzolara worked extensively on the ethnography and languages of the north, mainly the Luo-speaking peoples.[71]

A historical component – whether implicit or explicit – was critical to the functioning of indirect rule in Uganda, and elsewhere in British Africa, as described most effectively by Frederick Lugard in his 1923 treatise.[72] In many respects, indirect rule – the preferred principle of imperial governance in much of Africa, whereby colonial administrations governed via local, 'legitimate' elites – involved the recognition and co-opting of indigenous history and 'tradition' into the colonial

---

[68] J. Roscoe, *The Baganda: an account of their native customs and beliefs* (London, 1911), 3.

[69] J. Roscoe, *The Bakitara or Banyoro* (Cambridge, 1923); J. Roscoe, *The Banyankole* (Cambridge, 1923).

[70] J. Gorju, *Entre le Victoria, l'Albert et l'Edouard* (Rennes, 1920).

[71] Notably, see J.P. Crazzolara, *A Study of the Acooli Language: grammar and vocabulary* (London, 1938) and J.P. Crazzolara, *The Lwoo*, 3 vols (Verona, 1950–54).

[72] F.D. Lugard, *The Dual Mandate in British Tropical Africa* (Edinburgh & London, 1923), *passim*.

system of hierarchy, deference, history and 'tradition'.[73] The system at least *implied* some understanding of 'the native's' past – an understanding based, in the Ugandan context, on half a century of European historical writing and, increasingly, on local historical production, as we see further. An example of the supposed conjunction of Ganda and British histories/traditions is the case of King's College, Budo, a public school established by the British in 1905–6 on a hill near Kampala which had also been the site, in the past, of the coronation of Ganda kings.[74] Terry Ranger proposed that Budo was a striking instance of 'the invention of tradition' in the colonial context;[75] and although Ranger himself later modified his own 'invention' thesis and cautioned against overstating the case,[76] it is nonetheless noteworthy that historical (sub)consciousness was indeed a critical driver in the formation of the early colonial order.

Of course, this was not all one-way traffic. During this period Africans also created or revised histories, at least partly in response to new political markets and the demand for *historical knowledge*; Ganda historians themselves would respond to the opportunities presented by the late Victorian epistemological marketplace. Newly Protestant elites responded most successfully to the new opportunities, their intellectual engagement with the British at least as important as their military and political partnership in the 1890s and 1900s.[77] Yet this needs to be understood not only in the context of the competitive new political marketplace which had opened up as a result of the 'scramble' for Africa but also as coming at the end of a turbulent, often violent, and certainly transformative nineteenth century. Africa's nineteenth century had been an era of stress and change, and it was also characterised by intense historical interest, and continual historicisation. Societies

---

[73] See also D. Cannadine, *Ornamentalism: how the British saw their empire* (London, 2001).

[74] Ingrams, *Uganda*, 123–5.

[75] T.O. Ranger, 'The invention of tradition in colonial Africa', in T.O. Ranger & E. Hobsbawm (eds.), *The Invention of Tradition* (Cambridge, 1983), 221–3.

[76] T.O. Ranger, 'The Invention of Tradition Revisited: the case of Africa', in T.O. Ranger & O. Vaughan (eds.), *Legitimacy and the State in Twentieth-Century Africa* (Basingstoke, 1993); see also Spear, 'Neo-traditionalism'.

[77] See R.J. Reid, 'Ghosts in the Academy: historians and historical consciousness in the making of modern Uganda', *Comparative Studies in Society and History*, 56:2 (2014) and J. Rowe, 'Myth, Memoir and Moral Admonition: Luganda historical writing, 1893–1969', *Uganda Journal*, 33:1 (1969), 17–40 & 33:2 (1969), 217–19.

sought new ways of investigating, resurrecting and contextualising the past. In an era of upheaval and crisis, it had never been more critical to retrieve certain aspects of the past, and to reflect on their significance. Writing was novel, clearly, in the sense that as a form of representation and expression it was only introduced in the 1870s, and then haltingly; and it only began to become a mainstream (if elite) form of expression in the 1900s. Even so, written expression was, at least in the late nineteenth and early twentieth centuries, only an extension of a rich oral culture. Writing is oral; orality can be written; and the new forms of written text reflected, it can safely be assumed, much deeper cultures of history and testimony which had characterised much of the Ugandan region for a very long time. Still, there was something about the written text that lent itself to permanence and the 'definitive', as various parties sought to affirm long-held (or, indeed, recent) views of the region and the world, as far as it was understood, and it has become commonplace to suggest that because the first written texts introduced into Uganda were scriptures, the written word was associated with essential truth.[78] Thus our sources for much of this book – for the 'professional' reconstruction of the past – are also themselves key historical actors. They were not autonomous recorders of 'events', detached from the societies on which they wrote; they were partisan political and cultural leaders, for whom historical writing had *purpose*, and thus the Ugandan writers with whom we will become acquainted were deeply embedded within particular political projects. Yet in another sense they *were* also historians, not just latent primary sources awaiting a later generation of professional scholars to pick up their works, dust them down and deploy them in pursuit of historical 'truth'. *They* were scholars, too – the forerunners of the Ugandan academicians of the 1960s; and as such one or two of them have made it into the bigger scholarly surveys of global historical writing.[79] Above all, just as in the nineteenth century there was little distinction between political power and cultural knowledge, so in the early twentieth century there was no separation between historical work and political authority.

The father of African historical writing in Uganda is Apolo Kagwa, who had become *katikiro* or chief minister of Buganda in 1889 and

---

[78] Again, see Henige, ' "The disease of writing"'.
[79] For example, D. Woolf, *A Global History of History* (Cambridge, 2011), 443.

who would swiftly emerge as the dominant political figure of the age, both in Buganda and across the wider Protectorate. For Kagwa – Protestant convert and close ally of the early British administration – the writing of history was not merely the result of political dominance; it was one of its causes, and he seized with gusto the opportunities presented by his acquisition of a printing press which enabled him to create the vision of a Protestant Buganda. Kagwa wrote prolifically about the kings, customs and clans of Buganda, the kingdom which he implicitly or explicitly sought to place at the centre of regional history.[80] If Kagwa was the pioneer, others quickly followed, though they were not always willing to emulate him uncritically, and debates surrounding a range of historical issues unfurled in the pages of *Ebifa mu Buganda* ('Events in Buganda'), a monthly journal founded in 1907 by the CMS; and in *Munno* ('Your Friend'), a rival organ launched by the White Fathers in 1911.[81] Similar debates and interventions would later regularly appear in the pages of the English-language *Uganda Journal*, launched in 1934 as the organ of the Uganda Society. Newspapers proliferated in the 1920s and 1930s, too, though many disappeared as quickly as they had appeared.[82] In the 1930s, ageing representatives of the generation which had experienced the civil wars and the advent of British rule in the late nineteenth century went into print with an array of memoir, historical work and moral instruction: Albert Lugolobi, Bartolomayo Zimbe, James Miti and Kagwa's one-time secretary Ham Mukasa.[83]

Ganda writers dominated the literary scene in the early decades of the twentieth century, a reflection of – and underpinning – the political order in the British Protectorate. But in time authors from a range

---

[80] For example, A. Kagwa's *Basekabaka be Buganda* ('The Kings of Buganda') first appeared in 1901; the most commonly used English edition is that edited by Kiwanuka and published in 1971. Kagwa's *Empisa za Buganda* ('Customs of the Baganda') appeared in 1907, and his *Ebika bya Buganda* (dealing with the clans of the kingdom) in 1912.

[81] Complete runs of these early journals are available in Makerere University Library.

[82] Rowe, 'Myth', 23, 219; Reid, 'Ghosts', 359.

[83] Lugolobi's *Ekitabo Mbulire* ('Let me tell') was written in 1933, Zimbe's *Buganda ne Kabaka* in 1939 and Miti's three-volume *History of Buganda* around 1938. Mukasa's three-volume *Simuda Nyuma* ('Don't turn back') was written over several years, with volumes one and two dated 1938 and 1942 respectively, while the third volume was only rediscovered among his papers in 1964: Reid, 'Ghosts', 360.

of backgrounds – though invariably from an educated political elite – wrote up their own kingdoms' histories with an eye on the present. Y.K. Lubogo sought to carve out space for Busoga in the increasingly competitive political marketplace that was mid-colonial Uganda, and thus wrote up his mammoth history of Busoga between the early 1920s and the late 1930s. He intended to prove that the Soga had been 'a complete tribe for many generations now with firmly established boundaries', even though the narrative recounted extensive inter-clan warfare in careful detail.[84] In Bunyoro, chief minister Petero Bikunya sought to emulate Kagwa in 1927;[85] and the *mukama* of Bunyoro himself, writing under a pseudonym, tried to put the record straight with a series of more detailed historical essays in the *Uganda Journal* in the mid-1930s.[86] A decade later, John Nyakatura, a Nyoro official in the colonial administration, produced his monumental history of Bunyoro in large part to counter the Ganda-dominant historical and political narratives of the late colonial moment, and specifically to address the painful question of the 'Lost Counties' – territory which had been seized from Bunyoro in the 1890s and given to Buganda during the wars of Anglo-Ganda conquest.[87] At the same time, Princess Lucy Olive Katyanku wrote an admiring biography of Kabalega's son, Andereya Duhaga II, *mukama* of Bunyoro between 1902 and 1924.[88] Local historical writing elsewhere in Uganda was slower to develop, but mention might be made here of the first major vernacular study of Ankole, produced by Lazaro Kamugungunu and A.G. Katate in 1955.[89] Today, it is perfectly common for oral informants to point exasperated researchers in the direction of these great texts – Lubogo, Kagwa, Kamugungunu and Katate, and Nyakatura – which have apparently, in some ways, acquired the scriptural status which their authors intended at the outset.

---

[84] Y.K. Lubogo, *A History of Busoga* (translated & unpublished manuscript in Makerere University Library, Kampala, 1960), 3.

[85] P. Bikunya, *Ky'Abakama ba Bunyoro* (London, 1927).

[86] The three parts of 'The Kings of Bunyoro-Kitara' appeared in the *Uganda Journal* between 1935 and 1937.

[87] First published in 1947, the most accessible English translation is G.N. Uzoigwe (ed.), *Anatomy of an African Kingdom: a history of Bunyoro-Kitara* (New York, 1973).

[88] Princess L.O. Katyanku & S. Bulera, *The Life of Duhaga II* (Nairobi, 1950).

[89] L. Kamugungunu & A.G. Katate, *Abagabe b'Ankole* (Dar es Salaam, 1955).

Yet it was in the 1950s and 1960s that Ugandan history was born
as a professional discipline, in line with intellectual developments in
Africa – as well as in Europe and North America – more broadly. Much
of the work was undertaken by anthropologists and political scientists
as well as by a new generation of professional historians, each of whom
recognised the significance, and the richness, of the region's past.[90]
And again, Buganda was of particular interest to scholars, owing to
its prominence in the body politic, and indeed the comparative wealth
of sources available.[91] But increasingly there was interest – again
as much from anthropologists as historians – in Bunyoro, Busoga,
Ankole, Lango and Teso, and other, long-neglected parts of the late
colonial and early postcolonial state.[92] These in-depth studies, produced during what may be considered a 'golden age' for Ugandan and
African history, greatly expanded the corpus of historical knowledge
and interpretation. Moreover, this professional revolution – while
instigated to some extent by foreigners – was driven by the Africanisa-
tion of the academy, as in the course of the 1960s a new set of Ugandan
historians pioneered work on various aspects of the country's past,

---

[90] A.I. Richards (ed.), *East African Chiefs: a study of political development in
some Uganda and Tanganyika tribes* (London, 1959); Ingrams, *Uganda*; Apter,
Political Kingdom; Gulliver (ed.), *Tradition and Transition*.

[91] A selection would include: D.A. Low & R.C. Pratt, *Buganda and British
Overrule 1900–1955* (London, 1960), M. Southwold, *Bureaucracy and
Chiefship in Buganda*, East African Studies 14, (Kampala,1961), P.C.W.
Gutkind, *The Royal Capital of Buganda: a study of internal conflict and
external ambiguity* (The Hague, 1963), Fallers (ed.), *King's Men*, M.S.M.
Kiwanuka, *A History of Buganda: from the foundation of the kingdom to
1900* (London, 1971), Low, *Buganda in Modern History*, M. Wright, *Buganda
in the Heroic Age* (Nairobi, 1971).

[92] L.A. Fallers, *Bantu Bureaucracy: a century of political evolution among the
Basoga of Uganda* (Chicago, 1956, 1965); J.C.D. Lawrance, *The Iteso: fifty
years of change in a Nilo-Hamitic tribe of Uganda* (London, 1957); J. Beattie,
The Nyoro State (Oxford, 1971); S. Karugire, *A History of the Kingdom of
Nkore in Western Uganda to 1896* (Oxford, 1971); D.W. Cohen, *The
Historical Tradition of Busoga: Mukama and Kintu* (Oxford, 1972); J.
Lamphear, *The Traditional History of the Jie of Uganda* (Oxford, 1976); E.I.
Steinhart, *Conflict and Collaboration: the kingdoms of western Uganda
1890–1907* (Princeton, 1977); J. Tosh, *Clan Leaders and Colonial Chiefs in
Lango: the political history of an East African stateless society circa
1800–1939* (Oxford, 1978); J. Vincent, *Teso in Transformation: the political
economy of peasant and class in Eastern Africa* (Berkeley, 1982). D. Cohen
later edited a set of his original sources in *Toward a Reconstructed Past:
historical texts from Busoga, Uganda* (Baltimore, 1983).

including Semakula Kiwanuka, Samwiri Karugire and Phares Mutibwa. They often did so under the auspices of the mammoth 'History of Uganda' project run out of Makerere University's History Department, headed in the late 1960s by the dynamic Bertin Webster, which aimed at the retrieval of orally transmitted history by undergraduates and postgraduates in their home districts.[93] The department's output at this time was remarkable, including major historical work on northern Uganda for the first time,[94] a series of short books on 'Uganda's Famous Men',[95] and the Makerere History Papers, published by Longman.[96] Other vernacular work, aimed at the preservation of the 'traditional', was published under the auspices of the Uganda Literature Bureau.[97]

It might even be argued that Uganda was 'invented', on some levels, as a result of the great Makerere History project: this was the period when the nation was *conceived* as a historical entity and as the product of African agency in the deeper past as well as in more recent times. The 'History of Uganda' project sought, whether consciously or otherwise, to pull the disparate elements of the nation together and consider the shared experience of being Ugandan. Whether or not it succeeded is perhaps another question, and certainly the events of the next two decades would arguably demonstrate that all the historical work of the 1960s had done was provide the scholarly context for the bloody divisions that would soon open up across Uganda – and which in fact were already opening up even as the Makerere researchers were doing their finest work in the late 1960s and early 1970s. This basic paradox notwithstanding, however, it is worth noting that the especially intense interest in the past in Uganda in the 1950s and 1960s echoed that of the 1890s and 1900s, another similarly turbulent era – seeming to

[93] C. Sicherman, *Becoming an African University: Makerere 1922–2000* (Kampala, 2005), 91–2.

[94] J. B. Webster *et al.*, *The Iteso During the Asonya* (Nairobi, 1973); J.M. Onyango-ku-Odongo & J.B. Webster, *The Central Luo during the Aconya* (Nairobi, 1976).

[95] For example, A.R. Dunbar, *Omukama Chwa II Kabarega* (Nairobi, 1965), S.R. Karugire, *Nuwa Mbaguta* (Nairobi, 1973), M.S.M. Kiwanuka, *Muteesa of Uganda* (Nairobi, 1967).

[96] For example, M.S.M. Kiwanuka, *The Empire of Bunyoro-Kitara: myth or reality?* (Nairobi, 1968).

[97] An example, concerned with the kingdom of Toro, is Y.R.K. Mulindwa & V.K.K.G. Kagoro, *Engeso Zaitu Ez'Obuhangwa* [Our Traditions and Customs], (Kampala, 1968).

validate Jack Plumb's assertion that passions for the past run highest in periods of particular turmoil, even crisis.[98] The writers and researchers of Uganda's 'golden age' in the middle decades of the twentieth century shared much in common with those historians of half a century earlier. This observation is especially pertinent for local authors, but it holds, too, for their foreign associates.

Idi Amin's *coup d'etat* in 1971 brought the 'golden age' to an end, effectively, and for much of the next two decades historical research in, and therefore on, Uganda was almost impossible as a result of political turmoil. The History of Uganda project quickly collapsed, in large part through the disappearance of funds from the United States which had supported it. In the course of the 1970s, many of the pioneers of Ugandan scholarship and postcolonial culture fled into exile. The Ugandan cultural, intellectual and literary community was decimated. But in the late 1980s, with the relative stability engendered by the NRM, scholarship was once again possible. In the last quarter century, historians have continued to explore the intricacies of Buganda's evolution,[99] and, less commonly, modern Bunyoro's travails.[100] Our understanding of aspects of Uganda's socio-economic and cultural history has become immeasurably richer through work on clans, spiritualism, healing, health and gender.[101] Others have sought to reconstruct the distinctive experiences of societies in the northern part of Uganda,

---

[98] J.H. Plumb, *The Death of the Past* (London, 1973; 1st ed., 1969), 33–4.

[99] Ray, *Myth, Ritual and Kingship*; Wrigley, *Kingship and State*; R.J Reid, *Political Power in Pre-Colonial Buganda: economy, society and warfare in the nineteenth century* (Oxford, 2002); H. Hanson, *Landed Obligation: the practice of power in Buganda* (Portsmouth NH, 2003); H. Medard, *Le royaume du Buganda au XIXe siècle: mutations politiques et religieuses d'un ancien etat d'Afrique de l'Est* (Paris, 2007). Two excellent PhD theses have been produced which seek to explore in depth Buganda's twentieth-century political culture: see J.Earle, 'Political Theologies in Late Colonial Buganda', PhD thesis, University of Cambridge, 2012 and A. Stonehouse, 'Peripheral Identities in an African State: a history of ethnicity in the Ugandan kingdom of Buganda', PhD thesis, University of Leeds, 2012.

[100] S. Doyle, *Crisis and Decline in Bunyoro: population and environment in Western Uganda, 1860–1955* (Oxford, 2006).

[101] N. Kodesh, *Beyond the Royal Gaze: clanship and public healing in Buganda* (Charlottesville, 2010); D. Peterson, *Ethnic Patriotism and the East African Revival: a history of dissent c. 1935–1972* (Cambridge, 2012); R. Stephens, *A History of African Motherhood: the case of Uganda, 700–1900* (Cambridge, 2013); S. Doyle, *Before HIV: sexuality, fertility and mortality in East Africa 1900–1980* (Oxford, 2013).

on which much historical research is still needed;[102] some of the most compelling work has been done by intrepid anthropologists and journalists, particularly with a view to explaining the nature and fallout of the war in the north waged by the Lord's Resistance Army against the NRM state.[103] In terms of explicitly historical scholarship, a few have dealt with the very deep past,[104] though most have considered the significance of imperial partition and varied aspects of the colonial experience, and the postcolonial crisis which swiftly followed.[105] In the last few years, there has been a veritable explosion of writing on Uganda, driven in large part by a new cohort of younger scholars, and some of the central themes are usefully encapsulated in a series of special issues of the *Journal of Eastern African Studies*. The first considered 'Uganda from the margins', and includes contemporary analysis of northern Uganda as well as the western border.[106] Another, concerned with 'new themes in Ugandan history', offered insights into sexual behaviour, the politics of intellectual history, the evolution of political identity and colonial-era health policy.[107] A further special issue represented in many ways the most cogent attempt to date to understand the functioning of the state under Idi Amin.[108] In Uganda itself, a range of themes remain important in terms of scholarly output. Historical biography remains popular – such as Samwiri Lwamga Lunyiigo's recent study of Mwanga, which reads like an attempt to reposition the Ganda alongside the Nyoro as 'resisters',[109] and work on Edward Mutesa by

---

[102] R.R. Atkinson, *The Roots of Ethnicity: the origins of the Acholi of Uganda before 1800* (Philadelphia, 1994); M. Leopold, *Inside West Nile: violence, history and representation on an African frontier* (Oxford, 2005).

[103] See, for example, S. Finnstrom, *Living with Bad Surroundings: war, history, and everyday moments in Northern Uganda* (Durham NC & London, 2008), M. Green, *The Wizard of the Nile: the hunt for Africa's most wanted* (London, 2008).

[104] Notably, Schoenbrun, *A Green Place*, Stephens, *African Motherhood*, and Atkinson, *Roots of Ethnicity*.

[105] M. Twaddle, *Kakungulu and the Creation of Uganda* (London, 1993); G. Thompson, *Governing Uganda: British colonial rule and its legacy* (Kampala, 2003); D.A. Low, *Fabrication of Empire: the British and the Uganda Kingdoms, 1890–1902* (Cambridge, 2009).

[106] See the various papers in *Journal of Eastern African Studies*, 6:1 (2012).

[107] *Journal of Eastern African Studies*, 6:3 (2012).

[108] *Journal of Eastern African Studies*, 7:1 (2013).

[109] S.L. Lunyiigo, *Mwanga II: resistance to imposition of British colonial rule in Buganda, 1884–99* (Kampala, 2011).

Godfrey Nsubuga and A.B.K.Kasozi.[110] Charles Peter Mayiga's book on the restoration of Edward Mutesa's son to the throne is written from the author's perspective as the key lawyer involved.[111] And then there is the burgeoning world of memoir and autobiography, beginning with the President's own life story.[112] Museveni's autobiography begins with fond recollections of childhood, and a simpler, happier, often rural life, and has much in common with other recent political memoirs – those of *Kabaka* Edward Mutesa and Princess Elizabeth of Toro – in terms of the romantic imaginings of cattle and countryside, and simple folk, away from the hard complexities and conundrums of modern national politics.[113] Janet Museveni's life story presents, predictably, the strong campaigning woman of conscience, and reflects the fact that she has her own power base quite distinct from – even in competition with – her husband's.[114] Their son, Brig. Gen. Muhoozi Kainerugaba, has attempted a military history and wonders if there is indeed an 'African way of war', ranging back to Mbale in 1973 (the year before he was born) and of course up to the great deeds of his father.[115] Recent memoirs abound: experiences of life under Idi Amin, or under Obote; war memoirs from the NRA bush war, for example by Pecos Kutesa.[116] Others veer into the realms of hagiography, such as Ondoga ori Amaza's admiring study of Museveni.[117] At the very least it is a reminder of the darkness that lies just under Kampala's bustling surface. In 2012, a formerly close ally of Museveni published a book 'exposing' the failings of the regime.[118] Uganda in the 2010s is

---

[110] G. Nsubuga, *Sir Edward Muteesa: his life and politics* (Kampala, 2013); A.B.K. Kasozi, *The Bitter Bread of Exile: the financial problems of Sir Edward Muteesa during his final exile, 1966–69* (Kampala, 2013).

[111] C. P. Mayiga, *The King on the Throne* (Kampala, 2009).

[112] Yoweri Museveni, *Sowing the Mustard Seed: the struggle for freedom and democracy in Uganda* (Oxford, 1997).

[113] Princess Elizabeth of Toro, *African Princess: the story of Princess of Elizabeth of Toro* (London, 1983); The Kabaka of Buganda, *Desecration of My Kingdom* (London, 1967).

[114] J. Museveni, *My Life's Journey* (Kampala, 2011).

[115] M. Kainerugaba, *Battles of the Ugandan Resistance: a tradition of maneuver* (Kampala, 2010).

[116] P. Kutesa, *Uganda's Revolution, 1979–1986: how I saw it* (Kampala, 2006).

[117] Ondoga ori Amaza, *Museveni's Long March from Guerrilla to Statesman* (Kampala, 1998).

[118] Author's notes and informal interviews, 10 August 2012.

strikingly reminiscent of the 1930s, in terms of the concerns and interests of that decade, which was also a time when an ageing generation sought to write its place into history and society. There is also a similar interest in entrepreneurs of the past, big men who carved order out of chaos and opportunities for themselves in the wilderness – such as David Bakibinga's admiring study of Daudi Kintu-Mutekanga, who between c. 1900 and 1940 was established as a leading colonial figure, grabbing land and doing profitable business, in the Bugabula district in Busoga.[119]

In sum, there is a wealth of new research to get to grips with: this is scholarship which has continued to add to our understanding of Uganda's historical trajectory, or trajectories; and it is one of the core objectives of this book to pull these various specialist studies together and synthesise their findings, rendering them meaningful in the context of a *Ugandan* history in all its glorious complexity. It is a sad fact, however, that the vast bulk of the mainstream scholarship on Uganda is now undertaken by foreigners. There are numerous reasons for this, no doubt, but in sum, while the higher education sector in Uganda has stabilised and indeed expanded considerably over the last thirty years, its underpaid, resource-starved and teaching-burdened academic staff have little time for scholarly research. It is also the case that the current emphasis is very much away from the humanities and towards science, technology and business, at least in terms of government funding and encouragement; history, as a discipline, sits ill with the developmental agendas now dominant in Ugandan public life. Discussions about the state of the discipline with historians at Makerere University can be depressing affairs indeed.[120] The complaints are common, and multiple: students do not want to study history but are often made to; the History Department is largely a service department for secondary school teachers; there is a feeling that history as a discipline is declining in importance and receives no support from the government.[121] Academic staff, meanwhile, work long hours with huge classes and increasingly lack a research culture; publication is only an option for a few, and then mostly aimed at promotion.[122]

---

[119] D. Bakibinga, *Daudi Kintu-Mutekanga: administrator and entrepreneur* (Kampala, 2006).
[120] See also Reid, 'Ghosts'.
[121] Author's notes and informal interviews, 6 August 2010.
[122] Author's notes and informal interviews, 25 October 2013.

It is certainly an opportune moment to take stock. But it is also the case that since the 1960s, Ugandan historiography has become increasingly balkanised, reflecting a more general trend in Africanist scholarship. Historians, naturally, do what they do best, and focus on specific places at specific times while dealing with specific themes. There are no doubt a number of factors driving scholarly compartmentalisation, which is as much the product of the professional pressures facing historians as of intellectual considerations, but suffice to note here that it has been more than thirty years since the last attempts to produce histories of *Uganda* as a national entity over *la longue durée* were published, namely those by Samwiri Karugire (whose account in fact only goes up to c. 1970) and by J. J. Jorgensen.[123] In the interim, Phares Mutibwa's history covers the period of independence (up to the early 1990s),[124] while more recently Aili Mari Tripp has produced a fine survey of contemporary Uganda.[125] The latter is not explicitly a work of history but it offers some useful historical background to a series of current concerns. Otherwise, for large surveys of nineteenth- and twentieth-century Ugandan history and the wider regional context, one must revert to the relevant chapters in the ageing *History of East Africa*, a three-volume set published by Oxford University Press between 1963 and 1976.[126] Some of these are exemplary in scholarly terms, but they are, inevitably, increasingly out-of-date. Again, this no doubt reflects the specificity of the interests of scholars working on Uganda; but it also, perhaps, reflects a modern disinterest in – even a suspicion of – the conceptualisation of African history within the framework of the nation, and may even signify a lack of faith in Uganda itself as a viable unit of study; perhaps even a lack of faith in the nation itself.

---

[123] Karugire, *Political History*; J.J. Jorgensen, *Uganda: a modern history* (London, 1981).

[124] Mutibwa, *Uganda since Independence.*   [125] Tripp, *Museveni's Uganda.*

[126] R. Oliver, 'Discernible Developments in the Interior, c. 1500–1840' and D.A. Low, 'The Northern Interior, 1840–1884', in R. Oliver & G. Mathew (eds.) *History of East Africa*, vol. I (Oxford, 1963); D.A. Low, 'Uganda: the establishment of the Protectorate, 1894–1912', C. Ehrlich, 'The Uganda Economy, 1903–1945', and R.C. Pratt, 'Administration and Politics in Uganda, 1919–1945', in V. Harlow & E.M. Chilver (eds.), *History of East Africa*, vol. II (Oxford, 1965); C. Gertzel, 'Kingdoms, Districts, and the Unitary State: Uganda, 1945–1962', D.A. Lury, 'Dayspring Mishandled? The Uganda Economy, 1945–1960', and C. Wrigley, 'Changes in East African Society', in D.A. Low & A. Smith (eds.), *History of East Africa*, vol. III (Oxford, 1976).

Representation and Reverberation

Uganda's history is reflected in a multitude of things and words, in continually evolving cultural production. Through all the dramas of political upheaval, economic turmoil and social change, Ugandans represented their experiences in cultural forms of staggering variety. They have told and, later, written stories; performed plays; danced to and composed music; carved and painted. The reconstruction of cultural production in the deeper, precolonial, past can be problematic, of course, and the nature of its recovery a matter of serendipity, even irony. Take, for example, the Luzira Head, discovered in 1929 on the outskirts of Kampala together with fragments of other figures.[127] It has been dated to the ninth or tenth century CE. Made of clay, and apparently part of a pot, the elaborate hair arrangement – which looks like clay worked into the hair – may denote high status, as it was a coiffure associated with religious and political leadership elsewhere. It is regarded as a celebration of power, of leadership – as much subsequent craftsmanship and aesthetic endeavour did in the region. It may, for example, represent emerging power dynamics and structures on the northern shore of Lake Victoria which would eventually lead to the rise of centralised states. It is somewhat fitting, perhaps, that it was accidentally uncovered by the inmates of the nearby Luzira Prison – those who had fallen foul of a very modern form of centralised statehood, the British colonial order – assigned to undertake building work.[128] More broadly, artistic expression is difficult to historicise. We know – intuitively – that art, dance, music, all are part of the human experience, everywhere. But how to measure changes in expression over time in preliterate settings? The first contemporary recordings are in the texts of European observers, in which we are offered glimpses of dancing and drumming, which seemed to all Europeans the very essence of nerve-tingling savagery. Those sources reveal that war was fertile ground for aesthetic representation, as it remained into the twentieth century and beyond. Soldiers in Busongora around Kasese painted their

---

[127] It has long been a source of fascination, beginning with E.J. Wayland, M.C. Burkitt & H.J. Braunholtz, 'Archaeological Discoveries at Luzira', *Man*, 33 (1933), and rather more recently, A. Reid & C.Z. Ashley, 'A Context for the Luzira Head', *Antiquity*, 82:315 (2008).

[128] T. Phillips (ed.), *Africa: the art of a continent* (London, 1996), 140, 194–5; W. Gillon, *A Short History of African Art* (London, 1991), 323–4.

faces in war – one of the few Ugandan examples of proverbial 'war-paint' – while Nyoro soldiers decorated themselves with animal parts: leopard and monkey skins, cows' tails, antelopes' horns, and the false beards also used by chiefs.[129] The occasional glimpse afforded by earlier sources notwithstanding, we rely upon the ethnographic work done in the colonial period. From this, it may be possible, to some extent, to extrapolate backwards and trace patterns in the deeper past; but it is a problematic exercise, for the cultures thus collected are very much the product of the moment of their assembly, and inevitably contaminated, to a degree, by colonial representation. This is a question of selection and catalogue and narration. It was precisely the goal behind the establishment of the Uganda Museum to retrieve, preserve and display; and thanks to that project, we have access to a veritable treasure chest of material culture, and countless refractions of Uganda. The same culture of preservation and display is evident in a recent book on African art, in which we see the bonnet of human hair and beads, probably from Acholi, an example of the ornate coiffures associated with warrior initiation. Then there are the headrests of the Karamojong or a related group; and the milkpot from Bunyoro.[130] And there is evidence, too, of artistic networks following fast on the expansion of commerce in the nineteenth century: craftsmen on Ukerewe Island in the south of Lake Victoria were by the mid-nineteenth century producing distinctive carved figures which appear to have been dispatched to Buganda as diplomatic gifts.[131] Margaret Trowell – pioneer at Makerere's College of Art – along with her collaborator Karl Wachsmann produced a meticulously detailed and encyclopaedic tome on Ugandan arts and crafts.[132] But how much can we use these accounts – as typical as they are of the 'colonial library' – to reconstruct a nineteenth-century scenario, without reifying particular forms of 'traditional culture'? Can anything be said, for example, about the nineteenth century using twentieth-century descriptions of drums and instruments, as was attempted at a pioneering conference at Makerere in 1963?[133]

---

[129] Stanley, *Dark Continent*, I, 183; Baker, *Albert N'yanza*, II, 80–81.

[130] Phillips (ed.), *Africa: the art of a continent*, 139, 141.   [131] Ibid., 121.

[132] Margaret Trowell & Karl Wachsmann, *Tribal Crafts of Uganda* (London, 1953).

[133] See, for example, *First Conference on African Traditional Music*, Makerere University College, 15–19 December 1963 (Kampala, 1964).

External input can be problematic, and complicates the pursuit of 'authenticity' in the recovery of the cultural past. The story of Kasubi is particularly germane in this connection. The site of the royal tombs of Buganda – it contains the graves of Mutesa I, Mwanga, Daudi Chwa and Mutesa II – was badly damaged by a fire in March 2010 which provoked several days of trouble across the kingdom. Kasubi's history exemplifies the struggle around representation, authenticity and legitimacy. Originally built in 1874, it underwent major reconstruction in 1911, and again in the mid-1930s. On the occasion of each reconstruction, the challenge was – according to what model should it be rebuilt? What was 'authentic' and 'indigenous' and 'traditional'? At some point, and certainly by the 1930s, it became in effect a colonial mausoleum, as Andrew Reid has pointed out; but was that really its original purpose?[134] It is clear enough that the meanings and significance – and the design – of Kasubi may have changed over several decades, but that the 2010 fire reawakened fierce emotion about heritage and identity at a moment when the kingdom felt persecuted by the state.[135] In the months following the fire, the key issue has been the importance of local materials in the reconstruction of the tombs, and the identification of local historians and custodians who can advise on design and building. The problem was that between 1967 and 1993, when all kingdoms were abolished, vital skills and knowledge were lost. A search was launched for the special grass to make the thatched roof of the main enclosure, and for those who had the skills for the task. Meanwhile, old men sat around the edge of the ruins, all day, every day, as observers and guardians, making sure that everything proceeded according to convention and custom. Similar challenges in preservation and representation confronted the hard-pressed staff of Department of Antiquities in the 1960s and 1970s, as they struggled to protect historic sites against the predations of robbers and termites.[136]

Yet it seems – in a fascinating example of feedback – that at least some knowledge was to be gleaned from early European sources. At the

---

[134] See Remigius Kigongo & Andrew Reid, 'Local Communities, Politics, and the Management of the Kasubi Tombs', *World Archaeology*, 39:3 (2007).

[135] Interview, Remigius Kigongo, and site visit, Kasubi Tombs, 9 April 2013.

[136] For example: Kabale District Archives, 'Monuments Section – Monthly Report, August 1969', 2 September 1969, & 'Department of Antiquities Monthly Report, September 1974', 11 October 1974, COM 21, CD24, Culture & Activities.

main entrance of the Kasubi site, there was an arrangement of images and information, and plans of the layout; and use was made of the famous picture in Speke's *Journal* of 'King Mtesa holding a levee' at the entrance of his palace.[137] In fact this was originally a sketch by Speke's companion James Grant (both he and Speke are in the picture), and then drawn up in published form by the noted German illustrator based in London, Johann Baptist Zwecker. The problem is a fairly obvious one: the accuracy of the detail in Zwecker's final illustration is difficult to verify, and the question is – is the modern *kibuga* based on Zwecker's picture, or does Zwecker's picture accurately represent the nineteenth-century *kibuga*? Then there were later plans and maps, including some from Gutkind's noted studies from the 1950s.[138] The main building at Kasubi was a burnt-out shell after the fire; the only items still standing were a couple of supporting poles, the red brick wall erected beneath the grass and wattle by the British in 1938 to ensure (they believed) stability, and the iron roof support which dated to the same period. Many were shocked to see these architectural innovations, these manifestations of modernity under the vernacular design.[139] Those involved in the reconstruction work marvelled at the resolute intervention which had led colonial administrators in the 1930s to bolster the 'traditional' royal palace with bricks and metal: it seemed, in some ways, an apt metaphor for the relationship between Britain and Buganda. 'Tradition', indeed, can be rather more novel than might be assumed. The *Gomesi*, for example, is celebrated as the 'traditional' clothing for women, and lauded for its enduring appeal, despite modifications over the decades. Yet the *Gomesi* itself could be traced only to 1905, when its designer – the Goan Indian Caetano Gomes – first launched the dress, and it was only really in 1914, when the *Kabaka* Daudi Chwa's wife wore one at her husband's coronation, that it entered popular consciousness.[140] The 'traditional' *kanzu* outfit for men, meanwhile, at that point did not quite date back a century, and was only introduced in the 1840s and 1850s by coastal traders, when cotton cloth was increasingly supplanting bark-cloth as the indigenous textile of choice, although throughout the twentieth century bark-cloth continued to be deployed in 'traditional' activity.

---

[137] See Speke, *Journal*, opp. p.421.
[138] The work culminated in Gutkind, *Royal Capital*.
[139] Site visit, Kasubi Tombs, 9 April 2013.   [140] *Understand Uganda*, 24–5.

We cannot assess the significance of arts and crafts without noting the socio-political dimensions to both. There was a close association, notably, between forged metal and political leadership, as is clear from the earliest nineteenth-century descriptions of the artefacts kept in royal palaces. Much art was functional in that its chief purpose was to underscore political authority, especially royal power. One of the most clearly manifest instances of this is in the public usage of drums as a central component of material political culture. In Buganda, the *mujaguzo* was especially significant: this was a set of drums controlled by the *kabaka* which were used to issue messages across the kingdom, notably in terms of declaring military campaigns and issuing information about soldier collection points. It may have been *Kabaka* Mutebi – possibly in the mid-seventeenth century – who originated the drums,[141] but in some form or other they undoubtedly pre-dated this. Other drums were used by senior chiefs, particularly those on military campaign,[142] while similar sets of drums signifying political leadership were common across the region. They had an especial importance in Nkore where they were known as *Bagendanwa* and symbolised the kingdom's sovereign independence.[143] In Bunyoro, as in Buganda, drums were part of the *mukama*'s material estate and he also had a distinctive drum beat in issuing commands.[144] Art, then, was associated with stable political offices – regalia, chairs, etc., with distinctive visual design celebrating political authority. The association with political office is certainly the most public, visible representation of art that has survived. This was predominantly a male activity. The same is true of working in wood, where in the Ugandan area as elsewhere in Africa there is a link between the craft and the harnessing of spiritual power. Pottery perhaps tells a different story. Changes in pottery style in the deeper past, during the first half of the second millennium, suggested important shifts in social organisation: formerly ornate Urewe ware was probably the preserve of specialist craftsmen, but the simpler ware – apparently carried by pastoralists from the north – was likely made by most households, no longer specialist, and

---

[141] B.M. Zimbe, *Buganda ne Kabaka* [Buganda and the King], (tr. F. Kamoga, unpublished MS, Makerere University Library, Kampala, c.1939), 19.
[142] Stanley, *Dark Continent*, I, 337, 341.
[143] 'K.W.', 'The Kings of Bunyoro-Kitara, Part I', *Uganda Journal*, 3:2 (1935), 156.
[144] Speke, *Journal*, 478.

was perhaps the work of women.[145] Then there is cloth – notably bark cloth – which appears to have been predominantly male, though possibly women played a greater role in indigenous textiles. Overall, there was a reasonably clear relationship between gender, power and art or craftsmanship: for several decades into the twentieth century, as in the precolonial period, metal and wood were predominantly male activities and thus the production of things of beauty as well as power were in the realm of masculinity; and it seems fair to suggest that this only began to change in the middle decades of the twentieth century, when women begin to emerge as craftsfolk and artists.

For all these material achievements, Uganda's primary art forms were music, oral poetry and narrative performance, and therefore visual art was very much a product of the twentieth century.[146] In 1936, Margaret Trowell began organising informal painting classes in her home at Makerere; she was later able to secure funding to establish a Department of Fine Art at Makerere, which became the main centre in East Africa for formal art training.[147] This was the era in which the international market for African 'tribal' art expanded rapidly; ironically, as Sidney Littlefield Kasfir has pointed out, 'what was potent about African art in the eyes of European artists such as Picasso was derived from a past antithetical to the modernity newly prized in their own work'.[148] For a number of years the teachers at Makerere had at least partially been trained abroad – the Kenyan sculptor Gregory Maloba, the Tanzanian painter Sam Ntiro, for example – but by the 1970s there had emerged a generation of artists trained exclusively in Africa. In Uganda, as elsewhere, artists sought to capture the excitement and

---

[145] For a useful overview, see C. M. Kusimba & S. B. Kusimba, 'Mosaics and Interactions: East Africa, 2000 b.p to the Present', in Ann Brower Stahl (ed.), *African Archaeology: a critical introduction* (Malden MA, & Oxford, 2005). New work on Urewe culture is continuing under the auspices of the British Institute in Eastern Africa.

[146] R.-M. Rychner, 'The Context and Background of Ugandan Art', in Eckhard Breitinger (ed.), *Uganda: the cultural landscape* (Kampala, 2000), 263. For an excellent history with a grand sweep, see George William Kyeyune, 'Art in Uganda in the Twentieth Century', PhD dissertation, University of London, 2004.

[147] Rychner, 'The Context', 264–5.

[148] S. L. Kasfir, 'Visual Cultures', in J. Parker & R. Reid (eds.), *The Oxford Handbook of Modern African History* (Oxford, 2013), 438.

anticipation around new nationhood in painting.[149] As in other spheres the Amin and Obote years took their toll on artistic endeavour, but by the 1990s, the Ugandan art scene was flourishing, led by regularly exhibited artists such as Jak Katarikawe, Lydia Mugambi, Geoffrey Mukasa, Teresa Musoke, Fred Mutebi and Fabian Mpagi. The emergence of a small but successful cohort of female artists was particularly striking, given their previous invisibility in the field. Ugandan painters concerned themselves with the issues which dominated Ugandan public and political life: the devastation of the AIDS epidemic, marital infidelity, political disorder. Some – as in the case of Mpagi's 1994 oil on canvas 'Warriors' – approached distinctively African representation in new, visually powerful ways. This work has to some extent benefited from the continued expansion of the international art market.

It also reflected a growing individualism, with particular artists of note emerging in what had once been – certainly for much of the nineteenth and twentieth centuries – a community activity. Previously, artists and craftsmen had been largely anonymous, although oral histories collected in the early 1900s contain some brief glimpses into the 'fame' attached to particular workers in metal, or wood, bringing them to the attention of royal court or other chiefly figures. It is also clear that 'traditional' crafts were co-opted in new ways. Bark cloth, for example, was used in painting.[150] Among the notable instances of this is the use of bark cloth by women's campaign groups seeking to raise awareness of the impact of HIV/AIDS, with large segments of the cloth – once associated with royal power in Buganda, and to some extent elsewhere – being decorated with colourful designs and images. Modern Ugandan art was notable in particular for its vibrant colour, and its depictions of what might broadly be termed traditional scenes with a modern twist, or in a contemporary setting. The art scene, with its centre of gravity, inevitably enough, in Kampala, is arguably more dynamic in Uganda today than at any time since independence and involves a number of particularly celebrated artists who have moved Ugandan visual art decisively away from the utilitarian and towards a more abstract – 'art for art's sake' – deployment of the imagination and

---

[149] See also R. Woets, 'The Recreation of Modern and African Art at Achimoto School in the Gold Coast (1927–52)', *Journal of African History*, 55:3 (2014).
[150] See, for example, the excellent website http://ugandart.com/

subjective analysis. This has, perhaps, been the hallmark of the 'cultural revival' of the last twenty years, suggestive of liberation from troublesome 'traditional/modern' dichotomies, and of a more self-confident embrace of histories and cultures.

The central point to emphasise here is that throughout the twentieth century, artists and craftspeople linked past and present in ever more innovative ways, and several generations of them were joined together in a conviction, episodically inherited, that *the past mattered*, and was, indeed, inseparable from the present. Their work was often explicitly historical, as they sought to portray particular readings of the past, and to retrieve what was regarded at particular moments as valuable and, perhaps, lost. At the same time, they refracted contemporary issues and anxieties through historical depiction, and through stylised interpretations of 'traditional' culture, custom and narrative. The same was true of their literary counterparts.

A Flowering Barrenness

Taban lo Liyong once famously described East Africa as a literary wasteland.[151] Taban was a controversial and colourful figure, one of the leading lights of the Ugandan literary scene he so brutally disparaged, admired and lambasted in pretty much equal measure. But he had been one of the most vociferous advocates of the centrality of African oral tradition being positioned at the heart of literature curricula on the continent, and recommended the establishment of a 'counter-curriculum' of African literature which should take priority over 'English literature'. Only after the curriculum had been Africanised could students return to Western literature, which was then to be interpreted from African perspectives. In this he collaborated with Henry Owuor-Anyumba and Ngugi wa Thiong'o.[152] Ironically, however, much of the indignant opprobrium heaped on Taban consequent to his grim appraisal of the state of the East African literary

---

[151] T. l. Liyong, 'East Africa, O East Africa, I Lament Thy Literary Barrenness', *Transition*, 50 (1975), 43. See also 'Lo Liyong –Literary Icon Who Delights in Ruffling Feathers', 21 October 2011, http://allafrica.com/stories/ 201110240408.html

[152] 'On the Abolition of the English Department', in N. w. Thiong'o, *Homecoming: essays on African and Caribbean literature, culture and politics* (London, 1972).

landscape – including from no lesser a figure than fellow Acholi poet and scholar Okot p'Bitek – was based precisely on the fact that Taban had, as Ernesto Okello Ogwang points out, 'restricted his understanding of literature only to the written texts, at the expense of the oral literatures'.[153]

In any case, the period in which Taban made his summary pronouncement was something of a golden age for Ugandan literature. True, Uganda has often been overshadowed by its more celebrated Kenyan neighbour – and it was a shadow cast at the very outset of independence. The Kenyan writer Ngugi wa Thiong'o was a student at Makerere in the late 1950s, where he wrote some of his earliest works, works which Uganda would come to claim as its own, for Ngugi was regarded as having been steeped in the politics and culture of that exciting moment on the eve of independence. And it was a play by Ngugi which was the first by an African to be performed at the Uganda National Theatre in Kampala in 1963, claimed as a landmark moment for 'Ugandan' literature.[154] But Ugandan poets, novelists and playwrights were coming to the fore, too, wrestling with many of the same issues which gripped their contemporaries in other parts of the continent: decolonisation and 'African' identity; history and modernity; and, in time, the disillusion with postcolonial political culture and the emergence of dictatorship and censorship. Just as the trauma of the colonial experience and the meanings of modernity were the concerns of Camara Laye's *L'enfant noir* (1954) and Chinua Achebe's *Things Fall Apart* (1958), so they were, too, of Okot p'Bitek's pioneering Luo-language novel *Lak Tar* ('White Teeth'), published in 1953.[155]

There is some question as to whether this amounted to a 'national' culture, given the apparent bifurcation, as Eckhard Breitinger described it, between 'the Acholi North, standing for the form of poetry and epic, and the Baganda South/Centre representing drama and performance' – reflecting a crude ethnic division which was 'instrumentalised with devastating effect for national cohesion, national identity,

---

[153] E. O. Ogwang, 'Ugandan Poetry: trends and features, 1965–1995', in Breitinger (ed.), *Uganda: the cultural landscape*, 100.
[154] 'Ngugi wa Thiong'o: he wrote Uganda's independence play', *New Vision*, 1 February 2012.
[155] Remarkably, it was not until 1989 that an English translation appeared, published in Nairobi by Heinemann Kenya.

and...cultural development during the years of turmoil'.[156] And it
might be suggested that Okot was arguably Uganda's greatest writer
not *despite* being an Acholi himself, but precisely *because* of the distinctive 'northern' experience he was able to bring to bear on his writing.
Lak Tar dealt with themes to which many Ugandans could relate: in
this depressing and at times darkly comic tale, the young Acholi protagonist must travel to Buganda for work to earn money for brideprice,
and the novel describes a journey between the expectations of 'traditional', indigenous culture (in this case, gathering together brideprice
in order to achieve happiness and fulfilment) and the harsher, uncaring
and hazardous world of material modernity, manifest in the dangerous and grimy city of Kampala, brutal working conditions for migrant
labourers and criminality on the road. Our young, unfortunate hero
is robbed and loses everything, and he returns home empty-handed.
Likewise, Okot's greatest work – *Song of Lawino* (1966), followed by
the response, *Song of Ocol* (1967)[157] – is presented in distinctive song-
style Luo, and thus very much the product of Acholi cultural norms.
Yet it was again concerned with a set of anxieties and conflicts with
which all Ugandans were familiar: in the first song, Lawino, the wife,
lambasts her husband for having taken up with a 'Westernized' woman
and who has abandoned his traditional culture for all things foreign;
and in the second, the husband, Ocol, replies by mocking his own culture and refuting his wife's claims. The struggle to reconcile ideas about
'authenticity' and indigeneity with modernity – the 'foreign' – would
be a recurrent motif in much Ugandan writing, and in some respects
continues to be.

Writers of various hues, then – poets, novelists, dramatists – reached
back into the past in search of questions as well as answers, and the
struggle to describe and understand current problems was often framed
by historical allusion. Okot was at the centre of a veritable explosion
of literary and theatrical output in the years that followed. The work
of playwright John Ruganda – especially his plays *The Burdens* (1972)
and *The Floods* (1980) – captured the conflicts, tensions and ultimately
the tragedies of the immediate postcolonial era, including the Amin
years, frequently using the private lives of individuals and families as

---

[156] See his introduction to *Uganda: the cultural landscape*, 9–10.
[157] O. p'Bitek, *Song of Lawino & Song of Ocol* (Johannesburg, 1984); and see
   G.A. Heron, *The Poetry of Okot p'Bitek* (New York, 1976).

microcosms of larger challenges.[158] Ruganda himself, like many others, fled Uganda in the early 1970s and produced much of his most important work in Kenya. Ruganda's close contemporary (and fellow Catholic) was Robert Serumaga, whose novel *Return to the Shadows* was published in 1970, but he was especially celebrated as a playwright and as the founder of the National Theatre Company in 1967. His plays – *A Play* (produced 1967), *The Elephants* (produced 1970, published 1971) and *Majangwa* (produced 1971, published 1974) – were noted for their emphasis on the absurd and their lack of central narrative, but at the same time for their portrayal of a stagnating society under Obote. Under Amin, Serumaga developed a distinctive form of theatre, centred on the idea of the *Abafumi*, or storyteller, and relying on abstract physical movement, mime and dance which successfully conveyed postcolonial violence and disillusionment but which equally successfully escaped censorship. (Amin himself approved, apparently unaware of the criticism embodied in the form, and even invited Serumaga's troupe to perform at the OAU meeting in Kampala in 1974. Amin referred to it gratifyingly as 'gymnastics'.)[159] Ruganda and Serumaga are widely seen as among the founders of modern theatre in East Africa, and were instrumental in the early development of the National Theatre, housed in a modernist building in central Kampala, as the vehicle for emerging talent in the postcolonial epoch. But dramatic performance was mobile, too, witness the formation of the Makerere Free Travelling Theatre in 1964–5 which brought plays to rural areas.[160] Samuel Kasule has recently demonstrated that such popular performances can be dated to at least the 1930s, thanks to a corpus of archived Luganda recordings.[161] At the same time, however, the emergence of new forms of cultural output – alongside more deeply rooted traditions of poetry, song and story-telling – reflected a fundamental social shift: plays and novels, notably, implied relatively larger amounts

[158] See, for example, Francis Davies Imbuga, 'Thematic Trends and Circumstance in John Ruganda's Drama', PhD thesis, University of Iowa, 1991.

[159] Serumaga was involved in the liberation movement of 1979–80, and served briefly in Yusuf Lule's government – rather incongruously as commerce minister – but died suddenly in 1982.

[160] D. Cook, 'The Makerere Free Travelling Theatre: an experimental model', in Breitinger (ed.), *Uganda: the cultural landscape*.

[161] S. Kasule, '"Don't Talk into my Talk": oral narratives, cultural identity, and popular performance in colonial Uganda', in M. Banham, J. Gibbs, & F. Osofisan (eds.), *African Theatre: histories 1850–1950* (Woodbridge, 2010).

of 'private' time on the part of an educated, literate cultural elite, while also in some ways signifying the transition – as in the case of art and craft, noted above – from community to individual, and the normalisation of the self. All the while, the past was a critical reference point in literature which was frequently concerned with temporal journeys, whether personal or collective, and with the fundamental struggle to comprehend change.

There is a temptation to see the last thirty years as a kind of rebirth. This is certainly how the NRM would like to have it seen. We need, of course, to exercise caution here. Ugandan social and cultural life did not 'cease to be' between 1971 and 1986 – in fact, in all sorts of ways, it thrived. But there is no question that cultural life fell under some pretty dark shadows during that time, and was as much about survival as full expression; and just because the Movement has since pursued a 'rebirth' agenda does not mean there is not *some* kernels of truth in the basic idea – that since the late 1980s, Uganda has indeed entered a new period of cultural and artistic expression, arguably unprecedented, and certainly more vibrant than at any time since the 1950s. There was tremendous excitement when in 2014 the Ugandan writer Jennifer Nansubuga Makumbi won the Commonwealth Short Story prize. She evidently took enormous pleasure in proclaiming to a British newspaper: 'This is a dream. For Uganda, once described as a literary desert, it shows how the country's literary landscape is changing and I am proud to be a part of it'.[162] Uganda now had a thriving literary scene – including book-buying, book-writing and book-publishing.[163] Moreover the echoes of the deep past in the making of Ugandan literature were everywhere to behold, as also were the enduring influences of oral tradition: Makumbi's earlier work (as a doctoral student in the UK) had been based on the saga of Kintu, Buganda's culture-hero and mythical founding father. In many ways it was the culmination – or, at least, the latest stage – in Uganda's cultural revival since the 1980s and more especially the 1990s, an era characterised by growing self-confidence, even self-awareness. Yet it has also been an era in which writers have periodically tested the government's tolerance of dissent

---

[162] See 'Commonwealth Short Story Prize Goes to "Risk-Taking" Ugandan', *The Guardian* (London), 13 June 2014.
[163] 'Uganda's "Literary Desert" Is Back in Bloom', *Think Africa Press*, 17 September 2013.

and critique, and forbearance levels have varied according to political mood and context: in October 2012, the Uganda Media Council reflected a particularly heightened sensitivity in government when it banned a play, *State of the Nation*, for criticising political leadership at a time of celebration organised around Uganda's fiftieth anniversary of independence.[164] In broad terms, of course, Uganda's literary culture has – naturally enough – long positioned itself as a mirror to society and politics, and novelists, playwrights and poets have long been critics of incumbent regimes. This has been encouraged, no doubt, by the NRM – but only insofar as the critiques have been aimed past regimes and their odious antics. It has proven less tolerant of criticisms aimed at its own record.

A new generation of authors has come of age in recent years. In many ways the founding father of the Movement generation is Timothy Wangusa, whose novel *Upon This Mountain* (1989) described the colonial-era struggles with 'tradition' and modernity through the eyes of a young man and his imminent circumcision ceremony. In fact Wangusa's first collection of poems appeared in 1977 as *Salutations*, but it was in the 1990s that he became a leading figure in the Ugandan literary scene – with collections of poems such as *A Pattern of Dust* (1994), full of historical themes and images, followed by the ambitious *Anthem for Africa* in 1995, which set Amin's era in the context of Africa's entire modern history, and in 2006 *Africa's New Brood*, another poetry anthology.[165] Alongside him, and straddling several decades in a remarkable life, is Austin Bukenya, who was producing his first published work – *The People's Bachelor* (1972) – in the early years of the Amin regime, and who went on to write his most noted play, *The Bride*, in 1987; and most recently, reflections on modern environmental concerns, *A Hole in the Sky* (2013). Hailing from Masaka, in Buddu, Bukenya has often written in Swahili, and draws on Ganda traditions for inspiration for his work. Moses Isegawa, who lives in

---

[164] 'Uganda's Media Council Bans State of the Nation Play', BBC News, 31 October 2012.

[165] There is more to Wangusa than his literary output. He is an academic – he played a leading role in the creation of the department of Languages and Literature at Uganda Christian University in Mukono, and has been vice-chancellor of Kumi University in eastern Uganda – and has served as 'literary advisor' to the Ugandan President, demonstrating Museveni's enthusiasm for the co-option of a range of talent. In 1989, moreover, Wangusa was elected MP for Bubulo County in Mbale.

the Netherlands, represents a younger cohort of gifted and dynamic
Ugandan writers. His *Abyssinian Chronicles* (first published in Dutch
in 1998, and then in English two years later) is his most famous novel,
and won great acclaim in the years after its appearance – in many ways
it defies summary, but in broad terms it is a tumultuous story of modern Ugandan life. It rather overshadowed his second novel, *Snakepit*
(1999, 2004), which was set in Amin's Uganda and dealt with the
themes of corruption and dictatorship. While many of the older generation returned to Uganda in the late 1980s, Isegawa went in the other
direction: born into a middle-class Catholic family in Kampala (and
thus belonging to a lengthening Catholic literary tradition in Uganda),
he left for exile in the Netherlands in 1990, though he returned to
Uganda in 2006. Still, there is a conception among some, at least, that
the Ugandan 'creative industries' remain somehow defined by their
emulation of European models, and perhaps even by the desire to win
approval from Western audiences. At an event at Makerere organised
to mark the death of Nigerian writer Chinua Achebe, a senior figure
in academic administration made the point that 'as we become more
and more removed from *our culture*, we become less creative [italics
added]'....[166] It seems, given the canon of literature which Uganda
has produced in recent decades, an unnecessarily glum reading of the
situation.

And so, too, in the realm of popular media, where in Uganda – as
elsewhere across the continent[167] – there has been a veritable flourishing of reportage, analysis, opinion and argument, of multiple visions
of the nation, over the last half-century or more. The years after the
Second World War witnessed the emergence of the first truly 'national'
newspapers – the *Uganda Argus* was founded in 1955 as the main
organ of the colonial administration – and newspapers became ever
more important as 'national' organs but in pursuit of particular agendas or political visions. In time, after independence in 1962, it became
ever more important for the government to control the interpretation
of events and the flow of information relating to them. Soon after the
NRM seized power, the *New Vision* newspaper was launched – it was
basically a relaunch of the old *Uganda Argus* – as the government

---

[166] Author's notes and informal interviews, 6 April 2013.
[167] For an excellent overview, see J. Brennan, 'Communications and Media in
African History', in J. Parker & R. Reid (eds.), *The Oxford Handbook of
Modern African History* (Oxford, 2013).

organ. In the 1990s, however, the print media scene opened up some-what, with the founding of the independent *Daily Monitor* in 1994, and a few years later by the rather more salacious tabloid *Red Pepper*, launched in 2001. The *Pepper* appealed to the baser, more populist trends in Ugandan society, and would quickly become a thorn in the side of the government for its printing unseemly gossip about the antics of the NRM's top officials. Television broadcasting was also privatised, and the decade following Museveni's seizure of power in 1986 witnessed the launch of new channels alongside the government's own. Alongside these English-language initiatives in print media and broadcasting, there have been similar initiatives in the vernacular: newspapers such as *Bukedde* (Luganda), *Orumuri* (Runyoro), *Etop* (Ateso) and *Rupiny* (Luo) are published by the Vision Group, and there are others, each with powerful and occasionally provocative historical visions to promote and historical cultures to celebrate.[168]

Museveni appeared, for a number of years, to self-consciously welcome this robust new media, and had equally robust – even joking – relationships with newspaper editors, journalists and broadcasters. But in recent years there have been signs that the putative renaissance is under strain.[169] The President has become increasingly irritated by their tendency to criticise, and to run stories detrimental to his carefully crafted media image. There are worrying signs that he no longer believes a 'free press' is all it is cracked up to be, and has shown himself willing to use security forces to move in on wayward editors and journalists. The latter know, then, that history is a vital tool in social comment and political analysis, and as in other avenues of literary and aesthetic life, Ugandan print media is notably given to historical reflection, and frequently revels in discussions about the lessons and the precedents of the past. Historical reference points may remain relatively recent – most lie in Uganda's tumultuous twentieth century – but journalists, no less than their comrades in the arts and literature, are possessed of a historical consciousness which is invariably used to chastise, critique, even ridicule, on various sides of the political divide. It is this which often irritates those in power, when they are on the

---

[168] See 'A Mixed 50 Years for Uganda's Print Media', in *Independent Uganda*, 342–7.

[169] B. Tabaire, 'The Press and Political Repression in Uganda: back to the future?', *Journal of Eastern African Studies*, 1:2 (2007).

receiving end, though they are themselves no strangers to the deployment of strident historical vision in print and broadcast.

What is clear enough, however, is that representation and expression – whether spoken, sung, performed, written, sculpted – have been absolutely critical, from the precolonial to the modern eras, in enabling people to think about the past and its relationship to the present; to imagine the future; and to seek solace in that imagination. It has enabled Ugandans to interpret and represent tyranny, for example, while also offering protection and escape from that tyranny. It seems reasonable to suggest that the momentum towards a robust and critical commentary on Uganda's past and present, as well as its future direction, while always vulnerable to setbacks, is now unstoppable.

2 | *Pensive Nation*

The Age of Blood and Rebirth

1986: Year Zero

In January 1986, units of the National Resistance Army (NRA) entered the capital, Kampala, having spent the previous five years in 'the bush', conducting guerrilla war against the Ugandan state and its armed forces. As a movement its roots were in the west, in Ankole, although its major zone of operations had been to the north of Kampala, in Luwero, where it had won some of its greatest successes. At the time, there was no doubting the NRA's military credentials, and its remarkable achievement in having advanced after five years of bloody struggle to the heart of the Ugandan state.[1] What was less clear as its motorised units moved through the Kampala suburbs toward the city centre, however, was the extent to which the NRA heralded anything new, or whether it would be little more than yet another violent and ultimately hapless regime (there had been half a dozen since Idi Amin's ouster seven years earlier) which would only last as long as it took its enemies to organise themselves and overthrow it.

The ascent of the NRA was part of a wider phenomenon, a 'second wave' of liberation in eastern and southern Africa, in which a number of more or less professionalised, 'revolutionary' armed movements seized power between the mid-1980s and the mid-1990s following guerrilla wars of varying duration: the Zimbabwe African National Union in Zimbabwe, the Eritrean People's Liberation Front in Eritrea, the Ethiopian People's Revolutionary Democratic Front in Ethiopia, the RPF in Rwanda, the African National Congress in South Africa.[2] The leaders of these movements were political evangelists, promising

---

[1] They were assisted by units which would later found the Rwandan Patriotic Front (RPF), seizing power in Uganda's southerly neighbour in the midst of genocidal violence in 1994.

[2] P. D. Williams, *War and Conflict in Africa* (Cambridge, 2011); W. Reno, *Warfare in Independent Africa* (New York, 2011); R. J. Reid, *Warfare in African History* (New York, 2012).

national rebirth and revolutionary change; their leaders were on the whole urban middle class in provenance, and were often educated, imbued with the ideals and the revolutionary fervour of the 1960s and 1970s. They were famously heralded as Africa's 'new breed' of leaders, tough, intelligent and pragmatic, and better equipped than anyone since the era of decolonisation to take on the continent's seemingly endemic ailments in terms of political and economic development. Yoweri Kaguta Museveni, in his early forties when he led his forces into the capital, was foremost among them, and was soon feted by the international community – including the key financial institutions – as one of the great hopes for a troubled country, and a turbulent region. It is difficult to overstate how intense was the feeling – outside Uganda, at least – that Museveni was indeed something of a saviour after two decades of economic mayhem and political terror. He was sensible, but humorous; charming and persuasive; and very smart. Initially, Ugandans did not quite know what to make of him and the new political leadership more generally: seen by some as rather vulgar Nyankole, country bumpkins from the cattle-keeping far west of the country with their colourful language and undiplomatic public pronouncements, they were treated warily at first by many. But within a few months, traits which had been seen as bad manners initially were increasingly viewed as assets. There was a general sense that – despite the apparent rusticity and the fact that a perspiring Museveni had a tendency to wipe the sweat off his head with his cap in public – there was something different about this lot, that they were serious men, and soon quite a few women too, and that they meant business. The NRM would soon be confronted with more armed rebellions than either Obote or Amin had ever faced, and from different parts of the country; but these bitter malcontents aside, there was for many Ugandans a sense by 1987–8 that a new start, of some kind, had in fact been achieved. The challenges were enormous, but these only added to the notion – encouraged by the NRM government – that national cohesion was needed like never before, and that only collective effort, and the putting aside of multiple ethnic, religious and social differences, would rescue Uganda from the slough of despond into which it had sunk.[3]

---

[3] Wiebe & Dodge (eds.), *Beyond Crisis* and Twaddle & Hansen (eds.), *Uganda Now* and *Changing Uganda*. For a useful scholarly history which was very much of the moment, see also Mutibwa, *Uganda since Independence*.

What soon emerged was typical of what were sometimes termed 'hybrid regimes': as Aili Mari Tripp puts it, 'neither the autocracies of the past, nor ... fully democratic'.[4] 'No-party' politics were introduced – and enshrined in the 1995 constitution – meaning that elections were to be contested by individuals who stood on personal merit, rather than any party affiliation.[5] The rationale, comprehensible enough, was that formal political parties had been the root of violent disorder in Ugandan political life – beginning, indeed, in the late colonial period under the British; the only way to restore order was to abolish parties, until such time as Uganda had stabilised (or 'modernised', in NRM parlance) sufficiently to permit their reintroduction. People, in other words, could not be trusted to vote with the best interests of the nation at heart, but would instead be tempted once more into the shady realms of sectarianism, provincialism and tribalism. They were still ensnared by the past, and as yet unwilling and unable to leap free of the clutches of history – at least without some firm guidance. It is difficult to exaggerate the degree to which the NRM's early political discipline and focus seemed to embody the optimism and pragmatism of the moment. The political space appeared to open up considerably, as the Movement brought in allies and associates as well as potential political rivals in its stated attempt to broaden its base and form a genuinely representative coalition prioritising reconstruction in the run-up to the elections for the newly formed Constituent Assembly in 1994. Whatever criticism that would be later aimed at it, the new system of governance through Resistance Councils (RCs), renamed Local Councils in the 1995 Constitution, appeared to herald a new era of popular, grassroots participation.[6] At the same time, the government moved decisively towards the broadly popular restoration of the 'traditional' kingships in the south, abolished by Obote in 1967: Buganda, Bunyoro, Toro and Busoga; others would follow, some of which hadn't actually existed in quite this format previously. The only pre-existent monarchy of historical significance missing out was that in Ankole, for

---

[4] Tripp, *Museveni's Uganda*, 3.
[5] N. Kasfir, 'Ugandan politics and the Constituent Assembly elections of March 1994', in M. Twaddle and H. B. Hansen (eds.), *From Chaos to Order: the politics of constitution-making in Uganda* (Oxford, 1994); Nelson Kasfir, '"No-Party Democracy" in Uganda', *Journal of Democracy*, 9:2 (1998).
[6] See Articles 180 & 181 in the 1995 Constitution: http://www.parliament.go.ug/new/images/stories/constitution/Constitution_of_Uganda_1995.pdf

reasons to be examined in due course. These restored kingships were to be purely 'cultural' institutions, imbued with 'tradition' and draped in all the trappings of the reconstituted precolonial custom; but they would have none of the political authority.[7] The targeting of sectarian division – used by the Movement as an umbrella term encompassing anything remotely nefarious in Uganda's political past – through the practice of 'no-party democracy' and the restoration of the southern monarchies may seem contradictory, at first glance; but in fact the two broad policies revealed the central political vision of the new regime. Through no-party politics, the deadly toxins of historical division were being excised from Uganda's political culture; through the remaking of kingship as cultural institution, the past was being detoxified and safely quarantined from contemporary struggles and aspirations. Remove the past from the politics, and the politics from the past, and the future might start looking altogether more secure. Thus was '1986' considered 'year zero', with the moment of the NRM's capture of Kampala in January of that year supposedly marking the beginning of a process of rebirth. In order to fully appreciate the significance of the Movement's advent – and indeed the significance which the Movement has long attached to itself – we need to explore the recent past in a little more detail, to understand the immediate context and the environment of which the renascent NRM was a product.

Methods and Madness: The Rise and Fall of the Northern Military

The image of General Idi Amin scuttling around Kampala on the afternoon of 25 January 1971 in his open-topped jeep, which he drove himself, pistol poking out of its holster below his bulging waist, his 'boys' in uniform clinging on beside him and following up pensively in other vehicles, is an iconic and pivotal freeze-frame in the vivid pageantry that is contemporary Ugandan history.[8] The crowds lining the streets to catch a glimpse of the man who was apparently their new head of state were generally enthusiastic: Obote was gone (he was in fact out of

---

[7] See Chapter 16 in ibid. relating to the "Institution of Traditional or Cultural Leaders".

[8] 'Coup d'etat in Uganda, 25 January 1971, led by army commander, Major General Idi Amin', United Kingdom National Archives (hereafter UKNA), FCO 31/1023 & FCO 31/1024 (1971).

the country when the *coup* happened), and good riddance, said many – not least the Ganda, who despised Obote for his destruction of their kingdom and the exile of their king, and who were therefore among Amin's most eager supporters, initially – despite the fact that the soldiers who had attacked the palace had been under Amin's command.[9] Milton Obote, the wily and credible Langi who had dominated Ugandan politics for the past two decades, had proven himself incapable of managing the multiple forces at work in a rapidly changing Uganda, and his (temporary) political passing seemed to sound the death knell of the late colonial order of which he was so much a product.

Fast forward to the end of the decade, and Amin had been chased from Uganda with the same bullet-riddled indignity with which he had dispatched *Kabaka* 'Freddie' Mutesa years earlier, and the man whom he had overthrown was limbering up for a grand return. Hounding Amin into exile to Libya, briefly, and then to Saudi Arabia was the Tanzanian army bolstered by a coalition of various Ugandan opposition groups. In the interim, Uganda had been decimated by a chaotically brutal culture of violence, driven by a regime which fed off deep-rooted political and social insecurities, in the process pulverising an economy which at independence had been fragile but which had had some potential. Several hundred thousand Ugandans were dead, and many others were in exile. Nor were the nation's travails over yet, for the return of Obote at the end of 1980 perpetuated a vengeful and paranoid cycle of violence and precipitated full-scale civil war. Among the political movements involved in Amin's ouster and the complex aftermath was the group coalescing around the young revolutionary guerrilla and political science graduate Yoweri Museveni. It is crucial to grasp the extent to which he, and what would eventually become the NRA, were the products of this era of chronic violence and instability; and everything they have done since cannot be understood without a consideration of the 15-year period between 1971 and 1986 in which the nation itself appeared doomed to fail in the most basic of ways. This era witnessed the resurgence of the region's military tradition, and demonstrated the disruptive – and transformative – power of centrifugal forces, of the perennial struggle between expansionist centre and insurgent frontier. Idi Amin's decade in power and the regimes which followed in quick

---

[9] H. Kyemba, *State of Blood: the inside story of Idi Amin's reign of terror* (London, 1977), 26.

succession represented brutal and clumsy attempts at the political and economic reordering of Ugandan society, but they rendered Uganda a byword for bloody ineptitude – at least from the perspective of the outside world.

The more immediate sequence of events leading to Amin's *coup* is straightforward enough. He was the product of a botched decolonisation, of the deep-rooted and escalating tensions of the 1950s and the unhappy compromises various groups stitched together – the *ad hoc* politics – in the early 1960s. We will examine this period in more detail in a later chapter, but suffice to note here that the preceding decade had seen Uganda achieve independence through the short-term management of deep and multiple schisms which cut across the body politic in religious, regional and ethnic terms. The alliance between Obote's UPC and KY in Buganda was an unlikely partnership which sought not to bridge those profound divides, but to temporarily isolate them in the immediate pursuit of sovereignty, and to exclude others – chiefly the DP – from power. It was a coalition which had collapsed within two years of independence, and thereafter Uganda's politics were characterised by insecurity and anxiety at the centre, and a deepening sense of angry betrayal beyond it. This was the seedbed on which grew the relationship between Obote and his senior army officer, Idi Amin – a relationship which was intimate yet built on reciprocal distrust as well as need. It facilitated the expansion of the Ugandan army, and the increasing prominence of Amin himself, at the core of the political order. Theirs was a personal power struggle in many ways, but it was also emblematic of a deeper malaise within Ugandan political culture, and of a fundamental clash between visions of both the past and the future – two states which were, in any case, indivisible. Obote increasingly feared Amin's influence, and Amin was ever more contemptuous of his civilian boss; and by the end of the 1960s, the Ugandan political system was built on kindling. In the course of 1970, Amin's rift with Obote became complete: Amin was accused of supplying arms to the Anya Nya insurrection in southern Sudan, embezzling army funds and involvement in the killing of the deputy commander of the army, Brigadier Pierino Yere Okoya, in May 1970.[10] Amin's arrest

---

[10] Obote was a close friend of Okoya, a veteran of the KAR and regarded as one of Uganda's ablest soldiers, who had been promoted rapidly through the ranks since independence. He had been found murdered, along with his wife, at his

was ordered, but with Obote out of town – he was in Singapore for a Commonwealth summit – Amin made his move, occupying Kampala using the Malire Mechanised Regiment by the morning of 25 January 1971. It was an act motivated, at least in the first instance, by a powerful sense of self-preservation. But Amin had some political savvy, and it was demonstrated in the weeks that followed. At heart a populist, a showman, with a shrewd if variable sense of the pragmatic, he transformed himself into the great patriot, the friend of the poor, the saviour of Uganda. In time, too, he fashioned himself a pan-African liberator, conqueror of the British Empire and ultimately – much to the annoyance of his Western backers – Muslim crusader with a sworn hostility towards Israel. First, however, he needed to consolidate. Recognising the advantages of Ganda support – as Obote had before him – he permitted the return of the late *kabaka*'s body from the United Kingdom for interment at Kasubi.[11] Amin's takeover had been greeted with considerable jubilation in Kampala and Buganda at large, where Obote had been despised; now his popularity was secured, for the moment. He released dozens of political prisoners detained by Obote, including the leader of the opposition Democratic Party (DP), Benedicto Kiwanuka. As the secretary general of the DP, A.A.Latim, wrote with evident relief in February 1971:

I would like once more to congratulate Your Excellency...for having restored natural behaviour once more in our people of Uganda...I wish to assure Your Excellency that the coup has been accepted all over Uganda. Speaking as one of the leaders of the Democratic Party...I wish to assure you that we shall give you every support to enable you to re-establish true freedom and democracy in this country...Long live the Liberator of our freedom...Amin Dada.[12]

The 'Liberator' soon cut a humorous, amiable and humble figure, with a keen eye for media performance; however wary many parts of Uganda beyond Buganda might have been regarding his *coup*, he was quickly seen as a man with a plan, and a common touch to boot. By the

home in Gulu: 'Uganda mourns Brigadier Okoya', *DRUM*, May 1970, Kyemba, *State of Blood*, 30.

[11] 'Funeral of Sir Edward Mutesa, late Kabaka of Buganda at Kasubi Royal Tombs, 4 April 1971', UKNA FCO 57/307.

[12] A.A. Latim to Maj-Gen Idi Amin Dada, 13 February 1971, Papers of the Democratic Party, Makerere University Library Africana Section Archives (hereafter MUL).

middle of 1971 he felt confident enough to embark on his first over-seas trips – to Israel and the United Kingdom, and then to his first OAU summit in Addis Ababa. Amin seemed relatively unperturbed that the OAU conference was not held in Kampala, as had been planned, owing to the fact that several key members of the organisation – including Tanzania, Zambia, Guinea and Somalia – still refused to recognise the regime.[13]

If there was a honeymoon period – and the point is debatable – it was brief. By the end of 1972, a brutal (and increasingly *ad hoc*) authoritarianism was in place. Targeted but widespread killing had begun as early as July 1971, when Amin's forces had murdered several thousand Acholi and Langi soldiers for perceived or potential (and only occasionally actual) dissent.[14] Ethnically directed massacres continued through 1972, mostly of northern recruits. Yet in many ways the tipping point came in August–September. In August, Amin announced the imminent expulsion of some 50,000 Asians, on the grounds that they were not Ugandan but rather parasitic foreigners who for too long had controlled the Ugandan economy; it was an early indication – aside from the *coup d'etat* itself, of course – of Amin's cavalier approach to statecraft and diplomacy. It formed a central component in what Amin termed 'economic war',[15] but it was, it seems, a decision which was arrived at abruptly: as one government report put it a few months later, Amin's economic war 'had taken all people by surprise', but the new struggle 'received instantaneous, unwavering and total support. It very squarely answered the people's question of "After Political Independence, what next?"'[16] Then, in September, a small force of around 1,000 men loyal to Obote invaded from Tanzania and was massacred by Amin's Simba Battalion. While the Tanzanian high command denied knowledge of the attack, the Ugandan air force bombed the northern Tanzanian towns of Mwanza and Bukoba.[17] Significantly, by

[13] '1971 – a momentous year for Ugandans', *DRUM*, October 1971.
[14] Kyemba, *State of Blood*, 46–7.
[15] 'Message to the Nation by His Excellency the President General Idi Amin Dada, on British citizens of Asian origin and citizens of India, Pakistan and Bangla Desh living in Uganda . . . 12th/13th August, 1972', and also 'Midnight Address to the Nation by His Excellency the President on 17th December 1972', in *Speeches by His Excellency the President General Idi Amin Dada* (Government Printer, Entebbe).
[16] *Bunyoro District Annual Report 1972* (Uganda Government, 1972), 2.
[17] Mutibwa, *Uganda since Independence*, 97–101.

this point Libyan support to Amin was freely forthcoming, the beginnings of a close relationship between Amin and Muammar Qaddafi. The invading Ugandan force was wiped out, and there would be no serious attempt to dislodge Amin for another six years. In the same month, the first high-profile victim of Amin's unrestrained exercise of violence was Ben Kiwanuka, now Chief Justice, kidnapped and murdered just days after the ill-fated invasion attempt.[18]

Others would follow. Archbishop Janan Luwum was accused of involvement in a plot and, along with two senior ministers – Erinayo Oryema and Oboth-Ofumbi – was killed following a clumsily staged 'motor accident' one night in central Kampala.[19] There were many more murders, while Uganda's prisons swelled with political leaders, civil servants, playwrights, 'spies'. Amin's regime was underwritten by the chillingly euphemistic Public Safety Unit (PSU) and the State Research Bureau (SRB), both of which were refashioned out of Obote's General Service Unit and which acted – alongside the increasingly unruly army – with virtual impunity.[20] The fear that anyone could be an informant, and could deliver you into the dungeons of Nile Mansions, kept the populace remarkably cowed for much of the 1970s. Nonetheless, Amin's paranoia was not wholly unjustified. A coup attempt was foiled in March 1974, and there were two further assassination attempts: in February 1975, and again in June 1976, the latter incident marked by a large number of deaths as Amin's bodyguard opened fire into the crowds after hand grenades were thrown into his jeep.[21] Perhaps the most elaborate was the assassination attempt in June 1977, months in the planning, involving a group of men from the armed forces, the prison service and business, calling themselves the Uganda Liberation Movement. The most dramatic element in the plot was the planned bombing of State House from the air while Amin

---

[18] See a series of insightful *DRUM* magazine features from this period: 'Africa rallies to avert war', November 1972, 'The truth about Amin', May 1973, 'The mind of an African tyrant', May 1973.

[19] I. Grahame, *Amin and Uganda: a personal memoir* (London, 1980), 202; J. Kamau & A. Cameron, *Lust to Kill: the rise and fall of Idi Amin* (London, 1979), 246.

[20] This is attested to in numerous sources from the era: Kyemba, *State of Blood*, is illustrative, and for the extra-legal context, see M.S.M. Kiwanuka, *Amin and the Tragedy of Uganda* (Munich, 1979).

[21] Kyemba, *State of Blood*, 141–4; 'Opposition to President Idi Amin of Uganda', UKNA FCO 31/2043 [1976].

was in the building. He was tipped off, however, and the round-up which swiftly ensued led to summary executions (including a dozen plotters in front of a large crowd at Kampala's Clock Tower) and imprisonments.[22] Meanwhile low-level violent criminality – known as 'kondoism' – persisted, especially in the rural areas, and even Amin's security state struggled to impose itself on the quotidian business of armed robbery; but kondoism did provide a useful justification for curfews and round-ups.[23]

Personal testimonies are critical in shedding light on the brutal reality of Amin's state, such as those of the prominent political figure James Kahigiriza, arrested by the SRB in February 1977 while serving in the government. Extracts from his account are illustrative, and worth quoting directly:

I immediately knew this was my end. [The policeman] opened a door of a dark, virtually airless corridor, pushed me inside and locked the door.... Because I was breathless, I sat near the door to get whatever air was available... The floor of this tunnel was very slippery because of urine. It was unbearably hot, dirty, smelly and congested. As I tried to compose my thoughts about my ordeal, I heard people groaning. I knew they were being tortured and feared that it would soon be my turn...

Late in the afternoon, I heard another victim being pushed down the staircases, then the door opened... Later I learnt he was called Apollo Lawoko from Acholi. He was working in the Ministry of Information...

The following day... we heard people being pushed down the staircase at a terrific speed. These people turned out to be Erinayo Oryema, the Minister of Lands, Survey and Water Resources and Oboth Ofumbi, the Minister of Finance... Poor Ofumbi was just left in underpants. I was terribly shocked to see my minister Oryema, whom I had hoped would plead for me...

A little later, they are joined by still more fresh inmates, one of whom is the Archbishop, Janan Luwum:

This was the most shocking thing I had ever experienced in my life. For the head of the Church of Uganda to be so humiliated and treated like a common criminal was hard to believe...[His] garments had been removed...

---

[22] 'The plot that nearly worked', *DRUM*, September 1977.

[23] *Bunyoro District Annual Report 1972*, 2; and see A. Kayiira, 'Violence in Kondoism: the rise and nature of violent crime in Uganda' (PhD thesis, State University of New York at Albany, 1978). Andrew Kayiira would go on to lead the Uganda Freedom Movement, a guerrilla movement rivalling the NRA.

Then all of a sudden a State Research Bureau [official], one of those that had escorted them in, sarcastically asked the Archbishop questions: 'Who are you?' The Archbishop replied: 'I am the Archbishop.' The young man then slapped Luwum hard in the face, so much so that his false teeth fell on the ground. Tears started falling from my eyes . . .

The Archbishop courageously told this man that he was beating him because he had power, but that he should remember that this power was from God. The man who was speaking in Kiwahili said, '*We nakifiri wewe sheikh mufti?*' (Do you think you are Sheikh Mufti?) When the man who was serving us food, saw that we had failed to eat, he collected the plates and told us in Kiswahili '*Nyinyi najevuna, nakifiri nyinyi watu kubwa tutawona*' (You think you are big people, we shall see) . . . . Later, the Archbishop and his entire group as well as Oryema and Ofumbi were murdered.[24]

Today there are few outward, physical reminders of the violence of the period, though there is an exception to be found on Mengo Hill, inside what was, and is once more, the Ganda royal enclosure. Here, on one side of the hill facing Mwanga's lake, is a concrete bunker where both Amin (and Obote, second time around) killed indeterminate numbers of people; it is a small, disturbing, claustrophobic place, where bloody handprints can still be seen on the damp walls. It reeks of death and desperation.[25] This, then, was a shockingly violent state; and as with all such states there were opportunities for the unstable, the opportunistic, the ambitious – such as Colonel Maliyamungu, Amin's notoriously vicious and possibly psychotic right-hand man. Numbers are disputed but upwards of 300,000 died as the direct result of state-level violence.[26] In some ways the Ugandan state was the projection of Amin's own volatile and intemperate character but in other ways, too, the natural outcome of decolonisation a decade earlier. Government barely functioned in the normal sense; civil society was decimated; thousands fled Uganda, from the worlds of politics, academia, economics, medicine, the arts. As an article in the *Daily Monitor*, commemorating Uganda's fiftieth anniversary in 2012, reflected, 'the soul of the country was being ripped out'.[27]

---

[24] J. Kahigiriza, *Bridging the Gap: struggling against sectarianism and violence in Ankole and Uganda* (Kampala, 2001), 48–50.

[25] Author's field notes and informal interviews, 23 July 2014.

[26] International Commission of Jurists, UN Commission on Human Rights, *Uganda and Human Rights* (Geneva, 1977); Amnesty International, *Human Rights in Uganda* (London, 1978).

[27] 'Things we lost in the Amin fire', *Daily Monitor*, 27 September 2012.

For the outside world, meanwhile, and especially for a particularly sneering, faintly racist section of the foreign media, Idi Amin was a violent buffoon, a murderous joke, an African stereotype with its roots in the eighteenth and nineteenth centuries. Stories of his excesses and ludicrous pretentions, mingled with rumours of cannibalism and (on the part of his one-time foreign minister Princess Elizabeth of Toro) sexual depravity,[28] served to simultaneously titillate and horrify, in much the same way that crude representations of Africa had done for decades before colonial rule.[29] Such representation profoundly shaped the views of Amin's regime, and even of Africa more broadly. Amin's caricature as a manic, vaguely entertaining, brutal thug seemed to bear out the idea that decolonisation had not, after all, been a very good idea; 'they' (Ugandans, and Africans more generally) were clearly not up to the task of self-government.[30] Amin's apparently erratic and often (to foreign ears, at least) comical pronouncements only served to underline the point: declaring his desire to replace the Queen as the head of the Commonwealth, for example,[31] or laying claim to the putatively empty throne of Scotland.[32]

Meanwhile, Amin's foreign policy shifts amounted to a discernible 180 degrees.[33] On the face of it his relationship with the United Kingdom was never good: there was his self-awarded title 'Conqueror of the British Empire', and the deliberate humiliation of British (and other) expatriates who chose to live in Uganda following his seizure of power (they were forced to take an oath to him in public, on bended knee).[34] The expulsion of the Asian community was in part a deliberate insult to Britain, and an attack on what was presented as the enduring nefarious economic legacy of British rule – namely an effectively expatriate community with little apparent interest in the internal development of

---

[28] See her account of this in *African Princess*, 190–1.

[29] See, for example, P.D. Curtin, *The Image of Africa: British ideas and action, 1780–1850* (Madison WI, 1964), P. Brantlinger, 'Victorians and Africans: the Genealogy of the Myth of the Dark Continent', *Critical Enquiry*, 12:1 (1985).

[30] See, for example, D.N. Katono, 'Western Newspapers' Coverage of Idi Amin, 1971–1979', MA dissertation, Wake Forest University, 1990.

[31] Kiwanuka, *Amin and the Tragedy*, 168–9.

[32] Kamau & Cameron, *Lust to Kill*, 331. This book ends with a selection of Amin's colourful verbiage.

[33] Kiwanuka, *Amin*, 136–76; D. Gwyn, *Idi Amin: Death-Light of Africa* (Boston & Toronto, 1977), 152–72.

[34] Again, see Kamau & Cameron, *Lust to Kill*, 330–1.

Uganda itself. Yet for a couple of years the British nevertheless regarded him as a potential bulwark in the region, broadly pro-West, and certainly retained commercial as well as strategic interests in Uganda.[35] This changed fairly rapidly. The OAU, initially, had no particular problem incorporating the likes of Amin, and indeed he took up the chairmanship of the organisation as the latter convened in Kampala in June 1975, although this meeting was boycotted by Tanzania, Botswana and Zambia.[36] Relations with immediate neighbours deteriorated – including with Kenya, following Amin's territorial claims over the western part of Kenya in February 1976. In Tanzania, Nyerere remained a supporter of Obote and largely refused to deal with Amin. Further afield, the Unitd States closed its embassy in October 1973; Britain broke diplomatic ties in July 1976, a few weeks after the Israelis sent a commando mission to Entebbe airport to free the hostages of a commercial airliner hijacked by the PLO.[37] In the meantime, British Foreign Secretary James Callaghan had been forced to fly to Uganda to plead for the life of writer Denis Hills, arrested and sentenced to death as a result of a book he was writing in which Amin was portrayed as a 'black Nero' and a 'village tyrant'.[38] Amin enjoyed the grovelling of the UK government for a while, and then released Hills. By this time, in any case, he was moving decisively towards the Arab world, playing on his own Muslim identity and positioning Uganda accordingly, a reflection in part of his close ties – and the financial assistance these brought him – with Libya. Qaddafi's money shored up the military and led (eventually) to the building of an impressive mosque in the centre of Kampala.[39]

There are various interpretations of Amin's reign. Our comprehension of Amin's era – as well as the immediate aftermath – in many respects remains heavily dependent upon the grim analyses offered up at the time, both by Ugandan scholars and foreign commentators.

---

[35] Kyemba, *State of Blood*, 238; G. Arnold, *Africa: a modern history* (London, 2005), 368.

[36] 'Organisation of African Unity (OAU) Heads of State summit conference, Kampala, Uganda, 18 July – 1 August 1975', UKNA FCO 65/1596.

[37] 'Anglo-Ugandan relations: exchange of messages with President Idi Amin following James Callaghan's appointment as Prime Minister', UKNA PREM 16/1479, 6 April–20 May 1976; Kyemba, *State of Blood*, 166–78.

[38] Hills had himself drawn public attention to the contents of the book, which was later published as *The White Pumpkin* (London, 1975).

[39] Kyemba, *State of Blood*, 55, 240.

For Kiwanuka, Amin was a terrible anomaly, a one-man cyclone of bloody destruction;[40] a similarly singular idea pervades one of the most gripping accounts by a former insider turned political exile, that by the long-serving government minister Henry Kyemba who offered (according to the cover blurb) 'the shocking, brutal, story of the Hitler of our time'.[41] The somewhat unsubtle and misleading 'Hitler' analogy – though clearly desirable from a publisher's perspective – was also mobilised in a book by the former US ambassador to Uganda Thomas Melady.[42] The journalist Colin Legum, long-time friend and admirer of Milton Obote, offered a more nuanced critique which sought to expose the violent psychopath behind the jovial-featured, accordion-playing 'Big Daddy' image,[43] carefully cultivated by the man himself, for he watched keenly his representation abroad. Whatever the particular standpoint, this work tended – naturally enough, in some ways – to hone in on Amin himself, a mesmerising figure in the way that African dictators often are (or at least were, in the characterful 1970s). The emphasis was on his psychological makeup, his humble ethnic origins, his military background; Uganda was Amin, Amin was Uganda, and he dominated observers' line of vision absolutely. And so the Amin state has thrown a long shadow indeed over contemporary Uganda, and in many respects his legacy persists; there would be no NRM, no Museveni, perhaps even no neoliberal economics, without him. It is an era which remains shrouded in fear, guilt and simply ignorance. Yet within Uganda the ways in which the Amin regime was perceived were complex and nuanced. Recent pioneering work has begun to shed new light on the actual functioning of Amin's state and indeed on life beyond it.[44]

Idi Amin's seizure of power can be understood on various levels. A longer-term, thematic conceptualisation of events might focus on the north as the colonial centre of military gravity in Uganda, and as disproportionately powerful in the sense that northerners – despite being

---

[40] For example, Kiwanuka, *Amin*.   [41] Kyemba, *State of Blood*.
[42] T. Melady & M. Melady, *Idi Amin Dada: Hitler in Africa* (Kansas City, 1977). Other journalistic work of a more or less gory and sensationalist bent includes: D. Martin, *General Amin* (London, 1974), T. Donald, *Confessions of Idi Amin* (London, 1978), Kamau & Cameron, *Lust to Kill*, M. L. Richardson, *After Amin: the bloody pearl* (Atlanta, 1980), and a little later to reach the bookshelves, B. Measures & T. Walker, *Amin's Uganda* (London, 1998).
[43] For example C. Legum, 'Behind the Clown's Mask', *Transition*, 50 (Oct. 1975).
[44] D.R. Peterson & E.C. Taylor, 'Rethinking the state in Idi Amin's Uganda: the politics of exhortation', *Journal of Eastern African Studies*, 7:1 (2013).

demographically insignificant – made up the vast bulk of the Ugandan army, mainly Acholi.[45] It was, therefore, always a potential source of political intervention. Moreover, in the course of the 1960s, the Ugandan army had been expanding rapidly, becoming the seventh largest in Africa following the third-largest growth rate on the continent.[46] Reallocations to the defence budget had been significant under Obote, in part a response to a short-lived mutiny in 1964, but largely due to Obote's desire to shore up the hardware protecting his regime against internal opponents.[47] This was an increasingly unruly, ill-disciplined force, relatively easily mobilised in the event of political trouble, and in which Amin enjoyed considerable popularity.[48] Moreover, northern Uganda had long been a contested and militarised frontier zone, abutting and indeed seamlessly transitioning into southern Sudan; again, it was a frontier zone with the potential for political turbulence, with ramifications for the rest of the country (as well as for Sudan). Amin was a product of the turbulent frontier, and represented a distinctive pattern in the region's history, namely episodic military intervention in the political realm. He was, then, the creation of a historically marginalised and militarised periphery, but also an armed and ambitious leader in search of a state, a hardy frontiersman seeking to regenerate a flaccid and decaying political system. He was not, in that sense, particularly novel, or unusual in Ugandan or African history. But while some considered him the archetypal 'man on horseback', the warrior outsider come to rescue the nation from despair,[49] for others he was the embodiment of atavism, a version of the kind of tribal savagery which the younger Amin had himself helped suppress as a KAR soldier in Kenya in the 1950s.[50] His seizure of power was an atavistic scream, an eschewal of modernity, which seemed all the more compelling given the backwater – he was Kakwa, from the far northwest border area – from which he hailed. Kyemba in particular was clear that Amin's personality was shaped in large part by his 'tribal' background, rooted in the ungovernable north and, more specifically, the cannibalistic

---

[45] J.M. Lee, *African Armies and Civil Order* (London, 1969), 71.
[46] S. Decalo, *Coups and Army Rule in Africa: motivations and constraints* (New Haven & London, 1990), 158.
[47] Ibid.
[48] W.F. Gutteridge, *Military Regimes in Africa* (London, 1975), 158–61.
[49] A. Southall, 'General Amin and the Coup: great man or historical inevitability?', *Journal of Modern African Studies*, 13 (1975).
[50] Decalo, *Coups and Army Rule*, 171; Grahame, *Amin and Uganda*, 28*ff*.

'warrior' Kakwa.[51] Amin's state certainly came to be defined by ethnicity, with the army command in particular drawn from West Nile district; as Holger Bernt Hansen has influentially argued, however, this was to a large degree a reflection of the regime's chronic insecurity and incoherence, compelling it to carefully (and, increasingly, violently) distinguish between 'supporters' and 'enemies'.[52] At the same time, however, he might be seen, and was by political scientist Ali Mazrui, as an example of the kind of social mobility which might even be a cause for celebration – albeit social mobility which was particularly possible for the armed warrior of humble origins.[53] This interpretation, with its emphasis on individual agency as much as wider socio-historical pattern, is encapsulated in the common characterisation of Amin's rule as a 'personal dictatorship'.[54]

Amin was indeed idiosyncratic but he was also symptomatic of a nation profoundly uncertain of itself, its direction and its composition. It is likely that his leadership was no *less* certain than any of the possible alternatives, but it was certainly characterised by a preparedness to use, and an access to, violence which others would have lacked. As for the specific horrors of the Amin years, these were the product of a personality singularly ill-suited to political leadership, but more particularly they were related to the ethnic fissures evident in an ill-disciplined army and state-security service, dominated by northerners and Sudanese, whose willingness to carry out such brutal violence on the population can perhaps best be explained in terms of their marginalisation and disconnection from wider society. Meanwhile, more recent research has begun to offer us glimpses into the functioning and shaping of Amin's Uganda, especially on the edges – and indeed beyond the reaches – of the supposedly chaotically pervasive state itself. This was a regime which was paradoxically both gun-toting and pen-pushing: while the government pumped out official directives and sought to impose particular visions on the nation, these were diluted, modified and often

---

[51] Kyemba, *State of Blood*, 17, 109.
[52] H.B. Hansen, *Ethnicity and Military Rule in Uganda* (Uppsala, 1977) and a more recent revisiting of that argument in H.B. Hansen, 'Uganda in the 1970s: a decade of paradoxes and ambiguities', *Journal of Eastern African Studies*, 7:1 (2013).
[53] See, for example, A. A. Mazrui (ed.), *The Warrior Tradition in Modern Africa* (Leiden, 1977), A. A. Mazrui, 'The social origins of Ugandan presidents: from king to peasant warrior', *Canadian Journal of African Studies*, 8 (1974).
[54] Decalo, *Coups and Army Rule*, 139*ff.*

successfully contested at the outer reaches of the state, as Edgar Taylor has demonstrated for the Asians of Kabale. This community was not cowed by the bureaucratic state but rather used bureaucracy to fight for citizenship status and persuade local officials of their cause. And many other Asians, too, continued to live and work in the shadow of a regime that purportedly despised them, doing so by maintaining paperwork and hospitable relations with local bureaucrats.[55] There were many who quietly and courageously engaged with and resisted the predations of the agitated, violent state – none more so than the women described by Alicia Decker who testified to the internal commission of enquiry into human rights set up by Amin himself in 1974, and who mobilised sympathy for their plight as widows and relatives of the dead and missing in myriad ways.[56]

Naturally, some did very well out of the Amin years, not least those who gained access to land, and who benefited from economic mismanagement.[57] Meanwhile in Uganda itself, Amin was viewed ambivalently by some – how to weigh up the popularly received expulsion of the Asian community and the political and economic benefits accrued by some against the mass killing of Langi and Acholi and many others? In the three decades since his ouster, he continues to be considered in more nuanced ways inside Uganda than he ever was beyond it. Recently, he has even undergone something of a rehabilitation. At the time of his death in 2003, a live phone-in on Ugandan television involved callers lamenting the death of a man who was a great 'patriot', in contrast to the salesman Museveni;[58] and in more recent years, one informant remembered Amin as someone who 'wasn't all bad … he was a nationalist, and getting rid of the Indians was a good thing!'[59]

---

[55] E.C.Taylor, 'Claiming Kabale: racial thought and urban governance in Uganda' and A.K. Hundle, 'Exceptions to the expulsion: violence, security and community among Ugandan Asians, 1972–79', both in *Journal of Eastern African Studies*, 7:1 (2013).

[56] A.C. Decker, '"Sometime you may leave your husband in Karuma Falls or in the forest there": a gendered history of disappearance in Idi Amin's Uganda, 1971–79', *Journal of Eastern African Studies*, 7:1 (2013) and see also her excellent monograph on the experience of women during the 1970s, *In Idi Amin's Shadow: women, gender and militarism in Uganda* (Athens OH, 2014).

[57] Author's field notes and informal interviews, 10 August 2010.

[58] Author's field notes and informal interviews, August 2003.

[59] Author's field notes and informal interviews, 8 August 2010, also 10 August 2010.

This is a view which is often heard repeated.[60] A recent book, meanwhile, lays due stress on *The Other Side of Idi Amin*.[61] He is both a capricious tyrant and a well-intentioned patriot, and thus his remains an ambiguous kind of authoritarianism.

Still, his ouster at the time was received with general enthusiasm. Opposition forces were amassing beyond Uganda's borders by the latter end of the 1970s, some loyal to Obote, others bitterly opposed to Obote's return. But in the event it was a war with Tanzania which destroyed Amin, a war which escalated out of the latter's control and exposed his own inherent instability. His slow downfall began, in July 1978, with the decision to send an armoured unit of the Simba Battalion across the Tanzanian border following some skirmishes between pastoralists in the Mbarara border area.[62] A series of ostentatious manoeuvres followed, characterised by confusion in command and even exact position, while some units came under apparently friendly fire. Amin accused the Tanzanians of attacking Uganda but nonetheless withdrew in November, though he maintained a heavily armed presence at the border. Nyerere finally retaliated in January 1979, sending forces across the border which, combined with a coalition of Ugandan opposition forces – the Uganda National Liberation Front (UNLF) – numerically overwhelmed Amin's dwindling and archaically equipped army. The Ugandan army was compelled to continually withdraw, entrench and then withdraw again, abandoning Masaka and pulling back steadily towards Kampala.[63] There were some minor successes once Amin had handed command to his fellow Kakwa, Col. Godwin Sule, who abandoned trench war in favour of more mobile assaults – while Amin declared with each 'victory' that his advance would end in Dar es Salaam. But in a fitting endgame, Sule was apparently killed by his own mutinous troops, and Amin's last stand was at Mpigi, a few miles west of the capital. Some 3,000 Sudanese, plus smaller contingents of Libyans and Palestinians, failed to hold up the advance for more than a few days, and on 11 April, as Tanzanian and

---

[60] See also Peterson & Taylor, 'Rethinking the state', 63.

[61] C.C. Sembuya, *The Other Side of Idi Amin* (Kampala, 2009).

[62] For a detailed and at times first-hand account, see T. Avirgan & M. Honey, *War in Uganda: the legacy of Idi Amin* (Westport, CT. & London, 1982), chap 3.

[63] 'War on the border', *DRUM*, March 1979; 'The invasion that went wrong', *DRUM*, April 1979.

Ugandan opposition forces occupied Kampala, his overthrow was publicly announced.[64]

While Amin himself headed homeward to West Nile, eventually departing for Libya, many of his soldiers abandoned their weapons and likewise fled north, or sought to melt away; some fought on for the lost cause, such as the entourage that stuck with Mustapha Adrisi (who insisted on referring to himself, still, as Vice-President) in Sudan.[65] But the real danger was on the streets of Kampala after dark through 1979, for in the wake of the dissolution of the regime came a wave of apparently random violence, facilitated by abandoned small arms and carried out by an array of misfits, criminals, opportunists and the remnants of the old security forces.[66] Neither the presence of 20,000 Tanzanian troops, a large contingent of whom were based in and around the city, nor the curfew quickly introduced by the interim administration, could quell the backwash of the killing produced by the implosion of the regime; and it was this that formed the turbulent backdrop to eighteen months of political experimentation.[67] His ouster sparked close to a decade of violent turbulence and regime-change, a period of political experimentation and the politics of the stop-gap, and in many ways might be viewed as the final, bloody stage in Uganda's decolonisation. The successive regimes of Yusuf Lule, Godfrey Binaisa, Paulo Muwanga, Obote for the second stint – known locally as 'Obote II' – and Tito Okello were, with the exception of Obote II, short-lived, each lasting no more than a few months, and had the appearance in hindsight of doomed, ill-considered experiments in political management. Yet we must be careful not to be overly dismissive: to do so would be to fall, to some extent, under the NRM spell, and buy into Museveni's message that *devant moi, la catastrophe!* By that reading, everything was moving inexorably towards the salvation delivered to the Ugandan people by the Movement in 1986. That would be a mistake. Following Amin's ouster in April 1979, there were a series of sincere, if flawed, exercises in crisis management, and in damage limitation; they were not doomed to fail, although to be sure they were attended by chronic problems. Uganda reached its nadir in the early 1980s. But each

---

[64] Avirgan & Honey, *War in Uganda*, passim.

[65] 'Amin's legacy claims new victims', *DRUM*, August 1979.

[66] A vivid account of the immediate aftermath is in Avirgan & Honey, *War in Uganda*, chap. 11.

[67] 'Gun rule in Uganda', *DRUM*, October 1979.

failure brought new levels of experience, and each step some degree of clarification as to the scale and nature of the problems themselves – problems primarily related to a chronic lack of political confidence, ethnic mistrust, the erosion of social capital, economic collapse and an over-mighty, swollen and unruly army.

The appointment of Professor Yusuf Lule as president was the first attempt at stabilisation using a supposedly unifying figure.[68] He was a Muganda, which would bring the kingdom on side; he was an academic and a civil servant, and therefore seen as untainted by association with past regimes; and he had played a part – a modest one, admittedly – in organising against Amin. Yet the former principal of Makerere had very little room for manoeuvre. Real power lay with a triumvirate of political forces: UPC activist Paulo Muwanga, already planning for Obote's eventual return; the UNLF command; and Nyerere himself, who as Uganda's reluctant 'liberator' now had a significant say over any new dispensation of power in Kampala.[69] No sooner had Lule begun toying with army reform than he was removed by the quasi-parliamentary National Consultative Commission (NCC) in June, having served for 68 days. Against a backdrop of Ganda mass protests, he was replaced by another Muganda, though a rather more controversial one than Lule: Godfrey Binaisa, the lawyer who as Obote's Attorney-General had drafted the 1967 constitution abolishing the kingdoms – thus earning him the enduring animus of the Ganda.[70] Having spent much of the 1970s in exile – in the United Kingdom and the United States, practising law – he was now handed the opportunity to head the rickety structure that was Uganda's government. He had no intention, however, of serving as a largely impotent figurehead: by the beginning of 1980, he had begun to assert himself, proposing no-party elections (a move bitterly opposed by both the UPC and the DP) and seeking to break up the political-military oligopoly of Museveni, Muwanga and army chief Oyite Ojok. Museveni was moved from the defence ministry to regional cooperation, while there was a

---

[68] For an excellent overview of this period, see Mutibwa, *Uganda Since Independence*, chap. 10.

[69] Museveni, *Mustard Seed*, 109.

[70] Mutibwa, *Uganda since Independence*, 130. On Binaisa's death in 2010, there was a brief public debate over whether he should be allowed a 'hero's plot' in the state-owned cemetery. The government – and many Ugandans – thought not: author's field notes and informal interviews, 10 August 2010.

somewhat unsubtle attempt to have Muwanga dispatched as ambassador to Geneva and Ojok removed as army head. Yet Museveni's own recollection of the move – which he later asserted was 'an attempt to remove the freedom fighters from the core of the government' – was that it had been engineered by the Obote lobby, including Muwanga and Ojok, who shortly after fell out with Binaisa themselves.[71] This internal factionalism – essentially over the control of the army, and the future of Obote and the UPC – precluded effective government. Binaisa, who had overplayed his hand, was removed in May 1980, and the Military Commission, headed by Muwanga, took over. By now, there was deep apprehension about the power of the Commission and – especially in the ranks of the DP – the true openness of the forthcoming election. Yusuf Lule, in exile in Nairobi, warned of the need to 'work for unity among all people of Uganda regardless of their tribal affinity or religious beliefs' and made clear his conviction that only the DP could bring this about.[72] The DP itself feared the '[re]introduction of dictatorship...through the back-door'.[73] But between May and December, Muwanga prepared the way for Obote's return to office, and part of that groundwork involved the violent intimidation of the DP – notably in the north, where Acholi activists were targeted by Langi soldiers and militia.[74] The consensus is that the elections of December 1980 – the first in Uganda since 1962 – were rigged in favour of Obote and the UPC.[75]

It was a decisive moment, and in many ways continues to haunt – even define – electoral politics in Uganda. The DP claimed victory under Paul Ssemogerere, to little avail; Museveni's party, the third-placed Uganda Patriotic Movement (UPM), finally eschewed the fragile political process in place since Amin fled the country, and returned

---

[71] Museveni, *Mustard Seed*, 114–5.
[72] 'Press Statement by Prof. Y.K. Lule, 9 July 1980, Nairobi', Papers of the Democratic Party, MUL.
[73] 'Press Release' from the DP headquarters, Kampala, 7 May 1980, Papers of the Democratic Party, MUL.
[74] 'Press Conference: harassment and intimidation which will impair free and fair elections', n.d., probably August/September 1980, Papers of the Democratic Party, MUL.
[75] S. Karugire, *The Roots of Instability in Uganda* (Kampala, 1988), Appendix I, 84–100. The scandal and controversy surrounding the 'stolen elections' of 1980 remain intense. See, for example, J. Kabaireho, 'How UPC "rigged" the 1980 elections', *The Observer* (Kampala), 10 December 2008.

to the 'bush', opening guerrilla war in the Luwero area, although the main centre of recruitment and political gravity was in Ankole in the west.[76] A critical turning point, it effectively marked the end of even the pretence of serious electoral politics for a generation, and tilted the political scene in Uganda decisively towards violence as a means of resolution. This was of an altogether different hue from even Amin's violent reign, during which opponents had generally supposed that a single blow – a successful assassination – would allow Ugandans to recover their equilibrium and hammer out some kind of post-horror settlement. The new guerrilla war of the early 1980s was altogether different in ethos and objective, imbued as it was with current ideas about social as well as political revolution, facilitated by a profession-alised and ideologically conscious military.

Strikingly, Obote – ensconced once more in State House – seemed unaware of the political portents. His second stint arguably remains even murkier as a historical episode than Amin's period. Indeed, while it is understandable that there is a growing scholarly interest in the latter – just as he fascinated and repelled at the time – Obote II has received remarkably little sustained attention, and is shrouded by the smoke of battle and obfuscated by a kind of collective stress disorder. Yet he was, for many, the father of Ugandan nationalism – and who in recent years would be reconfigured and commemorated as such.[77] 'Love him or loathe him', began an assessment in the *New Vision* in 2012,

but Uganda's political history is incomplete without Dr Apollo Milton Obote.... Although many people [have] discredited him as a dictatorial leader who banned political parties, kingdoms, installed himself as presi-dent and abolished the 1962 independence constitution and drafted his own, many also credit him for development of infrastructure like schools, roads, establishment of cooperative societies and building of hospitals.[78]

Much was forgiven, if not forgotten.[79] In many ways, Obote represented continuity from Amin, and further utilised the role of

[76] Museveni, *Mustard Seed*, 118–20; Kutesa, *Uganda's Revolution*, 49.
[77] 'The rise of Dr Milton Obote', *Daily Monitor*, 9 July 2012.
[78] 'Obote: the man who did not need to please anyone', *New Vision*, 16 January 2012.
[79] See also the attempt at a more rounded assessment of Obote – the 'hero' as well as the 'villain' – in O.R. Anguria (ed.), *Apollo Milton Obote: what others say* (Kampala, 2006).

the military in politics; the militarisation of political culture arguably reached its apex in the early 1980s. For others, however, he represented a blessed relief from Amin, a 'second liberation' in his own words, and at the time there were optimistic and generally supportive assessments of the challenges facing his courageous leadership.[80] But it is difficult to contest, at least in terms of the basics, the accepted national narrative which describes an increasingly neurotic and illegitimate regime characterised by escalating violence, with progressive guerrilla forces – specifically those of the NRA – waging war against the forces of darkness, forces which threatened to consume the nation itself. The consensus is that his reign from the end of 1980 until the middle of 1985 was more brutal, and resulting in higher numbers of deaths, than the whole of Amin's. In large part this was the outcome of bloody counterinsurgency in the 'Luwero Triangle', the killing fields between Kampala and Lake Kyoga.[81]

A gloomy contemporary report at the outset of Obote's administration proclaimed that 'Uganda is in a terrible mess. The majority of her people have been . . . brought to a point of despair after years of suffering. Its north and northwest boundaries will be in a ferment for a generation. The army is divided. The economy has collapsed'.[82] A host of groups rejected the 1980 election result and took to the bush, including the joint forces of Yoweri Museveni and Yusuf Lule, whose respective groups, the Popular Resistance Army and the Uganda Freedom Fighters, combined in February 1981 to form the National Resistance Army/Movement.[83] But they were not alone: this was an increasingly crowded marketplace of violent enterprise. Andrew Kayiira's Uganda Freedom Movement and the Federal Democratic Movement of Uganda had links with the DP, which operated within the law 'by day', as it were, but which 'by night' – increasingly the most active hours in Ugandan politics – was involved with armed groups committed to the overthrow of the regime.[84] They even had links with disaffected members of the Ugandan army itself, not least those Catholic Acholi

---

[80] For example, V. Gupta, *Obote: second liberation* (New Delhi, 1983).

[81] The 'Triangle' took in the old frontier lands of Singo and Bulemezi *ssaza*s, long the battlegrounds of the Ganda and the Nyoro in the nineteenth century, and thus embodied a chilling degree of military continuity: see, for example, Amaza, *Museveni's Long March*.

[82] 'Obote wins rigged general election', *DRUM*, January 1981.

[83] Museveni, *Mustard Seed*, 133–4.   [84] Kutesa, *Uganda's Revolution*, 98, 207.

who responded to any encouragement of the idea that ethnically and religiously they remained on the despised peripheries of the political order.[85] But the Ganda too had reason to reach for the weaponry, for in the early 1980s there was a growing sense that after two decades of independence the great kingdom remained shut out of politics (the short-lived tenures of Lule and Binaisa was testament to the fact), while once again their nemesis Obote was back in office. Buganda's failure seemed complete. The NRA/M was keenly aware of this, and Museveni's appreciation of the value of the symbolic gesture in Ugandan politics led to him acceding to the appointment of Lule as chairman of the Movement (Museveni himself was deputy chairman and commander of the military wing), which duly proved enormously popular among the beleaguered Ganda.[86]

Violent contest now squirted in all directions. There had long been bloody recriminations against northerners in the wake of Amin's exodus, causing tens of thousands of Ugandan refugees to spill into southern Sudan – a crisis compounded by famine across the area.[87] These attacks continued into the early 1980s. Within the Ugandan army itself – arguably the single largest source of potentially explosive political change – there were major conflicts brewing between particular factions, loosely organised around Acholi and Langi ethnicity.[88] Meanwhile the NRA escalated its guerrilla war in the bush through the early 1980s, springing ambushes on government troops and buildings and laying landmines;[89] they even received some assistance from an unlikely source, Qaddafi's Libya, the latter hoping for greater influence in central Africa than they had been able to achieve through their support for Idi Amin.[90] In response, the National Security Agency organised counter-insurgency methods known in Swahili as *Panda Gari* – literally, 'get into the vehicle', which actually dated to the 1970s as a counter-insurgency tactic. It involved large-scale rounding-up of suspects and potential informants who were loaded onto trucks and pickups, and they tended to operate within the city of Kampala and its

---

[85] Museveni, *Mustard Seed*, 165–6.   [86] Ibid., 140–1.
[87] 'Amin's legacy claims new victims', *DRUM*, August 1979.
[88] A.B.K. Kasozi, *The Social Origins of Violence in Uganda, 1964–1985* (Montreal & London, 1994), 172–4; A. Omara-Otunnu, *Politics and the Military in Uganda, 1890–1985* (Basingstoke, 1987), 162–3.
[89] A useful first-hand account is Kutesa, *Uganda's Revolution*.   [90] Ibid., 85, 100.

environs, up to a radius of around fifty miles.[91] These operations, when successful, netted 'computers': the local slang for informants who provided information under duress, including torture, on known guerrillas and other urban insurgents.[92] More broadly, *Panda Gari* became a term denoting the fear and anxiety which characterised Kampala in the early 1980s, for as the bush war escalated, so in turn did the brutality of the state. The urban environment, as it always had, produced its own peculiar mix of politics and violence, characterised by darkness and concealment. But beyond the city limits, in the vulnerable rural setting, violence was even more overt. Security forces routinely retaliated against villages suspected of harbouring or abetting rebels of various hues, and all the while Obote preached reconciliation.[93]

Yet until the beginning of 1984 the NRA were largely contained by government forces, and seemed destined only to maintain Uganda in a state of unsettlement, rather than ever coming close to seizing power. This was in large part due to the talents of Obote's ruthless army chief of staff, fellow Langi David Oyite Ojok – war hero (he had played a prominent role in anti-Amin operations throughout the 1970s), womaniser, serial looter and embezzler, and a wealthy man due to his other job as chairman of Coffee Marketing Board. His success against rebel forces owed much to his relaxed attitude to his soldiers' own looting as well as his creation of counter-insurgency militia among the Langi, Acholi and Teso.[94] It was only Ojok's suspicious death in a plane crash in December 1983,[95] the NRA's increasing skill in attracting favourable foreign media attention, and perhaps above all the

---

[91] Kasozi, *Social Origins*, 146–8; S. Finnstrom, 'Fear of the Midnight Knock: state sovereignty and internal enemies in Uganda', in B. Kapferer & B. E. Bertelsen (eds.), *Crisis of the State: war and social upheaval* (New York, 2009), 134–5. See also the brief but informative segment, '1981–1985: The Panda Gari', in *Independent Uganda*, 76–7.

[92] Finnstrom, 'Fear of the Midnight Knock', 135.

[93] See the somewhat hagiographic assessment in K. Ingham, *Obote: a political biography* (London, 1994).

[94] Kutesa, *Uganda's Revolution*, 136, 183–4; Museveni, *Mustard Seed*, 142.

[95] By this time a rift had developed between Ojok and his self-styled 'patron' Obote. While some claimed the NRA had brought the aircraft down, including the Movement itself, there has long been a widely-held view that Obote had him killed. Notably, in 2010, Museveni declared his old foe a national hero, and during the jubilee celebrations in 2012 he was remembered as a formidable and worthy warrior: 'Oyite Ojok, one of Uganda's best soldiers', *New Vision*, 7 February 2012.

Movement's nurturing of links with discontented Acholi army officers which transformed their fortunes.[96] Catholic Acholi soldiers, supporters of the DP, ultimately provided the critical breakthrough against Obote in July 1985, when Acholi resentment at Obote's rule was manifest in a series of mutinies by troops under the overall leadership of Maj.-Gen. Bazillio Okello. Okello had also been threatened with retirement under plans to stand down semi-literate officers the year before, and he and fellow Acholi Lt.-Gen. Tito Okello joined forces to mobilise the simmering resentment of their subordinates. Meanwhile a Langi, Smith Opon-Acak, had been appointed as army chief of staff, a post rendered vacant by Ojok's death and one to which Bazillio Okello aspired. Langi-Acholi tensions intensified into the middle of 1985. In July, Bazillio Okello led a mutiny in Kitgum, marched on Gulu, and then dispatched units to Kampala to overthrow Obote – which they did, largely unopposed. For the second time, and this time never to return, Obote fled. Tito Okello was sworn in as head of state.[97]

However, Museveni refused to fully commit to peace talks taking place in Nairobi under the auspices of Daniel arap Moi, and Uganda endured tortuous negotiations – which collapsed and restarted on several occasions – for another six months between various rebel groups (the most important of which was the NRA) and the government. At one point, Museveni – now the undisputed leader of the NRA since Lule's death in London earlier in the year – refused to deal with Okello unless the latter was treated as merely the head of another armed faction; a revealing proposition, and not a wholly unjustified one.[98] All the while, the NRA strengthened its military position, especially in the west and in parts of Buganda, which were effectively sealed off from the rest of Uganda. Although a peace agreement was finally signed in December, and a coalition government formed in principle with various rebel groups represented on a Military Council, within days it was evident that the all-important ceasefire had not held. The NRA had little need for it to do so, in any case.[99] In January, its units entered Kampala, overcoming some brief but ferocious resistance from Okello's troops,

---

[96] Mutibwa, *Uganda since Independence*, 157*ff*.

[97] Ibid., 163–4; Museveni, *Mustard Seed*, 164–8; 'Obote toppled by Acholi officers', *DRUM*, September 1985.

[98] Museveni is naturally unequivocal on the point: *Mustard Seed*, 168–9; see also Omara-Otunnu, *Politics and the Military*, chap. 13.

[99] Omara-Otunnu, *Politics and the Military*, 175, provides a critical assessment of events.

and proclaimed a new political order. For the third time inside seven years, an insurgent force had entered the city proclaiming the death of the old regime and the birth of a new one.

Surveyed in the round, the era from 1971 to 1986 can be seen to represent a veritable explosion of violent entrepreneurialism – both at the level of the state and beyond it, including amongst groups who would supplant it. This was facilitated in particular by the collapse of the monopoly formerly maintained by the old army barracks, the early postcolonial military order embodied by veteran soldiers such as Tito Okello and Idi Amin himself who were ultimately products of the colonial military complex. Guerrilla groups of a rather different hue challenged this order – the product, ironically, of expanded education systems and educational opportunities, infused with revolutionary fervour and ideals and bolstered by an expanding white-collar class of political technocrats and professionals. Together, they now sought to capture the moral high ground. This was an era defined by multiple and overlapping vectors of violence: between Buganda and the north, and ultimately between north and south; within the north between Langi and Acholi, with the additional dynamic of West Nile groups to further destabilise a fragile coexistence; ultimately between the Nyankole and a host of enemies – Ganda reactionaries, Acholi chauvinists, *Ugandans* who had supposedly failed the nation. In many ways these conflicts were the product of militarised claustrophobia, and exacerbated by the emergence of sovereign nationhood.

Museveni's Time

Yoweri Museveni's inauguration speech would come back to haunt him. But it was a terrific performance at the time, one deserving of the new beginning which the Movement believed itself to have heralded. 'Nobody is to think', he declared,

that what is happening today, what has been happening in the last few days is a mere change of guards. This is not a mere change of guards. I think this is a fundamental change in the politics of our government. Any individual, any group or person who threatens the security of our people must be smashed without mercy. The people of Uganda should only die from natural causes which are not under our control, but not from fellow human beings.

Referring mockingly to the stereotype of the globe-trotting, disconnected African president, he intoned: 'His excellence is going to the United Nations, and he is there for meetings with Reagan and Gorbachev, and 90 per cent of his people have no shoes. They are walking on bare feet'.[100] No longer, these rank abuses of power and privilege; government must now serve the people, not the reverse. A quarter-century later, as Uganda celebrated its fifty years of independence, those who even remembered the speech could be forgiven for wondering what all the fuss had been about. The frustration was succinctly captured in a piece in the *Daily Monitor*, written following a visit by former US president Bill Clinton to Uganda in July 2012. 'Is Museveni still a "new breed" leader?', the piece wondered. It quoted a presidential spokesperson as saying yes, of course, with the trusty defence wheeled out: you need to remember where Uganda was in 1986. But the essay went on to outline the manifold failings of the regime, and quipped with reference to the inaugural oration: 'The President, in a coil of fate, cruises to New York in a Gulfstream V plane to attend UN meetings while jiggers kills villagers in the eastern Busoga region'.[101]

The central motif of the new government of the late 1980s was peace and development. The Movement itself was rooted in the revolutionary politics of the 1960s and 1970s; Museveni, a political science graduate of the University of Dar es Salaam, had sat at the feet of the great West Indian scholar Walter Rodney.[102] He had spent time with FRELIMO in Mozambique. But he and the 'Historicals', as the founding leaders were known, were more pragmatic than dogmatic, a realism forged in the challenging politics of the early 1980s and the slow painful death of the Obote regime. They were also, on the *prima facie* evidence, a talented bunch and won admiration for their approach and tactics: in their mobilisation of popular discontent against Obote; in their ability to recruit from rural areas and thus expand their numbers rapidly; in their internal structure and leadership organisation; in their self-reliance, a narrative familiar across other parts of eastern and northeast Africa among similar guerrilla forces.[103] The Movement was socially progressive, committed to socio-economic change

---

[100] 'Ours is a fundamental change', swearing-in address, 29 January 1986, in Y. K. Museveni, *What Is Africa's Problem?* (Minneapolis, 2000).

[101] 'Is Museveni still a "new breed" leader?', *Daily Monitor*, 23 July 2012.

[102] Museveni, *Mustard Seed*, 24–5 and Y. Museveni, 'Fanon's theory on violence: its verification in liberated Mozambique', in N.M. Shamuyarira (ed.), *Studies in Political Science*, 3 (Dar es Salaam, 1974).

[103] C. Clapham, 'Introduction: analysing African insurgencies', in C. Clapham (ed.), *African Guerrillas* (Oxford, 1998).

and the representation of 'historical minorities' (women and youth), and built around a clearheaded and evidently inspirational leader in Yoweri Museveni himself.[104] This was, in sum, a markedly successful military and political organisation with a programme designed to pull the bloodied nation back from the brink, and to facilitate its rebirth.[105]

There were indeed transformative elements to the NRM programme, though arguably the most significant *discontinuity*, certainly in terms of the period since independence, was in the realm of economics, with which we deal in more detail later in the book. The Movement's embrace of neoliberal economics led to a dramatic programme of privatisation and inward investment, and a parallel dismantling of the swollen public sector. Arguably, though, even here there was something of a resurgence of commercial dynamics dating back to the nineteenth century. But in the political arena the Movement also appeared to herald significant change. Museveni shared with the Obote regime, at least in terms of rhetoric, a fear of what was commonly termed 'sectarianism' – a conviction that there were too many ethnically- and regionally-identified groups organised noisily around 'tribe' and 'faith', squabbling (as the Historicals saw it) over needlessly destructive ideas about history. In pursuit of this agenda, the NRM eschewed party politics. There was no immediate appetite for elections within the Movement, and certainly not elections which might throw up any serious challenge. Of course the NRM would make a rather more compelling case than any Obote or Amin or Paulo Muwanga had ever made, which was that elections involving political parties were simply unsuited to Uganda's violent and deeply fissured political landscape. Given the shenanigans of the early 1960s, and the notorious 1980 election, the argument for that elusive creature, the 'benign dictatorship', and for democracy being a luxury of the developed world (Museveni routinely declared that Africa's problem was that it was primitive and undeveloped) was a powerful one. It was also one which many Ugandans were willing, for a time, to buy into – though the idea had, as the pastoralist president should have understood, a limited shelf life.

[104] For example, see P. Ngoga's admiring essay 'Uganda: the National Resistance Army', in Clapham (ed.), *African Guerrillas*.
[105] 'The National Resistance Movement Ten-Point Program', in Museveni, *What Is Africa's Problem?*, 257–61.

The Movement enjoyed, at the outset, a considerable stock of political capital.[106] But it was also able to take advantage of the relative weakness of rival political movements – including other armed groups and the major political parties, including the DP and the UPC – owing to the sudden collapse of the Okello regime. This meant that it had no need for the extensive negotiations over rapid democratisation that might otherwise have been necessary,[107] and was able to push its core idea of no-party politics under the pacifying influence of the NRM itself, although many would quickly become suspicious of the Movement's dismissiveness of the former 'winner takes all' political culture (of which the UPC in particular had been a beneficiary).[108] Still, the Movement aimed for inclusion: with the exception of the Former Uganda National Army (FUNA), led by a former Amin commander, and the UPC, still discredited by the sham election result in 1980, all major political groups were represented in Museveni's ever-growing cabinet.[109] But it seemed that inclusion was in fact a strategy designed to carefully control the fragile political environment, rather than a route to genuine democratic transition. Elections to the *de facto* national parliament, the National Resistance Council, in 1989 were tightly controlled (68 of the 279 members were actually appointed), while the much-vaunted reinvigoration of 'grassroots' participation was similarly stymied by the fact that local councils were actually under the close supervision of politically appointed district administrators.[110]

---

[106] The account which follows is partly based on a range of sources in the public arena, but it is worth making the broad point that while early contemporary assessments (i.e., between the mid-1980s and mid-1990s) tended to be sympathetic, later analyses are rather more critical, or at least sceptical, of the NRM 'project'. Compare, for example, the generally favourable discussions in P. Langseth, J. Katorobo, E. Brett & J. Munene (eds.), *Uganda: landmarks in rebuilding a nation* (Kampala, 1995), esp. Parts III & IV, with the later, more hostile, assessment in Joshua B. Rubongoya, *Regime Hegemony in Museveni's Uganda: Pax Musevenica* (New York, 2007), Part III, and indeed in Tripp, *Museveni's Uganda.*

[107] Nelson Kasfir, 'The Ugandan elections of 1989: power, populism, and democratization', in Hansen & Twaddle (eds.), *Changing Uganda.*

[108] J. Kiyaga-Nsubuga, 'Managing Political Change: Uganda under Museveni', in T.M. Ali & R.O. Matthews (eds.), *Civil Wars in Africa: roots and resolution* (Montreal & Kingston, 1999), 19.

[109] G. Hyden, 'The challenges of constitutionalising politics in Uganda', in H.B. Hansen & M. Twaddle (eds.), *Developing Uganda* (Oxford, 1998), 112.

[110] Kiyaga-Nsubuga, 'Managing Political Change', 22. See also Kasfir, 'The Ugandan elections of 1989' and J. Oloka-Onyango, 'The National Resistance

Meanwhile the whole system was guaranteed by the National Resistance Army itself, in effect the armed wing of the Movement.[111]

The story of Uganda's increasingly contested political space can be told simply, on one level, through its sequence of national elections over the past twenty years.[112] Full presidential elections – the first national election since the UPC-rigged ballot in 1980 – were held in 1996, with Museveni facing off against an old DP adversary, Paul Ssemogerere; the incumbent garnered an unassailable 75 per cent of the vote.[113] It was the last relatively 'civilised' election of the Movement System,[114] for by the time of the next one, in 2001, Museveni's former comrade (and personal physician) Kizza Besigye was the leading challenger, declaring that the Movement was veering dangerously off course and leading Uganda to disaster. Museveni still won 70 per cent of the vote, but the Supreme Court seriously debated the nullification of the result, accepting that there had been considerable discrepancies. In the end, the result stood, and just weeks later Besigye fled the country after being beaten up in police custody.[115] But he returned to contest the 2006 elections, which were the first to be held following a popular referendum in which Ugandans voted overwhelmingly in favour of a return to multi-partyism. Again, Museveni won, though this time managing barely 60 per cent of votes cast – more than enough for the expected landslide, but the tangible rise in support for Besigye's Forum for Democratic Change (FDC) sent a few ripples of discontent through the Movement's ranks. The 2006 election was marred by violence and intimidation on the part of the government, which also mobilised state funds for its campaign; but although Besigye alleged fraud, and the Supreme Court again ruled that there had been manifest irregularities, the result stood after a close vote by members of the Court (four in

Movement, "Grassroots Democracy", and Dictatorship in Uganda', in R. Cohen & H. Goulbourne (eds.), *Democracy and Socialism in Africa* (Oxford, 1991).

[111] E.A. Brett, 'Neutralising the use of force in Uganda: the role of the military in politics', *Journal of Modern African Studies*, 33:1 (1995).

[112] See ICG, *Uganda*, 10–13.

[113] Tripp, *Museveni's Uganda*, 28, 51, 60.

[114] However, see 'How free and fair was the 1996 election?', *Daily Monitor*, 30 January 2016.

[115] 'Uganda election arrests', BBC News, 12 February 2001; 'Uganda's Museveni leads in "rigged" elections', *The Guardian* (London), 14 March 2001; '2001 Elections: Supreme Court Judges ruling', *Daily Monitor*, 16 December 2005.

favour, three against).[116] Besigye ran a third time against his former patient in 2011. This time, Museveni's vote bounced back upward (he won 68 per cent), while the FDC's suffered a collapse, from 37 per cent in 2006 to 26 per cent in 2011. The ballot was widely regarded, including by external observers, as deeply flawed, marred by logistical failures and disenfranchisement.[117] This was against a background of popular uprising in North Africa, but there was to be no repeat of it here, with Kampala under heavily armed watch by the security forces and indeed a certain lack of vigour on the part of opposition forces. In the meantime, it is worth noting that Museveni was only able to run in 2006, 2011 and 2016 because of a constitutional amendment approved by parliament in 2005 removing the term-limits on presidential office. In between the clamour of elections, opposition parties – disorganised and ill-developed as a result of years in the political gloaming under the Movement System – struggle to make themselves heard in meaningful and articulate ways.[118]

In one particularly critical area, gender equality and related socio-political access and mobility, the NRM had much in common with other leftist revolutionary fronts in the 1970s and 1980s in foreground-ing women's rights as part of a socio-political programme.[119] This was a core component in the veritable postcolonial cultural revolu-tion which many such organisations across the region and beyond espoused, and in Uganda, as elsewhere, revolutionaries sought to mobilise women in the name of a struggle against historical patri-archy, and in pursuit of genuine social liberation and thus political deliverance. The Movement's champions pointed to the empowerment of women – more women in parliament, and serving as senior minis-ters (including, until her embroilment in a corruption scandal, as Vice

---

[116] Chr. Michelsen Institute, *Uganda's 2006 Presidential and Parliamentary Elections* (Bergen, 2006).

[117] 'Ugandan leader wins presidential election rejected as fraudulent by opposition', *The Guardian* (London), 20 February 2011; 'Uganda election: Yoweri Museveni wins fresh term', BBC News, 20 February 2011; J. Conroy-Krutz & C. Logan, 'Museveni and the 2011 Ugandan election: did the money matter?', *Journal of Modern African Studies*, 50:4 (2012).

[118] Tripp, *Museveni's Uganda*, chaps. 4 & 5, *passim*.

[119] For example, it formed a central part of socio-political strategy in Ethiopia and Eritrea in the same period: see A. Wilson, *The Challenge Road: women and the Eritrean revolution* (Trenton NJ, 1991) and J. Hammond, *Fire from the Ashes: a chronicle of the revolution in Tigray, Ethiopia, 1975–1991* (Lawrenceville NJ, 1999).

President in the case of Speciosa Wandira Kazibwe); more women enfranchised, and specifically protected by the constitution. The Movement prided itself on its 'gender equality' platform, and boasted that it had facilitated the advancement of women in economic and political life. In a recent publication assessing twenty-five years of the NRM – and it is generally a favourable assessment – attention was drawn to the idea that women had 'emerge[d] from the kitchen to take up political leadership', while another caption asserted somewhat tastelessly that 'more women have walked out of the bedroom into the boardroom in the last two decades', presumably because the sentence scanned rather nicely.[120]

Still, it is worth noting that women did not feature at all in the Movement's original 'Ten Point Programme' of the early 1980s,[121] and in the years following its seizure of power, the Movement sought to reinforce particular gender roles and relationships. Women voted overwhelmingly for Museveni in the 1996 election, although this support subsequently waned, in no small part owing to the government's failure to back legislation which would have allowed for spousal co-ownership of land.[122] Sceptical observers pointed out that the women promoted to positions of power through affirmative action had generally shown little interest in their gendered constituencies, and the accusation gathered force that the Movement had simply 'co-opted' women with the aim of strengthening political capital and extending client networks; that women had gratefully received the 'gift' of affirmative action by benevolent patriarchs, rather than owning it.[123] Neither Janet Museveni nor Winnie Byanyima, Kizza Besigye's high-profile wife, offered much succour in this regard. Men, it seemed, were the natural leaders in this deeply patriarchal society, and gender relations in political life appeared to replicate those in the idealised heterosexual marriage: the state, ultimately, was the public projection on an enlarged scale of the normative domestic environment. In the early twenty-first

---

[120] *NRM 25 Years. Uganda 1986–2011: politics, policies and personalities* (Kampala, 2011), 228, 230.

[121] 'The National Resistance Movement Ten-Point Program', in Museveni, *What is Africa's Problem?*, 257–61.

[122] Tripp, *Museveni's Uganda*, 106.

[123] M. R. Mugyenyi, 'Towards the empowerment of women: a critique of NRM policies and programmes', in Hansen & Twaddle (eds.), *Developing Uganda*; A.M. Tripp, *Women and Politics in Uganda* (Oxford, 2000).

century, successful middle-class, educated women were everywhere in evidence, but while some avenues had undoubtedly opened up for a few, most struggled for parity and independence and dignity in the face of a stubbornly androcentric political order. Meanwhile the extent to which they were expected to be at the centre of stable, heterosexual family life had scarcely altered in a century or more. And 'good' women were conservative ones, too: in early 2013, a so-called 'anti-pornography' bill was debated, and eventually passed, by the Ugandan parliament which revealed a markedly conservative turn in society and political culture, aiming to outlaw 'revealing clothing', and a range of putatively pornographic 'salacious cultural practices'.[124]

There was evidence, here, of a patriarchal state increasingly concerned about perceived shifts in gender roles. As in other spheres of political and cultural life, in an era of rapid social change ostensibly driven by 'liberalisation', the Movement strove to prevent the proliferation of alternative and nonconforming 'lifestyles' and aspirations, blocking paths to autonomy and individual realisation for women, and for others too. Uganda was by no means unique – in Africa or anywhere else – in providing evidence of a fundamental paradox in perceptions and expectations of women, but behavioural edicts were not confined to the latter. In the early twenty-first century, the conflict lines were drawn around the issue of homosexuality, which many Ugandans – women and men – felt strongly was both wrong and, moreover, a foreign cultural imposition, and that it had no place in Ugandan cultural and social behaviours or traditions. The *Red Pepper* tabloid, always eager to ridicule the ruling elite, nonetheless reflected a widely felt hostility to the gay community when it ran a story in early 2014, following the anti-homosexuality bill being signed into law, under the banner headline: 'Exposed! Uganda's 200 top homos named'.[125] These were culture wars of the most visceral kind. Still, the gay community survived in the face of popular and official hostility. For the political class, it was really only a question of approach: Museveni, for example, long asserted that he did not want to have homosexuals killed – the death penalty was proposed in an early draft of the anti-homosexual bill – but

---

[124] Author's field notes and informal interviews, 5 April 2013; 'Ugandan MPs pass law to ban miniskirts', BBC News, 19 December 2013.
[125] 'Uganda "homosexuals" named in Red Pepper paper', BBC News, 25 February 2014.

merely cured.[126] It was a stance which has drawn much criticism from Western donors, but to date it appears not to have seriously dented the government's resolve, nor indeed Uganda's role as key regional partner.[127] The age of rebirth did not extend to sexual aspiration or self-fulfilment.

In the realms of political culture, too, struggles were played out around virtuous tradition and histories of legitimacy and propriety. The traditional monarchies were restored in 1993 on condition that they were apolitical, 'cultural' bodies. Buganda in particular caused Museveni (as with every other leader of independent Uganda) serious trouble, not least in its continual lobbying for a federal constitution for Uganda, which would give the kingdom considerable autonomy – a struggle ongoing since the 1950s. Prior to an agreement between Mengo (the seat of the Kabaka's court) and State House in late 2013, which saw a slight thawing in relations, those relations had been dreadful for a number of years, with the Ganda elite perceiving Museveni's government as actively seeking to weaken and undermine it.[128] The fire which inflicted terrible damage on the Kasubi tombs in 2010 brought the nation to the point of crisis, highlighting the tensions between Buganda and the Presidency. The Ganda, as before, had the potential, more than any other single group, to rip the nation asunder; yet the kingdom appeared incapable of organising sustained opposition. More generally, however, 'kingdoms' and 'traditional' leaders proliferated as people sought to forge identities which were better equipped to combat the predations as well as the inefficiencies of the state. The NRM handled all this very badly, in some ways encouraging it – setting up cultural leaders against the Ganda, for example, and in providing sizeable stipends for officially recognised 'traditional' leaders[129] – but at the same time struggling to contain the consequences, and apparently

---

[126] 'Uganda drafts new anti-gay laws', *The Guardian* (London), 8 November 2014.

[127] I can recall, as a doctoral student in the mid-1990s, spending an unhealthy amount of time in the burgeoning Kabalagala suburb, and befriending a transvestite person who was known and 'open', and apparently at ease with his place in the world; I boasted to non-Ugandanists that it showed what a liberal society had been allowed to flower under the Movement. That now seems naïve.

[128] ICG, *Uganda*, 13–18.

[129] 'Too many kings for few people', *Saturday Vision*, 21 January 2012.

failing to appreciate how dysfunctional this had rendered the state itself. It might be argued that the national community had been actively undermined as a result, and that the Movement – despite its stated opposition to the forces of sectarianism and tribalism – had ended up facilitating deeply rooted ethnic loyalties competing within Uganda. Certainly there was a growing sense that Uganda itself was run by a Nyankole clique from the southwest which had simply taken over from the northern military and taken advantage of habitual Ganda inefficacy.[130] There is no doubt that the Nyankole – from Museveni himself downward – had occupied leadership positions in government, public sector and army.[131] Yet at the same time, continual reorganisation of local government led to a proliferation of districts, from around forty in 1986 to more than hundred at the last count.[132] The government claimed that these brought social services closer to the people, but they were often cash-strapped and compelled to appeal directly to Kampala for support. As for the 'grassroots' rationale, there was inconsistency: sometimes districts were organised along 'tribal' lines, but in other cases were apparently aimed at the deliberate destruction of ethnic identities.[133] State House continued to decentralise in order to centralise: in reality key resources, strategies, priorities and power lines ran to the centre, to the Presidency itself.[134]

Moreover, Uganda has experienced an extraordinary amount of outright violence in the form of a string of insurgencies in the last three decades. Uganda has been no more 'peaceful' since 1986 than under either Amin or Obote, but the violence has generally been safely quarantined in specific areas and mostly contained. The best-known instance is the war in the north, among the Acholi, fought first by the Holy Spirit Mobile Forces under self-proclaimed prophetess Alice

[130] I have heard this said in various forms and contexts over a number of years, but it is a view which has become especially pronounced over the past decade or so.

[131] For some authors, this has actually served to render Uganda *coup*-proof in that time, and therefore bring about much-needed stability: see S. Lindemann, 'The ethnic politics of coup avoidance: evidence from Zambia and Uganda', *Africa Spectrum*, 46:2 (2011).

[132] For example, Tripp, *Museveni's Uganda*, 113–20.

[133] Author's field notes and informal interviews, 6 August 2010.

[134] Author's field notes and informal interviews, 17 August 2012; and see also G. M.S. Lambright, *Decentralization in Uganda: explaining successes and failures in local governance* (Boulder CO, 2010).

Lakwena,[135] and then carried on by the Lord's Resistance Army (LRA) under Joseph Kony. The violence can be traced to the collapse of the Okello regime in 1985–6, at which point many former soldiers of the Ugandan army fled north, including a number of Acholi officers who felt betrayed by the NRM's failure to observe the ceasefire agreed in December 1985. The NRA chased them, and, on crossing what Finnstrom refers to as the 'symbolically significant border of the Nile',[136] behaved viciously towards the local population, engaging in wanton destruction of property and widespread killing amongst the Acholi, whom the Movement soldiers regarded in effect as an enemy people. Sexual violence, including rape, was especially prevalent, with women deliberately targeted in a manner which suggested that the desire was to rip apart the very fabric of community and culture, and to 'punish'.[137] There is no question that the local insurgencies which erupted there were driven at least partially in the first instance by the brutality of the NRA. Local bitterness at this occupying army was additionally mobilised by the Ugandan People's Democratic Movement (UPDM), an alliance of opposition elements which had regrouped in Sudan, and then by the Holy Spirit movement and later the LRA itself. In the course of the 1990s, the war escalated dramatically, and involved suffering among the Acholi on a terrible scale. They were caught between the brutally violent Ugandan army, which often acted with impunity towards the local populace, and the LRA which operated largely through the instillation of fear among isolated and beleaguered communities.[138] Children were kidnapped routinely and inducted as soldiers; physical punishments were meted out to supposedly recalcitrant communities and also to increase reliance on the LRA itself (attacks involved the removal of limbs as well as facial disfigurement).[139] Hundreds of thousands of Acholi ended up in

---

[135] H. Behrend, *Alice Lakwena and the Holy Spirits: war in northern Uganda, 1985–97* (Oxford, 2000).

[136] S. Finnstrom, '"For God and my Life": war and cosmology in Northern Uganda', in P. Richards (ed.), *No Peace, No War: an anthropology of contemporary armed conflicts* (Athens OH & Oxford, 2005).

[137] Amnesty International, *Uganda: the failure to safeguard human rights* (London, 1992).

[138] Finnstrom, *Living with Bad Surroundings*.

[139] See numerous reports, for example, by Human Rights Watch: *The scars of death: children abducted by the Lord's Resistance Army in Uganda* (New

IDP camps – reaching a peak of 800,000, more than half the Acholi population[140] – while the much-vaunted and newly professionalised UPDF appeared unable or unwilling to extend meaningful protection across a swathe of northern Uganda. And as with much else in Museveni's Uganda, it was a story of paradox and contradiction: while stories emerged of Ugandan soldiers selling weapons to the LRA,[141] Museveni spent a great deal of time in uniform, directing operations and positing Acholiland – as many had done before him – as a place of darkness and savagery and primitive barbarity which was holding out against modernity; Kony himself became the embodiment of those traits, certainly in the Western media – the 'wizard of the Nile', in the title of one popular account.[142] Despite periodic peace talks, sponsored by southern Sudanese leaders, the LRA remains essentially undefeated, if gradually weakened, and while it has largely abandoned its traditional hunting grounds in northern Uganda, it remains active in South Sudan, the Democratic Republic of Congo and the Central African Republic.[143]

The inability of the Movement to defeat the LRA is perhaps the single most significant military and political failure of Museveni's entire presidency. It is a crushing indictment of the regime; all the more remarkable, then, that its 'peace and development' agenda has ultimately attracted more international attention than the war in the north – in a sense compounding the idea of the marginalised and isolated Acholi, waging their nasty little war far away from the great exercises in state reconstruction in the south. But the LRA have by no means been the Movement's only armed opponents.[144] The UPDM was forged out of the remnants of the northern military. The Uganda People's Army was active in Teso in the late 1980s, while insurgencies persisted in West Nile throughout the 1990s and early 2000s.[145] The National Army for the Liberation of Uganda was behind an uprising

---

York, 1997), *Abducted and Abused: renewed conflict in northern Uganda* (New York, 2003), *Uprooted and Forgotten: impunity and human rights abuses in northern Uganda* (New York, 2005).

[140] K.C. Dunn, 'Uganda: the Lord's Resistance Army', in M. Boas & K.C. Dunn (eds.), *African Guerrillas: raging against the machine* (Boulder CO, 2007), 131.

[141] Author's field notes and informal interviews, August-September 2003.

[142] Green, *The Wizard of the Nile*. One of the best collective studies of the LRA is T. Allen & K. Vlassenroot (eds.), *The LRA: myth and reality* (London, 2010).

[143] See the 'LRA Crisis Tracker' at https://www.lracrisistracker.com/

[144] Tripp, *Museveni's Uganda*, esp. chap. 7.   [145] Leopold, *Inside West Nile*.

in the Rwenzoris from the late 1980s, drawing on historical memories of the earlier Ruwenzururu movement.[146] Herbert Itongwa's Allied Democratic Forces operated in Buganda in the mid-1990s.[147] Meanwhile in the northeast corner of Uganda, along the Uganda-Kenya border, 'low-level' violence of great local significance was habitual between pastoralist groups such as the Karamojong and the Pokot, who owned firearms and carried out violence with impunity far away from the reach of the 'peace-making' state.[148] The degree to which Karamoja could be objectified by the benignly maternal state is demonstrated by the fact that Janet Museveni herself would later become minister for the region, which unlike neighbouring Acholiland served as a useful showcase for the well-meaning regime.[149] It may or may not be the case that 'rogue elements' in the government actually *encouraged* local raiding and took a cut from the proceeds;[150] but it is certainly the case that the Movement benefits from the existence – at arm's length – of impoverished and insecure districts where it can demonstrate its developmental agendas to eager Western NGOs. Elsewhere across the benighted north, however, ethnicity drove local conflict, and vice versa, in a somewhat more violent variant of the phenomenon evident in Museveni's Uganda as a whole.[151] Little wonder that one commentator wrote nervously in the early 1990s: '... since independence northern Uganda has largely featured as the black sheep, or maybe even more accurately as a bull in a china shop, wrecking and spoiling all that came in its way'.[152] It reflected a deep anxiety on the part of many in the north about their newfound role as national scapegoats.

[146] G. Prunier, 'Rebel Movements and Proxy Warfare: Uganda, Sudan and the Congo (1986–1999)', *African Affairs*, 103:412 (2004).

[147] Tripp, *Museveni's Uganda*, 156–7; 'Herbert Itongwa: a soldier who turned guns on his own govt', *Daily Monitor*, 24 April 2013.

[148] Kennedy Agade Mkutu, 'Small arms and light weapons among pastoral groups in the Kenya-Uganda border area', *African Affairs*, 106:422 (2007); D. Eaton, 'The business of peace: raiding and peace work along the Kenya-Uganda border (Part I)', *African Affairs*, 107:426 (2008) & (Part II), *African Affairs*, 107:427 (2008).

[149] Museveni, *My Life's Journey*, chap. 15.

[150] Eaton, 'The business of peace (Part I)', 96.

[151] For example, T. Allen, 'Ethnicity and tribalism on the Sudan-Uganda border', in K. Fukui & J. Markakis (eds.), *Ethnicity and Conflict in the Horn of Africa* (London, 1994).

[152] A.G.G. Gingera-Pinycwa, *Northern Uganda in National Politics* (Kampala, 1992), 3.

It is clear that while the Movement has been seen as part of a con-
structively transformative wave of militarism in eastern Africa in the
1980s and 1990s – force deployed for 'good' – the reality is that
Uganda under its rule has been highly militarised and extremely violent. To an extent this has been the outcome of the NRM's own violent
advent, mirrored in other parts of the troubled region[153] – namely the
unleashing of frontier insurgency across Uganda, fuelled in part by the
proliferation of small arms and underpinned by historical grievances
and present opportunism of various kinds. Insurgencies in the NRM's
Uganda have been of various types: some are more the product of deep-
seated provincial or ethnically defined grievances, reaching back into
the mists of time; others, rather more the spasms of violent resistance to
the NRM, and symptomatic of the anxieties inherent in a state in transition. But practically all the insurgencies confronting the Movement
were in fact the product of *both* short-term and long-range dynamics. While the UPDF prides itself on its professionalisation, on the
progress it has made from the northern-run bandit rabble it was in the
1970s and 1980s,[154] this is a half-truth at best, albeit one central to the
Movement's image and eagerly consumed by Western donors. Uganda
since 1986 has been episodically violent, while 'peace', like many other
essential commodities in Uganda, has been accessible to only a relative
few. It is interesting that for some, the military, once so prominent in
Ugandan politics, has become much less so – such is the popular memory of Amin's army, or of the soldier-politicians of the early 1980s.[155]
Yet this view is perhaps confined to a southern, urban middle class; the
reality, the larger picture, suggests otherwise.[156] In many ways, this is
still a profoundly military state – perhaps more covert than overt in
terms of political culture, but the UPDF has played a pivotal role in
the maintenance and consolidation of the status quo for the last thirty
years, and will be critical in any post-Museveni transition.[157]

---

[153] For example, R. J. Reid, *Frontiers of Violence in Northeast Africa: genealogies
of conflict since c.1800* (Oxford, 2011).
[154] 'UPDF's 25 years of contribution towards political stability and
professionalization of the National Army', in *NRM 25 Years*, 50*ff*.
[155] Author's field notes and informal interviews, 10 August 2010.
[156] Author's field notes and informal interviews, 13 August 2012.
[157] The analysis here represents a development of the basic thesis in
Omara-Otunnu, *Politics and the Military*, regarding the prominent role played
by the army especially in postcolonial Uganda; and for an alternative
assessment, see again Lindemann, 'The ethnic politics of coup avoidance'.

And then there is the external adventurism, a foreign policy increasingly infused by ever-greater military confidence. While Uganda had occupied the role of regional troublemaker under Amin, the country had long been regarded, and regarded itself, as a crucial regional pivot – on a latitudinal axis between eastern and central Africa, and longitudinal between the Horn and sub-Saharan Africa. Obote certainly thought so, but so did Amin, who longed to be regarded as Big Daddy not simply in domestic terms but in the context of Africa's emerging struggle against foreign domination. Museveni's foreign policy ambitions were a little slower to develop, given his domestic preoccupations, but they were there from the beginning. His close but troubled relationship with Kagame and the RPF in the late 1980s and early 1990s led directly to involvement in Congo from the mid-1990s. Uganda and Rwanda backed the insurgency led by Laurent Kabila which eventually overturned the Mobutu regime, but they later found themselves supporting opposing rebel groups; in the meantime, amidst the deadly maelstrom of eastern Congolese political machinations, Uganda enriched itself through the exploitation of minerals there – doubtless one of the motivations for intervention in the first place.[158] It was an early indication of the NRM's outward looking and militarised opportunism – as befitted such an entrepreneurial and mobile organisation. Later, Ugandan troops would form the bulk of the African Union force in Somalia, where they have been credited – despite some glitches[159] – with significant advances against al-Shabaab and bringing greater levels of security to parts of southern Somalia, including Mogadishu, than has been the case for many years. Uganda has also become deeply enmeshed in the South Sudanese civil war, with Ugandan troops dispatched in support of the SPLM; its military involvement has led to its exclusion from regional peace efforts, while also demonstrating Museveni's far-reaching political ambitions beyond Uganda's immediate borders.[160] He is evidently keen to demonstrate regional muscle in the name of

[158] For one of the most vivid accounts, see G. Prunier, *Africa's World War: Congo, the Rwandan genocide, and the making of a continental catastrophe* (Oxford, 2009); and see also F. Reyntjens, *The Great African War: Congo and regional geopolitics, 1996–2006* (Cambridge, 2009).

[159] Human Rights Watch, 'Somalia: sexual abuse by African Union soldiers', 8 September 2014; 'Uganda army suspends 15 soldiers for alleged misconduct in Somalia', *Al Jazeera America*, 6 November 2014.

[160] International Crisis Group, *South Sudan: Keeping Faith with the IGAD Peace Process*, Africa Report No. 228 (Nairobi/Brussels, 27 July 2015).

'national interests'.[161] This may yet produce dangerous blowback for the Movement. Meanwhile, Kampala has been keen to advance the East African Community (EAC) project, resuscitated in 1993 by an agreement between Museveni, Mwinyi of Tanzania and Moi of Kenya after many years in abeyance.[162]

These initiatives – Congo, Somalia, South Sudan and the EAC – were representative of Museveni's growing ambition in foreign policy, and reflected two key goals. One was his positioning himself as the senior statesman of the region with military muscle to boot – an ambition which has often irritated Kenya, with whom Uganda has long had a kind of sibling rivalry, and Kagame's Rwanda. In many ways Museveni has been more successful – and in some respects more fortunate – than any of his predecessors in respect of situating Uganda at the centre of east and northeast African politics, arguably the fulfilment of ambitions harboured by Obote in the early 1960s. Yet of course his increasing confidence in foreign affairs was in many ways the outcome of political stability at home, and also the fact of Museveni's own longevity: he has now outlasted most of his peers in the wider region, including Meles Zenawi in Ethiopia and both Moi and Kibaki in Kenya, while South Sudan stumbles from one crisis to the next and the younger Kenyatta struggles to impose himself. This has enabled the achievement of the second key goal, namely the positioning of Uganda as a major partner of the West in the latter's regional security agenda. Long viewed as the great success in the area for neoliberal economic restructuring and stabilisation, Uganda is also now viewed by Washington as a strategic ally in terms of regional security – due in no small part to the presence of the UPDF in Somalia.[163]

As elsewhere in the region – including both Kenya and Ethiopia – the relationship between foreign policy and domestic politics has become ever more indelibly intertwined, as incumbent regimes marry internal and external exigencies in order to strengthen and diversify themselves. In 2010, two horrific bombs in Kampala killed dozens of people crowded into bars to watch the football World Cup. It was

---

[161] Author's field notes and informal interviews, 10 February 2014.
[162] See http://eac.int/about/EAC-history. This is a project with a long and tortuous history: for an earlier assessment see A.J. Hughes, *East Africa: the search for unity* (London, 1963).
[163] 'The consequences of the US war on terrorism in Africa', *Al Jazeera America*, 2 June 2014.

shocking, but of course the attacks also enabled Museveni to justify soldiers on the streets of Kampala in the weeks that followed, the greatly heightened security presence a timely reminder to would-be opposition groups – particularly well represented in the urban centre – of who was in charge. There could be little question that the government used the terror threat to tighten internal control.[164] That terror threat was no doubt real enough; but so too was the government's keenness to use al-Shabaab as an excuse to place Kampala – a centre of domestic opposition – under close watch.[165] Meanwhile the 2010 bombings also drove home to many the reality of Ugandan troops' involvement in Somalia; before July 2010, few had cared much, or even been aware of the fact. Now, they wanted to know why, and for how long, Ugandan troops had been patrolling the shattered streets of Mogadishu, and how long they would be there.[166] But Museveni was not especially interested in providing justifications for internal consumption: his eye was on a rather greater prize (as he saw it), which was his position as an invaluable ally to the United States in the wider region, in return for Washington's general ambivalence towards any domestic unrest in Uganda. It was the perfect *quid pro quo*, and something of a political nest-egg for Museveni himself.[167]

And indeed, in an increasingly insecure region, the NRM's Uganda began to look like an island of relative calm, although of course these things have a habit of altering fairly rapidly. The violence which followed the 2011 election was shocking, and for a period following the contested results the streets of Kampala were filled with burning debris, tear gas, heavily armed riot police and a large number of extremely angry people. The voices warning about creeping authoritarianism were impossible to ignore.[168] Meanwhile there was heightening concern about the levels of corruption in and around the government, at the highest levels, and of the inability or the unwillingness

---

[164] Author's field notes and informal interviews, 4 August 2010 and 10 August 2010.
[165] Author's field notes and informal interviews, 28 June 2011.
[166] Author's field notes and informal interviews, 10 August 2010.
[167] Author's field notes and informal interviews, 10 August 2010.
[168] 'Uganda's Muhoozi Kainerugaba denies "monarchy" plan', BBC News, 24 June 2013. Muhoozi is the President's son, and commander of the presidential guard. See also 'Ugandan police raid newspaper over Museveni succession letter', Reuters, Kampala, 20 May 2013.

of the President's Office to tackle a worryingly endemic problem.[169] In many ways, this appeared to be a direct result of the much-vaunted economic reforms introduced in the late 1980s which supposedly brought market-led growth to Uganda but which in fact had ushered in an era of chronic cronyism and state-led commercial rackets. Many were rightly worried about the prospects for the equitable sharing of imminent oil revenues.[170]

In many respects, Museveni in the second decade of the twenty-first century was at the apex of his power: a regional player, or certainly the most significant Ugandan leader in regional terms arguably since independence; a man who had honed his political skills to a remarkably nuanced degree – as evidenced by his sheer staying power; a man who ostensibly had lifted Uganda from the pits of laugh-stockery, where it wallowed in the mid-1980s, to the position of serious economic and political player; a president who had not allowed either himself or the Movement to be seriously challenged, but *had* given Ugandans back a considerable degree of self-confidence, and tolerated (at least until fairly recently) a feisty and critical press, read by an expanding and (relatively) well-off middle class. Above all, the central message was that Uganda would scarcely have survived without the Movement. *Remember where we were*, they said repeatedly, *remember where we were*. Yet it was an appeal which weakened with time. Museveni was increasingly seen to have failed on multiple levels – to ever hold himself properly to account, or to deliver meaningful democratic change; to seriously address the spiralling levels of corruption, or indeed the rank poverty that is its corollary; to seize the opportunity to become arguably one of the great postcolonial leaders, had he stepped down in 2001, or even in 2006, content with what he had contributed. Critics charge that Museveni will leave Uganda – when he leaves – a profoundly divided, unequal society.[171] He is no longer even in complete control of the NRM, which is riven with factions and discontent, and above all with a profound divide between the older generation around

---

[169] Human Rights Watch, '*Letting the Big Fish Swim': failures to prosecute high-level corruption in Uganda* (New York, 2013).

[170] Shepherd, *Oil in Uganda*.

[171] T.M. Shaw & P.K. Mbabazi, 'Two Africas? Two Ugandas? An African 'democratic developmental state' or another 'failed state'?, in A. Nhema & P. Tiyambe Zeleza (eds.), *The Roots of African Conflicts: the causes and costs* (Oxford, 2008).

Museveni himself – the 'Historicals' – and a rather younger generation weary of the old man and his blocking clique, and anxious for
change and opportunity.[172] The biggest actual threat to Museveni was
increasingly the Movement itself: always a loose coalition of interests,
and a broad church at best, it was now riven with factions and fester-
ing animosities.[173] Talk of his son Muhoozi being lined up as successor was profoundly destabilising in 2013, while a former key general,
David Sejusa, fled into exile and now talked openly about the dictatorship that the NRM had become.[174] The bad news for ordinary Ugandans was that these were not ideological splits – not great divides over
policy or direction, but personal camps and vendettas, driven largely
by personal ambition. At the same time, the NRM had unleashed a
genie from the bottle: liberalisation would be hard to claw back, as
boisterous openness increasingly defined Ugandan political life. Ultimately, many Ugandans still struggled with the NRM's balance sheet:
for many, even if legitimacy was now haemorrhaging away, there were
reasons, still, to buy into the basic 'peace and development' banner of
the regime, however much the quotidian reality suggested something
quite different.[175] Meanwhile the media pondered the encroachment
of 'failed state' status on Museveni's Uganda, while the President himself continued to blame the tribalism fostered by British colonial rule
for the country's periodic troubles.[176]

An enormous amount has been written on the Movement in the last
thirty years; but for us, now, as historians, we must suspend our con-
templation of contemporary Uganda and return to the past – for it will

---

[172] Tripp, *Museveni's Uganda*, passim; Lindemann, 'Just another change of
guard?'; ICG, *Uganda*, passim.

[173] Author's field notes and informal interviews, 20 July 2014. When Museveni
was formally endorsed by the NRM as its candidate for the 2016 elections,
many at the heart of the Movement were privately (and some not so privately)
shaking their heads in despair, and in truth desperately wanted rid of him:
author's field notes and informal interviews, 10 February 2014.

[174] Sejusa went on to formally endorse the DP, issuing a rallying cry for change in
the process. But not all Ugandans were impressed or inspired by his attempt to
morph into democratic champion: in his time as a senior figure in state
security, he had allegedly been responsible for the rounding up of opposition
suspects and their brutal mistreatment while in custody: Author's field notes
and informal interviews, 14 April 2015.

[175] Author's field notes and informal interviews, 16 August 2012; also 11 April
2013.

[176] 'Uganda as a failed state', *The Observer* (Kampala), 26 June 2011; author's
field notes and informal interviews, 27 June 2011.

be for future historians to assess much more accurately than I can do here the real significance of the NRM and of Museveni's time, as yet unfinished at the time of writing. Suffice to conclude here by suggesting that Uganda appears to be at a critical transitional 'moment' in its modern history. Rebirth, again, is central to the Movement's self-image. There is something akin to a secular political evangelism surrounding the armed liberation front, whereby the nation is depicted as 'born again', its past sins cleansed by the Movement, largely through blood sacrifice and martyrdom, its people urged never again to stray from the righteous path which has been laid by the Movement, rejection of which is akin to a kind of spiritual betrayal. Yet the paradoxes are everywhere. The Movement's self-appointed mission to bring light to darkness has resulted in an increasingly tense political space. Its emphasis on new beginnings has taken place against a background of greatly heightened historical consciousness; the past has been everywhere in Museveni's Uganda. The government has promoted peace and development, yet this has been a markedly violent era both internally and externally, and one defined by a widening chasm between rich and poor. This, then, is the pensive nation: a nation whose fragility had been established by the enclosure and claustrophobia of the late twentieth century, in which the capacity for violent ethnic conflict had been horrifically exposed, in which the dangers of the militarised polity had been clearly demonstrated, and in which the lack of real political leadership had been revealed.

Yet there had already been a millennium of political experience and experimentation, and it is to that which we must now turn. The last half-century of Uganda's history reads like a narrative of *coup* and counter-*coup*, of violent seizures of the state followed by distinctive patterns of militarisation within and on behalf of the state, and of war – or variations of it – influencing, indeed underpinning, political culture and hovering menacingly in the more shadowy corridors of power. It is a trajectory which seems to reflect a peculiarly *postcolonial* state of affairs, symptomatic of the flaws inherent in the design of Uganda itself by the British, and the inability of postcolonial elites to manage the place. But Amin and Museveni are only the latest manifestations of a much older *motif* in Uganda's history, for war, militarism and the violent capture and in some cases remaking of the political order are present in Ugandan history over *la longue durée*. It is a pattern which can be traced to the armed adventurers of the nineteenth century and earlier, a period which also saw the militarisation of political culture across Uganda and the growing significance of war as a driver, and an outcome, of political upheaval. The war bands of the 1970s and 1980s represented older, deeper dynamics, the latest manifestations of long-term violent transformation and military reorganisation, in the use of war as political, economic and ultimately cultural struggle. To fully understand the contemporary era, we must now wade rather deeper into those turbulent waters.

3 | *Rukidi's Children*

The Trials and Tribulations of Kabalega and Mwanga

A Tale of Two Kings

Kabaka Mwanga of Buganda and *Mukama* Kabalega of Bunyoro lived strikingly parallel lives, and their stories are inseparably intertwined – indeed, they embody some of the most salient themes in Uganda's modern history. Their relationship is one of both contrast and symbiosis. Each was born to a reigning king – Kamurasi in Bunyoro and Mutesa in Buganda – and each succeeded their fathers at a young age: Kamurasi was around 16 when he fought a short but intense war for the throne in 1869–70, and Mwanga was around 18 years old when he peacefully acceded to the throne of his late father in 1884. Kabalega spearheaded the resurgence of Bunyoro as a regional power in the 1870s, and spent almost the whole of his reign at war with Buganda: first against Mutesa, and then Mwanga himself in the later 1880s, and later still, against the Anglo-Ganda army which was suppressing resistance to the Protectorate in the 1890s. Then, Mwanga was – in a titular sense, at least – a key ally of the nascent British administration, and had been since he was returned to the throne at the end of the civil wars which ripped Buganda apart between 1888 and 1890. But the *kabaka* later turned again, in 1897–8, abandoning his post and fleeing to the bush in rebellion against the British, and indeed his own chiefs who had, it seemed, betrayed him. Though quickly captured by the Germans, he escaped their custody and headed north to throw himself into an alliance with Kabalega, then leading his rump of an army in a series of desperate last stands against the British and their Ganda allies. In 1899, they were finally seized by the British, and thus did they end up in exile together in the Seychelles, never to return to their respective kingdoms, though Kabalega at least died on his way home, at Jinja, in April 1923. He outlived his erstwhile partner and fellow exile Mwanga by twenty years: the latter died in 1903. In 1910, Mwanga's remains were interred at Kasubi royal tombs, alongside those of his father. Kabalega's were buried at his own home in Mparo, near Hoima, for he could not be laid to rest beside those of his ancestors: those old ghosts haunted the land which the Ganda had by now annexed – the 'Lost Counties'.[1] Their shared defeat and exile in 1899 was richly symbolic. It neatly stitched together, in a final act, the life trajectories of two very different men. Perhaps most poignantly of all, it signified the bathetic end to a coherent Ugandan precolonial past: the rulers of Bunyoro and Buganda were the progenies of ancient and intertwined political cultures in the area, yet as they were shunted coastward into exile, a wedge was driven into the Ugandan body politic from which it would struggle to recover. Uganda was now a more fractured place than at any point in the measurable past, and arguably the moment of the capture of Mwanga and Kabalega was the last act in a long, shared precolonial pageant.

The image-making around the pair was powerful from the very outset. Mwanga – according to most contemporary European accounts, at any rate – was a violent man rather than being in any sense a soldier or a statesman, although his story captures the illusion that has long been a part of Ugandan political culture, that of the skilled warrior, conquering the kingdom, protecting it from all enemies.[2] Mwanga, that 'weak, vain, and vicious man',[3] according to a typical European characterisation, had in fact spent much of his formative years hanging around mission compounds and befriending missionaries. But he was Alexander Mackay's 'negro Nero',[4] and to Gerald Portal, he was 'weak and invertebrate';[5] Gaetano Casati characterised him as 'a young man with a hard heart and a warped mind'.[6] A somewhat later assessment, more measured in tone but no less dismissive, described him as having 'more vices but far less courage and political acumen than his father'.[7] Mwanga has had an extremely bad press over the decades, and is surely

---

[1] Ingrams, *Uganda*, 240.
[2] According to Zimbe, Mwanga's accession ceremony involved the new *kabaka* stabbing a young Nyoro in the chest – whether symbolically or not is unclear – and swearing to 'fight and defeat the Banyoro', at which point he was 'now a grown up man who could even kill a man': Zimbe, *Buganda ne Kabaka*, 111–12.
[3] Mackay, *Pioneer Missionary*, 255.   [4] Ibid., 276.
[5] Portal, *British Mission*, 189.
[6] G. Casati, *Ten Years in Equatoria* (London, 1891), II, 16.
[7] Thomas & Scott, *Uganda*, 20.

ripe for a revisionist biography:[8] he is the callow, and callous, youth
who exceeds outrageously his royal prerogative; capricious and intemperate and indecisive, caught in the headlights of momentous change
and unable to make his mind up about anything much – at least until
it was too late; the murderer of Christian converts, as well as a hapless
British bishop, and quite possibly a paedophilic homosexual to boot –
though in truth it is difficult to decide which of these is the greater crime
in modern Uganda. At length he is a surly collaborator with the British,
until he throws in his lot, somewhat late in the day, with Kabalega. Yet
throughout Mwanga's era, it is his humanity – his inability to cope, his
vacillation, his vanity, his pretension and confusion – which is compelling, and illuminating; and his story, encompassing as it does much
of the era of revolutionary change, can on many levels be read as the
story of modern Ugandan political culture in miniature.

Kabalega, in keeping with the racial theory of noble (if ignorant)
savagery associated with honourable warriorhood, was less despised,
for all his insanely destructive resistance to the British, and Buganda:
Frederick Jackson noted his 'reputation for horrible cruelties, and cold-
blooded butchery...[but he] never grovelled when captured. In fact
he always kept his end up, and in some ways was at least a man'.[9] He
was 'vigorous and warlike', in Margery Perham's treatment of Lugard's
diaries.[10] But while Mwanga underwent no kind of retrospective reformation of character in Buganda, and has lain largely un-rehabilitated,
Kabalega was a hero in Bunyoro, and, later, in NRM-ruled Uganda.
To Nyakatura, he was 'among the most powerful and bravest kings of
Kitara':

Although he is said to have put many people to death, Kabalega still remains
one of the most respected and revered kings of Kitara. He was loved by his
chiefs, his servants, as well as by the ordinary people of Kitara. Today, the
people of Bunyoro recollect his name with pride and dignity. He brought
no shame on his country but, on the contrary, restored its former power
and prestige, which had declined considerably...And when in the end he
was faced with insurmountable problems and difficulties, he exhibited this
indefatigable spirit to the last.[11]

[8] See, for example, Lunyiigo, *Mwanga II*.
[9] Sir F. Jackson, *Early Days in East Africa* (London, 1930), 273.
[10] M. Perham (ed.), *Lugard: the years of adventure, 1858–1898* (London, 1956),
212.
[11] Nyakatura, *Anatomy*, 107.

In the 1920s and 1930s, there was some ambivalence within the British administration between the perception of Kabalega as the man whose 'folly' was responsible for Bunyoro's sorry state, and therefore best forgotten, on the one hand; and an admiration of his 'pride and vitality' as a model for Nyoro progress and development on the other.[12] In the early 1950s, the anthropologist John Beattie described a downcast, fatalistic people in the seemingly unbreakable grip of melancholic nostalgia for a glorious past, long gone;[13] and for the 'backward-looking' Nyoro, Kabalega, as the journalist Harold Ingrams found on the eve of Ugandan independence, was a 'national hero, almost a god' – a shimmering beacon for depressed times, if a sadly intangible one. Indeed the thoughtful Ingrams himself was moved to observe that 'I no longer felt Kabalega could be dismissed as a bloodthirsty savage only fighting civilising influences . . . A proud and brave monarch of ancient lineage but another world can have nothing but savagery left when the dignity of his freedom is taken from him'.[14]

During the bush war in the early 1980s, the NRA named two of its units, as Museveni himself described it, 'in honour of African heroic figures' – Kabalega and Mwanga. Both of them had been 'noted Ugandan opponents of British imperialism in the late 19th century'[15] – a somewhat selective view of Mwanga, at any rate. But it was only Kabalega who, in 2009, was declared a national hero and posthumously awarded the requisite medal,[16] although more sceptical observers pondered the need for the Movement to court electoral support in Bunyoro with its enormous potential oil wealth.[17] Mwanga, meanwhile, is now most likely to appear in the public eye only in connection with his homosexuality – proof that to be gay is indeed an intrinsic part of an African heritage, to the pro-gay rights lobby;[18] evidence of his flawed humanity and certainly of the sinister influence of 'Arab' merchants, in the eyes of the anti-homosexual political establishment, including Museveni and indeed the more 'traditionalist' core of the Buganda monarchy

---

[12] Doyle, *Crisis and Decline*, 165–6.

[13] Beattie, *Nyoro State*, 31–2, 58; Reid, 'Ghosts', 363–4.

[14] Ingrams, *Uganda*, 241–2.   [15] Museveni, *Mustard Seed*, 137.

[16] 'Kabalega named national hero', *New Vision*, 10 June 2009.

[17] 'Gen. Museveni woos Banyoro with medals', *The Observer*, 16 June 2009.

[18] R. Rao, 'Re-membering Mwanga: same-sex intimacy, memory and belonging in postcolonial Uganda', *Journal of Eastern African Studies*, 9:1 (2015).

itself.[19] And so the tales of these two kings, their lives strangely entangled, also continue to diverge: Kabalega, the lost hero and symbol of a glorious past; Mwanga, confused, fallible and ultimately sacrificed by his own chiefs as Buganda moved onto greater things – taking its place as the capstone of the colonial order at the expense of poor, defeated, devastated Bunyoro.

Yet how had these men arrived where they did, and come to the decisions they did? What do they represent more broadly? Their stories do not merely elucidate the vicissitudes of royalist history: kingship was contested and resisted, too, and monarchical narratives are only one way of reconstructing Uganda's modern history, and then only a part of it. Those narratives were eschewed by·others who refused to conform to normative ideas around territorial kingship. Kabalega and Mwanga are important, therefore, on multiple levels: what they represented, to some, and what they did *not*, to others. Yet what is clear enough is that between the 1850s and the 1880s, the wider region experienced dramatic flux, of which Mwanga and Kabalega were the outcomes. To fully understand their stories, and the wider significance of our two kings, we must travel back a little further in time.

Migrant Nation, 1: Kinetic Histories

Uganda is a land of migrants. The nature of those migrations, and the role played by migrants in social, economic and political terms – and the manner of their reception by those already there – has altered over time according to circumstances. In the deeper past, they played a vital role in the shaping of Ugandan political order and culture; they contributed folk heroes and mythologies of morality and might, as well as the stories of origin so important to emerging political elites; their presence engendered economic diversity and deepened prosperity, from the western edge of the Rift Valley to the Ruwenzori mountains. The primordial soul of Uganda, if we believe in such entities, is a migrant one, owing to its position on the upper Nile, and the well-watered

---

[19] 'When faith, state, and state-inspired homosexuality clash', *New Vision*, 2 June 2005; 'Uganda's President admits gays part of Africa's heritage', *Changing Attitude*, 3 April 2012; 'Gay Africa: casualty of a different power struggle', *African Arguments*, 4 March 2014; 'From Mwanga to Museveni: sex, politics and religion in Uganda', *African Arguments*, 24 March 2014; Rao, 'Re-membering Mwanga'.

arena formed by lakes Victoria, Albert and Kyoga, and their hinter-lands. It is, in sum, a regional fulcrum, a hothouse of intermixing and cohabitation, a crossroads of culture and economy, and in a very real sense a frontier zone of intense interaction and creativity. For the ear-lier period – that is, up to the first half of the second millennium – there is a host of detail which is currently beyond the historian's grasp, and in truth a great deal of it is likely to remain so. At times the best we can do is discern dim shapes and shadows, and try to engender clarity through available sources – oral history, linguistics and archaeology – and through the use of that trusty old implement, intelligent guess-work. But it is important to attempt to make sense of this complex epoch, even in broad outline, for three chief reasons. To begin with, this is when the foundations of modern Ugandan society and culture are laid, of which some basic understanding enables us to better appre-ciate some of the salient political and cultural dynamics of Ugandan history in the more recent past. Secondly, it illustrates the power of the past in a range of ways, both locally and externally mobilised, in the making of modern state and society. It clarifies for us, and compels us to reflect upon, the importance of differing interpretations of the past and the power these have for the societies involved (and indeed for foreigners too). And there is a third key driver behind this analytical focus, namely the desire to produce a *rebalanced* history of Uganda, one that shifts the centre of gravity away, even momentarily, from the southern monarchical states and incorporates the swathe of territory north of lakes Kyoga and Albert. An attempt to understand the migra-tory experiences which laid the groundwork for what became Uganda facilitates such a rebalancing exercise.

The first immigrants date back a millennium and a half. Our knowl-edge is patchy, and it remains the subject of debate and speculation. But Bantu-speakers had been expanding into the best-watered areas of the Great Lakes region, notably around Lake Victoria, from the early centuries CE.[20] They were iron-workers, and as they settled close to

---

[20] Accounts of this process have evolved over time, naturally enough, reflecting the research agendas – and to some extent the attitudes – of the time. G.W.B. Huntingford's 1963 essay, 'The Peopling of the Interior of East Africa by its Modern Inhabitants', in Oliver & Mathew (eds.), *History of East Africa*, I, makes for uncomfortable reading in places for a modern audience, with its jarring vocabulary and emphasis on racial types. For a more recent (and more compelling) study, see Schoenbrun, *Green Place*, especially chapters 2 and 3.

water – lakes and rivers – they cleared woodland in an attempt to push back the tsetse-fly frontier, meaning that in altering the landscape they were opening up the possibility of later pastoralist immigration. Beginning in the late first millennium CE, grain farmers with cattle moved into the higher and drier grasslands, and at this point there were major changes in political and economic organisation in the Great Lakes region, with the proliferation of terminology referring to political authority – increasingly centralised, and often rooted in ideas about health and ritual healing – and to the keeping of livestock.[21] In the centuries that followed, i.e. during the first half of the second millennium, pastoralism was increasingly important in local economies, although not at the expense of agriculture, which also remained central at the household level. It is clear that in this period, there was no specialist pastoralist class, elite or ethnic group, and that the radical changes which occurred were *not* the product of some great pastoralist invasion from the north. They were, rather, the product of changes within Uganda and across the wider lacustrine region. Archaeological work done at the large settlement of Ntusi, which flourished between c.1000 and 1400 CE, demonstrates this.[22] Only later, probably beginning in the sixteenth and seventeenth centuries, did distinctive pastoral ideologies emerge, reflecting the creation of larger-scale states out of the smaller chiefdoms of the earlier period, and reflecting too the social divisions based on economic practice. In other words, something happens in the middle centuries of the second millennium, leading to a greater emphasis on the essential ethnic difference between cattle-keepers and farmers, and in some places the reworking of history so that pastoral authority is extrapolated backwards into the deeper past. While the reality is that farming and pastoralism remained locally intertwined, including at the level of royal ritual, there were now clear associations between cattle-keeping and political authority.

So what had happened? From the early centuries of the second millennium, a series of small-scale but potent migrations took place involving specialist pastoralists from the north. The result of this interaction between Bantu and Nilotic populations was a series of small but

---

[21] Schoenbrun, *Green Place*, 74–9; Kodesh, *Beyond the Royal Gaze*, 81–6.

[22] A. Reid, 'Ntusi and the development of social complexity in Southern Uganda', in G. Pwiti & R. Soper (eds.), *Aspects of African Archaeology: papers from the 10th Congress of the Pan African Association for Prehistory and Related Studies* (Harare, 1996).

dynamic chiefdoms, rooted variously in agriculture or cattle-keeping; by the early fifteenth century, some of these little states had merged to form the larger state of Kitara, in western Uganda, ruled by a dynasty known as the Chwezi.[23] The Chwezi have long fascinated historians and archaeologists alike, as well as playing a central role in the public imaginary in modern Bunyoro and across western Uganda more broadly. Kitara was enormous, according to the standard traditions, improbably described as encompassing a swathe of territory from northern Tanzania to South Sudan, and from eastern Congo to western Kenya.[24] The empire was divine in origin, first ruled by the celestial Batembuzi dynasty, from whom it was inherited by the semi-divine Chwezi. The latter built impressive capitals, first at Mubende, and then at Bigo, and the latter is one of the earliest, and largest, discernible earthwork sites anywhere in eastern Africa. Work done by archaeologists which has uncovered similar types of pottery in a series of Iron Age sites from Bigo to the shores of Lake Albert suggests that Kitara may well have encompassed extensive grasslands, populated by tens of thousands of people and perhaps hundreds of thousands of cattle. Meanwhile work on the nearby site of Ntusi has revealed an extensive urban layout, a centre of iron-working as well as cultivation and cattle-keeping.[25]

So much for Kitara's material legacy, which is, by the archaeological standards of the region, impressive enough. Rather more striking is the fog of inscrutability which has long shrouded the Chwezi themselves, who flit ghostlike in the basement rooms of the Ugandan nation, many of whose more modern elements have drawn inspiration and legitimacy from those spectres of ancient civilisation. They are, variously, 'enigmatic' and 'mysterious'; they were certainly short lived, which

---

[23] Useful introductions include I. Berger, 'Deities, Dynasties and Oral Tradition: the history and legend of the Abacwezi', in Miller (ed.), *The African Past Speaks* and J.-P. Chretien (tr. Scott Straus), *The Great Lakes of Africa: two thousand years of history* (New York, 2003), chapter 2.

[24] 'K.W.', 'The Kings of Bunyoro-Kitara, Part I', *Uganda Journal*, 3:2 (1935), 158–9.

[25] However there have long been debates around the politics and economies of these sites. See P. Robertshaw, 'Archaeological Survey, Ceramic Analysis, and State Formation in Western Uganda', *African Archaeological Review*, 12 (1994) and J. Sutton, 'Ntusi and Bigo: farmers, cattle-herders and rulers in Western Uganda, AD1000–1500', in J. Sutton (ed.), *Archaeological Sites of East Africa: Four Studies. Azania*, 33 (1998).

somehow adds to their allure, and may not have lasted much more than fifty or sixty years (tradition claims for them three generations of rulers, two of whom were brothers).[26] They were said by some to be 'light-skinned', references to which were first picked up by Speke in the 1860s, enabling him to patch together a broad theory about the quasi-Caucasian roots of anything that looked a bit like civilisation in the region.[27] But it is true enough that the two major state systems which would come to dominate the area in the wake of their 'disappearance' in the early sixteenth century – Bunyoro and Buganda – each claimed, to varying degrees, to be the legitimate heirs of Kitara. In some respects that struggle for historical legitimacy tells us as much about the Chwezi as any shreds of evidence relating to their actual rule. Further, while there may or may not have been a Chwezi 'empire', their most enduring legacy has been in the eponymous spiritual cult which continues to thrive across western and southern Uganda today. The Chwezi cult celebrates an array of potent spirits, including Ndahura, Mulindwa and Wamala – the three named kings of the Chwezi period itself.[28] We know little about these figures as living men; but as ghosts and deities, they are hugely important.

Kitara was at least partially the product of long-range immigration into western Uganda. Elsewhere, the evidence suggests a series of interactions between northern Bantu-speaking farmers and incoming non-Bantu pastoralists and mixed farmers, who, wielding iron tools and weapons, may have been more bellicose (or at least appeared so) than the Bantu agriculturalists who often cleared out of their way. But these engagements are more properly understood as a series of competitive accommodations, involving integration, stratification and diversification. In the ferment of movement and interaction, cultures were shared and historical culture in particular took on new forms.[29] Nowhere was this more in evidence than in the story of Kintu, the Bantu-sphere culture hero – literally, 'the man', or perhaps more appropriately, 'of the man'. All along the northern shore of Lake Victoria, he emerges

---

[26] Berger, 'Deities', 62–5.   [27] Speke, *Journal*, 246–7.

[28] See, for example, J.-P. Chrétien, 'L'Empire des Bacwezi: la construction d'un imaginaire geopolitique', *Annales: histories, sciences sociales*, 40:6 (1985) and Cecilia Pennacini, 'Mubende Hill: preserving and transforming heritage in a Ugandan sacred site', special issue on 'Sacred Natural Sites and Cultural Heritage in East Africa', *Uganda Journal*, 53 (2013).

[29] For a neat summary, Schoenbrun, *Green Place*, 207.

apparently as the result of a movement of northern Bantu farmers, from around Mt. Elgon, into the lands of their southern, lakeshore Bantu neighbours – a population shift caused by earlier Nilotic southward movements. This swirl of population mobility became associated with, and personified by, Kintu who was thus the founder of a chain of small states – small, that is, in comparison with Kitara – from the east side of the Nile and across modern central Uganda, including the microstates of Buganda and Busoga in the early centuries of the second millennium CE.[30] In some forms of the tradition, Kintu is from heaven, the first person on earth and thus the father of all people; but in fact it is clear from other traditions that he is not *quite* the first person, but rather a kind of wise immigrant arbitrator, leading people into new areas and coming to agreements with already-resident clan heads in parcelling out land between the clans of the newcomers and those of the autochthones. In the small kingdoms thereby established, he co-opts clan heads by offering them key positions at his court, marries their daughters and attracts support for the new order through the introduction of new crops and economic specialisms; all the while he is sagacity and fertility incarnate, procreating impressively and dispensing wisdoms, before disappearing, moving on to repeat the performance elsewhere. In the little kingdoms that arose in his wake, rulers were probably figures imbued with sacred authority, originally concerned with ritual.[31]

In Buganda, he is now formally regarded as the first king, the founder of the current dynasty;[32] and based on the number of names in the kinglist, as well as guestimates for generation spans, for some time it was supposed by historians that the Kintu period dated to the fourteenth and fifteenth centuries. In fact, however, archaeological research suggests that Kintu is a stereotype encapsulating several centuries of political and demographic development, beginning around the eleventh century. Centrally, these were historical narratives arising out of population movement. Nowhere is this more evident than in Busoga, which in the precolonial era, according to David Cohen, comprised close to seventy individual chiefdoms. These microstates were the product of waves of immigration into the area – including Nilotic Luo-speakers

---

[30] Chrétien, *Great Lakes*, 111–13. [31] Wrigley, *Kingship and State*, 232.
[32] See Kagwa, *Kings*, for the more or less 'official' version of the kinglist. Again, however, Kintu was not always regarded as the founding monarch: in the 1860s, Speke does not mention him in what was the first recorded kinglist, though a decade later Stanley does.

coming from the north, and Bantu-speakers from the Mt. Elgon area. As Cohen explains, there thus developed in Soga historical culture a duality of traditions, evident by the early nineteenth century: the southern tradition was dominated by associations with Lake Victoria and upheld by ruling groups associated with the Kintu story; but the northern tradition was tied to another stereotypical founding father, Mukama, from the north, and was developed by descendants of the early Luo who emphasised the importance of the Luo pastoral contribution to the Soga cultural and economic world. In the duality of Kintu and Mukama, Busoga thus captures the competition inherent in emergent historical cultures.[33]

To be sure, gradual inward migration brought about political innovation, hugely significant over the long term. But it is worth emphasising the elements of continuity in this process. Neither Ndahura, nor Kintu, nor Mukama – despite some of the stories weaved around them and the meanings attached to them – arrived in virgin lands, untouched by human hands. Linguistic evidence as well as earlier traditions indicate that kingship, for example, predated the arrival of Nilotes into Kitara.[34] And as we have observed, in Buganda Kintu encountered not empty land, but a number of indigenous clans – *banansangwawo* – who claimed to have been governed by a remarkable thirty kings prior to Kintu's arrival, the last of which, Bemba, he is said to have defeated in battle.[35] Certainly, these were the original makers of early Iron Age political order in the Ganda heartlands of Busiro, Kyadondo and Mawokota, thriving from the middle centuries of the first millennium CE. We cannot always be certain how these earlier political traditions persisted in later centuries – how they manifested themselves, or the ways in which they were worked into the new, evolving forms of politics associated in large part with inward migration. What we do know is that in both Bunyoro and Buganda, clanship – which was in all probability the first basic building block of political authority north of Lake Victoria – remained enormously important as a signifier of identity, even as a vehicle of resistance, in the centuries that followed. Clans were not always compatible with muscular kingship, and in the early years of the twentieth century, for example, historical debates in Buganda centred around the figure of Kintu: specifically, whether

---

[33] Cohen, *Historical Tradition*, 1–2.   [34] Schoenbrun, *Green Place*, 184–95.
[35] In Kagwa's account, Bemba is a snake: *Kings*, 5.

he had indeed been an immigrant, which was the official position of the Ganda royal family, or whether he was in fact indigenous to the area, in which case, to whose clan did he belong?[36] These were not the marginal tussles of antiquarians, but arguments over the most central of perennially contemporary questions: how should we be governed, and what forms should legitimate authority take? More specifically, it was a debate which reflected a fundamental scepticism about, even rejection of, particular forms of kingly authority.

In later centuries, from c. 1400 onward, specialist Nilotic pastoralists appear to have moved in ever larger numbers from their homelands in southeast Sudan and southwest Ethiopia, into the ideal dry grasslands running across Uganda from the northeast to the southwest.[37] The immigrants – perhaps originally compelled to move by an expansion of Nuer communities in the plains around the confluence of the White Nile and Bahr-al Ghazal River – were mostly Luo-speakers, and while an earlier graphic description of them being like the Vikings in European history is not perhaps as accepted as it once was,[38] there is no doubt that they represented a remarkable phenomenon. Mobile and ferociously, if temporarily, militarised, small groups of Luo warriors successfully raided their unprepared Bantu adversaries, likely stealing people as well as cattle and crops; but perhaps more importantly, as they spread they were adept as incorporating people, setting up chiefdoms whose expansion soon developed its own momentum, and within which subject communities were integrated into Luo clans; distinctions were made between the people of the chief's enclosure (*jo-kal*) and the *lwak*, the conquered 'herd'. From their major military encampment at Pubungu, a few miles from the northern shore of Lake Albert, Luo radiated in various directions, raiding among the Lugbara, Lendu, and Madi populations and incorporating the captives.[39] We still do not know quite how this ongoing process of assimilation worked in practice, but between the sixteenth and eighteenth centuries, northern Uganda was absorbed into a Luo world, including the Acholi, Langi, Alur and Kumam; only pockets of the original Madi population and other tiny groups north of Lake Albert remained outside the Luo zone.

---

[36] Rowe, 'Myth', 218; Ray, *Myth, Ritual, and Kingship*, 99–103.
[37] C.C. Wrigley, 'The Problem of the Lwo', *History in Africa*, 8 (1981).
[38] R. Oliver & A. Atmore, *Medieval Africa, 1250–1800* (Cambridge, 2001), 143.
[39] B.A. Ogot, *History of the Southern Luo, Vol I* (Nairobi, 1967), 55–62.

These migrations were generally undertaken by a group categorised
by historians as 'Western' Nilotes. 'Eastern' Nilotes, including the
Karamojong and Teso, moved somewhat later, with a major impact
being felt by the late seventeenth and early eighteenth centuries: it
seems that some earlier Luo groups around Lake Albert were absorbed
by Teso moving from the northeast, and that others – like the Langi,
north of Lake Kyoga – were greatly influenced by the Eastern Nilotes,
even while retaining Luo speech.[40] Meanwhile the Ateker began to
move through the area of modern western Karamoja, during which
period they developed an agricultural economy (they became known
as *ngikatapa*, 'bread people') while retaining powerful cultural attach-
ments to cattle; and also southward into the hilly Koten-Magos country. As they moved, they carried with them distinct forms of historical
consciousness which were concerned centrally with the idea of a mythical place of origin, 'Longiro'.[41] These imaginaries were not (or not
only) the yearnings of the lost and homesick: they served as political
and cultural charters, and reflected ideas about the natural or pristine
state of affairs which might be emulated wherever the Ateker peoples
might settle.

Further south, among the Bantu populations, the process was a little different. Here, the immigrants were indubitably critical in the formation of new kinds of states and societies, including the centralised,
territorial monarchies of the southern forest; they were, for example,
the ancestors of the Hima in western Uganda (and of the Tutsi in
Rwanda and Burundi). Most notably, it was a Luo clan – the Bito –
which conquered Kitara, dispatching the Chwezi into the temporal
gloaming between history and myth, and infusing a new state, Bunyoro, with a remarkable and infectious political, economic and military
energy.[42] But although to some extent the pastoral lifestyle and associated culture remained discrete, there was considerable interaction
and integration between farmers and herdsmen, between immigrants
and residents; in time, notably, the former mainly adopted the Bantu

[40] Vincent, *Teso in Transformation*, 63–71; Webster et al., *The Iteso*, 1–19,
117–18; Ogot, *History*, 113–24.
[41] J. Lamphear, 'The evolution of Ateker "New Model" armies: Jie and Turkana',
in K. Fukui & J. Markakis (eds.), *Ethnicity and Conflict in the Horn of Africa*
(London, 1994), 65.
[42] Nyakatura, *Anatomy*, 51–6; Doyle, *Crisis and Decline*, 12–14; Beattie, *Nyoro
State*, 25 and passim.

languages of the latter. Nonetheless, the impact is undeniable. The case of Bunyoro is illustrative. Here, as Carole Buchanan demonstrated, the kingdom particularly absorbed immigrants from the north and west. Buchanan argued that assumptions that these clans were always Bantu-speaking were incorrect, and that in fact they traced their origins to the Luo-speaking region further north; by the early nineteenth century, Bunyoro may have been predominantly Bantu-speaking, but the northern and eastern parts of the kingdom retained Luo speech, while those cultural and linguistic connections had long enabled the Nyoro to extend influence to the east and north of the kingdom.[43] Worthy of mention, too, are the Padhola, Luo-speakers who ended up in the forests to the west of Mt. Elgon, and who – unlike many of the examples noted above – did not develop a centralised monarchical political tradition but retained a lineage-based system. Other smaller streams of Western Nilotic Luo travelled further south, ending up around the northeast corner of Lake Victoria, and included the Joka-Jok, Jok'Owiny, Jok'Omolo and Luo-Abasuba; in each case, though to varying degrees, they encountered and intermingled with existing Bantu speakers.[44]

There was therefore considerable local variation in terms of the impact of migration and the dynamics involved: more or less direct assimilation across much of northern Uganda, more indirect impacts further south, with the exception of the apparently violent seizure of Kitara. In the south, the emergent states of Buganda and Hinda-ruled Nkore would develop as responses to Luo aggression, rather than as direct products of Luo conquest. But the central point here is that Uganda is animated in extraordinary ways by the movement of people within and through its approximate confines; and that this process is continual and absolutely seminal in the creation of the place we today call Uganda, and in the creation of distinctive but connected cultures and politics, and vital in the expansion and diversification of economic systems. Moreover, the local histories which people constructed in the

---

[43] C.A. Buchanan, 'Perceptions of ethnic interaction in the East African interior: the Kitara complex', *International Journal of African Historical Studies*, 11:3 (1978).

[44] Karugire, *Political History*, 9; Oliver, 'Discernible Developments', 199*ff*; D.W. Cohen, 'The River-Lake Nilotes from the Fifteenth to the Nineteenth Century', in B.A. Ogot & J.A. Kieran (eds.), *Zamani: a survey of East African history* (Nairobi, 1968), 153–4.

wake of those migrations are part of the story – not simply quaint leg-
ends and at best 'sources' to be scrutinised and critiqued (though of
course they are that), but also expressions of identity and community,
and manifestations of culture. The region of Uganda is thus characterised by a remarkable shared historical and cultural heritage, however contested the precise lineage and direction of travel, and however entrenched ideas about difference (and superiority) became later
on. People migrated continually, over many centuries, and in so doing
they mobilised themselves and others in the creation of elaborate political systems, of ideas of origin, of economies, of innovative cultural
and intellectual processes. Status and particular categories of belonging
mutated continually.[45] By the early nineteenth century, these processes
were still in motion. But they would become arguably more significant
as states and societies' engagement with one another intensified in an
era of new catalysts.

Investments in Violence: The Rise of the Armed Entrepreneurs

In around 1500 – give or take a few decades – a man named Olum
Labongo seized power in the Chwezi state of Kitara. He was a war
leader, probably based originally in the nearby military camp of Pubungu, at the northern end of Lake Albert, and he arrived in Kitara at
the head of a Luo force of considerable size. In the southern Bantu traditions, he acquired a variety of names: 'Rukidi' – 'the naked man from
the north' (he was from 'Bukidi', a generic term for the land north of
Lake Kyoga); Isingoma, 'He of the Drum'; Mpuga, 'the spotted one',
or 'black and white'.[46] By whatever name he was known, his invasion
of the Chwezi state had far-reaching ramifications and fundamentally
remade the Ugandan political landscape – or so a particular historical interpretation would have it. In essence, he founded a new political
dynasty – the Bito – and was the ancestor of a chain of related dynasties which in time would come to rule much of southern Uganda. His
army apparently sent the short-lived Chwezi to flight – giving rise to
the oft-repeated notion that they 'mysteriously disappeared' – though
subsequent tradition emphasised the idea that the Bito had seized control with the full knowledge and approval of the Chwezi, thereby

---

[45] Chrétien, *Great Lakes*, 77–83.
[46] Ibid., 102; Oliver, 'Discernible developments', 182.

lending the new order legitimacy and continuity.[47] Later Nyoro historians may have greatly exaggerated the prior significance and extent of Kitara, and the antiquity of the royal line; they may even have largely invented the idea of a Chwezi state from which legitimacy was derived.[48] It is certainly difficult to know exactly what form the pre-Bito state took. But others have argued persuasively that the newly arrived Bito in fact harnessed pre-existing traditions to legitimate their rule, and this included respecting and protecting the Chwezi religious centres which almost certainly predated the Bito themselves, and by recognising the importance of those clans which served as guardians of Chwezi shrines.[49] Initially the Luo occupied Bigo and Ntusi, the sites of Chwezi governance, but later moved to the area around Mubende where they were able to practise agriculture on a larger scale; and it was in this region, in the northern half of the old Kitara kingdom, that Bunyoro was born – a new kingdom which appeared to signify a new political era, yet one which very much drew on the past for its moral authority. The bodies of the first few Bito kings of Bunyoro were apparently sent back north to Pubungu for burial,[50] though in due course there would be linguistic, social and cultural integration to the point that there was no meaningful 'racial' distinction between the Bantu-speaking Nyoro subjects and their Luo conquerors. Still, the rich oral traditions describing the regime change reflect a time of trauma and – as Schoenbrun has recently argued – deep emotion.[51]

The Bito, who also established themselves among the Soga states east of the Nile, certainly claimed to be the font of a new political order that reached around the northern shores of Lake Victoria, and whose influence – if indirect – could be felt far to the south, towards the Kagera River. Nyoro political culture was to a very large extent the taproot for much of the southern Ugandan history. In particular,

---

[47] Nyakatura, *Anatomy*, 50*ff.*
[48] See Wrigley, *Kingship and State.* In *The Chronology of Oral Tradition: quest for a chimera* (Oxford, 1974), David Henige also explores the idea of temporal innovation in oral tradition (driven often by necessity) in a West African context.
[49] R.Tantala, 'The early history of Kitara in western Uganda: process models of political and religious change', PhD thesis, University of Wisconsin, 1989.
[50] Nyakatura, *Anatomy*, 66–7; Oliver, 'Discernible Developments', 173.
[51] D.L. Schoenbrun, 'A Mask of Calm: emotion and founding the kingdom of Bunyoro in the sixteenth century', *Comparative Studies in Society and History*, 55:3 (2013).

Rukidi's younger twin, Kimera, was supposedly appointed to rule over the lesser kingdom of Buganda,[52] at this time little more than a huddle of patrilineal clans, no more than a few dozen miles across, probably originally centred somewhere to the north and west of present-day Kampala. This was disputed by the Ganda themselves – one of their eminent historians, Semakula Kiwanuka, described the idea as 'patriotic fiction' on the part of the Nyoro[53] – and Kimera, in Kagwa's account, is in fact the great-grandson of Kintu, the other founding father of the region, predating Rukidi by several generations.[54] The Ganda may originally have regarded themselves as Rukidi's own offspring, but in time they would come to eschew the Bito version of events and would elevate Kintu to the status of moral and political embodiment of the early kingdom.[55] As Christopher Wrigley pointed out in his final book, the battle over historical origins had very clear current political implications. Kiwanuka was writing at a moment – the 1960s – when the struggle between Buganda and Bunyoro was especially acute, and so it was difficult for him to stomach the idea of Buganda '[beginning] life as a mere colonial dependency' of Bunyoro.[56] And so Kimera – who may have some historicity as an actual person, unlike his hologrammatic predecessors Chwa and Kintu[57] – was made contemporaneous with, even a product of, Chwezi-ruled Kitara. It meant that Buganda, no less than Bunyoro, could *also* claim to be the legitimate heir of the idolised Chwezi.[58] What is certainly true is that Bito-ruled Bunyoro was soon the dominant power in the region, and that Buganda was on the receiving end of some devastating attacks, and had to learn quickly – perhaps by emulating the Nyoro themselves – in order to even survive as an autonomous political unit.

---

[52] Nyakatura, *Anatomy*, 50.   [53] 'Introduction', in Kagwa, *Kings*, xlii.

[54] Kagwa, *Kings*, 195, 203. The current *kabaka* of Buganda, Ronald Mutebi, is officially regarded as the thirty-sixth ruler in a line stretching back to Kintu.

[55] See H. Médard, 'Proto-Nationalism, Religion and Race: the many cloths of Kintu, first king of Buganda (18th-20th centuries)', in C. Panella (ed.), *Lives in Motion, Indeed: interdisciplinary perspectives on social change in honour of Danielle de Lame* (Tervuren, 2012) and Médard, *Le Royaume du Buganda*, 100ff; Ray, *Myth, Ritual and Kingship*, 99–103.

[56] Wrigley, *Kingship and State*, 194.

[57] In the first recorded kinglist, described by Speke, there is no mention of either Kintu or Chwa; but rather Kimera is noted as the founding king of Buganda: Speke, *Journal*, 252.

[58] Wrigley, *Kingship and State*, 194.

Meanwhile further to the southwest, the Hinda clan, which itself claimed descent from the Chwezi, established leadership and purpose among the pastoral groups which had fled before the Luo invasion. Confronted with a ferocious enemy in the Luo, the Hinda consolidated two major kingdoms – Nkore and, on the Tanzanian side of the Kagera River, Karagwe – and spawned several more. The precise origins of the Nkore dynasty are unclear, though again descent is claimed from the Chwezi persona Wamala, and the founding father of the state was Ruhinda, from whom, subsequently, direct descent was drawn by the royal clans, known as *Abahinda*.[59] In these Bito-era states, the process and ideology of kingship became more closely tied to the loaning of cattle to farmers who placed considerable stock by their milk and manure, and who thus began to enter into client-patron relations with the herders. In time, these tributary relations were enforced and managed by military leaders – probably drawn from both the agricultural and pastoral communities – and it was this fluid, entrepreneurial system which facilitated the spread of the Hinda dynasties. Yet at the same time Nkore and others expanded externally, at least in part driven by the military needs of defence against Nyoro aggression: Bunyoro targeted these southern states in pursuit of cattle.[60] And so the *quid pro quo* appears to have been external defence in exchange for tight internal control – another enduring theme of state-formation in the Ugandan region.

The political and economic history of Uganda in the seventeenth and eighteenth centuries bears witness to Charles Tilly's argument in the European context that the modern state arose as a result of the needs (and costs) of organised violence;[61] and echoes in the African context the wisdom of R.A. Brown's view that Europe was 'hammered out on the anvil of war'.[62] There has been a rather greater reluctance within the Africanist academy to place an emphasis on the role of violence in Africa's past to quite the same extent, at least in part reflecting a certain squeamishness about the continent's turbulent present.[63] But

---

[59] Karugire, *History of the Kingdom of Nkore*, 16, 28.
[60] H.F. Morris, *A History of Ankole* (Kampala, 2008; first ed., 1962), 9–12; H.F. Morris, *The Heroic Recitations of the Bahima of Ankole* (Oxford, 1964), 3–5.
[61] C. Tilly, *Coercion, Capital and European States, AD 990–1992* (Oxford, 1992).
[62] Quoted in M. Howard, *War in European History* (Oxford, 2009), 1.
[63] For example, R.J. Reid, *War in Precolonial Eastern Africa: the patterns and meanings of state-level conflict in the nineteenth century* (Oxford, 2007), 8–9.

war has been critical in African history over several centuries, and the Ugandan region illustrates this vividly. Across the south, Nyoro armies raided and harassed everyone in the vicinity, and established a political and military hegemony which would endure throughout the sixteenth and seventeenth centuries. This was a political and military project which allowed access to and accumulation of valuable resources, which underpinned royal and princely authority, and cemented wider loyalty. But key elements of Bunyoro's system were also emulated by those on the receiving end of military assaults – emulated, and indeed improved, for Bunyoro was in many ways something of a loosely run confederation in which violence was 'outsourced' to ambitious chiefs in borderland districts who extended the reach of the state by running warbands for their own benefit.[64] It was a brutally effective system when it worked, though a dangerously unstable one when it didn't.

Buganda, clinging to the shore of Lake Victoria, spent much of its early life enduring repeated attacks from their bigger, stronger neighbour through much of the seventeenth century. The story of *Kabaka* Nakibinge, killed fighting the Nyoro after calling on a famous warrior, Kibuka, to assist him – Kibuka, later the Ganda god of war, was also killed – seems to encapsulate the crisis of survival that confronted the kingdom for much of its early history. Notably, the last-ditch defence of the kingdom was organised by the late *kabaka*'s chief wife, Nanono, an early representation of the gendered politics which characterised the Ganda royal court.[65] At any rate Buganda did indeed survive, and in the course of the eighteenth century it did rather more than that, and actually began to flourish.[66] A series of *kabaka*s engaged in a twin-prong, long-term programme of external expansion and internal consolidation. External expansion involved carefully targeted military expeditions into neighbouring territories of economic and

[64] Doyle, *Crisis and Decline*, 15–16; E. Steinhart, 'The emergence of Bunyoro: the tributary mode of production and the formation of the state, 1400–1900', in Ahmed Idha Salim (ed.), *State Formation in Eastern Africa* (Nairobi, 1984), 82–5.

[65] Kagwa, *Kings*, 28–9 and see R.J. Reid, 'The reign of *Kabaka* Nakibinge: myth or watershed?', *History in Africa*, 24 (1997), for an early and rather clumsy attempt to consider the shadowy ruler as an actual historical figure and not, as Wrigley had it, an extended metaphor: Wrigley, *Kingship and State*, 162–3. For women and political power in Buganda, L. Schiller, 'The Royal Women of Buganda', *International Journal of African Historical Studies*, 23:3 (1990).

[66] R.J. Reid, 'Warfare and Militarism in Precolonial Buganda', *Azania*, XXXIV (1999).

strategic value, followed by full integration of conquered territory through the appointment of provincial governors, the destruction or at least sidelining of local ruling elites, and the systematic absorption of conquered populations into Ganda clans. The expansion of the clan system was arguably the most effective means of consolidating conquest, and allowed for the long-term rooting of a sense of *Kiganda* identity, however contested and locally interpreted that might be.[67] At the same time, ironically, within Buganda proper the kingship accrued ever more personal authority by actually undermining the *bataka* – the clan heads – and gaining access to clan land in order to distribute it to loyal followers, and in order to more readily mobilise material resources (wood, metal, textiles and above all people) in the service of the state. Clans became more about social connections than physical location.[68] The kingship belonged to no particular clan, but rather the *kabaka* relied on his mother's clansmen and, initially, was in essence little more than the *primus inter pares* in terms of political position. Increasingly, however, key chieftaincies were appointed directly by the *kabaka* whose power thus cut across 'traditional' centres of authority, with the royal court positioned at the heart of an increasingly centralised political network of fealty and obligation. At the court itself, political power and access to that power was ferociously competitive, and relatively open – and violent, too, witness the armed conflict that frequently attended fraternal and filial succession struggles over the kingship itself. Up to the end of the eighteenth century, succession was frequently contested between brothers who mobilised *bakungu* – key chiefs – and their armies to fight their causes, while their mothers utilised their own networks of political influence and leverage in support. In the nineteenth century, the throne passed to a son designated by agreement between *kabaka* and chiefs, with sibling rivals killed off to ensure a smooth succession – though this was still not always wholly guaranteed, witness the machinations surrounding Mutesa's succession in around 1857.[69]

---

[67] A close reading of A.Kagwa (tr. J.Wamala), 'A Book of Clans of Buganda' (ms. in Makerere University Library, c.1972) is richly rewarding in this respect, especially in conjunction with his *Kings*.

[68] One of the most compelling and original analyses in recent years is Kodesh, *Beyond the Royal Gaze*.

[69] Kagwa, *Kings*, 140–5; Stanley, *Dark Continent*, I, 295; R.J. Reid, 'Images of an African Ruler: *Kabaka* Mutesa of Buganda, c.1857–1884', *History in Africa*, 26 (1999), 274. See also M. Southwold, 'Succession to the throne in Buganda', in J. Goody (ed.), *Succession to High Office* (Cambridge, 1966).

Once in motion, it was a programme, built around a dynamic and highly political military system, which naturally enough fed off its own momentum, and nothing succeeded like success: the more military victory was achieved, the stronger the *kabaka*'s position and the more resource he had at his disposal to distribute among followers and reallocate to state-level projects, which in turn drove more ambitious projects of expansion. The more the kingdom grew, the greater the power of the kingship over clanship – for kin was no longer adequate in achieving effective administration, which was increasingly in the hands of centrally appointed provincial or specialised chieftainships, more or less meritocratic. At any rate, the most successful chiefs were those who could demonstrate *both* talent *and* love for the *kabaka*.[70] In the second half of the eighteenth century came two of Buganda's greatest territorial achievements: the capture and annexation of the wealthy Nyoro province of Buddu (also known as Bwera) to the southwest;[71] and the incorporation, under the leadership of an especially dynamic *kabaka* named Mawanda, of the richly forested district of Kyagwe to the east, extending Buganda's eastern frontier to the banks of the Nile.[72] Although further expansion west (into Mawogola) was checked at this time, Buganda entered the nineteenth century bristling with expansionist ambition and awash with the resources necessary to achieve it.[73] By around 1800, Buganda's formal territory stretched from the west bank of the Nile to the Kagera River, with periodic influence beyond these boundaries, especially among the Soga chieftaincies to the east.

Much of this expansion, though by no means all of it, came at the expense of Bunyoro, whose role as regional hegemon was increasingly under threat by the end of the eighteenth century. The image of the inexorable decline of Bunyoro, loosely and ineffectively organised, arthritic and unable to match the dynamism of smaller but more efficient and energised Buganda, is to a considerable extent the product of late nineteenth-century reworkings of the region's past. That history has been greatly influenced by two core dynamics: Nyoro efforts from the mid-twentieth century to position themselves as the heirs of

---

[70] There is a wealth of recent work dealing with Buganda in the nineteenth century in much more detail than can be provided here: see, especially, Hanson, *Landed Obligation*, Médard, *Le Royaume du Buganda*, Reid, *Political Power*.

[71] For example, Kagwa, 'Clans of Buganda', 71.

[72] 'Ebye Buganda: Entabalo za Sekabaka Mawanda', *Munno* (1921), 10–11.

[73] Reid, 'Warfare and Militarism', 47.

the Chwezi; and Ganda interactions with the British and their subsequent 'recalibrating' of their own history up to that point. Indeed, the actual extent of Bunyoro's decline may well be exaggerated, written into the accepted narrative by Ganda opportunist intellectuals keen to cement the place of Buganda itself in the colonial order around the turn of the twentieth century. Certainly, Kabalega's resistance to the British in that period cemented an enduringly hostile and negative image of Bunyoro among both British and Ganda administrators and intellectuals. Nevertheless, there is little doubt that by the 1800s and 1810s, Bunyoro was indeed facing a series of crises, not least of which was the challenge posed by Buganda, though just as important was the problem of territorial overstretch and internal insurgency.[74] There were apparently a series of major rebellions in the late eighteenth century, possibly the result of an aggressive attempt to exact tribute, while Nyoro politics was increasingly characterised by violent competition between Bito lineages. It has been suggested that localised clan resistance to a newly centralising regime in the eighteenth century was particularly important in weakening Bunyoro.[75] The Ganda, meanwhile, were able and willing to intervene in local conflicts in order to undermine Nyoro authority – as in Buddu, where they came to the protection of clan guardians of a Chwezi shrine under threat from Olimi (reigned 1710s and 1720s).[76] A few years later, *Kabaka* Junju of Buganda was able to take advantage of insurrection against *Mukama* Duhaga (1730s–70s) in the kingdom of Kkooki, which came under Ganda protection, and finally wrested Buddu away from Bunyoro.[77] All across Buganda's western borderlands, and Bunyoro's southern marches, Ganda armies provoked conflict, provided protection, intrigued with local rulers to erode Nyoro authority – which crumbled in outlying areas owing, therefore, to an insuperable combination of political overstretch, rebellious clans and princes, and an aggressively expansionist Buganda.

Buganda may have been the chief external cause and beneficiary of Bunyoro's relative decline, but it was by no means the only one: Nkore,

---

[74] For something of a 'classic' statement, see M.S.M. Kiwanuka, 'Bunyoro and the British: a reappraisal of the causes for the decline and fall of an African kingdom', *Journal of African History*, 9:4 (1968).

[75] Doyle, *Crisis and Decline*, 13–14; D. Cohen, *Womunafu's Bunafu: a study of authority in a nineteenth-century African community* (Princeton NJ, 1977), 75.

[76] Nyakatura, *Anatomy*, 82–4.   [77] Ibid., 85–6; Kagwa, *Kings*, 91.

too, expanded at Bunyoro's expense south of the Katonga River, taking advantage of the sequence of eighteenth-century Nyoro kings' fixation with the Ganda threat. Nkore had honed its own political order around a confederation of clans headed by the royal clan, in which the *Mugabe* – while in some respects projecting pastoralism as the ideal way of life, reflecting the growing class divide between cattle-keepers and farmers – nonetheless embodied both ways of life and was a unifying figure in a potentially riven society divided between status as aristocratic, ruling elite *Hima* or agricultural *Iru*. His holistic persona was reflected in his participation in the New Moon rituals, designed to guarantee the fertility of the land as well as of livestock.[78] Like Buganda, Nkore's early history was concerned with the endurance of regular Nyoro attacks,[79] but it too survived and then began to expand outward from its early core area of Isingiro, a few miles south of Mbarara. External adventures were facilitated by the implementation of large levies of soldiers, the *emitwe*, during the reign of Ntare IV in the middle of the eighteenth century, following which territory was conquered and annexed – notably Mpororo and at least parts of Buhweju – and larger herds could be protected from hostile raiders.[80]

So far, our discussion has been concerned primarily with the south – and it is broadly true that extant scholarship demarcates the south from the north in terms of political action, with the avatar of Rukidi obligingly carrying the torch of political drama and even progress southward from the Luo-speaking provinces, but in so doing leaving the latter in relative darkness and even stasis. There may be a crude truth in the dichotomy normatively posited between southern Uganda as historically more hierarchical, monarchical and territorial, and northern as altogether 'different', and more characterised by heterarchy and segmentary systems of social and political organisation. The boundary, again crudely, was Lake Kyoga and the Nile, which represented something of a marker between the two political zones. Land was at a premium in southern Uganda; and therefore territorial and hierarchical states were the outcome, and often at the centre of violent contest, and for these states systems were put in place to control both land and, thereby, people. In the north, it is not that land was

---

[78] Karugire, *History of the Kingdom of Nkore*, 89–92; see also Katate & Kamugungunu, *Abagabe*, in which this is a recurrent motif.
[79] Morris, *Heroic Recitations*.
[80] Karugire, *History of the Kingdom of Nkore*, 54–5.

unimportant – far from it. But emphasis was placed on the management of relatively meagre human resources through horizontal and segmentary systems of political administration and social organisation. Nonetheless, many of the themes in terms of political development and militarisation in the southern lake zone are also discernible in the north. In the Koten-Magos hills of northeast Karamoja, some Ateker groups experienced population growth in the early eighteenth century – in part owing to new types of cattle – and as they expanded into central Karamoja, they generated cycles, and cultures, of violence.[81] These were bristling, creative but often short-lived groupings which clashed along mobile and volatile frontiers, characterised by conflict over cattle and pasture – especially in times of natural disaster, for epizootics and drought, alongside hostile raiders, were constant pressures on the pastoralist communities of the northeast. And this was also true of the Ngikatapa groups of western Karamoja who were more inclined towards sedentary farming than the Koten-Magos communities but whose relatively intensive farming techniques could lead to catastrophic famines, which in turn led to the further population shifts. One such famine, the 'Nyamdere', remembered by J.B. Webster's Acholi informants as 'the greatest of all famines', probably ravaged the borderland between Karamoja and Acholiland between 1706 and 1733, and caused significant dispersal across a swathe of territory in northeast and central northern Uganda.[82] Some of these population movements involved the meeting of Koten-Magos and Ngikatapa groups, out of which grew new communities, including the Jie and the Karamojong. Other Ngikatapa moved further westward, beyond Karamoja and towards Lira, north of Lake Kyoga. But in this area, in turn, a prolonged and devastating famine, known as the 'Laparanat', between c.1770 and c.1800 led to the further dispersal of Ngikatapa – this time further west and southwest, where they contributed to the evolution of sections of the emerging Teso, Kumam and Langi groups.[83]

---

[81] For *longue durée* analysis, see Sandra J. Gray, 'A Memory of Loss: ecological politics, local history, and the evolution of Karimojong violence', *Human Organization*, 59:4 (2000); also John Lamphear, 'Historical Dimensions of Dual Organization: the Generation-Class System of the Jie and the Turkana' in David Maybury-Lewis & Uri Almagor (eds.), *The Attraction of Opposites: Thought and Society in the Dualistic Mode* (Ann Arbor, 1989).

[82] See Lamphear, *Traditional History*, 111, based on Webster's pioneering work on the 'historical texts' of the Acholi in the late 1960s.

[83] Lamphear, *Traditional History*, 159–70.

This was, therefore, one of the most dynamic, volatile and mobile zones of Uganda as the nineteenth century dawned, characterised by fission and fusion, and in many ways providing evidence in support of at least some parts of Kopytoff's interpretation of the frontier in African history as a place (and a process) of extraordinary creativity, assimilation and reinvention.[84] These were certainly dynamics which led more or less directly to political shifts similar to those unfolding further south. Up until the late eighteenth century, Ateker communities were mostly organised around age-class systems in which generational ties bound cohorts together more cohesively even than blood and territory, while the norm was a decentralised, 'egalitarian' politics in which elders exercised control over unruly youth – though the latter might, and often did, rebel by breaking away from gerontocratic authority and settling up camp elsewhere. In the course of the late eighteenth and early nineteenth centuries, however, violent conflict escalated among the Ateker, and also between the Ateker and both Bantu- and Nilotic-groups to the west and south. Wars over resource and space were fought between the Jie and Dodos on the one hand and the Ngikatapa in central Karamoja on the other; and between the Langi and the Madi, Alur and Jopaluo further west. The Langi also in time clashed with Teso, Acholi and Kumam to the south and west, and would come to supply mercenaries for service with Nyoro armies. The escalating violence of the nineteenth century led to a deepening sense of group cohesion among various Ateker clusters, as well as new forms of individual, charismatic leadership. Among both the Teso and the Langi, for example, military leadership became institutionalised and greatly expanded in scope, with 'big men' commanding both armies and military confederations and consolidating centralised authority which led to the virtual disappearance of gerontocratic systems.[85]

---

[84] I. Kopytoff, 'The internal African frontier: the making of African political culture', in I. Kopytoff (ed.), *The African Frontier: the reproduction of traditional African societies* (Bloomington & Indianapolis, 1987).

[85] These narratives are explored in depth in Crazzolara, *The Lwoo*, Vol. III and for a landmark revision of this earlier work, Ogot, *History*. John Lamphear's work remains the key reference point in terms of modern scholarship: see his *Traditional History*, chapter 2, 'Evolution' and 'Brothers in Arms: military aspects of East African age-class systems in historical perspective', in E. Kurimoto & S. Simonse (eds.), *Conflict, Age and Power in North East Africa* (Oxford, 1998). A useful summary of early Teso history is in Lawrance, *Iteso*,

A similar development is clearly discernible among the Acholi, for whom Atkinson has proposed a corporate ethnic identity far predating the period of colonial conquest: here, from the late seventeenth century, there was also an enlargement of political scale and military authority, even if centralisation in the hands of *rwodi* (sing., *rwot*, rulers of individual chiefdoms) was more limited than elsewhere and constrained by the continuing importance of lineage heads.[86] But the process of militarisation and centralisation was accelerated – as so often before – by a major drought, this time in the 1830s, which drove competition for resources across central northern Uganda and led to the emergence of military alliances and confederations of chiefdoms. As people moved, and as conflict escalated, corporate identities emerged which formed the basis of the ethnic groupings of modern Uganda: Acholi, Lugbara and Alur identities all expanded and consolidated as people clustered together for security, and invested in larger amalgamated communities within which the burdens of defence and food security could be shared. New types of war chiefs did not appear everywhere – they were largely absent, for example, among the Alur[87] – but it was indisputably a key feature of the wider region. Within Acholiland itself, the Payira chiefdom grew in particular importance, in no small part owing to its well-watered location and greater distance from Langi and Jie raiders.[88]

By the early years of the nineteenth century, across Uganda, there had emerged a series of potent political systems based, to a greater or lesser degree, on war as political and economic strategy and on centralised forms of leadership and identity. These were the dynamics which had shaped Uganda, in the profoundest of ways, over *la longue durée*, and which formed the backcloth to the dramas of the nineteenth century. In many ways, Bunyoro was the central pivot in these dramas. As the single most important conduit for the political influence of the Nilotic migrations into the southern half of the country, Bunyoro's influence was far-reaching – not only in terms of political culture, but in economic integration and cultural and cosmological frameworks across

---

9*ff* and see also J.H. Driberg, *The Lango, a Nilotic tribe of Uganda* (London, 1923).

[86] Atkinson, *Roots of Ethnicity*, 77–8.

[87] See, for example, 'The Alur', in Richards (ed.), *East African Chiefs*, 314 and A.W. Southall, *Alur Society: a study in processes and types of domination* (Cambridge, 1956), for a range of historical observations.

[88] Atkinson, *Roots of Ethnicity*, 265, 266–7.

a swathe of central and southern Uganda. So it is hardly surprising
that the fate of Bunyoro in the nineteenth century provides a crucial
entrée into wider turbulence across the region. Again, numerous scholars have assessed – and critiqued – the long-accepted narratives relating
to Bunyoro as the 'sick man of the lakes region' in the late precolonial period.[89] Nonetheless, the nature and course of Bunyoro's slow
but steady erosion of power is more complex than the linear processes
which are often presented in terms of declines and falls, and the rise of
'new kids' on various blocks.

In or around 1830, there were two major insurrections of note.
As Nyakatura records it, 'the principal reason for these rebellions
was because Nyamutukura had reigned for a very long time and had
become extremely old. His sons, too, had become old men and their
natural desire for the kingship became so great that they decided on
some drastic actions...'[90] *Mukama* Kyebambe III Nyamutukura had
indeed been ruling Bunyoro since the 1780s, and there is little doubt
that he had presided over some of the structural flaws noted above.
One particular son had gone to Buganda to seek military help from
Kabaka Kamanya, but the latter – at that point on friendly terms with
Nyamutukura – had sent a message to alert the *Mukama* to such filial disloyalty; yet he also counselled him to consider ceding power to
his children, for perhaps he had, after all, become too old to govern?
No, replied the ageing *Mukama* testily, and anyway, why should he be
deprived of all his belongings and a roof over his head, just because he
was old![91] In any event, Nyamutukura had bigger challenges. The first
was a princely rebellion in Paluo territory, a province in the north of
the kingdom located on the banks of the Nile where the river leaves
Lake Albert. It had long been an area of Luo-Nilotic settlement, perhaps as far back as the early fifteenth century.[92] Two princes – Kachope
and Isagara – had Paluo mothers and thus were more deeply rooted in
the local community, and better equipped to resist Nyoro attempts to
suppress their rebellion. We know relatively little about the rebellion
itself, save that its leaders and their progeny successfully warded off
reincorporation into Bunyoro for another half-century or more.[93] But
it was important in other ways, not least in terms of the symbolism

---

[89] Doyle, *Crisis and Decline*, 13–14.   [90] Nyakatura, *Anatomy*, 92.
[91] Ibid.   [92] Steinhart, 'Emergence', 77.
[93] One of the few specific studies ever undertaken is A.Adefuye, 'Political history
of the Paluo, 1400–1911' (PhD thesis, University of Ibadan, 1973).

of the Paluo as inhabiting – and facilitating – a critical corridor of influence to the north, at least since the late seventeenth century. For a century or more prior to their rebellion against Bunyoro, they had been the conduit of a number of core political ideas northward into the territory of the western Acholi who had increasingly absorbed and adapted them. Central among these new concepts were ideas related to centralised chiefship, a more organised and territory-wide tribute system, and the role of royal regalia, especially drums.[94] In other words, Paluo encapsulates the vitality with which political ideas spread across the region, but also the extent to which this involved stabilisation and continual headaches for those who would expand and consolidate. Bunyoro had been one of the great founts of political centralism, ideas which had clearly been absorbed by the Luo-speaking Paluo settlers of northern Bunyoro, which then increasingly passed it back northward to the Acholi. It was a striking case of revolutionary reverberation. The Paluo rebellion would also subsequently provide an entry point for the involvement of external forces in local conflict. Thirty years later, *Mukama* Kamurasi would welcome the traders and adventurers winding their way from Khartoum through South Sudan into northern Uganda – at least initially – as invaluable allies in the suppression of Paluo defiance.[95] The reality, however, was that the Khartoumers were rather more interested in sustaining rather than healing division – there was little profit to be made from unified and stable polities, but there *were* profits in conflict and instability, notably in terms of the pools of slaves such insecurity opened up, and the access to ivory likewise facilitated. Thus Paluo tells a story which is as much about the wider region as it is specifically about Bunyoro's own malaises in the middle decades of the nineteenth century.

Yet so, too, does the story of Toro – the other major rebellion against Nyoro rule in 1830. Toro was a province in the south of the kingdom which seceded under the leadership of Kaboyo, an apparently much-favoured son of Nyamutukura, after the former had apparently consulted with key groups in both Toro and Busongora.[96] Toro in itself

[94] Ronald R. Atkinson, ' "State" formation and language change in westernmost Acholi in the eighteenth century', in Ahmed Idha Salim (ed.), *State Formation*, 92; also Atkinson, *Roots of Ethnicity*, passim.

[95] Doyle, *Crisis and Decline*, 43.

[96] Nyakatura, *Anatomy*, 92–4; Beattie, *Nyoro State*, 64; Karugire, *Political History*, 43.

might not seem so noteworthy, save for the fact that it was able to maintain its independence until the later 1870s, when it was forcibly reincorporated into a resurgent Bunyoro. The point, rather, is that the appearance of Toro altered the power balance in southern and western Uganda, and – perhaps even more significantly for the longer term of Uganda – demonstrated the ability of particular groups to redesign new histories and identities for themselves even as they claimed legitimacy for themselves by connecting themselves with the old: in this case, the direct familial link with Bunyoro and thus the ancient seat of power in the region.[97] And like the Paluo, Toro demonstrates the power of Ugandan politics to pull in external forces, for the British under Lugard would later be so impressed by the claims of Kaboyo's grandson Kasagama – and the assistance which he had rendered them in their campaign against Bunyoro – at the beginning of the 1890s that they would restore Toro's independence as an autonomous kingdom within the Protectorate.[98] Not everyone eventually enclosed within the Toro kingdom would accept the new order, and that resistance in itself would involve new forms of history-making centred on a refusal to conform to imposed visions of monarchical authority in particular.

The beneficiary – and also the catalyst – for many of these shifts in the early decades of the nineteenth century was Buganda. By the time *Kabaka* Kamanya died, probably around 1830, he had brought a good deal of stability to Buganda, and arguably had presided over the kingdom's most successful phase in terms of regional dominance. Not until the early 1900s, in their partnership with the British, would the Ganda again enjoy such a hegemonic and largely unchallenged position across the Lake Victoria-Lake Kyoga zone. Kamanya's was no mean feat, considering how dangerously militarised the state had been when he first came to power, at the head of a restless and dissent-ridden army. In many respects he was also Buganda's last great warrior king, and certainly the last with genuine military credentials, having led the army personally on campaign – something increasingly rare in the course of the nineteenth century – and having had to deal directly with military affairs in the early years of his reign, probably in the 1790s and 1800s.[99] Kamanya was concerned primarily with the eastern frontier,

[97] K. Ingham, *The Kingdom of Toro in Uganda* (London, 1975), 23.
[98] Lugard, *Rise of Our East African Empire*, II, 187–8; Perham, *Lugard*, 261, 271.
[99] Kagwa, *Kings*, 103.

carrying out a series of attacks on the Soga principalities east of the Nile; but even now, in the 1810s and 1820s, as Buganda was arguably at the height of its power, it was clear that there were limits on that power, for no permanent control could be imposed on the Soga, but rather only tributary exactions which periodically had to be enforced following Soga 'rebellions'.[100] His son and successor, Suna, was rather more of a consolidator than a warrior. Nonetheless Suna, too, presided over the creeping militarisation of political culture, and he appears to have made a number of *batongole* appointments – chiefly positions with non-hereditary tracts of land attached to them – which involved, among other things, military responsibility and command at the local or regional level.[101] In all likelihood, this process of the militarisation of regional administration and the appointment in the 1830s and 1840s of a range of new political officers answerable directly to the centre represented an attempt to further consolidate the direct power of the *kabaka* ship, and perhaps to militate against the troubles in the army which his father had evidently had to contend. It is certainly also the case that rebel princes at the head of foreign armies – such as Kakungulu, son of *Kabaka* Semakokiro and brother of Kamanya, who over many years attacked the kingdom at the head of both Nyoro and Soga armies – posed a particular problem on Buganda's borderlands. It was in these frontier zones that the Ganda state sought to impose itself, and to create the architecture of military power through centrally appointed *batongole*.[102] Yet the defining feature of Suna's reign was the direct encroachment of an external world on his domain. The arrival of a group of coastal merchants at his court in 1844 permanently altered the kingdom.[103] Suna's response, apart from apparently welcoming the little group and immediately recognising the benefit of their guns and their goods, was to look southward with greater resolve. Buganda's geopolitical environment had suddenly altered: the vast lake, long a source of both material and spiritual sustenance, was now also something else – a zone of commercial, and military, interaction and

---

[100] Ibid., 105–6; Reid, *Political Power*, 187–8, 192–3. There was no unified 'Busoga' before the early 1900s, when the British brought together the several dozen micro-kingdoms of the nineteenth century into a single administration.

[101] Kagwa, *Kings*, 124.

[102] Ibid., 97–8, 100, 106–7; Reid, *Political Power*, 188–93.

[103] J.M. Gray, 'Ahmed bin Ibrahim: the first Arab to reach Buganda', *Uganda Journal*, 11 (1947).

opportunity. Under his patronage, the Ganda began to develop their maritime capability, in the form a fleet (or, more properly, fleets) of canoes with a view to long-range commercial, military and diplomatic missions down the western shore of the lake, and ultimately towards the south shore.[104] This was underway by the end of the 1840s.[105] Nevertheless, the fact that Suna was compelled to direct his energies towards the lake is also a reflection of the insecurity experienced by the kingdom on its landward side. It is clear from oral tradition that along critical stretches of borderland in the west and in the east, abutting the Soga and the Nyoro, Buganda could find itself overwhelmed by armed coalitions, and unable to impose itself in ways that its experience of dynamic expansion in the eighteenth century perhaps suggested it should.[106]

Yet it is also true that there was growing local resistance to the aggressive enlargement of the bigger state projects throughout the nineteenth century. A host of smaller states rebelled, repelled and seceded, and rejected the authority of kings. On the edges of, and in between, the larger players they were able, with difficulty and having to endure episodic military harassment in the process, to position themselves as regional pivots, and to negotiate for themselves autonomous spaces in which the power of the bigger, more 'ancient' states was mediated, diluted and refracted. This was the case in Toro and Paluo, and it was also true, for example, in Buhweju, west of Nkore, which was able to assert its autonomy against Bunyoro and later negotiate a tributary relationship with Nkore itself.[107] Buruli and Bugerere, on Buganda's northern peripheries under Bito rule, retained their autonomy until 1900 when they were incorporated into Buganda.[108] Similarly Kkooki, also under a Bito dynasty, had kept both Bunyoro and Buganda at bay, despite the growing power and influence of the latter with which it eventually entered into a tributary relationship. Kkooki variously allied itself with Buganda, and was itself raided by the Ganda mainly as an economic resource, but successfully retained its independence

---

[104] R.J. Reid, 'The Ganda on Lake Victoria: a nineteenth-century East African imperialism', *Journal of African History*, 39:3 (1998).

[105] See, for example, Stanley, *Dark Continent*, I, 285–8.

[106] This is evident from a close reading of the later sections of Kagwa, *Kings*.

[107] Karugire, *History of the Kingdom of Nkore*, 162–4.

[108] Nyakatura, *Anatomy*, 126; A.F. Robertson, *Community of Strangers: a journal of discovery in Uganda* (London, 1978), 47.

until the 1890s.[109] East of the Nile, the Soga microstates were, to be sure, vulnerable to both armed aggression and political influence from both Bunyoro and, later, Buganda;[110] but they too retained an autonomy which was simultaneously negotiated and asserted.[111] Such resistance and mediation was necessitated by the sheer aggression of the larger state projects themselves: the demands of centralising, militarising and authoritarian governments for food, labour, livestock and other commodities, whether through conquest or via tributary arrangements, prompted armed responses and diplomatic engagements in equal measure.

Further west, meanwhile, Nkore was able to take advantage of Ganda–Nyoro conflict and both expand and consolidate in its own right. Here, too, certain chieftaincies were explicitly military in nature, such as the offices of *Engangula* and *Abataunga*, normally occupied by soldiers.[112] Even beyond these military roles, there is evidence of the militarisation of political process, whereby favoured chiefs might be rewarded with command of armies, while success in battle brought them further material reward, notably in the form of cattle distributed by the *Mugabe*.[113] The collapse of the kingdom of Mpororo facilitated Nkore's expansion from the early nineteenth century, which was also made possible by the professional *emitwe* (regiments) headed by these royally appointed commanders; in this way did Nkore, an essentially pastoral kingdom, incorporate swathes of agricultural land on the western side.[114] In so doing, and in common with most other major state systems across the Ugandan region and beyond in this period, Nkore experienced a significant expansion in the use of slave labour, especially in agricultural production; indeed to a considerable extent

---

[109] For example, Kagwa, *Kings*, 131–2, Roscoe, *The Baganda*, 379, Oliver, 'Discernible Developments', 190–1, Twaddle, *Kakungulu*, 1. For an excellent examination of later Kkooki identity, and also that of other groups on the late nineteenth- and twentieth-century 'peripheries' of Buganda, see Stonehouse, 'Peripheral Identities'.

[110] For example, Cohen, *Womunafu's Bunafu*, 75–7.

[111] Lubogo's monumental *History of Busoga*, written in the 1920s and 1930s, avers that '[t]he Basoga secured this part of the world for themselves for ever' (3), although the bulk of the text is a rather fragmented set of individual histories of chieftaincies and clans.

[112] Roscoe, *The Banyankole*, 15.   [113] Ibid., 158, 160.

[114] Morris, *History*, 11–13, 17–22; Morris, *Heroic Recitations*, 4–5 and for analysis of a relevant praise-poem, 41–4; Karugire, *History of the Kingdom of Nkore*, 54–5.

the expansion of state power in the late eighteenth and early nineteenth centuries was most clearly manifest in the more systematic incorporation and exploitation of unfree labour.[115] Frontiers expanded and contracted even more dramatically in eastern Uganda, where in the early decades of the nineteenth century population movement gathered pace, especially among the Teso, who continued to push from Karamoja into the well-watered land around lakes Bisina and Kyoga.[116] Many of these folks turned to farming in order to support expanding populations, a development which in turn pushed Bantu-speakers across the Mpologoma and into northern Busoga. By the middle decades of the nineteenth century, northern Uganda was still experiencing large-scale population movement and the early consolidation of enlarged polities, while to the south we can discern a set of relatively established kingdoms with more or less stable populations; a balance of power in, say, the 1860s, with Buganda apparently more or less secure at its centre. But Buganda was already beginning to overreach itself, and experiments on the choppy waters of Lake Victoria were in part undertaken to offset incipient military decline on land: the reach of large Ganda armies was blunted in Busongora to the west, Kiziba to the south and the Soga to the east.[117] People either withdrew out of reach, or simply sought to absorb attacks and despoliations and waited for the enemy to withdraw – which, increasingly, they did, for Ganda policy in the nineteenth century was no longer to annex territory but to raid and withdraw. In part this shift in strategy was forced upon them, but it was also, coincidentally, driven by the demands of the slave trade. Extraction rather than conquest became the defining principle of war.

And so, in a sense, the seeds of a relative Ganda decline and a Nyoro resurgence had already been sown, even before various important political transitions in the course of the 1850s and 1860s. In Buganda, in around 1857, a young and seemingly somewhat headstrong *kabaka*, Mutesa, came to the throne. He would, in the fullness of time, demonstrate some skill in terms of balancing new forces entering the kingdom, but overall Mutesa's achievements have been greatly

---

[115] See, however, a careful assessment of the issue in E.I. Steinhart, 'Slavery and Other Forms of Social Oppression in Ankole, 1890–1940', in H. Medard & S. Doyle (eds.), *Slavery in the Great Lakes Region of East Africa* (Oxford, 2007).

[116] Vincent, *Teso in Transformation*, 62–75.

[117] For example, Kagwa, *Kings*, 134–5, 156.

exaggerated, perhaps magnified because of the relatively rich documentary record available on him and his reign.[118] He did not halt Buganda's diminution in regional standing, but rather presided over its acceleration; he also created tensions at the political centre through a combination of vacillation, unwise favouritism and the unrestrained exercise of violence, leading to a crisis for the kingship by the end of the century. Meanwhile, however, Bunyoro's fortunes were beginning to be reversed by Kamurasi, who seized power after overthrowing his brother Olimi in 1852.[119] Kamurasi's reign was in many ways profoundly troubled one: he was unable to control the predations and ambitions of the Khartoumers, the northern traders who had established a presence in the kingdom; he had continually to contend with political intrigue and the threat of princely rebellion, as many of his predecessors had done.[120] Nonetheless Kamurasi, who announced himself to Speke as 'the king of all these countries, even including Uganda',[121] also had ambitions of his own – not least to end the Paluo rebellion – and initiated important military reforms.[122] Yet if Bunyoro had been strengthened somewhat under Kamurasi, helped by a faltering Buganda, it was his son, Kabalega, who pushed those reforms even further to render Bunyoro once again a major actor in the regional power balance. He was the exemplar of the 'political warrior' in late precolonial Uganda, and in many respects the most remarkable victim of the culture of violence which pervaded the region in the nineteenth century.

These states and societies were many things. Their leaders needed to be possessed of many skills – or at least needed their advisors to have them: they were peace-makers and diplomats, builders of alliances, cultural and ritual nodes, avatars channelling historical legitimacy. The history of precolonial Uganda is to a very large extent the history of shifting networks and coalitions, the creation of multiple linkages and reciprocal relationships. Moreover, these were increasingly centred on new ideological constructions around motherhood, as Stephens has eloquently argued for this period, meaning that queen mothers were

---

[118] See Reid, 'Images'.
[119] This was not the view, however, in some older literature in which Kamurasi represents the nadir in a long, steep decline: see, for example, G.N. Uzoigwe, 'Succession and Civil War in Bunyoro-Kitara', *International Journal of African Historical Studies*, 6:1 (1973).
[120] Doyle, *Crisis and Decline*, 42–3, 50.   [121] Speke, *Journal*, 516.
[122] Nyakatura, *Anatomy*, 98–102; Doyle, *Crisis and Decline*, 155.

often critical in legitimating political power and in creating the socio-political linkages necessary to state-building.[123] At the same time, of course, monarchical authority also sought to reify gender roles – male and female – and to replicate the androcentric, patriarchal power relations intrinsic to the management of the family unit in the realm of public politics: kingship, according to this reading, was the projection of husbandly authority, undergirded by gender hierarchy.[124] Yet it is important, too, to remind ourselves of the significance of clans in these state-building exercises. In Buganda, Bunyoro and Nkore, clan support was critical to the growth of kingship and the consolidation of the state. In early Nyoro history, it was essential that the Bito *bakama* cultivated alliances with clans in order to secure their own positions; royal authority depended on clan support, hence the recognition of the role of clans in the guardianship of Chwezi religious sites, a recognition which served to legitimate Bito rule.[125] Likewise in Buganda, which started life as a confederation of clans under the loose suzerainty of the *kabaka* who had no clan, and whose very title indicated that he was the 'head of the clan heads' – the chair of a committee whose members were potentially rather more important than he himself was. This constitutional mechanism meant that the *kabaka* – taking his mother's clan in a patrilineal society – belonged to all clans, and none in particular; and because Ganda clans were exogamous, there was no possibility of a royal clan emerging.[126] He was, in a real sense, the incarnation of the kingdom itself, and thus a figure to whom all Ganda could offer loyalty. Ironically, however, this enabled the *kabaka* to accrue personal power at the expense of the clans, which by the nineteenth century found themselves increasingly marginal to political affairs, and indeed to some extent written out of the glorious history of the kingdom's expansion – something they would kick back against in the early decades of the twentieth century. As Kagwa

[123] Stephens, *African Motherhood*, deals with specifically with Buganda, Busoga and Bugwere.
[124] This was demonstrable, too, in the late twentieth century with the restoration of the kingdoms, as Mikael Karlstrom has argued powerfully in the context of Buganda: see his 'The Cultural Kingdom in Uganda: popular royalism and the restoration of the Buganda kingship', unpublished PhD thesis, University of Chicago, 1999.
[125] This is one of the central arguments in Tantala, 'Early history'.
[126] Roscoe, *The Baganda*, 137–8, 187.

himself demonstrated in his own work on Buganda, clans also represented economic forces, providing specialist skills and knowledge which contributed ineffably to the dynamism of the polities themselves.[127] This was particularly true in Nkore, where the major clans were associated with particular economic activities – herding, or iron-working – while clans also had important roles as guardians of ritual. In Nkore, clans maintained the kingship through ties of political and material reciprocity, and formed the major subnational component blocs of the polity. Notably, the *Mugabe*'s mother's clan was especially important – echoing the exercise of maternal authority elsewhere in the region – in any given reign in influencing political appointments and controlling access to the royal court, and this doubtless goes some way to explaining the regular succession disputes which marked the kingdom's deeper history.[128] More generally, it was within the clan structure in these three major southern states that the historical memory of the kingdom could be said to reside, and endure.

But perhaps above all, these leaders were the products of a distinctive military entrepreneurialism which itself was the outcome of dynamic interactions along the Nilotic-Bantu borderland. These states were formed by warriors of various hues, and maintained by military systems and processes of organised violence which were critical to both external security and to internal cohesion. To a very real degree, this was the age of the political warrior – a figure which would continue to dominate Ugandan political culture, and which continues to do so at the time of writing, even if the shadings and nuances of context change somewhat from time to time. The eighteenth and nineteenth centuries witnessed escalating militarisation and the development of the use of war as a means to the conceptual and physical expansion of the state, and as the clearest manifestation of 'national' identities. Moreover, in the increasingly crowded and dangerous political marketplace that was the zone between the Ruwenzori Mountains and lakes Victoria, Kyoga and Albert, the peoples of these emergent kingdoms entered into deals with their rulers: partnerships, as it were, for governance, and charters for the effective functioning of the state. Rulers would provide

---

[127] Kagwa, 'Clans' and for Bunyoro, see also J. Nyakatura, *Aspects of Bunyoro Customs and Traditions* (Nairobi, 1970).
[128] Karugire, *History of the Kingdom of Nkore*, 10–11, 72–4.

stability, protection and administration; the governed would offer loyalty, goods and services, and the legitimacy which flowed from an
engagement with public ceremony and 'tradition'. In effect, it was security abroad in exchange for fealty at home. Yet these were not relationships which would endure for all time, nor were they supposed to:
the putative providers of security were themselves resisted and their
positions contested when they were believed to have transgressed, and
leaders would find themselves challenged by those who were ready to
withdraw fealty at the perceived breaking of the contract – as more
recent regimes have discovered, too.

The figure of Rukidi, however we perceive his historicity, is crucial as historical emblem, and as theme; he is the incarnation of the
persistent, and in many ways undiminished, role of the military in
Ugandan history. Rukidi and his children were historical memories,
and legitimating ones – normalising the *coup* in political culture, the
seizures of power by relative outsiders, the regime ruptures that each
seizure brought. Still, the story contains an apparent paradox: regime-
rupture alongside selective elements of continuity, and indeed the quest
for legitimacy, in some respects, through a judicious combination of
eschewal of the previous regime, whether implicit or explicit, and
an emphasis on the threads of continuity. In the centuries following
Rukidi's seizure of power in Kitara, we have the increasing militarisation of political culture in Uganda, and the construction of ever
larger and more ambitious state systems, especially across the southern forests. Similar centralising and militarising tendencies can also be
espied in parts of the north, especially among the Acholi; but it is perhaps the single greatest irony of modern Ugandan history that while
northern infusions of political creativity provided the southern forest
zone with the energy and dynamism which has so characterised its centralised, territorial state systems in the last four hundred years, northern societies themselves would find it increasingly difficult to compete
with that peculiar monarchical vigour over the *longue durée* of political and economic development. Rukidi, in a sense, not only signifies the
role of militarism, arms and the politics of rupture in Ugandan political culture; he is also emblematic of a long-term shift in the centre of
political gravity from north to south.

Historical consciousness manifested itself in myriad ways. In
Nkore, Wamala and Ruhinda would come to be important spirits

associated with fertility, and whose mediums had powerful political connections;[129] but it is perfectly plausible that they were, in origin, especially noteworthy chiefs who became historicised and memorialised through their elevation to a spiritual pantheon. More broadly, traditions of origins and founding fathers, and later narrative histories, served to underscore the importance of social cohesion and health; to emphasise the weighty import of battle and the glories, as well as the tragedies, which were possible on the field of conflict; to provide moral guidance through allegory and allusion. And especial significance was indeed attached to war – a reflection, surely, of the violent roots of these states and societies. We have encountered this in some of the sources used in the reconstruction of the deeper past in this very chapter: *viz.*, the grand narratives of Kagwa for Buganda, and later Nyakatura and 'K.W.' (*Mukama* Tito Winyi's pseudonym) for Bunyoro, which place violence and redemption, war and transformation, at their centre. Indeed war was necessary even to historical visibility: as Tito Winyi wrote of one of his predecessors as *Mukama* of Bunyoro, Kyebambe, '[he was] not spoken of much, because he reigned in peace and died of old age'; and likewise Ochaki 'was not spoken of much as there was peace during his reign'.[130] Nyakatura's account of Winyi III was so short precisely because '[w]e have no tradition of any wars fought during his reign'.[131] By contrast, those who fought wars glorious and heroic received due attention in the twentieth-century accounts; and so, too, did those who fought valiantly but vainly, as in the case of Nakibinge and Kibuka of Buganda, remembered in Kagwa's account as tragic heroes killed fighting the Nyoro, but out of whose sacrifice would arise an ever stronger kingdom.[132] Karagwe had Luzenga, who died in an attempt to overthrow Nyoro rule in the late eighteenth century;[133] and in one narrative the kingdom of Nkore itself was forged through violence, the outcome of a rebellion against Kitara led by founding father Ruhinda.[134] The image of the peace-loving Kintu in

---

[129] For example, ibid., 84 and *passim*.
[130] 'K.W.', 'The Kings of Bunyoro-Kitara Part II', *Uganda Journal*, 4:1 (1936), 77, 83.
[131] Nyakatura, *Anatomy*, 76.   [132] Kagwa, *Kings*, 26–9.
[133] J. Ford & R.de Z. Hall, 'The history of Karagwe (Bukoba District)', *Tanganyika Notes and Records*, 24 (1947), 7.
[134] Nyakatura, *Anatomy*, 49.

Buganda may well have been utilised to critique the bloody tyranny of nineteenth-century *kabaka*s,[135] and contrasts sharply with the righteous, foundational violence of Ndahura, the first Chwezi ruler.[136] In a sense, war, and the exercise of violence, remained an ideal state and the purest and clearest manifestation of political leadership, long after rulers themselves had vacated the battlefield in favour of anointed specialist commanders, and affairs of court kept them from the battle itself – as happened in Bunyoro, over time;[137] and in Buganda, too, where no *kabaka* saw direct combat but where coronation ceremonies were nonetheless infused with military symbolism. For, as Zimbe had it, 'a Kingdom is always conquered not succeeded to'.[138] Everywhere, war is celebrated, its successful and righteous practitioners memorialised in oral text, while sinister transgressors and tyrannical aggressors are avatars against which the essence of national military prowess and morality can be measured.

This is especially true for the eighteenth and nineteenth centuries, a period characterised by nothing less than a revolution in military affairs.[139] It was an era in which across the Ugandan region the practice and organisation of warfare became professionalised in wholly novel ways, with soldiery and military structure becoming ever more effective; in which cultures of militarism and the celebration of arms increasingly underpinned political authority as well as wider political and cultural identities; in which the scale and purpose of war itself expanded dramatically, and hierarchies and heterarchies alike mobilised violence in pursuit of a range of interconnected objectives – political legitimacy, social cohesion, economic growth – in increasingly innovative and ambitious ways. It was an era of militarised mobility, and thus one of remarkable dynamism and energy, both north and south of the Nile – an era of big ambitious states, but also of

---

[135] Stanley, *Dark Continent*, I, 271, 276–81; J. Yoder, 'The quest for Kintu and the search for peace: mythology and morality in nineteenth-century Buganda', *History in Africa*, 15 (1988).

[136] Nyakatura, *Anatomy*, 25; 'K.W.', 'Kings of Bunyoro-Kitara Part I', 158–9.

[137] J. Roscoe, *Twenty-Five Years in East Africa* (Cambridge, 1921), 250; Roscoe, *The Bakitara*, 305–6.

[138] Zimbe, *Buganda ne Kabaka*, 83, 107.

[139] By the author, see *Warfare in African History*, 107–45 and 'The Fragile Revolution: rethinking war and development in Africa's violent nineteenth century', in E. Akyeampong, R.H. Bates, N. Nunn, & J.A. Robinson (eds.), *Africa's Development in Historical Perspective* (New York, 2014).

small ones mediating their power, and of some striking experiments in entrepreneurial violence and community-formation, especially across eastern and northern Uganda. The region was characterised by a complex weave of war and peace, friends and enemies, and continually morphing coalitions. Increasingly ideological states and chieftaincies, of various shapes and sizes, formed a belt of distinctive political engagement including violent interaction. It was an era in which centres of political and military gravity shifted, underpinned by political tectonics, and producing frontier zones across which states and societies forged their identities and against which the civilised defined themselves.

Yet militarisation was a good servant and an evil master. On the one hand, war served clear purposes and had definite advantages in the sense that it marked out the territorial state, generated external resources and provided external security, as well as tying people to institutions and personalities – the political fabric of life – which made for stable and safe environments. On the other, however, war and attendant systems of militarism unleashed cultures of organised violence upheld by the ambitious and the insurgent, the armed chief and the discontented princeling, which had the potential – frequently realised – to destabilise and undermine extant political authority, and act as an effective block on other routes to governance, and specifically more pacific decision-making. The basic story of the relationship between Buganda and Bunyoro, which in many ways defines southern Ugandan history, demonstrates the central theme: the role of the military in political culture, the primacy of arms as the basis of political expansion, advancement and aggrandisement, the central role of warrior heroes – and of course the inevitability that the young and able will challenge the old and infirm, and old heroes will be replaced with new. Yet there were dangers, too. Cyclically violent succession was profoundly destabilising, which is why in Buganda in the nineteenth century there was an attempt to regularise it; but in Nkore and Bunyoro succession was normatively a matter of rupture and conflict and, finally, reconciliation. 'The brothers fought for it', *Mukama* Kamurasi told Speke proudly in 1862, 'and the best man gained the crown'[140] – though Kamurasi's own brother, Omudaya, became 'very depressed by the terrible deaths which he and his soldiers had caused' when he successfully crushed a

---

[140] Speke, *Journal*, 547.

princely rebellion against Kamurasi: 'Let him not congratulate me for destroying all our family and our clan', he declared sadly in a message to his *Mukama*.[141] Even so, violent interregna served not only to allow the 'best man' to prove his mettle, but also seemed to have demonstrated the importance of the military order which the state (in theory) represented, such was the juxtaposition with the bloody lawlessness which erupted when the state rested.[142] This is not to say that kings themselves were not then capable of transgressions in violence while in power – in which case, they might expect equally violent resistance and perhaps bloody ouster, or, in the case of *Mukama* Winyi II in seventeenth-century Bunyoro, a good talking-to by his senior chiefs. As 'K.W.' pointedly explained (from the position of the Nyoro throne) in the mid-1930s, that king 'was fond of killing people for nothing', which meant that 'people did not love him', but after he was admonished by his chiefs, he reined in his behaviour and became rather more secure.[143] Kings could be cruel indeed – Ganda rulers sometimes seemed to inflict more physical damage on their own subjects than they did on external enemies – and in many ways that was expected, even desirable: it was reassuring to be physically abused by monarchs who needed above all to be *visible*; if they weren't, that meant they were either dead, dying or didn't care. But they were also ultimately held in check by popular pressure and political sanction.

More broadly, the expansion and professionalisation of violence in the late precolonial period had long-term implications for Uganda, not least in terms of an exaggerated faith in the primacy of arms to achieve cohesion and development, fostering the growth of a zero-sum political culture. Precedents were set long before the twentieth century for the great warrior-king whose role was salvation and transformation, or at least restoration; certainly the myth of such men (as men they invariably were) loomed ever larger. Processes of militarisation set in motion through the intense conflicts of the eighteenth and nineteenth centuries would not easily be extinguished, despite the best efforts of the colonial state. In sum, the political order which arose as a result of these dynamics could not necessarily control the forces thus unleashed – a long-term challenge, and in some ways a deep-rooted failure. Violent succession

[141] Nyakatura, *Anatomy*, 100.
[142] Roscoe, *Twenty-Five Years*, 254; Roscoe, *The Bakitara*, 314.
[143] 'K.W.', 'Kings of Bunyoro-Kitara Part II', 80.

may indeed have produced 'the best men' – the point is debatable – but more broadly it drove militarisation, and the militarisation of politics. It was sometimes easier to start a war than to end one; to assemble an army than to disband one. The states and societies of Uganda's eighteenth and nineteenth centuries were the victims of their own success. Militarisation often had a tendency to develop its own momentum, and it could influence politics in interesting and unexpected ways.

Oscillations and Outages

In 1869, *Mukama* Kamurasi of Bunyoro died, sparking a violent struggle for the kingship. In the months that followed, the young Kabalega defied the odds by organising an army against several of the most powerful political figures in the kingdom, demonstrating some of the skills he would later refine against the British and gaining the reputation of a fighter who was 'difficult to beat'.[144] Sometime in 1870, he sent for assistance from Buganda – which Mutesa granted, sending a force against Kabagumire, Kabalega's brother, the candidate favoured by many of the leading chiefs.[145] The utilisation of external assistance was by no means uncommon, and the history of the region is replete with armed interference in neighbours' affairs. Whether as a result of Ganda support or not, Kabalega prevailed, and was crowned *mukama* by 1871. If Ganda support had indeed been significant, it was ironic, for Kabalega's accession heralded a period in which the balance of power in the region changed dramatically at Buganda's expense.[146]

Kabalega did not singlehandedly engender a turnaround in Bunyoro's fortunes: the roots of the resurgence can be dated to his father Kamurasi, who skilfully made use of Langi mercenaries, marking the beginning of several decades of Nyoro-Langi military cooperation,

---

[144] Nyakatura, *Anatomy*, 108–110.
[145] Ibid., 110–11; Kagwa, *Kings*, 159. However, Nyakatura cannot resist the aside that the Ganda commander was really 'hoping to get Kabalega to fight without the assistance of Buganda' and was 'looking for cattle to raid': Nyakatura, *Anatomy*, 111.
[146] For extensive and still-penetrating analysis, see the work of G.N. Uzoigwe, one of the pioneers of the Africanist revolution in Ugandan historiography: *Revolution and Revolt in Bunyoro Kitara: two studies* (London, 1970), 'Precolonial Military Studies in Africa', *Journal of Modern African Studies*, 13:3 (1975) and 'The Warrior and the State in Precolonial Africa', in A.A. Mazrui (ed.), *The Warrior Tradition in Modern Africa* (Leiden, 1977), 32–3.

in securing his own succession in 1852, and who took advantage of
Mutesa's early insecurity on the throne in Buganda to expand Bunyoro's commercial and military presence across central and northern Uganda in the course of the 1860s. During this time Bunyoro
competed successfully for a share of the burgeoning Zanzibari trade
to the south and that with southern Sudan and Khartoum to the
north.[147] To Kamurasi's reign, too, can be traced the beginnings of
specialised military units – probably forming part of a royal bodyguard – fighting alongside the larger, more traditional military lev-
ees known as *bwesengeze*.[148] But Kabalega pushed reform much further in expanding some twelve *barusura* regiments into a professional
and permanent army, stationed in barracks across the kingdom, and
owing direct and personal loyalty to Kabalega himself: a 'national
army', as Nyakatura had it.[149] Its purpose, as was the case with much
nineteenth-century military reform elsewhere, was dual, both internal
and external. Internally, the *barusura* were positioned in troublesome
provinces, while simultaneously undermining older military and chiefly
centres of power which were evidently not trusted by the *mukama*.[150]
He embarked on a major programme of centralisation, and attempted
to impose the state on semi-autonomous outlying regions. In this, he
was only partially successful, but in the process he replaced a number of hereditary chieftaincies with his own kinsmen and those considered to be loyal to Kabalega himself. He also instigated public works
programmes, aimed at creating more efficient infrastructure and more
direct control over his subjects' labour. At the same time, externally,
the *barusura* were garrisoned on the kingdom's frontiers and represented a newly invigorated and aggressive outward policy. In around
1876, Kabalega reconquered rebellious Toro, bringing it back under
putatively rightful suzerainty;[151] and in the years that followed, Nyoro
forces captured the Paluo states of Chope and Bugungu which had
long taunted the old kingdom, thus rectifying the disasters of the early

---

[147] Doyle, *Crisis and Decline*, 43.
[148] Nyakatura, *Anatomy*, 133; Uzoigwe, *Revolution and Revolt*, 10–12; Doyle,
Crisis and Decline, 55–6. See also Baker's description of some of Kamurasi's
soldiers in *Albert N'yanza*, II, 347–9.
[149] Nyakatura, *Anatomy*, 131–3; also Doyle, *Crisis and Decline*, 55.
[150] Uzoigwe, 'Pre-colonial military studies', 473.
[151] See also a comprehensive dissertation by Peter Idowu Akingbade, 'The
History of the Kingdom of Toro, from its Foundation to 1928' (MA
Dissertation, University of East Africa, 1967), 50.

1830s. But the reformed army was also at the heart of a further key prong to Kabalega's outward policy, namely to take full advantage of the rapidly expanding commerce in slaves and ivory which was driving the region's economic transformation.[152]

Kabalega made use of external advisors – agents from Khartoum – in creating the *barusura*, and in his succession struggle; as a reward they 'demanded half of Kitara', at which point Kabalega drove them out of the country.[153] It was clear enough that while these growing links with the north represented opportunities on the one hand, they were also profound threats on the other.[154] The advancing presence of foreign forces from the north was rapidly transforming a broad arc of territory abutting present-day northern Uganda and South Sudan into a volatile and violent frontier zone. One of Kabalega's central concerns was to prevent his rival for the kingship, Rionga, from likewise enlisting Sudanese assistance; and into this mix was thrown the bumptious Samuel Baker, who had arrived in the region in 1872 as the representative of *Khedive* Ismail of Egypt with a view to extending Egyptian influence and suppressing the slave trade.[155] Initially Baker offered Kabalega armed support against Rionga in exchange for Bunyoro becoming an Egyptian protectorate – an early example of security assistance in return for alignment with an international order. Momentously, although it would not perhaps have seemed so at the time, Kabalega refused, at which point Baker switched his support to Rionga, but their combined forces were driven from Bunyoro by Kabalega's dynamic new army.[156] Bunyoro was indeed resurgent; but the cost – in terms of Baker's enduring interpretation of the Nyoro as savage obstacles to progress, in contrast to the semi-enlightened and cooperative Ganda – would only become clearer much later on.

---

[152] Beattie, *Nyoro State*, 68*ff*; Uzoigwe, *Revolution and Revolt, passim* and G.N. Uzoigwe, 'Kabarega and the making of a new Kitara', *Tarikh*, 3:2 (1970).

[153] Nyakatura, *Anatomy*, 111.

[154] E.A.Alpers, 'The nineteenth century: prelude to colonialism', in Ogot & Kieran (eds.), *Zamani*, 251.

[155] All of this is described in inevitably vivid detail in Samuel Baker, *Ismailia*, 2 vols. (London, 1874) and for an equally colourful overview, A. Moorehead, *The White Nile* (London, 1963), 143–62. See also Beattie, *Nyoro State*, 68–71.

[156] Nyakatura, *Anatomy*, 119–23; Beattie, *Nyoro State*, 68–9, 71. Baker's convoluted and self-promoting account of these events is in *Ismailia*, II, chapters X-XII.

Again, however, there were early indications that the militarisation of the polity was fraught with dangers. There is no question that the *barusura* were critical in the re-emergence of Bunyoro as a major regional power. They were deployed in expansionist campaigns into neighbouring territories – important in terms of the prestige and more specifically the revenue generated, revenue which was then distributed to loyal followers, thus creating a new political culture of royal authoritarianism. Competition heightened within new administrative and military classes for royal favour. The *barusura* enabled Kabalega to extend his reach over swathes of the population. Yet, despite the fact that Kabalega appears to have attached agents to clandestinely monitor the doings of his regiments and their commanders,[157] they gained a reputation over time for violent brutality and lawlessness, plundering and looting even within Bunyoro itself.[158] Moreover, the *barusura* were armed increasingly with firearms, the acquisition of which was the single most important commercial objective of Kabalega's reign.[159] Guns may have been rare enough in the mid-1860s to alarm the Nyoro with the noise they made,[160] but this certainly wasn't the case a few years later. Indeed the creation of specialised firearms units made Bunyoro much more effective in the use of the new technology than Buganda, where guns were rather distributed as political rewards, instead of as part of a larger, more coherent programme of military reform.[161] Enhanced firepower and military reorganisation enabled Kabalega to assert himself against the Egyptian and Sudanese threat from the north, and to achieve military success against Buganda in the course of the 1880s. Nyoro success at the battle of Rwengabi in 1886 placed the seal on Bunyoro as arguably the dominant military power in the area,[162] and soon after, Buganda itself was engulfed in civil war. However, this

---

[157] Roscoe, *The Bakitara*, 308.   [158] Doyle, *Crisis and Decline*, 55–6.

[159] The numbers reported by Stanley in 1888 – some '1500' guns – seem small by regional standards: Buganda had perhaps up to 10,000 at the beginning of the 1890s: Zimbe, *Buganda ne Kabaka*, 287. Nonetheless they were clearly more effectively used in Bunyoro than most places: Stanley, *In Darkest Africa*, I, 377, and II, 310 and see also Reid, *War in Precolonial Eastern Africa*, 46–52. In any case by the early 1890s the Nyoro apparently had rather more firearms at their disposal: Steinhart, *Conflict and Collaboration*, 63–4.

[160] Baker, *Albert Nyanza*, II, 82.

[161] Reid, *War in Precolonial Eastern Africa*, 52.

[162] Nyakatura, *Anatomy*, pp.134–6; Doyle, *Crisis and Decline*, 58; Twaddle, *Kakungulu*, 95.

very success would bring Kabalega unwelcome attention. Bunyoro's military success had closed off the north as an entry point for Europe into the region – meaning that Buganda was now the main platform for British expansion, and meaning in turn that Bunyoro was increasingly viewed through the eyes of a Ganda political establishment seriously anxious about Bunyoro's renaissance, compounding the influential judgment of Baker that the kingdom was a violent blot on the landscape.

By the late 1880s, Buganda had furthered its own military reforms, possibly even in emulation of the *barusura*, but certainly building on the militarisation of administrative authority underway since the 1830s and 1840s. There is evidence that the emergence of a military title, the *mujasi*, appointed directly by the *kabaka*, represented the appearance of an increasingly specialist armed force which probably evolved out of a royal bodyguard.[163] While it was also used as a kind of internal police force – and the *mujasi* inspired considerable fear around the Ganda capital as a result[164] – there is no question that this increasingly nationwide army was also being dispatched for the borders to fight the Nyoro, for example.[165] The success of these reforms was limited before the early 1890s, and they were at least partially prompted by the gradual decline in military performance in evidence by the 1870s – the moment of Kabalega's renaissance. Long-range expeditions, whether punitive or predatory or both, were increasingly ineffective as Ganda armies overstretched themselves. Ganda soldiers complained that the people of Gambaragara – the edge of the Ruwenzori Mountains – simply ran away and hid in inaccessible caves and hilltops when they saw them coming, and waited till the Ganda were forced to depart, which eventually they had to.[166] Another army headed for Buzinza at the south end of Lake Victoria was forced to turn back because

---

[163] Uganda National Archives (hereafter UNA) A1/1 IBEAC Report, 1891–2; A. Kagwa (tr. E.B. Kalibala), *The Customs of the Baganda* (New York, 1934), 90; Church Missionary Society Archives (hereafter CMS) G3/A6/0 1885/98 Mackay to Wigram, May 1885; White Fathers Rubaga Diary 2 / 14 May 1881. See also Low, 'The northern interior', 335 and C.P. Kottak, 'Ecological variables in the origin and evolution of African states: the Buganda example', *Comparative Studies in Society and History*, 14:3 (1972), 376.

[164] White Fathers Rubaga Diary 3 / 7 April 1886, 28 April 1886, 30 April 1886.

[165] CMS G3/A6/0 1885/98 Mackay to Wigram, May 1885; White Fathers C14/182 Lourdel to Superior-General, 12 September 1887.

[166] Stanley, *Dark Continent*, I, 336.

of lack of food.[167] Buganda was increasingly unable to impose itself
on the lacustrine political environment in quite the way envisioned at
the royal capital – which was, notably, in the same period increasingly
stationary in the heart of modern Kampala, when previously it had
been mobile and transient.[168] But this was not merely a question of
thwarted ambitions over excessive distances: Ganda armies were struggling closer to home, too, including against the Soga early in Mutesa's
reign.[169] One of the best illustrations of this is the war against the tiny
island of Buvuma, just off Buganda's eastern shoreline and in the little bay from which the Nile leaves Lake Victoria, a war fortuitously
(though not unproblematically) observed at first hand by Stanley.[170]
With its enormous fleet of canoes, and led by some of the leading military chiefs in the realm – as well as being overseen by Mutesa himself –
the Ganda army was for several weeks unable to subdue this stubborn
little community which defied the *kabaka*'s authority, raided for slaves
on Buganda's own shoreline, and disrupted grand plans for control
of Lake Victoria.[171] The symbolism would scarcely have been lost on
the Ganda political establishment, but other reverses were to come in
the final years of Mutesa's reign. While there were tangible successes
against the nearby Soga in the late 1870s – tangible in the sense that
the campaigns brought in the spoils of war, including slaves[172] – there
was also the calamitous defeat of a longer-range and rather more ambitious campaign apparently against Rwanda, although it is unclear if the
army ever got close to Rwanda. 'The prestige of Waganda warfare has
begun to fade', wrote one missionary based in the Ganda capital.[173] In
mid-1884, in what seems to have been the last major campaign before
Mutesa's death, a heavy defeat was inflicted on a Ganda army by the

[167] Kagwa, *Kings*, 163.
[168] H. Médard & R.J. Reid, 'Merchants, missions and the remaking of the urban
environment in Buganda, c.1840-c.1890', in D.M. Anderson & R. Rathbone
(eds.), *Africa's Urban Past* (London, 2000).
[169] Kagwa, *Kings*, 156.
[170] See, for example, Reid, 'Ganda on Lake Victoria' and R.J. Reid, 'Violence and
its Sources: European witnesses to the military revolution in
nineteenth-century eastern Africa', in P. Landau (ed.), *The Power of Doubt:
essays in honour of David Henige* (Madison WI, 2011).
[171] Stanley, *Dark Continent*, I, chapters 12 & 13.
[172] CMS CA6/010/48 Felkin's Journal, 14 February 1879 & 22 April 1879;
CA6/019/14 Pearson to Wright, 10 March 1879; CA6/019/15 Pearson to
Wright, 29 September 1879.
[173] CMS CA6/019/19 Pearson to Wright, 5 March 1880.

Langi or Teso – the enemy is simply described, as anyone from that direction usually was, as 'Bakedi'.[174] It is also worth noting Mutesa's ambivalent but increasingly uneasy attitude towards long-range foreign threats in the form of Sudan/Egypt to the north and Zanzibar to the south – resulting in foreign policy directives which only drove home the limitations on Buganda's ability to influence the external environment. On the one hand, at the beginning of the 1880s, Mutesa was reportedly planning to ally himself with the Arab community in Unyanyembe to achieve a crushing military victory over the Nyamwezi leader Mirambo who now controlled vital trade routes south of Lake Victoria; the plan, if indeed there ever actually was one, came to nothing, and soon Mutesa was instead offering Mirambo blood brotherhood (Mirambo accepted).[175] On the other hand, he was anxious to forge an alliance with Kabalega himself against the Sudanese to the north; yet Kabalega had that situation under control on his own – for the moment, at least.[176] It seems that Mutesa worried incessantly but largely impotently about looming foreign threats and also, ill as he was – possibly with syphilis – his own death.[177]

Yet some of the biggest problems were altogether closer to home, and concerned an increasingly introverted, riven and factious political-military class, more interested in status and position in and around the royal court than in achieving such status through armed endeavour. A good example is Stanley's companion Sambuzi, a favourite of Mutesa who was promoted and for a time was unbearably flushed with pride, but who – owing to his failure to bring the explorer to Lake Albert – was later stripped of his command and ruined. 'The Waganda', Stanley's servant supposedly told Mutesa, 'are very good before you, Kabaka, but when away from you, they forget your commands, and

---

[174] Zimbe, *Buganda ne Kabaka*, 85–6.
[175] CMS G3 A6/0 1881/22 Pearson to Mackay, 29 July 1880; LMS Central Africa, Incoming, Box 4: Southon to Thompson, 17 May 1881; CMS G3 A6/0 1882/14 O'Flaherty to Wigram, 25 December 1881. See also R.J. Reid, 'Mutesa and Mirambo: thoughts on East African warfare and diplomacy in the nineteenth century', *International Journal of African Historical Studies*, 31:1 (1998).
[176] White Fathers Rubaga Diary 1 / 19 December 1879; White Fathers C14/130 Lourdel to his brother, 4 May 1882.
[177] Reid, 'Images', 292, 294; Michael Tuck, '*Kabaka* Mutesa and Venereal Disease: an essay on medical history and sources in precolonial Buganda', *History in Africa*, 30 (2003).

steal people, cattle, and goats'.[178] It was a beautifully simple summation of the political crisis in Buganda on the eve of colonial rule. At the heart of the crisis was the fact that Mutesa himself was not a particularly imposing character, despite some of the good press he received at the time and subsequently (mostly in juxtaposition with his son), and struggled, towards the end, to manage or perhaps even to understand the changes taking place, and the cleavages opening up, within his own political establishment. Zimbe tells us that toward the end of his life Mutesa was aware that 'people were tired of him', and fearing assassination and rebellion, he continually dispatched the particularly dangerous chiefs on military campaign.[179] But the fact remained that a new class of younger chiefs was emerging by the 1880s which was politically ambitious but less interested in the more traditional means of achieving their goals – namely, military prowess – than in the opportunities offered by new religions, clothing and of course the guns which were indicators of prestige and status and quite useful in terms of internal pillage.[180]

There was also a gendered element to internal political shifts, in that women – at least elite women – were becoming powerful political actors in and around the royal court. The *namasole*, the king's mother, was evidently a potent character with her own extensive power networks and fully functioning court early in Mutesa's reign;[181] and by the 1870s and 1880s, royal women influenced political appointments, acted as counsellors and protected and promoted their menfolk.[182] This was symptomatic of the proliferation of alternative and competing centres of power even within the nominal hub of royal authority. Women had long been at the centre of polity and society, though expressions of masculinity in the nineteenth century contrasted sharply with the feminine: most emphatically in the realm of warrior courage, while cowardice was gendered. Nyoro soldiers who had demonstrated timidity were made to dress like female slaves in the midst of post-battle

---

[178] Stanley, *Dark Continent*, I, 349–51.
[179] Zimbe, *Buganda ne Kabaka*, 82.
[180] Reid, *Political Power*, 201, 216–17; CMS G3 A5/0 1888/241 Gordon to Mackay, 31 December 1887; Zimbe, *Buganda ne Kabaka*, 174.
[181] Speke's rather odd dealings with her are described at length in his *Journal*, 304–7, 310–19.
[182] Schiller, 'Royal Women' and for a more detailed study of women in the precolonial era – one of the few to be undertaken in the Ugandan context – see Stephens, *African Motherhood*.

celebrations, and Ganda men like pregnant women.[183] Yet this public representation of gendered hierarchy is contradicted by the evidently central role played by motherhood in social cohesion and economic development in the precolonial era, as demonstrated in the detailed work of Rhiannon Stephens, and by elite women at the top level of political life, as argued in some earlier work.[184]

Meanwhile, although the Nyoro-Ganda connexion arguably remained the defining axis along which modern Uganda was being forged in this period, the 'smaller' states across the southern region skilfully combined limited-range military action with pragmatic diplomacy to carve space for themselves in turbulent times – whether the comparatively modest, careful military campaigns of the Nyankore, who episodically raided cattle in Buganda's western borderlands;[185] or the defensive and pragmatic Soga states, which evidently managed Ganda incursions with some skill throughout the nineteenth century. Buganda could never claim to have achieved anything like complete dominance east of the Nile, and Lloyd Fallers' assertion that 'Busoga entered world history in the shadow of Buganda' now seems, though understandable in a Ganda-centric world, somewhat overstated and not a little dismissive.[186] For while, broadly speaking, the southern Soga were under Ganda influence and the northern communities were under Nyoro sway – reflecting the historic 'Kintu-Mukama' dichotomy – they were altogether more adept than has been fully acknowledged at mobilising external assistance in pursuit of local agendas, including limited political expansionism, as Lubogo's history of Bukoli, for example, demonstrates.[187] In the west, following the death of *Mugabe* Mutambukwa in 1878, Nkore warded off at least two significant Ganda invasions undertaken with a view to overthrowing his successor, Ntare.[188] Indeed Nkore continued to profit from the political and military obsession Buganda and Bunyoro had

---

[183] Speke, *Journal*, 312; Kagwa, *Customs*, 93.
[184] Stephens, *African Motherhood*; Schiller, 'Royal Women'. That essential ambiguity around gender roles has persisted through much of the twentieth century and beyond. See Christine Obbo, *African Women: their struggle for economic independence* (London, 1980), for example, which deals largely with Uganda.
[185] Roscoe, *The Banyankole*, 154–9.   [186] Fallers, *Bantu Bureaucracy*, 38.
[187] Lubogo, *History of Busoga*, 5–7.
[188] Karugire, *History of the Kingdom of Nkore*, 213–16; Low, 'The northern interior', 336–7.

with one another, and was able to expand its influence across the southwest, often through interventions in neighbours' wars in support of favoured princes. The biggest threat to the kingdom itself, however, came not from either Bunyoro or Buganda, but from Rwanda, which launched a series of attacks on Nkore down to the 1890s in an attempt to curb the latter's influence.[189] Yet much of this violence, in the end, was about cattle, the great prize of military success, and the great motivator of military action. Toro, meanwhile – the state which had so audaciously asserted itself against Bunyoro in the 1830s – fared less well, and was something of a focus for regional rivalries and ultimately outside intervention. After Kabalega reconquered it in 1876, Toro was a focus of Nyoro-Ganda rivalry: one of the exiled Toro princes, Namuyonjo, had fled to Buganda and was given an army with which to march back to power. According to Kiwanuka, Namuyonjo was indeed temporarily restored as ruler before Kabalega hit back and overthrew him.[190] It seems, however, that Nyoro administration of Toro was less than efficient, with only loose suzerainty achieved. In 1891, in one of the first major political initiatives in the area involving the British, Lugard's mobile force seized control of Toro, guaranteed its autonomy, and placed another exiled prince, Kasagama, on the throne.[191] Needless to say, these intricate dynastic politics were reflections of the relative strength or weakness of the influence of larger states in the area, and represented the entrepreneurial opportunism of the myriad descendants of Rukidi, carving out spaces for themselves in a turbulent age – as well as of those who eschewed these rigidified notions of monarchical power and refused to conform accordingly.

Further north – especially among the Acholi – the ongoing expansion of political and economic power was linked more or less directly to military capacity, while this was also the period, from the 1870s onward, in which the self-identification of 'Acholi' (or 'Shuuli' / 'Chuuli') clearly emerged.[192] Among the Jie, men of military talent and courage

[189] Karugire, *History of the Kingdom of Nkore*, 229–31.

[190] Kiwanuka's notes in Kagwa, *Kings*, 178; also Low, 'The northern interior', 337.

[191] Karugire, *History of the Kingdom of Nkore*, 217; however, Low suggests that Namuyonjo was in fact successfully placed on the throne and thus was Toro now ruled by a Ganda 'protégé': Low, 'The northern interior', 344–5. See also O.W. Furley, 'The reign of Kasagama in Toro from a contemporary account', *Uganda Journal*, 31:2 (1967).

[192] Atkinson, *Roots of Ethnicity*, 271–2.

(and doubtless luck) could bring about fundamental transformations in their status, as men of both material means and political leadership.[193] As the Teso continued to migrate and mutate, there were wars with the Langi, and exposure to the slave trade – carried into the area by both Ethiopian and Arab merchants – which itself involved heightened violence in turn and sharper political distinctions between formerly relatively friendly and certainly more flexible communities.[194] The Acholi, too, were from the 1860s onward increasingly caught up in the ravages of the slave trade, as traders and their entourages – the Khartoum merchant Abu Saud is especially noteworthy, and was Baker's *bête noire* in the latter's anti-slaving capacity – pushed their way into the area and carved out zones of entrepreneurial violence; some moved east into Langi territory, too.[195] Meanwhile the Acholi themselves were engaged in escalating violence, both against the Egyptian garrisons which had been placed there as part of the expanding Anglo-Egyptian presence in southern Sudan and northern Uganda, and between Acholi clans themselves – often involving the Sudanese soldiers of the Egyptian garrisons who were induced to support one side against another.[196] By the 1880s, there was also increasing Nyoro influence from the south, as Kabalega extended his network of allegiances among the southern Acholi, and sought to take advantage of an increasingly volatile and unstable political environment.[197] This was especially so following the disintegration and withdrawal of the Egyptian garrisons from the mid-1880s, with the area now isolated by the rise of the Mahdist state in central Sudan. Thus did 'Acholiland' begin its journey into the modern era violently insecure – and with a reputation for clannish and incessantly bloodthirsty feuding.

The oscillations and outages were internal, reflecting shifts *within* states and societies in terms of political process and indeed political and economic priorities. But they were also external – for this was the age of foreigners, of Zanzibari and Swahili and Sudanese and Egyptian traders, soldiers and administrators and of European missionaries; it

[193] Lamphear, 'Evolution', 68.   [194] For example, Lawrance, *Iteso*, 13–16.
[195] J.M. Gray, 'Acholi History, 1860–1901, Part I', *Uganda Journal*, 15 (1951); Driberg, *The Lango*, 33–4; Low, 'The northern interior', 326, 338–9.
[196] Gray, 'Acholi History, I', and 'Acholi History 1860–1901, Part II', *Uganda Journal*, 16 (1952); see also his 'Rwot Ochama of Payera', *Uganda Journal*, 12 (1948).
[197] M. de Kiewiet Hemphill, 'The British Sphere, 1884–94', in Oliver & Mathew (eds.), *History of East Africa*, I, 403–6.

was the era of new creeds and new commodities, and the destabili-
sation brought about by the ideas and aspirations increasingly associated with shifting material and spiritual horizons. In particular, the
economic dynamics of this era were seminal in this era of economic
crisis and opportunity, of which political change is to a large extent
the direct result. This is especially true in terms of the slave trade –
the seizure and control of people on an increasingly large scale which
underpinned political change and process – but also local commercial
rivalries, for example Bunyoro's dominance across central and parts
of northern Uganda, and Buganda's reach for the south, including its
struggle to enforce tributary relationships between the Nile, the Kagera
and the Ruwenzoris. External intrusions had internal political implications as the stakes involved in both war and diplomacy became ever
higher, and the resultant engagements between Ugandan states and
societies – whether peaceable or violent – became ever more fevered.
The late nineteenth and early twentieth centuries were a transformative era for Uganda, an era of martyrs, mercenaries, merchandise and
mutineers; of opportunists and entrepreneurs; of conversion and conquest and covenant. It saw the deposition of kings, or their careful
management; the reorganisation of land; extreme violence in the name
of causes old and new. And for that reason, too, the period between the
late 1880s and the early 1900s has received more scholarly attention
than virtually any other moment in Ugandan history. As a historical
'moment', it has subversion and rebellion and savage warfare; terrible
martyrdom and shimmering honour; heroic resistance and sly opportunism; the bringing of over-mighty monarchs to heel, and the making
of new political orders; sexual deviance; the encounter between thrust-
ing and restless indigeneity and the square-jawed, steely-eyed frontiers
of modernity. It is a story which has been told, and retold, countless
times.[198]

   Mutesa had done a reasonable job, overall, of balancing the various pressures and issues which now threatened to fundamentally
transform the northern Lake Victoria region – reasonable, though not
especially assured, and even this interpretation is debatable.[199] His vacillation and at times lack of clarity, and indeed his seeming inability or

[198] One of the most recent examples is Low, *Fabrication of Empire*, which offers
   much closer study than is possible here. But see also older surveys in Wright,
   Buganda in the Heroic Age, and Low, *Buganda in Modern History*.
[199] Reid, 'Images', 297–8.

unwillingness to stand up to older more conservative forces, probably rendered Buganda's internal structures more vulnerable than at any time since the civil wars at the beginning of the nineteenth century. At that time, his grandfather Kamanya had arisen to impose order on the chaos; but Kamanya had been a soldier, and a man with evidently much greater sway over a sizeable element of the army than Mutesa had had in the early 1880s. In many respects, Buganda was undergoing something of a quiet transformation: for close to three centuries, it had been an emergent, then dominant, military force. As recently as Suna's time, Buganda military innovation had been clear enough, manifest in the militarisation of political offices and then of the Lake itself, through the creation of a war fleet. But since then, Mutesa – no soldier himself, and evidently possessed of no particular gifts for reform – had effectively presided over the politicisation of the military order and thus its increasing impotence against better-organised, better-motivated and sometimes even better-armed enemies. By the 1880s, Buganda was increasingly run by a reformist intellectual and commercial class, a class with some military pretensions but little capacity to do much of a tangible nature, and certainly not in the face of the Nyoro military renaissance. Yet that class – divided within itself as it was – was offered two more opportunities to reinvent Buganda. The first came in 1888, when politico-religious factions moved against Mutesa's son Mwanga, and in the months that followed contingents within that class tested one another's strength in a struggle over effective control of the kingdom. The second opportunity, in some ways more fortuitous and certainly less rooted in precedent, presented itself in the form of the small British force which arrived in the early 1890s. Buganda retained enough institutional and military capacity – greatly bolstered by a deep-rooted tactical genius and a new intellectual engagement with the wider world – to render themselves indispensable to the British, and indeed to use the latter to its own advantage. Curiously enough, it was the last great military act of Buganda, but arguably one of the kingdom's greatest successes, for it cemented its place in the new political order and enabled its political and commercial elites to concentrate on what they regarded as the Anglo-Ganda alliance in the building of Uganda. Yet in the process profound internal cleavages were exposed – bitter disagreement over the meaning of kingship, clan and the nature of political power itself – while also provoking intense external hostility. The terrible backlash would only come much later.

Mutesa died in October 1884 and was succeeded by his son, Mwanga, who had spent much of his formative years in the mission compounds – he was a *musomi*, a Christian 'reader' – but who was apparently less committed than many of his fellow *bagalagala*, the pages attached to the royal enclosure who represented the indentured, apprenticed future elite of Buganda.[200] Mwanga now turned decisively against them – at least in part because he had been left with a rather toxic chalice, a dubious inheritance indeed, namely a kingdom struggling with internal fissure and external decline. Having spent time with his fellow *basomi*, he came to the conclusion that their adherence to new faiths, whether Christianity or Islam, was the internal manifestation of an external threat – the foreign forces beginning to circle Buganda.[201] The world was altogether a more dangerous place than the one in which Mutesa had become *kabaka* almost three decades earlier – and it was briefly, and unfortunately, embodied in the stubborn James Hannington, newly appointed (and the first) Anglican bishop of Equatorial Africa. Hannington decided to ignore the excellent advice he received from missionaries already at the Ganda capital, namely that he should not travel to Buganda via the east through Busoga; this would be perceived as a direct threat to the kingdom, not least owing to a 'tradition' that Buganda would one day be destroyed by an army coming from that direction. Whatever the origins or indeed veracity of this 'tradition',[202] any *muzungu* – especially one with authority – marching due west from the Kenyan coast was bound to create alarm at a sensitive time, and with a new *kabaka* sitting uncertainly on the throne. Hannington would have none of it. He duly reached Busoga, but was stopped and detained near the east bank of the Nile. After a few days, probably on Mwanga's direct orders, he was killed, in September 1885.[203] Naturally it was presented as the instinctive act of a disturbed and savage tyrant; it was in fact a rational and considered decision. Ugandan Christianity had its first martyr, but others – this time Ugandan – would soon follow. In 1886, enraged and panicked

---

[200] J.A. Rowe, 'The purge of Christians at Mwanga's court', *Journal of African History*, 5:1 (1964), 68; Médard, *Le Royaume*, 401–3.

[201] Ashe, *Chronicles*, 68.

[202] Zimbe suggested that it dated to the reign of Suna – *Buganda new Kabaka*, 126 – and it seems difficult to avoid the conclusion that it was directly related to a desire to control of burgeoning commerce.

[203] Mackay, *Pioneer Missionary*, 262, 265, 267–8.

by the audacity of Hannington's approach, and increasingly anxious about what Christian conversion meant in political terms, Mwanga rounded up dozens of young Christian readers and had them burnt alive at Namugongo, an existing execution site.[204] The act may also have been angry revenge for the rejection by a number of young court pages of his sexual advances. In the meantime, he attempted to assert his royal power in other ways, whipping his chiefs into line and most famously corralling them into supplying labour for the construction of a royal lake near the capital. His decrees and demands for labour and tax were regarded as excessive and ultimately illegitimate, and exacerbated simmering discontent against the *kabaka*.[205] These events occurred against a backdrop of periodic crop failure and livestock disease, evident throughout the latter half of the 1880s, undermining one of the key functions of the kingship as a key point of patronage and distribution.[206]

Yet this was also an era of continuity, or at least culmination. In fact, the forces of chiefly power versus royal prerogative was a fundamental political clash a long time in the making, and can be traced through the nineteenth century and earlier, in Buganda and elsewhere. Factionalism had long been a feature of life at the political centre of Buganda; Mutesa himself had had anxieties about the rising power of a chiefly class in the final years of his reign. And so what happened in the late 1880s and early 1890s needs to be seen as the culmination of long-term political dynamics. At the same time, these were dynamics awarded particular urgency by the arrival of the foreign faiths – Islam, Protestantism and Catholicism – around which particular groups of young chiefs now increasingly coalesced, and out of which there now emerged increasingly robust and ideological political factions.[207] Armed and dangerous, they constituted a very real threat to Mwanga, who attempted to co-opt them by appointing them to senior political positions, but to little avail. In September 1888, a coalition of

---

[204] C.C. Wrigley, 'The Christian Revolution in Buganda', *Comparative Studies in Society and History*, 2:1 (1959); Rowe, 'The purge'.
[205] Zimbe, *Buganda ne Kabaka*, 148, 153, 156; Ashe, *Chronicles*, 93. The *kabaka*'s lake, close to Mengo hill, can be visited today. See, for example, 'Kabaka's Lake: his highness Mwanga's positive legacy', *Daily Monitor*, 1 August 2013.
[206] Reid, *Political Power*, 35, 53.
[207] M. Twaddle, 'The emergence of politico-religious groupings in late nineteenth-century Buganda', *Journal of African History*, 29:1 (1988).

these new political actors overthrew Mwanga in what began, at least, as a palace *coup*, but which would swiftly destabilise the kingdom profoundly. For a few weeks, his successor was his brother, Nyonyintono Kiwewa, who was soon deposed by the dominant Muslim faction and replaced by another of Mwanga's brothers, Kalema, who had converted to Islam and taken the name Rashid. The marginalised Christians, with some irony, now rallied once more to Mwanga in exile as they perceived the attempted reformation of Buganda as an Islamic state. After a series of military campaigns, Mwanga was returned to power in October 1889, though Kalema remained at large – with Nyoro support – until his death from smallpox a few years later, and the situation remained fluid until the final Christian victory in February 1890, at which point Mwanga was more or less securely restored, at least for the time being.[208]

It was not the first time a *kabaka* had been ousted, and for similar reasons,[209] and certainly not the first time the kingdom had been wracked by violent unrest. But at a moment of encroaching foreign forces, this period was particularly significant. Those forces were British, with the connivance of Germany. At the moment in 1888 when Mwanga was overthrown, the Imperial British East Africa Company (IBEAC) was given its charter in London under the chairmanship of William Mackinnon.[210] In the age of imperial outsourcing, when private companies administered the expanding edges of empire on behalf of national governments, the IBEAC was granted the right to administer Uganda; and accordingly Frederick Lugard went to Uganda as a representative of the IBEAC, after the Anglo-German Agreement in July 1890 placed Uganda in the British sphere of influence. Lugard arrived at the Ganda capital in December 1890, whereupon he helped consolidate the Christian hold on power; and more specifically, Lugard was quickly sucked into Protestant-Catholic rivalries. By 1892, IBEAC forces were bolstering the numerically weaker

---

[208] Ibid.; Sir J.M. Gray, 'The Year of the Three Kings of Buganda, Mwanga–Kiwewa–Kalema, 1888–89', *Uganda Journal*, 14 (1950), and Wrigley, 'The Christian revolution'. For a contemporary narrative, see Ashe, *Chronicles*.

[209] In the eighteenth century, Mawanda had been assassinated following excessive demands for public labour from a number of leading princes: Kiwanuka's notes in Kagwa, *Kings*, 76.

[210] 'Charter: Imperial British East Africa Company (L.G., Sept. 7, 1888)', UKNA FO 881/5668X.

Protestant faction under the leadership of the young but dynamic and ambitious Apolo Kagwa.[211] By the time Gerald Portal arrived in the kingdom in 1893, he found a riven and fractious polity, where 'neither the one nor the other exercised any authority over more than a portion of the whole country': the Catholics were garrisoned in Buddu, and their leaders were refusing to come to the capital; Muslims, too, assigned three provinces by Lugard in the wake of the civil wars, sat back and regarded the royal capital 'with calm contempt' and largely ignored any orders emanating from it. Overall, Portal found 'the central administration in a very limping, dishevelled and unhappy condition of mind and body'.[212] Despite Mwanga's frequent ambivalence, indeed hostility, towards Lugard and his men, Lugard's interventions were both accidental and decisive. Beleaguered and unhappy, Mwanga was compelled to make use of the Company and its guns. From his modest fort in what is today 'Old Kampala', with a small force precariously equipped and severely buffeted by the winds of Ganda political change, Lugard found himself co-opted into Ganda politics, but also made decisions which fundamentally influenced what Uganda was to become.[213]

For all the disproportionate significance of Lugard's little army, the problem was that the IBEAC was bankrupt. The Company relinquished control in April 1893 and, after much deliberation and procrastination, and pressure from the missionary lobby, the British government declared a protectorate over Buganda in June 1894.[214] In the meantime, Mwanga – correctly identifying Lugard and the British as a potential ally against Bunyoro, as well as a means to bolstering his internal position – provided soldiers for the campaigns against the old enemy. The result, in the end, would be a British Protectorate, but these were very much Anglo-Ganda military operations, with the British co-opted into local dynamics of long standing. During 1891, Lugard relied heavily on Ganda expertise and manpower in his exploratory

---

[211] For this and the ensuing period, see correspondence in 'Imperial British East Africa Company', Vol 1 (UKNA FO 2/57), Vol 2 (UKNA FO 2/58), and Vol 3 (UKNA FO 2/59).

[212] Portal, *British Mission*, 190–1.

[213] One of the best and most detailed narratives is still Ingham, *Making of Modern Uganda*, 41–85.

[214] 'Notice. Protectorate over Uganda. (L.G., June 19, 1894)', UKNA FO 881/6489X.

expeditions towards the Ganda–Nyoro marches;[215] by early 1894, some 5000 Ganda soldiers – at least one thousand of them equipped with guns – were involved in the advance to Mruli.[216] This was, as Andrew Roberts memorably characterised it, classic 'sub-imperialism'.[217] Throughout the early 1890s, in addition to the wars against Bunyoro, Anglo-Ganda armies ranged across the southwest and west, imposing 'order' and securing treaties. By 1896, the Buganda Protectorate was extended territorially to include Bunyoro, Toro, Nkore and Busoga to the east, with Buganda established as the capstone of the colonial order.[218] The physical benefits were evident, too, in the seizure (in early 1894) and subsequent permanent transfer of Nyoro territory to Buganda – the ticking time bomb known as the 'Lost Counties' – as reward for Buganda's 'assistance' against the recalcitrant Kabalega.[219] This included all Nyoro territory south of the Kafu: Buyaga, Bugangaizi, Buruli and northern Bugerere.[220] It was indeed something of a stroke of genius for Buganda, a kingdom which over the preceding decade had undergone its worst crisis in a century, and yet whose salvation had lain in a timely strategic military and political alliance with a foreign power. For the Ganda political establishment there had been no 'conquest' of their kingdom by the British: the latter had been invited in, allowed to stay, and a partnership with them forged for the greater – and mutual – benefit. But for Mwanga, the arrangement swiftly soured, as he found his powers of decree greatly restricted, his entitlement to receive tribute from Busoga abolished, and his ability to distribute land as he saw fit summarily curtailed – curbs on royal power which were, to a greater or lesser extent, negotiated between the British and the Ganda chiefly oligarchy. For these reasons did Mwanga finally flee Mengo, in July 1897, in what was the first act in an attempt at armed insurrection. Defeated in Rakai, in the far southwest, he fled to German territory where he was captured and imprisoned at Mwanza; but he escaped once more the following year,

---

[215] UNA A26/4 Lugard to Admin.-Gen., IBEAC, 13 August 1891.
[216] UNA A2/2 Diary of expedition to Mruli, 29 April 1894.
[217] A.D. Roberts, 'The sub-imperialism of the Baganda', *Journal of African History*, 3:3 (1962).
[218] Thomas & Scott, *Uganda*, 36; Low, 'Uganda', 66–71.
[219] Low, *Fabrication of Empire*, 184–97.
[220] Nyakatura, *Anatomy*, 161–2; Beattie, *Nyoro State*, 74–5.

making his way to join Kabalega in Lango where they were both captured in April 1899.[221]

Within weeks of his rebellion, Mwanga had been formally deposed and replaced as *kabaka* by his infant son, Daudi Chwa. Three prominent chiefs were made his regents: Apolo Kagwa and Zakaria Kisingiri, both Protestants, and one Roman Catholic, Stanislaus Mugwanya. This was a political sequence which culminated in the 1900 'Uganda Agreement' – actually properly the 'Buganda Agreement' – which is widely regarded as one of the most significant and landmark pieces of colonial administration.[222] It was signed in March 1900 by Harry Johnston as British representative and newly arrived governor of Uganda assigned for the purpose,[223] and the three regents who led a much larger delegation of Ganda chiefs. The Agreement contained a number of salient issues, besides the formal recognition of Buganda as a province within the Protectorate of Uganda (rather than as an autonomous polity).[224] Above all, it created what was in effect a constitutional monarchy out of the ancient Ganda kingship – an act of treaty-making whose roots, nonetheless, can be traced much deeper into the kingdom's past, certainly long before the arrival of Lugard and his Maxim gun. The *kabaka*'s personal authority was greatly reduced in his role as an agent of the British administration, although he retained the power to appoint and dismiss his own chiefs. He was formally prevented from receiving tribute from outside Buganda – meaning a dramatic reduction in revenue, and one of the elements that had originally prompted Mwanga's last-ditch rebellion. Concurrently, a great deal of power shifted to the *Lukiiko*, the Buganda parliament. Just as important, if not more so, the Agreement initiated a new land tenure system, which in itself further weakened the kingship, which had previously 'owned' all land and had been able to distribute it to loyal

---

[221] Nyakatura's account of these events – *Anatomy*, 163–9 – manages to be both matter-of-fact and rather moving.

[222] 'Agreement. Kabaka, Chiefs and People of Uganda. Taxes, land, boundaries etc.' UKNA FO 93/4/6, 10 March 1900 (also FO 881/7620, Foreign Office Confidential Print Series). See also D.A.Low, 'The Making and Implementation of the Uganda Agreement of 1900', in Low & Pratt, *Buganda and British Overrule*. Appendix II contains the full text of the Agreement, extracts of which are also reproduced in Low (ed.), *Mind of Buganda*, 37–41.

[223] A classic study is Roland Oliver, *Sir Harry Johnston and the Scramble for Africa* (London, 1957), 299ff.

[224] See also Hanson, *Landed Obligation*, 129–33.

followers and political servants: it had been one of the planks of royal patronage. Now, a little over 9000 square miles were allocated to the *kabaka* and around one thousand chiefs on the basis of freehold. It became known, in Luganda, as *mailo* land, because the plots of land themselves were measured in square miles.[225] All other land – including supposed 'waste' land – was now owned by the British Crown. There was also recognition (in the sense that the territory was named as Ganda land) of Ganda occupation of Nyoro territory seized during the wars of the mid-1890s – although in fact the act of annexation had already been 'officially' recognised, both at the time (in April 1894) and by the British Foreign Office in late 1896.[226]

As Holly Hanson has argued, precolonial Buganda was characterised by delicate balances of power – reciprocal obligations – between the central kingship, chieftaincy and people, but the events of the 1890s and early 1900s profoundly unbalanced these interactions and introduced new and (to date) enduring conflicts over authority and land.[227] A modified view might espy the gradual build-up of political challenges to kingship even as the latter was putatively expanding and accumulating power, and therefore the 1900 Agreement as having a long gestation period, largely unconnected to the arrival of the British colonial state – but even so there is no question that disturbing new elements were indeed introduced into the arrangement of power and access to it. These elements were built upon the fundamental assumption of inequity and not only opened up conflicts within Buganda, but rippled outward across the wider territory with the application of the core ideas to other parts of the Protectorate. The Agreement represented the triumph of the political oligarchy – particularly its Protestant components – which had emerged over the preceding two decades, and which had succeeded, if bloodily and messily at times, in steering the kingdom through the crises of faith, monarchical authoritarianism and foreign intervention since the mid-1880s. As such, it placed the seal on a new dispensation of power within Buganda and beyond, for it provided the impetus for the imposition of the 'Buganda model' on other parts of the nascent Protectorate, a process often led, in the first instance, by Ganda chiefs themselves – the 'pride and joy of the British Administration', as

[225] 'Distribution of mailo lands in Buganda', UKNA CO 822/878 (1956).
[226] See Letters to the Editor, 'Was it an error of omission in the Agreements?', *Uganda Argus*, 14 January 1961.
[227] Hanson, *Landed Obligation*.

Low called them.[228] But while there were clear winners in terms of land and political appointments, there were losers – not least, in some ways, the boy *kabaka* and his successors, who now found themselves greatly reduced in authority and material circumstance. There were also the *bataka*, the clans who saw their access to land further diminished and the clan heads who found themselves further marginalised from the political centre – giving rise to new clan-based protest movements by the 1920s. In some respects these were 'new' forms of political and cultural organisation, but in fact they formed part of a much older and deeper pattern of anti-monarchical resistance. Many others found themselves with no access to land, or indeed to the histories now beginning to be written about it: for it was Kagwa, prime minister of Buganda, regent to the infant Daudi Chwa, and pillar of the new Anglo-Ganda political order, who now embarked on his vigorous writing career in order to root contemporary political realities in historical ones. Kagwa's Buganda was historically dominant, its kings glorious but kept in check by chiefly wisdom. Kagwa himself saw little distinction between his 'active' political role as a signatory to the 1900 Agreement and its implementation in the years that followed, and his job as a historian. More recently, the extent to which that history is a matter of bitter controversy has become clear. While the *Daily Monitor* celebrated the life of Stanislaus Mugwanya as 'the father of formal education in Uganda', placing emphasis on schooling for young Catholics,[229] Apolo Kagwa was considered in an essay which wondered whether he should be regarded as a reformer or a land-grabber,[230] indicating the extent to which such towering figures in Uganda's early history have become increasingly ripe for no-holds-barred revisionism. Indeed another piece in the *Monitor* robustly assessed 'the great Buganda land grab of 1900'.[231]

While the finer points of political settlement were being discussed around the hills of Kampala, the experience of the nascent political order was rather different further north. Kabalega was perceived as an obstacle to be summarily removed, especially following his invasions of Toro between 1891 and 1893, and his construction of a string of

---

[228] Low, 'Uganda', 97.
[229] 'Stanislaus Mugwanya: the father of formal education in Uganda', *Daily Monitor*, 18 April 2012.
[230] 'Apolo Kaggwa: reformer or land grabber?', *Daily Monitor*, 18 April 2012.
[231] 'The great Buganda land grab of 1900', *Daily Monitor*, 17 April 2012.

forts along the Nyoro-Toro border. It was also the case that his support for the Ganda Muslims – he had backed *Kabaka* Kalema – during the civil war led to his association, in the minds of the British, with militant Islam in the era of Mahdism in Sudan.[232] In truth, however, Kabalega was given little choice but to offer violent resistance. Following consultations with the Ganda chiefs, the British administrator Colonel Henry Colvile ordered the advance of a joint British and Ganda force into Bunyoro in December 1893.[233] At the beginning of January, this army had captured Kabalega's capital, and by the end of the month, attacks on his camps in Budongo had forced him into Langi territory, who also offered some support – although that assistance was half-hearted in light of the fact that during the 1890 campaign against Buganda, in which Nyoro-Muslim forces had suffered a heavy defeat, the bulk of the casualties were Bunyoro's Langi allies.[234] That diffidence among long-standing but wearying allies may have proved crucial in the unfolding British campaign. Nonetheless, despite early British success, Kabalega's overthrow proved rather more difficult than anticipated. He resisted for a further six years, his soldiers becoming skilled in guerrilla warfare and in the construction of defensive trenches and stockades; he defeated a British force at Kijunjubwa in March 1895, forcing the British back to Hoima to regroup. They brought in further reinforcements and made increasing use of vicious scorched earth policies; swathes of Bunyoro were devastated and depopulated by the late 1890s.[235] It may well be that there was little popular support for Kabalega's prolonged resistance, for all the subsequent lionising of the tragic hero.[236] In large part this was due to the awful nature of the war itself, involving as it did dislocation and despoliation at the hands of the marauding Anglo-Ganda force; it was destruction on (for the Nyoro) an unprecedented scale.[237] In July 1898, Kabalega was briefly joined by the mutinous Mwanga, but both men were captured the following April, thus ending the overt military campaign in Nyoro and one of the most brutal and nasty wars of

---

[232] White Fathers C14/192 Lourdel to Superior-General, 25 January 1890; also Doyle, *Crisis and Decline*, 59.
[233] Sir Henry Colvile, *The Land of the Nile Springs; being chiefly an account of how we fought Kabarega* (London, 1895), chapter VII.
[234] Tosh, *Clan Leaders*, 103.
[235] Beattie, *Nyoro State*, 73–5; Steinhart, *Conflict and Collaboration*, 58–97.
[236] Steinhart, *Conflict and Collaboration*, 96–7.   [237] Ibid., 51–2, 66.

imperial expansion undertaken by Britain anywhere during the era of high imperialism.

Bunyoro offers the starkest instance of military conquest and subsequent marginalisation from the political process of Uganda's formation; but there were many others. Among the most celebrated – and distinctive – examples of violent entrepreneurialism on the expanding imperial frontier is Semei Kakungulu, the armed adventurer from Kkooki who had made his warrior reputation in the 1880s and 1890s.[238] In the early 1900s, Kakungulu, using Ganda soldiers, conquered and administered a swathe of territory in eastern Teso, Busoga and Bugisu on behalf of the British, who trusted him – up to a point – owing to his Protestant faith and his connections in the Ganda political establishment. The town of Mbale itself was in large part the outcome of Kakungulu's expanding operations.[239] He fell foul of the colonial authorities, however, once the extent of his ambition became clear – he believed he was to be appointed king of Busoga – and he was soon restricted to a small area around Mbale with a dwindling but loyal number of followers. Later, in 1917, he shifted north to establish an idiosyncratic Judaic community in the western foothills of Mount Elgon.[240] Kakungulu's story is fascinating in itself, but it is also illustrative of the making of local administration, not least in the context of the somewhat rough-and-ready, frontier nature of the early Ugandan administrative and political arrangement of power – certainly beyond the metropolitan hub of central Buganda.

Further north still, in the early years of the Protectorate, beyond the range of a Kakungulu or anyone else, the problem facing British military units was the Ethiopian gun-runners who were at the outer edge of their long-range operations. In 1911–2, British units encountered Acholi who had purchased guns, mostly muzzle-loading muskets, from Ethiopian traders and who wielded them pretty effectively[241] – although their famous defeat at the hands of a much smaller and locally equipped Jie force in 1902 was an indication that the accoutrements of military modernity were not necessarily sufficient to achieve primacy in

---

[238] The best single study is Twaddle, *Kakungulu*.
[239] M. Twaddle, 'The founding of Mbale', *Uganda Journal*, 30:1 (1966).
[240] Arye Oded, *Religion and Politics in Uganda: a study of Islam and Judaism* (Nairobi, 1995), 75–87.
[241] Low, 'Uganda', 106–7.

the escalating conflicts across the area.[242] Indeed, as the British discovered, weapons of various kinds – though increasingly firearms – could be brought to bear on those conflicts, as through the early 1900s they struggled to impose 'order' by maintaining a patrolling, roving military presence in the northern borderlands.[243] In some cases, violence was provoked by the policy of applying the Buganda model of administration to areas to which it was singularly ill-suited. The model itself was based on the appointment of chiefs with enhanced status and authority, involving either selection from a pre-existing cohort of local chiefs or the imposition of Ganda agents brought in for the purpose. It was greeted with considerable opposition, not least because of the imposition of singular authority-figures among segmentary communities who bitterly resented the marginalisation of their elders. In the early 1900s, there was an upsurge in violence – including the murders of two Ganda evangelists and a tax-collector – in Padhola in response to the imposition of new forms of administration. As one missionary wrote in 1905: 'every Muganda and the whole of Mbale have for some time been living on the edge of a volcano'.[244] In Lango in 1910–11, there were armed skirmishes between locals and Ganda agents and their entourages,[245] while among the Teso, the forcible removal of chiefs in the 1920s who were seen to be champions of their own people led to violent protest.[246] When the Acholi murdered a loyal government chief in 1913, the acting district commissioner in Gulu made a show of force by capturing no less than eight culprits, executing four of them and sentencing the other four to long prison terms. It was swift and brutal justice that was welcomed by other Acholi chiefs, including the *rwot* of Atyak who lavished the British official with praise for having shown fortitude in the face of such criminal recalcitrance. Clearly, this was violent justice that offered opportunities for crafty (and lucky)

[242] Lamphear, 'Evolution', 76.
[243] See, for example, the detail in Lt.-Col. H. Moyse-Bartlett, *The King's African Rifles: a study in the military history of East and Central Africa, 1890–1945*, I (Aldershot, 1956), 228–56.
[244] Quoted in Michael Twaddle, 'Segmentary violence and political change in early colonial Uganda', paper presented at the University Social Sciences Council Conference, Nairobi, 8–12 December 1969.
[245] Tosh, *Clan Leaders*, 126.
[246] Vincent, *Teso in Transformation*, 251–259 and J. Vincent, 'Colonial Chiefs and the Making of Class: a case study from Teso, eastern Uganda', *Africa*, 47:2 (1977).

incumbents.[247] In Karamoja, relations between government and the Karamojong had been reasonably stable, as long as government was confined to occasional armed sorties and tax-collections – until the 1920s, that is, when restrictions were placed on cattle movement and new kinds of chiefs, again on the 'Buganda model', began to be appointed. Resulting skirmishes led to the death of one such chief, Achia.[248]

In Teso, violent upheaval in the 1900s, dating to earlier in the nineteenth century, laid the groundwork for aggressive Ganda expansion into the area with British backing. Ganda agents were able to take advantage of factions which were themselves the outcome of protracted migrations into the area, conflict over land for farming and periodic famine, including one between 1894 and 1896.[249] Elsewhere, the embryonic colonial state was confronted with a range of other types of political and spiritual action in defiance of the new order. This was not always overtly violent: witness the Nyangire 'revolt' among the Nyoro in 1907, for example, sparked in large part by the humiliation of the kingdom following the defeat of Kabalega and the appointment of overbearing Ganda chiefs to key positions. In physical terms the rebellion was manifest in the withdrawal of services provided to Ganda chiefs, as well as the burning of some property and destruction of crops – carried out by angry crowds which forced a number of Ganda chiefs to flee to Hoima for protection. But it is mostly noted for the articulacy of the Nyoro leaders' protests against brutal and high-handed treatment from the colonial administration. It was crushed, with little in the way of concession.[250] Similarly important in terms of local response to the early Protectorate was the spirit-possession Nyabingi cult in Kigezi, in 1910s, on the Rwanda-Uganda borderlands, based in Ndorwa just south of Kabale.[251] There wasn't always a

---

[247] J.R.P. Postlethwaite, *I Look Back* (London, 1947), 64–5; J.P. Barber, 'The moving frontier of British imperialism in northern Uganda, 1898–1919', *Uganda Journal*, 29:1 (1965), 37.

[248] J.P. Barber, 'The Karamoja District of Uganda: a pastoral people under colonial rule', *Journal of African History*, 3:1 (1962), 113, 116*ff*.

[249] J.B. Webster, 'The civil war in Usuku', in B.A. Ogot (ed.), *War and Society in Africa* (London, 1972).

[250] G.N.Uzoigwe, 'The Kyanyangire, 1907: passive revolt against British overrule', in Ogot (ed.), *War and Society*; Doyle, *Crisis and Decline*, 96–103.

[251] E. Hopkins, 'The Nyabingi cult of southwestern Uganda', in R.I. Rotberg & A.A. Mazrui (eds.), *Protest and Power in Black Africa* (New York, 1970).

particular military threat attached to it, but the cult spread across the west, and it was serious enough to cause concern in the local administration that the prophetess Nyabingi was episodically stirring up worrying levels of 'disaffection'.[252] Eventually quelled in the 1930s,[253] the Nyabingi cult nonetheless demonstrated in the most potent of terms a rejection of the compacting authority represented by the colonial state, and female agency in the articulation of alternative visions. These visions were, inseparably, both political and spiritual.

The Living and the Dead, 1

In 1879–80, the *lubaale* of Lake Victoria, Mukasa, brought commerce to a standstill while his representatives visited the royal capital to cure Mutesa of an illness. The *kabaka* himself was allegedly sceptical, at least in private, about the actual powers of the deity, but the latter was powerfully supported by Mutesa's own mother and her court, as well as by a number of his leading chiefs.[254] The *kabaka* appeared almost as a marginal figure as a result: this was particularly important in terms of public performance, for Mutesa – not in this scenario the omnipotent despot beloved of Eurocentric lore – could not be seen to tackle this most powerful of entities. There was consternation as eager buyers (and sellers) sat idle for many weeks, waiting for Mukasa to depart. The Ganda wrestled with a panoply of psychic elements – *bazimu* (spirits) and *balubaale* (gods) – which wielded enormous influence. More recently, too, cosmology has clashed with technology in developmental Uganda. The Bujagali Hydropower Project – Uganda's second largest dam when it was inaugurated in 2012, a few miles north of Jinja – had been delayed for a number of years because of the resistance of the representatives of a major Soga water spirit, Budhagaali, and in particular the most significant healer in the area, Jaja Bujagali, the embodiment of the spirit itself. Protracted negotiations were held between investors and Soga leaders to relocate the shrines owing to the fact that the area

---

[252] For example, Fort Portal District Archives, Report by the District Commissioner 310.1/16, 22 December 1914.

[253] The cult inspired Rastafarians in Jamaica to adopt 'Queen Nyabingi' as a spirit of liberation: P.B. Clarke, *Black Paradise: the Rastafarian movement* (Wellingborough, 1986), 49.

[254] Mackay, *Pioneer Missionary*, 148–50, 162, 164; White Fathers Rubaga Diary 1/14 August 1879; CMS CA6/016/43 Mackay to Wright, 7 July 1880.

was to be flooded by the dammed waters, although there was local disagreement about where, exactly, the spirit and its shrines might be located, and where they might be moved *to*. There was agreement in the end, amidst much relief on the part of the foreign backers of the project as well as the government itself.[255] Still, some continued to have misgivings about the weakening of the water spirits whose power rested in the waterfalls now extinguished by the dam; and many battles of a similar nature lie ahead, if, as is expected, further dam projects proceed downstream. The spirits themselves had become symbols of resistance in the clash between the deep past and the near future. It echoed the struggle over Mukasa in 1879–80 between developmental, globalised modernity and the cosmologies of the local.

Bodies, minds and spirits belonged to ever changing – and in many ways expanding – realms of identity. Amidst the episodic turmoil of political and economic change, people sought security and aspired to better lives, and they often did so through spiritual belief and observance. Here, too, were mobilisations of the past in innovative ways, in pursuit of more secure todays and better tomorrows. Holistic cultures around spiritual belief, well-being and consciousness were much in evidence, indeed had been central to most of the major state and political systems to emerge over the previous millennium. These spiritual cultures were both mobilised by political elites – and in some cases designed by them – and used by local communities as protection against those same political elites; as a means, in sum, to combat monarchical and other forms of authority. This ambivalence in the relationship between the governed and the governing is one of the central motifs of Ugandan social and political history.

Spirits, at least the 'good' ones, were agents of social mobility and facilitators of both security and aspiration – for the individual, and the wider community.[256] Ghosts of ancestors could withhold legitimacy and blessings from political leaders deemed to have transgressed, to have exceeded the limits of natural moral and physical order. In Uganda, it was often the case that the dead truly did govern, or at least were in possession of a substantial veto. The spheres of natural and

---

[255] Terje Oestigaard, *Dammed Divinities: the water powers at Bujagali Falls, Uganda* (Uppsala, 2015).

[256] For example, Stephen Ellis & Gerrie Ter Haar, *Worlds of Power: religious thought and political practice in Africa* (London, 2004), 49–69 & *passim*.

supernatural were indelibly interconnected. A great deal of public discourse was concerned with health, healing, remembrance, morality.[257]
It was concerned, ultimately, with social behaviour, respect for the past,
political legitimacy, and the well-being of the wider shared community.
In 1875, Stanley was apparently told a story by a Ganda informant and
companion, 'Sabbadu', about the encounter which a long-dead *kabaka*
of Buganda had with the ghost of an even longer-dead ruler. The story
involved *Kabaka* Mawanda, who perhaps reigned during the 1720s
and 1730s, Kintu, and a loyal but hapless chief minister. But the story
began – as a great many Ganda tales do – with a humble peasant, to
whom the ghost of Kintu appeared while he was performing his daily
tasks in the forest. Kintu, after a very basic quiz apparently to establish the peasant's credentials, told the startled man to go to the royal
palace and fetch the *kabaka*, and bring him to an appointed place to
meet with Kintu. But to these instructions was added the emphatic
order that the king must come alone, save for the peasant himself. The
kabaka set off to meet Kintu, following his instructions assiduously,
but was undone by his loyal *katikiro*, who followed unseen in order
to protect his master from any potential mishap. Kintu admonished
Mawanda for the violence stalking the kingdom, and then pointed
out that he had disobeyed his orders to come alone; horrified at the
sight of his chief minister lurking in the bushes, Mawanda speared
him to death, and spun around to beg Kintu's forgiveness, only to find
that the great founding father had vanished – never to return, as the
narrator imparted to Stanley.[258] In John Yoder's persuasive interpretation, the story was an indirect criticism of the current incumbent,
Mutesa, for whom Mawanda was presumably a safe proxy.[259] Above
all, though, it encapsulates the degree to which the dead were mobilised
in pursuit of political and moral order, by envisioning a plane of existence beyond that of the living; ghosts – often appearing in dreams
to kings, and presumably to many others, too – were commentators
on the state of things, offering counsel as to what might be done. The
past was reordered to critique the present, and ancestors and founding
fathers provided a direct link between the realm of history – a place of

---

[257] Neil Kodesh, 'History from the Healer's Shrine: genre, historical imagination,
and early Ganda history', *Comparative Studies in Society and History*, 49:3
(2007).
[258] Stanley, *Dark Continent*, I, 276–81.   [259] Yoder, 'The quest for Kintu'.

spiritual rectitude and sagacity, of moral order – and the living, contemporary, corporeal world in which Ugandans lived. When the *kabaka* of Buganda dreamt, he dreamt of the past, and his dreams were haunted by visitations of far-seeing ancestors who, elevated to a higher plane, could see further into the future than any mortal. The future, moreover, mattered more in the late nineteenth century than at any point in living memory, and for that reason alone there was heightened interest in the muscular spiritualism of Christianity and Islam and their seemingly omnipotent prophets.

A note of caution is perhaps in order at this juncture, which is that early twentieth-century commentaries often exaggerated the spiritual realm in African society and culture. John Roscoe famously overstated the spiritual case in his 1911 study of Buganda, and in most of his subsequent treaties on other groups.[260] The colonial library reflects an ongoing obsession with the role of the magical and the spiritual in African life and politics. Was Mutesa a god, wondered H.P. Gale in 1956;[261] and others, too, would ponder the relationship between royalty and deity – underlining the at least implicit notion that African kings, certainly those as supposedly potent as the *kabaka*, must be gods in some shape or form. Mutesa was not a god. But political leadership necessitated intimate connections with the divine and the transcendent. Mukasa may have been a particularly high profile deity – alongside Kibuka, the Ganda god of war – but a host of shrines to the significant departed were the very nodes of social existence in the precolonial era, and have continued to be through the twentieth century and beyond.[262] Nowhere were spirits more important than in the sphere of war. In Buganda, Kibuka – the spirit of the sixteenth-century warrior from the Sesse Islands – was responsible for wars against Bunyoro and other enemies to the west, while Nende was invoked for conflicts to the east.[263] War usually required spiritual sanction, up and to including the advice of gods in the choice of commander, for example,

---

[260] See his *The Baganda*, *The Bakitara*, and *The Banyankole*. Earlier, he had written specifically on Kibuka: see 'Kibuka, the War God of the Baganda', *Man*, 7 (1907). For critical analysis, see D. Richards, *Masks of Difference: cultural representations in literature, anthropology and art* (Cambridge, 1994), 158*ff*.

[261] H.P. Gale, 'Mutesa I: was he a god?', *Uganda Journal*, 20:1 (1956).

[262] See Roscoe's exhaustive, though not unproblematic, survey in *The Baganda*, chapter IX.

[263] Zimbe, *Buganda ne Kabaka*, 84.

to lead a particular campaign, as well as on the righteousness of the campaign itself.[264] For the Nyankole, the *mugabe*'s dreams of war set in motion consultations with spirit-mediums about tactics, command, the strength of the enemy; charms were deployed to weaken the latter, and once the army had been dispatched, women carefully attended shrines to ensure the safe return of their menfolk.[265] In Bunyoro, mediums were similarly consulted during military preparations, and directly involved in certain tactical manoeuvres.[266] Again, we need to be careful about Roscoe's obsession with these things, but his is not the only evidence, and in any case, the flourishing of shrines and spiritualism in the more recent past – while in part perhaps pointing to an indigenous religious 'revival' – suggest a deeper significance of the spiritual, the supernatural, in the most practical and prosaic of human activities.[267]

Deities held up robustly against the arrival of new faiths. Indeed they proved quite compatible, for they each performed many of the same functions and each borrowed heavily from the other's tropes and messages and cosmological architectures. Spirits were omnipresent, as moral judges, interpreters of the past and harbingers of things to come. As Kodesh has powerfully demonstrated, their shrines were places of public healing and political order, and indeed were at the heart of the emergence of centralised statehood. Those who tended the shrines of *balubaale* were guardians of national well-being in eighteenth-century

---

[264] Zimbe, *Buganda ne Kabaka*, 84; Roscoe, *The Baganda*, 348.

[265] Roscoe, *The Banyankole*, 33, 155, 157–8, 161; Speke, *Journal*, 500.

[266] Roscoe, *The Bakitara*, 306–7, 309.

[267] It is worth noting that in the 1960s and early 1970s, Makerere University published a series of papers on 'traditional religion and philosophy', which was very much emblematic of the *zeitgeist* – the idea of retrieval and preservation of complex spiritual and philosophical achievement, especially, perhaps, against a backdrop of contemporary stress and looming spiritual (and material) 'failure' with the late Obote years and the early period of Amin. These papers undergirded the notion that meaning was provided in rich, complex and sophisticated ways prior to the advent of foreign faiths – and, indeed, afterwards alongside them. See 'Occasional Research Papers in African Religions and Philosophies', published by the Department of Religious Studies and Philosophy, Makerere University, available in Makerere University Library. A number of these were edited by A.B.T. Byaruhanga-Akiiki, whose own PhD thesis was on 'Religion in Bunyoro' (unpublished PhD thesis, Makerere University, 1971). One of the leading figures in this scholarly surge was the writer Okot p'Bitek, who during this period wrote one of the most important books on 'traditional' religion, *Religion of the Central Luo* (Nairobi, 1971).

Buganda, notably, and *balubaale* themselves became national spirits of the kingdom itself as it reached its zenith.[268] Spirits had variegated levels of power and responsibility, and spirit mediums – again, often women[269] – channelled their wishes and counsel, and dedicated their lives to the maintenance of particular shrines, which became critical nodes of moral, historical, and political order. They were also frequently the foci of resistance to transgressive authority. The role of clanship was vital in this context, for clans bore responsibility for the protection of particular shrines and through spiritual veneration and intermediation did clans remain at the centre of political order. The Chwezi cult, rooted in the earlier history of Kitara and centred on the key royal personages of the short-lived dynasty, demonstrates very clearly the idea across western and central Uganda.[270] The reality of the Chwezi is apparent today in the spirit possession cult *Embandwa*, involving a pantheon of Chwezi characters including Mugasa, Mulindwa, Wamala and Ndahura who operate through a network of spirit mediums who are either itinerant, or located at specific fixed shrines.[271] In Nick Twinamatsiko's novel *The Chwezi Code*, the protagonist of the story, in order to escape the security apparatus closing in on him, hides himself as a Chwezi spirit medium (he names himself 'Mugu'), only to discover that the Chwezi spirits are in fact *real*. The book is an indictment of corruption and oppression in modern Ugandan history, but also describes a struggle between the deep past and the ancestors, on the one hand, and the teachings of missionaries on the other.[272]

People sought assistance and succour from these potent spiritual forces, and relief from physical and emotional ailments. In Buganda alone, an array of spirits were propitiated in order to guard against famine and to ensure rainfall and abundant harvests: Mukasa, *lubaale* of Lake Victoria, the guarantor of plenty and fertility; Kitaka, of the

---

[268] Kodesh, *Beyond the Royal Gaze*, esp. chapter 5.

[269] Iris Berger, 'Fertility as Power: spirit mediums, priestesses, and the precolonial state in interlacustrine East Africa', in D.M. Anderson & D. Johnson (eds.), *Revealing Prophets: Prophecy in Eastern African History* (London, 1995).

[270] See, for example, Marie Pierre Ballarin, Herman Kiriama, and Cecilia Pennacini (eds.), 'Sacred Natural Sites and Cultural Heritage in East Africa', special issue of the *Uganda Journal*, 53 (2013).

[271] E.I. Steinhart, 'The Resurrection of the Spirits: archaeology, oral history, and the Bacwezi at Munsa', *Uganda Journal*, 48 (2002); Pennacini, 'Mubende Hill'.

[272] *The Chwezi Code* (Kampala, 2010).

fecundity of the land; Nagadya, the female spirit approached particularly in times of drought. The shrine of Nagawonyi in Bulemezi, in
northern Buganda, was likewise the focus of anxious petition during
times of poor rainfall, for she also had the power to end hunger.[273]
Certain figures of greater or lesser historicity became key points of
connection between the living and the dead, the natural and the preter-
natural. Spirits were historical; history, in turn, was often seen in spiritual terms.[274] And all of this, together, was in the name of keeping the
present in order. These were, literally, haunting histories, histories of
life, death and the past in precolonial society; ghosts provided moral
order but could also reflect social and political conditions, and thus
were conduits and commentators on the contemporary moral shape of
things. And the past, thus filtered through stories and spirit mediums,
was didactic and instructive, creating a vortex of past and present and
of the dead and the living. At the same time, watchfulness was needed
against witchcraft and the omnipresence of malevolent spirits.[275] Yet
change was continual. Shrines themselves were continually reinvented
and had changing roles according to circumstance, not least in terms
of the historical imaginary that played such a vibrant role across the
shared cultural space. Arguably, indeed, this became more intense in
periods of profound change – as in the last four decades of the nineteenth century, for example, with the arrival of Europeans and above
all of new gods, alongside changing material standards and expectations.[276] In the case of the Nyabingi cult in Kigezi and Kabale, an
ancient spirit was reinvigorated by colonial invasion in the early 1900s
and channelled into prolonged anticolonial resistance which drew on
the cult's older history of administering to the sick and offering sanctuary to the poor and oppressed.[277] The agents of Nyabingi herself –
apparently an historical figure who was ruler of Karagwe in c.1700,

[273] Roscoe, *The Baganda*, 290, 313, 315.
[274] See a number of germane contributions to Anderson & Johnson (eds.),
Revealing Prophets.
[275] See chapters by John Beattie (Bunyoro), Jean La Fontaine (Bugisu), and John
Middleton (Lugbara) in John Middleton & Edward Winter (eds.), *Witchcraft
and Sorcery in East Africa* (London, 1963).
[276] For a similar argument made in the European context, see Shane
McCorristine, *Spectres of the Self: thinking about ghosts and ghost-seeing in
England, 1750–1920* (Cambridge, 2010).
[277] 'Giharo Mutalla Survey Report, 1937', Kabale District Archives, ADM67, File
No. 193, 27.

though her spirit later reappeared in Rwanda – were always women, the *bagirwa* or priestesses who sustained their order by dedicating their daughters to the cult through a process known as *okutweija*.[278] Between the 1910s and the 1930s, various *bagirwa* claimed to be possessed by Nyabingi and dedicated themselves to the eradication of European colonial rule in the hilly territory straddling the Uganda–Rwanda border. At the same time, Nyabingi was the crystallisation of a core theme in Uganda's history over *la longue durée*, namely resistance to the monarchical and territorially delineated politics of hierarchy and settlement.[279] For Nyabingi's followers, kings and their promoters were to be robustly opposed: this was dissension which was especially marked in this period of Kigezi's history, but which was evident elsewhere across Uganda as the twentieth century unfolded, and notably as kingship itself was increasingly posited as a normative part of the political architecture of colonial rule.

Yet spiritual change was rarely uniform. Archaeologists have observed that in newly Christian Buganda in the early decades of the twentieth century, iron-working skills largely disappeared – quite possibly because these skills were associated with particular spirits which no longer had a place in a Uganda where missionaries actively worked against them.[280] Still, in recent years, shrines have proliferated along the roadsides of rural Uganda. They continue to be of use and attract large communities, even within Kampala itself. Along Mityana road, for example, a veritable shrine industry is in motion – with various groups being served by various spirits.[281] The significance of the spiritual in the public sphere – in gaining access to succour and protection, and indeed to political and moral power – is clear enough. We see, again, the mobilisation of spirits as critics of incumbent regimes, while political leaders sought legitimacy through the co-option of shrines and deities – most dramatically, perhaps, in the case of the Chwezi. The redemptive, curative and temporal power of evolving spiritual systems

---

[278] Hopkins, 'The Nyabingi cult'; Holger Bernt Hansen, 'The Colonial Control of Spirit Cults in Uganda', in Anderson & Johnson (eds.), *Revealing Prophets*.

[279] David Schoenbrun, 'A Past Whose Time Has Come: historical context and history in Eastern Africa's Great Lakes', *History and Theory*, 32:4 (1993).

[280] Jane Humphris, Marcos Martinon-Torres, Thilo Rehren, and Andrew Reid, 'Variability in single smelting episodes: a pilot study using iron slag from Uganda', *Journal of Archaeological Science*, 36 (2009), 360.

[281] Author's field notes and informal interviews, April 2013.

helps explain why so many Ugandans also embraced imported faiths and took up ostensibly novel forms of belief.[282]

Introduced by coastal merchants in the 1840s, Islam began to penetrate the Ganda capital in the course of the ensuing two decades. While there is no indication in the accounts of Speke and Grant that the young Mutesa was particularly drawn to Islam in the early 1860s, within a few years he was evidently observing at least some aspects of the faith, including Ramadhan.[283] He continued to do so until around 1875. Islam thus won an increasing number of converts at the royal court, and no doubt for many of the same reasons that Africans elsewhere, over many centuries, had converted: intellectual curiosity and a preparedness to engage with dynamic new ideas; in emulation of rulers who, at the same time, used new faiths to enhance their own authority; in pursuit of commercial advantage, for Islam provided an arena of connection between buyers and sellers in the new global marketplace opening up around Lake Victoria.[284] In much the same period, Muslim slavers from Egypt and Sudan were escalating their operations among the Acholi and Langi, though Kabalega in Bunyoro – wary of the threat from the north – was scarcely interested in new creeds.[285] Mutesa, by contrast, embraced Islam with a brutal vigour, as Kagwa explains:

... [T]he king began to observe his ninth Ramadhan in 1875. On the following day, there was a mass arrest of all the people who did not practice Mohamedanism. The king ordered all the chiefs to hand over to him all the 'unbelievers'. The chiefs arrested very many people on the pretext that they were unbelievers, but as a matter of fact, they were men against whom they had grudges. All the captives were taken to Nakinziro execution place and done to death ... From that time forward, the whole country became

[282] Michael Twaddle, 'The Ganda receptivity to change', *Journal of African History*, 15:2 (1974); Oliver, *Missionary Factor*; see also Wrigley, 'Christian Revolution'; by Twaddle, 'The Muslim revolution in Buganda', *African Affairs*, 71 (1972), and 'The emergence of politico-religious groupings'; Rowe, 'The purge of Christians'; J.D.Y. Peel, 'Conversion and tradition in two African societies: Ijebu and Buganda', *Past and Present*, 77 (1977).

[283] Kagwa, *Kings*, 158–60.

[284] See classic studies of conversion to Islam among the city-states and 'empires' of the early modern West African savannah: for example, Nehemiah Levtzion, *Ancient Ghana and Mali* (London, 1973) or E.W. Bovill, *The Golden Trade of the Moors* (London, 1958).

[285] Nyakatura, *Anatomy*, 113–16. He was, at best, equivocal, going by his shifting attitudes toward Christian and Muslim causes in the 1880s and 1890s: see Sir John Gray, 'Kabarega and the CMS', *Uganda Journal*, 35:1 (1971), 81–2.

very devoutly Mohamedan and many more mosques were built in every village.[286]

But not for long, it seems. This kind of brutal purge was indubitably driven by a range of political and personal agendas, and the flexibility of his (and many chiefs') adherence to Islam *per se* is indicated by the facility with which Mutesa experimented with another new faith, Christianity. In the months following Stanley's visit in 1875, Mutesa apparently poured his energies into a translation of the Pentateuch, much to the disgruntlement of those who had long been rather more devout Muslims than Mutesa ever was. Their zeal, seemingly piqued by the arrival of some Egyptian clerics, led to protests that Mutesa's mosque faced west rather than east; that he was uncircumcised and therefore so, too, were his cooks, which meant that the meat at the royal court was not *halal*; and ultimately that Mutesa had no authority to conduct prayers at the royal court, nor could the ardent young pages be expected to eat there. Mutesa was furious, and he rounded up some seventy Muslim converts and had them burnt to death at Namugongo.[287] It was by no means the first time a king had been challenged and had responded with a killing spree; it was, however, the first religious martyrdom of the modern era. It was also one which to some extent would become overshadowed by the story of the Christian martyrs a decade later, but which would form a critical component in the Ugandan Muslim historical imaginary in the decades to come.[288]

Still, Mutesa almost certainly continued to regard himself as a practising Muslim for a number of years, although Christianity was winning its share of hearts and minds. From the mid-1870s, European explorers, as part of an escalating process of cultural engagement with the wider world, were the first to brandish bibles, and from the late 1870s, the first missionaries arrived in Buganda, British Anglicans represented by the Church Missionary Society, swiftly followed by French Catholics. The Christian factions grew with remarkable speed from the late 1870s onward, and the White Fathers in particular proved adept at drawing young, ambitious, excited Ganda to their compound. These 'readers', *basomi*, as they became known, formed part of the

[286] Kagwa, *Kings*, 166–7.   [287] Ibid., 171–2.
[288] For example, 'The untold story of the Muslim martyrs', *Daily Monitor*, 6 July 2013.

emergent privileged class of chiefs' children, and thus they were powerful disproportionate to their actual numbers. But the White Fathers decided to evacuate Buganda in 1882 owing to local tensions, and they would not return for three years.[289] It was a critical period in which the Anglican mission was able to make considerable headway, not least by demonstrating apparently rather greater commitment to the cause, and to their small but expanding community of converts. They were also proving quite useful in terms of the skills they offered, including reading and carpentry. It was a community which survived the vicious pogrom carried out by an anxious Mwanga who made connections between the injudicious advance of Bishop Hannington, a vaguely defined external threat, and the growing insolence of the *basomi* at home. In 1886 he had several dozen burnt to death – like their Muslim compatriots ten years earlier – at Namugongo.[290] The courage with which both Muslim and Christian converts faced horrific execution has elicited much analysis over many years. It certainly seems to have been an expression of the concept of *ekitiibwa* in Ganda culture: honour, dignity, self-respect, a requirement to be stoical in the face of personal suffering.[291] Such defiance of worldly authority was also an expression of aspiration – deeply rooted in Uganda's political cultures and social behaviours, and now provided an additional zest by the belief in bodily resurrection, though that too was compatible with extant spiritual convictions. These were dramatic episodes, but in many ways they were especially intense distillations of more quotidian and long-standing struggles between the living and the dead. At the same time, of course, Mwanga was perfectly within his rights – he believed – to punish by death those who would defy his authority and thus offend the dignity of the kingdom itself; yet his problem was not global religion *per se* but rather the cultural shift it had encouraged, in terms of socio-political aspiration and expectation which led to factionalism and mounting defiance of the *kabaka* in the first place. The martyrdoms were also about personal vendetta, and – probably – the sorry consequence of resistance to the king's sexual predations.[292]

---

[289] R.F. Clarke (ed.), *Cardinal Lavigerie and the African Slave Trade* (London, 1889), 167.

[290] Mackay, *Pioneer Missionary*, 276–7.

[291] John Iliffe, *Honour in African History* (Cambridge, 2005), 168–80.

[292] J.F. Faupel, *African Holocaust: the story of the Uganda martyrs* (London, 1965); H. Médard, 'L'homosexualité au Buganda, une acculturation peut une cache une autre', *Hypothèses*, 1 (1999); Rao, 'Re-membering Mwanga', 1–4.

When Mwanga was overthrown in 1888, his immediate successor was a Muslim, Kalema/Rashid, and there was no reason to suppose that Buganda would *not* become an Islamic state of some kind. That it did not owed something to the serendipitous arrival of Lugard's guns which gave considerable encouragement to the Christian camps who had managed to dispatch Kalema and replace him with Kiwewa. Muslims would thereafter play a losing hand, and in the course of the 1890s would come to be both maligned and marginalised by an Anglo–Ganda Protestant alliance which would have lasting repercussions (for numerically superior Catholics, too) deep into the twentieth century.

Conversion to Protestantism, Catholicism and Islam in the late nineteenth and early twentieth centuries was in some ways representative of the quest for personal and collective redemption and security in a brutal, turbulent era. In the elaboration of new forms of eschatology, there was the militant defence of personal dignity, as found in both the Bible and the Quran. These were powerful messages and motifs in an era of war, and political and economic transformation; they resonated at the end of a long nineteenth century of material, ideological and cultural change. It is also the case that both Christianity and Islam – but especially the former, in terms of its relatively linear narrative – provided many with a template of *history* into which the moral pasts of particular groups and peoples could be inserted. At any rate, these were powerful messages, and attractive opportunities, and by the early 1900s Christianity of the Anglican variety had formed the very architecture – physical, in the 'place of peace', Namirembe Cathedral, as well as moral and political – of the British colonial state.[293] A short distance from Namirembe was Rubaga Cathedral, centre of the Catholic faith. If it could not be strictly said that any one denomination represented the Ugandan elite at prayer, then Anglicanism certainly came close, with Roman Catholicism second; Islam was a rather distant third. The outcome was an intimate, if at times uneasy, alliance of colonial officialdom and Christian mission;[294] the emergence of a new governing class, steeped in Anglicanism, and a political consciousness among the expanding Catholic population; and an initially cowed but increasingly assertive Muslim population. In each case, the

---

[293] Ashe, *Chronicles*, 228, 343–4; C.W. Hattersley, *The Baganda at Home* (London, 1908), 201; J.D. Mullins, *The Wonderful Story of Uganda* (London, 1908), esp. chapters X & XII.

[294] Holger Bernt Hansen, *Mission, Church and State in a Colonial Setting: Uganda, c.1890–1925* (London, 1984).

Ugandan agency was paramount, and by the 1930s and 1940s, the age-ing converts and their offspring had moved to take control – morally and politically, if not yet in terms of church hierarchy – of their respec-tive sects, and had travelled some distance from the foreigners who had first imparted their sacred knowledge.

From the 1890s and 1900s, mission stations proliferated across the Protectorate, and consummated the imperial project in ways which sought to emphasise rupture and rebirth. 'The last time we came to you here in this country', proclaimed Petero Kasuju, a recent Nyoro con-vert to the Gospel, to the missionary A.B.Lloyd in around 1900, 'we came with shields and spears in our hands and hatred in our hearts; now we stand before you with God's Word in our hands and His love in our hearts'.[295] Kabalega's son and successor as *Mukama* of Bunyoro, Andereya, waited anxiously for the news that his father had redeemed himself in exile by accepting baptism and renouncing his (and thus Bunyoro's) evil past: 'I have heard that my father Kabarega has been baptized', he wrote excitedly in 1907. 'The Lord be praised . . . ' But the story was untrue, for the Civil Chaplain of the Seychelles was as yet unconvinced as to the old warrior's ingenuity.[296] In 1911, however, Kabalega had indeed reportedly converted.[297] From Toro, *Mukama* Kasagama wrote a letter to 'the elders of the Church in Europe', help-fully rendered in blank verse by the Rev. Canon Rawnsley:

> For round about is darkness – Abakonjo,
> Abamba, Abahoko, Abaega,
> Abasagola, Abasongola, all
> Are nations still in darkness, send them light![298]

Missionary doings – their successes and their setbacks – were faithfully recorded in a series of publications created for the purpose, including, on the Anglican side, *Mengo Notes* and the more general *Church Mis-sionary Gleaner*. In Bunyoro, missionaries depended on the support of Paulo Bwabachwezi, whose 'private life is not all one could wish' but whose financial contribution to the building of a new church was criti-cal. Fortunately, his wife Damali 'is a splendid woman, and in her quiet

---

[295] Mullins, *Wonderful Story*, 154.
[296] *Church Missionary Gleaner*, XXXV (1908), 92.
[297] *Church Missionary Gleaner*, XXXVIII (1911), 139.
[298] *Church Missionary Gleaner*, XXIV (1897), 187.

way has a good influence'; his sister, however, 'was a terrible drunk-
ard and worse'.[299] Post-conquest Bunyoro was not an especially happy
assignment, as a Miss Chadwick wrote from Hoima in 1905: 'To one
accustomed to the gay friendliness of the Baganda the cold and indif-
ferent, if not suspicious manner of their Banyoro sisters comes with
something of a shock'.[300] More generally, African agency in conversion and control remained paramount: in Busoga, chiefs were critical
in the spread and consolidation of the church, and local refraction and
regulation were similarly central to religious conversion in Ankole.[301]
Ganda teachers were critical in the spreading of the Word, as they
were in Bukedi under Kakungulu's leadership: here, they fanned out
across the countryside in military fashion, doing God's work among
'unevangelised tribes'.[302] 'The Baganda are well adapted to become
light bearers to the inhabitants of the countries around them, thousands of whom are still naked savages, utterly uncivilised', suggested a
review of the situation in Uganda in 1906.[303] But they did not always
do so with much enthusiasm, witness the Ganda teachers in Toro who
were agitating to return home by early 1900.[304] Meanwhile missionaries themselves wrestled heroically with other quotidian challenges:
'Frailty, thy name is [a] Katwe canoe', wrote one anxiously.[305]

But a rather more significant anxiety for missionaries was the expansion of Islam, which by 1906 was 'making serious advances' owing
in part to the 'influx of ... Swahili traders and workmen, interpreters,
masons, carpenters, &c.'; in a curious distortion of Livingstone's old
nineteenth-century battle-cry, this writer lamented that 'the efforts
of commerce have outstripped those of the Christian missionary in

---

[299] *Mengo Notes*, September 1900, 19 and March 1901, 44.
[300] *Church Missionary Gleaner*, XXXII (1905), 70; also *Church Missionary
Gleaner*, XL (1913), 100.
[301] Tom Tuma, 'African Chiefs and Church Work in Busoga Province of Uganda,
1900–1940' (unpublished paper, Makerere University, Kampala, n.d.); J.K.
Bamunoba, 'A reconstruction of the history of the Christian Church in
Ankole; based on original sources, oral and written', unpublished paper,
Makerere University, c.1966. See also John Waliggo's superlative study, 'The
Catholic Church in the Buddu province of Buganda', unpublished PhD thesis,
University of Cambridge, 1976.
[302] *Mengo Notes*, June 1901, 58.
[303] *Church Missionary Gleaner*, XXXIII, (1906), 190.
[304] *Church Missionary Gleaner*, XXVII (1900), 27.
[305] *Mengo Notes*, January 1902, 6.

the Protectorate!'[306] Islam did indeed spread in the early twentieth century, but its adherents found themselves marginalised from the centres of power and opportunity.[307]

War and Peace: Culmination and Revolution

This, then, was a nation forged in war, the product of a nineteenth-century military revolution combined with a generation of co-option and conquest in the approximately two decades either side of 1900. Yet it is important to draw out the crucial differences in regional experience in this period – differences which weaved fissures into the organic arena of interaction that became Uganda. The wars in which the British became embroiled marked a decisive watershed: the British did not enable the nation; they retarded it. While the British were to a considerable extent co-opted into local dynamics, the outcome nonetheless was a deeply inequitable power (and resource) relationship. The violence north of the Nile, especially, would mean decades of underdevelopment and marginality, and pose enormous challenges for future Ugandan national elites. While there is no doubt that to some extent the expanding scope and scale of war was facilitated by the flood of firearms into Uganda since the mid-nineteenth century,[308] guns were not the cause of widening political and military and economic visions which characterised late precolonial Uganda. These were the product of endogenous and deep-rooted struggles over polity, society and economy, over people and ideas, intensified by foreign intrusions. This was a time of violent oscillation and outage of power, the culmination of many decades' militarisation of political culture intersecting with – and in many ways facilitating – the expansion of foreign forces and the military transformation in Europe itself, manifest in British imperialism. The latter was initially tentative, brittle, and its representatives were co-opted into *Ugandan* conflicts and dynamics and relationships; but it was also probing and increasingly robust, and ultimately proved potent and transformative in its own right. This was the era which witnessed the elevation of the Buganda state to dominance in the emerging entity of Uganda, based on a partnership – as the Ganda themselves

---

[306] *Church Missionary Gleaner*, XXXIII, (1906), 190.

[307] One of the best single accounts remains A.B.K. Kasozi, *The Spread of Islam in Uganda* (Nairobi & Khartoum, 1986).

[308] This was an obsession with many missionaries: see, for example, Mackay, *Pioneer Missionary*, 437.

saw it – between them and the British administration, who had arrived in much the same way as other invaders in the past. Mwanga's kingdom became the gateway to Uganda, and the platform on which it was built. And problems were stored for the future in that such a fractious and troubled polity was now the capstone of the colonial territory. Within Buganda itself, the rise of a chiefly oligarchy had its roots in the deeper nineteenth century and indeed earlier, but was provided with new impetus by the arrival of foreign faiths which themselves opened up new fissures and factions within the political class. This was true in terms of Protestants, Catholics and Muslims; but it was also the case between a royalist camp coalescing around the *bwakabaka* – the kingship which was at the centre of Ganda political life – and the *bataka*, the clans which felt sidelined by the colonial arrangement of power. The latter, no less than the coalescence of resistance around Nyabingi, represented the long-standing contestation around the role of kingship, and the articulation of other visions of political organisation and entitlement. It was the era which saw widespread destruction of, and the marginalisation of, Bunyoro – the historic fount of political culture in the region but now displaced and punished for its resistance to Anglo-Ganda hegemony. And then there was the militarised north, treated as 'the land beyond', the unstable appendage to the southern forest core of the Protectorate. This would create a long-term dynamic in terms of the political balance in Uganda, with implications that would only become apparent several decades later.

It is important to emphasise two particular elements in this story: First, revolutionary though the period is, it needs to be understood as part of the *longue durée* of Ugandan history, comprising both dramatic disjuncture and some striking continuities; and to understand the stories, and representations, of Kabalega and Mwanga not just for the doubtless characterful personalities themselves, but in terms of what these avatars embody in terms of precolonial – and ongoing – political dynamics. Second, what was happening beyond the central regions, to the east and north of Lake Kyoga, was at least as important as what was happening around Mengo and the vectors emanating out of that great political hub, notwithstanding the fact that the scholarly gaze has long been fixed on the south in this period.[309] Scholarly interest

---

[309] There is a striking comparison to be made with Shoa and the Amhara areas of central Ethiopia in much the same period: the academy would come to reinforce the political elevation of the group itself in an oddly perpetuating

essentially followed the political nodes established at the end of the nineteenth century, hence perpetuating the nodes themselves. And so, political power was directly connected to the ability to capture and broadcast knowledge, in whatever form it came. In the 1890s and 1900s, the Ganda political elite drew on the antiquity and order of a deep past to reverse national decline, bring under some degree of control the internal political crisis, and cement their place in a new political order based on control of historical 'knowledge'. The intellectual implications of these events were profound, and long-lasting, in terms of the memory and celebration of the struggles for Christian Buganda. Early European writers were greatly struck by the struggle for Christian truth among the Ganda, giving rise to a celebration of the triumph of the church in the heart of Africa;[310] more importantly, the young Ganda pages, members of the emerging elite who had lived through the trials of this era and seen many of their fellows killed for their faith, would later seek to emphasise that epic journey and their part in the creation of modern Uganda.[311] Moreover, the violence among the Langi and Acholi, and that experienced by the Nyoro, in the course of the 1890s and 1900s enabled the Ganda to co-opt the British into a particular vision of the north – cementing the idea that Buganda was the stable and civilised hub, and the lands north from Bunyoro and beyond Lake Kyoga as perennially backward, unstable, violently primitive and in need of aggressive and often militarised control. Those places were in stark contrast to the boisterous but urbane forested zone, a place of sophisticated political discourse, and intellectual endeavour. And thus the north became frozen in a militarised moment; and this would soon after intersect with the colonial military system, and was both cause and effect of British recruitment into the colonial army. The roots of the northern military

cycle of cause and effect, while outlying areas and peoples huddled in the shadows of Semitic civilisation with its enormous, bureaucratic, and well-articulated presence. Ethiopia has recently undergone something of a scholarly remapping; Uganda, not yet. See, for example: D. Donham & W. James (eds.), *The Southern Marches of Imperial Ethiopia: essays in history and social anthropology* (Cambridge, 1986) and W. James, D. Donham, E. Kurimoto & A. Triulzi (eds.), *Remapping Ethiopia: socialism and after* (Oxford, 2002).

[310] For example, Ashe, *Chronicles* and Stanley's Preface to the 1899 edition of *Dark Continent*.

[311] Rowe, 'Myth'; Reid, 'Ghosts'.

complex lie in this striking conjunction of the nineteenth-century military revolution and a localised, pragmatic application of British martial race theory.

As for Mwanga and Kabalega, our two kings are symptomatic of long-term dynamics in Uganda's history. They both reflected the deeper past, and anticipated the future; as actors and icons, they are pivots, hinges on which the modern history of Uganda hang. Each encapsulated the ambiguous utility of violence; the story of each represented the growing power of chiefly oligarchy and the constraints which were being imposed on monarchy; each told a distinct story of responses to, and the harnessing of, external forces, and the consequences of those actions, for good or ill. Mwanga, then, is not only the troubled *kabaka*, somehow perennially childlike and confused, caught in the crossfire of historical dynamics. He is also profoundly emblematic in terms of the *longue durée* of Ugandan history: his wrestling with outside forces over which, it seems, he has very little control (he ends his life as Daniel Mwanga, the resigned convert to a faith which a few years earlier he had loathed and feared); his tyranny, and vain attempts at absolutist omnipotence; his failure to manage an increasingly unruly and discontented chiefly class, an oligarchy which was a long time in the making but which now, at the turn of the twentieth century, would come to dominate Ugandan political culture. He was, in sum, a symbol of the era, characterised by struggles around the interpretation and imposition of political order, and the meanings attached to that order. Kabalega, meanwhile, invites a rather different set of narratives. He is the exemplar of the nineteenth-century African military revolution, who revives a putatively moribund state-system in remarkable – if remarkably violent – style, but who discovers that timing, as they say, is everything: Bunyoro's renascence happens at a moment of extraordinary external pressure, and the *Mukama*, vigilant and astute in so many other aspects of his public life, makes the wrong call – he chooses war against the old enemy, the Ganda, who have rather more cleverly partnered themselves with the British. Thus, unlike the vacillating Mwanga, who is crushed in a pincer movement between his own chiefs and the forces of British imperialism, Kabalega faces down the new order valiantly but hopelessly, and in unleashing total war he presides over the almost-total destruction of his kingdom which is thus marginalised as an obstacle to progress for the foreseeable future, and has swathes of its territory colonised by the Ganda in what would become known as the issue of the 'Lost Counties'. Violence had served him well in reasserting Bunyoro in the 1870s and 1880s; it was his people's undoing in its deployment against the wrong enemy, at the wrong moment, in the course of the 1890s. Even his great champion, John Nyakatura, wrote: 'It must, however, be pointed out that he lacked good advisers who could have explained to him the new forces which had come to Africa'.[312] The idea of the brave and honourable ruler undone by lack of wise counsel – for he would surely have acted otherwise had he possessed such guidance – was an echo of earlier monarchical tradition, and has continued to echo in more recent times, too.

The revolutionary generation which oversaw such profound change in Uganda between the 1880s and the 1900s resonates today as perhaps never before. Uganda in the 2000s and 2010s is confronted with many of the issues which wracked Buganda at the close of the nineteenth century: the anxieties and exigencies of political transition, Uganda's place in the world and its relationship with it, social and sexual propriety and behavioural norms. Kabalega has the President's medal, but it is Mwanga who is very much a man for our times: he presided precariously over a fractious and ambitious political and military class; found himself caught in the crosshairs of personal ambition, domestic need and external pressure; was ultimately overthrown by an alliance of domestic and foreign forces which he had imagined he could control. The pensive nation of today echoes the tumult of the 1890s. Moreover, these were the dynamics with which the NRM was confronted in the late 1980s. The Uganda of the late nineteenth and early twentieth centuries was in many respects the Uganda inherited by Museveni and his guerrillas, and they made as their task – so they stated – to complete the decolonisation of that order and remake the nation in new ways.

[312] Nyakatura, *Anatomy*, 107.

4 *The Adventures of Zigeye and Atuk*

The Age of Opportunity and Disparity

'The Hairy One' and 'White Teeth'

In the Hijri year 1260 of the Islamic calendar – 1844 in the Gregorian –
a small group of foreign merchants arrived at the capital of Buganda,
then at Nabulagala hill, present-day Kasubi, on the outskirts of modern Kampala. Among them was Ahmed bin Ibrahim, whose account of
this and two subsequent visits to the kingdom is left to us through an
apparently first-hand account in Emin Pasha's diary.[1] In Kagwa's version, there were 'three Arabs, Kyera, Lusukwa and Zigeye, and the two
Swahilis were Muina and Lukabya'.[2] These were Luganda nicknames
for the strangers; and one of these, Zigeye, referred to the fact that he
was extremely hairy. In fact, his real name was Isa bin Hussein, and he
appeared in Burton's account a few years later. Burton describes him
as hailing from Balochistan, in present-day Pakistan, and as in origin
a 'mercenary', by which he probably meant trader, in the service of the
Sultan of Zanzibar. However:

He had fled from his debtors, and had gradually wandered to Uganda, where
the favour of the sovereign procured him wealth in ivory, and a harem containing from 200 to 300 women. 'Mzagayya' – the hairy one, as he was
locally called, from his long locks and bushy beard – was not permitted, nor
probably did he desire, to quit the country...

He became one of Suna's favourites, and 'used constantly to sit by him
on guard, matchlock in hand'. When Suna died in 1856 or 1857, 'he
fled to independent Unyoro, having probably raised up, as these adventurers will, a host of enemies [in] Uganda'.[3] This may be true, but

---

[1] Gray, 'Ahmed bin Ibrahim'; also J.M. Gray's editorship of 'The Diaries of Emin
   Pasha', *Uganda Journal*, 25:1 (1961) and his 'Trading Expeditions from the
   Coast to Lakes Tanganyika and Victoria before 1867', *Tanganyika Notes and
   Records*, 49 (1957).
[2] Kagwa, *Kings*, 120.   [3] Burton, *Lake Regions*, 402–3.

we know nothing more of his adventures. Meanwhile Speke mentions 'Eseau' – almost certainly the same character – who travelled into the interior with a great deal of merchandise, much of which, as in Burton's account, he lost on the way to Buganda, possibly as a result of exorbitant local taxation. Unable to return to Zanzibar, he 'instead made great friends with the late King Sunna, who took an especial fancy to him because he had a very large beard, and raised him to the rank of Mkungu'. Interestingly, Speke's character did not live at the capital – as implied in Burton's account – but in Buddu, where he was apparently a personage of some significance; for when he died (Speke makes no mention of him fleeing to Bunyoro on Suna's death), he 'left all his family and property to a slave named Uledi, who now, in consequence, is the border officer'.[4] This is corroborated by Miti's version of events, in which 'Isa bin Ushen . . . found much favour with the king' who gave him 'a whole village, called Kituntu, in the district of Buddu'.[5]

Thus is Isa bin Hussein – aka 'Zigeye', 'the hairy one' – glimpsed intriguingly in a handful of sources. In his characteristically deadpan style, Kagwa tells us why this visit in 1260/1844 was so important: 'Coming from the direction of Karagwe, they brought with them harps, clothes, mirrors, and many other things. The king stored his presents of clothes for a long time before he started wearing them'.[6] These strangers laid before the *kabaka* gifts of high value, soon to become prestige commercial imports, and initiated a veritable revolution in material and commercial culture with far-reaching political and social implications. We may know little about 'the hairy one', but his role in the history of Uganda is of ineffable significance. Similar dynamics were unfolding at the opposite end of Uganda, coming from the direction of Egypt and Sudan. In this case, we have even less in the way of detailed evidence on which to hang our analysis; few specific characters, hirsute or otherwise, to use as *entrées* into a changing commercial world. Still, we know that in 1841 a Turkish sailor, named Selim, found that that he could navigate the Nile as far as Gondokoro, just a few miles north of the present-day Uganda–South Sudan border; and that in the 1850s, a Maltese merchant named Debono was operating among the Acholi.[7] Just as in the 1830s and 1840s, a new commercial frontier had begun to fan out across the interior from Zanzibar towards lakes

---

[4] Speke, *Journal*, 276.   [5] Miti, *History of Buganda*, I, 124.
[6] Kagwa, *Kings*, 120.   [7] Low, 'Northern Interior', 324–5, 326.

Tanganyika and Victoria, so in much the same period did new commercial impulses encroach from the north. Egypt was expanding into central and southern Sudan, edging towards what would become Uganda's northern border from the 1820s onward. Opportunities were opening up for ivory (and, later, slaves) south of the Bahr al-Ghazal; and thus traders known as 'Khartoumers' – the term for a motley collection of adventurers and chancers and entrepreneurs – were by the middle decades of the nineteenth century drawing the Acholi and the Langi into a larger economic arena based on the Sudanic Nile and Khartoum itself, and beyond that still, Egypt, the eastern Mediterranean and the Levant.[8]

Uganda was caught up in the transnational explosion of trade which, it is broadly accepted, formed one of the salient characteristics of the global nineteenth century.[9] The political and military transformations examined so far were to a large extent driven by economic change. This was not merely a matter of an increase in the *volume* of trade, although clearly this was an important dynamic. The *nature* of international commerce – driven as it was by a focus on a handful of commodities, foremost among which were slaves and ivory – transformed Ugandan states and societies, and the trade itself involved a more intense, indeed intimate, penetration of outside actors into the region itself, culminating in Indian merchant capital and British commercial concerns at the end of the nineteenth century. Yet Uganda was not – in the conceptualisation of later British imperial ideologues and missionaries, inspired by Livingstone[10] – a tightly closed little kernel nestling in the dark heart of an isolated region, only awaiting the revelations of good Christians bringing commerce and, by default, civilisation to benighted folks. Uganda was a region with a deep history of economic migration, exchange and wider connectivity. Thus the nineteenth-century commercial revolution was several centuries in the making: its provenance

---

[8] Edward Thomas, *South Sudan: a slow liberation* (London, 2015), 58–60, 66–7; P.M. Holt & M.W. Daly, *A History of the Sudan: from the coming of Islam to the present day* (Harlow, 2000), chapter 4.

[9] C. Bayly, *The Birth of the Modern World, 1780–1914* (Oxford, 2004); R. Cameron & L. Neal, *A Concise Economic History of the World* (Oxford, 1989); R. Austen, *African Economic History: internal development and external dependency* (London, 1987).

[10] 'Dr Livingstone's Cambridge Lectures [December 1857]', in B. Harlow & M. Carter (eds.), *Archives of Empire, II: The Scramble for Africa* (Durham NC & London, 2003), 253–78.

lay in centuries of commercial interaction with the wider region, and indeed further afield. Excavations at Ntusi have revealed glass beads from the Indian Ocean coast, dating to the fourteenth century or even earlier;[11] and while such connections doubtless ebbed and flowed over time, patterns of long-distance trade are discernible over the longer term. Moreover, Isa bin Hussein may have been among the first party of coastal merchants to make it to the north end of Lake Victoria, but the Ganda in the 1840s were no strangers to the kinds of commodities they brought with them; new and fancy imports had been arriving into Buganda since the middle of the eighteenth century. It is more difficult to say for certain what form trade took further north, where archaeological work has been much more limited, and where indigenous sources describing commerce are lacking. But it seems reasonable to suppose that commercial contacts had long existed, if organised in small-scale, local stages, between northern Uganda and Sudan and Ethiopia, and perhaps beyond, for some considerable time; the picture that has emerged regarding population movements across this area certainly imply as much.[12] And so there was no abrupt moment of material revelation, no sudden expansion of economic horizons; but rather, the gradual escalation of long-range communication and commodification.

Still, as notional watershed dates go, 1844 looks a decent bet, marking the beginnings of the economic transformation of Uganda. And in one other respect, finally, the story of 'the hairy one' is important; and that relates to the apparent receptivity of the Ganda to this odd foreigner with his funny beard. He embodied the ideas of social mobility, of how fortune might smile on the adventurer and the entrepreneur and of how the open and flexible society of Buganda could welcome a foreigner to the very centre of the political system – ideas which were present, of course, in Buganda's own oral traditions. These ideas persist in Ugandans' socio-economic imaginary, although in the century and a half since the appearance of 'Zigeye' at Kasubi hill social mobility has only been possible for a relative few, entrepreneurialism has not always been rewarded and indeed has often been greeted with hostility, and foreigners – broadly defined – have not always been

---

[11] John Iliffe, *Africans: the history of a continent* (Cambridge, 2007), 110.
[12] Christopher Ehret, *Ethiopians and East Africans: the problem of contacts* (Nairobi, 1974).

especially welcome. Nonetheless, the arrival of 'Zigeye' at the royal court of Buganda is both culmination and departure: culmination of several decades, indeed centuries, of long-range commercial contacts with distant horizons – indirect but gathering momentum; and a new point of departure in terms of direct global trade and transformative commerce. 1844, therefore, is a pivot, and a symbolic point of temporal mediation in the *longue durée* economic history of Uganda.

A century later, it is another journey that draws our attention – a fictional one, this time, but no less significant for that. In Okot p'Bitek's 1953 novel *Lak Tar* ('White Teeth'), set some time in the recent past – probably the second half of the 1940s – the lead character is a young Acholi man named Okeca Ladwong, though his *mwoc*, his nickname, is Atuk. His father's *mwoc* had been Lak Tar, and the boy's cheerful demeanour causes people to recall his father's *mwoc*: *Lak tar miyo kinyero wilobo* ('White teeth make us laugh on earth'). But in fact, he spends much of his time worrying about bridewealth. He and his friends fret that with the costs of bridewealth spiralling upwards, and with so few economic opportunities in their own village, they will never be able to afford to get married. Their parents cannot help. So the young man decides to head south, first to Kampala, where he lands himself in all sorts of scrapes – including a spell in jail – and is overwhelmed by the crush and noise and rudeness of this city full of strangers, chancers, paupers. After some time staying in a miserable and overcrowded house, full of fellow migrants scraping a living, he travels east, taking a job on a sugar plantation near Jinja. Here, he finally begins to make a little money, something approaching what he needs to marry; he escapes the indentured labour system binding so many young men to the plantation, and via Kampala he begins the bus journey back north. Tragically, however, a series of unforeseen costs and mishaps – including, ultimately, being robbed on the bus home – means that he ends the novel defeated, trudging wearily on foot the last stretch of the road to his village, his prospects of marrying and living a fulfilled life crushed utterly.

The book is full of insight and moments of dark comedy about the 'human condition'. But above all it is a bleak indictment of the colonial economy, describing a Uganda which is a deeply divided, increasingly difficult place to live; a place underwritten by cash crop economics, founded on – indeed dependent upon – a system of underpaid migrant labour, often drawn from outside Uganda itself, but also from the more impoverished territories within it. The nineteenth-century economy has morphed into a more rigid, oppressive material order characterised by opportunity for a few, but mostly by an awful, gaping disparity. There has been plenty of foreign investment, but not the kind that generally trickles downward, and Zigeye's descendants have come and gone regularly, growing and selling on the back of a cheap workforce. The story is centrally concerned with the changes taking place around bridewealth, with the introduction of a monetary economy driving up prices to exorbitant levels. But the overarching theme is economic transformation. As Lubwa p'Chong put it in a foreword to the 1989 English translation of *Lak Tar*: '...the book was...a condemnation of corruption in Kampala; of the breakdown of the clan system, and of the exploitation of Africans by Asians in those material days'.[13] Atuk's journey is a story of modern Ugandan economic history. In our own age, he is still very much alive, and in search of his place in the putative brave new world of neoliberal economics. Economic despair has driven political action throughout the twentieth century, of course, pushing forward protest, nationalism and tightening ethnic identity. It has driven many to violence, including in Atuk's own homeland. His children – imagining that he did go on to have them – continue to wrestle with the same issues; they might even have it worse.

The Frontiers of Economy: Commercial Revolution

African economic history has been enjoying a resurgence over the last decade or so.[14] It is no coincidence that this has happened in the era of the supposed great African economic revival – the era of eye-watering annual GDP growth rates, of waves of inward investment (mostly from China and India), of developmental and thus often state-led capitalism. The preoccupations of modern economic historians have ranged away from the old influential 'vent for surplus' model and towards critical assessments of the kinds of numbers traditionally used to describe African economic performance while simultaneously seeking to introduce new numbers on which bold new theses can be

---

[13] 'Foreword', to *White Teeth* (1989 ed.).

[14] A.G. Hopkins, 'The new economic history of Africa', *Journal of African History*, 50:2 (2009).

securely hung.[15] Precolonial eastern Africa is comparatively marginal in much of the 'new' economic history, with its emphasis on econometrics and macroeconomics at the expense of fine-detail, bore-hole reconstructions of local economic history. The account which follows here draws inspiration and succour, rather, from an older – some might say old-fashioned – kind of locally focused and painstakingly reconstructed economic and socio-economic history: Law on Dahomey and the Slave Coast in the sixteenth and seventeenth centuries, for example; Wilks' classic treatise on Asante in the nineteenth; Hopkins on West Africa; Ambler on central Kenya.[16]

The headline story of Uganda's nineteenth century is the expansion of the export trades in slaves and ivory. Longer-range trading contacts were already intensifying in the eighteenth century, most clearly in southern Uganda. By that time, cowries – again, naturally, coming from the coast – were in wide circulation in Buganda, and chiefs were able to build up their own stores of them through trading contacts.[17] In the middle of the eighteenth century, *Kabaka* Kyabaggu is recorded by Kagwa as having been the 'first king to buy cups and plates', strongly suggestive of a long-distance trade in relative luxury items with Zanzibar and the coast.[18] By the 1790s and 1800s, while ivory had probably declined in importance as a local currency in Buganda, demand

---

[15] The hardy perennial 'vent for surplus' model – according to which access to foreign markets facilitates the exploitation of surplus productive capacity and ultimately brings about economic growth, which arguably applies to much of nineteenth-century southern Uganda – has been reassessed and modified: see Gareth Austin, 'Resources, techniques and strategies south of the Sahara: revising the factor endowments perspective on African economic development, 1500–2000', *Economic History Review*, 61:3 (2008). See also a useful assessment of the model in Keith Fuglie, ' "Vent-for-surplus" as a source of agricultural growth in northeast Thailand, 1950–1986', *Economic Development Center* (University of Minnesota), *Bulletin 89–3* (March 1989). Hla Myint's original thesis failed to take into account the actual operation of local economies: this is not a question of underused labour or resource being mobilised for the export trade, but rather diversion of thriving regional and domestic economies into it, with long-term consequences. See Hla Myint, 'The Classical Theory of International Trade and the Underdeveloped Countries', *Economic Journal*, 68 (June 1958).

[16] R.C.C. Law, *The Slave Coast of West Africa 1550–1750* (Oxford, 1991); I. Wilks, *Asante in the Nineteenth Century* (Cambridge, 1975); A.G. Hopkins, *An Economic History of West Africa* (London, 1973); C.H. Ambler, *Kenyan Communities in the Age of Imperialism* (New Haven & London, 1988).

[17] Reid, *Political Power*, 149–50.   [18] Kagwa, *Kings*, 99.

for it as an export commodity from south of Lake Victoria was escalating rapidly. *Kabaka* Semakokiro, noted as being especially wealthy
in ivory, was described as having his own 'royal salesman' whose job
it was to sell the royal ivory, and by the late eighteenth and early nineteenth centuries such traders were operating in Kiziba, south of the
Kagera River.[19] It is almost certainly no coincidence that Semakokiro
was the first Ganda ruler 'to buy cotton cloth from Karagwe', which at
the beginning of the nineteenth century was Buganda's main southern
trading partner.[20] A seismic commercial shift had begun: the Ganda
were selling ivory for imported cotton cloth, heralding the beginning
of a fundamentally transformative commercial relationship with the
outside world that would come, for better or worse, to define Uganda.
These were largely luxury imports, aimed at engaging the political
establishments of the region, and thus did commerce mark a shift away
from small-scale local exchange towards oligopolistic elitism. Political
elites sought to control, if not to achieve outright monopoly on, the
trade in these valuable new commodities, and certainly to manage their
distribution once they were in the area. Cloth was certainly a prestige
good,[21] and one that increasingly replaced barkcloth in Buganda as the
garment of the elite: Semakokiro, notably, presided over an expansion
in barkcloth production within Buganda, strongly suggestive that it
was becoming more common and more accessible.[22] The Ganda political establishment, increasingly interested in long-distance commerce,
had shifted its gaze further afield.

The commercial revolution would not have been possible without
well-established local and regional trade networks. This was not a
question of the harbingers of economic modernity penetrating the
primordial forest, and conquering the natives through a combination of shock and awe. Local agency, local partnership, was essential. Upcountry caravans, composed of and led by a motley array of
Swahili, 'Arab', and other assorted adventurers, followed well-trodden
roads of often considerable antiquity, snaking around the southern

---

[19] Ibid., 100–1.   [20] Ibid., 99.

[21] Nonetheless, there were gradations in quality and the generic term 'cotton
cloth' disguises a more sophisticated local market: *bugibugi* and *kafiifi* were
cheaper types, while more valuable and desirable were *kaniki*, a dark blue
calico; *amerikaani*, a hard, glossy, unbleached calico; and *bafuta*, a thin cotton
cloth.

[22] Kagwa, *Kings*, 99.

and western shores of Lake Victoria, skirting the forests of Kigezi and Mbarara. They walked on roads used by traders from Kkooki, Buddu, Buganda; and before them, by the Nyoro and their more ancient predecessors. Buganda's famous road network may have been relatively new, attributed by one missionary source to *Kabaka* Suna – a plausible supposition, given that it was during Suna's reign that long-distance commerce escalated, making infrastructure an attractive investment.[23] But for sure many roads had remained more or less constant for decades, perhaps centuries. In other words, this was a commercial zone of longstanding – already well integrated in material and commercial terms, long before the British demarcated the territory with the appellation 'Uganda'. Frameworks of production and exchange had long existed on which longer-range commerce could be superimposed; foreign merchants followed African roads, not vice versa.

Nonetheless, what transpired in the 1840s and the 1850s heralded a veritable revolution in how commerce was practised, and in terms of its impact – not just in indigenous economic terms, but in the realm of politics and society too. It was driven by a series of wider regional dynamics: chief among them, the relocation of the Omani capital to Zanzibar in the 1830s, providing impetus to a new commercial network based on slaves and ivory.[24] From Zanzibar – or more precisely, from Bagamoyo on the adjacent mainland coast – emanated a multitude of caravans every year, and in increasing numbers, snaking their way inland along recently discovered highways into the interior. This led to the establishment of a permanent coastal merchant settlement at Tabora by the end of the 1840s, and the dispatch northward, around the western shore of Lake Victoria, of exploratory trade missions towards Karagwe and ultimately, as we have seen, Buganda itself.[25] There was a permanent Arab quarter at the Ganda capital from the end of the 1850s onward. Trade was transformative in those areas it reached. Buganda in particular – singularly well placed at the top end of Lake Victoria to take advantage of burgeoning commercial opportunities – became one of the key regional commercial actors in the second half of the nineteenth century, exporting both slaves and ivory, and experiencing rapid

[23] Felkin, 'Notes', 754.
[24] Abdul Sheriff, *Slaves, Spices and Ivory in Zanzibar: integration of an East African commercial empire into the world economy, 1770–1873* (London, 1987).
[25] Iliffe, *Modern History of Tanganyika*, 41.

social and political change as a result of transformations in material expectation and aspiration, at least among the kingdom's elite. We have less detail about the northern passages, the area transiting modern day northern Uganda and South Sudan. But the impact here from the middle of the nineteenth century was also seismic: particularly among the Acholi and the Langi, the increasingly intense connections with Sudan and the commercial hub of Khartoum were of enormous significance, and again involved the export of human beings and elephant tusks.[26] In exchange, Ugandans received various types of cloth, jewellery and precious stones, miscellaneous manufactured items and firearms. Exports of slaves and ivory peaked in the 1870s and 1880s, whereupon they dwindled rapidly. It was a story of brutal commercial transformation: brief but intense, it was as nasty an introduction to a global marketplace as that experienced by millions of West Africans from the sixteenth century onward. However, the rapid expansion of long-range trade between the 1840s and the 1890s was to a very considerable degree an extension – and, no doubt, an escalation – of what had been long been happening to local economies in the Ugandan area. In short, Ugandan economies had long been dynamic and violent, based on an indelible interconnection between economic expansion – whether we call it 'growth', or 'development' – and warfare. Moreover, slavery was, by the early nineteenth century, a well-established economic system in the Great Lakes region,[27] and thus Arab merchants were able to tap into an extant system of unfree labour, and to harness a series of military cultures which had evolved in large part to meet domestic economic need.

The commercial revolution of the long nineteenth century was based on a variety of 'internal', domestic economics and their interchange, which formed the absolute bedrock of any kind of large-scale economic change. Several centuries of inward migration and socio-cultural intermingling meant that by the early decades of the nineteenth century, the area was economically complex, characterised by specialisation and stratification, and underpinned in most communities by a mixed and diversified economy. Above all, the Ugandan region's economic history is very much the history of immigration and integration, of skills and

---

[26] For example, Low, 'The northern interior', 326, Atkinson, *Roots*, 267–8.

[27] H. Médard, 'Introduction', in H. Médard & S. Doyle (eds.), *Slavery in the Great Lakes Region of East Africa* (Oxford, 2007), 13–14.

labour being imported, exported, adopted and adapted. This is most obviously true of Buganda, and in the early history of Bunyoro-Kitara, but it is reflected across the region – often encapsulated in oral tradition through stories of individuals coming with particular skills and winning favour with the king. Later economic histories might make much play of certain stereotypes: the Ganda and their *matooke*, the Nyoro and their sweet potatoes;[28] but in reality their economies were mixed, shared, defined by population movement, settlement and incorporation. By the early nineteenth century, discernible economic patterns had been established across Uganda:[29] rain-fed and riverine agriculture in the lush southern areas between lakes Victoria, Albert and Kyoga, gradually giving way, in westerly and northerly directions, to a greater reliance on livestock, particularly cattle. The Karamojong, in the open savannah and brush land of the northeast, were heavily dependent on cattle, which had cultural as well as material value; the Soga and the Ganda made extensive use of cattle, but these were people socially as well as economically defined by their crowded habitat, with compact homesteads surrounded by banana groves, carefully demarcated from those of their neighbours. Yet economic connections were extensive and of considerable antiquity. Adjacent groups traded items which were rare in their respective home districts, and regional import and export was well-established long before the tentacles of global commerce began to curl around, and through, particular communities.

These foundations allowed for continual innovation and expansion – as well as episodic contraction – in which the relationship between war and production, and even between war and trade, was fundamental, if at times apparently paradoxical. The major military and political entities from the sixteenth century onward were also economic empires; Rukidi's children were not only warriors, but farmers, cattle-keepers, merchants, iron-workers, craftsmen and craftswomen. The cultural and political complexes which stretched out across the region – the Luo migrations, the Chwezi, Bunyoro-Kitara, Buganda – were also commercial networks, signifying economic relationships based on reciprocity, exchange and investment, and made

---

[28] Stanley, *Dark Continent*, I, 274.
[29] One of the best accounts of early economic history – perhaps something of an indictment of recent scholarly neglect – remains Oliver, 'Discernible developments'.

possible by economic specialisation and social stratification. They were also underpinned by networks of spirits and their shrines, as we noted in the previous chapter, one of whose many functions was to safeguard against hunger and dearth, and ensure the fecundity of the earth itself. The earliest foundations had been laid by the first of all the major economic migrations: those of the Bantu-speaking clusters, who must surely be counted amongst Iliffe's memorable 'frontiersmen' of African and indeed global history,[30] moving across the lacustrine zone of eastern Africa in the early centuries CE. They worked iron, were less reliant on livestock and moved onto fertile land close to the lakes and in river valleys, cutting back forest to keep the tsetse fly at bay and clearing land for agriculture. They transformed the environment, and by the early second millennium CE mixed-farming communities had appeared across Uganda.[31] Their patterns of settlement meant more open, relatively dry grassland for occupation by more specialist pastoralists from the north over the next few centuries. They moved in from the northeast from around the fifteenth century onward, and thus did the Luo-speakers become the economic pioneers of these drier lands which were less suited to the agricultural systems of the Bantu-speakers – with whom, nonetheless, there was considerable intermixing.[32] While distinct groups of specialist cattle-keepers became known as Hima in western Uganda, and the pastoralist lifestyle remained discrete in many places, there was intermarriage and interdependence and a good deal of economic fusion.[33] Indeed it was the requirements of coexistence between farmers and herdsmen which advanced the need for new political forms between the fifteenth and seventeenth centuries: as pastoralists moved onto the edges of adjacent farmland, they began to lend cattle to cultivators who prized their manure and milk, and who in turn provided food and other services; and this emergent reciprocity provided opportunities for political entrepreneurs who enforced the arrangement and built on it, leading to more elaborate patron–client systems based on socio-economic distinctions – often framed in ethnic terms – and backed up by increasingly centralised military force. The Hinda state of Nkore, for example, almost certainly has its roots in this entrepreneurial dynamic, a

---

[30] Iliffe, *Africans*, 1.   [31] Schoenbrun, *Green Place*, chapters 1 & 2.
[32] This is a subject explored at length in Ogot, *History*.
[33] Karugire, *History of the Kingdom of Nkore*, 37.

political order which arose in the first instance on an economic frontier.[34]

Certainly Bunyoro's rise took place on the back of economic wealth, including cattle, grains and plantation; the sites of Bigo and Ntusi suggest a regional economy centred on cattle, and imply power over labour.[35] Moreover, the Bito state had access to iron ore and wood for charcoal, and its iron hoes dominated the region for several hundred years. And there was salt, one of the staple commodities in the early modern history of the regional economy. Salt production at Kibiro, on the shore of Lake Albert, underpinned Nyoro expansion in the seventeenth century, and was the focal point of an extensive regional trade over several centuries – though the women who dominated production were granted a fair amount of autonomy over the process, notwithstanding the fact that Kibiro was under Nyoro control and the inhabitants liable to pay tribute to the *mukama*. The women themselves were probably organised according to household or kin, and were in charge of their own plots where they prepared this most precious of commodities before packaging it into small individual loads for transport to local markets.[36] Kibiro was particularly significant, but another important source of salt was at Katwe, near Lake Edward; here, in the nineteenth century, the salt trade made an enormous contribution to the economy of Toro, under whose jurisdiction it fell from the 1830s. Salt was certainly exported far and wide.[37] In Nkore, economic specialism came to denote social and political status, and there was an increasing emphasis on the distinction between Hima herdsmen and Iru farmers; by the eighteenth century, cattle-keeping and farming were almost mutually exclusive and unquestionably represented the parameters of class formation.[38] While the clans were associated with various economic specialisms, the king was arbiter and ritually the embodiment of unity, seeking to represent both farming and herding in ceremonial

---

[34] For example, ibid., chapter 3.

[35] Doyle, *Crisis and Decline*, chapter 1; J. Sutton, 'Ntusi and Bigo: farmers, cattle-herders and rulers in Western Uganda, AD1000–1500', *Azania*, 33 (1998).

[36] G. Connah, E. Kamuhangire, & A. Piper, 'Salt production at Kibiro', *Azania*, 25 (1990) and G. Connah, 'The Cultural and Chronological Context of Kibiro, Uganda', *African Archaeological Review*, 14:1 (1997).

[37] Schweinfurth *et al.* (eds.), *Emin Pasha in Central Africa*, 74, 121–2; UNA A8/1 Tomkins to Comm., 3 October 1901.

[38] Doornbos, *The Ankole Kingship Controversy*, 12–14.

terms. The symbolism of milk and cattle were powerfully represented in the ritual of the royal clan, seeming to suggest the purity of the pastoral lifestyle, but the *mugabe* sought to remain above these socio-economic fault lines – indeed it was critical for the vigour and success of the kingdom that he did so, and the lunar rituals performed by the king were designed to ensure the fecundity of both land and livestock.[39] In the late eighteenth and early nineteenth centuries, it seemed to be working, for Nkore expanded outward from its pastoralist core and took control of swathes of farmland to the west, strengthening central authority over labour – including slave labour – in the mobilisation of agricultural production in the service of the state.[40]

Such economic expansionism – driven by, and in turn maintaining, a political-military complex at the centre of the state – is evident in Buganda, too.[41] From its prosperous agricultural foundations – an inner core of banana plantations on fertile, well-watered land and a cluster of clans whose identities were at least partially defined by skill and renown in a particular sphere of material life – Buganda expanded in the seventeenth and eighteenth centuries, its drive for access to resources indivisible from the development of centralised royal authority. A thriving domestic economy meant thriving local markets in each county or *ssaza*, facilitating economic specialisation and diversification, while chiefs at various levels of administration derived tax revenue from produce and trade.[42] In terms of outward policy, Ganda expansionism was driven in particular by a desire for iron – stemming, perhaps, from the bitter experience of sixteenth-century *kabaka* Nakibinge, who apparently prized his blacksmiths greatly for their role in defending the kingdom.[43] Over the next two hundred years, access to iron underpinned much military adventurism, and was one of the primary motivations in the annexation of Buddu in the mid-eighteenth century. But of equal importance was the seizure of people, and Buganda's success was based on the seizure and incorporation of people from immediate neighbours and across the region. Women in particular were critical, and significant numbers of women were absorbed into the kingdom as concubines in the course of the

[39] Karugire, *History of the Kingdom of Nkore*, 89–90; Patrick G.N. Kirindi, *History and Culture of the Kingdom of Ankole* (Kampala, 2008), 26–7.
[40] Karugire, *History of the Kingdom of Nkore*, chapters 3 & 4.
[41] Médard, *La Royaume*, esp. chapter 1.
[42] Reid, *Political Power*, 21.   [43] Kagwa, *Customs*, 160.

eighteenth and nineteenth centuries – making, involuntarily, an ineffable contribution to its productive and reproductive capacity, for
women both worked in agriculture and produced children for their
new masters.[44] Buganda is perhaps the most visible example of the
significance of the large-scale forcible importation of labour, but it was
common across the region.

These exercises in large-scale economic acquisition and control
in some ways contrasted with developments further north, notably
among the Ateker groups; but here too there were rolling economic
frontiers and evolving systems of livelihood in the seventeenth and
eighteenth centuries.[45] Those Ateker moving through the wetter parts
of western Karamoja may have retained powerful cultural associations with livestock, but they became known by the nickname
Ngikatapa – 'bread people' – because of their development of farming. They were distinguished from a separate Ateker stream inhabiting the drier eastern parts of Karamoja who remained primarily
pastoral, though they too cultivated some grains and supplemented
their diets through hunting-gathering. These tough environments produced distinctive economic as well as cultural identities, and mobile
Ateker communities were continually prone to fissure and fusion and
thus, however productive, were inherently unstable in political terms.
Nonetheless, population increases in the Koten–Magos area – probably the result of improved breeds of cattle – led to the migration of
some groups into central Karamoja in the early eighteenth century;
and in order to offset the constant threats to their cattle of raiding,
drought and disease, these populations developed complex systems of
cattle exchange and mutual assistance which provided some degree of
cohesion between family groups which were essentially self-sufficient
economic units.[46] Meanwhile, the *Ngikatapa* further west struggled
to sustain themselves through more sedentary systems of farming on
land which was not always fit for the purpose. Over-cultivation led
to awful famines, which themselves led to further economic migrations. Yet these could in turn produce new communities, such as the
Jie, Dodos, and Karamojong, the products of a learning process in
which migrants developed more effective and stable mixed-farming

---

[44] For example, Gorju, *Entre*, 123.
[45] Lamphear, *Traditional History*, chapters. 1 & 3; Oliver, 'Discernible
developments', 175–8.
[46] Lamphear, *Traditional History*, 72–90.

systems.[47] Thus, again, were political and cultural identities formulated in the first instance on the frontiers of economic distress and/or opportunism in a pattern which would be repeated through the twentieth century and beyond.

The eighteenth century witnessed a series of economic expansions and contractions in a fertile and vibrant zone between the Nile, lakes Edward and George and Lake Victoria as polities sought access to local trade networks, local industry, local assets.[48] In the age of global commerce in the nineteenth century, states and societies sought comparative advantage at a time of flux while also seeking to cultivate commercial relations as widely as possible. Despite having lost ground to Buganda in the course of the eighteenth and early nineteenth centuries, the Nyoro actually consolidated their position as the dominant economic force in northern and central Uganda in the middle decades of the nineteenth century, taking advantage of the Ganda fixation with Lake Victoria and the merchants coming up from the south. Bunyoro was still a major producer of salt and iron, and through these exports was able to draw Lango and the northern Soga states into an economic system centred on Lake Kyoga. At the same time, Nyoro iron hoes facilitated the expansion of agriculture among the Teso and Langi.[49] Moreover, farming among these populations was diversified through the introduction of groundnuts and sweet potatoes from Bunyoro, which imported ivory, livestock and sesame in exchange.[50] Bunyoro was in effect taking advantage of the dramatic population movements which shaped eastern Uganda in the early decades of the nineteenth century: the Teso in particular, according to oral traditions, were moving in significant numbers out of Karamoja and onto the shores of Lake Kyoga following rapid population increase which in turn necessitated more intensive agriculture.[51] Pastoralists turned increasingly to farming, and pushed south and west, driving competition for land

---

[47] For example, see B.A. Ogot, *Economic Adaptation and Change Among the Jii-speaking Peoples of Eastern Africa* (Kisumu, c.1991).

[48] See, for example, the excellent summation in A.C. Unomah & J.B. Webster, 'East Africa: the expansion of commerce', in John E. Flint (ed.), *The Cambridge History of Africa: Vol 5, from c.1790 to c.1870* (Cambridge, 1976), esp. 289–94.

[49] Low, 'Northern interior', 326–7.

[50] Doyle, *Crisis and Decline*, 44. At least some of the ivory acquired by Bunyoro appears to have been in the form of tribute from the north: see Beattie, *Nyoro State*, 28 and Speke, *Journal*, 530.

[51] Lawrance, *Iteso*, 8–12.

south of Kyoga in northern Busoga. These were fluid and competitive economic frontiers, shaping in the most fundamental ways the communities caught up on them. An arms trade flowed across the frontiers between Buganda and Bunyoro: while Nyoro spear blades were highly valued by the Ganda, Ganda blacksmiths hawked their skills in repairing firearms in Bunyoro. Those markets along the Ganda–Nyoro borderlands also attracted weapons from Karagwe.[52] Kkooki had long been a key regional exporter of iron, not least to Buganda, and in the nineteenth century iron was unquestionably one of the key factors behind Ganda interest in the small kingdom.[53] On the other side of Lake Victoria, iron was imported from Kavirondo to the east by the Soga and the Ganda, who worked it into hoes, and who evidently regarded it as superior in quality to much of the iron found closer to home.[54] In the mid-1870s, Emin Pasha named Rubaga in Buganda, Mpara Nyamoga in Bunyoro and Werhanje in Karagwe as the three major markets in the region. At Mpara Nyamoga, near Hoima, a fabulous array of commodities was exchanged from across the region – including some from considerable distance (copper wire) alongside Ganda bark cloth, and one of the less glamorous factors behind the kingdom's regional economic dominance.[55] A broad arc of borderland reaching from the Nile to Lake Edward linked the Soga, Buganda, Bunyoro, Toro, Nkore and many others in commercial exchange: dried fish, salt, skins, hoes and other iron goods, ivory, livestock, bark cloth, ornaments, jewellery and charms, often purchased with the regional currency, cowry shells, rather than traded in kind. The sources for the second half of the nineteenth century reveal a flourishing regional economy – sometimes centred in established market towns where it might be supervised (and taxed) by local authorities, but just as often carried out along the road, in tiny hamlets, at bends in rivers and anywhere where opportunity presented itself. When the British began to establish forts across southern Uganda in the 1890s and 1900s, sure enough these too became the target of local traders eager for business.[56] At the same time, however, certain commodities – and

[52] J.A. Grant, *A Walk Across Africa* (Edinburgh & London, 1864), 271, 293.
[53] Roscoe, *The Baganda*, 379.
[54] UNA A2/1 Owen to Rhodes, 29 March 1893; G.F. Scott Elliot, *A Naturalist in Mid-Africa* (London, 1896); UNA A2/3 Ansorge to Colvile, 5 October 1894.
[55] Schweinfurth *et al.* (eds.), *Emin Pasha in Central Africa*, 112, 119, 120-1.
[56] Speke, *Journal*, 476, 487; Roscoe, *The Baganda*, 456; UNA A8/7 Paske-Smith to Sub.-Comm., 3 December 1905; UNA A8/7 Manara [?] to Sub.-Comm., 3 November 1905, UNA A2/3 Owen to Colvile, 16 November 1894.

their sites of production – were the source of violent contest, for example the Katwe salt-producing area where in the late nineteenth century there were regular armed tussles between Bunyoro, Nkore and Busongora, seeking to wrest control of this most lucrative business from Toro.[57] Livestock, too, was at the heart of much conflict – a desire to expand herds and control pasture drove Ganda expansion north- ward and westward, and underpinned Nyoro wars against Nkore.[58]

By the late eighteenth century, then, there had emerged across Uganda a network of polities and communities organised around the drive for ever greater control over labour and access to resources. Competition for resource was fierce in the more pastoral north, and there was escalating violent conflict within the Langi and Teso popu- lations from the early nineteenth century, producing further waves of economic migration; for the Teso, indeed, the late nineteenth century was a period of bitter 'civil' war.[59] In southern and central Uganda, large states developed economic strategies aimed at the maximisation of assets both within existing boundaries and beyond them. And it was soon a circular and self-feeding dynamic: resources were needed to fund expanding royal courts and the architectures of power within which they sat, and to feed the armies necessary to defence as well as further adventurism. War was often essential in the pursuit of economic gain in the first instance; but wars themselves could be costly – and in the case of the larger states like Buganda, increas- ingly and sometimes unbearably so – and therefore economic systems became conjoined with military complexes so that the two were indeli- bly intertwined, each serving the other in inseparable nexus. In the realm of commerce, this nexus could seem all the more paradoxical – war can destroy trade, but it can also provide commercial opportuni- ties, and facilitate its control. It also inspired resistance to economic exploitation in various forms – demands for tribute and enslavement in particular – and this resistance would in itself give rise to new polit- ical identities. At the same time, states were not able to directly control swathes of economic activity in any case, and trade and production often carried on beyond the reach of centralised authority.

War and economic policy, again, had long been indelibly inter- twined in the region. Buganda's increasingly aggressive policy towards

[57] Stanley, *In Darkest Africa*, II, 316.   [58] K.W., 'Kings', Part II, 81.
[59] Vincent, *Teso in Transformation*, chapter 1.

the lucrative trade corridor running along the western side of Lake Victoria can be dated to the middle decades of the eighteenth century – during the same period when long-range commerce was expanding – and was focused in large part around the Kagera River and adjacent Kiziba on its southern bank. When Semakokiro's trade representative, Mangagala, was killed in Kiziba towards the end of the eighteenth century – the locals believed he had been cheating them – the *kabaka* dispatched a punitive expedition.[60] In the mid-nineteenth century – possibly after the arrival of the first coastal merchants at his court, the timing is unclear – Suna likewise dispatched a military expedition against Kiziba in what can only have been an attempt to assert control over burgeoning long-distance trade.[61] It was unsuccessful, but it was a signal of intent, and an aspect of a policy which culminated in the formation of a long-range fleet of canoes whose purpose was again to assert Ganda hegemony over Lake Victoria itself.[62] For the same reason was Suna induced to intervene in the Karagwe civil war in a nineteenth-century East African variation of nefarious international funding for military adventures. Suna was given a 'large present of ivory' to send soldiers against the insurgent Rumanika in the mid-1850s – and apparently the bribe was supplied by an Arab merchant, Musa Mzuri, based at Unyanyembe but now resident in Karagwe, a kingdom located on the thriving western trade route. Suna was presumably interested in both securing access to that commerce (and bringing influence to bear on Karagwe politics), while Musa Mzuri evidently believed that Rumanika was the less attractive candidate for the kingship from a commercial viewpoint.[63] Soon after, Mutesa sought to smash commercial links between Karagwe and Bunyoro along Buganda's western flank in the early 1860s,[64] while in later years Mutesa demonstrated the same grand ambition as his father in seeking (again unsuccessfully) a sweeping alliance with the Arabs of Tabora against the Nyamwezi leader Mirambo in the early 1880s in order to dominate commerce west and south of Lake Victoria, or at least to guarantee the security of Ganda caravans in the area.[65] In the end this was achieved through diplomacy rather than armed force – a

---

[60] Kagwa, *Kings*, 97–8, 100.   [61] Ibid., 134–5.
[62] See Reid, 'The Ganda on Lake Victoria'.
[63] Burton, *Lake Regions*, 396–7, 424.   [64] Speke, *Journal*, 544.
[65] See Reid, 'Mutesa and Mirambo', 82–5, CMS G3 A6/0 1881/22 Pearson to
   Mackay, 29 July 1880, Stanley & Neame (eds.), *Exploration Diaries*, 71.

resolution arrived at by necessity, as Buganda was incapable of such an ambitious military operation.[66] To be sure, successful war-making could reap rich rewards, but war was frequently inimical to economic benefit, and could indeed involve great costs – as the frequent disturbances along the critical commercial artery west and south of Lake Victoria demonstrated in the course of the 1870s. And armies themselves were expensive, not least in food terms: an expedition dispatched by Mutesa towards the south end of the Lake had to turn back because it was starving.[67] Nonetheless, viewed over *la longue durée*, we can see the steady escalation of Ganda militarism in response to widening commercial opportunities from the mid-eighteenth to the late nineteenth centuries. It wasn't always met with the kind of success envisaged by strategists at the royal court, but these were the economics of violence aimed at the control of communities and commodities, of people and produce. Ganda warfare, and the military policy of a number of states and societies across Uganda, was at least partially motivated by the opportunities presented by the slave trade, and while there was always a political dimension to military expansionism, the seizure of captives for export was increasingly the object and purpose of military campaigns.

The existence of a permanent coastal merchant 'quarter' in the Ganda capital is testament to the importance of exogenous commercial forces, though familiarity bred a certain contempt over the longer term. When the trader Snay bin Amir, an acquaintance of Burton's at Tabora, visited Suna in the early 1850s, he was (according, presumably, to Snay's own account) feted, much encouraged and provided with all the essentials of life and more. The possibility of an alliance between Buganda and Zanzibar was even discussed: Suna was apparently excited by the prospect, though it evidently came to nothing.[68] Then, in the late 1850s, there was a brief period in which coastal merchants were denied entry into Buganda, probably as a precaution during a time of political vulnerability, namely the death of Suna and the accession of Mutesa.[69] From the early 1860s, however, there was

---

[66] London Missionary Society (LMS) Central Africa, Incoming, Box 4: Southon to Thompson, 17 May 1881, CMS G3 A6/0 1882/14 O'Flaherty to Wigram, 25 December 1881.

[67] Kagwa, *Kings*, 163.   [68] Burton, *Lake Regions*, 404.

[69] Speke, *What Led to the Discovery*, 259, Low, 'The Northern Interior', 334, Speke, *Journal*, 187, Rowe, 'Revolution in Buganda', 50, Reid, *Political Power*, 154.

a permanent merchant presence at the royal capital, though Mutesa now treated them rather more contemptuously: the merchant community lived in fear of the *kabaka*, in an unhealthy part of the capital, and often in hand-to-mouth circumstances.[70] In 1888, Mwanga even briefly prohibited the sale of food and water to foreign traders, apparently as punishment for their sale of guns to Bunyoro – a dangerous game, indeed.[71] These often precarious conditions doubtless prompted foreign residents to grow their own crops, in the process introducing a new number of new ones to the region – including onions and rice, and a range of fruits.[72] Meanwhile, perhaps in an attempt to offset a growing dependence on the resident merchant community, the Ganda regularly dispatched their own long-range trade missions – initially as far as Karagwe, and then by the 1870s further still, to Tabora and even Zanzibar itself.[73]

Still, many others were regular visitors to Buganda in the meantime, such as Hamed Ibrahim, whom Stanley met in Karagwe in 1876, and who had travelled frequently between Buganda and Unyanyembe for many years, using Kafuro in Karagwe as his main base.[74] Of course these representatives of global commerce presented opportunities for profit, but they were frequently regarded with ambivalence, owing to their potential for troublemaking and political interference. The energetic entrepreneur Songura in Buganda was one such character, accused in the mid-1880s – by a missionary source, admittedly – of trying to induce a Ganda canoe flotilla to make war along the lake shore.[75] In Bunyoro, in the early 1870s, a group of Khartoumers who had helped Kabalega gain the throne, were expelled from the kingdom after they tried to claim a rather excessive reward – 'half of Kitara', according to Nyakatura – for their efforts.[76] Bunyoro's relations with northern traders remained strained, and volatile; the Egyptian evacuation of Mruli on the banks of the Nile west of Lake Kyoga by the beginning

[70] Miti, *History of Buganda*, I, 124, Speke, *Journal*, 288, 303, Schweitzer (ed.), *Emin Pasha*, I, 60.

[71] CMS G3 A5/0 1888/244 Gordon to Parker, 6 March 1888.

[72] Schweitzer (ed.), *Emin Pasha*, I, 35, A.R. Tucker, *Eighteen Years in Uganda and East Africa* (London, 1908), I, 88.

[73] Speke, *Journal*, 188, H. Waller (ed.), *The Last Journals of David Livingstone in Central Africa* (London, 1874), II, 226, White Fathers C13/282 Livinhac to Lavigerie, 20 November 1878.

[74] Stanley, *Dark Continent*, I, 356–7.

[75] White Fathers Mission du Bukumbi, I, 17 August 1885.

[76] Nyakatura, *Anatomy*, 111.

of the 1880s brought to an end the thriving trade in which cattle and bark cloth were exchanged for cloth and other items of 'exotic' clothing, such as fezes and slippers.[77] If Kabalega was often suspicious of the intentions of his Sudanese and Egyptian neighbours, so too was Mutesa further south – seeing military threat rather more than commercial opportunity.

International commerce involved the increasing material integration of Uganda. Communities, whether close neighbours or at somewhat further remove, became more closely entwined, and exchange – and movement – between them all the more intimate. This is, after all, something of a truism about the power of commerce. But there are two important caveats to add, which alter the picture somewhat of Uganda's involvement in inexorable globalisation. The first is that trade also meant war: heightened commercial competition led to greatly heightened levels of violent conflict over the apparent benefits of involvement in trade, and thus over territory and communications and above all *access*. This was nothing new in the East African region, but its intensification – and the attendant military and political reform it involved – meant that violence increased in tandem. Secondly, trade meant greater regional division, and differentiation: in terms of the *capacity* to diversify internally, finding the human resources to maintain internal growth and thus absorb demand for key commodities such as ivory and slaves; and in terms of the *access* to trade and its putative benefits. These two fundamental dynamics – the variation in capacity and access – are critically important in understanding the making of the nation. Commerce forged the nation but in violently competitive and unequal ways. This was not only true *between* states and societies, but also *within* them. These developments intersected with the geopolitical accidents of birth which were to the advantage of the Ganda but the disadvantage of the Madi, the Acholi and the Karamojong: by century's end the attitudes of the British towards Buganda and 'the rest' were the outcome of racialised dogma and sheer sociopolitical pragmatism. But the commercial dynamics outlined here suggest that in terms of violence and inequity Uganda appears to be very much a precolonial, not a colonial, creation. Above all it was an era defined by fluid exchange and specialisation, often underpinned by militarised state and social systems. It was, arguably, a commercial golden

---

[77] Wilson & Felkin, *Uganda*, I, 191.

age – mirrored, too, in the political and military innovations of the era – and certainly more 'open' and dynamic than anything that has followed since. There were certainly more opportunities for a lot more people. States sometimes sought to impose restrictions on *who* could trade in what items, and again there were growing social inequalities in the second half of the nineteenth century. Yet this was the era of dynamic, energetic, accomplished and sophisticated productive and commercial networks, which demonstrate the existence of a markedly discrete precolonial zone of interaction and which contradict some of Yoweri Museveni's more scathing comments about the lack of African initiative in the 'pre-modern' age.[78]

Migrant Nation, 2: 'The Traffic in Human Flesh, with all its Accompanying Miseries'[79]

Earlier migratory movements created the seedbeds on which Uganda was founded. Yet there is no point at which the clock of the nation starts ticking, once everyone is present and correct, and history can begin properly. This was a continually evolving, organic, living process, a dynamic which took on new forms in different periods. In the eighteenth and nineteenth centuries, it was the institution of slavery and thus the slave trade itself which involved the mass movement of people in and around the Ugandan region, and, increasingly, out of it, particularly from the 1850s onward. 'Stolen people', to borrow Holly Hanson's phrase,[80] came in the form of local slaves and, perhaps above all, women as concubines and domestic slaves; and this culminated in the export of people, both out of northern Uganda into Sudan and beyond, and across Lake Victoria towards the south and in many cases the East African coast in the second half of the nineteenth century. Remarkably little is understood about the long-term dynamics, operation and impact of the East African slave trade; in comparison with its well-documented and much-studied Atlantic counterpart,

---

[78] See speeches made in 1989 and 1990 – not coincidentally, supposedly the moment of capitalism's greatest triumph – quoted in Museveni, *What is Africa's Problem?*, 172–3, 189.

[79] Clarke (ed.), *Cardinal Lavigerie*, v.

[80] H. Hanson, 'Stolen People and Autonomous Chiefs in Nineteenth-Century Buganda: the social consequences of non-free followers', in Médard & Doyle (eds.), *Slavery*.

the region is poorly served – a discrepancy which is to a large extent linked to methodological challenges and a relative paucity of reliable source material.[81] In some ways, too, the East African slave trade is rather more complicated, involving multiple actors at any given time, driven in several different directions, and overlapping in complex ways with 'domestic' or 'internal' demand. The 'export' of slaves from the region is also complicated, as while a growing number of slaves in the nineteenth century were destined for Zanzibar and Pemba off the Indian Ocean coast, and a few were transported to the Middle East, Arabia and even central Asia, many more probably remained within eastern Africa, to be absorbed – as were their children – into host societies. In this way have a multitude of slave stories disappeared from the historian's view.[82] Epistemological challenges notwithstanding, the movement of slaves both within Uganda and beyond it was a critical dynamic in the making of the modern region. While slavery itself may be of considerable antiquity in the region, we know little about it until more recent centuries. Slave-ownership began to expand dramatically in some areas in the course of the eighteenth century – *before* the major impetus for long-distance export developed from Zanzibar and Khartoum in the early nineteenth century. Many of these slaves were women. In Buganda, for example, for which we have arguably the best (though still sketchy) pre-1800 data, it looks as though the number of women attached to the royal court increased significantly in this period, including foreign female slaves who had been seized in war.[83] This certainly fits with the picture we have of eighteenth-century Buganda as an aggressively expansionist state, arguably at its most potent in terms of regional dominance.[84] One direct outcome of that expansionism – and it may well have been its key motivation – was

---

[81] An selection of older work would include: E.A. Alpers, *The East African Slave Trade* (Nairobi, 1967), N.R. Bennett, *Arab versus European: diplomacy and war in nineteenth-century East Central Africa* (New York & London, 1986), G.W. Hartwig, 'The Victoria Nyanza as a trade route in the nineteenth century', *Journal of African History*, 11:4 (1970).

[82] The methodological challenges – and opportunities – are explored in Médard, 'Introduction'.

[83] Kagwa, *Customs*, 18ff, Gorju, *Entre*, 123. See also the wider social implications of this for women and motherhood in Stephens, *African Motherhood*, esp. chapter 4.

[84] R.J.Reid, 'Human Booty in Buganda: some observations on the seizure of people in war, c.1700–1890', in Medard & Doyle (eds.), *Slavery*.

a huge increase in the number of foreigners arriving in the kingdom and, in one way or another, incorporated into it. As Hanson has argued, this influx profoundly affected forms of economic production and socio-political relations, as the increase in the numbers of non-free people reduced the need of chiefs to compete for the goodwill of 'free' followers.[85]

The Ganda may well have referred contemptuously to all northern peoples as *mudokolo*, and, according to Bartolomayo Zimbe, had a tendency to 'despise other tribes, and any person of any of the other tribes they called him Munyoro'.[86] (For their part, the Nyoro called Buganda *Mhwahwa*, 'land of the wild dogs'.[87]) But the fact is that the Ganda were rather adept at drawing in foreigners and making them their own, whether those outsiders were 'free' migrants or – as was increasingly the case in the eighteenth and nineteenth centuries – captured in war and enslaved. Great value was attached to particular skills, such as iron-working: blacksmiths from Bunyoro, and in particular from the former Nyoro province of Buddu, annexed by Buganda in the mid-eighteenth century, were brought to the capital to work, and many of these were probably war captives in the first instance.[88] Kagwa tells what must in part have been an allegorical story about the enslaved Nyoro potter whose talents made a deep impression on *Kabaka* Kamanya.[89] In the nineteenth century, most slaves in Buganda were 'foreign', whether first-generation or by descent.[90] But Buganda was by no means unique: in Bunyoro, too, considerable stock was placed on the acquisition of foreign slaves – both fertile women and productive male labour – to meet the challenges, demographic and political, of the nineteenth century.[91] This is not to say, of course, that all 'foreign migration' in Uganda in the nineteenth century was coerced; much 'free' movement took place, and was again highly valued.[92] But it is important to emphasise that the incorporation of enslaved labour, mostly through war but also presumably through regional trading networks, was of long-standing in the Ugandan region.

[85] Hanson, *Landed Obligation*, 59–60.
[86] Zimbe, *Buganda ne Kabaka*, 53, Reid, 'Human Booty', 154.
[87] S.Doyle, 'Bunyoro and the Demography of Slavery Debate: fertility, kinship and assimilation', in Médard & Doyle (eds.), *Slavery*, 241.
[88] Kagwa, *Customs*, 160, Reid, 'Human Booty', 155.
[89] Kagwa, *Customs*, 159.   [90] For example, Roscoe, *The Baganda*, 14–15.
[91] Doyle, 'Bunyoro and the Demography of Slavery Debate'.
[92] Médard, 'Introduction', 25.

In the nineteenth century, the influx of people escalated further, but now it was complicated by the fact that many merely passed through various entrepots on their way *out* of Uganda. The escalation of the export trade in people is well attested for the nineteenth century, though further research is doubtless needed to fully understand its operation and impact.[93] The wider East African slave trade escalated dramatically between the 1820s and the 1860s, driven from two main sources: the first, and comparatively better-documented, was the development of Zanzibari commercial interests on the Indian Ocean coast and, later, in the central east African interior itself; the second was the Khartoum-centred trade, organised by Sudanese and Egyptian traders coming from the north. In the 1860s, for example, some 20,000 slaves per annum may have been sold at Zanzibar, according to Sheriff,[94] although Lovejoy warns us that in the 1870s many of these will have come from the southern routes, via Kilwa, not from the northern lacustrine zone.[95] For Uganda itself, we only have the glimpses afforded by contemporary observers – mostly missionaries, and mostly reporting on the Lake Victoria route. Slave exports via the southern route probably cannot be dated much earlier than the 1850s. In return for the sheets of cloth, beads and sundry items offered by coastal merchants, the Ganda, for example, offered solely ivory initially; one Ganda source asserts that Suna 'would never allow the sale of any of his subjects to foreigners'.[96] That, of course, did not preclude the sale of Buganda's neighbouring peoples. By the 1860s, slaves arriving in Unyanyembe from Buganda and Karagwe were regarded as the finest on the market – especially Hima women.[97] While it is questionable whether more wars were actually fought for the purposes of slave gathering, there is no doubt that large-scale extractive state systems such as Buganda used extant patterns of warfare to do just that – although it did not represent a significant shift in terms of a key long-standing objective, namely the capture and absorption of people. Some of these were

---

[93] For example, see the older scholarship in J. Tosh, 'The Northern Lacustrine Region', in R. Gray & D. Birmingham (eds.), *Pre-Colonial African Trade: essays on trade in central and eastern Africa before 1900* (London, 1970) and relevant essays in Ogot & Kieran (eds.), *Zamani*. For a more recent set of studies, Médard & Doyle (eds.), *Slavery*.

[94] Sheriff, *Slaves, Spices and Ivory*, 60, 224–30.

[95] P. Lovejoy, *Transformations in Slavery* (Cambridge, 1983), 151–2.

[96] Zimbe, *Buganda ne Kabaka*, 79.   [97] Grant, *A Walk*, 48.

now earmarked for export.[98] In particular, the export trade tapped into an existing domestic market for female slaves, and women were commonly seized – sometimes individually and opportunistically, at other times by armies on the move – and sold between the 1860s and 1880s, whether to Lake Victorian Arabs or Sudanese further north. Again, Hima women fetched especially high prices.[99] In the course of the 1870s, prices paid for slave exports increased significantly – they quadrupled, according to one source – and especially those for young women, preferred by coastal traders.[100] Missionaries described fresh batches of slaves arriving regularly at the Ganda capital, such as 'old women, and women with children, some of them in the most shocking condition', from Busoga; and in the same group, young boys, 'lean, lank & hungry looking, some mere skeletons'.[101] The 'best' women were often taken by the *kabaka* and his chiefs, such as the 'three hundred wretched creatures', again from Busoga, who had originally been five hundred 'but death by hunger and fatigue had so reduced them'.[102] At the beginning of the 1880s, one missionary source suggested 1,000 slaves per annum were leaving via Buganda's lake ports.[103] The energetic anti-slavery campaigner Alexander Mackay estimated that for the 1880s some 2,000 slaves a year were leaving Buganda via the lake route alone, transported by 'Arab' merchants.[104] These figures do not include any slaves that may have gone overland via Karagwe on the western side of the lake, though by the late 1870s it may be that canoe transported was greatly favoured by the coastal buyers; it was reported in 1879, in any case, that the western land route was to all intents and purposes closed.[105]

Meanwhile estimates for the northern routes are even more difficult to provide any confidence, and what evidence there is, is largely impressionistic. According to John Tosh, the Langi were engaged in regular

---

[98] M. Twaddle, 'The ending of slavery in Buganda', in R. Roberts & S. Miers (eds.), *The End of Slavery in Africa* (Madison WI, 1988), 119, 122, Reid, *Political Power*, 162.

[99] Grant, *A Walk*, 258, Wilson & Felkin, *Uganda*, II, 32, White Fathers Rubaga Diary 1/18 January 1880, Peters, *New Light*, 402, Junker, *Travels*, 550.

[100] Felkin, 'Notes', 746, Schweinfurth *et al.* (eds.), *Emin Pasha in Central Africa*, 117.

[101] CMS CA6/019/13 Pearson to Wright, 29 September 1879.

[102] CMS G3 A6/0 1881/22 Pearson to Mackay, 29 July 1880.

[103] Wilson & Felkin, *Uganda*, I, 189–91.

[104] Mackay, *Pioneer Missionary*, 435.

[105] CMS CA6/016/42 Mackay to Wright, 2 November 1879.

slave raids against the Nyoro from the 1850s onward, targeting women and children especially, and presumably selling large numbers of them northward.[106] Arriving at the key trading settlement of Gondokoro (in present-day South Sudan) in the mid-1860s, Baker described 'a perfect hell . . . The camps were full of slaves, and the Bari natives assured me that there were large depots of slaves in the interior belonging to the traders that would be marched to Gondokoro for shipment to the Soudan . . .'.[107] Ronald Atkinson explains how in the 1850s the arrival of Arabic-speaking traders from Sudan, known among the Acholi as *Kutoria*, marked the beginning of an era of capture and export of people from the region – with the Acholi themselves assisting in raids on their neighbours – while incidentally further spurring the evolution of Acholi ethnic identity.[108] In all probability some slave raiding and kidnapping, even on a low level, continued in northern Uganda and on the borderlands with Sudan until the early years of the twentieth century, owing to the presence of the Mahdist state directly to the north, and Ethiopian raiders pushing across the Rift Valley into Karamoja.

Mackay asserted that '[t]he demand for slaves in Uganda itself is very great, it being only the surplus which is carried off by the Arabs'.[109] Domestic slavery was extremely important across the Ugandan region throughout the nineteenth century, underpinned by routine military expeditions for the purpose. The Nyoro stole Ganda along the Singo and Bulemezi borderlands: in the 1890s, a number of Ganda slaves in Bunyoro, including several hundred women, were 'liberated' by the invading Anglo–Ganda army.[110] Ganda living along the eastern lake shoreline of the kingdom were also vulnerable to enslavement at the hands of the islanders of Buvuma, who frequently dispatched raiding parties right under the nose of the great kingdom.[111] Some Ganda female slaves were freed in Toro in the mid-1890s.[112] The Teso also commonly acquired both male and female slaves, especially from Busoga.[113] The Ganda seized Nyoro and Soga in particular.[114] During the wars of Anglo–Ganda expansion in the mid-1890s, the

---

[106] Tosh, *Clan Leaders*, 86.   [107] Baker, *Albert N'yanza*, I, 68–9.
[108] Atkinson, *Roots*, 267.   [109] Mackay, *Pioneer Missionary*, 435–6.
[110] Macdonald, *Soldiering*, 149, 159, 320, Colvile, *Land of the Nile Springs*, 134, 188.
[111] Stanley, *Dark Continent*, I, 238, 303, Macdonald, *Soldiering*, 149, 159.
[112] A.B. Lloyd, *In Dwarf Land and Cannibal Country* (London, 1900), 163.
[113] Lawrance, *The Iteso*, 97.   [114] See also Reid, *Political Power*, 117, 161–2.

Ganda relished the opportunity, in the words of one British officers, of 'replenishing their harems and slave establishments'.[115] Some of these were retained for domestic usage; others were sold to coastal merchants. The escalation of the export trade brought its own anxieties for the Ganda in particular: anticipating discussions around the role of immigrant labour a generation later, one source remarked in the early 1880s that the Ganda 'are beginning to feel that the exportation of slaves must cease, for if not, they will be compelled to do manual labour work themselves, which . . . they strongly object to'.[116] Undoubtedly, as the export trade reached its apex in the 1880s, major slave-holding societies such as Buganda struggled to balance external demand against internal requirements.[117] Again, it was a looming crisis which foreshadowed the labour shortages of the early colonial period. Even so, by now the future of the export trade was uncertain. There was something of a final throw in the political turmoil at the end of the 1880s, when coastal merchants may have raided on their own account for captives. Large numbers of slaves were also being sold to the north, in Bunyoro, in exchange for ever-rarer ivory.[118] In March 1890, the reinstated Mwanga – displaying a certain amount of cautious contrition – announced the end of the slave trade.[119] It had little immediate effect – in the first half of the 1890s, again, Ganda forces took advantage of the war against Bunyoro to seize slaves[120] – but it was the beginning of the end. A similar dynamic may be assumed for the northern route via Sudan, too, though here it seems safe to suggest that the proportion retained locally was lower, given the nature of local economic systems, and considering that slave-raiding here appears to have been much more directly stimulated by external demand. Overall, the capture and control of people was paramount to economic – and political – success, and represented one of the mainstays of what we might term the precolonial Ugandan economy. It is worth reminding ourselves that the export trade tapped into an existing regional dynamic whereby the seizure of people, followed by various degrees of absorption into host

---

[115] A.B. Thruston, *African Incidents* (London, 1900), 129.
[116] Felkin, 'Notes', 746.
[117] White Fathers C13/5 Livinhac to Lavigerie, 24 September 1879, White Fathers C14/139 Lourdel to his brother, 15 October 1886.
[118] White Fathers C14/190 Lourdel to Superior-General, 8 June 1889.
[119] White Fathers Rubaga Diary 4/12–16 March 1890.
[120] For example, White Fathers Rubaga Diary 4/4–9 August 1890.

societies, formed a core part of the regional economy. External demand now required diversification in terms of captives earmarked for internal and external destination.

It is unclear just how significant the export slave trade really was, quantitatively speaking – however awful for those caught up in it, it may even have been relatively insignificant in quantitative terms. What is important, however, is the import materials received in return – particularly cloth and guns, fundamentally shaping local economy, material culture and systems of warfare; and equally important was the internal system by which people were seized and controlled, and the political, economic and military culture which underpinned it. Slavery within Uganda and the export of slaves itself had its own logic, as these dynamics did elsewhere in Africa. There can be no denying the logic inherent in the acquisition of people with none of the rights of comparatively 'free' farmers and craftsmen and merchants; of controlling labour which brought about the greater productivity of land; of the enhancement of political position through the enlargement of unfree retinues, not least in terms of their deployment at chiefly enclosures in an array of positions and ultimately in their mobilisation for war; in the utilisation of female slaves for the expansion of personal kin and clan groupings. Control of people, in the end, was wealth and political clout; it was also, of course, a potential liability, as all responsibility is – for big men (and not a few women) were required to manage and provide for their expanded enclosures – but it was a risk worth taking. And if that risk was worth it, then the capture and sale of nearby foreigners to merchants from beyond the region was equally so, for here the logic was even more unassailable. For neither the Ganda nor the Acholi nor the Langi – arguably the three biggest handlers of slave exports in the nineteenth century – there was nothing to be lost by the sale of Nyoro, Soga or Madi, and in fact only pecuniary and political gain. The only consideration, especially in Buganda but also in other societies which had come to rely on extensive slave holdings for much of their internal economics, was striking the balance between the opportunities presented by external demand and internal need.

Thus the Ugandan region was characterised by inter-ethnic mobility during this seminal era: forced labour and a sex trade involved the movement of captives within Uganda, and their children frequently adopted the identities of their hosts from the 1900s onward. Tragic though the story is from a purely human standpoint, one could make the case that the regional slave trade and long-standing practice of slavery itself – the forcible incorporation of productive and reproductive labour – is further evidence of integration in much the same way that colonial economies are considered integrative. The absorption of foreign skills and labour was deeply rooted. As with earlier migrations, slavery and the slave trade facilitated both economic growth and the consolidation of political and military authority, rooted in the control of people. Control of people allowed more muscular forms of political authority, military expansion and economic diversification. Thus war in the nineteenth century can be seen to have been circular: the seizure and incorporation of slaves meant bigger retinues and army support systems, the 'easier' control exercised by chiefs over people – people who had fewer 'rights' over land and their own labour. This arguably hardened regional disparity and class status – a situation which would continue into the twentieth century, in terms of a culture of an 'elite' political class having access to labour. Thus the integrative dynamic did *not* mean equitable distribution of power and resource, which is quite a separate issue. Viewed over the long term, this is mostly the story of a drainage of people towards Buganda in particular, notably, as Médard has argued, in conjunction with the collapse of Nyoro hegemony in the course of the eighteenth century.[121] We have noted evidence from Toro and Busoga in the late nineteenth century that this was not all one-way traffic. But there is little question that Buganda was the major beneficiary and despite its gradual military decline in the nineteenth century it remained the single most successful importer of labour. The legacies of the trade and of slavery itself, moreover, were evident in the decades that followed, not least in attitudes towards particular forms of labour, and classes of labour; and in the regional imbalance that it had cemented, for it ultimately involved the chronic underdevelopment of those regions from whence most people had been stolen – the northwest and Bunyoro, in particular. By the same token, there can be little question that its operation had rigidified ideas about ethnic superiority and chauvinism, especially among the kingdoms of the southern forest, and specifically within Buganda, not least with regard to the value and contribution of the northern peoples. Hardened concepts about the hierarchy of culture implicit within the geographical order would endure, indeed harden further, into the twentieth century. These ideas

---

[121] Medard, 'Introduction', 13.

would now intersect with new migratory patterns which are just as important in understanding the making of modern Uganda.

The Road to *Magendo*

On the eve of decolonisation – that moment, in the early 1950s, between the hardships of the Second World War and the brave new world of sovereign statehood – the economic prospects of much of Africa were bright, or were at least cause for some optimistic projections.[122] The post-war boom pushed up world prices for a range of cash crops, and while African farmers were by no means 'wealthy' – in any case a relative and thus problematic term – neither were they among the world's poorest; the rural economy was booming. In industry, too, the outlook was positive in the 1950s. Even beyond the exceptional cases such as industrialised South Africa, there had been a post-war investment in mining across the continent, and manufacturing increased accordingly; there were developments, too, in energy supply.[123] Does this generalisation hold true for Uganda? On the face of it, yes. *Prima facie*, the Ugandan economy looked set fair in c. 1950, overall, despite some difficulties: it had a thriving and well developed commercial sector, based on a robust export economy which was centred on coffee and cotton; it had a decent railway and road infrastructure; labour was mobile and cheap; new sources of electricity were being developed, harnessing the power of the Nile north of Jinja; and while mineral exploitation was still, relatively, in its infancy, there were moves in this direction and a light manufacturing sector was emerging. For the colonial administration, the 'pearl of Africa' was becoming its little nugget of economic prosperity in the heart of British East Africa. Indeed, Uganda's annual GDP growth (depending on which source we believe) averaged 5.9 per cent between 1962 and 1971, anticipating more recent, much-celebrated rates.[124]

---

[122] Iliffe, *Africans*, 260.

[123] Frederick Cooper, *Africa since 1940: the past of the present* (Cambridge, 2002), 92ff.

[124] Vali Jamal, 'Changes in poverty patterns in Uganda', in Hansen & Twaddle (eds.), *Developing Uganda*, 74. A figure of 5.8 per cent is given in Andrew Byerley's entry for Uganda in John Middleton & Joseph Miller (eds.), *New Encyclopaedia of Africa* (Detroit, 2008), Vol. V, 120. From the perspective of the mid-1960s, E.J. Stoutjesdijk, *Uganda's Manufacturing Sector: a*

This is, however, a somewhat superficial reading – as macroeconomic assessments often are. It is certainly true that within a generation, by the middle of the 1970s, the Ugandan economy had been to all intents and purposes destroyed – its assets wasted, its foreign exchange depleted, the public sector bloated and ineffective, and the thriving commercial sector replaced by a black market – known locally as *magendo* – in which goods and services were exchanged in the shadows of the swollen and corrupt state.[125] Was this the outcome of indigenous incompetence, of the wilful and wanton destruction wreaked on the economy by kleptomaniacs in uniform? Or did it suggest, in fact, that the economic system bequeathed to the Obote regime by the British had not been as robust as it apparently seemed at the time? The answer, to an extent, was a political one – native ineptitude, said those apologists for British rule who shook their heads in indignant horror at the statist dogma espoused by Milton Obote and then the economic illiteracy of Idi Amin; the long-term structural flaws inherited from the colonial economy, claimed those who believed imperialism had intrinsically disadvantaged African economies from the outset, and who argued that only now, in independence, were those weaknesses cruelly exposed. What is certainly true is that the colonial economy had been nowhere near as 'open' as might be supposed. It had excluded the vast majority of Africans from the lucrative export sector, and reduced most to the role of marginalised and exploited manual labour. A burgeoning Indian community had been favoured by the British in terms of export markets and a range of other investments in retail, cash crops and light industry. Within the African economy itself, social mobility had, if anything, decreased under the British; for ultimately it was those with access to land and political as well as financial resources who 'benefited' from colonial economics, and an increasingly rigidified plutocracy characterised the Ugandan social structure, limiting the ability to engage profitably with the economy and to effect positive economic change in the longer term to a narrow social group of landholders and lineages close to the British administration.

By the 1950s, the Ugandan region, especially southern Uganda, had undergone a century and a half of economic transformation – a

---

contribution to the analysis of industrialisation in East Africa (Nairobi, 1967), 3, offers 3.9 per cent for the period between 1954 and 1964.

[125] For example, Nelson Kasfir, 'State, Magendo and class formation in Uganda', *The Journal of Commonwealth and Comparative Politics*, 21:3 (1983), 85.

veritable revolution in terms of global contact and exchange, and of dramatically changing values in land and labour. In many ways, the 1950s was the 'moment' when Ugandans might have consolidated the putative gains of that revolution in economic affairs, but also modified and improved the extant system in anticipation of independence so that many more Ugandans might enjoy its benefits. It is, therefore, something of a watershed, a moment between past and future in which Ugandan economic agency is paramount but in which, at the same time, certain processes and dynamics of long-standing – notably the disproportionate influence wielded by 'external' actors, including foreign markets and buyers, and the inequality of access which had been the hallmark of the commercial revolution from the late eighteenth century onward – become evident in the starkest of ways. Certainly, it is worth noting the apparent ease with which successive postcolonial regimes actually managed to decimate the economy itself, a feat achieved in little more than a couple of decades after independence; this suggests an economy which was, indeed, rather more fragile and built on rather less secure foundations than our opening gambit might indicate.

The roots of that fragility lie in the crises and upheavals of the late nineteenth century, which were as much the outcome of economic policies and shifts as of political affairs. In Buganda, Mwanga's overthrow in 1888 was the culmination of an economic crisis – albeit one with obvious political dimensions, given that the young *kabaka* was testing the boundaries of his own authority in an increasingly uncertain world. His violent and predatory collection of livestock across the kingdom in 1887 demonstrated a desperation to impose himself as king, as well as revealing the potential fragility of the state's economic system.[126] And then there was his 'royal lake' project, in which '[e]verybody in the country, chief and commoner' – Zimbe records, with perhaps a little hyperbole – was commanded to dig and carry soil, or face heavy fines.[127] It was an exercise in royal excess, and though the artificial lake was indeed created – it is still there today – it prompted an alliance of young chiefs keen on his ouster. These young chiefs, identifying themselves variously in Christian and Muslim camps, moved against Mwanga in September 1888, and though there were numerous

---

[126] Zimbe, *Buganda ne Kabaka*, 156.
[127] Ibid., 148, 153, 156, Ashe, *Chronicles*, 93.

factors – not least his murder of converts two years earlier – Mwanga's abuse of his economic prerogatives was unquestionably one of the most significant. There was trauma, too, in terms of wider economic shifts. It is a broadly accepted wisdom that much of eastern Africa – Uganda included – experienced the onset of colonial rule in economic terms very differently from, and rather more traumatically than, elsewhere in Africa, notably much of coastal West Africa.[128] Merchant peoples along swathes of the Atlantic coast had long been involved in commercial agriculture by the late nineteenth century, and so the establishment of a colonial economy was marked by a fair amount of continuity. In the eastern African interior, including around Lake Victoria, the situation was markedly dissimilar. Here, there was no commercial agriculture in the conventional sense – beyond the selling of crops to resident merchants – and entire export economies were based on two ultimately finite resources: people and elephants. Ivory was indeed a rapidly disappearing commodity by the 1880s; between the late 1870s and the mid-1880s in Buganda, Mutesa and Mwanga were already struggling to get hold of it, reflecting their political inability to enforce tributary relationships (for example, with the Soga chieftaincies) but also the long-term depletion of elephant herds themselves.[129] In this sense economic stress precipitated political crisis for Buganda, which by the 1890s was marginal as coastal traders headed to Bunyoro and Busoga for ivory; the Ganda themselves gave the Soga firearms in exchange for it.[130] Moreover, by the early 1890s, the export of slaves was becoming next to impossible, owing in part to the greatly weakened position of coastal merchants in Buganda following the civil war, and in part to the increased European presence – both British and German – around Lake Victoria and beyond. That brought an abolitionist dynamic to bear on the region, even though in the case of both the British and the German colonial administrations there would be rather greater flexibility towards – and, in effect, tolerance of – forms of servitude itself. And so neither slaves nor ivory were commodities with a future: 'progress towards an inevitable dead end', as Andrew Roberts

---

[128] See, for example, Hopkins, *Economic History*.

[129] CMS CA6/010/48 Felkin's Journal, 17 March 1879, CMS G3 A6/0 1884/55 Mackay's Log, 5 January 1884, CMS G3 A6/0 1885/98 Mackay to Wigram, May 1885.

[130] UNA A2/1 Munworthy to Williams, 1 February 1893, UNA A2/1 Memo by Williams, 1 March 1893.

characterised the economic situation of the Nyamwezi further south in the same period.[131] The onset of colonial rule in the 1890s and early 1900s, in that sense, was characterised by discontinuity and rupture.

In other ways, too, the 1890s were a turbulent period for the regional economy – not least in those areas where the great cattle epidemic known as rinderpest decimated herding communities in particular but also the mixed economies characteristic of the Ugandan region.[132] Herds in Bunyoro and Buganda, for example, were devastated; we have less data about the pastoralist communities further north for this period, but the impact can be guessed at. Moreover, rinderpest, compounding the political upheavals and the impact of long-term slaving activities of recent years, led to depopulation as communities moved in search of pasture, food and water; as a result, bush and wildlife encroached, bringing with them the tsetse fly and contributing to the outbreak of sleeping sickness around the Lake Victoria shoreline by the beginning of the 1900s.[133] Tens of thousands of people died, notably in Busoga and on the offshore islands, and the British launched one of their earliest large-scale public health campaigns, evacuating entire communities from the worst affected areas. The human variant of sleeping sickness was regarded, in the early 1900s, as one of the most terrible blights affecting Africa – with a public presence akin to HIV-AIDS in more recent times – and as justifying imperial intervention; it came, again, at a time of remarkable political and economic transformation across southern Uganda.[134] Elsewhere, political actions had profound economic consequences. Nowhere was this more dramatically or tragically demonstrated than in Bunyoro, where Kabalega's war with the Ganda and the British in the 1890s wrought economic catastrophe – not least because the British themselves waged a deliberately economic war, burning crops and destroying villages, while their Ganda allies generally despoiled the country with impunity. Thus was Bunyoro – one of the pillars of the regional economy, long the fount

---

[131] A.D. Roberts, 'Nyamwezi trade', in Gray & Birmingham (eds.), *Pre-Colonial African Trade*, 73.
[132] UNA A26/4 Lugard to Admin.-Gen., IBEAC, 13 August 1891, F.D. Lugard, 'Travels from the East Coast to Uganda', *Proceedings of the Royal Geographical Society*, 14 (1892), 823.
[133] CMS G3 A5/0 1892/89 Baskerville's Journal, 18 November 1891, Thomas & Scott, *Uganda*, 299.
[134] Eric M. Fèvre, *et al.* 'Re-analysing the 1900–1920 sleeping sickness epidemic in Uganda', *Emerging Infectious Diseases*, 10:4 (2004), Low, 'Uganda', 111–12.

of economic innovation and material culture, and one of the centres of commerce, resurgent since the 1870s – laid waste at the close of the nineteenth century and the outset of the colonial era. While the Ganda had their problems, these were as nothing compared to the devastation countenanced by the Nyoro at the dawn of the twentieth century.[135]

For perhaps a century, between the 1770s and the 1870s, imported cotton cloth had been largely monopolised by socio-political elites: Burton tells us of Buganda that there were tight restrictions on the import of cloth, while Speke likewise suggests that terrible penalties awaited anyone outside the royal court who managed to get hold of it.[136] But in the last decades of the nineteenth century it became something of a common currency – and one which was characterised by a great deal of local variation in value and popularity, certainly in Buganda, where tastes were highly sophisticated, the outcome of long-term exposure to cloth itself.[137] The rapid growth of imported cotton cloth as a prized and increasingly common commodity would eventually undermine one of the mainstays of the local economy, the production of bark cloth, but it was not an overnight process. The displacement and ravaging of communities during the Ganda civil wars meant the collapse in the making of bark cloth in the early 1890s in what was a clear sign of socio-economic distress.[138] Yet in the early 1900s, trade between Buddu and Ankole – bark cloth carried from the former in exchange for cattle from the latter – was flourishing, if now vulnerable to the strictures of zealous German and British colonial officials.[139] Still, by the 1930s, bark cloth production was in decline, limited to a small group or even a single individual in every village, and bearing out the more general observation that imported cloth did great damage to East Africa's textile industry.[140]

For many Ugandans, however, involved in neither slaves or ivory, this was the age of seamless continuity, not rupture; old economies

---

[135] Doyle, *Crisis and Decline, passim*; it is an overarching theme which is quickly evident in interviews with Nyoro today.

[136] Burton, *Lake Regions*, 404–5, Speke, *Journal*, 345.

[137] UNA A26/4 Lugard to Admin.-Gen., IBEAC, 13 August 1891, UNA A4/13 Smith to Comm., 7 November 1898.

[138] For example, WF C14/192 Lourdel to Superior-General, 25 January 1890.

[139] UNA A8/1 Prendergast to Jackson, 3 September 1901, UNA A8/4 Anderson to Sub.-Comm., 6 January 1904.

[140] For example, Lucy Mair, *An African People in the Twentieth Century* (London, 1934), 95.

persisted, thriving underneath the colonial economic order and largely irrelevant to it. The ancient trade in salt, for example, continued well into the twentieth century, notably that between the production sites at Katwe and Kibiro and Toro and Ankole. Therefore, while the introduction of cash crops in the 1900s – chiefly cotton, to begin with – was indeed transformative, two elements are important to highlight. The first is that the economic shift tended to benefit many of the same types of people who had in fact been beneficiaries under the *ancien régime* economy of the nineteenth century – that is to say, unsurprisingly, the royal court, those with access to chiefly power as well as chiefs themselves. There was no profound social shift towards ordinary producers, even if some of these would seek to exercise power in the years ahead; no 'opening up' of the economic system towards wider participation and control. The international export economy of the 1920s would look very similar to that of the 1860s, in terms of its hierarchical nature. The most dramatic difference, indeed, was not in terms of the African structures, but in the influx of Asian businessmen and investors who came to dominate the actual export side of things. In that sense, later economic-driven political protest aimed at the Indian control of the export economy was led by Ugandans who were not interested *per se* in the opening up of the economy, but largely in their exclusion from its benefits. The second issue to highlight is that in the early twentieth century Uganda returned to a situation in which demand for labour for internal use was high. In other words, understood over *la longue durée*, the export of slaves was both remarkably short-lived – lasting little more than half a century, in effect, between the 1830s and the 1880s – and historically anomalous, in that in the broadest possible terms the imperative had long been to attract and incorporate labour locally. Following a hiatus in the 1890s and 1900s, Uganda reverted to a situation of labour *shortage* in which labour was needed to fuel and maintain an expanding economy – as had been the case across much of southern Uganda, especially Buganda, between the sixteenth and nineteenth centuries.

As elsewhere in early colonial Africa, there was quickly an imperative to make newly founded territories pay for themselves. Colonies now became economic units, and increasingly most other realms of life were subordinate to financial exigencies. Southern Uganda seemed ripe for economic transformation, given that its previous commercial staples – slaves and ivory – had shuddered to a halt, and that there was in place by 1900 a viable and (relatively) stable political system which could be harnessed in pursuit of an equally viable and stable cash economy.[141] It was also identified as having rich agricultural potential, with high rainfall and fertile soil cover. First, however, there was the issue of communications and transport; Uganda was, after all, land-locked. Economic transformation was to be engendered by the single metre-gauge railway line – known as the 'Uganda railway', even though the vast bulk of the line ran through Kenya – approved by the colonial government in 1895, and on which work began at Mombasa in 1896. In 1901, the line reached Kisumu, on the northeast corner of Lake Victoria. Within a few years, it was extended to Kampala itself, and thence out west, towards Fort Portal.[142] In the 1920s, branch extensions were completed to Soroti in Teso district, and to Jinja. In sum, the railway would slash transportation costs and ultimately enable Uganda to pay for its own administration.[143] It ensured that bulky items of relatively low value could be produced in Uganda itself and exported towards the coast, demonstrating in the most vivid of terms – despite considerable scepticism, even ridicule, in Britain itself – the power of British imperialism to 'open up' the clenched interior of the continent and expose it to the civilising power of commerce. It was richly appropriate indeed that the chief export, cotton, was to be cultivated on the land of a class of Protestant Ganda chiefs who had become the pillars of the colonial project: Uganda was the fulfilment, if anywhere was, of Livingstone's mid-nineteenth century vision. The willingness of the notoriously parsimonious British Treasury to advance the funds (on the promise of tremendous profits to come) in the first place was a reflection of the impact which the Ganda in particular had had on the British imperial psyche.

---

[141] For a more detailed account than is possible here, see Ehrlich, 'The Uganda Economy'.

[142] 'Uganda Railway Construction', UKNA CO 614/7 and subsequent through to CO 614/12, 'Railways: proposed Kampala-Mubende railway extension', UKNA CO 536/166/2, 18 March 1931–14 September 1932.

[143] Nonetheless, the financing of construction was a continual source of discussion and, at times, anxiety: 'Loans from imperial funds for the improvement of East African and Ugandan railways', UKNA T 1/11651/14814 [1914], 'Financing of loan construction on branch lines...', UKNA CO 533/376/7 [1928–29], Liability for cost of construction...', UKNA CO 533/472/7, 1 May 1936–30 June 1937.

And so, enter the British Cotton Growing Association, established in 1902 to foster the expansion of cotton production across the empire; and as Ehrlich pointed out, the early 1900s was a good moment at which to experiment with raw materials, with the global markets for the latter buoyant in the years before the First World War.[144] In 1904 the colonial government and the Uganda Company distributed several different types of cotton seed among chiefs in Buganda, Bunyoro and Busoga in an attempt to discover which were best for which local conditions. Ganda chiefs in particular took up the opportunities with gusto, although the early results were disappointing: cotton arriving from Uganda in 1906–7, for example, was often badly stained (several varieties being mixed in the same bale). In 1908 the administration intervened decisively, identifying one seed to be cultivated which the government itself would distribute, and standardising production procedures. After a season of uncertainty, by 1910 cotton output had increased significantly and the standard had improved markedly.[145] In the years to come, thanks to a combination of robust colonial intervention and Ganda entrepreneurialism, Uganda became established as a major producer of quality cotton – no mean feat in a discerning and competitive global marketplace.[146] Cotton would force the pace of social and economic change until the 1940s. To a very considerable extent, moreover, the central purpose behind the creation of Native Authorities was the harnessing of commercial forces which could act as the authorities over and guarantors of economic production: they were responsible for the collection of tax (on which chiefs were carefully briefed[147]), the distribution of cotton seed and the encouragement of peasant farmers to cultivate cotton itself. To lubricate the wage-labour system, a cash economy was introduced in 1901, with the Indian rupee used as currency throughout the territory. The overarching emphasis of the colonial economy was on agricultural production, rather than

---

[144] Ehrlich, 'The Uganda Economy', 399 and Torbjörn Engdahl, *The Exchange of Cotton: Ugandan peasants, colonial market regulations and the organisation of the international cotton trade, 1904–1918* (Uppsala, 1999).

[145] Ehrlich, 'The Uganda Economy', 404–5.

[146] 'Cotton Industry: reports on state of industry and cotton policy in Uganda', UKNA CO 536/155/6, 12 March–28 November 1929, 'Cotton industry: proposed abolition of the Cotton Board in favour of the Uganda Cotton Association...', UKNA CO 536/156/5, 15 April 1929–18 February 1930.

[147] See, for example, *Instructions re. Collection of Poll Taxes by Chiefs in the District of Toro (translated into Lutoro)*, (Entebbe, c. 1913).

anything that might be termed 'industrial'. Within a few years
the economy had diversified to include coffee, rubber, tobacco and
sugarcane.[148]

With the railway, and with cash crops, came the Ugandan Asian
community – the conceptual descendants of the Baloch 'Zigeye' half a
century earlier, beginning with Allidina Visram, who opened a supply
store near Lugard's fort in 1900 and who went on to open branches
in Jinja, Mbarara, Masaka, Hoima and as far north as Nimule and
Gondokoro.[149] The forerunners of this most controversial of modern
immigrant communities had been the Sikh soldiers – the clearest manifestation of British 'martial race' thinking – serving in the colonial
army from the 1890s. Soon, other Sikhs came, as skilled labourers and
professionals; the gel in the British Empire.[150] Many of these were comparatively affluent, and were soon setting up business across the Protectorate and taking advantage of the opportunities offered by the colonial economic frontier. They did so alongside another community with
an increasing presence, Shi'a Muslims from Gujarati state in India –
less affluent, at least initially, and mostly part of the indentured labour
force brought in to build the Uganda railway in the late 1890s and
early 1900s. Many stayed, and formed entrepreneurial business communities in the decades ahead, as their compatriots did in neighbouring
Kenya and Tanzania. Their presence, however logical in an imperial
context, would prove to be profoundly destabilising in terms of Ugandan economic opportunities and social mobility, and many Ugandans
would come to behold them with simmering resentment.[151]

Within a generation, the regional imbalance in terms of economic
'development' had largely crystallised. By the end of the 1920s, southern and central Uganda – Buganda, Eastern Province and Western
Province (minus Kigezi) – had become the main zones of cash crop
production, while Kigezi and the vast region north of the Nile was a
labour reserve for the cotton and coffee farms and sugar plantations

---

[148] For example, C.C. Wrigley, 'The changing economic structure of Buganda', in
Fallers (ed.), *The King's Men* and Ingham, *Making of Modern Uganda*,
chapter 3.

[149] Ingham, *Making of Modern Uganda*, 98.

[150] See, for example, S. Constantine, 'Migrants and Settlers', in J. Brown & W. R.
Louis (eds.), *The Oxford History of the British Empire, Vol IV: the twentieth
century* (Oxford, 1999), 178–9.

[151] A good overview is to be found in J.S. Mangat, 'The Immigrant Communities:
the Asians', in Low & Smith (eds.), *History of East Africa*, III.

spreading across the Lake Victoria zone. The expanding railway network ensured that cotton could be transported in bulk to British textile
mills, but of greater relevance in terms of local economics was the fact
that the purchase, ginning and exporting of cotton was highly regulated and circumscribed.[152] It was dominated by the burgeoning Asian
community and Africans were largely excluded from it, chiefly as a
result of the cost of the requisite licenses and fees which were excessive
for the vast majority of Africans.[153] Any further attempts by African
producers to enter the export sector were blocked by government regulation. Still, ironically enough, land remained largely in African hands:
even Ugandan Asians were prohibited from owning land, and while
settler agriculture was toyed with as an idea for a few years before the
First World War,[154] it was largely abandoned by the beginning of the
1920s, in large part because the 1900 Agreement – the landmark treaty
between Britain and Buganda which formed the constitutional bedrock
of the Protectorate – precluded foreign ownership of land on the scale
necessary. In any case, it was hardly needed given Buganda's success as
a centralised economic engine – unlike the situation in Kenya, where
there were none of the state-systems of southern Uganda which might
be harnessed in pursuit of economic growth. In the end, less than 1 per
cent of land in Uganda was allocated to non-Africans. Within Buganda,
meanwhile, a new class of cotton chiefs did very well out of the new
economic system. The 1900 Agreement had established private land
ownership in Buganda – the only territory in the Protectorate where
this was the case. Elsewhere, defined 'tribal groups' had land for the use
of its inhabitants, but in Buganda, private landlords could compel the
production of cotton by a peasant class and reap the benefits through
rent and sales of cotton to ginners.[155] The Ganda were, of course, the
masters of a particularly favourable environment with enormous commercial potential; but they themselves were regarded as worthy of this
act of supposed British technological and economic benevolence.

---

[152] 'Cotton Ordinance, 1926: proposed introduction of legislation to regulate and
control the Uganda cotton industry', UKNA CO 536/141/7, 30 March-29
June 1926.
[153] Thomas & Scott, *Uganda*, Appendix III, 510.
[154] Ehrlich, 'The Uganda Economy', 410, Pratt, 'Administration and Politics',
477–8.
[155] Engdahl, *Exchange*, passim, Hanson, *Landed Obligation*, chapter 6.

The arrival of the first steam locomotives in eastern Uganda in the early 1900s was the culmination of a process of economic transformation beginning in the late eighteenth century, when contacts with external commercial forces had begun to intensify. In effect, the period between the 1760s and the 1900s may be considered, in the round, as encompassing a series of commercial *revolutions* which define modern Uganda. The first, broadly, was that between roughly the 1760s and the 1830s, the era of heightened, if indirect, long-range commerce intersecting with a vibrant local and regional network of production and exchange which was itself made possible by the expansion of political scale across the region. The second, from the 1840s to the 1880s, was the age of direct global commerce and the integration of Uganda with larger commercial and productive systems – a process made possible both by African entrepreneurialism and by the physical presence of merchants from considerable distances at key entrepôts and political centres across the region. The third transformative stage, flowing directly out of the first and second, was characterised by the creation of a colonial economic system between the 1890s and the 1910s – a putatively 'new' system but one which in fact resembled, and drew upon many of the mores and operandi of, the trading and productive (and extractive) dynamics of the long nineteenth century. Therefore the 'disjuncture' thesis – the argument for a fundamental restructuring of the Ugandan economy from slaves and ivory to cash crops – must not be exaggerated. In many respects, what happened in the early years of the twentieth century was a continuation of processes and dynamics underway of the previous century. Still, for sure there were some novel elements. Arguably, while there was a reversion to a reliance on mobile reserves of immigrant labour, the economy became even less 'open', and in fact was even more rigid than had been the case during the era of innovative commercial frontiers between the sixteenth and the nineteenth centuries. There is little doubt that while this was the era of globalisation, in which local economies became in one way or another contingent upon distant markets and economic actors, this was not in itself a positive development for most ordinary Ugandans with limited access to land and power. It was, at best, ambiguous; and we do not espy, nor ascribe to, some kind of inexorable if uneven march towards economic modernity. There were some very clear downsides to the commercial revolution in the era of globalisation; and if the roots of Museveni's much-vaunted neoliberalism and market-oriented economics lie, oddly enough, in the commercial shifts of the mid-nineteenth century, then so, too, do the deleterious consequences of that economic philosophy: a sharp increase in inequality, and a marked slowdown in social mobility.

Still, there was indeed disjuncture of a particular kind in the infrastructure that now snaked its away across the Protectorate, and the modern (colonial) economic history of Uganda can in many ways be told in the history of roads and railways. And these tracks of empire were also emblematic of a particular economic vision – in the case of Uganda, the vigorous exploitation of southern cash crops using a class of landholding chiefs as commercial pioneers to encourage their tenant farmers to cultivate cotton, tea, sugar, coffee. The colonial state was not averse to admonishing those chiefs when they were seen to be absent landlords – witness the intervention in 1928 to cap the rents which could be imposed on farmers by chiefs.[156] Still, soon much of the business of large-scale production and marketing was in the hands of Asian merchants and investors, whose domination of the export market would lead, in time, to profound strains within Ugandan society. A successful export economy depended, it seemed, on the concentration of commercial land in relatively few hands; and thus one especially dramatic long-term consequence of the colonial economy – and, as we have seen, of the early constitutional settlement – was the politicisation of land not only as a tangible resource, but also as a battleground for culture, identity and rights. Nonetheless, peasant production – African labour – remained at the heart of the economy. Between 1945 and 1960 coffee and cotton contributed over 75 per cent of Uganda's export earnings – in the 1950s, coffee surpassed cotton as the chief cash earner[157] – and Buganda and Eastern Province, where the vast bulk of cash crop acreage was located, alone generated a similar figure, around 75 per cent, of total monetary income.[158] The trajectory of the

---

[156] C.P. Youe, 'Peasants, planters and cotton capitalists: the "dual economy" of Uganda', *Canadian Journal of African Studies*, 12:2 (1978) and for the wider context, see Michael Twaddle, 'The *Bakungu* chiefs of Buganda under British colonial rule, 1900–1939', *Journal of African History*, 10:2 (1969).

[157] The development can be traced, for example, in 'Reorganisation of the coffee industry in Uganda', UKNA CO 822/336 [1952–3] and 'Uganda: coffee prices', UKNA FCO 141/18462 [1961–2].

[158] 'Cotton industry in Uganda', UKNA CO 822/1756 [1957–9], Colonial Office, *Uganda: report for the year 1956* (London, 1957), 50–1, Uganda Protectorate, *Annual report for the Eastern Province, for the year ended 31 December 1959* (Entebbe, 1959), 15. The single best account of this later period remains Lury, 'Dayspring mishandled?'.

colonial economy reinforced a very basic north-south dichotomy. Uganda north of the Nile was essentially seen as economically unviable, except as a pool of migrant labour necessary to the functioning of the southern cash crop economy. Men from West Nile, Madi, Acholi and Lango travelled south periodically, as we see below, to earn the cash to pay their taxes as well as increasingly expensive bridewealth. By the end of the 1920s, indeed, cash crops were actively discouraged across much of northern Uganda in order to ensure the steady supply of labour to the southern economy. More generally, development initiatives in the north were infrequent and limited in scope; for example, there was no attempt to regulate and thus enhance the livestock economy, or to master livestock disease in the way that sleeping sickness had elicited such a dramatic programme of action on the shore of Lake Victoria. Elsewhere, economic investment was noticeably absent, as in Bunyoro, where development was largely non-existent before the 1930s and where farmers eked out a harsh existence in the face of outbreaks of disease, notably sleeping sickness.[159]

Colonial economic policy was for several decades essentially agrarian, rooted in a vision of rural development which would somehow benefit all concerned, if in different ways and at different speeds.[160] It was also feared that local industrialisation would eventually lead to a reduction in crucial revenue from import duties on manufactured goods, while also disrupting organic African 'development'.[161] Industrialisation had been limited through the first half of the twentieth century, confined to some small-scale mining projects in western Uganda, and periodic interest in possible oil reserves in the Albertine basin beginning in the 1920s.[162] The sugar refinery at Kakira and the production for market of tea and cotton had involved light industrial works in support of an essentially plantation economy. This only began to change in the 1940s, in the wake of Colonial Development and Welfare acts (1940 and 1945) which signalled something of a gear-change in British attitudes towards economic growth, in part

---

[159] See, for example, Nyangabyaki Bazaara, 'The Food Question in Colonial Bunyoro-Kitara: capital penetration and peasant response', unpublished MA dissertation, Makerere University, 1988.

[160] For the classic underdevelopment thesis, see E.A. Brett, *Colonialism and Underdevelopment in East Africa, 1919–1939* (London, 1973).

[161] Ibid., 75–7.

[162] For example, 'Oil: potentialities of Lake Albert oilfields...', UKNA CO 536/143/4, 29 September 1926–7 January 1927.

spurred by the stresses and strains of the Second World War.[163] Now
there was state-led industrialisation, implemented in 1946 under the
umbrella of a Ten Year Development Plan which sought to create
processing industries in particular:[164] textile mills, breweries, cement
factories and paper manufacturing were among the projects initiated under the auspices of the Uganda Development Corporation,
founded in 1952, and a copper ore processing plant was built at
Kilembe, near Kasese, which in turn had significant implications for
the railway network in western Uganda.[165] Leading the private investment charge were the big Ugandan Asian corporations, Madhvani
and Mehta, using funds acquired through years in the lucrative sugar
sector.[166] Yet Uganda had neither coal nor oil, and thus perhaps the
most dramatic and visible manifestation of late colonial industrial
technology was the Owen Falls Dam at Jinja, completed in 1954
with the aim of producing electricity to further power the minor
industrial revolution envisaged for the territory.[167] Still, the hoped-
for industrial hub around Jinja never quite materialised, and on the
eve of independence, the Uganda Electricity Board was mainly producing for some light local industry – the copper smelting plant, and
textile and cement factories – streetlights for the major towns, and
neighbouring Kenya, which was an eager purchaser of Nile power.[168]
Alongside industrial expansion, as part of what has been termed
a 'second colonial occupation',[169] there was renewed vigour in the
agricultural sector, too, with a drive towards increased production,

[163] 'Colonial Development and Welfare Act: progress reports', UKNA CO
852/865/4 [1948].
[164] K.A. Davies, 'Background to Development', *Uganda Review*, June 1952.
[165] 'Industrial development: reports on various schemes, including Owen Falls
hydro-electric scheme, development of iron and steel industry, mining at
Kilembe and Sukulu, Tororo mineral deposits...', UKNA CO 536/224/3,
17 October 1950–12 July 1951, 'Industrial development: mineral resources;
possibility for establishing iron and steel industry in Uganda', UKNA CO
536/224/5, 5 July 1950–17 July 1951. See also 'Railway to the West', *The
Uganda Herald*, 19 April 1951.
[166] Mangat, 'Immigrant communities', 482–3.
[167] B.S. Hoyle, 'The Economic Expansion of Jinja, Uganda', *Geographical
Review*, 53:3 (1963); also 'Commercial and industrial development: East
Africa Royal Commission [Dow Commission]', UKNA CO 892/15/10 [1953].
[168] Still, cross-subsidy was critical: 'Loans to the Uganda Electricity Board by
Uganda Development Corporation', UKNA CO 822/308 [1953].
[169] D.A. Low & J.M. Lonsdale, 'Introduction: towards the new order,
1945–1963', in Low & Smith (eds.), *History of East Africa*, III, 12–16.

diversification through new cash crops, the introduction of some mechanisation and new technologies and larger-scale farming.[170] Plans were developed for cattle ranching, for example in Bunyoro, which was also targeted for bush clearance and agricultural development.[171]

It was in the towns – again, especially Kampala – that economic protest was most likely, and most visible. The urban environment witnessed the emergence of the first associations, quasi-trade unions and ultimately formalised organisations in the 1930s, and it is important to reiterate that the roots of later political parties lay in economic grievance. The Uganda Motor Drivers' Association and the Uganda African Farmers' Union, founded in the 1930s and early 1940s, sought to represent the grievances of key economic constituents working in the transport and agricultural sectors respectively.[172] Protest movements, unions and associations of various kinds of workers were in some ways ostensibly political but were actually economic in their anxieties and aspirations, and organised labour protest was an important barometer of economic discontent, although they intersected with political ideas and identities. Nor was this simply about the petition and the manifesto, and the written word, however impassioned: it was grievance which was manifest in street protest and violence, as in the case of the riots in Buganda in 1945 and again in 1949, which demonstrated, among other things, the depth of anger around farmers' exclusion from cotton marketing.[173] Protest could produce results: for example, the Lint Marketing Board was established by the Protectorate government to protect African producers from the predations of

---

[170] 'Budget Session of Legislative Council', *The Uganda Herald*, 5 December 1945, 'The Development Plan: extracts from Dr Worthington's report', *The Uganda Herald*, 4 June 1947.
[171] 'Development in Bunyoro', *The Uganda Herald*, 3 July 1951, 'Big cattle ranch scheme approved for Bunyoro', *Uganda Argus*, 13 December 1955, 'Bunyoro scheme turns thick bush into fine farm lands', *Uganda Argus*, 17 March 1956.
[172] 'Petitions and memorials: representations from the African Produce Growers and Uganda African Farmers Union raising various grievances . . .', UKNA CO 536/216/1, 19 June 1948–22 August 1949.
[173] 'Deportation and detention of Samwiri Wamala . . . and four others following the disturbances in Buganda in January 1945', UKNA FCO 141/18160 [1945–6], 'Civil disturbances in Buganda, April 1949', UKNA FCO 141/18131 [1949]; also Low, *Buganda in Modern History*, 148–49.

expatriate control.[174] Economic and political protest was sharpened in many ways by the experience of the Second World War, characterised as that was by severe economic pressures, including shortages of basic commodities and inflation.[175]

Particular anger was increasingly reserved, meanwhile, for the ever more powerful and prominent Asian community, growing in economic significance by the 1920s and 1930s, particularly in the retail and export sectors.[176] At the top end of the socio-economic scale they were major investors in plantations and in processing and marketing ventures, and especially in the industrial projects around Kampala and Jinja in the later years of colonial rule. While they clearly enhanced the economic capacity of the territory, and employed large numbers of Africans in their various enterprises, they were also a source of socio-economic and ultimately political tension from the 1930s onward.[177] Their economic dominance generated resentment which was harnessed by nascent nationalist movements in the 1950s. In 1959, for example, the Uganda National Movement under the chairmanship of Augustine Kamya organised a trade boycott of 'non-African' shops across Buganda and beyond.[178] There was also the mounting sense that they held themselves apart, that they were possessed of some fairly unabashed and strident racist views of the lowly 'native', arguably at times even worse than any view held by the average British official, who in any case would have taken great pains to conceal it. For the Asian businessman, trapped in the middle tier of an imperial racial hierarchy, his worst contempt was often reserved for the uneducated and dim-witted African at the bottom of that hierarchy. Increasingly, too, it was believed – correctly, in many cases – that their loyalties to India or Bangladesh were altogether stronger than any relationship they might

[174] 'Uganda Protectorate Ordinance No 10 (Lint Marketing Board [Amendment] Ordinance) of 1951 . . .', UKNA CO 536/225/10, 2 June 1951–8 January 1952.

[175] Thompson, *Governing Uganda*, offers a wealth of detail, esp. Part Two.

[176] J.S. Mangat, *The History of the Asians of East Africa: c. 1886–1945* (Oxford, 1969).

[177] Godfrey Asiimwe, 'The roots and dynamics of the Indian question and inter-racial relations in Uganda', unpublished conference paper, Mukono, Uganda, July 2015.

[178] 'Uganda National Movement and trade boycott in Buganda: sessional paper', UKNA FCO 141/18298 [1959], Dharam P. Ghai, 'The Bugandan Trade Boycott: a study in tribal, political, and economic nationalism', in Mazrui & Rotberg (eds.), *Protest and Power*.

have with Uganda *per se*. This became a much bigger issue as independence loomed, and thus the question of the Asian community would come to dominate much economic planning in the first Obote administration and, notoriously, Amin's early regime.[179]

The economics of decolonisation and early independence, thus, can be understood as involving several overlapping and in some ways paradoxical dynamics.[180] There were plenty of hopes and expectations – in some ways economic nationalism intersected with political nationalism, and all the political parties had economic plans and visions for Uganda. On one level, increased levels of private and government investment in development projects had seen an increase in Uganda's gross domestic product in the course of the 1950s. Cash crops were lucrative in the post-war period, and there were considerable cash profits on offer for small-scale cultivators of cotton, for example – even if increased cash income did not translate into 'development', as farmers tended to hoard their money, much to officials' irritation.[181] In the decade prior to independence, the share of the industrial sector in the economy averaged 10 per cent per annum under the supervision of the Uganda Development Corporation, an increase from the previous half-century, though still a markedly small percentage.[182] At the same time, however, the basic structure of the national economy in the making was unaltered:[183] skewed towards commercial agriculture which was in the hands of small groups of expatriates, whether Asian or European, and which was based on African labour which had been excluded from the benefits normatively associated with international trade. Roughly half of the annual industrial share in the economy still came from sugar processing, coffee curing and cotton production. In addition to a weak industrial base, newly independent Uganda faced a problem common to many new nations across the continent – a heavy reliance on the export of a limited range of cash crops to overseas markets. This made the nascent national economy inherently brittle, and its supply of foreign currency precarious. Skilled African labour was in short supply, too, owing to decades of educational provision which was

---

[179] H.S. Morris, *The Indians in Uganda* (London, 1968).
[180] Lury, 'Dayspring mishandled?', *passim*.
[181] 'Increased cash income not raising living standards', *The Uganda Herald*, 20 February 1951.
[182] Colonial Office, *Uganda: report for the year 1961* (London, 1962), 70–5.
[183] Lury, 'Dayspring mishandled?', 236, 239, 243–4.

skewed either towards the learning of low-level craft skills or towards largely unsuitable academic achievement;[184] Asians, again, had long filled the role of skilled and semi-skilled labour.

Thus in 1963, Uganda's first full year as an independent state, the country could be safely depicted by a contemporary economist as 'the text-book description of a low-income country'. Its GDP was £176.1 million, which meant that output per head amounted to £24.5 per annum, 'among the lowest per capita income figures in the world'. Nearly 27 per cent of GDP was derived from subsistence activity, and agriculture alone accounted for more than 50 per cent of monetary GDP. National income was heavily dependent on export earnings, accounting for over 46 per cent of GDP. Most Ugandans were 'self-employed' – as farmers and herdsmen, operating at small-scale, subsistence level – while less than 6 per cent of Ugandan adults were classified as wage- and salary-earners. By sharp contrast, Asians and Europeans – constituting 1.4 per cent of the total population – were in receipt of approximately 26 per cent of monetary incomes.[185] Manufacturing, meanwhile, made a markedly small contribution to GDP.[186]

A sharp sense of injustice and inequity therefore unquestionably informed the first Obote administration's view of economic policy. From the outset, the government's development strategy prioritised industrialisation and aimed at a greatly reduced role for export crops;[187] meanwhile, as part of the independence celebrations in October 1962, Obote had opened a 'science and industry' pavilion at the Uganda Museum which signposted its determination to enter the brave world of economic modernity[188] – a modernity which eschewed the clutches of vested outside interests and which was increasingly conceived of within socialist parameters. By the mid-1960s, much to the alarm of Uganda's external economic partners, including the British, Obote had begun a decisive shift to the left, in the belief that only

---

[184] For a fascinating contemporary exploration of this, see Cyril Ehrlich, 'Some social and economic implications of paternalism in Uganda', *Journal of African History*, 4:2 (1963).

[185] D. P. Ghai, *Taxation for Development: a case study of Uganda* (Nairobi, 1966), 13–14.

[186] Stoutjesdijk, *Uganda's Manufacturing Sector*.

[187] Uganda Government, *The First Five-Year Development Plan 1961/62 – 1965/66* (Entebbe, 1962).

[188] This section of the Museum is now mournfully run down and greatly depleted in terms of actual exhibits.

a statist approach to the economy could bring about 'Africanization' and enable the country to realise its full material potential.[189] The belief in the power of state intervention, central planning and industrial socialism was at least in part justified by a cursory glance at twentieth-century global history – most recently in Britain's own, albeit limited, state-led experiments in industrialisation in late colonial Uganda. It was a logical conclusion to reach, and one that was common across in numerous newly independent nations across the continent. This was the rationale behind the nationalisation programme across the financial and commercial sectors, and the beginnings of a re-examination of the status of the Asian community in terms of citizenship rights and their role in the economy.[190] But it also led to greater interest in rural development, and to the sponsoring of research on the part of the Ministry of Agriculture into peasant farming technologies and use of labour.[191] It was an economic programme which in many ways culminated in the putatively radical 'Common Man's Charter' in 1969.[192] Much-derided consequently,[193] it nevertheless represented an attempt to constitutionally enshrine a batch of entitlements and protections for the 'ordinary citizen'. At an enthusiastic reception for the Charter in Kigezi, one speech-maker stressed how important it was 'that we share what we have...Individualism...should give way to group-living', and the state should 'own all or the major means of production'. There was also a critique of the deep divide opening up between town and countryside, with the former breeding greed, selfishness and sectarianism; 'people developed the erroneous feeling that agriculture was for the uneducated and the poor and the old', declared the speaker gravely and, in many ways, pretty accurately.[194]

---

[189] 'His Excellency the President's Communication from the Chair of the National Assembly, on 9 June 1967', Kabale District Archives, ADM30/ADM22/ 'Legislative Council – National Assembly, Proceedings and Policy Speeches'.

[190] 'Possible expulsion of Asians from Uganda', UKNA FCO 50/268 [1969].

[191] For example, *An Economic Survey of Farming in a Wet, Long-Grass Area of Toro* (Ministry of Agriculture and Forestry, Entebbe, 1968).

[192] Apollo Milton Obote, *The common man's charter*. No.1. Government Printer, 1970.

[193] Ali Mazrui sceptically referred to it as 'documentary radicalism', reflecting a fixation on the part of African leaders with the text and paperwork of 'reform': Ali Mazrui, *African Thought in Comparative Perspective* (Cambridge, 2014), 30.

[194] 'A speech given to Kigezi District Councillors on Thursday 6 August 1970', Kabale District Archives, MISC BOX 13, File No. CD/112A, Speeches General

There was considerable continuity between Obote and Amin in economic terms. A similar combination of economic patriotism and historical injustice informed Amin's 'war' on parasites and foreign influences; and it was further complicated by the specific regional disparity represented by a succession of northern governments with deeprooted and simmering resentments around the southern domination of the national economy. Amin's was not in itself a ludicrous economic programme: he was addressing – in the expulsion of the Asians in 1972 – an issue of long-standing importance in Uganda, i.e. economic inequity, and a chronic imbalance in commercial opportunity, around which grievances had been crystallising since the 1930s. But it heralded two decades of economic disorder, not least the result of Amin's short-termism and highly emotional approach to deep-rooted structural problems. When Amin declared his 'economic war' in August 1972, his declared enemies were those non-citizen Asians who owned too much and contributed too little, who sent their savings abroad (or 'home', to India and Bangladesh), and had for too long stood haughtily apart from (even above) Ugandan Africans.[195] For sure, these were the politics of envy; but it is also widely accepted, again, that the Asian community harboured often ill-disguised racial attitudes towards Ugandans.[196] In the 'new Uganda' – which for Amin was all about African economic empowerment and liberation from the increasingly arthritic grasp of greedy foreigners – there would be, could be, no place for such people. And so, he gave those who were unwilling to renounce their British or Indian citizenship and adopt Ugandan citizenship ninety days to settle their affairs, make their arrangements and get out. In the event, however, the hostility towards even those who were Ugandan citizens intensified through August and September, and many of those were compelled to leave, too.[197] In many cases, Asians were forced to abandon homes and businesses as there was noone legitimate to hand over to, thus unleashing a bonanza for Ugandan

---

[195] Speech by His Excellency the President of the Republic of Uganda General Idi Amin Dada on the occasion of the conference . . . on the transfer of economy into the hands of Ugandans', 29 August 1972, Kabale District Archives, ADM89, C/MIS 3/1, Presidential & Ministerial Speeches.

[196] See the extensive writings of Ugandan-born expellee Yasmin Alibhai-Brown, now a prominent British journalist. For example, 'Starting over', *FT Magazine*, 24 August 2012.

[197] 'Expulsion of UK passport-holders of Asian origin from Uganda', UKNA FCO 31/1375 [1972] and subsequent.

employees and houseboys, as well as for the Treasury, as the expelled were permitted to remove a maximum of £50 (Sterling) from the country. Bank accounts and assets were seized, and for a while, Amin enjoyed his windfall. While ad hoc committees were set up to ostensibly redistribute Asian businesses, a rather more haphazard 'system' also operated, involving government ministers (or even Amin himself) making pronouncements on the street surrounded by crowds waving claim forms.[198]

Beneath the economic directives pouring forth from the relevant government ministries, and Amin himself, a shadow realm operated involving plunder, extraction and redistribution throughout the 1970s. To describe this as mere 'economic mismanagement' perhaps does no justice to the social complexity and psychological pressure involved in its operation, and to the myriad ways which ordinary Ugandans – their protection under the terms of the Common Man's Charter long forgotten – managed to survive amidst the destruction. And it is also the case that the Amin government's proclaimed aim of 'self-reliance' produced some interesting initiatives – such as the attempt in the mid-1970s to revive the disappearing skills in iron-working for which Kigezi was once renowned.[199] More serious for the national economy was the crippling of industry, the decay of essential infrastructure, the collapse of crop marketing systems and shocking inflation amidst shortages of essential goods.

Uganda had long been an entrepreneurial economy – which is not the same as suggesting it was an equitable one, for there were both political limitations to economic activity and social inequities which often acted as brakes on social mobility. But there *were* opportunities, and a culture of entrepreneurialism which dated to the nineteenth century and earlier continued to flourish. Amin's reign represented opportunities for some, not least of course for those close to Amin himself, but also for the black marketeers, smugglers and others who were in a position to profit from supplying necessities (and sometimes luxuries) at increased prices. These were the *Mafuta Mingi* – literally, those who are

---

[198] For example, Melady & Melady, *Idi Amin Dada*, 90–1, Kyemba, *State of Blood*, 63–4.

[199] Culture officer Kigezi Districts to the Ministry of Culture, Kabale, 28 August 1975, Kabale District Archives, COM 21, File No. CD24, 'Culture and Activities'.

dripping with oil[200] – who thrived in the *magendo* economy, which had its own rules, parameters and opportunities. Still, beyond the essential truth that someone's economic distress is always another's economic opening, it is nonetheless the case that Amin's reign profoundly damaged the embryonic middle class and caused greater material damage than anything in the region since the war in Bunyoro in the 1890s. It also exposed the chronic frailties which the British colonial state had bequeathed to the UPC government in 1962.

Ontological Journeys, 1: The Urban Ugandan

Urbanisation has both driven and reflected economic and social change in the most fundamental of ways. In the course of the eighteenth and nineteenth centuries, we see the emergence of concentrated centres of population as places where the ambitious go to get things done and pursue personal achievement. Royal capitals emerged as fulcrums, as gravitational centres, of political and economic power. Before the nineteenth century, 'urban' living, however we define it, was limited to a handful of concentrated centres of population from the Chwezi period onward, mostly between lakes Victoria and Albert, and at most probably containing a few hundred people. This began to change in the course of the nineteenth century, around the northern shore of Lake Victoria, with the stabilisation and expansion of urban centres such as the royal capital of Buganda, and other centres such as Masaka and Jinja.[201] Masaka began to grow in significance following the Ganda conquest of Buddu in the second half of the eighteenth century, and Speke in the 1860s found a substantial regional headquarters laid out in very similar ways to the Ganda capital.[202] At the other end of the kingdom, Jinja grew in the same period into a highly significant frontier garrison on the Nile, the base for eastward wars against the Soga, and occasional temporary royal capital, as it was for both Suna and Mutesa, when it swelled to house tens of thousands of soldiers,

---

[200] Kasfir, 'State, Magendo and class formation', 90.
[201] Reid, *War in Precolonial Eastern Africa*, 165–6, R.J. Reid, 'Warfare and Urbanisation: the relationship between town and conflict in pre-colonial eastern Africa', in A. Burton (ed.), *The Urban Experience in Eastern Africa, c. 1750–2000* (Nairobi, 2002), 54*ff.*
[202] Kiwanuka's notes in Kagwa, *Kings*, 91, Speke, *Journal*, 275–6.

administrators and their various attendants and entourages.[203] In line with developments across the wider East African region, proto-urbanism was characterised by fortification in an age of political and military turmoil, as people drew together for protection; the Teso, for example, may have begun to build fortified villages towards the end of the eighteenth century,[204] while a century later, in Busongora, land was increasingly enclosed by euphorbia as defence.[205] But precolonial urbanisation was most dramatic in the case of the Ganda capital itself, which from the reign of Suna onward ceased being a mobile royal feast – which was relocated several times during particular reigns, as well as between them, for ideological, economic and sanitary reasons – and became rooted around a lucrative inlet off Lake Victoria and spread out permanently across several hills at the heart of modern Kampala. This was related only partly to militarism and the consolidation of political authority, and increasingly to the commercial opportunity represented by proximity to the lake.

Commerce drove urbanisation in the course of the nineteenth century, at least in the southern zone, building on older economic patterns of concentrated population at sites such as Bigo and Ntusi. The importance of the Lake Victoria trade meant, from the 1840s onward, the gradual rootedness, consolidation and expansion of the Ganda royal capital across the hills of modern day central Kampala. Urban growth reflected the expansion of economic scale, certainly in the case of Kampala; they comprised larger markets, housed more or less permanently resident trading communities, both foreign and indigenous, and represented the desire to maximise both profit and control. But of course the Ganda capital and other centres – notably Jinja and Masaka – were also the products of the expansion of political and military scale over the same period, and reflected the needs of government and garrison in an era of socio-political transformation. These urban, and proto-urban, sites were physical symbols of the confluence of war and economy in Uganda's nineteenth century.[206] From the early twentieth century, urban growth resulted from a long-term combination of economic

---

[203] Kagwa, *Kings*, 85–7, Stanley, *Dark Continent*, I, 235–7, 238–9, 242–3, 292–3.
[204] Stanley, *Dark Continent*, I, 283.   [205] Stanley, *In Darkest Africa*, II, 309.
[206] R.J. Reid, 'Traders, chiefs, and soldiers: the pre-colonial capitals of Buganda', *Les Cahiers de l'Institut Français de Recherche en Afrique*, 9 (1998), Reid & Médard, 'Merchants, missions and the remaking of the urban environment', Reid, 'Warfare and Urbanisation'.

drivers, with towns becoming stable centres of commerce and industry, the locations of major regional markets, and pools of labour, as
well as being sites of socio-economic opportunity. As Kampala, in particular, expanded, it had a wider economic impact: by the beginning
of the 1950s, farmers surrounding the city tended to grow less cotton
and more food for sale in town.[207] Towns were the target of labour
migration, mostly men, but increasingly women, too, which was much
more worrying to colonial and chiefly patriarchy. As the local economy
changed, providing opportunities as well as introducing new hardships,
women sought new ways of earning their own living, including moving
to town in the process of asserting their economic independence from
men.[208]

As elsewhere in Africa, the twentieth century was the urban
century.[209] By the time of the 1911 Census, a little over 40 per cent
of the African population of Buganda Province lived in Mengo district – in, or on the peri-urban edges of, the township of Kampala.
In the 1930s, however, the actual population which might be defined
as 'urban residents' remained fluid, and relatively small; several thousand labourers entered and left Kampala daily, and those that lived on
the edges of the town – as in other smaller centres – lived quasi-rural
lifestyles, keeping some animals and growing crops on small plots of
land.[210] By the 1950s, there had been some dramatic changes: Kampala
had begun to sprawl, and was home to a bustling, mixed African (and
Asian) population. There was an excitement, and a vibrant excitability,
to the city which was captured in Southall and Gutkind's work, which
describes, in the mid-1950s, an emergent urban character defined by
jostling entrepreneurialism, particularly in the suburb that was the
focus of their study, Kisenyi.[211] In 1969, the population of Kampala

---

[207] E. S. Munger, *Relational Patterns of Kampala, Uganda* (Chicago, 1951), 35.
    See also A.W. Southall & P.C.W. Gutkind, *Townsmen in the Making: Kampala
    and its suburbs* (Kampala, 1957), for a superb contemporary (mid-1950s)
    snapshot.
[208] Obbo, *African Women*, 26–7.
[209] D. M. Anderson & R. Rathbone, 'Introduction. Urban Africa: histories in the
    making', in Anderson & Rathbone (eds.), *Africa's Urban Past*, Burton (ed.),
    The Urban Experience.
[210] Thomas & Scott, *Uganda*, 273, 276.
[211] Southall & Gutkind, *Townsmen in the Making*. This is an especially rich and
    compelling account which one can still read for genuine pleasure, for example
    their 'daily scene in Kisenyi', 22–6, which contains much more detail than can
    possibly be included here.

was recorded in the census of that year at 330,700, with a total of 634,952 Ugandans recorded as living in fifty-eight urban centres. In 2012, the population of the capital was estimated – rather vaguely – at between 2 million and 3.15 million, with a further million living in seventy-three other urban centres.[212] The disparity appeared to be the definition of the Greater Kampala Metropolitan Area, but the disparity itself – the apparent inability of the urban authorities to be clear how many people actually lived in Kampala – is striking. What is certainly clear is that between the 1980s and 2010s, Kampala was one of the fastest growing cities in Africa, with an annual growth rate of 5.6 per cent – in keeping with phenomenal population rates more broadly, but in fact urban growth was twice the level of rural population expansion.[213] Such rapid expansion far outran the ability of municipal authorities to provide adequate social services, and the growth of urban poverty was palpable in the early years of the twenty-first century. In other towns, there were similar levels of growth, and the general pattern in Uganda matched that across much of sub-Saharan Africa – namely, in the second half of the twentieth century, an escalating rural drain, signifying long-term agrarian decline.[214]

Despite the poverty that often awaits them, there has been a continual and escalating drainage of people from the rural to the urban environment in Uganda. As elsewhere, too, urbanites regarded themselves as more sophisticated than the bumpkins who annually flooded into the city in search of work and schooling from impoverished villages, and who – like Okot p'Bitek's Okeca Ladwong, confused and frightened by the traffic in downtown Kampala in the late 1940s – wander the streets looking dazed and bewildered. Today's inward migrants have to contend with the swarms of *boda-bodas*, customised motorcycles carrying passengers across the city, and a multitude of other quotidian threats to life and limb. As elsewhere in postcolonial Africa, too, Uganda's first-generation political elite – though in most cases hailing from the countryside in terms of birth and formative years – were decidedly urban and industrial in their prejudices, and saw the future in terms of the industrial, capital-backed

---

[212] *Independent Uganda*, 2–3, *Understand Uganda*, 120–3.
[213] K. Vermeiren, A. van Rompaey, M. Loopmans, E. S., & P. Mukwaya, 'Urban growth of Kampala, Uganda: pattern analysis and scenario development', *Landscape and Urban Planning*, 106:2 (2012).
[214] Iliffe, *Africans*, 264–6.

projects directed by urban centres overcoming the inherent backward-
ness of rural peasantries.[215] This also tended to reinforce the difference between the south and the north. But links between the urban
and the rural remain robust; for many, despite their modernist biases,
there is something pure and idyllic about the rural setting which is
conceptualised in terms of 'soul' and 'provenance', with cities the products of imposed but unavoidable modernity and the sites of iniquity.
Urban folk still have their ancestral homes, and the urban professional
will still often have their plot of land 'back home', to which they will
one day retire to grow some crops, and keep some livestock, and in
which they will eventually be buried by their kin. If it was often said of
Nairobi in neighbouring Kenya that this was a city of transients – that
no-one was ever 'from' Nairobi – then it is perhaps only a little less true
of Kampala, which does have organic roots in the nineteenth century
but which has grown into a hub of people who are increasingly disproportionately from somewhere else. And that somewhere else is usually
the place to which they will return towards the end of life. Indeed, especially in the urban centres, but more generally too, one of the unfortunate outcomes of rapid population growth is that land – perennially contentious in Uganda's modern history – has become extremely
expensive, prohibitively so for many.[216] For millions of Ugandans, as
middle age approaches, the overpowering focus of work and life is to
secure a plot of land in one's own district to where one will retire, one
day; and to have on that land everything to secure a reasonably com-
fortable old age.

   Yet it is interesting to note that as the region's capital cities go, Kampala has long been known as a remarkably safe place – no more (or
less) crime than the average inner-city London estate, and compared to
Nairobi, a veritable haven. That this is true is all the more remarkable
given Uganda's violent modern history compared to that of relatively
stable Kenya; and it is a source of great pride among Ugandans that it is
so. But Kampala splurges outward across a wider and wider area, con-
suming small townships and semi-rural districts which were formerly
a good bus ride from the city. In just the last two decades, visitors who
have not been for a while will be shocked at how much Kampala has

---

[215] For example, R. Bates, *Markets and States in Tropical Africa: The Political
    Basis of Agricultural Policies* (Berkeley CA, 1981).
[216] Author's field notes and informal interviews, 8 August 2010.

grown, eating into the surrounding hills and countryside and seeping towards the lake edge; and in particular at the congestion on its roads, especially in the city centre and on any of the major highways in and out of the city – congestion that is more commonly associated with Nairobi. At the same time, more recently, the city's population has been swollen massively by an influx from South Sudan, the DRC, Rwanda and Burundi; Kampala has become a regional hub, and the congested streets are testament to the fact. Thousands of Eritreans, too, have flooded to Kampala in recent years; Eritrean (and 'Ethiopian') restaurants have proliferated across the city.[217] The question of whether or not urbanisation represented greater social mobility and opportunity is not an easy one to answer. On one level, the answer must be that it has, as people break away from the constraints of rural life and shape new identities in the urban setting, in the process gaining access to material opportunities, belief systems, education. In a sense, it was ever thus – witness the naked entrepreneurialism in evidence in the Ganda capital in the 1880s. Urban life had long signified aspiration of a kind, and certainly material prospects. Towns and cities offered varied compensations for the rigours of urban living – as they do the world over. Towns offer a range of opportunities and experiences, and freedoms, away from the putative cloying control of custom and behaviour, especially for women, but for young men, too.[218] Yet this is not a straightforward picture, for cities like Kampala have also become places where people are ensnared in poverty, in which opportunities are extremely limited, and in which people lack access to kinship support networks – especially important in an environment in which social services are limited. State-sponsored behavioural expectations of women contrasted sharply with the expansion of prostitution across nocturnal Kampala, though it is worth noting that many of the women driving this surge were from across the wider region, including Rwanda, Kenya and Congo.[219] True, Kampala today boasts a substantial educated, well-heeled, cosmopolitan middle class, within which reside some of the sharpest ideas about the nation and its identity. But beyond this, there is a large, disaffected urban population living on the edge of destitution or at best scraping by – evidenced by the fact that

[217] Author's field notes and informal interviews, 5 August 2010.
[218] For example, John Lonsdale, 'Town life in colonial Kenya', in Burton (ed.), *The Urban Experience in Eastern Africa*.
[219] Author's field notes and informal interviews, 1 July 2011 & 26 October 2013.

support for opposition movements against the NRM is most visible in Kampala.

Ontological Journeys, 2: Wellbeing and Aspiration

Amidst so much socio-economic transformation and, indeed, hardship, Ugandans sought the means to achieve security and comfort, both drawing on older experiences and institutions, and building on these by way of innovation. The church had long been the driver of social intervention and welfare, providing a range of medical and educational services. The Catholic Church, for example, prided itself on its work in all aspects of community life, from health provision to printing presses to the creation of family study groups aimed at the 'improvement of family life'.[220] This had deep roots, of course. The spiritual realm had long provided critical access to fundamental social resources, to physical, emotional and intellectual wellbeing. Faith and sect provided Ugandans with access to medicine and education, for spiritual organisation and faith-based institutions had long been indelibly intertwined with ideas about healing and learning: these, too, are central to an understanding of histories of expectation and aspiration. At the same time, self-knowledge and awareness of the world – its perils, its opportunities and what was required to achieve security and cohesion – had long been an intrinsic role of spiritual observance. This was essentially about access to fundamental social resources: education and health provided reasons to flock to mission stations, manifesting aspiration, as had long been the case with shrines and an endogenous spiritual universe. Only over time was there at least a partial detachment of medicine and education from the realm of religion; but the former remained a matter of social security and aspiration.

In the twentieth century, healthcare was the realm in which 'modernity' was often held to have made significant inroads into African society: modern medicine, distributed either via small scale local clinics, or through large-scale campaigns in state intervention, involved the diagnosis of Africans (and their livestock), their treatment and their cure, demonstrating in no uncertain terms the power of the colonial mission to transform Africans' lives. Initially, however, there was little direct

---

[220] See the special issue celebrating Ugandan independence of the *Catholic News Bulletin*, published by Uganda Catholic Information, 5 September 1962.

interest on the part of the state in providing for Ugandans' physical well-being. This was the work of mission stations, and in particular of energetic missionary medics – most famously, in the early years of the Protectorate, Albert Cook, who was the driving force behind the establishment of a clinic at Mulago, on the edge of Kampala, in 1917.[221] When the colonial state did become involved, it was with the aim of tackling major diseases – such as the large-scale intervention to eradicate sleeping sickness along the Lake Victoria shoreline and numerous islands in the early 1900s, involving the evacuation and resettlement of tens of thousands of people in what was a muscular exercise in diagnosis, treatment and the demonstration of the medical state's power to administer modernity.[222] A later example was the eradication in the early 1950s of black fly – *Simulium damnosum* – from the forests of Bugerere, giving rise to new communities which flooded to the area to farm.[223] Sexual health was another persistent concern: while external intrusions brought a sharp rise in syphilis and other STDs, the colonial state also brought with it the power to treat these diseases, and to improve female fertility.[224] In so doing, the colonial state was able, if inadvertently, to exercise some control over African bodies and behaviours, and Ugandans themselves became medical subjects in the colonial laboratory.[225]

Meanwhile, the gradual introduction of 'formal' education – in the normative Western sense of institutional schooling – in many ways built upon long-standing practices of social learning and vocational training in precolonial communities. As girls learnt from mothers and other older female relatives, so boys received instruction from fathers in history, culture, politics and economics; and boys, too, were frequently apprenticed to economic specialists to learn particular crafts, and – in the case of political elites – were sent to serve time as attendants in

---

[221] Sir A. R. Cook, *Uganda Memories (1897–1940)* (Kampala, 1945).

[222] 'Sleeping Sickness and Small Pox in Uganda Protectorate', *Mengo Notes*, January 1902, 6–7.

[223] The story is powerfully told in Robertson, *Community of Strangers*.

[224] For example Doyle, *Before HIV*; also C. Summers, 'Intimate Colonialism: the imperial production of reproduction in Uganda, 1907–1925', *Signs: the journal of women in culture and society*, 16:4 (1991).

[225] M. Tuck, 'Syphilis, Sexuality, and Social Control: a history of venereal disease in colonial Uganda', unpublished PhD thesis, Northwestern University, 1997.

the compounds of chiefs or the courts of rulers. Early mission education built upon this basic model, and mission compounds – and later
schools – served much the same purpose.[226] Missionaries, for whom
schooling was the central plank of expanding, or at least maintaining,
the faith and the faithful, sought to work in Luganda, initially, in order
to create a written language from which converts could learn scripture,
and the link between conversion and literacy remained robust for many
years, as the key aim among both Catholic and Protestant missions
was for converts to read a catechism with a view to eventual baptism.
From the early 1900s, some more general education was introduced
in a handful of schools – geography, for example, or selected aspects
of world history – alongside more vocational training.[227] But the colonial state remained aloof from much of this before the 1920s, with
religious orders remaining in control of schools which were loosely
supervised by the authorities and supported through small grants-in-
aid. Schools themselves ranged from Catechist schools, to village or
'bush' schools (usually under the management of a Ugandan teacher),
to high schools and technical schools.[228] The chasm between the
best and least appointed schools was marked. Makerere College was
established in 1922 as a technical school, offering vocational training
courses, though it would in time evolve into an institute of higher general education.[229] 'Bush' schools were common in the north – such as
those in Arua in the mid-1920s, which combined Christian worship
with training in 'certain crafts, such as brickmaking, brick-laying, carpentry, clerical work, tanning and leatherwork, boot repairing, printing and dispensary work', while a women's school – attended by Lugbara, Madi, Kakwa and Alur women – involved 'instruction in sewing,
machining, and dress and mat-making'.[230]

In the course of the 1920s and 1930s, the colonial state became more
actively involved in the provision of both healthcare and education. In

---

[226] Hansen, *Mission, Church and State*, 224–58.
[227] A. K. Tiberondwa, *Missionary Teachers as Agents of Colonialism in Uganda*
(Kampala, 1977, 1998), chapter 3.
[228] J.C. Ssekamwa, *History and Development of Education in Uganda* (Kampala,
1997), 40–42.
[229] The best dedicated history of Makerere is Sicherman, *Becoming an African
University*.
[230] Uganda Protectorate, *Annual Report of the Education Department, for the
year ended 31 December 1925* (Entebbe, 1926), 17.

the wake of the establishment of Mulago medical school in 1923, hospitals were built at the administrative headquarters of districts, as well as in the larger towns, while district medical officers were appointed to administer health services across the Protectorate.[231] Meanwhile the Phelps-Stokes commission into African education in the colonies in the mid-1920s had the effect of spurring greater state involvement in the provision of education, with the colonial authorities sensitive to criticism that it had been negligent in this realm, and increasingly aware of the need to work more closely with religious organisations.[232] As a result a full department of education was set up in 1925,[233] thus marking a clear shift towards an expanded role for the state in the delivery of social services – one that would come to haunt the postcolonial state. The central issue with which officials struggled – and which was never fully resolved – was the degree to which any curriculum should be 'Westernised': 'a few natives, especially in Buganda ... blind themselves to the possibility of developing a system of higher education in their own country and would like to see the whole education of the country moulded on European lines', warned a 1926 report, which went on to caution against 'a policy of ruthless Westernization'.[234] There was certainly now a greater impetus in the provision of particular kinds of curricula, and of teaching materials: by the end of the 1930s, H.B.Thomas had produced one of the first school textbooks specifically designed to inculcate in students the idea of 'Uganda' and its historical connections with the wider region.[235] Even so, the government did not assume direct control over education provision, only direct involvement, and the debate intensified through the 1930s and 1940s, and beyond, over what *kind* of education should be provided to *whom*, and for what *purpose*. Many in government believed that too

---

[231] Thomas & Scott, *Uganda*, 303, 304.

[232] See T. J. Jones, *Education in East Africa: a study of east, central and south Africa by the second African Education Commission under the auspices of the Phelps-Stokes Fund, in cooperation with the International Education Board: report* (London & New York, 1925) and discussions of evolving education policy in the British colonial territories in Hailey, *African Survey* (1938 and 1957 editions).

[233] Uganda Protectorate, *Annual Report of the Education Department ... 1925.*

[234] Uganda Protectorate, *Annual Report of the Education Department, for the year ended 31 December 1926* (Entebbe, 1927), 5.

[235] See H.B. Thomas, *The Story of Uganda* (1st ed. 1939, revised ed. by Samwiri Karugire, Nairobi & Oxford, 1973).

many schools were providing an excessively literary, academic education which only produced dislocated and discombobulated 'natives'
who no longer belonged to, and therefore could not serve, their home
communities; and that, officials believed, was bad for Uganda. Advocates of that position argued for the expansion of technical and vocational education. Yet many Ugandans – especially the aspirant upper
and middle classes in the 1930s and 1940s – earnestly desired academic
education for their children, who would thus have access to better-paid
jobs in administration, in business and in education itself. A more academic curriculum was introduced even for girls in some schools by
the end of the 1930s, and young women were able to enter Makerere
after 1945, though they were small in number and restricted to the
usual 'feminine' subjects.[236] Still, despite spasmodic attempts to raise
standards in girls' education, and to change attitudes towards them,
core problems remained around their perceived role in society. At the
beginning of the 1950s, an education department report noted that the
biggest single issue vexing educated men was

the status of women in the new society which is emerging. For it is still
true that a single woman in this country has no recognised place and that
her character is assumed to be undesirable, as witness the almost universal
condemnation of a woman occupying a room or house on her own...In
co-educational schools there is often only one woman teacher posted, who
ought, of course, to be a married woman, but frequently is not. There are
many African chiefs who have much to answer for, failing lamentably in
giving the women of their area protection or in showing them respect.[237]

Patriarchy was proving remarkably robust.

Already in the 1900s, meanwhile, the first boarding secondary
schools were established with a view to educating the sons of the chiefly
oligarchy. This elitist stratum would continue to flourish, producing
in essence a Western-educated ruling class, although the opportunities were rather more limited for girls: while the first schools for girls
began to appear in the 1900s and 1910s, these graduates were confined to the fields of nursing, midwifery, teaching and of course home-
making, for they would make (it was supposed) good mates for the

[236] Sicherman, *Becoming an African University*, 25–6.
[237] Uganda Protectorate, *Annual Report of the Education Department, for the
year ended 31 December 1951* (Entebbe, 1952), 65.

graduates of the boys' schools. In the mid-1930s, it remained a matter of concern that the number of girls enrolled in school across the Protectorate was 'negligible'.[238] For boys, however, the situation was rather different. In the early years of the twentieth century, a number of schools – most of which exist at the time of writing – were established: King's College Budo, Namilyango Technical College, St Joseph Technical School Kisubi, Nsambya Technical School, Nagongera, Rugarama, Layibi, Mbale.[239] The schooling system expanded across the Protectorate, but Ganda children were particular beneficiaries, owing to the economic immigration from Rwanda, or Kigezi, or Acholiland, which freed up time and labour and enabled access to education.

Over the space of a generation, this privileged – or, perhaps more accurately, bolstered – a political class with the academic equipment and the spare time to dominate literary visions of their own communities and, moreover, of Uganda as a whole. Competition over the written past had begun almost as soon as imported faiths had taken root. Kagwa's own *Basekabaka ba Buganda* was an early case in point: a notice in the missionary press announced its appearance – 'at five rupees per copy, a high price' – and observed: 'It is a curious fact that the Baganda, like most other nations, put down the origin of all their troubles to a woman, just as Eve brought trouble to the world. Before the Baganda knew of this, their own story was of the same nature'.[240] The possibility was not entertained that Kagwa may have actually gained inspiration from the Old Testament tale; but at any rate, there followed a proliferation of historical writing in the form of newspapers and pamphlets, and in the pages of mission journals.[241] Protestants and the Namirembe establishment, led by Kagwa, may have dominated in the early years, but exposure to education and literacy facilitated the emergence of a range of historical visions. By the 1930s, the generation which represented the cohort of young converts in the 1880s was going into print with memoirs which underscored the righteousness of their struggle against barbaric and heathen tyranny.[242] In many ways their work bears out the argument made by numerous

[238] Uganda Protectorate, *Annual Report of the Education Department, for the year ended 31 December 1936* (Entebbe, 1937), 36.
[239] Tiberondwa, *Missionary Teachers*, 36.
[240] *Mengo Notes*, January 1902, 4.   [241] Rowe, 'Myth', Reid, 'Ghosts'.
[242] Most notably, Lugolobi, *Ekitabo Mbulire*, Zimbe *Buganda ne Kabaka*, Miti, *History of Buganda*, Mukasa, *Simuda Nyuma*.

authors about the relationship between biblical education and historical writing.[243] The bible itself was a powerful handbook for the nation-
in-the-making.[244] Adrian Hastings made the case compellingly for the
role of religion in particular visions of ethnicity and nationalism, and
he used the experience of the Ganda as an especially potent illustration. For Hastings, '[t]he impressive histories of his people written [for
example] by Apolo Kagwa ... symbolise the way in which a political
identity and oral history are bound together through the development
of literature, grounded on scripture translation, to stabilise a specific
national consciousness'.[245] Ganda intellectuals would use their the-
ological knowledge to think deeply about the kingdom's own past,
as Earle has brilliantly demonstrated.[246] Resistance to Luganda texts
would lead to the emergence of writing in other Ugandan vernaculars;
but the central point here is that a particular educated group at the apex
of Ugandan society – very largely, but by no means exclusively, rooted
in Buganda – was able and willing to dominate public discourse about
the history and nature of Uganda to the exclusion of those other voices
which belonged to those lacking education, visibility, access. Christians
sought to write their own historical truth, and it is not wholly unproblematic that many of the sources underpinning this book are written by
those very people. The role played by King's College Budo is an interesting illustration of what Ranger once described as an 'Anglo-Ganda'
institution based on an 'invention' of tradition; and even if Ranger
himself later modified the 'invention' argument, the fact remains that
Budo quickly took its place as the training college of the power elite.[247]

---

[243] One of the author's research team in Uganda once went to interview an
elderly priest in Toro. When asked about the significance of the precolonial
past, he instructed the researcher to go to a shelf and fetch a book. The book
was the Bible. The old man said simply, 'Start reading'. When he had
obligingly skimmed through to Leviticus, the researcher paused. The priest
said, 'Now, you understand everything.'

[244] By A.D. Smith, see *Myths and Memories* and *The Ethnic Origins of Nations*
(Malden MA & Oxford, 1986); see also Adrian Hastings, *The Construction
of Nationhood: ethnicity, religion and nationalism* (Cambridge, 1997).

[245] Hastings, *Construction*, 156. See also D. Maxwell, 'Christianity', in Parker &
Reid (eds.), *Oxford Handbook*.

[246] Earle, 'Political Theologies'.

[247] Ranger, 'The invention of tradition' and 'The invention of tradition revisited'
and see, for example, Gordon McGregor, *King's College Budo: a centenary
history, 1906–2006* (Kampala, 2006). The first cohort of students could
expect two sessions of manual labour per week, alongside history lessons
dealing with Ulysses and the Cyclops – stories which generated 'real
excitement': 'King's School Budo Report', 20 April 1908.

With its associations with ancient royal power, Budo sat at the centre of what was quite literally an old school tie network, in many ways replicating the role played by the precolonial Ganda royal court, to which the chiefly elite sent its sons in pursuit of political apprenticeship. Those who attended over the decades were inculcated with a particular Ganda-centric view of the nation; little coincidence that the first ever African history text in Luganda was produced at Budo, 'An Introductory History of the Entire World' by Samusoni Bazongere and the Reverend Weatherhead, the bulk of which was dedicated to the history of Buganda.[248] To some extent it bears out Benedict Anderson's observation concerning the relationship between education and nationhood in the colonial territory, and certainly reinforced the southern-centric shape of the polity.[249]

Owing to more limited educational opportunities, it would be several decades before Muslim historiography would emerge to challenge some of those narratives, but through the 'revisionist' writings of Sheikh Sekimwanyi, Bakale Mukasa bin Mayanja and Sheikh Nyanzi, among others, emerge it would by the 1940s and 1950s.[250] Still, even now, it is not at all clear that Muslim historical writings have succeeded in seriously modifying the image of late nineteenth-century Uganda as an inexorably Christian polity – an idea galvanised by the Christianised accoutrements of independence in 1962. Muslim children had long been especially poorly served, with many Muslim parents reluctant to send them to Christian schools and confining their education to the Quranic schools which proliferated across the territory.[251] But by the 1950s, under the auspices of the Ugandan Muslim Education Association, secondary schools for Muslims were established, as well as the government-run non-denominational schools set up in 1952.[252] Yet even the Muslim population of the south appeared relatively well served alongside the deprivation evident in the north: before the 1920s, statistical analysis of school attendance across northern Uganda was virtually impossible because there were so few statistics; by the Second World War, there was neither a full secondary school nor a vocational

---

[248] Rowe, 'Myth', 218.
[249] Benedict Anderson, *Imagined Communities: Reflections on the Origins and Spread of Nationalism* (London, 1991, 1983).
[250] Rowe, 'Myth', 25–6.
[251] For example, Uganda Protectorate, *Annual Report of the Education Department . . . 1936*, 38–9.
[252] J.C. Ssekamwa & S.M.E. Lugumba, *A History of Education in East Africa* (Kampala, 2001), 58*ff.*

training institute in either Acholi, Lango, West Nile or Madi. Only in the 1950s did this situation begin to improve.

In the last years of colonial rule, education was a critically important issue for political and social activists – to some extent spurred by the new emphasis on the part of the colonial state on social services through the Colonial Development and Welfare Acts of 1940 and 1945.[253] '[N]othing is so urgent in the minds of the people of Uganda as education', Eridadi Mulira wrote in the *Uganda Herald* in 1940, in the wake of a meeting on the subject in Mukono. But the problems were numerous:

Schools in Uganda are not yet satisfactory. Teachers are not satisfied and are discontented, and this...has driven many of them away from the profession...The standard of girls is below that of the boys...and there are not enough Secondary Schools for the poorer class, with the result that only the sons and daughters of the well-to-do can receive this kind of education....There is not enough equipment in schools, and the curriculum at Colleges is lacking in some valuable subjects such as African Studies, Philosophy and Law.[254]

These pressures would only continue to grow in the years running up to independence, as the task of building a national education system for every citizen passed to a Ugandan educated elite. Private schools proliferated in the 1940s and 1950s, mostly in Buganda.[255] Yet in the early 1950s, a detailed memorandum by the students of Mbarara Teacher Training College complained about the 'low standard' of education in Uganda compared to Kenya, largely due to 'too few teachers...some of them being incompetent'. The Kabalega Parents' Association noted that underpaid and discontented teachers, moreover, often took on 'petty trades so as to enhance his total income' while more generally

[253] During the course of the war 'the development of education and social services [was] recognised as necessary to sound economic development': Overseas Development Institute, *Colonial Development: a factual survey of the origins and history of British aid to developing countries* (London, 1964), 10.

[254] 'Education: the African view', by E.M.K. Mulira, *The Uganda Herald*, 14 February 1940.

[255] Uganda Protectorate, *Annual Report of the Education Department, for the year ended 31 December 1950* (Entebbe, 1952), 4, Uganda Protectorate, *Annual Report of the Education Department, for the year ended 31 December 1957* (Entebbe, 1958), 11.

their attitude towards teaching became 'negative'.[256] Toro district was identified as a particular problem, and was 'lagging behind the rest of the Protectorate in educational development'.[257] Across the territory as a whole, there was sufficient concern to prompt the setting up of a commission of enquiry, leading to the 'Bunsen report', which expressed anxiety that Uganda might be falling behind its neighbours in educational practice and attainment.[258] In the decade that followed, there was significant expansion in education provision: eight times more children in senior secondary schools by the time of independence, a doubling of children in primary schools and an increase in spending on the part of central government from £1,100,000 in 1952 to £5,500,000 in 1962.[259]

Yet this was not merely a question of resources. Colonial education had produced a metropolitan elite but it had not been sufficient to inculcate a cogent, unified, shared view of the nation and its past; or conversely to 'breed out' a sense of locality and ethnicity which invariably pitted particular groups against all the others. Witness, for example, the emergence of the Bukedi Makerere Students Union in the 1950s which aimed at unity among the young generation from the area, even if it did struggle, in 1961, to mobilise everyone into pulling their weight in running the organisation, prompting a chastisement from the union president in the occasional magazine.[260] The government of newly independent Uganda duly appointed a commission in 1963 – the first since the Bunsen report a decade earlier – to examine the nation's educational needs. Some positives were identified, including the great enthusiasm for learning among parents who made countless sacrifices

[256] 'Memorandum No.23: Submitted by the Students, Government Teacher Training College, Mbarara', & 'Memorandum No.6: Submitted by the Kabalega Parents' Association, Masindi', 1952, MUL.

[257] Uganda Protectorate, *Annual Report of the Education Department … 1950*, 20.

[258] Uganda Protectorate, *African Education in Uganda: being the report of a committee set up by His Excellency the Governor to study and make recommendations on the future of African education in the Uganda Protectorate* (Entebbe, 1953), 1 and see the Government's response in Uganda Protectorate, *Memorandum by the Protectorate Government on the Report of the African Education Committee* (Entebbe, 1953).

[259] Uganda Government, *Education in Uganda: the report of the Uganda Education Commission* (Entebbe, 1963), 3.

[260] 'The Bukedi Student: the magazine of Bukedi Makerere Students Union', 1961–62.

for their children; but the major problems included a distorted system which fed youth unemployment and which militated against essential agricultural and manual work, and the absence of 'the stabilising influence of a prosperous and self-respecting middle group of citizens, composed largely of well-paid and highly skilled artisans and producers'.[261] Education must be directed towards the creation of such a group, which would in turn feed Uganda's industrial development.[262] It was a lament which would be echoed by the NRM three decades later – as would the exhortation in 1963 'to encourage Uganda's citizens to think beyond the confines of race and tribe, for Uganda as a nation now exists in an international world where parochial thinking is at a discount. We hope, therefore, that sound education will help heal division and promote national harmony'.[263]

The late colonial state had – belatedly – placed much greater emphasis than previously on development through medicine and education, marking a significant shift in the emergence of the idea that the state itself might provide, and accordingly facilitate greater cohesion and mobility. It was to prove chimeric, but had a powerful hold at a critical moment in the middle years of the twentieth century. The independent Ugandan state did indeed take very seriously the provision of social services, and it was one of the hallmarks of the Obote government of the 1960s.[264] But appropriate levels of investment in health and education would prove to be an enormous financial and logistical challenge, and was vulnerable to political instability. Even prior to independence, the costs of healthcare were sometimes seen to be prohibitive – as in when, in 1958, Mengo CMS Hospital had to close down two thirds of its beds and cease general nursing courses owing to rising debts, despite financial assistance from the government.[265] Still, while the hospitals built between the 1920s and the 1950s by the British formed the foundation of the Ugandan health service, the new government was energetic: by 1970, some twenty new hospitals had been built, and until his arrest for allegedly plotting against Obote in 1966, Dr Emmanuel Lumu, Uganda's first health minister, was the driving force behind much of this expansion and brought a marked

[261] Uganda Government, *Education in Uganda*, 2.
[262] Ibid., 40.   [263] Ibid., 3–4.
[264] Uganda Government, *The First Five-Year Development Plan*, 42–6.
[265] 'Mengo reducing beds by two thirds', *Uganda Argus*, 11 January 1958.

degree of dynamism and vision to the role.[266] Nonetheless, despite the efforts of the Obote regime, facilities remained basic in outlying rural areas, away from the shiny and well-appointed urban hospitals which served as the medical flagships of the new Uganda. Clinics were small and poorly equipped, and struggled to administer large numbers of potential and actual patients spread over large areas. The strains on the system would only increase in the years to come.

Social services, including health, collapsed in the course of the 1970s and 1980s, coinciding catastrophically with the HIV-AIDS epidemic.[267] The first victims of HIV appeared in the early 1980s, when little was known about the virus either in Africa or anywhere else. The number had escalated significantly by the end of the decade. By the early and mid-1990s, AIDS in Uganda had become a full-blown crisis, killing tens of thousands every year – peaking in the mid-1990s, when 50–60,000 AIDS-related deaths were recorded annually – and to date killing over a million Ugandans in total and leaving many more orphaned and chronically debilitated.[268] The virus reached epidemic proportions in Uganda earlier than most other places in Africa, which meant it was both an early focus for AIDS relief and research, and a showcase for what might be done at the level of the state. Museveni's and the NRM's approach was openness: he declared that AIDS was a major problem, that it had to be tackled, and launched one of the most successful efforts anywhere in the world to bring the crisis under control.[269] The government tended to focus on sexual behaviour, with campaigns emphasising the importance of abstinence, monogamy and (almost as a last resort) the use of condoms. But the Ugandan success story has since come in for critical reassessment in some quarters, with a number of analysts believing that the government exaggerated declining infection rates, for example. By the 2010s, Uganda still had a disturbingly high infection rate – in 2015, it had increased slightly to

---

[266] He is certainly remembered as such: 'Lumu headed the best ever health system in Uganda', *New Vision*, 16 April 2012.

[267] For a concise summary, see J. Iliffe, *The African AIDS Epidemic: a history* (Oxford, 2006), 19–32.

[268] For example, see M. Lyons, 'AIDS and development in Uganda', and C. Obbo, 'Who cares for the carers? AIDS and women in Uganda', in Hansen & Twaddle (eds.), *Developing Uganda*, also Sandra Wallman, *Kampala Women Getting By: wellbeing in the time of AIDS* (London, 1996).

[269] J. Kinsman, *AIDS Policy in Uganda: evidence, ideology, and the making of an African success story* (New York, 2010).

around 7 per cent of the total population, including adult men and women, and children born with HIV[270] – but the government had claimed a major victory in the battle.[271] It was a battle which, however significant the role of the state in creating the parameters for action, was fought on several fronts. NGOs – both international and local, the latter often supported by external funds – played a major role in health provision and in the struggle against AIDS, especially in dealing with the terrible fallout for tens of thousands of orphaned and sick children. As in other spheres, NGOs stepped in where the state's capacity was stretched, or absent. Some of these organisations were religious, and faith-based bodies remained prominent in social services. Yet the Movement was also keen to involve the private sector, and Museveni frequently pointed to the government's success in attracting inward investment in the development of a sustainable pharmaceutical sector: witness the establishment of Quality Chemical Industries in 2005, a joint venture involving Ugandan and Indian investors, with some additional funding from South Africa and the UK. The company's major concerns included anti-retroviral drugs for those infected with HIV, but also those equally critical health concerns which were often overlooked in the global rush to tackle AIDS – notably malaria, which remained a major killer in Uganda. More broadly, however, clinics and hospitals faced quotidian financial struggles and the frailties of the health system were exposed by episodic outbreaks of Ebola which also highlighted the difficulties in extending public information campaigns to rural areas.

Whatever the strains on the system, female fertility is high, child mortality falling and this means that in the decades ahead there will be ever more pressure on a health and social services infrastructure which was fragile and under-equipped to begin with, but which will find increasing numbers of people in need of basic medical care. In 1970, Uganda's population stood at 9.45 million, up a little over 2 million since independence eight years earlier – an annual growth rate of around 3 per cent. Although the growth rate dipped below 3 per cent in the course of the 1970s – reaching a low of 2.6 per cent in 1973 – it soon recovered

[270] For example, 'Uganda battles increase in HIV infections', VoA, 21 July 2015 and see also http://www.avert.org/professionals/hiv-around-world/ sub-saharan-africa/uganda

[271] Uganda AIDS Commission, 'HIV and AIDS Uganda Country progress report, 2013', *Uganda AIDS Commission* (Kampala, 2014).

and has remained buoyant ever since: it reached a high of 3.6 per cent in the second half of the 1980s, and since then has hovered between 3.1 and 3.4 per cent.[272] At the time of writing, Uganda's population is around 37.5 million, and growing fast, with among the highest growth (3.4 per cent) and fertility (approximately six children per woman) rates in the world since 2012.[273] The global average growth rate is 1.2 per cent, and the average number of children per woman globally is 2.7. In effect, this relatively small country's population has increased more than five-fold since independence. Recent projections suggest that Uganda's population will increase a further five times in the next 30–35 years, reaching 130 million by the middle of the twenty-first century.[274] The strain on Uganda's limited resources is already a cause for concern, and the government's current lack of serious family planning policies has been identified by various quarters as a major problem. Museveni himself, indeed, apparently delights in Uganda's spiralling population, referring to it as a great resource.[275] But this is a young population – the median is below sixteen years at the time of writing – with little or no access to opportunity or employment. Arguably, this is the biggest crisis on Uganda's horizon in the early twenty-first century. Without both adequate family planning and improvements to the healthcare system, the Uganda described in this book over the past two hundred years will become unrecognisable – and not in positive ways.

As in medical care, so in education, an arena in which the independent state has struggled to rebuild since the 1970s and 1980s, and in which ambitions – and priorities – have proven, perhaps inevitably, to be controversial. By the mid-1970s, a more Africa-centred curriculum had been introduced in schools and faculty itself had been thoroughly Africanised.[276] But as the Amin and Obote II regimes unravelled, the education sector was hard hit, as resources evaporated and teaching staff struggled to get by, or fled the country. Under the Movement,

---

[272] See the excellent website http://countrymeters.info/en/Uganda

[273] 'Uganda population at record 37 million', *New Vision*, 23 June 2013.

[274] See the report in http://www.worldwatch.org/node/4525

[275] 'Uganda faced with high and unsustainable population growth – Parliamentary report', Radio One FM, 10 July 2014, http://radioonefm90 .com/uganda-faced-with-high-and-unsustainable-population-growth- parliamentary-report/

[276] 'Inaugural Address by the Honourable Minister of Education Brigadier Barnabas Kili, DSO', in National Curriculum Development Centre, *The Inaugural National Curriculum Conference Report* (Kampala, 1973).

in the 1990s, education was prioritised: schools were rebuilt and the government pursued a programme of universal primary education.[277] But it struggled with how to pay for such a commendable policy, and one of the obvious options – increased student fees at Makerere, and at secondary schools – has inevitably provoked protest.[278] In many ways just as contentious was the question over what kind of education would best serve Uganda. It was Museveni's conviction that a liberal arts education (of which the President himself was a recipient) was ill-suited to Uganda's requirements. The overwhelming priority, as in the economic sphere, has been identified as 'development'; as a result, considerable emphasis was quickly placed on science subjects, including agriculture, veterinary science, engineering, medicine. Education resources were redirected accordingly – a new university at Mbarara was established with the purpose of supporting rural development – and humanities and 'liberal arts' subjects have suffered accordingly. History in particular has come in for sustained criticism from the President himself, who has described it as badly taught and in any case of no use in the pursuit of national development – much to the detriment of the morale of those who teach it, both in schools and at university.[279] In the attempt to overcome the long-term failings in history education, and in place of it, the government has aggressively promoted a patriotism agenda, with patriotic clubs in schools providing flattened out, ahistorical summations of the nation's struggles and achievements.[280] And young Ugandans, too, eschew subjects which promise no opportunity, no material gain, no job (other than a teaching post) and instead apply to study business, development studies, economics, information technology, media. Meeting – and indeed fuelling – this demand is a plethora of private schools, colleges and universities, which very much push the science-and-economics agenda and generally eschew the liberal arts and humanities subjects.

[277] Museveni, *Mustard Seed*, 200.

[278] Author's field notes and informal interviews, 2010–15 and see, for example, '40 Makerere University students arrested over strike', *Daily Monitor*, 7 October 2015.

[279] Reid, 'Ghosts', *passim*, and author's field notes and informal interviews, 2010–15.

[280] 'Museveni wants patriotism clubs, scouts fused', *Daily Monitor*, 21 August 2015, and see 'The National Secretariat for Patriotism Clubs Statement', Office of the President / Uganda Media Centre, http://www.mediacentre.go .ug/press-release/national-secretariat-patriotism-clubs-statement

Stephen Kiprotich, the long-distance runner from Kapchorwa district in Sebei sub-region on the Uganda–Kenya border, hadn't had much schooling in his earlier life; in fact a serious illness had prevented him from attending school for several years. But at the 2012 Olympic Games in London, he won gold in the marathon and was an overnight national hero, accorded an uproarious reception on his return. The Entebbe road was blocked by the crowds of people who turned out to welcome him home, and a state banquet was given in his honour at State House. President Museveni gave him 200 million Ugandan shillings (around US $80,000), and promoted him several ranks in his job as a prison warden, making him assistant superintendent. Kiprotich was grateful, but asked the President to build a house for his impoverished parents. Museveni agreed to do so.[281] Kiprotich was the hero of the hour, but he belonged to a long line of champions and icons and avatars who embodied the idea of social mobility; uniting the community in celebration, and appealing to political authority which bestows great rewards upon them. It was one of the surest ways of protecting oneself from the hardships of the world. These heroes exemplified the serendipity of talent and opportunity, undergirded by courage and mettle, and they resonate across time and space in Ugandan history.

Kiprotich drew perhaps his immediate inspiration from the example of Uganda's previous gold medal-winner, the 400m hurdler John Akii-Bua from Lango, who had won gold at the Munich Olympics in 1972 and who had been given a state funeral upon his death in 1997.[282] But the line stretched back further than that, and emblematic characters appear throughout oral tradition and folklore as heroes from humble backgrounds who nonetheless seize the day and come to the attention of the great and the powerful. It is an idea perhaps best encapsulated in the story of Kasindula, as told to Stanley: the modest sub-chief of an insignificant district in mid-nineteenth century Buganda, Kasindula goes out of his way to prove his loyalty to the *kabaka* by outdoing all the great courtly chiefs in the capture of enormous amounts of war booty from Busoga. He is granted an audience with Suna, where he describes himself as poor and deprived in contrast to the well-appointed chiefs surrounding the *kabaka*, and with

---

[281] 'Uganda Olympic champion Kiprotich given hero's welcome', BBC News, 15 August 2012.
[282] 'John Akii-Bua, 47, is Dead, Ugandan won Olympic gold', *New York Times*, 25 June 1997.

none of their socio-political advantages; thus his achievement was all the greater, and purer. Suna, profoundly moved by this humble servant's courage and ambition, agrees, and lavishes him with riches and political position. He becomes a *mukungu*, a great chief.[283] Uganda's modern history is replete with stories of aspiration and expectation, of the drive for social mobility. Kasindula went about becoming socially mobile in the 'right' way, and was duly rewarded. There was not such a happy ending for the two young men in the late 1880s who also captured the aspirational spirit of the age: they were attached to the royal court, perhaps as pages, and they were condemned to death for seizing and selling a slave to a coastal trader in return for some much-prized cotton cloth. Unfortunately for them, the slave had belonged to the *katikiro*, the king's chief minister.[284] Expanding global trade excited material passions in new ways, and ignited struggles over access to the benefits it was seen to offer – in material comfort and personal security, but also in terms of the social prestige which possession of certain imported commodities was seen to involve. Of course, trade of this kind was only made possible by pre-existing divisions of labour and cultures of economic specialisation. Buganda, famously, had long been a markedly competitive society in which mobility – upward and downward – was part of the fabric of life, and such cultures can be identified in all of the southern monarchies. But differentiation increased fairly dramatically as a result of global commerce, to which some had access and many others not. Imported goods produced new cultures of materialism and disparity. It is worth reiterating the fundamental paradox of Uganda's nineteenth century that while economic change involved material integration, pulling disparate places together and making economic links and relationships across the region viable and durable, it also drove stratification and differentiation, heightened difference, and bolstered the redistributive power of gatekeeping. One of the earliest examples of this, perhaps, is the impact the import of cotton had on the bark cloth economy in late eighteenth-century Buganda. As the Ganda elite shifted increasingly to cotton cloth, beginning a long-term trend towards coastal fashions, bark cloth production apparently became more widespread, its popularity the result of official encouragement and widening access to a commodity which was previously

---

[283] Stanley, *Dark Continent*, I, 289–94.
[284] White Fathers C14/185 Lourdel to Directeur, 1 June 1888.

restricted.[285] At the same time, indigenous histories of Bunyoro and Buganda, reaching back far beyond the era of long-range commerce, are replete with stories of men undone by greed, of over-mighty individuals (among them kings as well as their subjects) known for their great material wealth in land, in people, in cattle, and in goods and who are often laid low by the ambition which drove them. Modern bitterness about the gluttony and insatiability of the ruling class is nothing new, therefore; material accumulation, often through vice, may now be on a scale undreamt of by any precolonial *mukama* or *kabaka*, but its moral and social dimensions are something with which Ugandans have been wrestling for centuries, reflected in oral histories and literatures.

Of course economic endeavour was only one route by which to achieve social mobility. More generally, war, cultures of militarism and the practice of violence have likewise been attractive to the aspirational and ambitious, both socially and politically. Among the Ateker groups of northeast Uganda, as Lamphear has eloquently argued, individual warrior prowess led to positions of leadership, and successful young men could become commanders of what were in effect small private armies which often collaborated with others to form temporary large armies but which were above all vehicles for individual and small-group social and political and ultimately material mobility.[286] Nyoro and Ganda oral histories offer up tales of derring-do and martial prowess, which brought great wealth and position to those lucky enough to bring their tales before the *kabaka* and – perhaps more important – have others corroborate those tales. Successful and courageous Nyoro and Ganda soldiers might expect considerable material reward and honour, and while pusillanimous soldiers in Nkore were not punished, according to one source, they knew they might never expect 'promotion'.[287] We can only speculate as to the precise ways in which such cultures of militarism persisted into the twentieth century and beyond, but persist they certainly did. For all the social and psychological trauma experienced by countless communities and individuals as a result of nineteenth-century political upheaval and warfare, many others joined the colonial army for many of the same reasons that their forebears had joined campaigns in the nineteenth century:

---

[285] Roscoe, *The Baganda*, 403, Reid, *Political Power*, 73–5.
[286] Lamphear, 'Evolution', 69.
[287] Roscoe, *The Bakitara*, 312; Kagwa, *Customs*, 93; Roscoe, *The Banyankole*, 160–1.

for pecuniary gain, social recognition, security. Moreover, the idea persisted – down to the NRM itself, and a host of its opponents who
have taken to the bush in armed defiance – that participation in armed
combat was a route not only to political transformation, but also to
personal advancement and achievement, to a realisation of the *self*,
in both material and spiritual ways. Much of this was driven by, and
manifest in, generational conflict. Military and political leaders had
episodically used the young in pursuit of larger aims – most dramatically in the form of 'child soldiers'. In the early nineteenth century,
Kabaka Kamanya was noted for his 'restless warfare' involving children as young as fourteen;[288] two centuries later, one of the central
modus operandi of Kony's LRA, notoriously, was the use of children
in its ranks. But more generally, each generation struggled with the one
preceding it for a redistribution of political and material resources, and
for a different interpretation of the past. That conflict has been profoundly destabilising but, as with the succession wars of precolonial
Bunyoro, it has been essential in guaranteeing social movement, creativity and – so the thinking goes – the entry of the best people into
the most important positions. Our slave-stealing youths noted above
were one manifestation of a wider phenomenon in late nineteenth-
century Buganda, namely the young, privileged class of pages – the
sons, and some daughters, of chiefs of varying rank – who had not
necessarily proven themselves in war but who were able to use political (and religious) intrigue for self-advancement. They had access to
guns and to the *kabaka*, and the insignia of political status, and in the
decade between the late 1880s and 1900 would wrest control of the
kingdom from the generation born in the 1840s. Some of those caught
up in these changes – for example the Kagwa generation, born in the
Mutesa era between the 1850s and the 1870s – would emerge in the
later nineteenth century as a new elite, shaping early colonial Buganda
and Uganda more broadly. This was a process of commercial change
and aspiration which can be dated to the middle years of the nineteenth
century, though of course it can also be argued that the fact that Kagwa,
Mukasa *et al* period began their careers as pages at the royal court in
the first place demonstrates a certain continuity in terms of a specifically political elite which was emerging in the same period. Arguably,
Kabaka Suna's reforms in creating new groupings of *batongole* in the

---

[288] Kagwa, *Customs*, 43.

1830s and 1840s gave rise to a new political elite which was then in a position to take advantage of commercial change.[289] Thus we can discern a prevalent theme in modern Ugandan history, namely the fact that political elites were able to take advantage of the social and economic opportunities on offer – so long as they did not fall foul of the prevailing political winds of their particular eras.

Out of similar processes of political change and realignment would emerge, as we have noted, an educated, literate, articulate political class which was the product of the Christian mission in Uganda. The turbulent and dangerous events of the late nineteenth century would have an abiding influence on the generation caught up in them, as they overthrew an older monarchical order in pursuit of a new one – and again the recollections of that cohort as they attained venerable old age in the 1930s drew attention to their contribution to the evolution of a civilised Uganda, and revealed anxiety about the feckless, immoral, amnesiac young who copied European ways and in so doing eschewed propriety.[290] The epoch of Kagwa and Kakungulu was the age of opportunity, and opportunism; their youth had been spent engaged in the great struggle for Christian truth. But they in their turn would be challenged a younger, differently educated generation weary of their dominance of literary output and political position. In some cases these struggles were played out between educated young men and those holding chiefly positions within the colonial order, to which youth were increasingly hostile. Even so, as the ethnographic work of Audrey Richards and others into the nature and composition of chiefship in the 1950s revealed, in the late colonial period local political position was often inherited; a particular level of wealth was qualification for office, but education was increasingly expected to be of a certain standard – a standard which was out of reach for most Ugandans. Among the Gisu, for example, 'the higher chiefs are drawn from the social elite. They have more education and generally come from wealthier families. The two are closely connected, because it is only the wealthier families who can afford a good education for their sons'.[291] The opportunities for a Kasindula still existed, but in some ways he

---

[289] Kagwa, *Kings*, 124, 128 and Southwold, *Bureaucracy and Chiefship*.
[290] 'Education, Civilization and "Foreignisation" in Buganda', pamphlet by the *Kabaka* (1935), in D.A. Low (ed.), *The Mind of Buganda: documents of the modern history of an African kingdom* (London, 1971).
[291] Richards (ed.), *East African Chiefs*, 270.

was less likely to emerge as the twentieth century drew on, owing to the inequity of access to education and thus the closing of the political ranks as a result.[292]

But the idea persisted, and persists still, in the stories which fill the shelves of bookshops in early-twenty-first century Uganda – books about the overcoming of adversity, self-made achievement blessed by God, rags-to-riches. Inspiration memoir proliferated, including that penned by such a high-profile personage as Janet Museveni herself, who followed her husband into print with her life history, her Oprah-style 'journey', which sought ultimately to highlight her role as the great campaigner and political idealist.[293] Other examples of motivational and confessional literature included the autobiography of Gilbert Bukenya, which ended not with the corruption scandals in which he was later ensnared but with the poor boy from the village becoming vice-president.[294] In a similar vein was Pius Bigirimana's memoir, describing his transformation – made possible through 'positive thinking' – from barefoot child to Permanent Secretary in the Prime Minister's Office.[295] Positive thought and the power of dreams – as well as the importance of some help from above – underpinned the autobiography of successful businesswoman Rehmah Kasule, liberally sprinkled with motivational quotations from the great and the good.[296] In many respects this literature was representative of the 'new' Uganda – the Uganda that had been wrought by the NRM, neoliberalism and indeed relative security. The rise of the nation appeared to have something of an echo in the increasingly prevalent story of the *individual*; or, put another way, the rise of the individual, facilitated by neoliberal economics, paralleled the reconstruction of Uganda itself. The rise of a sense of individualism perhaps indicated a greater capacity for personal reflection, and a wider sense of odyssey, and this in turn appeared to be connected to the increasing confidence of the individual's place in the collective. The individual, according to this reading, had been empowered, and was able to engage in a direct, personal relationship

[292] For a still-highly-readable account of socio-political change across the region, see Wrigley, 'Changes in East African society'.

[293] Museveni, *My Life's Journey* and see the President's own *Mustard Seed*.

[294] G. Bukenya, *Through Intricate Corridors to Power* (Kampala, 2008).

[295] P. Bigirimana, *Abundance Mentality: my autobiography* (Brighton, 2011).

[296] R. Kasule, *From Gomba to the White House: the journey of an African woman entrepreneur* (Kampala, 2010).

with the nation, as well as taking responsibility for his or her contribution to it. But as an idea it drew on some much older tropes and visions.

This literature sat alongside countless books on success in business, on making money and getting ahead, which themselves complemented neatly work on spiritual well-being and fulfilment, on God moving in mysterious ways to transform lives, often rewarding hard work and devotion with the material security which the emergent Ugandan middle class so craved. What loomed into view was a complex tapestry of consumerism and spiritualism, of God and mammon indelibly intertwined, of mall culture and increasingly global tastes and aspirations. And that expanded middle class was greatly in evidence in Kampala in particular: these were the people holding down white-collar jobs across the public and private sectors, running several cars, sending their children to good schools, but worrying about the future, about what would happen in the event of regime change, about the very stability of the foundations on which the 'new' Uganda was built. And in Kampala, they stood out amidst the quotidian (and equally expanding) poverty: here, in the increasingly cramped, congested city, the contrast between the relatively rich and the extremely poor was stark and visible. For many young Ugandans, men and women alike, the only way to cross that divide was, again, through education. And so they sought to scrape the money together to attend one of the rapidly growing number of private colleges and universities across the country, with their focus on business studies and the like, and their overriding goal of material improvement. The fees in many of these institutions could be lower than in a big public institution like Makerere University, but they often remained prohibitively high, and parents struggled to earn enough money to give their children the education they so desperately craved for them; drop-out rates were high as a result.[297] And so, not for these young people the insane indulgence of the humanities, which could only lead to a life of impoverished reflection and an underpaid job as a teacher; for the 'NRM babies', the products of neoliberal economics, it was about business management, computing, or commerce, following the Government's own aggressive agenda promoting those subjects which would generate revenue, and facilitate opportunity.

---

[297] Author's field notes and informal interviews, 26 June 2011.

Nonetheless, financial challenges notwithstanding, a host of opportunities continued to open up in terms of leisure and entertainment.
Ugandans had long known how to organise leisure as an expression of
aspiration, and as a means to social cohesion and fulfilment. Music,
central to all Ugandan cultures, developed in ways which reflected
both socio-economic change, indeed celebrated it, while also providing much-needed diversion from the harsher realities of life: Congolese
music, for example – first taking root in the early 1930s – provided the
soundtrack to socio-economic and political tumult in the late colonial and early postcolonial eras, and was central to the energetic band
culture which dominated the new clubs and bars proliferating across
southern Uganda in the middle decades of the twentieth century. People danced as society mutated, and often in the face of calamity, as
they did in the 1980s to the music of Philly Lutaaya, whose public battle with AIDS greatly assisted the government's efforts. In the 1990s,
Kampala in particular witnessed the re-emergence of a thriving live
music scene as the ever-popular Congolese vibe was augmented by the
sound of South African artists as well as adaptations of Western influences, including hip-hop, rap and R&B.[298] For those who could afford
it, there were widening prospects for leisure time, underpinned by an
increasingly ubiquitous corporate sponsorship. Likewise in the realm
of sport, and in particular football, which had been played in an organised way ever since the founding of the Uganda Football Association in
1925. In the second half of the twentieth century, football was played
the length and breadth of Uganda with passion and joy in pursuit of a
host of local trophies – a love for the game and its champions which
transcended class, ethnicity and faith, and indeed national boundaries,
for while the fortunes of the Cranes, the national side, were keenly
followed, so too were those of the top-flight English clubs.

And thus sport and music facilitated the elevation of heroes and idols
in many forms, and Kiprotich took his place in a long tradition of
diversion and entertainment, and of dreams of achievement and bet-
terment. Above all, perhaps, it represented Ugandans' innate capacity for fun, and their ability to channel desire, in an era of profound
change and often violent tumult. But while young people continued to

[298] *Independent Uganda*, 378*ff*, is a mine of information. The history of popular
music in Uganda has yet to be written, but whoever does so will have a
wonderful time in the process.

aspire, their own confidence levels and drive to succeed may be seen to have been directly linked to cultural and ethnic background: as one recent study of Konzo and non-Konzo girls studying in science subjects in Busongora-Kasese district demonstrated, Konzo girls suffered as a result of low self-esteem and self-confidence, the result (the author suggested) of decades of marginalisation, neglect and conflict in the area.[299] Even more broadly, there is chronic regional inequity: the vast majority of schools, and institutions of further and higher education, located in the south, and in or close to the urban centres, reinforcing rural and northern marginalisation. It has never been truer that one's life opportunities in modern Uganda depend very much on where, and to whom, one is born.

Migrant Nation, 3: Immigrants and Citizens

The expulsion of the Indian community represented the culmination of an especially difficult, and very visible, dynamic in terms of immigration and, eventually, citizenship in modern Uganda. But more broadly it is an issue of critical significance in understanding modern society and economy. In the second half of the nineteenth century, the Ugandan region witnessed a significant upsurge in the number of people being exported to the wider East African area and beyond. In the early 1900s, this situation was reversed, sharply, with the beginnings of what would become an enormous expansion of immigrant labour *into* the territory. Just as in Uganda's deeper past migration was absolutely critical to the evolution of political culture, and to economic and social development, so in the twentieth century, too, migration played an enormously important role – if in some respects an even more contentious one. Immigrant labour across the region was nothing new; it had a deep and profoundly important history in Uganda. The potential crisis brought about by the death of slavery and the slave trade – on which many of the southern kingdoms had come to rely – in the 1890s was mitigated by the influx of foreign labour in the early twentieth century, labour which performed much the same role as slavery

---

[299] J. M. Mateso, 'Cultural Identity and Self Esteem as Factors in Self Efficacy in Sciences among Bakonzo and Non Bakonzo Girls in Busongora-Kasese District', unpublished Masters thesis in Educational Psychology, Makerere University, 2008.

had in the nineteenth century: enhancing political authority and economic power, and freeing up the owners of land and capital to engage in politics and education and social advancement. The greatest shift, perhaps, in this context was not the rupture between slaves/ivory in the late nineteenth century and cash crops in the early twentieth; it was the fact that the experiences of the transition among the Ganda and the Acholi, for example, were so markedly divergent.

Our history of immigration in Uganda's long twentieth century begins at the close of the nineteenth, with the arrival of a series of communities – and communities in the making – as part of the new political order associated with colonial rule, or in response to the socio-economic opportunities opening up. An example of the former was the Nilotic Nubi, originally the southern Sudanese soldiers deployed by the British in the founding of the Ugandan Protectorate in the 1890s.[300] Exemplifying the latter, and arguably of greater long-term significance, was the Asian community – mostly Bangladeshis and Indians – who began to arrive in the 1890s and 1900s, and who may have numbered as many as 80,000 in the 1950s and 1960s before their expulsion by Idi Amin in the early 1970s; a comparatively small number has returned, perhaps around 12,000 at the time of writing, though still economically significant. For the moment, however, our concern is with a range of other groups – both within Uganda and from outside the territory – who moved and frequently resettled in the course of the twentieth century in search of work. These economic migrants were in many ways the bedrock of the modern Ugandan economy, and played a fundamental role in urban growth in the south, especially Kampala. The key driver was the expansion of commercial agriculture across southern Uganda, especially in Buganda, which in time attracted the vast bulk of immigrant labour. The booming cash crop sector, and the greatly heightened demand for manual labour, drew in hundreds of thousands from various parts of Uganda, as well as transregional migrants from Rwanda, Congo and Kenya. Labour shortage was a constant concern for the colonial administration, and increasingly for the Ganda themselves. In the early 1900s, the expansion of the cotton economy meant that the Ganda could earn enough money for taxes and all the

---

[300] Their descendants are now largely Muslim urban dwellers. Nubi soldiers and functionaries would play a key role in shoring up Idi Amin's regime in the 1970s: see Leopold, *Inside West Nile*, 15.

necessities of life (and a few luxuries, too) without having recourse to wage labour;[301] but this was a period, in Kampala and the surrounding area, when demand for labour on plantations and for head porterage was fast exceeding supply, while Christian influence on women in particular was discouraging them from engaging in cotton cultivation, at least full-time, and placing more pressure on men to support family homesteads.[302]

While the south was identified early on by the British administration as being the key to the Protectorate's economic development, the north, by contrast – West Nile, Madi, Acholi and Lango provinces – was officially perceived as economically unviable save as a vast labour reserve. By the beginning of the 1920s, increasing numbers of northern migrants were heading south to find the kind of wage labour needed to pay taxes, get married, set up home. In that sense, many were 'wage raiders', travelling south for short periods before returning home; but many stayed, and settled across the south. In the early 1930s, the anthropologist Lucy Mair noted:

As a result partly of the decline of voluntary co-operation and partly of the disappearance of slavery wage-labour has become a normal feature of Baganda life. The labourers are almost entirely drawn from other tribes....The Baganda regard themselves as belonging to the employing class.[303]

Some of these migrants stayed just long enough to earn money to pay their taxes, save some cash, and return home; but others 'settle permanently, building their own houses and sending for their families. One often sees a little village of some alien tribe standing by itself not far from the Baganda village where the first arrivals worked'.[304] The north was also a hunting ground for army recruiters: during the First World War, the British began recruiting among the Alur, for example, and the experience of these pioneers motivated other Alur to migrate south. At the same time, a major famine occurred in 1919–20, which prompted many to leave their homeland and head for work to the south.[305] When

---

[301] Hattersley, *Baganda at Home*, 114.
[302] P.G. Powesland, 'History of the migration in Uganda', in A.I. Richards (ed.), *Economic Development and Tribal Change: a study of immigrant labour in Buganda* (Cambridge, 1954), 21–2.
[303] Mair, *An African People*, 127.   [304] Ibid.
[305] A.W. Southall, 'Alur migrants', in Richards (eds.), *Economic Development*.

the young Kakwa Idi Amin joined the King's African Rifles in around 1946, he would have been all too aware of the presence of significant numbers of northern compatriots in the army, many from neighbouring and rival 'tribes', following a well-travelled route to adventure and security.

In fact many Alur travelled to Bunyoro, initially, but towards the end of the 1920s, following the decline in commercial agriculture there, they began to target Buganda, as did thousands of others.[306] Many poor young men, and quite a few women, trudged along the paths first tread by their Nilotic ancestors centuries earlier, but this time in pursuit of wages which were unavailable in the increasingly underdeveloped north of the Protectorate. These 'other Ugandans' – the Acholi and Langi, Madi and Alur, Lugbara and Kakwa – flooded the sugar and cotton plantations across the shore of Lake Victoria, particularly after the major Lugazi and Kakira sugar plantations opened either side of Jinja in 1924 and 1929 respectively.[307] They crammed into houses in the ever-sprawling suburbs of Kampala and Jinja and elsewhere in search of jobs as policemen, construction workers, domestic helps, casual labourers. By the time eager student Milton Obote, a Langi, arrived at Makerere College in 1947, he would have been acutely aware that most Langi were in Kampala doing menial jobs, doubtless exacerbating in his young mind a growing sense of the regional disparity which now characterised Uganda. It was the tale, again, of Atuk; yet this was by no means a singularly 'northern' experience. Labour arrived from the far southwest, from Kigezi and Ankole, and from the east, Soga and Gisu. Toro and Nyoro migrant labourers were present in Buganda by the time of the First World War.[308] And then were those from beyond Uganda's borders, chiefly from Belgian Ruanda-Urundi and eastern Congo. They increasingly crossed into Uganda at established points along the Kagera River, with particular surges at times of famine in Rwanda itself (as in 1928), but mostly driven by the generally better conditions and wages on offer in Buganda. Comparatively smaller numbers of Tanganyikans and Kenyans came too, chiefly the

---

[306] Ibid., 141–2.
[307] T. Mushanga, 'Notes on migration in Uganda', in D. Parkin (ed.), *Town and Country in Central and Eastern Africa* (London, 1975), 160–1.
[308] Powesland, 'History of the migration', 21.

Haya and Ziba from northwest Tanganyika,[309] and Luo from Kavirondo province just across Uganda's eastern border.[310] The demand for migrant labour increased further from the early 1930s with the expansion of coffee alongside cotton as a key cash crop in Buganda and the Eastern Region.[311]

Inevitably, these population movements had political implications, and prompted increasing concern for a colonial administration wary of the potential for political disruption both within Uganda and across the wider region.[312] Certainly in 1956 Thomas Hodgkin, in his pioneering work on African nationalism, could write of 'a gradual political awakening' among the Nyarwanda and Rundi who had migrated to Uganda and later returned home.[313] Meanwhile, the emergence of 'tribal' associations and linkages on the part of migrants in the urban environment was well attested in Kampala in the 1960s, even in comparatively 'mixed', middle-class surburbs; David Parkin's work highlighted the dynamics, for example, leading to the growth of the Luo Union – formed among Kenyan immigrants – and the importance of it and other ethnic associations around the period of Ugandan independence, an anxious time for migrants. Many of these organisations appeared in Kampala East, an area of the city with concentrated immigrant settlement.[314]

Much of the migration was by definition rural, in the sense that migrant workers headed towards plantations where there was demand, and these were distributed across rural Buganda. But increasingly migrants came to towns, for the same reasons that people have always been attracted to them – in search of paid work, opportunity and better lives, the 'pull' factor, as well as the 'push' factor, namely the desire to escape the drudgery and poverty of rural home life. They headed toward Kampala, Jinja and Mbale-Tororo.[315] In particular, from the 1930s and 1940s, there was significant migration into Kampala, and

---

[309] J.M. Fortt, 'The distribution of Immigrant and Ganda population within Buganda', in Richards (ed.), *Economic Development*, 109–10.

[310] D. Parkin, *Neighbours and Nationals in an African City Ward* (London, 1969), esp. chapter 1; and David Parkin, 'Tribe as Fact and Fiction in an East African City', in Gulliver (ed.), *Tradition and Transition*, 287–91.

[311] Mushanga, 'Notes', 160.

[312] A.I. Richards, 'The problem and the methods', in Richards (ed.), *Economic Development*, 7.

[313] Hodgkin, *Nationalism in Colonial Africa*, 13.

[314] Parkin, *Neighbours and Nationals*, passim.   [315] Mushanga, 'Notes', 160–1.

the city swelled as a result. If the capital had its roots in Ganda political and commercial ambition in the second half of the nineteenth
century, it was now expanded by the influx of 'strangers', and not
always in healthy ways. The growth of the city was often rapid and
disorderly, with the uncontrolled expansion of 'slum' areas – such as
Kisenyi – of particular concern to colonial administrators and sociolo-
gists alike in the 1950s.[316] The place was soon a microcosm of Uganda,
with the emergence across the city of zones of residency by particular
migrant groups, often in multiple clusters, with particular neighbour-
hoods emerging for Acholi, Lugbara, Nyoro and so on.[317] These urban
communities were by the 1960s arriving by well-established routes
from the north, the west, and the east and were being formed by ethnic
association and probably a range of other dynamics, including occupation and broadly socio-economic status. Migration meant social and
economic diversification – even, arguably, facilitating political thought
and ambition – among the Ganda whose personal time was significantly freed up as a result. An emerging Ganda middle class was thus
enabled to generally 'get on' and claim moral and intellectual leadership, and send their children to school, hence perpetuating a kind
of class revolution begun in the late eighteenth and early nineteenth
centuries with the expansion of slavery and the slave trade. At the
same time, however, migration greatly complicated and problematised
ideas about identity, belonging and ultimately citizenship in independent Uganda. The roots of citizenship are thus entangled and often
obscured. Many of the children of migrants who arrived in the 1940s
and 1950s – especially from Rwanda – would come to 'conceal' their
immigrant origins and 'become Ganda'. An intensive anthropological
survey in Kabale district in the late 1930s revealed that 'the older men
still feel themselves as belonging to the kingdom of Ruanda; but ... the
younger ones consider the immediate advantages of British rule, economic and social, are sufficient to make the separation worthwhile'.[318]

Immigrant status would become, for many, something to be con-
cealed, connoting illegitimacy: one of the surest signs of Museveni's

---

[316] Southall & Gutkind, *Townsmen in the Making*.
[317] M.A. Hirst, 'The distribution of migrants in Kampala, Uganda', in Parkin
(ed.), *Town and Country*; also Parkin, *Neighbours and Nationals*, passim.
[318] 'Giharo Mutalla Survey Report, 1937', Kabale District Archives, ADM67, File
No. 193, 33.

waning popularity was the fact that rumours began to spread regarding his foreign origins – Tanzania, said some; Burundi, whispered others – which was a way of explaining incompetence and corruption.[319] More recently, in an age of terrorism but also in an age of pressed resources and growing poverty, there has been a growing fear and suspicion of strangers and foreigners – for example, of Congolese and Somalis getting through borders with ease and turning up in unexpected places.[320] The question of who was 'truly Ugandan' was one that was raised repeatedly, not least by government itself. While a popular self-image among many Ganda is that they are hospitable and welcoming and will 'accept everyone' into their ranks, the strictures contained in an unofficial 'Buganda passport' – a little piece of propagandist ephemera – suggest otherwise: a 'true Muganda' should be able to answer a long list of questions, relating to clan, ancestry and lineage. For those Nyarwanda who came to Buganda in the 1940s, and whose descendants now claimed to be 'pure Ganda', some degree of invention would presumably be required.[321] This sensitive subject requires more work, and certainly complicates received wisdoms about the purity of clan and ethnic identity, and above all has serious implications for claims on land. While the idea of the permanence of clan, ethnic group, or kingdom retained an elevated, idealised status, the fact remains that Uganda is a nation of migrants, porous and selectively absorbent, its cultures and essences indelibly linked to, even drawn from, the surrounding region. The politics of enclosure in the course of the long twentieth century has complicated matters, rendering the sharper demarcation of particular types of belonging altogether more urgent, and more contested. And in this respect, too, histories and identities have become at once more prone to being massaged and cultivated, and more rigid in their public projection. In the migrant nation, the past is simultaneously perilous and yet fundamental, often with certain issues deliberately obscured, and an especial emphasis on matters of tradition and origin. There is, today, still a place in Uganda for the foreign immigrant, an echo of the fluidity and mobility of the deeper past, in which arguably – and the point is always arguable – states and societies were more porous, more receptive and more adaptable. But

---

[319] Author's field notes and informal interviews, 6 November 2012.
[320] Author's field notes and informal interviews 27 October 2013.
[321] Author's field notes and informal interviews, 10 February 2014.

there can be little doubt that ideas about class and status – even race – have indeed hardened up over time.

The implications of migration have been enormous for modern Uganda: most obviously in areas of Buganda itself, but no less in the migrant areas themselves in terms of a labour drain, economic inequity, and in some cases, ultimately, ethnic and political mobilisation. Modern Uganda is largely the product of the movement and resettlement of people both within and from outside the territory, just as in the deeper past. Mobility has clearly had advantages, for both migrant and host, personally and collectively, in terms of both material benefit as well as life experience, widening horizons, political consciousness. Yet there are less positive implications. Over the last century, generations of inward migration have kept wages low for a range of 'menial' and unskilled labour occupations. It has served, again, to heighten ethnic chauvinism within Uganda itself. And of course over the long term it has served to impoverish the home districts of the migrants themselves. As a result of labour movement, such underdevelopment takes on its own momentum, self-perpetuates, and is ultimately extremely difficult to reverse. The twentieth-century political and economic inequity driving migration has actually served to *undermine* the modern nation, to balkanise and fragment it. It has served to harden the sense of self among host communities (and indeed among migrants), while perpetuating and stiffening stereotypes about 'other tribes'. It is no great stretch of the imagination to propose that northern domination of the army and the police, for example, would ultimately intersect with a sense of national division and more specifically a long-term grievance against the 'prosperous' south among various northern actors. We live in an era in which sensitivity about the immigrant and the indigenous, about citizenship and the rights and duties it might entail, and ultimately over strangers who might seek to do us harm, has become greatly heightened.[322] The modern era is one of increasingly political exercises in origin and difference and belonging. These are certainly debates of considerable urgency in Uganda today. But almost all Ugandans are immigrants of one kind or another, and the vast bulk of putatively rooted, indigenous societies are the product

---

[322] See, for example, essays by Preben Kaarsholm, James Brennan, Jonathon Glassman and Jeremy Prestholdt on Africa and the Indian Ocean in *Journal of African History*, 55:2 (2014).

of interaction with strangers who settle in their midst, or the progeny of mobile strangers. This is the story of appropriation and adaptation, of intermixture and integration – of conflict and stratification, but also of the forging of ties through difference. Over *la longue dureé*, Uganda is the migrant nation *par excellence*; and the quest for an integrated set of histories, therefore, is simultaneously more challenging and more rewarding than might be supposed at first glance.

'Who is More Patriotic – the one who Builds up the Economy, or the one who Runs it Down?'[323]

By the middle of the 1980s, the Ugandan economy was in a raddled state. The export economy had deteriorated significantly, the public finances were in dire straits, infrastructure had withered dramatically, and in many ways what economic activity there was remained under the control of the *Mafuta Mingi* which had arisen in the wake of the Indians' expulsion in the early 1970s. This was true despite emergency aid from the UK and Kenya, and the fact that the new global neoliberal orthodoxy had already been adopted by the UPC government: it was Milton Obote who early in his second administration had begun to implement the austerity measures demanded as part of the IMF's proposed aid package and structural adjustment programme.[324] He was now willing to embrace liberalisation and confessed, many years later, that he regretted nationalisation and the shift to the Left in the late 1960s.[325] In fact between 1981 and 1983 some stability had returned to the economy, but amidst political violence, little real progress had been achieved since the meltdown under Amin in the course of the 1970s. Moreover, the northern parts of the country were ravaged by famine as a result of the prolonged Sahelian drought: in the early 1980s, Karamoja province was starving to death while Obote waged war on the NRA further south.[326]

---

[323] Museveni, *Mustard Seed*, 181.

[324] G. Mwakikagile, *Obote to Museveni: political transformation in Uganda since independence* (Dar es Salaam, 2012), 127.

[325] 'Milton Obote: telling his own lifetime story', *Daily Monitor*, 24 October 2005.

[326] 'While the politicians squabble the children starve', *DRUM*, September 1980. See also a historical perspective in Mahmood Mamdani, 'Karamoja: colonial roots of famine in North-East Uganda', *Review of African Political Economy*, 9:25 (1982), and an important critique of that piece by Beverly Gartrell,

For Museveni and the Movement, and many of their allies, the causes of contemporary catastrophe were to be found in Uganda's deeper economic history, or rather two broadly discernible phases of it. First, the 'precolonial' era – a time of petty tribalism, of virtually no commercial value whatever when set alongside the achievements of eighteenth- and nineteenth-century Europe. Museveni was certainly much more enthusiastic about the latter, especially in terms of the rise of a dynamic, industrial middle class and the demonstrable power of free market economics.[327] And then there was the colonial economy, for which Ugandans might be grateful in terms of some basic infrastructure and some of the accoutrements of modernity but which otherwise had wilfully buckled indigenous economic development and produced an under-skilled labour force – and no useable middle class to speak of.[328] Museveni would certainly make a hobby of blaming British rule for all of Uganda's contemporary problems. These historical disasters represented the baselines for contemporary malaise, the reference points against which all subsequent achievements must be measured.

As in politics, so in economics: the NRM would rebirth the nation, and it would do so through the supposedly transformative power of the global market, of which the country's new leadership was seemingly in awe. In the late 1980s and early 1990s, the Movement went much further than Obote in taking up the recommendations of the now-(in)famous Berg Report to the World Bank in 1981 which enshrined the need to scale back the state and throw up ravaged economies to the private sector – though Museveni himself had rather more in common with Obote in undergoing something of an ideological conversion from Left to Right. He was in good company, of course: all manner of political insurgents and ideologues in Africa in the 1960s and 1970s were broadly on the Left, or regarded themselves as such, only to transfer their convictions in the 1980s and 1990s. They did so, often, quite independently of any structural adjustment programmes arising from the Berg Report, for by this time, across the continent, the limitations of the state had been brutally exposed. In the late 1980s and early 1990s, Uganda moved with extraordinary speed from conflict-wracked basket-case to poster-boy for the success of structural

'Searching for "The Roots of Famine": the case of Karamoja', *Review of African Political Economy*, 33 (1985).

[327] Museveni, *Mustard Seed*, 14.
[328] Museveni, *What Is Africa's Problem?*, 182, 191.

adjustment, liberalisation and developmental agendas.[329] Under the NRM, the country became the exemplar of the free-market restructuring embraced by (and indeed imposed upon) a large number of African governments, involving large-scale privatisation and the retraction of the state in economic affairs. This combined with relative political stability, the 'good governance' component in the international development agenda, to burnish the nation with favoured status in the global north. Uganda was 'opened up' – in a way echoing the experience of the nineteenth century, and certainly redolent of the language of colonial strategists – to foreign investment, massive injections of aid and a freer, more liberal economy. Market forces ruled, and Uganda's economy grew steadily over the next twenty years – problems arising from the post-2008 global recession notwithstanding. The stated aim – in many respects wholly comprehensible – was the creation of a vibrant, entrepreneurial middle class, unburdened by state control, and freed up from the clutches of history and tribalism. The nation's economic salvation would lie in the emergence of people who would not only sell and consume, but produce.[330]

Development was once more overwhelmingly southern-focused. In most of the south, the Movement enjoyed relative peace and security, and was thus able to introduce wide-ranging economic reforms as laid out in the Economic Recovery Programme agreed upon between the government and the IMF in 1987.[331] Over the next few years, these reforms were introduced against a backdrop of economic catastrophe: rampant inflation, mass unemployment and extreme hardship even for those with jobs, for the value of their wages had plummeted. Measures included deregulation of pricing and marketing controls, privatisation of major state assets, reform of the civil service and the devaluation of the currency.[332] The result, evident by the early 1990s, was a stabilised financial sector and a more attractive environment for inward investment. Museveni courted the expelled Asian community whose return in the course of the 1990s provided a much-needed fillip to the retail and

---

[329] The most lucid accounts of this are in Tripp, *Museveni's Uganda*, 181–5; and in the economic discussions contained in two Hansen & Twaddle volumes, *Changing Uganda* (1991) and *Developing Uganda* (1998).

[330] The Movement's economic visions are laid out in some detail in Museveni, *What Is Africa's Problem?*

[331] K. Sarwar Lateef, 'Structural adjustment in Uganda: the initial experience', in Hansen & Twaddle (eds.), *Changing Uganda*, 26.

[332] Ibid., 25–37.

tourism sectors, although it was a profoundly unpopular move among many Ugandans who quietly resented their reappearance as key economic actors.[333] Still, there were costs: at the core of structural adjustment was the rolling back of the state's responsibilities in the provision of social services, which suffered as a result, at the very moment when the population was increasing in spite of the AIDS epidemic. The space vacated by the state was soon filled by NGOs, which now became significant socio-economic actors.[334] Cost sharing was introduced in the realms of education and health care, while subsidies were curtailed.[335] The drive towards increased exports and a reduction in the reliance on imports – all with a view to the repayment of international debt – were, again, logical in many respects, but it meant that the national economy remained vulnerable to global price fluctuations for coffee, tea, sugar and cotton, which remained the country's chief exports. It was thus with great excitement that the government escalated the search for oil and gas in the Lake Albert basin, and production promised to bring considerable revenue to state coffers (and of course, to the companies involved) for many years to come.[336] The feeling in Museveni's circle was that this was Uganda's moment, a remarkable opportunity to develop its position as an economic hub, and an exporter of ever more precious resources. The question of who would actually benefit from oil and gas revenues was, as ever, an open one, though many Ugandans remained healthily sceptical.[337] Still, the eagerly anticipated mineral revolution fitted with the government's evangelism around science and technology, as it envisioned a Uganda of the future complete with hydroelectric dams, new cropping technologies, high-speed railways, garden cities and solar power.[338] But for the moment, the most visible manifestation of Ugandan economic growth was Kampala itself, which from the 1980s spread inexorably outward and upward. What

---

[333] This view was first expressed to me in April 1995, and I have heard complaints ever since.

[334] Lateef, 'Structural adjustment', 29, 30.

[335] D. Maxwell, 'Urban agriculture: unplanned responses to the economic crisis', in Hansen & Twaddle (eds.), *Developing Uganda*, 98. Some of these initiatives, however, dated to the Obote administration in the early 1980s: E.O.Ochieng, 'Economic adjustment programmes in Uganda, 1985–89', in Hansen & Twaddle (eds.), *Changing Uganda*, 44.

[336] Shepherd, *Oil in Uganda*, 'Museveni gets his refinery', *Africa Confidential*, 56:5, 6 March 2015.

[337] Author's field notes and informal interviews, July 2015; also ICG, *Uganda*.

[338] See, for example, the 'Uganda in 2062' feature in *Understand Uganda*.

were formerly dusty, peri-urban trunk roads out of town – such as on Kira Road, passing through Kitante and Mulago – became lined with shiny new office complexes and high rises, and in the case of Kira Road, the tinted-glass-fronted Victoria University, a private institution emblematic of neoliberal education policy with its emphasis on business studies. Chronic congestion, meanwhile, gave rise to the *boda-boda* phenomenon, arguably the single most potent manifestation of entrepreneurialism as well as of economic desperation.

The *boda-boda* riders encapsulate a larger issue, which is that, despite impressive GDP growth rates – averaging around 6 per cent since the Movement took power[339] – the informal sector has long accounted for the majority of Ugandans' economic activity, making an accurate assessment of national performance and incomes extremely difficult, if not impossible. Beyond the light-industrial and urban hubs, millions of Ugandans still operate at subsistence level, growing agricultural produce, or performing manual labour. Poverty has not only persisted but increased as a result of privatisation and the attendant proliferation of 'market rates' for everything from housing to schooling and healthcare, meaning the cost of living has increased dramatically but wages have not kept pace. Overall, economic reform has benefited government and party officials themselves and other well-connected elites who have been able to take advantage of major economic projects instead of regulating them. An emergent middle class was quickly in evidence in the urban centres; but so, too, was the gap between those who have benefited from neoliberal economic orthodoxy and those who have been marginalised by it. The government has shown markedly little interest in the growing divide between regions, or in the protection of that enormous group at the bottom of all neoliberal economies, the dispossessed and the vulnerable and the voiceless. Unemployment is rife, especially among the burgeoning youthful population – a major problem for any future government. However, arguably the biggest single problem, in the immediate term, is rampant cronyism and corruption which has become institutionalised under the NRM to a shocking extent.[340] Museveni has singularly failed, for all the frank and colourful rhetoric, to address corruption at the highest levels: from time to time, selected members of the administration have been targeted in much-publicised anti-corruption drives,

---

[339] Tripp, *Museveni's Uganda*, 181–5.   [340] HRW, *'Letting the Big Fish Swim'*.

but very rarely the people closest to the President himself.[341] Corruption had reached such alarming levels that by the early 2010s, the UK, among Uganda's key donors, had suspended aid as a result of the 'disappearance' of millions of dollars from the Prime Minister's office.[342]

Even leaving aside electoral malpractice, it is single most important issue in explaining ordinary Ugandans' loss of faith in the government, with popular perception hardening that Museveni's entire circle (including his family) 'eat too much' – a euphemism for grand fraud; own too much, from shopping malls to housing complexes; and do too little in terms of meaningful investment in Ugandans' lives.[343] For a long time, Museveni himself managed to remain aloof from the problem;[344] but increasingly he is seen as the root of it. The truth of the matter was that while, arguably, the Movement in the late 1980s had little choice but to buy into the so-called 'Washington consensus', given that Uganda was broke and desperate for outside investment and donor assistance,[345] this was never actually about the 'free market': privatisation favoured those could afford to get hold of major assets, and thus this was an economic system that really only benefited a comparatively tiny socio-economic elite with which international financial institutions were content to deal. Nor was this only about financial dominance: land, again, was a critical battleground in early twenty-first Uganda, with the law courts increasingly congested by land disputes, as people sought security and inheritance. And in this realm, too, government expropriation of land bred increasing resentment, with large tracts seized and sold to investors, including those from China and India.[346] Much was to be sacrificed to appease hungry overseas

---

[341] 'Uganda ministers resign over corruption allegations', BBC News, 12 October 2011.

[342] 'UK suspends aid to Uganda as concern grows over misuse of funds', *The Guardian* (London), 16 November 2012.

[343] Author's field notes and informal interviews, 8 November 2012, 20 July 2014, and April 2015.

[344] Author's field notes and informal interviews, 8 August 2010.

[345] This is certainly Museveni's own robust defence of the strategy: see *Mustard Seed*, 180–2.

[346] Author's field notes and informal interviews, April 2015. Moreover, Ugandan retailers have protested the flood of cheap goods from China into local markets: 'Between Extremes: China and Africa', *Africa Research Institute: Briefing Note 1202*, October 2012.

creditors and investors; and perhaps, in the long-term, there will be larger, more tangible benefits. But for many, Ugandan economic growth is ultimately a mirage, based on precisely nothing except access to putatively free money and political power; there is no real economic security, and the growth is not yet based on internal expansion of industry, or anything self-sustaining. For millions of Ugandans, life is extremely tough and often very short, and there are deep socio-economic cleavages which readily become ethnic and religious fissures; modern Uganda should be characterised, in economic terms, not by high growth rates, which in many respects are ultimately meaningless for most Ugandans, but by the stark inequities which now define people's lives. Since the 1990s, choice has proliferated with deregulation and privatisation: choice of schools and universities, of mobile phone network and internet service provider, of eateries and nightclubs and radio stations. The *Mafuta Mingi* class gave way in the 1980s to a group of eager and artful traders known colloquially as the 'Kibanda Boys', a 'Kampala mafia', as novelist Moses Isegawa described them;[347] and they in turn made room for the 'Kikuubo Boys' of downtown Kampala, the rough-hewn kings of import–export in neoliberal Uganda.[348] But the process involved a deep division between those who could take advantage of such choice, and those who were not in a position to do so.

In the broadest terms, the NRM believed that colonial rule had excluded Ugandans from the benefits of the modern global economy. This was certainly a compelling interpretation of the more recent past, but in many ways Uganda's modern economic history could be traced directly to the experience of global commerce in the nineteenth century, during which time the commercial revolution was driven by and for a range of political and socio-economic elites. The NRM believed, ultimately, in particular forms of privatisation and market economics, but in fact the economy remained in the hands of a very few and was open to chronic abuse as a result. This could be seen to represent continuity from the nineteenth century, when, for example, the big slaving export economies were ultimately in the hands of large state-led or otherwise centralised, militarised organisations. What the NRM *had* done was

---

[347] See *Abyssinian Chronicles*, ix and *passim*. 'Kibanda' means black market.
[348] *Independent Uganda*, 263.

to broaden the range of people with access to the economic 'boom'. While the 'elite' expanded in the course of the 1990s and 2000s, mostly based on credit and access, so, too, had the population as a whole, a population explosion which is among the most dramatic in the world in relative terms and which paradoxically the Movement government gleefully celebrated. Ultimately, most people remained 'poor' by any normal definition. Neoliberal economics had *not* addressed the fundamental inequity which could be traced to the second half of the eighteenth century. Zigeye and his equivalents in the decades to follow would come to exercise a remarkable degree of economic influence, although it is important to recall that what had attracted him to the region in the first place was the diversity and vibrancy of extant cultures of production and exchange; but ultimately he needed particular kinds of goods, and those could only be produced on the back of Atuk's labour. So Atuk headed south, like so many before him, and so many since.

Uganda's modern history is characterised by the expansion and intertwining of networks of belonging, and the mobilisation of those networks in pursuit of individual as well as collective security and aspiration. There is plenty of evidence of a history of ambivalence towards the modern nation-state in the realms of healthcare, education and faith. In many cases, the hope exists that the state might provide the services needed for livelihood and well-being – but this sits alongside the mobilisation of deeper ideas around faith, in particular, as a means of protection *against* the state and even circumvent it. The territorial enclosure of the twentieth century has a direct bearing on the contours of ontology, both experience and expectation; but a number of these patterns can be traced into the nineteenth century, and in some ways into the deeper past still. There have been many ways of being Ugandan, and many histories to draw upon. Rendering these compatible and in the interests of – or at least not to the detriment – other members of the national community has been a larger struggle, ongoing. In Uganda – in common with most other human societies – stories of individual heroes, whether historical or supernatural or both, have played a critical role as models and inspirations. Yet powerful and emotive though such narratives and icons are, they have tended to obscure the deeper historical trajectory of heightening inequality and restricted opportunity. The history of Uganda over *la longue durée* demonstrates the ineffable significance of access to well-being: spiritual, physical, psychological. And thus histories of faith, demography, health and learning provide the signposts to Uganda's future – in particular the critical need to provide access to well-being, to satisfy aspiration (which is, for most people, fairly modest), and to permit Ugandans a reasonable degree of expectation. The provision of access and the encouragement of aspiration will be a challenge given spiralling population levels and the finite resources available to future governments; but this is critical to the future stability, even the very survival, of the nation itself.

5 | Kings and Others

History and Modernity

The Return of the Kings

In July 1993, Buganda celebrated. For the first time since *Kabaka* Edward Mutesa had limped through the bush into exile in May 1966, chased by the soldiers of Milton Obote, the king was back. 'Freddie's' son, Ronald Mutebi, had been allowed to return as *kabaka*, and his coronation marked the restoration of the kingdom.[1] The focus of much of the preceding discussion in government circles had been Buganda, but the constitutional amendment passed by the National Resistance Council – then the *de facto* parliament – encompassed the kingdoms of Bunyoro and Toro, as well as the comparatively more recent confederation of Busoga, and within months their kingships had been restored with much the same joyous pageantry as that of Buganda. Thus Bunyoro's new *mukama* was Solomon Gafabusa Iguru; in Toro, *Mukama* Patrick David Matthew Koboyo Olimi III died soon after his accession, in 1995, and was succeeded by his infant son Oyo Rukidi IV; Busoga's new *kyabazinga* was Henry Wako Muloki. Constitutionally, they were not actually 'kings' at all, but rather 'cultural leaders', and were strictly prohibited from involvement in politics. Of the big southern monarchies, only Ankole remained unrestored, owing to popular opposition to the return of oppressive kingship.[2] In November 1993, however, in a secret ceremony, John Barigye was crowned *Mugabe* Ntare VI, but this was not recognised by the government on the grounds that it had not had the endorsement of the district councils of Ankole. Barigye remains a 'king in waiting', with local Nyankole politics

---

[1] The festivities, activities, and general excitement are conveyed in the *Coronation Special Souvenir* (Kampala, 1993).

[2] Museveni's supporters have claimed that he is only following the wishes of the Iru majority and acting according to the constitutional amendments. His critics argue that as a Munyankole he would never have countenanced a restored king in his own district.

dominated by competition between the royalist and pro-restoration Nkore Cultural Trust and the anti-restorationist Banyankore Trust Foundation.[3]

The troubled situation in the west demonstrated that restoration and the role of 'traditional' monarchy was by no means uncontested terrain; royalism was neither unproblematic nor monolithic in its local conceptualisation, while episodes of resistance and a refusal to accept territorial, monarchical narratives were much in evidence throughout the nineteenth and twentieth centuries. Nonetheless, the mid-1990s was a period of enormous significance for the ancient kingdoms which had formed the bedrock of state-formation – of political consolidation, the marshalling of human, animal and mineral resources, the taproots of culture and art and spiritual process – in the Ugandan region for several centuries: their reappearance on cultural and constitutional maps was momentous to those who had long believed that herein lay truly legitimate authority, far removed from the falsehoods of unitary state-level governance. It began with Buganda, Bunyoro, Toro and Busoga; but soon all sorts of communities wanted their 'traditional' leaders, too. This was, of course, one of the oldest conundrums in modern African history, namely the struggle to reconcile the 'tribe' and the 'nation', precolonial identities and the putatively modern force that is the nation-state. How can the nation survive, as Samora Machel wondered in the context of Mozambique, if the tribe does not die?[4] The implication of that, in turn, is that History must be severed at the root, or at least severely pruned back. To an extent this has been overlooked in the modern scholarship on nationalism, perhaps reflecting the ongoing fixation with the 'modern' itself, the impact of colonial rule, the machinations of decolonisation and the emergence of the African nation-state as a novel form. To be sure, 'tribe' and nation have not proven especially compatible, at least superficially; but the rise of these ostensibly new forms of historical consciousness represented only the latest manifestation of the struggle over the past and its implications for the future.

[3] See, for example, Doornbos, *The Ankole Kingship Controversy*, especially chapter 8.
[4] M. Mamdani, *Citizen and Subject: Contemporary Africa and the Legacy of Late Colonialism* (Princeton, 1996), 135.

Uganda and the British

In 1902, Apolo Kagwa and his secretary, Ham Mukasa, went to England. Mukasa recorded the epic journey in a carefully kept diary, in which he described the pair's amazement at the various spectacles before them – not the least of which was the coronation of King Edward VII, the centrepiece of the expedition.

> We climbed to the top of the Tower, and looked over the city and the River Thames, and saw many houses, and many ships on the Thames. We saw also a most wonderful thing. They have made a bridge across this River Thames which flows through the middle of the city of London, and this bridge is made of iron, and they put on it great hinges, so great that I can compare them to nothing in our country . . . [M]y friends, you ought to be struck with that wonderful bridge that goes up by itself as you have heard; such a breadth and length is a marvellous thing [sic]. It is called the 'Tower Bridge'.[5]

It was the culmination of a remarkable four decades of intense interaction between the Ganda and the British. As Kagwa and Mukasa travelled the length and breadth of the kingdom, they may well have reflected on the remarkable journey which, beginning in the 1860s, had led them to this place; it was an experience which surely had a profound influence on the historical writings of each in the years to come, as they sought to cement Protestant Buganda's place in the new spatial and temporal firmament. Yet while these two luminaries of an emerging Ganda political class may have symbolised cooperation between Buganda and the British, just a few years earlier a British-led force had laid waste to Bunyoro, with catastrophic consequences. Depending on where you were from in Uganda, you had a very different perception of the *muzungu* and his representatives. Some eighty years later, as Ugandans surveyed their shattered political landscape, strewn with bodies and long-defunct ideas, and deserted by a generation of political and military leaders, many pointed to the colonial period as the root of all the nation's ills – and it is an angry indictment of the British that is reflected in Timothy Wangusa's 1989 novel, *Upon This Mountain*. The protagonist, Mwambu, is haunted by fear of 'the knife', a visceral allusion to the circumcision ceremony that looms unavoidably before

---

[5] H. Mukasa (ed. S. Gikandi), *Uganda's Katikiro in England* (Manchester & New York, 1998, 1st. ed., 1904), 104–5.

him as the painful but necessary passage to manhood. In the end, facing down the outraged mocking of his peers and elders, he opts for an anaesthetised hospital procedure – a blessing, it seems, of modernity. Yet along the way, he encounters sexual impropriety and duplicity on the part of one of the European masters at the mission school:

The main section of the chapel was in darkness . . . He could vaguely make out the low voices of the chapel wardens. On impulse, he decided to give Nambozo and her friends a pleasant surprise by entering like a ghost without knocking first. Quietly turning the knob, he gently opened the door with the slightest squeak and eased himself in. It was therefore several seconds before those inside saw with horror that they had not locked the door, and by the end of those seconds Mwambu's shocked eyes had taken in the spectre of half-naked Nambozo and the Reverend James Graves intertwined on the floor upon the Holy Table cloth for the season of Lent.[6]

It reads as a blunt indictment of colonial rule, and certainly the weakness and hypocrisy of Europeans. It is an awkward, tense dualism – simultaneously a celebration of modern medicine and a sneering critique of those who brought it.

Criticism of the British has certainly been a recurrent theme for successive postcolonial regimes. The problem, surely, was that the British had set up a political system doomed to fail: rooted in armed force, both real and implied and the militarisation of political culture; a system of staggering geopolitical inequity, with Buganda as the capstone and outlying areas as marginalised zones of conquest; and thus a system which institutionalised ethnic competition and the politics of zero-sum. Moreover, political reform had come much too late to make any difference in terms of preparing civil society and the political class for the division of powers and conception of 'loyal opposition' so intrinsic to the functioning of the Westminster model.[7] Whether consciously or not, Ugandans routinely think of the British in terms of a balance sheet, with pros in one column and cons in the other. In Bunyoro, and elsewhere, the British were violent and destructive and allowed the Ganda to seize land and political position; more broadly, they governed on profoundly racist principles and underdeveloped Uganda economically, while effectively preventing anything approaching

---

[6] Timothy Wangusa, *Upon This Mountain* (2005 Bow and Arrow Publishers edition), 101–2.
[7] Cooper, *Africa since 1940*, 156–61, Davidson, *The Black Man's Burden*.

democracy from taking root. They allowed tribalism to flourish, especially in their privileging of Buganda at the expense of everyone else.
Yet their very presence – beginning with the intrepid explorers of the
mid-nineteenth century – gave life to Uganda itself, and they brought
the salvation of both faith and science. They facilitated the material
integration of the future nation in their thin, rickety but vital railway
lines and in their spidery roads, some of which were even tarmacked.
Contrasting views, then, depending on mood and experience and location. 'The British should apologise and compensate Bunyoro for the
atrocities committed, [and] should sponsor an affirmative action [sic]
to develop Bunyoro', according to one Nyoro informant,[8] making a
point repeated by many interviewees, that Britain was directly responsible for Bunyoro's tragic plight in the modern era and should be held
accountable. Colonial rule 'made' Uganda; yet the British had often
behaved despicably. The obliging tour guide at the national mosque
in Kampala will happily tell his British charges how wonderful were
their pith-helmeted ancestors, for they made Uganda possible;[9] yet a
senior Museum official will mischievously wonder why it is Japan, and
not the UK, which is so forthcoming with funds to help repair the fire-
damaged Kasubi Tombs.[10]

There was certainly nothing predestined about Britain's acquisition
of the territory. While Mwanga struggled to consolidate his return
to power in 1889–90, he had initially flirted with the IBEAC, on the
eastern side of Lake Victoria; but then he had signed a vague 'treaty
of friendship' with the opportunistic and energetic German explorer
Karl Peters.[11] By the time the IBEAC arrived at Mengo in April 1890
Mwanga felt secure enough not to be tempted by anything the British
had to offer. But he was stranded by the mysteries of global diplomacy, and in July 1890 the Anglo–German agreement awarded the
area of Kenya and Uganda to Britain.[12] Lugard arrived on behalf of the
IBEAC in December 1890, and signed a treaty with Mwanga, allowing him involvement in Buganda's internal affairs. In the early 1890s,
this was mostly about shoring up Mwanga's position and keeping the

---

[8] Interview, Selesti Kakongoro, Kagadi, Uganda, 10 January 2015.
[9] Author's field notes and informal interviews, July 2014.
[10] Author's field notes and informal interviews, 9 April 2013.
[11] Sebastian Conrad, *German Colonialism: a short history* (Cambridge, 2012), 50.
[12] R. Robinson & J. Gallagher, with A. Denny, *Africa and the Victorians: the official mind of imperialism* (London, 1961), 292–3.

peace amidst the growing Protestant–Catholic tensions which made the unfortunate *kabaka*'s position increasingly difficult. It was also the case in a broad sense, despite Lugard's apparently sincere attempts at even-handedness, that the Protestant chiefly faction was favoured by the intervention of the IBEAC and its little armoury on the hill beside Mengo.[13] And so the age of the imagination had morphed into that of charters and chancers, populated by an array of missionaries, investors, company officials and ultimately governors and commissioners charged with the fashioning of Uganda into a full member of the British Empire with all the responsibilities and opportunities that supposedly entailed – Lugard's 'dual mandate'.[14] From the perspective of the British metropole, Uganda was, in the first instance, a buffer protecting the headwaters of the Nile, and so incipient Ugandan nationhood was the result of strategic planning around a bunch of places a long way away from it: India, the Red Sea, Egypt, Suez.[15]

The single most remarkable 'fact' about the creation of British Uganda is the weird and wonderful conversion of a bunch of ill-resourced, precarious clingers-on to formal administrators in the space of a decade; from the signing of the agreement with Mwanga in December 1890, which was in some respects scarcely worth the paper it was written on, to the signing of the Buganda Agreement, one of the landmark pieces of colonial treaty-making, in March 1900. It had been a remarkable transformation. It was driven by a chance meeting of Ganda cultural, economic and political aspiration on the one hand, and British racial and strategic thought on the other. The area that became known as 'Uganda' in the late nineteenth century was to be dominated by the major monarchical and territorial states of the well-watered, fertile and comparatively densely populated southern half of the country, while the more dispersed communities in the northern half of the territory, those which inhabited the drier, less populated provinces of West Nile, Acholi, Lango and Karamoja, were assigned markedly subordinate roles. In the years that followed, especially with the crushing of the Nyoro, the Ganda were at the centre of it all, as confident in their ability

---

[13] Perham, *Lugard*, 209–10, 226–7, Ingham, *Making of Modern Uganda*, 43–8.

[14] In *Dual Mandate*, Lugard argued that the colonial project involved benefit for both Africans and Europeans, and responsibilities for each, too.

[15] See T. Pakenham, *The Scramble for Africa, 1876–1912* (London, 1991), 353, 356–7. One of the best accounts of these events and dynamics remains Robinson & Gallagher, *Africa and the Victorians*, 307–11, 314–23, 326–30.

to work alongside the British in the great civilising project among the surrounding savage tribes as Harry Johnston was in Buganda's capacity for intelligent and swift self-improvement, and in their utility as agents of colonial rule.[16] The relationship between the British and Buganda would soon, within a couple of decades, become desperately complicated and profoundly troubled; but this was the moment – the early 1900s – when Ganda chiefs fanned out beyond the kingdom to serve as agents and administrators and economic entrepreneurs in Busoga, Bugisu, Teso, Lango, Bunyoro and elsewhere, and the great partnership was forged which would so shape the future of the nation. For the British, above all, this was indirect rule in action, as envisaged and later articulated by Lugard himself: the privileging of the best-equipped group, allowing them a degree of self-governance and even a stake in the political administration and economic development of the territory.

In purely administrative terms, in 1902 the Uganda Order in Council had brought Buganda, Busoga, Bunyoro, Toro, Ankole (as the expanded territory with the historical state of Nkore at its core was now known) and 'Bukedi', which included Teso, Bugisu and Lango, under formal British governance.[17] Kigezi was added in 1911. It was not until 1911 that any serious attention was paid to administration in the north, and to effectively incorporating the region north of the Nile into the Protectorate territory.[18] In August of that year, Lango district was established,[19] and at the same time a military force was assembled with responsibility for operations in Acholiland, Karamoja and West Nile. In 1913, Acholiland was created, and Karamoja in the same year, complete with military station (there would not be a civilian administrator until 1921);[20] West Nile was formed in 1914 as a result of a boundary adjustment between Uganda and Sudan, though the inhabitants would retain close links with communities in the latter.[21] Outlying territory would be released to neighbouring territories – the Lado Enclave, the remnants of Emin Pasha's old Equatoria province,[22] and

---

[16] Oliver, *Sir Harry Johnston*, 332–3.
[17] Contained in 'East Africa and Uganda: Orders in Council', UKNA FO 2/549.
[18] Low, 'Uganda', 103–110.   [19] Driberg, *The Lango*, 35–6.
[20] Neville Dyson-Hudson, *Karimojong Politics* (Oxford, 1966), 6–9.
[21] *A Handbook of the Uganda Protectorate*, prepared by the Geographical Section of the Naval Intelligence Division, Naval Staff, Admiralty (London, 1920), 371–2.
[22] Leopold, *Inside West Nile*, 10–12.

the western Rift Valley. Uganda came to be divided into Northern, Eastern and Western Provinces, plus Buganda – the only extant kingdom
awarded provincial status. Local government, in terms of shape and
form and political outcome, was diverse. In some cases, administrative
units were artificial, amalgamated territories that bore no relationship
to ethnic or any other kind of identity: West Nile, Bukedi and Kigezi
districts, notably, were ethnically heterogeneous. Other districts tended
to be ethnically defined, and there is a correlation between those forms
of local administrative structure and the emergence of more 'militant'
ethnic consolidation and identity, especially from the 1920s onward.
In other words, in a variation of the argument made by John Iliffe
about tribalism in Tanganyika,[23] to some extent it can be argued that
the British built local administrative units, and Ugandans built local
identities around those units and sought to use them to compete in
a hostile political environment. British colonial administration can be
seen to have effectively balkanised Uganda. However, it is important to
temper this image of colonial transformation of local identities, on two
levels. First, plenty of identities were already pretty well entrenched: the
Nyoro and the Ganda needed no artificial stimuli, foreign or otherwise,
to the appearance of a finely articulated sense of self, however shifting
and contested that may have been at particular moments. Secondly,
it is important to note that there had been growing ethnic consolidation, centralisation and militarisation throughout the nineteenth century, and in some places earlier, and so the British phase was simply the
latest stage in a markedly long-term development. This had been the
story of Uganda's political *longue durée*, not just of its comparatively
brief colonial moment.

The overriding aim of the British, to make an obvious but critical
point, was the creation of viable order: the creation of lines of hierarchy and authority, between subject peoples and upper echelons of
the governorate in leafy Entebbe, preferably through the recreation of
'traditional' authenticity – that is, through local rulers. The corner-
stone of Protectorate policy was the relationship with the major southern kingdoms – Buganda, most obviously, but also Bunyoro, Ankole
and Toro. The big states would come to be well served by the intellectual and moral class that formed the literary and spiritual fibre of
the colonial project: missionaries, ethnographers, anthropologists and,

[23] Iliffe, *Modern History of Tanganyika*, 324.

eventually, historians. There would be separate agreements with Bunyoro, Toro and Ankole, moreover, similar to that signed with Buganda but lacking the autonomous powers given to the latter.[24] The relationship with these capstone rulers was critical to the political management of the populous, fertile south, the centre of political and economic gravity. With that aim in view, agreements were updated from time to time – that with Bunyoro, for example, in 1933, allowed the *mukama* greater powers over his chiefs (greater, indeed, than had been the case in the nineteenth century) and brought the relationship more into line with that between Britain and Buganda.[25] Moreover, the British mission – especially between the world wars – to 'improve' African society through traditional authority required the careful training of a chiefly class and intervention to ensure the elevation of the 'right kind' through the ranks, or at least some influence over the process by which chiefs were appointed.[26] The basic principles of indirect rule rested on the mobilisation of particular visions of the past in the pursuit of political stability. Still, while the popularity of monarchs may have remained more or less robust, notwithstanding some local variation – the precise role and meaning of kingship was always contested – chiefs were often seen as altogether more problematic, mistrusted by their own communities who saw them as increasingly distant and ineffectual, and despised by nationalists who regarded them as collaborators with the British.[27]

At the level of local government, therefore, the overriding aim was the imposition, or at least adaptation, of the 'Buganda model' of administration whereby (in simple terms) kings ruled counties through appointed chiefs. Yet there was a striking disparity between the north and the south. Where putatively great monarchs did not exist, versions of them needed to be invented.[28] Of course, in many places north of the

---

[24] G.N. Uzoigwe, 'The Agreement States and the Making of Uganda: II. Tooro, Ankole, and Bunyoro-Kitara', in G.N. Uzoigwe (ed.), *Uganda: the dilemma of nationhood* (New York, 1982).

[25] 'Bunyoro native administration: Bunyoro Agreement 1933 . . .', UKNA CO 536/178/10, 26 August 1933–2 January 1934. Also R.J. Southall, *Parties and Politics in Bunyoro* (Kampala, 1972), 6–7.

[26] Richards (ed.), *East African Chiefs*, 14.

[27] For example, L. Mair, *African Societies* (Cambridge, 1974), 191–2.

[28] This is the topic of a vast and restless body of Africanist scholarship. For a classic study of the situation in Nigeria, see A.E. Afigbo, *The Warrant Chiefs: indirect rule in SE Nigeria* (Harlow, 1972) and more broadly, two influential

Nile – among the Acholi, for example – the trend towards centralising, militarising leadership had been evident in the course of the nineteenth century, and so the 'invention' thesis must not be overblown. Nonetheless, the imposition of chiefs proceeded across swathes of the north (and elsewhere) where they were unfamiliar figures in the form now presented. As Thomas and Scott described it in a sanguine assessment from the mid-1930s:

Where . . . the hereditary principle has long-standing validity (as, apparently, in Busoga), or certain clans have furnished certain sections of the community with their leaders (as among the Acholi), every endeavour is made to ensure that each chief appointed shall possess, in addition to administrative ability and some measure of educational attainment, the personal status which makes him a natural guide to his people.[29]

Initially, however, there was nothing less familiar – or in fact the focus of greater hostility – than the imposition of Ganda agents and administrators across the Protectorate. Hatred of alien rule meant that the British frequently resorted to violence to enforce peace, especially in northern Uganda; and subsequently the administration was compelled towards discretion and the official position that Ganda agents should be withdrawn as soon opportunity permitted. The most famous example, again, was that of Kakungulu and his Ganda entourage in Busoga and Bugisu and later in Teso.[30] Elsewhere, there was the creation of councils in various districts: in Acholiland, a Central Native Council was formed in Gulu in 1914, comprising prominent Acholi, and awarded judicial and executive powers.[31] A similar body was set up in Lango in 1919.[32] Such councils were favoured because they created a vertical relationship with the administration, but they quickly became centres of anticolonial activity, pressure points on the administration itself. Elsewhere, British manipulations of the chiefly class caused considerable resentment. Among the Alur, for example, from the 1920s,

and wide-ranging tomes in Mamdani, *Citizen and Subject*, and Young, *The African Colonial State*.

[29] Thomas & Scott, *Uganda*, 84.

[30] Low, 'Uganda', 104–5. In fact in 1896 a Teso delegation had requested formal Ganda protection against the Langi: G. Emwanu, 'The reception of alien rule in Teso, 1896–1927', *Uganda Journal*, 31:2 (1967).

[31] H.R. Wallis, *The Handbook of Uganda* (London, 1920, 2nd ed.), 106–7, Low, 'Uganda', 107.

[32] Low, 'Uganda', 107.

the British reduced the number of '*wakungu*' – the chiefly rank derived from the Ganda nomenclature – leading to discontent among an Alur aristocracy, some members of which had to be in effect pensioned off. The British policy was to eliminate 'unsuitable' hereditary candidates, replacing them with educated relatives, or in some cases non-hereditary chiefs based on merit or loyal service to government.[33] In Busoga, although in theory district commissioners had the authority to make or unmake such promotions unilaterally, in reality the appointment and dismissal of chiefs was a matter of delicate consultation at the local level.[34] Across the Protectorate, but especially among the segmentary and quasi-segmentary societies of eastern, northern and northwest Uganda, the position of such chiefs was considerably enhanced by the 1919 Native Authority Ordinance which awarded them wider powers with a view to maintaining law and order.[35] In some ways this may be contrasted – ironically, given the significance of the Buganda model – with the constraints placed on the *kabaka* by the 1900 agreement, although in theory the *kabaka* continued to rule Buganda through the chiefs. The 1910 Native Laws Agreement stipulated that the *kabaka* and the *lukiiko* would 'make laws governing the Baganda in Buganda', although with the consent of the Governor.[36] But the British had trouble with particularly powerful individuals, such as Buganda's prime minister Apolo Kagwa, who resigned in high dudgeon in 1926 following a dispute with the Governor.[37]

Just as stark a regional difference lay in the deployment of force in northern Uganda, the militarised northern districts and the continual military operations by the British through the 1900s and 1910s – especially among the Acholi communities on the Sudanese frontier, exposed to raids from across the border into the 1920s.[38] Northern Uganda

---

[33] Richards (ed.), *East African Chiefs*, 318–19.

[34] D. Mudoola, 'Colonial Chief-Making: Busoga, a case-study, 1900–1940', unpublished paper presented at the Universities of East Africa Social Science Conference, December 1970. See also his 'Chiefs and Political Action: the case of Busoga, 1900–1960' (unpublished PhD thesis, Makerere University, 1974).

[35] Low, 'Uganda', 93, Mamdani, *Citizen and Subject*, 166.

[36] Hailey, *An African Survey: a study of the problems arising in Africa south of the Sahara* (London, 1938), 444.

[37] 'Sir Apolo Kagwa, Katikiro . . . of Buganda: arrangements for proposed visit to England during 1926; resignation due to ill health . . . ; submission of petition of complaint against the acting Provincial Commissioner of Buganda . . . ', UKNA CO 536/141/8, 26 April 1926–22 September 1926.

[38] Sir H. Macmichael, *The Anglo-Egyptian Sudan* (London, 1934), 177–8.

necessitated a greater degree of militarisation than in the south where, certainly by the 1920s, the overt militarism of the era of conquest had largely receded.[39] This also meant a marked shift in the military gravity of Uganda itself. Buganda, one of the great military states of the last three hundred years, still produced some recruits for the colonial army; but the reality was that the British now did most of their recruitment in the far north.[40] The same circumstances that required a military presence across unsettled northern territories – their propensity for violence and aptitude as warriors – made the inhabitants of those lands ideal recruits.[41] In part, at least, this was linked to martial race theory: the essentialised idea that certain groups, notably pastoralists and those hardy folks of the uplands and savannah lands, made better soldiers.[42] British recruitment policy in northern Uganda in some ways built on the militarisation of the region through the eighteenth and nineteenth centuries and indeed reflected the new geopolitical north/south imbalance of power within the territory. It had enormous implications for the future of Uganda, but those implications would only become clear towards the end of the 1960s. In 1897, an Indian army battalion had been necessary in the suppression of a revolt by a contingent of Sudanese soldiers,[43] but from the early 1900s, large numbers of Acholi and Langi were recruited.[44] The Uganda Rifles joined with the Central Africa Rifles and the East Africa Rifles to form the King's African Rifles (KAR), of which the fourth battalion was Ugandan. The KAR saw service during the First World War, and Uganda produced large numbers of porters for the regional campaign.[45] 'Waganda warriors'

---

[39] See the general point made by Bill Freund, *The Making of Contemporary Africa: the development of African society since 1800* (Basingstoke, 1998), 112, 118.

[40] Reid, *Warfare in African History*, 149.   [41] Lugard, *Dual Mandate*, 574–5.

[42] It was an idea that was still in vogue during the Second World War: D. Killingray, *Fighting for Britain: African soldiers in the Second World War* (Woodbridge, 2010), 42. See also Heather Streets' excellent *Martial Races: the military, race and masculinity in British imperial culture, 1857–1914* (Manchester, 2004), which is not concerned with Africa but which explores the subject in compelling style.

[43] Johnston, *Uganda Protectorate*, I, 237–42.

[44] Omara-Otunnu, *Politics and the Military*, 31–2, Decalo, *Coups and Army Rule*, 158.

[45] See E. Paice, *Tip and Run: the untold tragedy of the Great War in Africa* (London, 2007), 281, 284, 286 and R. Anderson, *The Forgotten Front: the East African campaign* (Stroud, 2004).

may have come in for special mention in German commander von Lettow-Vorbeck's 1914–18 war memoir,[46] but most Ugandan askaris spoke Nubi until 1927 until, in line with the other regional battalions, they were required to use Swahili;[47] still, it remained the most Muslim battalion in the KAR.[48] During the Second World War, when Uganda was expected to play its part as the loyal colonial territory, northerners – and westerners – once more joined up in large numbers, almost certainly owing to the fewer economic opportunities at home and the promise of both wages and status in service.[49] In the meantime, however, the British were able to claim the loyalty of their Ugandan subjects in two world wars. Governor Philip Mitchell, at the outbreak of war in September 1939, ordered the raising of an extra KAR battalion to serve as a territorial unit in order that Ugandans – including many Makerere graduates – could demonstrate their loyalty. Most of the new battalion were Ganda recruited from around Kampala and Jinja. Later, however, the battalion was given frontline status, which caused considerable distress among its formerly eager recruits who had regarded their service as part-time.[50] Such was the demand for recruits by 1941–2 that the administration moved beyond their traditional Acholi hunting grounds into Toro, Teso, Busoga and Bugwere.[51]

To some extent, those wars were catalysts of political change for the colonial administration. Loyal service and significant contributions in men and material during the 1914–18 at least in part prompted Daudi Chwa to demand an end to the practice of *kasanvu*, or forced labour;[52] and in 1920, in an attempt to regularise the administrative affairs of the territory, the Legislative Council (LegCo) was established, designed to be a kind of parliamentary body advising the Governor.[53] But it was not until 1946 that the first Africans were allowed to sit on it, as part of a wider post-war process of quasi-democratic reform aimed at

---

[46] General von Lettow-Vorbeck, *My Reminiscences of East Africa* (London, 1920), 47.
[47] T.H. Parsons, *The African Rank-and-File: social implications of colonial military service in the King's African Rifles, 1902–1964* (Portsmouth NH, 1999), 112.
[48] Ibid., 125.   [49] Thompson, *Governing Uganda*, 104–5.
[50] Parsons, *Rank-and-File*, 24–5.
[51] Colonial Office, *Annual Report on Uganda for the year 1946* (London, 1948), 3, Killingray, *Fighting for Britain*, 63.
[52] Paice, *Tip and Run*, 395.
[53] See 'Sessional Papers. Legislative Council', UKNA CO 685/18 [1921–1934].

opening up local government and awarding it greater responsibility.[54]
Revisions to the organisation of local government in 1949–50 gave
wider powers and responsibilities to district councils – that is, in those
areas where there had been formal agreement, as in the case of the
southern monarchies – and allowed the governor to establish district
councils anywhere in the Protectorate.[55] Local elections now enfranchised communities which were able to send representatives to district councils, although these tended to congeal around ethnic identity. Meanwhile, as decolonising impulses gathered pace in the 1950s,
LegCo was further opened up by an extension of the franchise, with
30 Ugandan representatives present by 1956.[56] Yet these piecemeal
initiatives took place against a background of political crisis: riots in
Buganda in 1945 and 1949, the emergence of more militant political
action across the territory, and the *kabaka* crisis of 1953–5. Britain
sought – largely unsuccessfully, and much too late in the day – to
present LegCo as a national parliament in the making, but the reality was that by the late 1950s LegCo had already been superseded
in actual political importance by the parties proliferating across the
Protectorate. As elsewhere, from the British perspective, as they now
looked to withdraw from formal administration in Africa – if not from
the exercise of informal influence – the objective was the management
of disarray, and the putting in place of a functioning system from which
Her Majesty's Government could retreat, after the appropriate cere-
monials, with a modicum of confidence. In Hailey's mammoth revised
Survey, the assessment reflected soberly the overriding British aim: to
retain Uganda as a unitary state, assuage the wilder assertions and aspirations of the Ganda, and act as – in Hailey's own phrase – an 'impartial
arbiter' in the debates of the enlarged and more boisterous LegCo.[57]
What is striking in Hailey's account is the passive voice, and the odd
intonation which implies no British responsibility in the facilitation of
Ganda nationalism, nor in the creation of such an imbalanced political
territory. The end of British rule came, according to one official based in

[54] 'Legislative Council: question of future African representation', UKNA CO
    536/211/5, 12 June 1944–12 December 1944.
[55] 'Uganda Protectorate Ordinance No.33 (African Local Governments
    (Amendments) Ordinance) of 1950 . . .', UKNA CO 536/224/2, 2 January
    1951.
[56] Colonial Office, *Annual Report: Uganda 1957* (London, 1958), 149, 150–2.
[57] Hailey, *African Survey* (1957 ed.), 294–5.

Toro, 'in a peaceful, orderly, unemotional kind of way'.[58] That was certainly not true for everyone involved, but it was a fairly typical British
conclusion that 'few Britons or Ugandans were willing to guess how
this fragile collection of wildly disparate tribes would fare'.[59] It was a
rather prosaic and again curiously detached position to take after more
than half a century of administration.

The upshot of the British 'moment' is that Buganda – and adjacent
bits of the south – became the hub of the nation, and the north and
east become the borderlands and peripheries. This was a fundamental switch – a reversal of fortune in which regions which had been
the historic founts of culture and ideology had now become borderlands and peripheries. In a sense, it pitted pastoralism versus sedentary
regimes. Buganda, most obviously, was helped by the fact that its big
state structure was organisationally better equipped to work with their
foreign 'partners'; by its geopolitical and economic location; and by
the fact that the nature of the changing external contact – slavers to
begin with, but then a more sympathetic and indeed empathic European state-building culture – differed favourably from the more predatory, informal contact that emanated from southern Sudan. But there
is no doubting the terrific irony that Buganda – a state based on large-
scale violence and slavery in the eighteenth and nineteenth centuries –
became the preferred partner of the British in the colonial project not
despite that unsavoury past but precisely *because* of it. The significance
of the external in shaping Ugandan politics is undeniable – not least in
the geopolitical advantages it involved for some, and in the scholarly
attention which ensued. Yet we need to be careful not to exaggerate the
significance of British rule *per se*: colonial rule can only be understood
as one strand in a long and complex story. The colonial moment clearly
has become the preoccupation of the Africanist historical academy; our
line of vision has been drawn inexorably to the twentieth century, and
in particular to the transformative power of the colonial era. There are
particular reasons for this, no doubt.[60] But in truth the era between
the 1890s and the 1960s was one in which precolonial dynamics

---

[58] R.M. Purcell, 'A turning point', in D. & M.V. Brown (eds.), *Looking Back at
the Uganda Protectorate: recollections of District Officers* (Dalkeith, 1996),
264.

[59] Ibid.

[60] R. Reid, 'Past and Presentism: the "precolonial" and the foreshortening of
African history', *Journal of African History*, 52:2 (2011), 136–7.

continued to reverberate and refract, albeit through many of the prisms created by colonial administration.

Reimagining Uganda and Ugandans

In the course of the 1910s and 1920s, new kinds of struggle began to emerge over the nature and form of Uganda, which was continually reinvented as a result of these early but increasingly potent manifestations of subnational identity. The nation, meanwhile, was by and large indistinct, though it hovered spectrally and aloof above public debate and political protest. Yet the various movements which emerged all shared a profound concern with the past, their protagonists were historically conscious, and history was a means of debating the present and arguing over the future. These historical visions were both rooted in the deep past – the epoch of Kintu and Rukidi – while also drawing on the turbulent experiences of the nineteenth century, using these experiences to get to grips with the new dispensation of political and economic power in the twentieth century. These dynamics intensified in the 1930s and 1940s, especially in Buganda, where in some respects it was most visible, but where particular generational and social conflicts were deeply rooted and expressed in ever more sophisticated ways.

The expansion of political scale discernible in the course of the nineteenth century in some ways escalated in the twentieth, driven by the exigencies of the colonial order. In essence, the proliferation of 'tribalism', as it was acceptably known in academic circles until the 1960s,[61] meant the appearance of militant identities around rigidified notions of 'ethnicity'; it implied the *invention* of tribes, the instrumentalist mobilisation of ethnic identities as a specific *political* response on the part of local elites to the challenges as well as the opportunities of the colonial order. There is a vast literature on this subject, often with a focus on the kinds of 'tribes' supposedly constructed in the early twentieth century and 'imagined' by the British – for example, Acholi, Madi, Gisu, Kiga, Teso.[62] But a note of caution is required here. Scholars have often been more interested in the innovative elements to the colonial moment than anything else, reflecting a deeper (even unconscious) tendency to

---

[61] It was a term which was recognised as increasingly problematic and provocative even in the 1960s, though it was still deployed as an analytical tool in, for example, Gulliver (ed.), *Tradition and Transition*, published in 1969.

[62] See, for example, Young, *The African Colonial State*, 234.

see the modern era as fundamentally transformative.[63] Claustrophobia and entrapment unquestionably, in many cases, produced more competitive, militant identities – identities which were less porous, it is argued, less flexible, more 'otherising' and exclusive, than anything which existed in the broadly defined 'precolonial' era. However, this was also a process of some antiquity, and a multitude of groups were palpably and demonstrably *not* 'invented' during colonial rule in any meaningful sense, but which were evolving long before 1900 – more permeable at certain moments than at others, sometimes flexible and open, at other times exclusive and defensive.[64] Colonial rule made ethnic identity a zero-sum game, in many cases, and the fragile nation suffered as a result; but 'ethnic identity' itself has become reified as a modern phenomenon, and nuance is needed in considering the twentieth-century evolution of political culture.

Groupings that previously had some degree of internal cultural and linguistic affinity now began to consolidate, and cohere more closely: like the Langi clans, for example, who from the 1940s began to emerge as the 'Lango *people*', asserting a unity of purpose and identity which was used as leverage against the late colonial state.[65] Within administrative districts, clusters of small groups might coalesce into larger aggregations, as happened with the Kalenjin-speaking 'Sebei' north of Mt. Elgon; 'Sebei' had previously been the name of but one of the groups, but by the 1940s was being used self-consciously to describe a larger cluster.[66] It was a phenomenon well attested in other parts of eastern Uganda, too. Among the Gisu, the anthropologist J.S. La Fontaine observed the rise of 'tribal policy' by the 1950s, and she described the emergence of 'tribalism' in Bugisu, usefully, as having occurred in two stages:

The first stage was that of the development of a truly tribal awareness of common cultural features and common interest, which had existed before only in a ritual context. Second, there emerges what I have called (somewhat

---

[63] Ranger, 'The invention of tradition' and 'The invention of tradition revisited', Spear, 'Neo-traditionalism and the limits of invention', 16*ff*, Reid, 'Past and Presentism'.

[64] Again, see, for example, Atkinson on the pre-nineteenth century roots of the Acholi in *Roots of Ethnicity* and, in terms of a distinctive borderland environment over *la longue durée*, Leopold, *Inside West Nile*.

[65] Low & Lonsdale, 'Introduction: towards the new order', 25.

[66] Ibid., 27–8, W. Goldschmidt, *Sebei Law* (Berkeley, 1967), 7.

misleadingly, because it was never clearly formulated) Gisu tribal policy. This is action by Gisu leaders on behalf of the tribe as a whole over issues which appeared to them either to threaten their new identity or seemed to deny them rights accorded to other tribes. *Tribalism in Bugisu is thus the mobilisation of loyalties which, in the traditional system, were latent and expressed only ritually, into a political pressure group.* [italics added].[67]

In the same area, 'tribalism' among such formerly loose affiliations as the 'Bakedi' – which is previously how the Ganda, and thus the British, referred to a number of groups clustered around the eastern shore of Lake Kyoga – and the Teso emerged as a result of several stimulants: Ganda sub-imperialism (against which local 'tribalism' was initially a defence), British administration, and economic dynamics. For example, the Teso identified closely with cattle and cotton, while the Gisu were, in Twaddle's words, 'the most productive suppliers of coffee' in eastern Uganda.[68] Busoga, formerly a loose confederacy of chieftaincies, was amalgamated into a larger, unitary realm under a greatly expanded notion of kingship. The stimuli were both the exigencies of British administration and the need for the Soga to reinvent themselves through royalism and political identity against the overbearing influence of the Ganda.[69] Busoga was directly adjacent to Buganda, which could take much of the credit for 'inventing' Busoga as a broadly cohesive unit, beginning in the nineteenth century and, in the early twentieth, through its role in the administration of the region. The Soga had spent much of the nineteenth century attempting to manage the influence as well as the physical incursions of the Ganda, and so in the early decades of the twentieth, there was something of a political imperative to cohere, but it was a profoundly unsatisfactory and in many respects dysfunctional project – which had, after all, begun with Kakungulu's administration between 1906 and 1913, during which time the Ganda political entrepreneur had been president of Busoga's *Lukiiko*.[70] Even once the role of president passed to hereditary Soga chiefs on a rotational basis during the 1920s and 1930s, it was profoundly

---

[67] J.S. La Fontaine, 'Tribalism among the Gisu', in Gulliver (ed.), *Tradition and Transition*, 187.

[68] M.Twaddle, '"Tribalism"' in eastern Uganda, in Gulliver (ed.), *Tradition and Transition*, 204.

[69] The classic study is Fallers, *Bantu Bureaucracy*, see also W.F. Nabwiso-Bulima, 'The evolution of the Kyabazingaship of Busoga', *Uganda Journal*, 31:1 (1967).

[70] Twaddle, *Kakungulu*, chapter 8.

unpopular, as it came with no financial perks, an expanded workload and the need to spend too much time near Jinja (which was never popular). Nonetheless, the presidency of the *Lukiiko* evolved, in 1939, into the *kyabazinga* – although the British did not intend for the role to be hereditary, but rather fixed-term, and would develop the habit of interfering in Soga politics thereafter.[71]

Busoga was not the most convincing of corporate identities, but it did demonstrate a larger issue pertaining to other more historically rooted southern kingdoms, paralleling developments further north and east, namely the consolidation and sometimes extension of territory and centralised authority. Ankole was expanded to absorb peripheral and buffer areas, and it became much larger as a territorial 'unit' than it had been before the 1890s, with the British formally adding Igara, Buhweju, Bunyaruguru and Kajara.[72] Buganda itself of course had been swollen to include swathes of Nyoro territory, but there was a variation on the theme here, for in at least one case, that of the incorporated kingdom of Kkooki, Adrian Stonehouse has uncovered evidence of a desire in the early decades of the twentieth century to 'become Ganda' – associated as that was with the accoutrements of modernity, civilised behaviour and access to status. There was a significant distinction, in Stonehouse's view, between the 'Lost Counties' – where there was an aggressive programme of absorption against the defeated Nyoro – and the 'Acquired Counties', such as Kkooki, where voluntary 'Gandaisation' was much in evidence by the midway point of colonial rule.[73] More generally, of course, Buganda sat squarely at the heart of the imperial order, and there was no clearer, and no more dramatic, exemplar of the expansion and consolidation of a political identity: simply put, however successful and dynamic Buganda had been in the previous century, its position in the twentieth century was considerably more powerful than anything it had previously experienced. The

---

[71] D. Sseppuuya, 'Why Busoga's Kyabazingaship is not a kingdom', in *Understand Uganda*, 106. The Soga chiefs themselves longed for parity with their counterparts in other parts of the Protectorate: 'Land: policy in Busoga; proposal that Busoga Chiefs be given opportunity for entering an agreement with government upon lines of Bunyoro Agreement...', UKNA CO 536/85/15, 27 March 1935–17 March 1936.

[72] Richards (ed.), *East African Chiefs*, 156–7, Roscoe, *The Banyankole*.

[73] Stonehouse, 'Peripheral Identities' and also A. Stonehouse, 'The Bakooki in Buganda: identity and assimilation on the peripheries of a Ugandan kingdom', *Journal of Eastern African Studies*, 6:3 (2012).

Ganda sense of ethnic superiority was pronounced, manifest in a sense, as Doyle puts it, 'that Uganda was an extension of Buganda',[74] and also in the idea – still cherished – that the relationship with the British was one of partnership between equals. Better educated, manual work was beneath them – they had immigrant labour for that;[75] and they were the political and historical hub of the territory. 'Of all the peoples of the Protectorate', wrote political activist Eridadi Mulira in 1950,

the Baganda…have been at the forefront in the shaping of things, and almost all the dramatic happenings in the Protectorate have taken place in Buganda. In fact, it is safe to say that Buganda has not only given to the Protectorate its name…but also its history, its culture, its education, its religion.[76]

Yet that sense of supremacy came at a cost – a growing backlash against the Ganda across the rest of the territory, and an increasingly difficult, fractious relationship with their supposed partners, the British themselves.

To varying degrees, these escalating ethnic and regional identities were manifest in more or less formal political organisations and associations. If time was important, so too was space: the issue of land underpinned militant identity-formation among groups which perceived themselves to be under attack. Again eastern Uganda provides a useful illustration. In 1918–19, a group of prominent Ganda figures, formerly followers of Kakungulu, formed the Baganda Association of Mbale with a view to lobbying for more *mailo* freehold estates to be granted them in the area. In response, in 1930, a number of Gwere 'new men' – those created by missionary education – including teachers, junior chiefs and independent-minded church leaders formed the Young Bagwere Association; their aim, simply, was to push back domineering Ganda authority in the area and prevent the Ganda from taking control of Mbale Township.[77] These young activists were successful – the Ganda themselves were regarded as a nuisance by local colonial officials – certainly in comparison to the comparatively

---

[74] S. Doyle, 'Immigrants and indigenes: the Lost Counties dispute and the evolution of ethnic identity in colonial Buganda', *Journal of Eastern African Studies*, 3:2 (2009), 288.

[75] Mair, *An African People*, 11.

[76] E.M.K. Mulira, *Troubled Uganda* (London, 1950), 6.

[77] Twaddle, '"Tribalism"', 197.

stranded Nyoro who had to lobby for many more decades over the issue of the Lost Counties. Here, too, systematic oppressive attempts at acculturation and assimilation met with organised resistance.[78] The Mubende Banyoro Committee (MBC) was formed in 1921 to lobby for the return of the Lost Counties,[79] the latter peppered with *amagasani* – the shrines of the Bito kings of Bunyoro – which were now separated from the homeland through foreign occupation.[80] Yet it is also important to note that many of the ostensibly 'political' organisations were in fact driven, at least in the first instance, by economic and material grievance. The Young Busoga Association, notably, was established in 1929 with the primary aim of preventing cotton cultivators in Eastern Province from selling their crop to members of the British Cotton Growing Association, which increasingly acted in monopolistic fashion against the interests of African farmers.[81] Meanwhile the purpose of the Bataka movement in Buganda, established in 1921 and generally regarded as the first recognisable political movement in Uganda in the colonial era, was twofold: to challenge the growing Asian monopoly on the processing and marketing of cotton; and, more immediately relevant for our purposes here, to fight the oligarchy which had risen to power in the 1890s and whose place in the new political order had been cemented by the 1900 Agreement. The *bataka*, it may be recalled, were the clan heads, and they had been badly served by the land dispensation of the early 1900s. The Bataka movement represented, on one level, the latest stage in a long history of resistance to over-mighty monarchy and the over-privileged establishment which surrounded it. Now, the clan, such a critical element in the early political and social construction of the Buganda kingdom, became emblematic of a lost glorious past, a moral as well as political order rooted in the rightful access to ancestral land which had been demolished by the Protestant oligarchy's pact with the British. The fundamental drivers behind the formation of the Bataka movement were omnipresent in the decades to come: contemporary grievances (in the Bataka case, the marketing of cotton and the redistribution of land) which nonetheless drew on particular visions of the deeper past as markers of identity. The movement argued in the

---

[78] Stonehouse, 'Peripheral Identities', Doyle, 'Immigrants and indigenes'.
[79] Southall, *Parties and Politics*, 11.
[80] K. Ingham, 'The *Amagasani* of the Abakama of Bunyoro', *Uganda Journal*, 17:2 (1953), 144.
[81] Ehrlich, 'The Uganda Economy', 447, 466.

1920s and 1930s for a revision of the 1900 Agreement which would see the inclusion of a clause allowing for ancestral land to remain the property of clans.[82] It even won the support of *Kabaka* Daudi Chwa, but the colonial administration stymied the move in favour of the existing chiefly order.[83]

The Bataka movement failed in its stated goal of land reform, but it set the tone and ethos for subsequent movements likewise seeking to challenge the colonial order through the mobilisation of historical consciousness.[84] Thus in 1938 the Sons of Kintu – a more poignant historical reference point is difficult to imagine – was formed with the specific goal of representing the grievances of traders and farmers to the colonial administration, and of overthrowing the unpopular government of Martin Nsibirwa, who was seen as an obstacle to progressive reform.[85] For David Apter, the appearance of this organisation – led by Ignatius Musazi, father and son Samwiri and Shem Mukasa, and James Kivu (later to found the Uganda Motor Drivers' Association) – signified the birth of a putatively 'modern' form of nationalism in Buganda, marked by a departure from the earlier forms of intrigue and lobbying and a shift towards more regular forms of political organisation.[86] Notably, *père et fils* Mukasa had been prominent in the Bataka movement: Shem had lost land when the government decided to expand Mulago Hospital.[87] Meanwhile Musazi it was, too, who was the leading figure behind the formation in 1941 of the UAFU – not quite, as the name suggests, a territory-wide organisation, but rather again Buganda-focused, and representing cultivators across the kingdom.[88]

Not only did Buganda have its 'external' struggles – its relationship with Britain, and its role within the wider territory – but that these

---

[82] For example: 'Bataka lands in Buganda: further petition from Bataka representatives...', UKNA CO 536/185/18, 24 March 1935–22 May 1935, 'Petitions and memorials: Bataka of Buganda', UKNA CO 537/4666 [1949].

[83] M.S.M. Kiwanuka, 'Uganda under the British', in Ogot & Kieran (eds.), *Zamani*, 324.

[84] J. Earle, 'Reading Revolution in late colonial Buganda', *Journal of Eastern African Studies*, 6:3 (2012).

[85] P. Kavuma, *Crisis in Buganda, 1953–55: the story of the exile and return of the Kabaka, Mutesa II* (London, 1979), 8–9.

[86] Apter, *Political Kingdom*, 202–3.   [87] Ibid., 203.

[88] 'Petitions and memorials: representations from the African Produce Growers and Uganda African Farmers Union raising various grievances...', UKNA CO 536/216/1, 19 June 1948–22 August 1949.

increasingly intersected with internal fissures and contests. Some of these have been explored in depth in the work of Carol Summers, for example, who points towards a new kind of political dissidence in the 1940s which was defined by religious difference – in particular, that of Catholic Ganda, prominent in the popular politics of the 1940s – and generational conflict, expressed in the emergence of specific movements challenging the old order and its perceived failings.[89] This was not in itself especially novel: as early as the 1910s and 1920s, many were challenging the Kagwa generation, including the Young Baganda Association which identified a champion in the relatively powerless Daudi Chwa.[90] Kagwa's own hubris had led to his downfall in 1926, and the British had become all the warier of allowing the emergence of such dominant personalities with the sense that they were somehow more important than the system they ostensibly served – as Kagwa, pre-eminent in Ganda politics since the revolution of 1889–90 and creator of Protestant Buganda through his extensive literary output, evidently believed. Daudi Chwa had warned in the 1930s of the dangers of seeking to act like Europeans;[91] but when he died in 1939, he was succeeded by his son Edward Mutesa II, a man who seemed a product of that very generation. Two key precolonial dynamics are worth noting here. One had been the system of clientage by which young men (as male they mostly were) sought socio-political advancement through the patronage of senior chiefs and office-holders. But the other was generational conflict, the episodic conviction that particular cohorts had had their day, and must be ejected from office, in order that better-skilled – and, increasingly, better schooled – young men might take their place. This was the motif of Ugandan politics in the 1930s and 1940s, reflected in the youthful nomenclature of many politic-economic associations, and

---

[89] By Carol Summers, see, for example, 'Young Buganda and Old Boys: youth, generational transition, and ideas of leadership in Buganda, 1920–1949', *Africa Today*, 51:3 (2005) and 'Grandfathers, Grandsons, Morality, and Radical Politics in Late Colonial Buganda', *International Journal of African Historical Studies*, 38:3 (2005).

[90] See early, and very courteous, expressions of intent in 'The Secretary, The Young Baganda Association to the Reverend C.F. Andrews, 22 December 1919' and 'The Secretary, The Young Baganda Association, to the Negro Farmers' Conference, Tuskegee Industrial and Normal Institution', Alabama, USA, 13 September 1921', in Low (ed.), *Mind of Buganda*, 52–4; also Apter, *Political Kingdom*, 213, who noted its 'very admirable and progressive purposes'.

[91] 'Education, Civilization, and "Foreignisation" in Buganda . . . by the *Kabaka* (1935)', in Low (ed.), *Mind of Buganda*.

driven by those born after the wars of the late nineteenth century and the coming of the British.

By the 1940s, there had been half a century of some profoundly difficult changes and challenges – a violent internal political revolution, and a new and problematic partnership with an external force, Britain; large-scale immigration, both from outside the Protectorate and from various bits within it; urban growth and rapid economic change. Little wonder, then, that the 1940s witnessed a visceral escalation in the intensity and force of public politics. It began in 1941, around the same time as the foundation of the UAFU, with a public scandal over an ostensibly private matter – the desire of the *namasole*, the *kabaka*'s mother, to remarry, and to a commoner – although of course when it came to royal matters nothing was essentially 'private', and certainly not when it came to the behaviour of women in the public arena.[92] Public opinion was deeply divided, and when the chief minister and the church permitted the marriage, eruptions of popular anger in Kampala led to the resignation of the former, pressured by British officials. A few months later, there was a disturbance at King's College Budo, when a number of the children of the elite effectively led a 'strike', which seemed to herald emerging tensions at the very heart of the Anglo-Ganda social elite.[93] These events took place alongside the emergence in the religious realm of the *Balokole*, 'the saved ones', part of a wider East African religious revival involving those who believed that they heard the voice of God directly. It represented a profound rift with the established churches.[94]

This was certainly a period of increasing rumbustious and clamorous politics in Buganda,[95] as dangerous and tumultuous in its way as the

[92] By Nakanyike Musisi, see: 'The politics of perception or perception as politics? Colonial and missionary representations of Baganda women, 1900–1945', in J. Allman, S. Geiger & N. Musisi (eds.), *Women in African Colonial Histories* (Bloomington IN, 2002) and 'A personal journey into custom, identity, power and politics: researching and writing the life and times of Buganda's Queen Mother Irene Drusilla Namaganda, 1896–1957', *History in Africa*, 23 (1996).
[93] 'Disturbances at King's College, Budo . . .', UKNA CO 536/210/5, 16 May 1943–12 July 1944.
[94] K. Ward & E. Wild-Wood (eds.), *The East African Revival: history and legacies* (Kampala, 2010) and Peterson, *Ethnic Patriotism*.
[95] See Low's chapter on 'The Advent of Populism in Buganda', in his *Buganda in Modern History*, C. Summers, 'Radical Rudeness: Ugandan social critiques in the 1940s', *Journal of Social History*, 39:3 (2006).

last years of the nineteenth century, and indeed in some respects a re-run of many of the issues of that period. In 1945, a strike and series of riots erupted, essentially caused by rumours of the financial incompetence of the chief treasurer Serwano Kulubya, accused of selling off land to the British, rumours which were at the very least harnessed by a group of chiefs aiming to get rid of Kulubya and advance their own careers in the administration. Kulubya resigned with a mob surrounding the royal palace, and _Katikiro_ Martin Nsibirwa was assassinated.[96] The following year, the Bataka Party appeared, again drawing on the symbolism of clan and awarding it renewed populist lustre, and under the slogan 'Every Muganda is a Mutaka' championed access to land and economic justice, as well as representing effectively an assault on the seemingly soporific and ineffectual government of Mutesa II.[97] However atavistic the Bataka Party seemed to some, it represented a distinctive strand of angry and disenchanted Ganda politics, its fire directed as much at the incumbent royal regime as at the grasping iniquities of the British. The movement sent one of their own, Semakula Mulumba, to London to lobby; refused access to the Secretary of State at the Colonial Office, Mulumba forwarded a petition to the UN, outlining popular Ganda grievances. The move enflamed and divided political opinion back home: one faction of chiefs advised the British that the Bataka was not a legitimate movement – they weren't even real _bataka_, they claimed[98] – and that Mulumba should be arrested. Another faction pressured the _kabaka_ to defend Mulumba, and to dismiss those chiefs plotting against the Bataka Party.[99] The _kabaka_ proved singularly unable to comply. In 1949, more riots erupted across Buganda, this time engineered by the Bataka Party and by members of

---

[96] 'Report of the Commission of Inquiry into the Disturbances which occurred in Uganda during January 1945', UKNA CO 536/215/9, 'Assassination of Martin Luther Nsibirwa...5 September 1945', UKNA FCO 141/18156.

[97] 'Bataka agitators and supporters', UKNA FCO 141/18185 [1949–50], Low, _Buganda in Modern History_, 94, 176.

[98] 'Baganda chiefs disown Bataka', _The Uganda Herald_, 19 August 1948. It is certainly true that the movement was not _solely_ comprised of clan leaders: L.A.Fallers, 'Social stratification in traditional Buganda', in Fallers (ed.), _The King's Men_, 90–1.

[99] 'Actions of Semakula Mulumba, representative of the Bataka community in England', UKNA FCO 141/18212 [1948–51]. Mulumba was a controversial character, landing in trouble a few years later when he allegedly wrote to King Farouk of Egypt requesting Egyptian protection for Uganda: 'Mahommed and the Mountain', _The Uganda Herald_, 1 July 1950.

the UAFU,[100] necessitating the arrival in Uganda of the Kenyan fifth battalion of the KAR.[101] It was a sad moment for a kingdom which had been the platform of the 'new' political order: Mulira, again, could only lament that while 'the past 25 years have seen immense material and intellectual advances in Uganda . . . these advances have not been accompanied by true progress, which expresses itself in love, understanding and fair play'.[102] Mulira's yearning for 'progress' was very much of its time, of course, but the problems to which he alluded were manifest on multiple levels: between the Ganda and the British, and the Ganda and the rest of Uganda; and among the Ganda themselves. The kingdom he described in 1950 was one in tremendous flux, cut across by conflict around economic rights, moral practice, legitimate authority and proper political representation.

There were internal struggles, too, within Bunyoro – between traditionalists surrounding the *Mukama* who sought to strengthen the kingship, and the modernisers who believed that the historic institutions and relationships of power in Bunyoro had become distorted and bore no resemblance to the rightful order of things, as reflected in the precolonial kingdom. The 1933 Agreement greatly strengthened the *Mukama* at the expense of the chiefs, rendering the kingdom – to internal critics, frequently educated men of thwarted ambition – an oppressively authoritarian state in which the king, in alliance with the British, had no reason to consult the parliamentary assembly, the *Rukutaro*, on any issue.[103] The struggle between history and modernity therefore took on a particular twist in the context of Bunyoro, for here the contest was between a chiefly class which believed that the colonial state had grossly distorted the legitimate powers of the kingship – something of a contrast to Buganda, where chiefs built on the constitutional monarchism of the late nineteenth century to further constrain the actual authority of the *kabaka*. Meanwhile, the main formal political party organisation in Bunyoro remained the MBC, dedicated to the 'Lost Counties' issue, until the emergence (briefly) of the

---

[100] 'Civil disturbances in Buganda, April 1949', UKNA FCO 141/18131 [1949].

[101] It seems that the administration did not trust the Ugandan 4th battalion to fire on the local population, if required to do so. Notably, the Ugandan unit had reinforced the Kenyan police two years earlier during the Mombasa dockworkers' strike: Parsons, *Rank-and-File*, 36.

[102] Mulira, *Troubled Uganda*, 27.

[103] Beattie, *Nyoro State*, 157–8, Southall, *Parties and Politics*, 6–7.

Bunyoro People's Party in the late 1950s and early 1960s, and then more importantly the Democratic Party's establishment in Bunyoro from 1960.[104] Southern Uganda was certainly an arena of especially intense, and escalating, political activity in the 1940s, but it was in evidence elsewhere, too. While there were fewer 'formal' political outlets in northern Uganda prior to the 1950s, there was fierce competition over the nature of chieftaincy, as elsewhere in Uganda: in the 1930s and 1940s in Lango, for example, a handful of key families competed for influence, especially following the introduction of a new council administration by the British, and in particular there was heightened agitation for increased powers for county chiefs.[105]

The result of the claustrophobically combative politics fostered by the colonial state, especially from the 1940s onward, then, was hardened local identity and increasingly entrenched conflict around rights and privileges. Indeed, this is one of the core strands of Uganda's colonial story – namely the reinforcement of new forms of identity in order to compete in the political marketplace. This was not, again, purely a matter of 'invention', but rather of evolution and adaptation. For the Gisu, there were now clear markers between members of a community who 'regard themselves as mutually allied', versus 'strangers (non-Gisu) who could be expected to be hostile'. Particular emphasis was placed on the importance of initiation rituals, which further strengthened 'in-group' cohesion.[106] Approaches to 'strangers' in Buganda were complex, even contradictory: for while in the former Nyoro territories there was a clear drive to assimilate the 'indigenous' population, there was heightening anxiety about the escalation of immigration into Buganda. While some Ugandans were regarded as able to assimilate into Ganda culture (mostly southerners, for example Haya and Nyoro), others – notably northerners – were emphatically not.[107] And so the era of nascent 'nationalism', characterised by street protest as well as petition and civic association, combined the 'modernity' of structure and organisation, of message and media, with

---

[104] The main purpose of the BPP was in fact to raise funds for the MBC: Southall, *Parties and Politics*, 26–7.

[105] Uganda Protectorate, *Annual Report on the Northern Province, for the year ended 31 December 1949* (Entebbe, 1950), 117–8, C. Gertzel, *Party and Locality in Northern Uganda, 1945–1962* (London, 1974), 25–7.

[106] La Fontaine, 'Tribalism', 187.

[107] Doyle, 'Immigrants and indigenes', 288–90.

'neo-traditionalism', the force of historical consciousness and visions of the past in the modern era. Activism reflected increasingly complex realities by the beginning of the 1950s: economic grievances, social flux and generational conflict. Meanwhile, Uganda loomed into view through the smoke of battle, a spectral prospect of the independent nation, carrying all of these fissures and factions within it.

History Wars, 1

In the course of the 1950s, these various tensions and conflicts threatened to completely derail the national project, and decolonisation itself. When in 1952 the Uganda National Congress (UNC) was founded, it appeared to indicate the culmination of something – the coming together of a hitherto fragmented arena of sectional and sectarian interest and grievance, the riots of 1945 and 1949 and the collapse of the UAFU.[108] It was not such a simple, nor such a linear, story. There is a growing body of scholarship which seeks to re-examine the late colonial state and the seminal 'moment' of decolonisation from new perspectives.[109] Cooper, notably, argues that there was nothing 'inevitable' about the emergence of the nation-state, and that various options were just as viable to African political leaders in the 1950s.[110] Among those options, notably, was a neo-traditionalist monarchism which contradicted conventional European narratives of how modern political discourse should evolve; at the same time, 'patriotic' ideas crystallised around religious interpretations of *ethnie* to defy the supposed 'logic' of the unitary nation. Such identifications, moreover, were often transnational.[111] Decolonisation, in other words, was complicated. Yet, even at the time, there was little adherence to a 'textbook' interpretation of decolonisation. Thomas Hodgkin in the mid-1950s was quite clear about the challenges confronting would-be nationalists, including the importance of monarchical politics, nor was it even particularly clear whether nationalists saw these things as 'challenges' at all – they were, rather, obvious opportunities and certainly facts of

---

[108] 'Original Correspondence: Uganda National Congress', UKNA CO 822/849 [1954–56] & 822/850 [1956–57].

[109] A.G. Hopkins, 'Rethinking Decolonisation', *Past and Present*, 200:1 (2008).

[110] Cooper, *Africa in the World* and also his *Citizenship between Empire and Nation: remaking France and French Africa, 1945–1960* (Princeton NJ, 2014).

[111] Peterson, *Ethnic Patriotism*, Earle, 'Political Theologies'.

life.[112] Nonetheless, a 'Ugandan nation' – while alien in many of its presumed modern manifestations – was not quite as artificial as might be supposed, and in some ways the travails of the 1950s were emblematic of a loss of temporal vision, a curious exercise in foreshortening in which interconnectedness in the deeper past had been obscured by the *pax colonia*.

Uganda was ill-served by its putatively 'nationalist' class. There were significant structural tensions within the UNC, rooted in the very provenance and leadership of the movement itself. On the face of it, the UNC – under a gifted and dynamic core of leaders including Musazi, Joseph Kiwanuka and Abu Mayanja – had much to offer people across the territory: it was socialist-leaning, interracial, cosmopolitan.[113] It was, in many respects, a typically pan-African movement in that it looked beyond Uganda towards the succour of a distinctive African identity and historical experience: the key vehicle for nationalist aspiration relied to an extent on imagined external identities for its legitimacy, as though the nation itself was not enough, and certainly not to be relied upon. But there were other problems, too. It was dominated by Protestant Ganda, mostly the product of Budo public school, and thus part of an old network of social and political hegemony; its ancestry, after all, could be traced to the UAFU in the 1940s, one of whose leaders, Ignatius Musazi, had also been a key figure in the Kintu movement.[114] Indeed it is broadly true that the impetus for the broad nationalist movement came from intellectual Ganda, who also sought to harness protest elsewhere in their political endeavours. At the same time, however, while purportedly a national movement, the UNC played self-consciously to local concerns and issues: the Mbale branch agitated against the Asian community, for example, and across the north more generally, popular political activism was centred on the historic lack of social and economic development. In Lango, the UNC received considerable support as a result of its promotion of education

---

[112] Hodgkin, *Nationalism in Colonial Africa, passim.*
[113] Low, *Buganda in Modern History*, 178*ff* and see 'Freedom Charter and Manifesto of the Uganda National Congress, by the President-General, I.K.Musazi [1952]', in Low (ed.), *Mind of Buganda*, 181–3. Also 'Joseph W. Kiwanuka, Chairman of the Uganda National Congress (UNC)', UKNA FCO 141/18248 [1956–61], and 'Abubakar Kakyama Mayanja, prominent member of the Uganda National Congress (UNC)', UKNA FCO 141/18246 [1952–58] & 141/18247 [1957–62].
[114] Karugire, *Political History*, 148.

and promises of speedy development in the future.[115] Many Acholi came to see the UNC as the only viable alternative to a chiefly class which had become the tool of the British administration; but by the same token it was the arena within which intra-Acholi conflicts along clan and faith lines were pursued, and so its 'nationalism' was somewhat subsumed by local dispute and contest.[116] In the 1950s and early 1960s, politics in both Acholi and Lango was increasingly dominated by nationalist parties – culminating in the Democratic Party (which soon developed Acholi strongholds), the UNC and the Uganda People's Congress (popular among the Langi, and led by one of their own, Obote) – whose agendas were readily refracted in pursuit of local interests, including economic development and hostility to chiefs seen to be part and parcel of the Protectorate government.[117]

Particular visions of the past and, by extension, of the future now dominated the political arena – an arena, crudely summarised, which was contested between Ganda political activism on the one hand, and those purporting to represent the unitary nation on the other. In Buganda, *Kabaka* Edward Mutesa II had long been seen as aloof and disinterested – a weak character, out of touch, even irrelevant in the putatively 'new' politics of the late colonial moment. He was transformed in the mid-1950s through his public hostility to the idea of the unitary nation, the stated objective of the colonial administration, as well as to the idea of East African federation, floated casually by the British Colonial Secretary Oliver Lyttleton.[118] The *kabaka* declared that Buganda would never accept this, and moreover that a clear timetable should be laid out for independence. In any case, Buganda, argued the *kabaka*, should deal with the Foreign Office – with whom the 1900 Agreement had been made – and not the Colonial Office, which only took over in 1902.[119] Relations between Edward Mutesa and the Governor Andrew Cohen deteriorated in the latter part of 1953, and in November, the *kabaka* was bundled aboard a

---

[115] Uganda Protectorate, *Annual Report on the Northern Province for the year ended 31 December 1957* (Entebbe, 1958), 107–9.

[116] Ibid., 105; Gertzel, 'Kingdoms, Districts, and the Unitary State', 80–1.

[117] Uganda Protectorate, *Annual Report on the Northern Province for the year ended 31 December 1959* (Entebbe, 1960), 91–2, Gertzel, *Party and Locality*, 77.

[118] Hughes, *East Africa: the search for unity*, 168.

[119] Kabaka of Buganda, *Desecration*, 118–19.

plane and exiled to England.[120] It was a crisis of considerable magnitude, and one which produced profound shock and indeed mourning in Buganda itself, for the head of the family had been in effect been summarily removed – a savage decapitation which was interpreted by the Ganda as an assault on the central pillar of the gendered political order, leading to women weeping in public and men withdrawing from the political and social fabric of colonial life.[121] It also destabilised the wider territory, and further undermined the prospects for the unitary nation. At length, compromise was reached: the federation idea was placed to one side, but the *kabaka* was to be rendered even more of a constitutional monarch under the terms of a new agreement in 1955. The *kabaka* returned to Uganda in October of that year, but new crises continued to emerge. In essence, the Buganda government trusted neither LegCo, nor the British, nor any of the political parties now proliferating across the territory – even though many of them were led by Ganda. Buganda wanted a federal arrangement with the rest of Uganda, and regarded itself as quite distinct from the territory at large. As the *kabaka* described it years later:

Buganda's relationship with Uganda had never been important before. We had dealings with the British and we had friendly neighbours...At first we thought we would be held back by our more backward neighbours; later we feared that a combination of the rest of the country might from motives of self-interest and jealousy seek to destroy us. Both fears proved well-founded...Legco, larger and more African, was designed to become the National Assembly, and we had lost none of our suspicions of a body that could claim our participation and ignore our voice...We did not consider Legco to be important. The Lukiiko disapproved of the whole idea of political parties, and it can indeed be argued that it is an un-African concept.[122]

Buganda, in other words, wanted no part in the political scrum forming in the lead-up to independence, held itself apart culturally and politically, and regarded any attempt at national integration as a fundamental assault upon the dignity of the kingdom and the kingship.

---

[120] A detailed justification was written by Governor Cohen and circulated to administrations across the Protectorate: 'Statement by the Governor', Kabale District Archives ADM95/JUD8/Deporters, distributed 21 December 1953. See also Kavuma, *Crisis in Buganda*.

[121] A.I. Richards, *The Multicultural States of East Africa* (Montreal & London, 1969), 47–8, Tripp, *Women and Politics*, 36–7.

[122] Kabaka of Buganda, *Desecration*, 149–50.

In the second half of the 1950s, not all the parties set up in the febrile political atmosphere were destined to survive.[123] The Progressive Party was one such, founded earlier in 1955, before the *kabaka*'s return, and led by Mulira; it comprised members of the Lukiiko, prominent churchmen and businessmen, and a number of those who had been involved in another very active civil society organisation, the Uganda Teachers' Association.[124] It was, in essence, a party of intellectuals with little of the popular support which was now becoming increasingly essential in a busy and clamorous political marketplace. It soon collapsed, but at around the same moment, another appeared – this time more robust, and longer-lived (it lives still, if subdued). Religious affiliation had long been important in shaping, and reflecting, political identity – dating to the late nineteenth century – and now this came ever more sharply to the fore, adding to the unstable mix of ethnicity and provincialism that characterised Ugandan national politics in the late 1950s. Catholic Ganda, who had long felt discriminated against by the predominantly Anglican Mengo establishment, seized the opportunity presented by Edward Mutesa's exile to form the Democratic Party (DP) in 1955–6, founded under the leadership of the prominent Catholic politician Matayo Mugwanya.[125] Mugwanya's defeat in elections for the post of *katikiro* in 1955 seemed the latest manifestation of Catholic exclusion from the key chieftaincies in the kingdom.[126] The Catholic cause was now given new impetus by the DP, which also sought to reach out beyond Buganda as well as redefine the relationship between Buganda and Uganda. The DP was by no stretch of the imagination 'republican', but it was much less wedded to the idea of monarchical authority and territoriality, and did not accept, in simple terms, that the *kabaka* alone was the embodiment of Buganda; it claimed for itself a role akin to that of the American revolutionaries of the late eighteenth century and positioned itself as the party with the widest

---

[123] One of the best accounts remains Gertzel, 'Kingdoms, Districts, and the Unitary State'.

[124] 'The Progressive Party Manifesto 1955', in Low (ed.), *Mind of Buganda*, 183–90.

[125] 'Original correspondence: Uganda Democratic Party', UKNA CO 822/858 [1956].

[126] 'Elections to the Buganda Lukiiko . . . , refusal of the Kabaka . . . to appoint Matayo Mugwanya as a member of the Lukiiko', UKNA FCO 141/18188 [1956–57].

democratic and national embrace of all the movements proliferating at that moment.[127]

Buganda, meanwhile, withdrew its representatives from LegCo in 1957. Despite this, elections were held across Uganda in 1958,[128] with the result that the UNC won five seats on the Council, the DP one seat and four seats by independent candidates. As the new-look LegCo met, another party was formed – the Uganda People's Union (UPU), comprising African members of the Legislative Council. In 1959, frustrated by Ganda intransigence, Obote split from the UNC, and in March 1960 founded the Uganda People's Congress (UPC), merging with the UPU, drawing mainly on northern and Protestant support, and challenging his old movement over education and the provision of a range of social services.[129] Obote and the UPC regarded northern Uganda as of particular strategic importance, and sought to mobilise extensively across Acholi and Langi territory: here, the UPC tapped into deep-seated hostility to Buganda, dating to the hegemony of Ganda agents in the early years of the twentieth century.[130] More broadly, both the DP and the UPC won support across the north, owing in large part to the perception, at least, of both Kiwanuka and Obote as genuine 'nationalists' with little patience for Ganda ambition.[131] Yet elsewhere the success of the big parties was often connected to the individual local standing of candidates – as in the case of Gaspare Oda in West Nile, who stood as a DP candidate in the 1958 LegCo elections but whose triumph was the result of his local standing and popularity among Catholics, rather than any extensive party activity in the area.[132] West Nile was generally regarded as stony ground for the national parties compared to Acholi and Lango, owing to a combination of geographical isolation and 'ethnic complexity'.[133] But both DP and UPC tapped into widespread anxiety and anger across the north around Buganda's ambitions both for itself and for Uganda as a whole. As a resolution in Lango district council put it in 1958: 'We fear that what Mengo Lukiko

---

[127] Explicit reference was made to both the American and the French revolutions in Ben Kiwanuka's preface in *Forward to Freedom, being the Manifesto of the Democratic Party* (Kampala, 1960).

[128] 'Detailed arrangements for elections in Uganda', UKNA FCO 822/1537 [1957–59].

[129] Low, *Buganda in Modern History*, 189–92.

[130] C. Leys, *Politicians and Policies: an essay on politics in Acholi, Uganda, 1962–65* (Nairobi, 1967), 11–12.

[131] Gingera-Pinycwa, *Northern Uganda*, 12.

[132] Gertzel, *Party and Locality*, 79.   [133] Ibid., 80.

are doing, they want to spoil the relationships among the people of the Uganda Protectorate. They are opening a wide gap of hatred among the tribes...'[134] Such anxiety seemed justified when in 1961 the *Kabaka Yekka* party (KY, 'The King Alone') was founded in Buganda as an essentially ethno-nationalist movement expounding the separation of Buganda from Uganda.[135] KY was both exemplar and pioneer of the royalist, neo-traditionalist spirit which would come to define Ugandan politics in the decades ahead; it embodied the presence of the past in the political present. Its existence exemplified in the starkest of ways the splintered vision of the nation: Buganda, after all, was a ready-made nation within the artificial construct of Uganda. By late 1961 Mengo had shifted from that extreme position to one of willingness to partici-pate in discussions about the future of Uganda;[136] still, its position with regard to the kingship itself was unambiguous enough: '1. The Kabaka shall not be in an inferior position to anybody on Buganda soil. 2. It is inconceivable that a commoner should ever "sit over" the Kabaka'.[137] But of course KY also represented deep fissures within Buganda itself, not least in terms of the juxtaposition with the DP's vision for Uganda/Buganda as inclusive, integrative, outward-looking. KY boy-cotted the elections of 1961, but were horrified as the DP – drawing much of its support from the south, and from Catholics – triumphed as a result, allowing its leader Benedicto Kiwanuka to become chief minister at the head of internal self-government from May 1961 to April 1962. It was electoral arithmetic, rather than any deeply rooted reconciliation of opposing political visions, that prompted KY to enter into its alliance with Obote's UPC.[138] Kiwanuka would be denied the opportunity to lead Uganda to full independence, achieved in October 1962 with Obote as prime minister and *Kabaka* Edward Mutesa as executive president of Uganda.[139] It seemed a reasonable compromise, to the outsider at least; and though fundamentally unstable, it reflected,

---

[134] Quoted in ibid., 82.
[135] 'Kabaka Yekka ('king only') movement', UKNA FCO 141/18392 [1961–62], I.R. Hancock, 'Patriotism and neo-traditionalism in Buganda: the Kabaka Yekka ("the King Alone") movement, 1961–62', *Journal of African History*, 11:3 (1970), Apter, *Political Kingdom, passim*.
[136] See 'The Lukiiko Memorandum' and 'Kabaka Mutesa II to the Lukiiko, 16 September 1961', in Low (ed.), *Mind of Buganda*, 200–211.
[137] 'KY election pamphlet, 1962', in Low (ed.), *Mind of Buganda*, 214.
[138] 'General election, April 1962', UKNA FCO 141/18356 [1962].
[139] 'Governor's consultations with new Prime Minister of Uganda, Apolo Milton Obote', UKNA FCO 141/18402 [1962].

to an extent, the desire by Obote – in the face of opposition from some in the UPC – to accommodate Buganda within Uganda, and to offset the fundamental problem confronting all political leaders that there was no single dominant movement in Uganda.[140]

Many Ganda believed Buganda to be a nation in its own right, and Uganda to be an entirely unwanted, artificial and indeed illogical construct. But they were not alone in their disenchantment with the putative nation, nor in the ferocious debates they had around the role of monarchy. In the far west, on the edges of the Toro kingdom, another movement appeared around the same time as KY to defy the unitary impulse, drawing on its own interpretation of the 'national past' in pursuit of a very different political agenda. In August 1962, a violent rebellion erupted in Toro involving Konzo and Amba who rejected their incorporation into that kingdom and in particular the Toro kingship as reified by the late nineteenth-century political settlement.[141] They drew on a multi-layered historical argument – including an earlier insurgency in 1919, as well as resistance to centralising violence in the nineteenth century – to justify their claim to a separate 'kingdom' named Ruwenzururu.[142] Kings and kingdoms, again, were problematic for many. Armed resistance would rumble on – intermittent, and at times low-level – for the next two decades before an agreement with the second Obote regime in 1982; it would reignite once more in the

---

[140] The electoral detail and the political narrative are well enough known, and very effectively told elsewhere: for example, see Low, *Buganda in Modern History*, chapter 6 and several chapters in Uzoigwe (ed.), *Uganda: the dilemma of nationhood*, including: O.Furley, 'The Legislative Council, 1945–1961: the wind of change', Benoni Turyahikayo-Rugyema, 'The development of mass nationalism, 1952–1962' and Phares Mutibwa, 'Internal self-government, March 1961–October 1962'.

[141] Uganda Government, *Report of the Commission of Inquiry into the Recent Disturbances amongst the Baamba and Bakonjo People of Toro* (Entebbe, 1962), published the day after Uganda became independent, 10 October. There is a rich seam of material on the insurgency – and on historical claim and counter-claim – in the Fort Portal district archives.

[142] M. Doornbos, 'Kumanyana and Rwenzururu: two responses to ethnic inequality', in Mazrui & Rotberg (eds.), *Protest and Power*, M. Syahuka, 'The Origin and Development of the Rwenzururu Movement, 1900–1962', *Mawazo*, 5:2 (December 1983), D.R.Peterson, 'States of Mind: Political History and the Rwenzururu Kingdom in Western Uganda', in Peterson & Macola (eds.), *Recasting the Past*. For an engaging contemporary account, see T. Stacey, *Summons to Ruwenzori* (London, 1965), a book notably dedicated to Milton Obote.

late 1980s and 1990s.[143] In Bunyoro in the 1950s there was historical vision of a slightly different sort, but no less intense, and no less
impassioned. On the occasion celebrating thirty years of his reign in
1954, *Mukama* Tito Winyi might point to the great socio-economic
progress made in the kingdom under his guidance;[144] but the contestation within Bunyoro between 'traditionalists' and 'modernisers'
entered a new phase as a result of the 1955 agreement with the colonial government. This ostensibly marked a victory for the modernisers
in that the *Mukama*'s powers were theoretically curtailed by a more
muscular council, though in reality Tito Winyi continued to exercise
substantial personal influence.[145] The 1955 Agreement also, incidentally, stipulated that the Kingdom was entitled to share in any future
mineral wealth generated within its borders.[146] Yet the great struggle
was yet to be won, for now, during the years of politicking around
the future of Uganda, there was renewed activity around the issue of
the Lost Counties.[147] It was a political struggle which was foremost in
the mind of the Nyoro historian John Nyakatura when he produced
his great work on the kingdom's glorious past in the late 1940s; and
the *Mukama* had used the occasion of a speech following the signing of the 1955 Agreement to pointedly demand their return.[148] That
vigour, even to the point of recruiting British legal expertise to look
into the question, contrasted with the melancholic sense of nostalgia
and resignation memorably captured by the anthropologist John Beattie – the idea that Bunyoro had a long-lost, glorious past but one which

[143] A. Syahuka-Muhindo, *The Rwenzururu Movement and the Democratic
Struggle* (Centre for Basic Research, Kampala, 1991), Augustine
Kyaminyawandi, *The Faces of the Rwenzururu Movement* (n.p., 2001).
[144] 'Omukama's 30 year's rule', *The Uganda Herald*, 4 May 1954. In truth, the
essentials of the *Mukama*'s speeches barely changed from one prominent
anniversary to the next: see, for example, 'Twenty-five years ruler of Bunyoro',
The Uganda Herald, 23 April 1949 and '20th anniversary of the accession of
Rukirabasajja T.G. Winyi IV, CBE, Mukama of Bunyoro-Kitara', *The Uganda
Herald*, 19 April 1944.
[145] The full text of the Agreement can be viewed at http://www.bunyoro-kitara
.org/resources/Bunyoro$2C+Agreement+1955.pdf; also Doyle, *Crisis and
Decline*, 176–7.
[146] 'Why is Bunyoro demanding a share of oil money?', *New Vision*, 1 May 2009.
[147] See, for example, 'Bunyoro's Claim for Mubende', *The Uganda Herald*, 30
May 1955, 'Memorandum by the Katikiro of Bunyoro Kingdom', Uganda
Constitutional Conference 1961: Restoration of Bunyoro's Lost Counties,
Appendix 2 in Karugire, *Political History*.
[148] 'Bunyoro Agreement Signed', *Uganda Argus*, 5 September 1955.

would never be rekindled.[149] It also contrasted with the sense that many Ganda had of their history being a living, dynamic energy that *entitled* them to – even guaranteed – a distinctive and glorious future. But in the late 1950s, despite initial British recalcitrance,[150] the Lost Counties campaign gathered legal momentum, and physical impetus, too, with attacks on Ganda settled in the disputed territories escalating during the final years of colonial rule. Research commissioned by the British government into the dispute led to the conclusion that at least some of the territory needed urgently to be transferred to Bunyoro, and that there was a very real threat of serious unrest if this failed to happen; Ganda resistance, meanwhile, needed to be faced down and overcome sooner rather than later – not least because Buganda was likely to be even more powerful after independence, according to the chair of the commission.[151]

Historical consciousness was forcefully and politically visible in Buganda, Bunyoro, and Toro; but elsewhere, too, historical thinking represented the emergence of a territorial, cultural politics forged in the unstable late colonial era. The Masaaba Historical Research Association had its origins in the mid-1950s in Tororo, though it was not until 1962 that a formal constitution was produced. The aims of the Association were to 'collect the past' of Bugisu, produce books in the vernacular, and develop geographical knowledge. As for membership, this was – a little defensively – 'open to the Sebei, Babukusu and Balegeni, should they wish to do so', while other 'non-Bamasaba may be granted membership provided they have lived in Bugisu for a considerable period and are familiar with Kigisu customs and way of life'.[152] The crackle of political electricity can be detected between each line, and the Association belonged to a literary lineage – beginning with Kagwa himself – characterised by the mobilisation of historical work in pursuit of political projects. It was no coincidence that interest in 'historical research' spiked during a boundary dispute with neighbouring Bukedi, a commission of inquiry into which had to wrestle with

---

[149] Beattie, *Nyoro State*, 31, also Ingrams, *Uganda*, 238–9.
[150] '"Lost Counties" plea rejected', *Uganda Argus*, 17 November 1955, 'No delegation on the "Lost Counties"', *Uganda Argus*, 12 December 1955.
[151] Colonial Office, *Uganda: Report of a Commission of Privy Counsellors on a Dispute between Buganda and Bunyoro* (London, 1962).
[152] 'The Masaba Historical Research Association Constitution, 1962', 1–2, copies in MUL.

the thorny questions of migration, settlement and the provenance of place-names.[153] Nor was it a coincidence that 'historical research' was prioritised at a time of factional conflict and, as the annual report for 1961 had it, 'personal animosities' *within* Bugisu. There was a certain paradox in that while the late colonial period bred zero-sum politics, the insularity involved in strengthening local identities simultaneously weakened their hand at the national level, according to a prescient assessment on the eve of independence: '[u]nless the Bagisu can...escape from preoccupation with solely parochial affairs it will be difficult for the tribe to play an influential and decisive role in the life a self-governing Uganda'. And then, with that peculiar lack of irony that marked colonial judgments: 'It is significant that no Mugisu has yet achieved any major prominence in the national political field due it would appear to an inability to develop a true national spirit and a sense of common purpose'.[154]

Against a backdrop of feverish politicking, the newfound cynicism integral to electoral politics, the various forms of political movement, and political party, which were established from various directions to represent particular constituent groups: amidst all this, Uganda became independent. People were invited to write to the organising committee through 1962 with their ideas for the national anthem, the design of the flag, suggestions for stamps.[155] What emerged was a set of emblems for the new nation, a self-conscious fusion of African and European iconography of statehood.[156] The nation had its signs and symbols,

---

[153] Uganda Protectorate, *Sessional Paper on the Report of the Commission of Inquiry into the Disturbances in Certain Areas of the Bukedi and Bugisu Districts of the Eastern Province during the month of January 1960* (Entebbe, 1960), *Report of the Commission appointed to Review the Boundary between the Districts of Bugisu and Bukedi* (Entebbe, 1962).

[154] Bugisu District Annual Report, 1961, UNA Eastern Province (EP) Annual Reports, A46 series.

[155] For example, Letter from King's College Budo to the Secretary, Uganda National Anthem Consideration Committee, 23 February 1962, A.J. Owino to the Secretary, Uganda National Anthem Committee, 15 February 1962, Makerere College School to the Secretary, National Flag Committee, 17 February 1962. Thanks to Christopher Muhoozi of Makerere University for giving the author access to these documents.

[156] 'Uganda's anthem was inspired by Christianity', *New Vision*, 11 January 2012, *Uganda Independence: the Celebrations and the Royal Tour* (Kampala, 1962), 13, 29, 'The Crested Crane: Uganda's emblem of beauty and serenity', *Daily Monitor*, 23 July 2012.

but Obote's challenges were manifold as the nation stumbled blinking into the light following its brief but poignant ceremonial recess. Earnest and intelligent, he was nonetheless at the centre, and in some ways was the incarnation, of a balkanised politics. The British had played their part in this, to be sure; but Obote's energetic paranoia was symptomatic of a wider malaise among Uganda's first generation of national leadership. There was much talent in Obote's early cabinets, and Uganda's nascent political elite was arguably no less equipped or prepared for sovereign government than anywhere else in the reborn Africa of the early 1960s. But a series of great clefts lay at the centre of Uganda, a set of tectonic plates underlying the political order which left it profoundly vulnerable to chronic instability. The fissure of greatest significance was that between Buganda and Uganda – not because the others were less important in their own terms, but because this was the fault line with the capacity to destroy Uganda at its very centre. The UPC was increasingly socialist and republican in political orientation, and comparatively radical in its embrace of an Afrocentric and pan-African view of the continent's, and Uganda's, future. KY was monarchist, essentially inward-looking, in some ways even solipsistic, with little interest in becoming a national movement. For two years, there had been some compromise and evidence of goodwill on the part of both Edward Mutesa and Obote. But it was a doomed match, unsustainable over the longer term, and had already begun to unravel in the middle of 1964, by which time Obote had dissolved the parliamentary alliance between UPC and KY.[157] Later that year violence erupted in Kampala and elsewhere in protest at the Lost Counties referendum, as a result of which Bunyoro was given its territory back, 70 years after it was seized.[158] The referendum had been recommended by the British commission of enquiry but it was pushed through by Obote in the face of Ganda opposition, and was an early indication of Obote's growing confidence in dealing with Buganda.

Obote had sent overenthusiastic troops to quell the Lost Counties riots, and indeed a parallel development alongside mounting political crisis was the militarisation of the polity from the mid-1960s. The British had bequeathed Uganda a comparatively tiny army in 1962 – a few hundred men – but in January 1964 a mutiny had taken

---

[157] Low, *Buganda in Modern History*, 237.   [158] Beattie, *Nyoro State*, 94.

place (along with similar mutinies in Tanganyika and Kenya) at the barracks in Jinja over pay and conditions.[159] It was over after a few days, and the soldiers' concerns were addressed; but it was a reminder to Obote of the potential threat from an army which might otherwise be transformed into an invaluable political ally. It was a critical moment, providing the impetus for the (re)emergence of soldiers in public life. As a direct result, Obote embarked on a rapid expansion of the Ugandan army, recruiting from the usual northern groups including from among his own Langi community. The growth of the army to one of the largest in sub-Saharan Africa involved the elevation of one Idi Amin, a veteran of the KAR and one of the first (along with his Teso rival Shaban Opolot) African commissioned officers prior to independence.[160] If Obote hoped he could use Amin to shore up his position, he was in fact dealing with an opportunistic and shrewd operator who was soon made the head of army recruitment, giving him close links with Sudanese and Congolese rebel groups through whom he also established advantageous links with British and Israeli intelligence services.[161] Obote had ordered Amin to establish military camps in Congo with a view to supporting Patrice Lumumba's adherents. Indeed it was this military adventurism – and Amin's increasing over-ambition – which escalated the political standoff between Obote and Buganda, and the history wars which would shape Uganda over the next half-century. In early 1966, a KY member of the National Assembly introduced the 'Gold Allegations Motion', accusing Amin of stealing large amounts of gold – as well as ivory and coffee – from Congo for the purchase of arms. It implicated Obote himself and two other cabinet ministers. Obote's response was to announce his own commission of enquiry, and that a plot against him had been uncovered; five ministers were arrested, and Buganda was accused of being involved in the plot.[162] In May, Idi Amin was placed in charge of the armed force that attacked the *kabaka*'s palace at Mengo. Mutesa and a small contingent of men managed to escape, fleeing into eventual

---

[159] The outstanding study is Timothy Parsons, *The 1964 Army Mutinies and the Making of Modern East Africa* (Westport CT & London, 2003), also Parsons, *Rank-and-File*, 45–6.
[160] There were growing tensions between the two: Lee, *African Armies*, 77.
[161] Kyemba, *State of Blood*, 23–5.
[162] Mutibwa, *Uganda since Independence*, 35–6.

exile in London.[163] The following year, Obote declared the kingdoms formally abolished under a new republican constitution according to which Obote himself was executive president at the head of a newly strengthened, central UPC government.[164] As for Amin, he was now commander of the armed forces, and increasingly, it seemed, unassailable. Together, they represented the resurgence of a northern bloc in Ugandan political and military culture, and the assault on the southern kingdoms – Buganda in particular – signified the apparent culmination of a set of deep-rooted history wars now waged in the name of republican unity.[165] As Low put it in a contemporary analysis:

[Obote] was expressing the deep-seated hostility of the traditionally acephalous peoples of his own northern region against the hierarchical values which the Buganda model had displayed . . . The attack upon the Kabaka of Buganda's palace represented . . . not just an attack upon the structural features of the Buganda model, or upon its religious accompaniments. It was an attack as well upon the hierarchical, elitist values which were so closely associated with them.[166]

A little later, one Ugandan political scientist would use the example of Busoga – its kingship abolished along with the rest – to make an implicit argument against traditional authority more generally. It was precisely because the '*kyabazinga*ship' had become 'monarchised' that its downfall was both inevitable and desirable: it was divisive, imitative (based on Buganda), ostentatious and extravagant, he proposed.[167] The academic was none other than Apolo Nsibambi, later one of Museveni's long-serving prime ministers (1999–2011).

Meanwhile Obote shifted significantly to the left, and the government's programme took on an emphatically socialist hue through,

---

[163] A compelling, if naturally one-sided, account is provided in Edward Mutesa's *Desecration*; also 'The Kabaka's flight into exile', *DRUM*, August 1966.

[164] The vision is laid out (in overwhelming detail) in Republic of Uganda, *His Excellency the President's Communication from the Chair of the National Assembly on 9th June 1967* (Government Printer, Entebbe).

[165] For example, Secretary-General's speech on 'Mukago' ceremony, and the Republic celebrations at Kikungiri – Ndorwa, 1 January 1968, Kabale District Archives, COM13 / NAF 2.

[166] Low, *Buganda in Modern History*, 245–6.

[167] A. Nsibambi, 'The monarchization of the kyabazingaship and the passing of traditional leaders in Uganda', *Nigerian Behavioural Sciences Journal*, II (1979), 98.

among other pieces of legislation, the Common Man's Charter. If the abolition of the kingdoms had been justified in the name of republican modernity, the Charter – somewhat paradoxically – emphasised the need to restore 'traditional values' at the centre of Ugandan social and political life.[168] In reality, authoritarianism was not so much creeping as rapidly materialising, and to be a member of the opposition – notably that offered by the beleaguered and harassed DP – was an increasingly perilous business.[169] Six months after the bloody attack on Mengo, which involved hundreds of deaths and the mutilation of an entire political community, Obote announced that he could not envisage elections for another five years.[170] He could remind Ugandans that independence meant belonging to one country, and admonish them, setting a precedent for heads of government using independence-day speeches to tick off their ignorant compatriots, that

[u]nfortunately ... some of our citizens did not take seriously this fundamental meaning of our Independence. The result of this has been that we faced a series of situations caused by some of our citizens who held the idea that Uganda was merely a collection or a confederation of tribesmen ...

He went on to declare how 'two victories of the people over forces of external and domestic colonialism have given citizens a new mission'.[171] The DP would hardly have agreed with the latter assertion, but certainly concurred with the prime minister in its eschewal of tribalism: 'The founders of this Party looked at Uganda as one entity and to her inhabitants, albeit composed of many tribes, as people with one destiny', asserted Paul Ssemogerere in 1969.[172] Yet the DP lamented bitterly – and, by 1968–9, rather courageously – the collapse of whatever nascent democratic culture had been nurtured a decade earlier,

---

[168] 'The Common Man's Charter: a speech given to Kigezi District Councillors on Thursday 6 August 1970, at Kikungiri Rural Training Centre', Kabale District Archives, MISC BOX 13, CD/112A.

[169] See also Tabaire, 'The Press and Political Repression', 195–202.

[170] For example, 'Mr Obote and Elections: Press Statement', 15 December 1966, Papers of the Democratic Party, MUL.

[171] 'Address to the Nation by the President Dr A. Milton Obote on the occasion of the sixth anniversary of independence on 9th October 1968', Kabale District Archives COM18 / CMI57 / Independence and Republic Celebrations and Labour Day.

[172] The first issue of *The Democrat: Uganda's messenger of truth and justice*, the monthly newsletter of the DP, February 1969, 6.

and positioned itself as the champion of human rights and democracy. Obote declared in September 1969: 'During the last two years the people of Uganda have shown positive signs of full realisation and appreciation of the fact that it is better to build an integrated home for themselves rather than live in the divided Uganda of the past . . . We are building a new society, [and] one homogenous and united nation'.[173] A month later, on the occasion of Uganda's seventh anniversary, in October 1969, Kiwanuka matched Obote's portentous speech with a statement of his own, in which he declared:

The seven years of UPC rule since independence are nothing but a record of injustice, arbitrary rule and broken promises. We have a society in which citizens are the victims of discrimination on the basis of their political opinions, religion or tribe . . . . Uganda's seventh independence anniversary has come at a time when tyranny and political persecution dictate Government policy. Detention without trial has been inscribed in our Statute Book . . . Such being the situation in which this year's independence anniversary finds us, we see no good reason to join the celebrations and festivities . . . Such merriment and jubilation is, in the circumstances, best reserved for the Cabinet Ministers, the UPC Members of Parliament, and the nominated Secretaries General, Mayors and Councillors . . . [174]

In the course of the decade, the DP shaped itself as the self-conscious representative of political modernity, rooted in the disappointment of Obote's brave new world and drawing on the language of the fundamental rights and principles enshrined in the internationalism of the United Nations. In 1967, in requesting amendments to the government's constitutional proposals, the DP declared: 'We believe, like the United Nations, in the fundamental human rights, in the dignity and worth of the human person and in the equal rights of all people . . .'; and in 'a Government of the people, by the people and for the people'.[175] This included women, on whose status as equal citizens the DP placed increasing emphasis as political actors and agents

[173] 'Message to the Nation from His Excellency the President of the Republic of Ugannda Dr A. Milton Obote on the second anniversary of Republic Day, 8th September 1969', Kabale District Archives COM18 / CMI57 / Independence and Republic Celebrations and Labour Day.

[174] 'Uganda's 7th Independence Anniversary: Press Statement', 7 October 1969, Papers of the Democratic Party, MUL.

[175] 'The Democratic Party and the Constitutional Proposals', 7 July 1967, Papers of the Democratic Party, MUL.

of both social change and social cohesion.[176] At the same time, however, Obote's own internationalist modernity had involved the courageous decision to confront the lately departed British at home and abroad: condemning British arms sales to South Africa, and nationalising British firms in Uganda.[177] It was a principled stand, on the face of it at least. But by the end of the decade, Obote's abrupt and alarming embrace of socialist authoritarianism had produced a growing backlash, among other political parties and civil society and indeed within the UPC itself. Amin was restless, the army was discontented, and Buganda was seething; Kiwanuka was arrested and detained for sedition in September 1969.[178] Obote, meanwhile, fearful of Amin's growing power, placed him under house arrest in 1970, but to little avail. And thus in January 1971, as Idi Amin announced Obote's overthrow, there was open jubilation in some quarters; quiet relief in others; though many more still would wonder anxiously what was still to come.

Despite its early advantage in the colonial order, Buganda had in some ways squandered that advantage and had not come to terms with the pan-Ugandan nation or its place in it. To a large extent, too, this was the direct outcome of the crises of the late nineteenth century, from which the kingdom never really recovered. At the same time, of course, Buganda was really only doing what many others were doing across the continent – consolidating, retrenching, seeking to define itself more sharply against others – against the backcloth of the fragile, illusory nation. In the grand sweep of Ugandan history, Buganda (and other kingdoms) enjoyed key advantages in terms of political structures, processes and institutions, certainly when it came to engaging in 'nation-building' exercises. But in other respects, there was the curse of antiquity: Buganda's increasingly defensive sense of self, exclusive and excluding, as developed in and around Mengo, which marginalised

---

[176] For example, 'Uganda women march to freedom: the Democratic Party policy statement about the status of women', n.d., Papers of the Democratic Party, MUL.

[177] A. Gavshon, *Crisis in Africa: battleground of East and West* (Harmondsworth, 1981), 61.

[178] 'Ben's arrest etc – from the publicity desk', 17 September 1969 and Paul Ssemogerere to the Inspector General of Police, Kampala, re. Democrats recently detained under the emergency regulations, 30 September 1969, Papers of the Democratic Party, MUL.

that deeper history of openness, flexibility and inclusivity as championed by the DP under the leadership of Ben Kiwanuka.[179] Meanwhile, Obote's administration had sought, like so many of its counterparts in the newly formed Organisation of African Unity, to consign the 'tribe' to the past, and create a nation of the future – which often meant, in the late 1960s and early 1970s, a leftist vision of socialist modernity. But this only served to encourage subnational identity, and the political culture fostered by Obote and the UPC was characterised by growing uncertainty and anxiety. In 1964, Basil Davidson could write with bubbling optimism about how

a few outsiders had predicted . . . that Uganda would fall apart with independence, and become the victim of its own 'tribal conflicts'. But what in fact has happened there? By mid-1963 the shrewd Milton Obote, prime minister of a government struggling hard against internal separatism, could reasonably claim a large and perhaps decisive measure of success. The [UPC] which he leads was already emerging as a dominant unifying force, and was making inroads even into Baganda separatism . . . [180]

It was a rash judgement, if an understandable one. A few years later, George Bennett noted how Obote 'was determined to build a nation', and quoted him with implicit approval: '"[T]he problems of people putting the tribe above national consciousness is a problem that we must face, and an issue we must destroy"'.[181] Edward Mutesa's position was rather different, as he made clear in a letter to the UN Secretary-General in March 1966, as the constitutional crisis was unfolding: '[T]he stability of the whole country – the nation – largely depends on the continued existence of their traditional institutions, upon which the new and foreign national institutions must be built; loyalty to the nation is only forming, where tribal loyalty is an accomplished and ingrained fact'.[182] Yet for the DP, this was precisely

---

[179] In essence, the great struggle of this stage of Kiwanuka's political life was against the cloistered unaccountability of Mengo and the subsequent disenfranchisement of the Ganda people: see, for example, Albert Bade, *Benedicto Kiwanuka: the man and his politics* (Kampala, 1996), esp. chapter VI.

[180] B. Davidson, *Which Way Africa? The search for a new society* (Harmondsworth, 1964), 129.

[181] G. Bennett, 'Tribalism in Politics', in Gulliver (ed.), *Tradition and Transition*, 71.

[182] 'Annexure to the Appeal by Kabaka Mutesa II to the Secretary-General of the United Nations, 11 March 1966', in Low (ed.), *Mind of Buganda*, 222.

the problem, as the party asserted at the same moment that Edward Mutesa was complaining to the UN: 'This country is getting bitterly divided tribally [sic]. It appears to us that you yourself as a leader and guardian of this country for the time being, are not helping to stop this development'.[183] At any rate, Obote's ouster at the hands of his long-time lieutenant Idi Amin in January 1971 represented, in many ways, the end of the 'colonial moment': the reassertion of the frontier against the centre; the re-emergence of the violent entrepreneurialism which had defined the region's nineteenth century; and, briefly at least, the restoration of northern dominance in Ugandan politics. Yet it is also the case that the period between 1950 and 1970 bore some similarity – as a defining one of turbulent upheaval and ultimately political transformation – to that of the 1890s and 1900s. Both were moments in which political mobilisation involved historical interpretation, and in which fractious instability produced crises of leadership. Processes begun in the late nineteenth century appeared to have come full circle by the end of the 1960s.

The Living and the Dead, 2

In the realm of faith, too – inseparable as it was from political culture – the events of the late nineteenth century had abiding influence. In colonial Uganda, public faith of the 'new' kind continued to expand, and took on an increasing social and political significance; the architecture of state and society was in many ways defined in terms of spiritual allegiance. The leader of the Muslim community in the wake of the colonial settlements of the 1890s and early 1900s was *Omulangira* Mbogo, a brother of Mutesa's who was awarded land and status through the 1900 Agreement in return for his renouncing his claim to the kingship. He was the most senior Muslim at the royal court until his death in 1921, when he was replaced by a young prince, Badru Kakungulu.[184] Badru was not universally supported – owing at least in part to his limited education – and when his position as spiritual leader of the

---

[183] A.A. Latim & G.O.B. Oda to The Prime Minister, re. Disunity in Uganda, 19 March 1966, Papers of the Democratic Party, MUL.

[184] T.W. Gee, 'A century of Muhammadan influence in Buganda, 1852–1951', *Uganda Journal*, 22:2 (1958), 141–3 and see A.B.K. Kasozi, *The Life of Prince Badru Kakungulu Wasajja, and the development of a forward looking Muslim community in Uganda, 1907–1991* (Kampala, 1996).

Ugandan Muslim community was confirmed on the occasion of his twenty-first birthday in 1928 by Daudi Chwa, that community began to splinter. Initially the main divide was between the Kibuli sect (pro-Badru) and the Magato sect, under the leadership of Sheikh Sekimwanyi, but others would open up in time, including within the Kibuli sect itself, mostly over leadership and doctrinal questions around prayer. It was a sad and desperate time for the Ugandan *umma*, as one local writer described it:

Before the division, other religious groups desired to be like us. Among the Moslems there was no thieving, no adultery. But [after the splits] all such things became common... There was stealing, prostitution and a Moslem could send away a Moslem, they started drinking and accusing one another. Those who had envied us started to laugh at us, claiming they were drinking with our young men.[185]

The various parties were not reconciled until 1948, by which time the Ugandan Muslim Education Association had been established to overcome factionalism and promote much-neglected education pro-grammes for young Muslims.[186] Decades of fissure and faction had not, in any case, slowed the rate of expansion of the Muslim commu-nity as a whole: by the 1950s, there were an estimated 180,000 Mus-lims in Uganda (in comparison to 445,000 Protestants and 579,000 Catholics), and their size had increased substantially, year on year, pro-portionate to the larger Christian groups. One commentator would warn in the late 1950s that such an expansion 'will undoubtedly give rise to greater pressure by the Muslim leaders on Government to set to rights their long-standing grievances', especially in regard to land allo-cation, political representation and educational opportunities. Mean-while, Ugandan Muslims had already begun to reach beyond their bor-ders, establishing links with the Emirs of Northern Nigeria and with spiritual leaders in Cairo.[187]

These were vibrant, evolving systems of belief, producing local variations and transnational movements which incorporated worship, political activism and social reformism. This was most dramatically

---

[185] M. M. Katungulu, 'Islam in Buganda', unpublished translated manuscript in Makerere University Library, c. 1962, 17.

[186] Kasozi, *Spread of Islam*, 106–7. The organisation is still thriving: http://umeauganda.org/home.

[187] Gee, 'A century', 148–9.

manifest in the East African revivalist movement which emerged across
the wider in the 1930s, driven by new churches in Uganda, Rwanda
and Tanganyika. In its early stages it was known as 'the Ruanda movement', as it originated in Gahini, but it was a Luganda word – *Balokole*,
or 'the saved people' – by which it became more widely known as
it spread. East African revivalists had much in common with American evangelical revivalism in their emphasis on sin and repentance, for
example, and a quest for moral and spiritual sanctity.[188] In Uganda, it
was fuelled at least in part by a disillusion with the Anglican Church
and, by implication, with the colonial order of which the latter was
such an integral part. Yet revivalists did not embrace the anticolonial nationalism of the 1950s, whether KY in Buganda or the wider
Ugandan nationalist movements, but rather saw themselves as part of
a transnational community aiming at the improvement of social (and
political) behaviour; as Kevin Ward puts it, they saw themselves 'as
modelling a non-racial, non-tribal, non-ethnic solidarity with those
who were saved'.[189] The *Balokole* were especially visible, but there
were a multitude of local manifestations of similar phenomena: divergent and often radical (and literal) readings of the Bible, leading to
new groupings organised around charismatic figures. The evolution of
Kakungulu's distinctive Judaism around Mbale was an early instance,
as was the *Bamalaki* movement – named after one of its founding figures, a small-scale chief and certified Church teacher named Malaki
Musajjakawa. Another of its leading lights was Joswa Kate Mugema,
who eschewed the use of Western medicine in the belief – and he
had plenty of evidence from the Old Testament in support – that
true faith alone was enough to overcome bodily perils.[190] It was a
remarkable example of a localised interpretation of global faith, and
the embrace of those elements which seemed most potent in pursuit
of self-realisation and true enlightenment, and the rejection of those
components dogged by association with European high-handedness
and indeed wrong-headedness. Ugandan Christians took the Gospel
and deployed it according to their needs; in some cases, it amounted
to a contemptuous rejection of the European colonial order, and pity

---

[188] 'Abalokole movement: activities', UKNA CO 536/215/4 [1944].
[189] See his 'Introduction' to Ward & Wild-Wood (eds.), *The East African Revival*
and see also Peterson, *Ethnic Patriotism*.
[190] F.B. Welbourn, *East African Rebels: a study of some independent churches*
(London, 1961), 31–58.

for compatriots who merely emulated Europeans and operated within their spiritual paradigms. In more recent, extreme cases, this could lead to outright political and social violence: most notably, the rise, in the mid-1980s, of the Holy Spirit Movement under the leadership of Alice Lakwena, whose idiosyncratic interpretation of Old Testament scripture and militant rejection of the evil serpents (the NRM) who had taken control of Uganda in the south, chimed with the anxieties of defeated Acholi army officers to produce the most serious armed challenge yet faced by the incumbent regime.[191] In March 2000, in the village of Kanungu in southwest Uganda, hundreds of people belonging to a charismatic Christian sect, the Movement for the Restoration of the Ten Commandments of God, burned to death in an apparent mass suicide; other mass graves were discovered later.[192] What had led to these tragic events, as Richard Vokes has powerfully argued, was a long history in the area of political trauma, disease and spiritual innovation (including around the Nyabingi cult) in pursuit of security and salvation.[193] It was the latest episode in a deep-rooted tradition of nonconformity, and of considered rejection of imposed, normative political and spiritual order.

This, then, was the age of both conflict and communion, as Ugandans of different hues, persuasions and backgrounds sought both historical trajectory and revelation, mobilising eschatological messages in pursuit of political morality as well as eventual bodily deliverance. God brought folks together in solemn conviction; but he also provided organisational frameworks for political and social action. Late nineteenth-century Buganda's political landscape was characterised by violent factionalism, when ambitious men of newfound passion and faith organised themselves around imported religions as tools of political expression, as well as spiritual succour. In the decades that followed, this pattern was replicated: religious conviction often, if never precisely, played out along political lines, with Catholics, Protestants and Muslims generally supporting, as religious groupings, one particular political party or another – the 'Catholic' DP; the more 'Protestant' UPC – even if the reality was a little muddier than those rigid designations suggest. Religious adherence was inextricably political. This was especially

---

[191] Ellis & Ter Haar, *Worlds of Power*, 99.

[192] 'Quiet cult's doomsday deaths', BBC News, 29 March 2000.

[193] R. Vokes, *Ghosts of Kanungu: fertility, secrecy and exchange in the Great Lakes of East Africa* (Woodbridge, 2009).

evident in the 1950s, in the years before decolonisation, when political fractures often reflected religious ones, and Ugandans frequently signed up to one or other of the burgeoning political movements in the late colonial era based on the perception – real or imagined – that they were inclined towards Anglicanism or Catholicism, at least in terms of leadership. And of course there is no question that religion was indeed politics: most famously, perhaps, the Catholic leadership of the DP was the product of a longstanding conviction that the Anglican establishment in Buganda had been dominant for far too long, to the detriment of millions of Ganda, and Ugandans. Less well known, perhaps, is the vigour with which Muslim leaders worked within KY as they sought to refashion the precolonial kingdom and their place in it.[194] More generally, Muslims were also prominent social activists and trade unionists – a reflection of the fact that, lacking the educational chances of their Christian compatriots, they tended to occupy lowlier roles in the economy (small shopkeepers, taxi drivers, butchers, bus drivers), and were therefore more responsive to emerging socio-economic inequities in the course of the twentieth century, and were disproportionately more visible as a result.[195]

In the 1960s Muslims remained anxious about, and resentful of, the ambivalence of Obote's government in dealing with them. Using his cousin and political colleague Hajj Nekyon, Obote set up the National Association for the Advancement of Muslims in 1965, but many eschewed it, perceiving in the NAAM (correctly, to some extent) an attempt by Obote to stabilise support for the UPC among Ganda Muslims in particular.[196] Many angrily rejected the attempt to co-opt the Muslim community and expressed outrage at the vaguely threatening language emanating from Government about the inevitable triumph of NAAM.[197] 'As non-supporters of NAAM', read one public statement issued by leading Muslim figures including Abu Mayanja, 'we of the Uganda Muslim Community wish to state emphatically that we resent the implication...that somehow we are not loyal to the

---

[194] Earle, 'Political Theologies'.

[195] A. Chande, 'Radicalism and Reform in East Africa', in N. Levtzion and R.L. Pouwels (eds.), *The History of Islam in Africa* (Athens OH & Oxford, 2000), 354.

[196] Kasozi, *Spread of Islam*, 113–116.

[197] For example, Joint Secretary of the Uganda Muslim Community, Kibuli, to the News Editor, *Uganda Argus*, 16 September 1969.

state'.[198] But their fortunes seemed to change fairly dramatically with the coming to power of Amin, and especially with his more overtly Islamic stance in the course of the 1970s. NAAM was abolished and replaced by the Uganda Muslim Supreme Council, which was awarded substantially more land,[199] while many of the confiscated Asian properties were also handed to the UMSC to be 'looked after'.[200] During the 1970s, Islam returned to the centre of political power in the region for the first time in a century, as Amin sponsored Islam domestically, proclaimed Uganda a Muslim state, and shifted his foreign policy accordingly towards the Muslim world. Amin's Muslim identity became more visible as the decade wore on, and he was increasingly keen to be seen as a Muslim leader, much to the nervousness of the Christian leaders. He planned and began building what he hoped would be the biggest mosque in Africa, though it was not completed until 2007, and only then with Col. Gaddafi's financial assistance (now known as the Uganda National Mosque, it was originally designated the Gaddafi National Mosque[201]). It is a stunning building, with equally stunning views across the city from the minaret. Still, those grand vistas notwithstanding, Amin's overthrow was followed by the retreat of the Muslim community to some extent, and in some respects they have remained in retreat, damaged in many ways by their problematic associations with Amin and the decade of northern military dominance, as well as by the increasingly charged debate around loyalty and citizenship.

In recent decades, religion has continued to play a central role in Ugandan public life, infusing politics, culture and social behaviour. It has also continued to diversify, whether through the powerful influence of Pentecostal and charismatic churches, the robustness with which 'traditional' shrines has retained their place in the Ugandan cosmology, or the transnational religiosity of Ugandan Islam. Catholics have become more prominent as political and cultural leaders – a subversion of the idea that historically it was Anglicans who had long been

---

[198] 'All Muslims are Loyal: Uganda Muslim Community replies to NAAM allegations', Press Release, by Abubaker Mayanja MP, Sheikh Ali Kulumba, and Sheikh Yusufu Sirimani Matovu, n.d. MUL.

[199] Secretary for Religious Affairs to Lt. Col. K.Saafi, re. Land for the Uganda Supreme Council [sic], 26 April 1973, MUL.

[200] General Idi Amin Dada to Minister of Mineral and Water Resources, 27 September 1973, MUL.

[201] 'Old Kampala mosque drops Gaddafi name', *The Observer* (Kampala), 19 June 2013.

groomed for leadership, while Catholics were taught subservience and deference.[202] Protestantism has fragmented in various directions and forms, serving particular constituencies and needs. Yet Anglicans, Pentecostals and Catholics are generally united within Uganda in terms of their role in upholding particular visions of national culture – most notably, in recent years, in the muscular, even xenophobic, dealings with the West over the issue of gay clergy and of gay rights more broadly.[203] To some extent, however, this may also reflect external linkages with likeminded evangelical movements, especially in the US. Uganda remains a powerful magnet for what we might describe as religious tourism. Board any given flight from London, or Amsterdam, heading for Entebbe, and it will be crammed full of Christian missionaries, activists, NGO workers and school parties heading to the equator to commune with their fellows in God and in the process achieve those life-changing experiences that apparently cannot be found closer to home. There is something powerful about Uganda in the Western Christian imagination, and there has been for a century and a half.

Meanwhile, since the mid-1980s, reformist Salafi Islam has been growing in Uganda as a result of a strengthening network of external relationships, and there has been a deepening divide between the young people who tend to gravitate towards Salafi mosques and the older generation which attends those run by more traditional ulama.[204] The Chairman of the Uganda Muslim Youth Assembly, Dr Abasi Kiyimba, would claim (understandably) in 2005 that there were 7 million Muslims in Uganda – some 25 per cent of the population[205] – but normally the percentage was given as somewhere between 10 and 15 per cent.[206] Still, whatever the precise figure, the sense that they are marginalised and discriminated against is deeply rooted in the Muslim community – as evidenced, for example, by a 2012 petition by Muslim MPs which accused the Government of routinely excluding Muslims from political office and the civil service, reflecting an institutional mistrust of

---

[202] Author's field notes and informal interviews, 11 April 2013.
[203] For example, 'Uganda archbishop responds to Welby on anti-gay laws', BBC News, 1 February 2014.
[204] Chande, 'Radicalism', 355.
[205] A. Kiyimba, 'Islam in Uganda: a situational report', unpublished paper for the Uganda Muslim Youth Assembly, 2005, 3.
[206] For example, Chande, 'Radicalism', 354.

Muslims as fellow citizens.[207] To a considerable extent, this mistrust undoubtedly speaks to a deeper fear of an Islamic radicalism which is transnational in its orientation and inspiration. The 2010 bombings in Kampala brought home to Ugandans the implications of their military presence in Somalia, and raised anxieties – largely, to date, unfounded – about an imminent wave of Islamic terrorism, and doubts about the loyalties of some members of the Muslim community. In fact, Uganda's experiences of Muslim extremism remain insignificant compared to those of neighbouring Kenya, where a number of the alleged perpetrators of the 2010 bombings were apparently radicalised. But in truth this is only really the latest stage, for Muslims, in a long history of marginalisation.[208] Muslims in many ways continue to struggle with their role in Ugandan society, and their contributions to its history.[209] The killing of several Muslim clerics by unknown assailants on *boda-bodas* in 2015 prompted feverish speculation that the government was behind it, thus enabling the latter to point to the internecine violence of the Muslim community; others worried that it demonstrated the spread to Kampala of the violent internal struggles of the Allied Democratic Forces in the far west of Uganda, formed originally by members of the hard line Tabliq sect. More worryingly, there was talk of the ADF now developing links to both *al-Shabaab* in Somalia and Islamic State in Syria and Iraq.[210] Again, in keeping with a more general theme, it was those untrustworthy foreign links, the fear of strangers in the midst, which informed – or misinformed – much of the public and private discussion on these issues.

What is certainly clear is that faith and the spiritual realm have been indelibly connected to the political and economic traumas of the last two hundred years or more, as they provided not only – in

---

[207] 'Petition by Muslim Parliamentarians to halt the vetting process for members of the National Citizenship and Immigration Board', addressed to the Speaker of Parliament, no. 20/17/2012, MUL.

[208] Author's field notes and informal interviews, 11 April 2013, also Yusuf Kasumba, 'Islamophobia in Uganda: Myths and realities. A historical study of illusions of persecution complex among the Muslim community in Uganda from 1888 to 1985', unpublished conference paper, Mukono, Uganda, 19 July 2015.

[209] This is reflected in local writing: see, for example, K. Tibenderana, *Islamic Fundamentalism: the quest for the rights of Muslims in Uganda* (Kampala, 2006) and G. W. Kanyeiharuba, *Reflections on the Muslim Leadership Question in Uganda* (Kampala, 1998).

[210] Author's field notes and informal interviews, July 2015.

common-sense terms – the supernatural succour against the predations and vagaries of the material world; they have offered real opportunities in terms of social aspiration and expectation, nodes of political mobilisation, expanded horizons of intellectual endeavour and – crucially – ways of thinking about both the past and the future. They have also intersected in very potent ways with other realms of public life which facilitate aspiration and nourish expectation.

History Wars, 2

In the mid-1980s, there were ghosts in the politics, demons in the history, perils in returning to the kind of cultures of public debate and slander and tribalism which had given rise to the state of blood. For all of the efforts of Museveni and his circle to manage the politics of the past, and the history of the politics, the era from the late 1980s witnessed the resurgence and reinterpretation of some deep-rooted dynamics. The self-consciously progressive and modernising regime of the NRM pitted its modernist and developmental visions against the 'traditional' authority which the regime itself had encouraged. It is a story which deserves some attention on two main levels. First, it reveals a great deal about how this ostensibly 'new' country remained deeply rooted in a precolonial past, or various versions of it, and about how the echoes and shades of history continued to dominate Ugandan political culture despite the Movement's doggedly 'modern' agenda and emphasis on development. Yet it is not quite as simple as that, for the second point is that 'traditional' leaders proliferated in unexpected ways – and this was not always a straightforward matter of *restoration*. It was, rather, also a matter of refashioning, for monarchical and other 'traditional' systems have taken forms which seem to differ markedly from anything that existed previously. Therefore it tells us a great deal about many Ugandans' relationship to the state itself, and of the uses of 'tradition' and 'culture' in the face of the Movement's style of governance.

In the early 1980s, the NRM began to discuss the issue of restoration while still in the bush. Of primary importance was the Movement's need for Ganda support, should it succeed in advancing to Kampala. Buganda was, once more, at the heart of the political 'problem' in Uganda, and therefore it had to be rendered part of the Movement's programme of national recovery once in power. Thus in the mid-1990s

Buganda, Bunyoro, Toro and Busoga reappeared on the political land-scape, with the significant caveat, already noted, that these entities in fact had no formal or constitutional political presence but were, rather, purely 'cultural' artefacts. It was, in a sense, the reinvention of an indigenous form of indirect rule, with the state – now an extension of the inner circle of the Movement itself – seeking to govern, or at least administer, in part by using cultural intermediaries, the latter supposedly possessed of deeply rooted and organic authority in a way which the state, alternately khaki-draped and sharp-suited, was not. Newly fashioned and reinvented forms of 'organic' community leadership caught on elsewhere, too, and in fact spread rapidly to the furthest corners of Uganda. Nor was this solely about 'monarchy', as normatively understood; republican forms of leadership were also embraced. Royalism and neo-traditionalism now proliferated like spirits unleashed and uncontainable. Among the Acholi, the Payira – the biggest clan – furnished the wider Acholi community with *Rwot* David Onen Achana II, while *Emorimor* Paphras Imodot Edimu was crowned ruler of the Teso; the Alur enthroned Obimo Jobi II as their *Rwoth*, while the Jopadhola were now under the reign of *Tieng Adhola* Moses Stephen Owor. And still further: the Gwere had their *Nagwere*, George William Koire, crowned in 2003 though in 2009 he was replaced acrimoniously with Kintu Mubbala under the new title of *Ikumbania*. The Gisu had *Umukuuka* Wilson Weasa Wamimbi, and the Langi had *Won Nyaci* Yosam Odur. And in the far west, the Konzo of Rwenzururu, triumphantly rejecting the jurisdiction of Toro, declared their *Musinga* to be Charles Wesley Mumbere.

There were obvious political and financial benefits – not least the provision of a state stipend and a four-wheel-drive vehicle. More profoundly, the absence of meaningful political parties and thus viable outlets for opposition meant that people invested political energy in kingdoms and monarchism in order to better protect themselves from the state itself. In many respects the restoration of the kingdoms was, paradoxically, an indication of both the confidence of the Movement that it could manage the expectations which would inevitably accompany the reappearance of cultural leaders in public life; but also its insecurity, as it sought to broaden its base of popular support and in particular to court the Ganda as partners in the new state project. For the Movement, this was as much as about the restoration of the nation as it was about historical cultures, and 'traditional' leaders would need to be a core part of that national project. As throughout the twentieth century, however, that co-option quickly became a site of conflict, as visions of traditional legitimacy were once again pitted against those of putative modernity. Leaders from Buganda to Acholiland, Rwenzururu to Bugisu, became the embodiments of social capital, engaging in an array of ostensibly apolitical activities: conservationism and environmental awareness, health and immunisation, education work especially among youth.[211] But other public activities were undeniably and increasingly politicised, such as the large-scale cultural festivals which were often used to raise funds for cultural leaders' work as a means to getting around government edicts prohibiting the direct raising of taxes by the kingdoms themselves. Meanwhile, tightening group identities were forged around particular cultural or supposedly historic traits and characteristics, with due emphasis on the things that bound the group together and made them distinctive: for Busoga, it was the idea of a history of democratic unity, making the Soga distinct from 'other traditional institutions';[212] for the Gisu, there was the culture of circumcision which ensured the passage to manhood, and – as the Masaaba Historical Research Association had it – the ineffable significance of Mt. Elgon, their cultural and spiritual, as well as physical, ballast.[213]

Moreover, the government had apparently not anticipated the resurgence of Ganda nationalism, fuelled by the kingdom's mounting disappointment with what restoration actually entailed. In simple terms, Buganda wanted *federo* – a federal rearrangement of power and territory, echoing demands made in the 1950s, meaning in effect self-governing status. This was clearly never a realistic prospect under the NRM, which nevertheless had evidently made a fundamental strategic miscalculation in failing to foresee that restoration combined with political obstinacy would lead inexorably to crisis. The relationship between kingdom and state reached that crisis point – the worst since 1967 – over the space of a few months in 2009–10. In 2009, a local

---

[211] This is true for 'traditional' leaders across the continent: for example see 'Kings: Adapt or Die!', *The Africa Report*, No. 54 (October 2013).
[212] Letter from the Katukiro of Busoga to His Excellency the President of Uganda, 25 July 1994. Copy in author's possession.
[213] 'Bagishu proud of circumcision culture', *Weekly Topic* (Kampala), 15 January 1993; also Masaaba [Gisu] Historical Research Association, *For the Land and Culture of Bamasaaba* (privately published & distributed, c. 1992). Copy in author's possession.

'traditional' leader of the Banyala community in Kayunga, Bugerere district, Baker Kimeze, indicated to the government that his community wished to secede from Buganda. It echoed a similar request a few months earlier when increasingly militant traditionalists in Buruli county had demanded their secession from Buganda, into which their district had been incorporated by the British.[214] The *kabaka*, however, wished to visit Kayunga – he regularly toured the kingdom – and it was announced that the *katikiro* would embark on a preparatory visit to the area. The government advised against it, on security grounds, considering Kimeze's stance and the resultant tensions in the area. Mengo was outraged that the *kabaka* was effectively being blocked from visiting a part of his rightful realm, while many Ganda believed that in any case Kimeze was merely a government stooge, representative of an anti-Buganda agenda. The call went out via CBS-FM, the radio station closely affiliated to Mengo and known as 'Radio Buganda', for all loyal Ganda to converge on Kayunga. The *katikiro* duly travelled there, only to find his entry to the area blocked by a heavy police presence, and riots erupted, both in Kampala and across the kingdom. The government, apparently fearing some form of mass breakdown of order and certainly taken by surprise by the rioting, responded to the violence with characteristic force, and closed down CBS-FM as well as three other FM radio stations for several months.[215] And then, six months later, in March 2010, came the fire at Kasubi which all but destroyed the traditional palace containing the tombs of Mutesa, Mwanga, Daudi Chwa and Mutesa II. Tensions reached new heights as distraught Ganda struggled to come to terms with how this awful thing had happened – the blaze wiping out a UNESCO heritage site but more importantly obliterating a place of ineffable spiritual and cultural significance in the kingdom's historical landscape. The fire itself was certainly a terrible accident, but as the flames roared into the night sky amid equally heightened emotion, some quickly came to the conclusion that the government might even have had a hand in it. An extraordinary security presence was required when Museveni himself visited ground zero hours after the fire.[216]

---

[214] ICG, *Uganda*, 14.   [215] Tripp, *Museveni's Uganda*, 120–1.
[216] For example, 'Why Kasubi fire might backfire', *The Observer*, 21 March 2010, ICG, *Uganda*, 18.

In the months that followed, Ronald Mutebi saw his relationship with Yoweri Museveni as strained as his father's had been with Milton Obote. It only slowly improved; meetings took place, and reassurances made. But the government continued to prove itself willing and able to provoke Ganda ire by actively encouraging the 'secession' of precolonial kingdoms which were not 'organically' part of Buganda – such as Kkooki, whose separatism was publicly supported by Museveni in 2013.[217] At the same time, one of the longest-running political arguments in Uganda's history – that over land reform – continued to rage, with the government continually seeking to push through land reform legislation that would address the unequal distribution of land by the British to the Ganda royal court under the terms of the 1900 agreement. These were history wars at the highest level, the past mobilised in pursuit of contemporary power struggles. Yet for some, the fraught relationship was as much about personalities as about public policy. It was often privately blamed on the bad advice the President was receiving from his Buganda advisors – who were 'not the right kind', according to an informant – while on the other side Mutebi was regarded as being surrounded by some serious hardliners who regarded the kingdom's dignity as utterly inalienable and whose position more generally had long been that Uganda should be grateful to have Buganda in it at all.[218]

Buganda was not the only monarchy in which government intervention or otherwise difficult relationships with the state have led to trouble. In Busoga, following the death of Wako Muloki in 2008, there was a bitter standoff between two camps: the government supported the candidacy of Muloki's son, Prince Edward Columbus Wambuzi, while the bulk of Soga political leaders favoured Prince William Gabula Nadiope IV, son of the former *kyabazinga* Nadiope who had reigned in the 1950s and 1960s (and served as Uganda's Vice-President). Each was in fact crowned in a separate ceremony and there remained disagreement over which was the 'legitimate' cultural leader of Busoga.[219]

---

[217] Author's field notes and informal interviews, 14 June 2013.
[218] Author's field notes and informal interviews, 14 August 2012.
[219] Another candidate, Patrick Izimba Gologolo of the Kigulu chiefdom, declared in his pitch for the kingship: 'Busoga is currently under the threat of disintegration, because of selfish self-seekers [sic], who are bent on manipulating this hitherto straightforward process, by complicating it with frivolous machinations to divert the peaceful process of enthroning the next

Indeed, such a fissure is perhaps richly symptomatic of the ambiguity surrounding the Soga 'kingdom' itself: while the introductory section in Busoga's 'constitution' makes clear that prior to colonial rule each of the 'eleven independent chiefdoms' had its own 'completely independent' chief who was 'equivalent to a King', still the preamble indicates that each of these eleven

Hereditary Traditional Chiefdoms [is] desirous of preserving and maintaining their old culture/tradition of unity and solidarity under one central/overall cultural/traditional ruler of Busoga viz. Isebantu Kyabazinga ... under whom they are thus united.[220]

The Nyoro faced a somewhat different struggle, in that their continued search for assurances from government that the kingdom should receive a percentage of forthcoming oil revenues was greeted with, at best, ambivalence. *All* Ugandans would share in these God-given fruits of the earth, Museveni proclaimed routinely. Elsewhere, the government retreated in the face of local pressure, and here the long-running Rwenzururu saga is informative. In 2005, Museveni finally ordered a formal investigation into the claims of Konzo leaders to a kingdom. The report was headed up by Deputy Prime Minister Henry Kajura, after whom it was known, and the Kajura Report, when it was finally concluded, revealed the finding that there was no historic basis for Rwenzururu, or for a group people termed 'Banyarwenzururu'. *However*, Kajura recommended that for the sake of local peace and security – the insurgency had rumbled on and off for the better part of half a century – the government should acknowledge the wishes of the Konzo population, and permit the creation of a cultural institution known as 'Rwenzururu'.[221] At this point, the government recognised Charles Mumbere as king (earlier research had suggested that he had the overwhelming support of both Konzo and Amba populations), but in fact his appointment came as a blow to several other contenders. In

Kyabazinga of a united Busoga': 'Towards a progressive and prosperous Busoga kingdom in a united and stable Uganda', Jinja, 17 October 2008. Copy in author's possession.

[220] *The Constitution of Obwa Kyabazinga bwa Busoga*, promulgated by the Isebantu Kyabazinga of Busoga at Bugembe Headquarters, 30 December 2000, 7, 9.

[221] 'Rwenzururu kingdom has never existed', *New Vision*, 3 October 2007.

the years that followed, there was episodic violence in the area around Kasese, often involving quite shocking numbers of casualties – in mid-2014, dozens were killed over several days of skirmishes.[222] A tightened monarchical system may have been perceived as a defence against aggressive outsiders, the state included, but local debate over the nature of that system spilled over into slaughter.[223] These contests were fundamentally over identity and land, the creation of rival kingships and the claims of jurisdiction over supposed subjects who viscerally rejected it. The western borderland encapsulated, at the local level, the wars over the past and the present, and ongoing clashes over belonging and land. These were complex and shifting issues, and indicated the contests which took place over the nation at its very edges – though conversely this was also emblematic of the marginalisation of the nation at the local level.

Of course, restoration was more broadly about the government seeking to manage deep-rooted political and social forces. 'The Kingdom which was declared dead in 1967 in actual fact never died', wrote David Kihumuro Apuuli in the brief preface to his 1994 book on Bunyoro-Kitara. 'The enthusiasm with which the people greeted [the] NRM government's decision to allow the people who once had kingdoms to revive them if they so wished is testimony enough'.[224] And as a Nyoro source quoted in a recent political assessment of Uganda put it: 'If the king says plant a tree, everyone will plant one; but if the president asks, everyone will say, "where's the seed money?"'[225] For many in Bunyoro, the kingdom was the fundamental historical building block – the decrepit stage from which they survey the grim wreckage of their recent past, and rail against the predations of a succession of centralising states.[226] Interviews, again, revealed many of the same glum complaints and grievances that were being expressed in the 1950s: we are marginalised, and underdeveloped, and were destroyed by the British;

---

[222] Author's field notes and informal interviews, July 2014.

[223] For a passionate and sceptical assessment of the emergent kingdom, see M.M. Caleb & M.P. Baluku, *Obusinga Bwa Rwenzururu: a critical analysis and revealing facts about the 'institution'* (n.p., March 2005).

[224] D.K. Apuuli, *A Thousand Years of Bunyoro-Kitara Kingdom: the people and the rulers* (Kampala, 1994), ii.

[225] Quoted in ICG, *Uganda*, 13.

[226] Y.N. Nsamba, *Breaking Chains of Poverty: Bunyoro-Kitara Kingdom Advocacy Publication* (Hoima, c. 1999).

we need, indeed deserve, recompense.[227] For many, too, there was simply the fear – another longstanding one through Uganda's twentieth century – that the young had forgotten, or worse, they had never known, the culture and history that made this community great, once. As Patrick Kirindi explained it in his book on Ankole's customs and culture, published in the author's ninetieth year: 'Unfortunately, due to colonialism and especially the impact of Christianity, our young people have shown little or even no interest at all in our culture ... Our misguided obsession with things foreign has gradually eroded the vibrancy of our own history and culture'.[228] Whatever the case, genies had long since departed bottles, forces unleashed and expectations heightened. The most contentious area amidst this frenzy of neo-traditionalism was, again, Museveni's own backyard, Ankole. The President certainly did not want troublesome potential rivals on his own turf, and steadfastly refused to countenance the restoration of the *Mugabe*. His position – that this was in the interests of an egalitarian politics which aimed to destroy old Hima-Iru divisions and inequities – found support among many.[229] It was also the case that many Ugandans, under whatever 'traditional' authority, could be quite wry about their 'cultural' leaders, and were often no more enamoured of kings than they were of those who have episodically occupied State House over the years. Still, controversies in Ankole, and Ugandans' natural scepticism about *all* authority, aside, monarchism and other forms of putatively traditional power were everywhere rampant in early twenty-first-century Uganda; and it thrived alongside hardening ideas around ethnic belonging and cohesion – the very thing that the current regime swore to banish, and condemned as having brought the nation to the brink of extinction. The government continued to ponder new laws regulating the activities of traditional cultural leaders, and to even more stringently separate the politics from the culture, and the culture from the politics. The apparent cult of the 'traditional leader', and of imagined precolonial roots, was symptomatic of an age in which the modern state was not entirely to be trusted – if at all. On this view, our putative nation seems fragmented, virtual, ghostly. Kings had proven durable, and 'history' continued to hold out against 'modernity' – for many of

---

[227] Interview, Aramanzani Banturaki, Hoima, Uganda, 7 January 2015.
[228] Kirindi, *History and Culture*, iv.
[229] Author's field notes and informal interviews, 18 August 2012.

the same reasons across the colonial and postcolonial periods, namely that they have flourished in the absence of alternative political and cultural sources of power. Where the state was untrusted, and the political party that supposedly represents political modernity could not thrive, communities had time and again nurtured particular visions of putatively 'traditional' authority, and embraced visions of the past as forms of defiance and protection and identity against the state. In that sense, in the end, 'modernity' had come to be a meaningless phrase – much bandied about in elite circles, and favoured by those ahistorical patriots who sought, as Francis Fukuyama had it, the end of history and all the past represented.[230] In truth, for millions of Ugandans, historical culture was all that mattered, and all they could trust.[231]

History wars will carry on more or less destructively, and inimically to the nation, until there is a more robust engagement with 'Uganda' as an authentic, legitimate and of course complicated historical space. The central point is that the power and passion that surrounds the kingship in Buganda, and royalty and 'traditional' chieftaincy elsewhere, can be explained at least on one level by the fact that there is no other political space within which to organise against an increasingly rapacious and uncaring state.[232] But it is important to remind ourselves that this is nothing new. The consolidation, and often expansion, of group identity – and the associated continual reinvention and reinvigoration of visions of the political past – is a long-term process in Ugandan history. It is also the case that visions of 'tradition', and the role and even the very existence of kingship, have long been vehemently contested. Alternative ideas about political culture have deep roots. And yet: an organic, integrated, *horizontal* nation – a temporal as well as spatial

---

[230] F. Fukuyama, *The End of History and the Last Man* (London, 1992).

[231] A useful recent example is the successful campaign to have UNESCO recognition of *Empaako*, a naming system for children practised in Bunyoro and Toro and elsewhere whereby the use of particular names is supposed to build far-reaching social relationships and promote reconciliation within and between communities: see, for example, Engabu za Tooro (Tooro Youth Platform for Action), *Towards Celebrations of UNESCO's Inscription of Empaako Tradition in 2013* (Fort Portal, n.d.). UNESCO placed *Empaako* on its list of 'intangible cultural heritage in need of urgent safeguarding', and noted that '[t]he transmission of Empaako through naming rituals has dropped dramatically due to a general decline in appreciation of traditional culture and the diminishing use of the language associated with the element': see http://www.unesco.org/culture/ich/index.php?USL=00904

[232] Author's field notes and informal interviews, April 2015.

entity – is also discernible, defined by reciprocity and borrowing and interdependency, and multiple sites of inspiration and power. This is something remarkable, in many respects. But it is less remarkable once we are able to break beyond the idea that before the NRM all was mayhem and blood.

Epilogue
Managing Time and Space

Uganda is a nation governed by the past – sometimes in the form of shadows and ghosts, a kind of politics of the gloaming; often in bold, vivid colours. The connectivity between the past and the present is palpable, and the significance of the former has been especially blatant in moments of turmoil and change, at those critical points of transition and disjuncture which populate Uganda's history at regular intervals. As this book goes to press, it is difficult not to conclude that Uganda stands at such a crossroads.[1] The failures of time management on the part of the Movement mean that particular visions of the past continue to trouble the nation: in Buganda, barometer of stability within the country as a whole, and emblematic of the troubled relationship between historic centre and modern statehood; in the proliferation of a multitude of neo-traditional institutions and sentiments in Busoga, Bunyoro, Toro and elsewhere; in the chronic and entrenched inequity between the north and the south, the result of distorted processes of development and redistribution over *la longue durée*. In many ways the period between 1979 and 1986, leading to the rise of the Movement itself, bore some resemblance to those other key 'moments' in the making of modern Uganda, in terms of its seminal political shifts: the 1890s, involving the civil war in Buganda, the Anglo–Ganda alliance and the creation of the Protectorate, and the brutal war against Bunyoro; and the 1950s, incorporating the return of the *kabaka* from exile, the escalation of nationalist politics, and the opening up of profound rifts in the interpretation of Uganda's past and future. Those periods had produced fundamental realignments of political power; and by the mid-1980s, something similar was the outcome of a decade and more of violent uncertainty. The 1890s and 1950s witnessed the creation of new and supposedly robust political orders which would come, in time,

---

[1] For an excellent overview, see ICG, *Uganda*; and also Tripp, *Museveni's Uganda*.

to be forcefully challenged. It is no coincidence that the past matters so much now, at a moment of aggressive, ahistorical, economic developmentalism on the part of an increasingly authoritarian, securitised state. There persists among Uganda's political leaders a deep-seated fear of the past, a horror of what it purportedly represents – namely division, mayhem, violence. The emphasis, rather, is on 'modernity', on marching onward from the savagery of the past, and a concentration on 'development', usually measured in terms of economic output and more specifically annual GDP growth rates. This is no doubt understandable, on many levels. Yet 'economic growth', as currently defined in the context of neoliberal economic thought, is hardly in itself unproblematic. Growth rates and ever rising office blocks in Kampala are one thing; confronting the past, celebrating past achievements and incorporating these into more robust and inclusive political systems, is quite another. If the NRM's primary goal was to face 'forwards' and demonise the past, the next frontier in Uganda's long-term development is to look 'backwards', too. There needs to be a recognition of what Ugandans of various hues have achieved and contributed to what the nation has become; a recognition that Uganda has not merely survived but has in many respects flourished, both because of, and despite, the history which is the country's bedrock. If that happens, then Uganda can indeed continue to move forward with increasing confidence.

This in itself will depend on Ugandans and their leaders continuing to get to grips with the past, and to engage with history at the national level. Successive governments have so far struggled to do so. The diversity enclosed within Uganda's modern borders has long represented a challenge: the area has comprised markedly different, and at times actively hostile, political and cultural systems, some of which – notably the more centralised monarchies in the south – were rather more inclined to aggressive expansion and characterised by a capacity to dominate than others, in political, economic and cultural terms. And yet diversity has, equally, long represented an opportunity. This is no mere cliché, resorted to by those desperate to see a way out of apparently inextricable conflict. The area of modern Uganda has for centuries been characterised by population movement, both local and over longer distances, giving rise to intense interaction: mutual borrowing, interdependency, inclusivity and flexibility. It is precisely the *absence* of uniformity that has been Uganda's great strength in the quest for economic diversification, successful and adaptable systems of governance, aesthetic and spiritual expression. Ugandans, of whatever cultural and regional provenance, have amassed a remarkable wealth of experience in all these discrete but interconnected spheres of human activity. Since the early decades of the nineteenth century, there has been violent conflict and social trauma as well as marked levels of coexistence; open, pluralistic and inclusive cultures as well as systems rooted in authoritarianism and fear. Certainly, even a cursory glance at Uganda's modern history suggests enough accumulated knowledge to make the nation 'work', and sufficiently deep pools of experience on which to draw in the search for solutions for enduring problems. Too often, the excuse is offered (by African politicians as well as outsiders) that modern African nations 'fail' on various levels because of too little experience in governance; that colonial rule left African political elites ill-prepared and ignorant. But this view – politically convenient though it may often be – tends oddly to overlook centuries of political, economic and social evolution, aeons of experience in addressing the hardy perennials of what is often lazily referred to as the 'human condition'. At any rate, ignorance and ill-preparedness are no longer excuses for failure, if they ever were. History, in this regard, is a matter of inspiration and encouragement.

And what an inspiration. Uganda's history comprises a truly remarkable cast of characters, whether they inhabit the worlds of fact or fiction, or somewhere in between, for in truth the lines between the two are often blurred: Kabalega and Museveni; Ocol and Lawino; Nyabingi and Irene Drusilla; Kintu and Idi Amin. They are tethered together by both space and time, a boisterous assemblage representing the rich social, cultural and material fabric from which the nation of Uganda is weaved, and the processes, dynamics, vectors and cycles, the tides and seasons of Ugandan history: Kintu, or the Chwezi, incarnations of ideologies forged around political order and moral conscience; Nyabingi, champion of the poor and the dispossessed in an uncaring world; Kabalega, doomed warrior and emblem of faded glory. Violence has its role to play in this story, of course. It seems uncontroversial to venture that all nations are the product of violence, in one way or another, and in their turn deploy violence in their development and consolidation and struggles for survival. So it is, too, with Uganda. And it is important to remember that war divides, of course, but it also binds; in our crucible of interaction, the organic nation is the product of violence over *la longue durée*, as well as of the history of troubled coalescences and alliances.

Everywhere, in often unexpected ways, the past is present in Uganda, and some of the long-term continuities are clear enough: the persistent and seminal role played by migration; the episodic militarisation of political culture, and often at times of troubled transition; ongoing struggles around extraversion, and the varying and competitive responses to the opportunities presented by external forces; the recurrent forging of militant local identities designed to offer protection against hostile neighbours and predatory others; and perhaps, above all, the making and remaking of historical knowledge in pursuit of a multitude of aims. Like their sixteenth-century predecessors, the NRM arrived to proclaim a new order; but virtually every regime in modern Ugandan history has been assessed contemporaneously according to the public measurement of the one immediately preceding it, and so each defunct regime has a curious, extended afterlife, living on in the political pronouncements and historical visions of the one that replaced it. All of which leads us back once more to the role of history in the modern education system, and the push, albeit understandable, towards a technocracy at the expense of reflective, considered histories of Uganda. The neglect of, indeed hostility towards, history in secondary and tertiary education means that historical consciousness resides not in the nation but in those ethnic and religious communities where it is susceptible to angry mobilisation and demagoguery. A national historical identity is strikingly absent, often, or at least one free of European inputs and epithets; an informant of the author's was shocked when he asked one of his children what made Uganda a special part of Africa, to which the reply was – learned at school – that Churchill had described Uganda as the 'pearl of Africa'.[2] But is it really the case that the Movement's ahistorical developmental agenda will alone bring about stability and coherence? The answer is surely no, but only alongside a greater public effort to make connections between the past and the present, and the future; and while of course no one can be so naïve to think that this is ever in the interests of incumbent regimes, one can only endorse the view of colleagues in Nigeria that such connections are vital.[3]

[2] Author's field notes and informal interviews, 9 April 2013.
[3] For example, Y A. Ochefu & C. B.N. Ogbogbo, 'The role of historical societies in Nigeria's development', *Afrika Zamani*, 13 & 14 (2005–6).

Uganda has witnessed the creation and indeed the crystallisation of some major regional reversals of fortune and imbalances in terms of access to economic and political resources: specifically, the relative advantage of the south at the expense of the north. This has transpired slowly over the past four hundred years or so, but the process has quickened dramatically in the past century and a half. In the last century or so, moreover, the north has been marginalised and militarised as a frontier zone. In many respects, this has been very much driven by the reification of – in addition to the relative natural advantages enjoyed by – particular economic, cultural and political forms at the expense of others, notably sedentary agriculture over more dispersed pastoralist or agro-pastoralist groups; centralised hierarchy over segmentary, decentralised and heterarchical communities. In cultural terms, carefully compiled, if contested, 'traditions' have led to access to literacy and social mobility, and the consolidation of material and political power. Thus were Obote and Amin the products of long-term historical processes of geopolitical and economic change, and representative of an attempt to re-centre a nation which was anchored, seemingly immovably, around the shore of Lake Victoria. Of course all modern nations are, to a greater or lesser degree, brittle, contested, characterised by shifting patterns of inclusion and exclusion; Ugandans' capacity to build and destroy simultaneously is the story of humanity in microcosm. There is no denying the degree to which Uganda has been undermined by deep-rooted identities which cut across and are often inimical to the nation. Yet those identities themselves are neither fixed, nor impermeable, and are themselves multi-layered. Religious adherence, for example, has never been a matter purely of the soul, or private conviction about the spiritual world. Faith has always been linked directly and robustly to various spheres: it underpins, drives, informs (and is itself influenced by) ideas about civic duty, political culture, nationalism, historical consciousness and the manifestation and interpretation of the past. All this considered, it is not, perhaps, especially surprising that postcolonial Uganda has been profoundly shaped by spiritual adherence – unsurprising, that is, in terms of the solace and cohesion provided by the realm of the divine in an era defined by political violence, social conflict, economic collapse and inequity. Ethnicity, moreover, has not been the sole agency of either access, or lack of it, to resources. It *has* been enormously significant, of course – and the perception that it matters has remained powerful among

Ugandans themselves. Nonetheless, it intersects with class and gender in providing the parameters of social experience and expectation: ethnicity, gender and class are the key social categories and identifications which have at times been mobilised in pursuit of the nation but which otherwise have tended to neutralise it, if not actively undermine it. In other words, these are socio-economic dynamics and experiences, rather than overtly political ones, though they have indeed been mobilised for political causes.[4] As a prominent body of scholarship has argued, of course, the mere 'fact' of ethnic identity cannot ever be simply 'assumed'. Despite what leaders of various provenance, in various parts of Uganda, have sought to argue since at least the 1940s and 1950s, ethnicity is *not* an unchanging thing in the lives of people but an evolving, morphing, living entity; now expanding, then contracting; at certain moments and in certain circumstances, more important than at others. We do not have to invest in either primordial or modernist camps to understand this, and to recognise that 'ethnicity' – defined in the broadest sense as a collective with a shared set of cultural norms, language and historical narratives – is plainly evident in the nineteenth century and earlier, but that it is also given new meanings in the twentieth century and beyond by the exigencies of political entrapment, resultant claustrophobia and the failures of the 'nation' as a viable political space. In truth, considered within the analytical parameters of the modern nation, ethnicity is less important than political geography: the geographical imbalance which is omnipresent throughout our narrative, influencing the central ideas of access and mobility.

Yet the construction of balanced and comprehensive histories of nations is – as I have discovered – a tremendous challenge; and so it must inevitably be for political leaders, too, who across the continent have long wrestled with the issue of national histories.[5] For the Movement and any future Ugandan government, the challenges are manifold, and given Uganda's recent past, it is perhaps hardly surprising that the NRM eschews history as a useful means of national reconstruction. Nations are places of secrets. Postcolonial Uganda is a deeply secretive place, a place of shadows and dark recesses: the question of migration and origin, for example, is a perilous and contested one, tied as it is to ideas about citizenship, entitlements and land ownership.[6] More generally, fears about the elephant-traps lying in the gloomy

---

[4] See also Kasozi, *Social Origins of Violence.*   [5] See Reid, 'States of Anxiety'.
[6] Author's field notes and informal interviews, 28 June 2011.

past have produced a flattening out of national history into an ahistorical patriotism, in which schoolchildren are well versed. Ugandans have struggled even – or perhaps especially – to get to grips with contemporary history, never mind the more ancient kind; Idi Amin and the 1970s is a case in point, still shrouded in darkness, still with the power to make Ugandans who lived through it anxious and suspicious. Nations are nothing if not a bunch of contrasts and paradoxes. The Kalashnikov-wielding pastoralists of hot, arid Karamoja district, and the smartly dressed drivers of Land Cruisers on the well-kept tarmac roads around Nakasero in central Kampala: these are not the images of two different countries, but are both Uganda, and distinctively so. Yet the dichotomy reflects a power relationship, too: those porous and sporadically violent frontiers far from political centres are not anomalies and anachronisms, but necessary and even desirable elements in the political lives of nations. The latter often *need* them, monitored more or less at a distance, to demonstrate contrast and progress; they permit the militarisation of political culture, and the expenditure necessary to demonstrate action and to keep the military estate busy, in ways which would otherwise be unthinkable. Fountain Publishers' enduring and glossy production *Peoples and Cultures of Uganda* – which we first encountered in the Prologue – displays the various peoples of the country in all their traditional tribal glory. These are risk-free exercises in living museology, stripped of their political content and packaged as traditional culture safely removed from the everyday stresses and distractions of political modernity. But they are very much part of that 'modernity' – with all its multiple meanings and contradictions.

In the end, perhaps the best that we can say is that the attempt to reconstruct the history of the nation as a shared space presents opportunities as well as challenges. A popular view may be that all Ugandans are thankful to the British for giving them their nation – 'before that, we were just tribes and kingdoms'[7] – but a rather different perspective is possible, one which depicts Uganda as more organic and long-term. Still, there is no linear journey for Uganda, no straightforward 'story'. As one might expect from the 'tale' of tens of millions of people over several centuries, paradox is everywhere. War is destructive and devastating, and the militarism which underpins it murderous, but it has also, in the past, proven cohesive and integrative. There is, from the late eighteenth century, an expansion of political scale, and evidence of

---

[7] For example, author's notes and informal interviews, 23 July 2014.

a remarkable politico-military revolution; and yet alongside this, and in the borderlands and spaces between the territorially large units, we see a proliferation of small but potent pivots and local identities. Religious adherence, providing meaning and unity to millions of Ugandans, nonetheless drives deep fissures in the body politic, and is the source of profound disunity. Economic integration can be discerned over the last two hundred years, involving material interconnection and exchange; yet this has unfolded in parallel with growing inequity at the national level and underdevelopment in some areas. In other words, our 'story' is riddled with contradiction. One looks eagerly for clarity of narrative, but instead finds the conjunction of the supposedly incompatible. And yet, while there was nothing inevitable about Uganda, there does not need to be anything inherently illogical about it. Uganda persists – indeed flourishes, at least for some, as an idea and as a political, cultural, economic reality – and is characterised by accommodation, reciprocity and interdependency, as much as by histories of distrust and antagonism. And Uganda's past, as much as its 'journey', continues. The historian of the future *History of Modern Uganda* has their work cut out, on what will undoubtedly be a rather different book.

Glossary

Note on orthography: Prefixes in Bantu languages are as follows: Ba-, indicating the plural, so *Baganda*, the Ganda people; Mu-, indicating the singular, so a *Muganda*, a Ganda person. While it is difficult, depending on circumstances, to be wholly consistent, this book follows the orthographic convention of dropping the Bantu prefix when using these terms in English.

ADF	Allied Democratic Forces
askari	colonial soldiers
Bagendanwa	royal drums, Nkore
bakungu	great chiefs, orig. Buganda
Balokole	the saved ones
banansangwawo	indigenous or original clans of Buganda
barusura	professional soldiers, Bunyoro
basomi	'readers', early Christian converts
bataka	clans, Buganda
batongole	non-hereditary rank of chieftaincy, Buganda
bazimu	spirits
bazungu	plural of *muzungu*
boda-bodas	motorcycle taxis
CMS	Church Missionary Society
DP	Democratic Party
Embandwa	spirit possession cult
FDC	Forum for Democratic Change
'Historicals'	founding members of the NRA/M
IBEAC	Imperial British East Africa Company
kabaka	'king' of Buganda
Kabaka Yekka (KY)	'The King Alone'
KAR	King's African Rifles
Katikiro	chief minister, Buganda; applied elsewhere from 1900s

kibuga	*kabaka*'s enclosure; inner core of the royal capital
kyabazinga	paramount chief of Busoga
LegCo	Legislative Council
LRA	Lord's Resistance Army
lubaale	major deities
Luganda	language of Buganda
Lukiiko	parliament of Buganda
Lunyoro	language of Bunyoro
magendo	black market
MBC	Mubende Banyoro Committee
mugabe	'king' of Nkore
Muganda	Ganda person (sing.)
mujaguzo	royal drums, Buganda
mukama	'king' of Bunyoro, and used elsewhere across region
muzungu	European, foreigner
NAAM	National Association for the Advancement of Muslims
namasole	mother of the *kabaka* in Buganda
ngikatapa	'bread people', Ateker groups
NGO	non-governmental organisation
NRA	National Resistance Army
NRM	National Resistance Movement
OAU	Organisation of African Unity
Panda Gari	counter-insurgency technique, lit., 'get into the vehicle'
Runyankole	language of Nkore/Ankole
rwot	ruler of individual Acholi chiefdom
SPLM	Sudan People's Liberation Movement
ssaza	county, province, orig. Buganda
UAFU	Uganda African Farmers' Union
UNC	Uganda National Congress
UNLF	Uganda National Liberation Front
UNM	Uganda National Movement
UPC	Uganda People's Congress
UPDF	Uganda People's Defence Forces
UPDM	Uganda People's Democratic Movement
UPM	Uganda Patriotic Movement

Sources and Bibliography

I. Interviews and Fieldwork

Much of the book is drawn from a wide range of oral informants with whom the author talked over a number of years, but especially between 2010 and 2015. For reasons of confidentiality and security, most of these sources – unless otherwise stated – have been anonymised. On the whole I also eschewed formal interviews in favour of informal conversations which enabled people to talk more freely about a range of political, economic and cultural issues. In footnotes, these have been rendered as 'Author's field notes and informal interviews', complete with date.

II. Archival Collections

Church Missionary Society Archives (CMS), University of Birmingham, UK
Fort Portal District Archives, Uganda
Kabale District Archives, Uganda
London Missionary Society Archives (LMS), SOAS, London, UK
Makerere University Library Africana Section Archives (MUL), Kampala, Uganda
National Archives of the United Kingdom (UKNA), London, UK
Uganda National Archives (UNA), Entebbe, Uganda
White Fathers Archives, Rome, Italy

III. Official, Institutional and 'Grey' Literature

Africa Research Institute. 'Between Extremes: China and Africa', *Africa Research Institute: Briefing Note 1202*. London: October 2012.
Amnesty International. *Human Rights in Uganda*. London: Amnesty International, 1978.
  Uganda: the failure to safeguard human rights. London: Amnesty International, 1992.
Bukedi Makerere Students Union. 'The Bukedi Student: the magazine of Bukedi Makerere Students Union', 1961–2.
Caleb, M.M. & M.P. Baluku. *Obusinga Bwa Rwenzururu: a critical analysis and revealing facts about the "institution"*. Unpublished, March 2005.

Chr. Michelsen Institute. *Uganda's 2006 Presidential and Parliamentary Elections*. Bergen: Chr. Michelsen Institute, 2006.

Church Missionary Society. *Church Missionary Gleaner*. London: CMS, various years.

Mengo Notes. London: CMS, various years.

Colonial Office. *Uganda Annual Reports*. London: HMSO, various years.

Uganda: Report of a Commission of Privy Counsellors on a Dispute between Buganda and Bunyoro. London: HMSO, 1962.

Democratic Party. *Forward to Freedom; being the Manifesto of the Democratic Party*. Kampala: Uganda Bookshop Press, 1960.

The Democrat: Uganda's messenger of truth and justice, the monthly newsletter of the DP, February 1969.

Engabu za Tooro (Tooro Youth Platform for Action). *Towards Celebrations of UNESCO's Inscription of Empaako Tradition in 2013*. Fort Portal.

Geographical Section of the Naval Intelligence Division, Naval Staff, Admiralty. *A Handbook of the Uganda Protectorate*. London: 1920.

Gologolo, P.I. 'Towards a progressive and prosperous Busoga kingdom in a united and stable Uganda', Jinja, 17 October 2008.

Hailey. *An African Survey: a study of the problems arising in Africa south of the Sahara*. London: Oxford University Press, 1938.

An African Survey: a study of the problems arising in Africa south of the Sahara. London: Oxford University Press, 1957.

Human Rights Watch. *The scars of death: children abducted by the Lord's Resistance Army in Uganda*. New York: Human Rights Watch, 1997.

Abducted and Abused: renewed conflict in northern Uganda. New York: Human Rights Watch, 2003.

Uprooted and Forgotten: impunity and human rights abuses in northern Uganda. New York: Human Rights Watch, 2005.

'Letting the Big Fish Swim': failures to prosecute high-level corruption in Uganda. New York: Human Rights Watch, 2013.

Somalia: sexual abuse by African Union soldiers. New York: Human Rights Watch, 8 September 2014.

'Inaugural Address by the Honourable Minister of Education Brigadier Barnabas Kili, DSO', in National Curriculum Development Centre, *The Inaugural National Curriculum Conference Report*. Kampala: Government Printer, 1973.

International Commission of Jurists, UN Commission on Human Rights. *Uganda and Human Rights*. Geneva: United Nations, 1977.

International Crisis Group. *Uganda: no resolution to growing tensions*. Africa Report No. 187, Nairobi/Brussels, 5 April 2012.

South Sudan: Keeping Faith with the IGAD Peace Process. Africa Report No. 228, Nairobi/Brussels, 27 July 2015.

Isebantu Kyabazinga of Busoga. *The Constitution of Obwa Kyabazinga bwa Busoga,* promulgated by the Isebantu Kyabazinga of Busoga at Bugembe Headquarters, 30 December 2000.

Jones, T.J. *Education in East Africa: a study of east, central and south Africa by the second African Education Commission under the auspices of the Phelps-Stokes Fund, in cooperation with the International Education Board: report.* London & New York: Phelps-Stokes Fund, 1925.

Katukiro of Busoga. Letter from the Katukiro of Busoga to His Excellency the President of Uganda, 25 July 1994.

Kavuma, M., *et al. Coronation Special Souvenir.* Kampala: World of a Woman Publications, 1993.

King's College Budo. *'King's School Budo Report',* 20 April 1908.

Kiyimba, A. *'Islam in Uganda: a situational report',* unpublished paper for the Uganda Muslim Youth Assembly, 2005.

Kyaminyawandi, A. *The Faces of the Rwenzururu Movement.* n.p., 2001.

Low, D.A. (ed.), *The Mind of Buganda: documents of the modern history of an African kingdom.* London: Heinemann, 1971.

Makerere University College. *First Conference on African Traditional Music,* 15–19 December 1963. Kampala, 1964.

Masaaba [Gisu] Historical Research Association, *For the Land and Culture of Bamasaaba* (privately published & distributed, c. 1992).

Ministry of Agriculture and Forestry. *An Economic Survey of Farming in a Wet, Long-Grass Area of Toro.* Entebbe: Government Printer, 1968.

Ministry of Tourism, Trade and Industry, Government of Uganda. *The East African Trade Centre Project Proposal,* Kampala, n.d. [c. 2011].

Nsamba, Yolamu Ndoleriire Nsamba. *Breaking Chains of Poverty: Bunyoro-Kitara Kingdom Advocacy Publication.* Hoima, c. 1999.

Obote, A.M. *The common man's charter.* Entebbe: Government Printer, 1970.

Overseas Development Institute, *Colonial Development: a factual survey of the origins and history of British aid to developing countries.* London: ODI, 1964.

Republic of Uganda. *His Excellency the President's Communication from the Chair of the National Assembly on 9th June 1967.* Entebbe: Government Printer, 1967.

Uganda AIDS Commission. *'HIV and AIDS Uganda Country progress report, 2013'.* Kampala, 2014.

Uganda Government. *The First Five-Year Development Plan 1961/62 – 1965/66.* Entebbe: Government Printer, 1962.

Report of the Commission of Inquiry into the Recent Disturbances Amongst the Baamba and Bakonjo People of Toro. Entebbe: Government Printer, 1962.

Education in Uganda: the report of the Uganda Education Commission. Entebbe: Government Printer, 1963.

Bunyoro District Annual Report 1972. Entebbe: Government Printer, 1972.

Speeches by His Excellency the President General Idi Amin Dada. Entebbe: Government Printer, 1972.

Uganda Protectorate. *Instructions re. Collection of Poll Taxes by Chiefs in the District of Toro (translated into Lutoro).* Entebbe: Government Printer, c. 1913.

African Education in Uganda: being the report of a committee set up by His Excellency the Governor to study and make recommendations on the future of African education in the Uganda Protectorate. Entebbe: Government Printer, 1953.

Memorandum by the Protectorate Government on the Report of the African Education Committee. Entebbe: Government Printer, 1953.

Sessional Paper on the Report of the Commission of Inquiry into the Disturbances in Certain Areas of the Bukedi and Bugisu Districts of the Eastern Province during the month of January 1960. Entebbe: Government Printer, 1960.

Report of the Commission appointed to Review the Boundary between the Districts of Bugisu and Bukedi. Entebbe: Government Printer, 1962.

Annual Reports on the Kingdom of Buganda, Eastern Province, Western Province, Northern Province. Entebbe: Government Printer, various years.

Annual Reports of the Education Department. Entebbe: Government Printer, various years.

Wallis, H.R. *The Handbook of Uganda*, 2nd ed. London: Crown agents for the colonies for the government of Uganda, 1920.

IV. Newspapers and Other Media

A range of print media sources were consulted. In Uganda:

Munno
New Vision
The Daily Monitor
The Observer
Red Pepper

Saturday Vision
Uganda Argus
Uganda Review
The Uganda Herald
Catholic News Bulletin
Weekly Topic
Other media & commentary sources include:
BBC News
AllAfrica
Think Africa Press
The Guardian (London)
DRUM Magazine (Johannesburg)
Al Jazeera America
Reuters
Changing Attitude
African Arguments
Voice of America
New York Times
Africa Confidential
The Africa Report
Additional websites consulted:
Art:
http://ugandart.com/
Contemporary politics: http://www.parliament.go.ug/new/images/stories/
    constitution/Constitution_of_Uganda_1995.pdf
http://www.mediacentre.go.ug/press-release/national-secretariat-
    patriotism-clubs-statement
LRA:
https://www.lracrisistracker.com/
East African Community:
http://eac.int/about/EAC-history
HIV-AIDS:
http://www.avert.org/professionals/hiv-around-world/sub-saharan-
    africa/uganda
Demography:
http://countrymeters.info/en/Uganda
http://www.worldwatch.org/node/4525
Islam in Uganda:
http://umeauganda.org/home
UNESCO and *empaako*:
http://www.unesco.org/culture/ich/index.php?USL=00904

V. Select Bibliography (i): Primary & Secondary Texts

Independent Uganda: the first fifty years. Kampala: Fountain, 2012.

NRM 25 Years. Uganda 1986–2011: politics, policies and personalities. Kampala: Tourguide Publications, 2011.

Peoples and Cultures of Uganda. Kampala: Fountain, 2011.

Uganda: a picture history, 1857–2007. Kampala: Fountain, 2009.

Adefuye, A. 'Political history of the Paluo, 1400–1911', unpublished PhD thesis, University of Ibadan, 1973.

Akingbade, P.I. 'The History of the Kingdom of Toro, from its Foundation to 1928', unpublished MA Dissertation, University of East Africa, 1967.

Alibhai-Brown, Y. 'Starting over', *FT Magazine*, 24 August 2012.

Allen, T. 'Ethnicity and Tribalism on the Sudan-Uganda Border', in K. Fukui & J. Markakis (eds.), *Ethnicity and Conflict in the Horn of Africa*. London: James Currey, 1994.

Allen, T. & K. Vlassenroot (eds.), *The LRA: myth and reality*. London: Zed Books, 2010.

Alpers, E.A. 'The Nineteenth Century: prelude to colonialism', in B.A. Ogot & J.A. Kieran (eds.), *Zamani: a survey of East African history*. Nairobi: East African Publishing House, 1968.

Amaza, O.o. *Museveni's Long March from Guerrilla to Statesman*. Kampala: Fountain, 1998.

Anderson, D.M. & D. Johnson (eds.), *Revealing Prophets: prophecy in Eastern African history*. London: James Currey, 1995.

Anderson, D.M. & R. Rathbone. 'Introduction. Urban Africa: histories in the making', in D.M. Anderson & R. Rathbone (eds.), *Africa's Urban Past*. London: James Currey, 2000.

Anderson, R. *The Forgotten Front: the East African campaign*. Stroud: Tempus Publishing, 2004.

Anguria, O.R. (ed.), *Apollo Milton Obote: what others say*. Kampala: Fountain, 2006.

Apter, D. *The Political Kingdom in Uganda: a study in bureaucratic nationalism*. Princeton: Princeton University Press, 1961.

Apuuli, D.K. *A Thousand Years of Bunyoro-Kitara Kingdom: the people and the rulers*. Kampala: Fountain, 1994.

Ashe, R.P. *Chronicles of Uganda*. London: Hodder & Stoughton, 1894.

Asiimwe, G. 'The Roots and Dynamics of the Indian Question and Interracial Relations in Uganda', unpublished conference paper, Mukono, July 2015.

Atkinson, R.R. '"State" Formation and Language Change in Westernmost Acholi in the Eighteenth Century', in A.I. Salim (ed.), *State Formation in Eastern Africa*. Nairobi: Heinemann, 1984.

The Roots of Ethnicity: the origins of the Acholi of Uganda before 1800. Philadelphia: University of Pennsylvania Press, 1994.

Avirgan, T. & M. Honey, *War in Uganda: the legacy of Idi Amin.* Westport, Conn. & London: Lawrence Hill, 1982.

Bade, A. *Benedicto Kiwanuka: the man and his politics.* Kampala: Fountain, 1996.

Baker, S. *The Albert N'yanza: Great Basin of the Nile and Explorations of the Nile Sources,* 2 vols. London: Macmillan & Co, 1866.

Ismailia, 2 vols. London: Macmillan & Co., 1874.

Baker, S.J.K. 'The East African Environment', in R. Oliver & G. Mathew (eds.) *History of East Africa Volume I.* Oxford: Oxford University Press, 1963.

Bakibinga, D. *Daudi Kintu-Mutekanga: administrator and entrepreneur.* Kampala: Professional Books Publishers, 2006.

Ballarin, M.P., H. Kiriama, and C. Pennacini (eds.), 'Sacred Natural Sites and Cultural Heritage in East Africa', special issue of the *Uganda Journal,* 53 (2013).

Bamunoba, J.K. *'A reconstruction of the history of the Christian Church in Ankole; based on original sources, oral and written',* unpublished paper, Makerere University, c. 1966.

Barber, J.P. 'The Karamoja District of Uganda: a pastoral people under colonial rule', *Journal of African History,* 3:1 (1962).

'The Moving Frontier of British Imperialism in Northern Uganda, 1898–1919', *Uganda Journal,* 29:1 (1965).

Bazaara, Nyangabyaki. *'The Food Question in Colonial Bunyoro-Kitara: capital penetration and peasant response',* unpublished MA dissertation, Makerere University, 1988.

Beattie, J. *The Nyoro State.* Oxford: Oxford University Press, 1971.

Behrend, H. *Alice Lakwena and the Holy Spirits: war in northern Uganda, 1985–97.* Oxford: James Currey, 2000.

Berger, I. 'Deities, Dynasties and Oral Tradition: the history and legend of the Abacwezi', in J.C. Miller (ed.), *The African Past Speaks.* Folkestone & Hamden: Dawson, 1980.

'Fertility as Power: spirit mediums, priestesses, and the precolonial state in interlacustrine East Africa', in D.M. Anderson & D. Johnson (eds.), *Revealing Prophets: Prophecy in Eastern African History.* London: James Currey, 1995.

Bigirimana, P. *Abundance Mentality: my autobiography.* Brighton: Pen Press, 2011.

Bikunya, P. *Ky'Abakama ba Bunyoro.* London: Sheldon Press, 1927.

p'Bitek, Okot. *White Teeth. A novel.* Nairobi: Heinemann Kenya, 1989 (1st pub. as *Lak Tar,* 1953).

Song of Lawino & Song of Ocol. Johannesburg: Heinemann, 1984 (1ˢᵗ pub. 1966, 1967.)

Religion of the Central Luo. Nairobi: East African Literature Bureau, 1971.

Breitinger, E. 'Introduction', in Eckhard Breitinger (ed.), *Uganda: the cultural landscape*. Kampala: Fountain, 2000.

Brett, E.A. *Colonialism and Underdevelopment in East Africa, 1919–1939*. London: Heinemann, 1973.

'Neutralising the Use of Force in Uganda: the role of the military in politics', *Journal of Modern African Studies*, 33:1 (1995).

Brown, D. & M.V. (eds.), *Looking Back at the Uganda Protectorate: recollections of District Officers*. Dalkeith: privately published, 1996.

Buchanan, C.A. 'Perceptions of Ethnic Interaction in the East African Interior: the Kitara complex', *International Journal of African Historical Studies*, 11:3 (1978).

Bukenya, A. *The People's Bachelor*. Nairobi: East African Publishing House, 1972.

The Bride. Nairobi: Heinemann Kenya, 1987.

A Hole in the Sky. Nairobi: Oxford University Press, 2013.

Bukenya, G. *Through Intricate Corridors to Power*. Kampala: Fountain, 2008.

Burton, R.F. *The Lake Regions of Central Africa*, 2 vols. London: Longman, Green, Longman & Roberts, 1860; republished in one volume: New York: Dover, 1995.

Byaruhanga-Akiiki, A.B.T. *'Religion in Bunyoro'*, unpublished PhD thesis, Makerere University, 1971.

Byerley, Andrew. 'Uganda', in J. Middleton & J. Miller (eds.), *New Encyclopaedia of Africa, Vol V*. Detroit: Thomson Gale, 2008.

Casati, G. *Ten Years in Equatoria*, 2 vols. London: Frederick Warne & Co., 1891.

Chande, A. 'Radicalism and Reform in East Africa', in N. Levtzion and R.L. Pouwels (eds.), *The History of Islam in Africa*. Athens & Oxford: Ohio University Press, 2000.

Chrétien, J.-P. 'L'Empire des Bacwezi: la construction d'un imaginaire géopolitique', *Annales: histories, sciences sociales*, 40:6 (1985).

(tr. Scott Straus). *The Great Lakes of Africa: two thousand years of history*. New York: Zone Books, 2003.

Churchill, W.S. *My African Journey*. London: Hodder & Stoughton, 1908.

Clarke, R.F. (ed.), *Cardinal Lavigerie and the African Slave Trade*. London: Longmans, Green & Co., 1889.

Cohen, D.W. 'The River-Lake Nilotes from the Fifteenth to the Nineteenth Century', in B.A. Ogot & J.A. Kieran (eds.), *Zamani: a survey of East African history*. Nairobi: East African Publishing House, 1968.

    The Historical Tradition of Busoga: Mukama and Kintu. Oxford: Clarendon Press, 1972.

    Womunafu's Bunafu: a study of authority in a nineteenth-century African community. Princeton NJ: Princeton University Press, 1977.

    Toward a Reconstructed Past: historical texts from Busoga, Uganda. Baltimore: Johns Hopkins University Press, 1983.

Colvile, Sir H. *The Land of the Nile Springs; being chiefly an account of how we fought Kabarega*. London: Edward Arnold, 1895.

Connah, G., E. Kamuhangire, & A. Piper, 'Salt production at Kibiro', *Azania*, 25 (1990).

Connah, G. 'The Cultural and Chronological Context of Kibiro, Uganda', *African Archaeological Review*, 14:1 (1997).

Conroy-Krutz, J. & C. Logan, 'Museveni and the 2011 Ugandan election: did the money matter?', *Journal of Modern African Studies*, 50:4 (2012).

Cook, D. 'The Makerere Free Travelling Theatre: an experimental model', in Eckhard Breitinger (ed.), *Uganda: the cultural landscape*. Kampala: Fountain, 2000.

Cook, Sir A.R. *Uganda Memories (1897–1940)*. Kampala: The Uganda Society, 1945.

Crazzolara, J.P. *A Study of the Acooli Language: grammar and vocabulary*. London: Oxford University Press, 1938.

    The Lwoo, 3 vols. Verona: Museum Combonianum, Missioni Africane, 1950–4.

Daily Monitor, *Understand Uganda: 50 years of independence, 9 October 1962 – 9 October 2012*. Kampala: Daily Monitor Publications, 2012.

Decker, A.C. '"Sometime you may leave your husband in Karuma Falls or in the forest there": a gendered history of disappearance in Idi Amin's Uganda, 1971–79', *Journal of Eastern African Studies*, 7:1 (2013).

    In Idi Amin's Shadow: women, gender and militarism in Uganda. Athens OH: Ohio University Press, 2014.

Donald, T. *Confessions of Idi Amin*. London: W.H. Allen & Co., 1978.

Doornbos, M.R. 'Kumanyana and Rwenzururu: two responses to ethnic inequality', in R.I. Rotberg & A.A. Mazrui (eds.), *Protest and Power in Black Africa*. New York: Oxford University Press, 1970.

The Ankole Kingship Controversy: regalia galore revisited. Kampala: Fountain, 2001.

Doyle, S. *Crisis and Decline in Bunyoro: population and environment in Western Uganda, 1860–1955.* Oxford: James Currey, 2006.

Bunyoro and the Demography of Slavery Debate: fertility, kinship and assimilation', in H. Médard & S. Doyle (eds.), *Slavery in the Great Lakes Region of East Africa.* Oxford: James Currey, 2007.

'Immigrants and indigenes: the Lost Counties dispute and the evolution of ethnic identity in colonial Buganda', *Journal of Eastern African Studies*, 3:2 (2009).

Before HIV: sexuality, fertility and mortality in East Africa 1900–1980. Oxford: Oxford University Press, 2013.

Driberg, J.H. *The Lango, a Nilotic tribe of Uganda.* London: T.F. Unwin, 1923.

Dunbar, A.R. *Omukama Chwa II Kabarega.* Nairobi: East African Literature Bureau, 1965.

Dunn, K.C. 'Uganda: the Lord's Resistance Army', in M. Boas & K.C. Dunn (eds.), *African Guerrillas: raging against the machine.* Boulder CO: Lynne Rienner, 2007.

Dyson-Hudson, N. *Karimojong Politics.* Oxford: Clarendon Press, 1966.

Earle, J. *'Political Theologies in Late Colonial Buganda'*, unpublished PhD thesis, University of Cambridge, 2012.

'Reading Revolution in late colonial Buganda', *Journal of Eastern African Studies*, 6:3 (2012).

Eaton, D. 'The business of peace: raiding and peace work along the Kenya-Uganda border (Part I)', *African Affairs*, 107:426 (2008) & (Part II), *African Affairs*, 107:427 (2008).

Ehrlich, C. 'Some social and economic implications of paternalism in Uganda', *Journal of African History*, 4:2 (1963).

'The Uganda Economy, 1903–1945', in V. Harlow & E.M. Chilver (eds.), *History of East Africa, Vol. II.* Oxford: Clarendon Press, 1965.

Elizabeth, Princess, of Toro. *African Princess: the story of Princess of Elizabeth of Toro.* London: Hamish Hamilton, 1983.

Emwanu, G. 'The Reception of Alien Rule in Teso, 1896–1927', *Uganda Journal*, 31:2 (1967).

Engdahl, T. *The Exchange of Cotton: Ugandan peasants, colonial market regulations, and the organisation of the international cotton trade, 1904–1918.* Uppsala: Acta Universitatis Upsaliensis, 1999.

Fallers, L.A. *Bantu Bureaucracy: a century of political evolution among the Basoga of Uganda.* Chicago: University of Chicago Press, 1956, 2nd ed. 1965.

(ed.), *The King's Men: leadership and status in Buganda on the eve of independence*. New York: Oxford University Press, 1964.

L.A. Fallers, 'Social Stratification in Traditional Buganda', in L.A. Fallers (ed.), *The King's Men: leadership and status in Buganda on the eve of independence*. New York: Oxford University Press, 1964.

Faupel, J.F. *African Holocaust: the story of the Uganda martyrs*. London: Geoffrey Chapman, 1965.

Felkin, R.W. 'Notes on the Waganda tribe of Central Africa', *Proceedings of the Royal Society of Edinburgh*, 13 (1885–6).

Fèvre, E.M. *et al.* 'Re-analysing the 1900–1920 Sleeping Sickness Epidemic in Uganda', *Emerging Infectious Diseases*, 10:4 (2004).

Finnstrom, S. '"For God and My Life": war and cosmology in Northern Uganda', in P. Richards (ed.), *No Peace, No War: an anthropology of contemporary armed conflicts*. Athens OH & Oxford: James Currey, 2005.

Living with Bad Surroundings: war, history, and everyday moments in Northern Uganda. Durham NC & London: Duke University Press, 2008.

'Fear of the Midnight Knock: state sovereignty and internal enemies in Uganda', in Bruce Kapferer & Bjorn Enge Bertelsen (eds.), *Crisis of the State: war and social upheaval*. New York: Berghahn, 2009.

Fortt, J.M. 'The Distribution of Immigrant and Ganda Population within Buganda', in A.I. Richards (ed.), *Economic Development and Tribal Change: a study of immigrant labour in Buganda*. Cambridge: W. Heffer & Sons, 1954.

Furley, O.W. 'The Reign of Kasagama in Toro from a Contemporary Account', *Uganda Journal*, 31:2 (1967).

'The Legislative Council, 1945–1961: the wind of change', in G.N. Uzoigwe (ed.), *Uganda: the dilemma of nationhood*. New York: NOK Publishers International, 1982.

Gale, H.P. 'Mutesa I: was he a god?', *Uganda Journal*, 20:1 (1956).

Gartrell, B. 'Searching for "The Roots of Famine": the case of Karamoja', *Review of African Political Economy*, 33 (1985).

Gee, T.W. 'A Century of Muhammadan Influence in Buganda, 1852–1951', *Uganda Journal*, 22:2 (1958).

Gertzel, C. *Party and Locality in Northern Uganda, 1945–1962*. London: Atholone Press, 1974.

'Kingdoms, Districts, and the Unitary State: Uganda, 1945–1962', in D.A. Low & A. Smith (eds.), *History of East Africa*, Vol. III. Oxford: Clarendon Press, 1976.

Ghai, D.P. *Taxation for Development: a case study of Uganda*. Nairobi: East African Publishing House, 1966.

'The Bugandan Trade Boycott: a study in tribal, political, and economic nationalism', in R.I. Rotberg & A.A. Mazrui (eds.), *Protest and Power in Black Africa*. New York: Oxford University Press, 1970.

Gingera-Pinycwa, A.G.G. *Northern Uganda in National Politics*. Kampala: Fountain, 1992.

Goldschmidt, W. *Sebei Law*. Berkeley: University of California Press, 1967.

Gorju, J. *Entre le Victoria, l'Albert et l'Edouard*. Rennes: Imprimerie Oberthur, 1920.

Grahame, I. *Amin and Uganda: a personal memoir*. London: Granada, 1980.

Grant, J.A. *A Walk Across Africa*. Edinburgh & London: William Blackwood & Sons, 1864.

Gray, J.M. 'Ahmed bin Ibrahim: the first Arab to reach Buganda', *Uganda Journal*, 11 (1947).

'Rwot Ochama of Payera', *Uganda Journal*, 12 (1948).

'The Year of the Three Kings of Buganda, Mwanga–Kiwewa–Kalema, 1888–89', *Uganda Journal*, 14 (1950).

'Acholi History, 1860–1901, Part I', *Uganda Journal*, 15 (1951).

'Acholi History 1860–1901, Part II', *Uganda Journal*, 16 (1952).

'Trading Expeditions from the Coast to Lakes Tanganyika and Victoria before 1867', *Tanganyika Notes and Records*, 49 (1957).

(ed.), 'The Diaries of Emin Pasha', *Uganda Journal*, 25:1 (1961).

'Kabarega and the CMS', *Uganda Journal*, 35 (1971).

Gray, S.J. 'A Memory of Loss: ecological politics, local history, and the evolution of Karimojong violence', *Human Organization*, 59:4 (2000).

Green, M. *The Wizard of the Nile: the hunt for Africa's most wanted*. London: Portobello, 2008.

Gulliver, P.H. (ed.) *Tradition and Transition in East Africa: studies of the tribal element in the modern era*. London: Routledge & Kegan Paul, 1969.

Gupta, V. *Obote: second liberation*. New Delhi: Vika Publishing, 1983.

Gutkind, P.C.W. *The Royal Capital of Buganda: a study of internal conflict and external ambiguity*. The Hague: Mouton, 1963.

Gwyn, D. *Idi Amin: death-light of Africa*. Boston & Toronto: Little, Brown, 1977.

Hancock, I.R. 'Patriotism and Neo-traditionalism in Buganda: the Kabaka Yekka ("the King Alone") movement, 1961–62', *Journal of African History*, 11:3 (1970).

Hansen, H.B. *Ethnicity and Military Rule in Uganda*. Uppsala: Scandinavian Institute of African Studies, 1977.

Mission, Church and State in a Colonial Setting: Uganda, c. 1890–1925. London: Heinemann Educational, 1984.

'The Colonial Control of Spirit Cults in Uganda', in D.M. Anderson & D. Johnson (eds.), *Revealing Prophets: Prophecy in Eastern African History*. London: James Currey, 1995.

'Uganda in the 1970s: a decade of paradoxes and ambiguities', *Journal of Eastern African Studies*, 7:1 (2013).

Hansen, H.B. & M. Twaddle (eds.), *Uganda Now: between decay and development*. London: James Currey, 1988.

(eds.), *Changing Uganda: the dilemmas of structural adjustment and revolutionary change*. London: James Currey, 1991.

(eds.), *From Chaos to Order: the politics of constitution-making in Uganda*. Kampala: Fountain, 1994.

(eds.), *Developing Uganda*. Oxford: James Currey, 1998.

Hanson, H. *Landed Obligation: the practice of power in Buganda*. Portsmouth NH: Heinemann, 2003.

'Stolen People and Autonomous Chiefs in Nineteenth-Century Buganda: the social consequences of non-free followers', in H. Médard & S. Doyle (eds.), *Slavery in the Great Lakes Region of East Africa*. Oxford: James Currey, 2007.

Hartwig, G.W. 'The Victoria Nyanza as a Trade Route in the Nineteenth Century', *Journal of African History*, 11:4 (1970).

Hattersley, C.W. *The Baganda at Home*. London: Religious Tract Society, 1908.

Henige, D. '"The Disease of Writing": Ganda and Nyoro kinglists in a newly literate world', in J.C. Miller (ed.), *The African Past Speaks*. Folkestone & Hamden: Dawson, 1980.

Heron, G.A. *The Poetry of Okot p'Bitek*. New York: Heinemann, 1976.

Hills, D. *The White Pumpkin*. London: Allen & Unwin, 1975.

Hirst, M.A. 'The Distribution of Migrants in Kampala, Uganda', in D. Parkin (ed.), *Town and Country in Central and Eastern Africa*. London: Oxford University Press, 1975.

Hopkins, E. 'The Nyabingi Cult of Southwestern Uganda', in R.I. Rotberg & A.A. Mazrui (eds.), *Protest and Power in Black Africa*. New York: Oxford University Press, 1970.

Hoyle, B.S. 'The Economic Expansion of Jinja, Uganda', *Geographical Review*, 53:3 (1963).

Hughes, A.J. *East Africa: the search for unity*. London: Penguin, 1963.

Humphris, J., M. Martinon-Torres, T. Rehren, and A. Reid, 'Variability in Single Smelting Episodes: a pilot study using iron slag from Uganda', *Journal of Archaeological Science*, 36 (2009).

Hundle, A.K. 'Exceptions to the Expulsion: violence, security and community among Ugandan Asians, 1972–79', *Journal of Eastern African Studies*, 7:1 (2013).

Huntingford, G.W.B. 'The Peopling of the Interior of East Africa by its Modern Inhabitants', in R. Oliver & G. Mathew (eds.), *History of East Africa*, Vol. I. Oxford: Clarendon Press, 1963.

Hyden, G. 'The Challenges of Constitutionalising Politics in Uganda', in Holger Bernt Hansen & Michael Twaddle (eds.), *Developing Uganda*. Oxford: James Currey, 1998.

Ibingira, G. *The Forging of an African Nation: the political and constitutional evolution of Uganda from colonial rule to independence, 1894–1962*. New York: Viking, 1973.

  Bitter Harvest: a political novel. Nairobi: East African Publishing House, 1980.

Iliffe, J. *Honour in African History*. Cambridge: Cambridge University Press, 2005.

  The African AIDS Epidemic: a history. Oxford: James Currey, 2006.

Imbuga, F.D. 'Thematic Trends and Circumstance in John Ruganda's Drama', unpublished PhD thesis, University of Iowa, 1991.

Ingham, K. 'The *Amagasani* of the Abakama of Bunyoro', *Uganda Journal*, 17:2 (1953).

  The Making of Modern Uganda. London: George Allen & Unwin, 1958.

  The Kingdom of Toro in Uganda. London: Methuen, 1975.

  Obote: a political biography. London: Routledge, 1994.

  Uganda: a crisis of nationhood. London: H.M. Stationery Office, 1960.

Isegawa, Moses. *Abyssinian Chronicles*. New York: Alfred A. Knopf, 2000.

  Snakepit. New York: Alfred A. Knopf, 2004.

Jackson, Sir F. *Early Days in East Africa*. London: Edward Arnold, 1930.

Jamal, V. 'Changes in Poverty Patterns in Uganda', in Holger Bernt Hansen & Michael Twaddle (eds.), *Developing Uganda*. Oxford: James Currey, 1998.

Johnston, Sir H.H. *The Uganda Protectorate*, 2 vols. London: Hutchinson & Co., 1902.

Jorgensen, J.J. *Uganda: a modern history*. London: Croom Helm, 1981.

'K.W.' 'The Kings of Bunyoro-Kitara', *Uganda Journal*, 3:2 (1935).

'K.W.' 'The Kings of Bunyoro-Kitara, Part II', *Uganda Journal*, 4:1 (1936).

'K.W.' 'The Kings of Bunyoro-Kitara, Part III', *Uganda Journal*, 5:2 (1937).

Kabaka of Buganda. *Desecration of My Kingdom*. London: Constable, 1967.

Kagwa, A. (tr. E.B.Kalibala). *The Customs of the Baganda*. New York: Columbia University Press, 1934.

  (tr. & ed. M.S.M. Kiwanuka). *The Kings of Buganda*. Nairobi: East African Publishing House, 1971.

  (tr. J.Wamala). 'A Book of Clans of Buganda', unpublished manuscript in Makerere University Library, c. 1972.

Kahigiriza, J. *Bridging the Gap: struggling against sectarianism and violence in Ankole and Uganda*. Kampala: Fountain, 2001.

Kainerugaba, M. *Battles of the Ugandan Resistance: a tradition of maneuver*. Kampala: Fountain, 2010.

Kamau J. & A. Cameron. *Lust to Kill: the rise and fall of Idi Amin*. London: Corgi Books, 1979.

Kamugungunu, Lazaro & A.G. Katate. *Abagabe b'Ankole*. Dar es Salaam: Eagle Press, 1955.

Kanyeiharuba, G.W. *Reflections on the Muslim Leadership Question in Uganda*. Kampala: Fountain, 1998.

Karlstrom, M. 'The Cultural Kingdom in Uganda: popular royalism and the restoration of the Buganda kingship', unpublished PhD thesis, University of Chicago, 1999.

Karugire, S. *A History of the Kingdom of Nkore in Western Uganda to 1896*. Oxford: Clarendon Press, 1971.

Nuwa Mbaguta. Nairobi: East African Literature Bureau, 1973.

A Political History of Uganda. Nairobi: Heinemann, 1980.

The Roots of Instability in Uganda. Kampala: New Vision, 1988.

Kasfir, N. 'State, Magendo and Class Formation in Uganda', *The Journal of Commonwealth and Comparative Politics*, 21:3 (1983), 85.

'The Ugandan Elections of 1989: power, populism, and democratization', in H.B. Hansen & M. Twaddle (eds.), *Changing Uganda: the dilemmas of structural adjustment and revolutionary change*. London: James Currey, 1991.

'Ugandan Politics and the Constituent Assembly Elections of March 1994', in Michael Twaddle and Holger Bernt Hansen (eds.), *From Chaos to Order: the politics of constitution-making in Uganda*. Kampala: Fountain, 1994.

'"No-Party Democracy" in Uganda', *Journal of Democracy*, 9:2 (1998).

Kasozi, A.B.K. *The Spread of Islam in Uganda*. Nairobi & Khartoum: Oxford University Press, 1986.

The Social Origins of Violence in Uganda, 1964–1985. Montreal & London: McGill-Queen's University Press, 1994.

The Life of Prince Badru Kakungulu Wasajja, and the Development of a Forward Looking Muslim Community in Uganda, 1907–1991. Kampala: Progressive Publishing House, 1996.

The Bitter Bread of Exile: the financial problems of Sir Edward Muteesa during his final exile, 1966–69. Kampala: Progressive Publishing House, 2013.

Kasule, R. *From Gomba to the White House: the journey of an African woman entrepreneur*. Kampala: Xlibris Publishing, 2010.

Kasule, S. '"Don't Talk into My Talk": oral narratives, cultural identity, and popular performance in colonial Uganda', in M. Banham, J. Gibbs, & F. Osofisan (eds.), *African Theatre: histories 1850–1950*. Woodbridge: James Currey, 2010.

Kasumba, Y. *'Islamophobia in Uganda: myths and realities. A historical study of illusions of persecution complex among the Muslim community in Uganda from 1888 to 1985'*, unpublished conference paper, Mukono, Uganda, 19 July 2015.

Katono, D.N. *'Western Newspapers' Coverage of Idi Amin, 1971–1979'*, unpublished MA dissertation, Wake Forest University, 1990.

Katungulu, M.M. *'Islam in Buganda'*, unpublished translated manuscript in Makerere University Library, c. 1962.

Katyanku, Princess L.O. & S. Bulera. *The Life of Duhaga II*. Nairobi: Eagle Press, 1950.

Kavuma, P. *Crisis in Buganda, 1953–55: the story of the exile and return of the Kabaka, Mutesa II*. London: Rex Collings, 1979.

Kayiira, A. *'Violence in Kondoism: the rise and nature of violent crime in Uganda'*, unpublished PhD thesis, State University of New York at Albany, 1978.

de Kiewiet Hemphill, M. 'The British Sphere, 1884–94', in R. Oliver & G. Mathew (eds.), *History of East Africa*, Vol. I. Oxford: Clarendon Press, 1963.

Kigongo, R. & A. Reid. 'Local Communities, Politics, and the Management of the Kasubi Tombs', *World Archaeology*, 39:3 (2007).

Killingray, D. *Fighting for Britain: African soldiers in the Second World War*. Woodbridge: James Currey, 2010.

Kinsman, J. *AIDS Policy in Uganda: evidence, ideology, and the making of an African success story*. New York: Palgrave Macmillan, 2010.

Kirindi, Patrick G.N. *History and Culture of the Kingdom of Ankole*. Kampala: Fountain, 2008.

Kiwanuka, M.S.M. *Muteesa of Uganda*. Nairobi: East African Literature Bureau, 1967.

The Empire of Bunyoro-Kitara: myth or reality? Nairobi: Longman, 1968.

'Bunyoro and the British: a reappraisal of the causes for the decline and fall of an African kingdom', *Journal of African History*, 9:4 (1968).

'Uganda under the British', in B.A. Ogot & J.A. Kieran (eds.), *Zamani: a survey of East African history*. Nairobi: East African Publishing House, 1968.

A History of Buganda: from the foundation of the kingdom to 1900. London: Longman, 1971.

Amin and the Tragedy of Uganda. Munich: Weltforum Verlag, 1979.

Kiyaga-Nsubuga, J. 'Managing Political Change: Uganda under Museveni', in T.M. Ali & R.O. Matthews (eds.), *Civil Wars in Africa: roots and resolution*. Montreal & Kingston: McGill-Queen's University Press, 1999.

Knighton, B. 'Globalizing Trends or Identities through Time? The *longue durée* in Karamojong ethnography', *Journal of Eastern African Studies*, 1:3 (2007).

Kodesh, N. 'History from the Healer's Shrine: genre, historical imagination, and early Ganda history', *Comparative Studies in Society and History*, 49:3 (2007).

Beyond the Royal Gaze: clanship and public healing in Buganda. Charlottesville: University of Virginia Press, 2010.

Kottak, C.P. 'Ecological Variables in the Origin and Evolution of African states: the Buganda example', *Comparative Studies in Society and History*, 14:3 (1972).

Kusimba, C.M. & S.B. Kusimba, 'Mosaics and Interactions: East Africa, 2000 b.p. to the present', in Ann Brower Stahl (ed.), *African Archaeology: a critical introduction*. Malden MA & Oxford: Blackwell, 2005.

Kutesa, P. *Uganda's Revolution, 1979–1986: how I saw it*. Kampala: Fountain, 2006.

Kyemba, H. *State of Blood: the inside story of Idi Amin's reign of terror*. London: Corgi Books, 1977.

Kyeyune, G.W. *'Art in Uganda in the Twentieth Century'*, unpublished PhD dissertation, University of London, 2004.

La Fontaine, J.S. 'Tribalism Among the Gisu', in P.H. Gulliver (ed.) *Tradition and Transition in East Africa: studies of the tribal element in the modern era*. London: Routledge & Kegan Paul, 1969.

Lambright, G.M.S. *Decentralization in Uganda: explaining successes and failures in local governance*. Boulder CO: Lynne Rienner, 2010.

Lamphear, J. *The Traditional History of the Jie of Uganda*. Oxford: Clarendon Press, 1976.

'Historical Dimensions of Dual Organization: the generation-class system of the Jie and the Turkana' in D. Maybury-Lewis & U. Almagor (eds.), *The Attraction of Opposites: thought and society in the dualistic mode*. Ann Arbor: Michigan University Press, 1989.

'The Evolution of Ateker "New Model" Armies: Jie and Turkana', in K. Fukui & J. Markakis (eds.), *Ethnicity and Conflict in the Horn of Africa*. London: James Currey, 1994.

'Brothers in Arms: military aspects of East African age-class systems in historical perspective', in E. Kurimoto & S. Simonse (eds.), *Conflict, Age and Power in North East Africa*. Oxford: James Currey, 1998.

Langseth, P., J. Katorobo, E. Brett & J. Munene (eds.) *Uganda: landmarks in rebuilding a nation*. Kampala: Fountain, 1995.

Lateef, K.S. 'Structural Adjustment in Uganda: the initial experience', in Holger Bernt Hansen & Michael Twaddle (eds.), *Changing Uganda: the dilemmas of structural adjustment and revolutionary change*. London: James Currey, 1991.

Lawrance, J.C.D. *The Iteso: fifty years of change in a Nilo-Hamitic tribe of Uganda*. London: Oxford University Press, 1957.

Legum, C. 'Behind the Clown's Mask', *Transition*, 50 (Oct. 1975).

Leopold, M. *Inside West Nile: violence, history and representation on an African frontier*. Oxford: James Currey, 2005.

von Lettow-Vorbeck, General. *My Reminiscences of East Africa*. London: Hurst & Blackett, 1920.

Leys, C. *Politicians and Policies: an essay on politics in Acholi, Uganda, 1962–65*. Nairobi: East African Publishing House, 1967.

Lindemann, S. 'Just Another Change of Guard? Broad-based politics and civil war in Museveni's Uganda', *African Affairs*, 110/440 (2011).

'The Ethnic Politics of Coup Avoidance: evidence from Zambia and Uganda', *Africa Spectrum*, 46:2 (2011).

Lloyd, A.B. *In Dwarf Land and Cannibal Country*. T. Fisher Unwin: London, 1900.

lo Liyong, T. 'East Africa, O East Africa, I Lament Thy Literary Barrenness', *Transition*, 50 (Oct. 1975).

Low, D.A. & R.C. Pratt. *Buganda and British Overrule 1900–1955*. London: Oxford University Press, 1960.

Low, D.A. 'The Northern Interior, 1840–1884', in R. Oliver & G. Mathew (eds.), *History of East Africa*, Vol. I. Oxford: Clarendon Press, 1963.

'Uganda: the establishment of the Protectorate, 1894–1912', in V. Harlow & E.M. Chilver (eds.), *History of East Africa*, Vol. II. Oxford: Clarendon Press, 1965.

Buganda in Modern History. London: Weidenfeld & Nicolson, 1971.

Fabrication of Empire: the British and the Uganda Kingdoms, 1890–1902. Cambridge: Cambridge University Press, 2009.

Low, D.A. & J.M. Lonsdale, 'Introduction: towards the new order, 1945–1963', in D.A. Low & A. Smith (eds.), *History of East Africa*, Vol. III. Oxford: Clarendon Press, 1976.

Lubogo, Y.K. *A History of Busoga*. Translated & unpublished typescript in Makerere University Library, Kampala; Jinja, 1960.

Lugard, F.D. 'Travels from the East Coast to Uganda', *Proceedings of the Royal Geographical Society*, 14 (1892).

The Rise of our East African Empire, 2 vols. Edinburgh & London: William Blackwood & Sons, 1893.

Lunyiigo, S.L. *Mwanga II: resistance to imposition of British colonial rule in Buganda, 1884–99*. Kampala: Wavah Books, 2011.

Lury, D.A. 'Dayspring Mishandled? The Uganda economy, 1945–1960', in D.A. Low & A. Smith (eds.), *History of East Africa*, Vol. III. Oxford: Clarendon Press, 1976.

Lyons, M. 'AIDS and Development in Uganda', in Holger Bernt Hansen & Michael Twaddle (eds.), *Developing Uganda*. Oxford: James Currey, 1998.

Macdonald, J.R.L. *Soldiering and Surveying in British East Africa*. London: Edward Arnold, 1897.

Mackay, A.M. (ed. by his sister). *A.M. Mackay, Pioneer Missionary of the Church Missionary Society to Uganda*. London: Hodder & Stoughton, 1890.

Macmichael, Sir H. *The Anglo-Egyptian Sudan*. London: Faber, 1934.

Mair, L. *An African People in the Twentieth Century*. London: George Routledge & Sons, 1934.

Makumbi, J.N. *Kintu*. Nairobi: Kwani Trust, 2014.

Mamdani, M. 'Karamoja: colonial roots of famine in North-East Uganda', *Review of African Political Economy*, 9:25 (1982).

Mangat, J.S. *The History of the Asians of East Africa: c. 1886–1945*. Oxford: Clarendon Press, 1969.

'The Immigrant Communities: the Asians', in D.A. Low & A. Smith (eds.), *History of East Africa*, Vol. III. Oxford: Clarendon Press, 1976.

Martin, D. *General Amin*. London: Faber, 1974.

Mateso, J.M. '*Cultural Identity and Self Esteem as Factors in Self Efficacy in Sciences Among Bakonzo and Non Bakonzo Girls in Busongora-Kasese District*', unpublished Masters thesis in Educational Psychology, Makerere University, 2008.

Maxwell, D. 'Urban agriculture: unplanned responses to the economic crisis', in H.B. Hansen & M. Twaddle (eds.), *Developing Uganda*. Oxford: James Currey, 1998.

Mayiga, C.P. *The King on the Throne*. Kampala: Prime Time Communications, 2009.

Mazrui, A.A. 'The Social Origins of Ugandan Presidents: from king to peasant warrior', *Canadian Journal of African Studies*, 8 (1974).

(ed.) *The Warrior Tradition in Modern Africa*. Leiden: Brill, 1977.

African Thought in Comparative Perspective. Cambridge: Cambridge Scholars Publishing, 2014.

McGregor, G. *King's College Budo: a centenary history, 1906–2006*. Kampala: Fountain, 2006.

Measures, B. & T. Walker. *Amin's Uganda*. London: Minerva, 1998.

Médard, H. 'L'homosexualité au Buganda, une acculturation peut une cache une autre', *Hypothèses*, 1 (1999).

Le royaume du Buganda au XIXe siècle: mutations politiques et religieuses d'un ancien etat d'Afrique de l'Est. Paris: Karthala, 2007.

'Introduction', in H. Médard & S. Doyle (eds.), *Slavery in the Great Lakes Region of East Africa*. Oxford: James Currey, 2007.

'Proto-Nationalism, Religion and Race: the many cloths of Kintu, first king of Buganda (18th–20th centuries)', in C. Panella (ed.), *Lives in Motion, Indeed: interdisciplinary perspectives on social change in honour of Danielle de Lame*. Tervuren: Koninklijk Museum voor Midden-Afrika, 2012.

Médard, H. & S. Doyle (eds.), *Slavery in the Great Lakes Region of East Africa*. Oxford: James Currey, 2007.

Melady T. & M. Melady. *Idi Amin Dada: Hitler in Africa*. Kansas City: Sheed Andrews and McMeel, 1977.

Middleton, J. & E. Winter (eds.), *Witchcraft and Sorcery in East Africa*. London: Routledge & Kegan Paul, 1963.

Miti, J. *A History of Buganda*, 3 vols. Unpublished manuscript, School of Oriental and African Studies Library, c. 1938.

Mkutu, K.A. 'Small Arms and Light Weapons Among Pastoral Groups in the Kenya–Uganda border area', *African Affairs*, 106:422 (2007).

Moorehead, A. *The White Nile*. London: Penguin, 1963.

Morris, H.F. *A History of Ankole*. Kampala: Fountain, 2008 (1st pub., 1962).

The Heroic Recitations of the Bahima of Ankole. Oxford: Clarendon Press, 1964.

Morris, H.S. *The Indians in Uganda*. London: Weidenfeld & Nicolson, 1968.

Mounteney-Jephson, A.J. *Emin Pasha and the Rebellion at the Equator*. London: Sampson Low, Marston, Searle & Rivington, 1890.

Moyse-Bartlett, Lt.-Col. H. *The King's African Rifles: a study in the military history of East and Central Africa, 1890–1945*, 2 vols. Aldershot: Gale and Polden, 1956.

Mudoola, D. '*Colonial Chief-Making: Busoga, a case-study, 1900–1940*', unpublished paper presented at the Universities of East Africa Social Science Conference, December 1970.

'*Chiefs and Political Action: the case of Busoga, 1900–1960*', unpublished PhD thesis, Makerere University, 1974.

Mukasa, H. (ed. S. Gikandi). *Uganda's Katikiro in England*. Manchester & New York: Manchester University Press, 1998 [1st pub., 1904].

Mugyenyi, M.R. 'Towards the Empowerment of Women: a critique of NRM policies and programmes', in H.B. Hansen & M. Twaddle (eds.), *Developing Uganda*. Oxford: James Currey, 1998.

Mulindwa, Y.R.K. & V.K.K.G. Kagoro, *Engeso Zaitu Ez'Obuhangwa [Our Traditions and Customs]*. Kampala: Uganda Literature Bureau, 1968.

Mulira, E.M.K. *Troubled Uganda*. London: Fabian Publications, 1950.

Mullins, J.D. *The Wonderful Story of Uganda*. London: Church Missionary Society, 1908.

Munger, E.S. *Relational Patterns of Kampala, Uganda*. Chicago: University of Chicago Press, 1951.

Museveni, J. *My Life's Journey*. Kampala: Fountain, 2011.

Museveni, Y. 'Fanon's Theory on Violence: its verification in liberated Mozambique', in N.M. Shamuyarira (ed.), *Studies in Political Science, 3*. Dar es Salaam: Tanzania Publishing House, 1974.

Sowing the Mustard Seed: the struggle for freedom and democracy in Uganda. Oxford: Macmillan, 1997.

What Is Africa's Problem? Minneapolis: University of Minnesota Press, 2000.

Mushanga, T. 'Notes on Migration in Uganda', in D. Parkin (ed.), *Town and Country in Central and Eastern Africa*. London: Oxford University Press, 1975.

Musisi, N. 'A Personal Journey into Custom, Identity, Power and Politics: researching and writing the life and times of Buganda's Queen Mother Irene Drusilla Namaganda, 1896–1957', *History in Africa*, 23 (1996).

'The Politics of Perception or Perception as Politics? Colonial and missionary representations of Baganda women, 1900–1945', in J. Allman, S. Geiger & N. Musisi (eds.), *Women in African Colonial Histories*. Bloomington IN: Indiana University Press, 2002.

Mutibwa, P. 'Internal Self-Government, March 1961–October 1962', in G.N. Uzoigwe (ed.), *Uganda: the dilemma of nationhood*. New York: NOK Publishers International, 1982.

Uganda since Independence: a story of unfulfilled hopes. London: Hurst, 1992.

Mwakikagile, G. *Obote to Museveni: political transformation in Uganda since independence*. Dar es Salaam: New Africa Press, 2012.

Nabwiso-Bulima, W.F. 'The Evolution of the Kyabazingaship of Busoga', *Uganda Journal*, 31:1 (1967).

Ngoga, P. 'Uganda: the National Resistance Army', in Christopher Clapham (ed.), *African Guerrillas*. Oxford: James Currey, 1998.

Nsibambi, A. 'The Monarchization of the Kyabazingaship and the Passing of Traditional Leaders in Uganda', *Nigerian Behavioural Sciences Journal*, II (1979).

Nsubuga, G. *Sir Edward Muteesa: his life and politics*. Kampala: Nissi Publishers, 2013.

Nyakatura, J. (ed. G.N. Uzoigwe). *Anatomy of an African Kingdom: a history of Bunyoro-Kitara.* New York: Doubleday/Anchor Press, 1973.

   Aspects of Bunyoro Customs and Traditions. Nairobi: East African Literature Bureau, 1970.

Obbo, C. *African Women: their struggle for economic independence.* London: Zed Press, 1980.

   'Who Cares for the Carers? AIDS and women in Uganda', in H.B. Hansen & M. Twaddle (eds.), *Developing Uganda.* Oxford: James Currey, 1998.

Ochieng, E.O. 'Economic Adjustment Programmes in Uganda, 1985–89', in H.B. Hansen & M. Twaddle (eds.), *Changing Uganda: the dilemmas of structural adjustment and revolutionary change.* London: James Currey, 1991.

Oded, A. *Religion and Politics in Uganda: a study of Islam and Judaism.* Nairobi: East African Educational Publishers, 1995.

Oestigaard, T. *Dammed Divinities: the water powers at Bujagali Falls, Uganda.* Uppsala: Nordiska Afrikainstitutet, 2015.

Ogot, B.A. *History of the Southern Luo, Vol I.* Nairobi: East African Publishing House, 1967.

   Economic Adaptation and Change Among the Jii-speaking Peoples of Eastern Africa. Kisumu: Anyange Press, c. 1991.

Ogwang, E.O. 'Ugandan Poetry: trends and features, 1965–1995', in Eckhard Breitinger (ed.), *Uganda: the cultural landscape.* Kampala: Fountain, 2000.

Oliver, R. *Sir Harry Johnston and the Scramble for Africa.* London: Chatto & Windus, 1957.

   'Discernible Developments in the Interior, c. 1500–1840', in R. Oliver & G. Mathew (eds.), *History of East Africa,* Vol. I. Oxford: Clarendon Press, 1963.

   The Missionary Factor in East Africa. London: Longmans, 1965; [1st. pub., 1952].

Oloka-Onyango, J. 'The National Resistance Movement, "Grassroots Democracy", and Dictatorship in Uganda', in R. Cohen & H. Goulbourne (eds.), *Democracy and Socialism in Africa.* Oxford: Westview, 1991.

Omara-Otunnu, A. *Politics and the Military in Uganda, 1890–1985.* Basingstoke: Macmillan, 1987.

Onyango-ku-Odongo, J.M. & J.B. Webster, *The Central Luo during the Aconya.* Nairobi: East African Literature Bureau, 1976.

Paice, E. *Tip and Run: the untold tragedy of the Great War in Africa.* London: Phoenix, 2007.

Parkin, D. *Neighbours and Nationals in an African City Ward*. London: Routledge & Kegan Paul, 1969.

'Tribe as Fact and Fiction in an East African City', in P.H. Gulliver (ed.), *Tradition and Transition in East Africa: studies of the tribal element in the modern era*. London: Routledge & Kegan Paul, 1969.

Parsons, T.H. *The African Rank-and-File: social implications of colonial military service in the King's African Rifles, 1902–1964*. Portsmouth NH: Heinemann, 1999.

The 1964 Army Mutinies and the Making of Modern East Africa. Westport CT & London: Praeger, 2003.

Peel, J.D.Y. 'Conversion and Tradition in Two African Societies: Ijebu and Buganda', *Past and Present*, 77 (1977).

Pennacini, C. 'Mubende Hill: preserving and transforming heritage in a Ugandan sacred site', *Uganda Journal*, 53 (2013).

Perham, M. (ed.), *Lugard: the years of adventure, 1858–1898*. London: Collins, 1956.

Peters, K. (tr. H.W. Dulcken). *New Light on Dark Africa*. London: Ward, Lock, 1891.

Peterson, D. 'States of Mind: Political History and the Rwenzururu Kingdom in Western Uganda', in D. Peterson & G. Macola (eds.), *Recasting the Past: history writing and political work in modern Africa*. Athens OH: Ohio University Press, 2009.

Ethnic Patriotism and the East African Revival: a history of dissent c. 1935–1972. Cambridge: Cambridge University Press, 2012.

Peterson, D. *et al.* (eds.) Special issue: 'Rethinking the State in Idi Amin's Uganda: the politics of exhortation'. *Journal of Eastern African Studies*, 7:1 (2013).

Peterson, D.R. & E.C. Taylor. 'Rethinking the State in Idi Amin's Uganda: the politics of exhortation', *Journal of Eastern African Studies*, 7:1 (2013).

Portal, G. *The British Mission to Uganda in 1893*. London: Edward Arnold, 1894.

Postlethwaite, J.R.P. *I Look Back*. London: T.V. Boardman, 1947.

Powesland, P.G. 'History of the Migration in Uganda', in A.I. Richards (ed.), *Economic Development and Tribal Change: a study of immigrant labour in Buganda*. Cambridge: W. Heffer & Sons, 1954.

Pratt, R.C. 'Administration and Politics in Uganda, 1919–1945', in V. Harlow & E.M. Chilver (eds.) *History of East Africa*, Vol. II. Oxford: Clarendon Press, 1965.

Prunier, G. 'Rebel Movements and Proxy Warfare: Uganda, Sudan and the Congo (1986–1999)', *African Affairs*, 103:412 (2004).

Africa's World War: Congo, the Rwandan genocide, and the making of a continental catastrophe. Oxford: Oxford University Press, 2009.

Rao, R. 'Re-membering Mwanga: same-sex intimacy, memory and belonging in postcolonial Uganda', *Journal of Eastern African Studies*, 9:1 (2015).

Ray, B. *Myth, Ritual and Kingship in Buganda*. New York: Oxford University Press, 1991.

Reid, A. 'Ntusi and the Development of Social Complexity in Southern Uganda', in G. Pwiti & R. Soper (eds.), *Aspects of African Archaeology: papers from the 10th Congress of the Pan African Association for Prehistory and Related Studies*. Harare: University of Zimbabwe Publications, 1996.

Reid, A. & C.Z. Ashley. 'A Context for the Luzira Head', *Antiquity*, 82:315 (2008).

Reid, R.J. 'The Reign of *Kabaka* Nakibinge: myth or watershed?', *History in Africa*, 24 (1997).

'The Ganda on Lake Victoria: a nineteenth-century East African imperialism', *Journal of African History*, 39:3 (1998).

'Mutesa and Mirambo: thoughts on East African warfare and diplomacy in the nineteenth century', *International Journal of African Historical Studies*, 31:1 (1998).

'Traders, Chiefs, and Soldiers: the pre-colonial capitals of Buganda', *Les Cahiers de l'Institut Français de Recherche en Afrique*, 9 (1998).

'Warfare and Militarism in Precolonial Buganda', *Azania*, XXXIV (1999).

'Images of an African Ruler: *Kabaka* Mutesa of Buganda, c. 1857–1884', *History in Africa*, 26 (1999).

Political Power in Pre-Colonial Buganda: economy, society and warfare in the nineteenth century. Oxford: James Currey, 2002.

'Warfare and Urbanisation: the relationship between town and conflict in pre-colonial eastern Africa', in A. Burton (ed.), *The Urban Experience in Eastern Africa, c. 1750–2000*. Nairobi: British Institute in Eastern Africa, 2002.

War in Precolonial Eastern Africa: the patterns and meanings of state-level conflict in the nineteenth century. Oxford: James Currey, 2007.

'Human Booty in Buganda: some observations on the seizure of people in war, c. 1700–1890', in H. Médard & S. Doyle (eds.), *Slavery in the Great Lakes Region of East Africa*. Oxford: James Currey, 2007.

'Violence and its Sources: European witnesses to the military revolution in nineteenth-century eastern Africa', in P. Landau (ed.), *The Power of Doubt: essays in honour of David Henige*. Madison WI: Parallel Press, 2011.

'Ghosts in the Academy: historians and historical consciousness in the making of modern Uganda', *Comparative Studies in Society and History*, 56:2 (2014).

Reid, R.J. & H. Médard. 'Merchants, Missions and the Remaking of the Urban Environment in Buganda, c. 1840-c. 1890', in D.M. Anderson & R. Rathbone (eds.), *Africa's Urban Past*. London: James Currey, 2000.

Reyntjens, F. *The Great African War: Congo and regional geopolitics, 1996–2006*. Cambridge: Cambridge University Press, 2009.

Richards, A.I. (ed.), *Economic Development and Tribal Change: a study of immigrant labour in Buganda*. Cambridge: W. Heffer & Sons, 1954.

'The Problem and the Methods', in A.I. Richards (ed.), *Economic Development and Tribal Change: a study of immigrant labour in Buganda*. Cambridge: W. Heffer & Sons, 1954.

(ed.), *East African Chiefs: a study of political development in some Uganda and Tanganyika tribes*. London: Faber, 1959.

The Multicultural States of East Africa. Montreal & London: McGill-Queens University Press, 1969.

Richardson, M.L. *After Amin: the bloody pearl*. Atlanta: Majestic Books, 1980.

Roberts, A.D. 'The Sub-Imperialism of the Baganda', *Journal of African History*, 3:3 (1962).

Robertshaw, P. 'Archaeological Survey, Ceramic Analysis, and State Formation in Western Uganda', *African Archaeological Review*, 12 (1994).

Robertson, A.F. *Community of Strangers: a journal of discovery in Uganda*. London: Scolar Press, 1978.

Roscoe, J. 'Kibuka, the War God of the Baganda', *Man*, 7 (1907).

The Baganda: an account of their native customs and beliefs. London: Macmillan, 1911.

Twenty-Five Years in East Africa. Cambridge: Cambridge University Press, 1921.

The Bakitara or Banyoro. Cambridge: Cambridge University Press, 1923.

The Banyankole. Cambridge: Cambridge University Press, 1923.

Rowe, J. 'The purge of Christians at Mwanga's court', *Journal of African History*, 5:1 (1964).

'Myth, Memoir and Moral Admonition: Luganda historical writing, 1893–1969', *Uganda Journal*, 33:1 (1969) & 33:2 (1969).

Rubongoya, J.B. *Regime Hegemony in Museveni's Uganda: Pax Musevenica*. New York: Palgrave Macmillan, 2007.

Ruganda, J. *The Burdens*. Nairobi: Oxford University Press, 1972.

The Floods. Nairobi: East African Publishing House, 1980.

Rychner, R.-M. 'The Context and Background of Ugandan Art', in Eckhard Breitinger (ed.), *Uganda: the cultural landscape*. Kampala: Fountain, 2000.

Schiller, L. 'The Royal Women of Buganda', *International Journal of African Historical Studies*, 23:3 (1990).

Schoenbrun, D. 'A Past Whose Time Has Come: historical context and history in Eastern Africa's Great Lakes', *History and Theory*, 32:4 (1993).

   A Green Place, A Good Place: agrarian change, gender, and social identity in the Great Lakes region to the 15th century. Portsmouth, NH: Heinemann, 1998.

   'A Mask of Calm: emotion and founding the kingdom of Bunyoro in the sixteenth century', *Comparative Studies in Society and History*, 55:3 (2013).

Schweinfurth, G. *et al.* (eds.) *Emin Pasha in Central Africa*. London: George Philip, 1888.

Schweitzer, G. (ed.) *Emin Pasha: his life and work*, 2 vols. London: Archibald Constable, 1898.

Scott Elliot, G.F. *A Naturalist in Mid-Africa*. London: A.D. Innes, 1896.

Seligman, C.G. *Races of Africa*. London: Thornton Butterworth, 1939.

Sembuya, C.C. *The Other Side of Idi Amin*. Kampala: Sest Holdings, 2009.

Serumaga, R. *Return to the Shadows*. London: Heinemann, 1970.

   The Elephants. Nairobi: Oxford University Press, 1971.

   Majangwa: a promise of rains and a play. Nairobi: East African Publishing House, 1974.

Shaw, T.M. & P.K. Mbabazi. 'Two Africas? Two Ugandas? An African 'democratic developmental state' or another 'failed state'?, in A. Nhema & P. Tiyambe Zeleza (eds.), *The Roots of African Conflicts: the causes and costs*. Oxford: James Currey, 2008.

Shepherd, B. *Oil in Uganda: international lessons for success*. London: Chatham House, February 2013.

Sicherman, C. *Becoming an African University: Makerere 1922–2000*. Kampala: Fountain, 2005.

Southall, A. 'Alur Migrants', in A.I. Richards (ed.), *Economic Development and Tribal Change: a study of immigrant labour in Buganda*. Cambridge: W. Heffer & Sons, 1954.

Southall, A. *Alur Society: a study in processes and types of domination*. Cambridge: W. Heffer & Sons, 1956.

   'General Amin and the Coup: great man or historical inevitability?', *Journal of Modern African Studies*, 13 (1975).

Southall, A. & P.C.W. Gutkind. *Townsmen in the Making: Kampala and its suburbs*. Kampala: East African Institute of Social Research, 1957.

Southall, R.J. *Parties and Politics in Bunyoro*. Kampala: Makerere Institute of Social Research, 1972.

Southwold, M. *Bureaucracy and Chiefship in Buganda*, East African Studies 14. Kampala: East African Institute of Social Research, 1961.

'Succession to the Throne in Buganda', in J. Goody (ed.), *Succession to High Office*. Cambridge: Cambridge University Press, 1966.

Speke, John Hanning. *Journal of the Discovery of the Source of the Nile*. Edinburgh & London: William Blackwood & Sons, 1863.

What Led to the Discovery of the Source of the Nile. Edinburgh & London: William Blackwood & Sons, 1864.

Ssekamwa, J.C. *History and Development of Education in Uganda*. Kampala: Fountain, 1997.

Ssekamwa, J.C. & S.M.E. Lugumba, *A History of Education in East Africa*. Kampala: Fountain, 2001 [1st pub., 1973].

Stacey, T. *Summons to Ruwenzori*. London: Secker & Warburg, 1965.

Stanley, H.M. *Through the Dark Continent*, 2 vols. London: George Newnes, 1899; 1st ed., 1878.

In Darkest Africa, 2 vols. London: Sampson Low, Marston, Searle & Rivington, 1890.

Steinhart, E.I. *Conflict and Collaboration: the kingdoms of western Uganda 1890–1907*. Princeton: Princeton University Press, 1977.

'The Emergence of Bunyoro: the tributary mode of production and the formation of the state, 1400–1900', in Ahmed Idha Salim (ed.), *State Formation in Eastern Africa*. Nairobi: Heinemann, 1984.

'The Resurrection of the Spirits: archaeology, oral history, and the Bacwezi at Munsa', *Uganda Journal*, 48 (2002).

'Slavery and Other Forms of Social Oppression in Ankole, 1890–1940', in H. Medard & S. Doyle (eds.), *Slavery in the Great Lakes Region of East Africa*. Oxford: James Currey, 2007.

Stephens, R. *A History of African Motherhood: the case of Uganda, 700–1900*. Cambridge: Cambridge University Press, 2013.

Stephens, R. *et al.* (eds.) Themed section: 'New Themes in Ugandan history'. *Journal of Eastern African Studies*, 6:3 (2012).

Stonehouse, A. *'Peripheral Identities in an African State: a history of ethnicity in the Ugandan kingdom of Buganda'*, unpublished PhD thesis, University of Leeds, 2012.

'The Bakooki in Buganda: identity and assimilation on the peripheries of a Ugandan kingdom', *Journal of Eastern African Studies*, 6:3 (2012).

Stoutjesdijk, E.J. *Uganda's Manufacturing Sector: a contribution to the analysis of industrialisation in East Africa*. Nairobi: East African Publishing House, 1967.

Summers, C. 'Intimate Colonialism: the imperial production of reproduction in Uganda, 1907–1925', *Signs: The Journal of Women in Culture and Society*, 16:4 (1991).

'Young Buganda and Old Boys: youth, generational transition, and ideas of leadership in Buganda, 1920–1949', *Africa Today*, 51:3 (2005).

'Grandfathers, Grandsons, Morality, and Radical Politics in Late Colonial Buganda', *International Journal of African Historical Studies*, 38:3 (2005).

'Radical Rudeness: Ugandan social critiques in the 1940s', *Journal of Social History*, 39:3 (2006).

Sutton, J. 'Ntusi and Bigo: farmers, cattle-herders and rulers in Western Uganda, AD1000–1500', *Azania*, 33 (1998).

'Ntusi and Bigo: farmers, cattle-herders and rulers in Western Uganda, AD1000–1500', in J. Sutton (ed.), *Archaeological Sites of East Africa: Four Studies. Azania*, 33 (1998).

Syahuka, M. 'The Origin and Development of the Rwenzururu Movement, 1900–1962', *Mawazo*, 5:2 (December 1983).

Syahuka-Muhindo, A. *The Rwenzururu Movement and the Democratic Struggle*. Kampala: Centre for Basic Research, 1991.

Tabaire, B. 'The Press and Political Repression in Uganda: back to the future?', *Journal of Eastern African Studies*, 1:2 (2007).

Tantala, R. *'The Early History of Kitara in Western Uganda: process models of political and religious change'*, unpublished PhD thesis, University of Wisconsin, 1989.

Taylor, E.C. 'Claiming Kabale: racial thought and urban governance in Uganda', *Journal of Eastern African Studies*, 7:1 (2013).

Thomas, H.B. & R. Scott. *Uganda*. London: Oxford University Press, 1935.

Thomas, H.B. *The Story of Uganda*. 1st ed. 1939, revised ed. by Samwiri Karugire. Nairobi & Oxford: Oxford University Press, 1973.

Thompson, G. *Governing Uganda: British colonial rule and its legacy*. Kampala: Fountain, 2003.

Thruston, A.B. *African Incidents*. London: John Murray, 1900.

Tibenderana, K. *Islamic Fundamentalism: the quest for the rights of Muslims in Uganda*. Kampala: Fountain, 2006.

Tiberondwa, Ado K. *Missionary Teachers as Agents of Colonialism in Uganda*. Kampala: Fountain, 1977, 1998.

Tosh, J. 'The Northern Lacustrine Region', in R. Gray & D. Birmingham (eds.), *Pre-Colonial African Trade: essays on trade in central and eastern Africa before 1900*. London: Oxford University Press, 1970.

Clan Leaders and Colonial Chiefs in Lango: the political history of an East Africans stateless society circa 1890–1939. Oxford: Clarendon Press, 1978.

Tripp, A.M. *Women and Politics in Uganda*. Oxford: James Currey, 2000.

Museveni's Uganda: paradoxes of power in a hybrid regime. Boulder CO: Lynne Rienner, 2010.

Trowell, M. & K. Wachsmann. *Tribal Crafts of Uganda*. London: Oxford University Press, 1953.

Tuck, M. *'Syphilis, Sexuality, and Social Control: a history of venereal disease in colonial Uganda'*, unpublished PhD thesis, Northwestern University, 1997.

'*Kabaka* Mutesa and Venereal Disease: an essay on medical history and sources in precolonial Buganda', *History in Africa*, 30 (2003).

Tucker, A.R. *Eighteen Years in Uganda and East Africa*, 2 vols. London: Edward Arnold, 1908.

Tuma, T. *'African Chiefs and Church Work in Busoga Province of Uganda, 1900–1940'*, unpublished paper, Makerere University, Kampala, n.d.

Turyahikayo-Rugyema, B. 'The Development of Mass Nationalism, 1952–1962', in G.N. Uzoigwe (ed.), *Uganda: the dilemma of nationhood*. New York: NOK Publishers International, 1982.

Twaddle, M. 'The Founding of Mbale', *Uganda Journal*, 30:1 (1966).

'The *Bakungu* Chiefs of Buganda under British Colonial Rule, 1900–1939', *Journal of African History*, 10:2 (1969).

'"Tribalism" in Eastern Uganda, in P.H. Gulliver (ed.), *Tradition and Transition in East Africa: studies of the tribal element in the modern era*. London: Routledge & Kegan Paul, 1969.

'Segmentary Violence and Political Change in Early Colonial Uganda', unpublished paper presented at the University Social Sciences Council Conference, Nairobi, 8–12 December 1969.

'The Muslim Revolution in Buganda', *African Affairs*, 71 (1972).

'The Ganda Receptivity to Change', *Journal of African History*, 15:2 (1974).

'The Emergence of Politico-Religious Groupings in Late Nineteenth-Century Buganda', *Journal of African History*, 29:1 (1988).

'The Ending of Slavery in Buganda', in R. Roberts & S. Miers (eds.), *The End of Slavery in Africa*. Madison WI: University of Wisconsin Press, 1988.

Kakungulu and the Creation of Uganda. London: James Currey, 1993.

Twinamatsiko, N. *The Chwezi Code*. Kampala: Pilgrims Publications, 2010.

Unomah, A.C. & J.B. Webster. 'East Africa: the expansion of commerce', in John E. Flint (ed.), *The Cambridge History of Africa: Vol 5, from c. 1790 to c. 1870*. Cambridge: Cambridge University Press, 1976.

Uzoigwe, G.N. *Revolution and Revolt in Bunyoro Kitara: two studies*. London: Longman, 1970.

'Kabarega and the making of a new Kitara', *Tarikh*, 3:2 (1970).

'The Kyanyangire, 1907: passive revolt against British overrule', in B.A. Ogot (ed.), *War and Society in Africa*. London: Frank Cass, 1972.

'Succession and Civil War in Bunyoro-Kitara', *International Journal of African Historical Studies*, 6:1 (1973).

(ed.), *Uganda: the dilemma of nationhood*. New York: NOK Publishers International, 1982.

'The Agreement States and the Making of Uganda: II. Tooro, Ankole, and Bunyoro-Kitara', in G.N. Uzoigwe (ed.), *Uganda: the dilemma of nationhood*. New York: NOK Publishers International, 1982.

Vermeiren, K., A. van Rompaey, M. Loopmans, E. Serwajja, & P. Mukwaya, 'Urban Growth of Kampala, Uganda: pattern analysis and scenario development', *Landscape and Urban Planning*, 106:2 (2012).

Vincent, J. 'Colonial Chiefs and the Making of Class: a case study from Teso, eastern Uganda', *Africa*, 47:2 (1977).

Teso in Transformation: the political economy of peasant and class in Eastern Africa. Berkeley: University of California Press, 1982.

Vlassenroot, K. *et al.* (eds.) Special issue: 'Uganda from the Margins'. *Journal of Eastern African Studies*, 6:1 (2012).

Vokes, R. *Ghosts of Kanungu: fertility, secrecy and exchange in the Great Lakes of East Africa*. Woodbridge: James Currey, 2009.

Waliggo, J. '*The Catholic Church in the Buddu province of Buganda*', unpublished PhD thesis, University of Cambridge, 1976.

Waller, H. (ed.), *The Last Journals of David Livingstone in Central Africa*, 2 vols. London: John Murray, 1874.

Wallman, S. *Kampala Women Getting By: wellbeing in the time of AIDS*. London: James Currey, 1996.

Wangusa, T. *Salutations: poems 1965–75*. Nairobi: East African Literature Bureau, 1977.

Upon This Mountain. Oxford: Heinemann, 1989.

A Pattern of Dust: selected poems 1965–1990. Kampala: Fountain, 1994.

Anthem for Africa. Turin: La Rosa, 1995.

Africa's New Brood. Kampala: Bow and Arrow Publishers, 2006.

Ward, K. & E. Wild-Wood (eds.), *The East African Revival: history and legacies*. Kampala: Fountain, 2010.

Wayland, E.J., M.C. Burkitt & H.J. Braunholtz. 'Archaeological discoveries at Luzira', *Man*, 33 (1933).

Webster, J.B. 'The Civil War in Usuku', in B.A. Ogot (ed.), *War and Society in Africa*. London: Frank Cass, 1972.

Webster J.B. *et al. The Iteso During the Asonya*. Nairobi: East African Publishing House, 1973.

Welbourn, F.B. *East African Rebels: a study of some independent churches.* London: SCM Press, 1961.

Wiebe P.D. & C.P. Dodge (eds.) *Beyond Crisis: development issues in Uganda.* Kampala: Makerere Institute of Social Research, 1987.

Wilson, C.T. & R.W. Felkin. *Uganda and the Egyptian Soudan*, 2 vols. London: Sampson Low, Marston, Searle & Rivington, 1882.

Wright, M. *Buganda in the Heroic Age.* Nairobi: Oxford University Press, 1971.

Wrigley, C.C. 'The Christian Revolution in Buganda', *Comparative Studies in Society and History*, 2:1 (1959).

'The Changing Economic Structure of Buganda', in L.A. Fallers (ed.), *The King's Men: leadership and status in Buganda on the eve of independence.* New York: Oxford University Press, 1964.

'Changes in East African society', in D.A. Low & A. Smith (eds.), *History of East Africa*, Vol. III. Oxford: Clarendon Press, 1976.

'The Problem of the Lwo', *History in Africa*, 8 (1981).

Kingship and State: the Buganda dynasty. Cambridge: Cambridge University Press, 1996.

Yoder, J. 'The Quest for Kintu and the Search for Peace: mythology and morality in nineteenth-century Buganda', *History in Africa*, 15 (1988).

Youe, C.P. 'Peasants, Planters and Cotton Capitalists: the "dual economy" of Uganda', *Canadian Journal of African Studies*, 12:2 (1978).

Zimbe, B.M. (tr. F. Kamoga). *Buganda ne Kabaka.* Unpublished manuscript, Makerere University Library, c. 1939.

VI. Select Bibliography (ii): Comparative, Theoretical and Contextual Literature

Acemoglu, D., S. Johnson & J. Robinson, 'Reversal of Fortune: geography and institutions in the making of the modern world income distribution', *The Quarterly Journal of Economics*, 117:4 (2002).

Achebe, C. *Things Fall Apart.* London: Heinemann, 1958.

Afigbo, A.E. *The Warrant Chiefs: indirect rule in SE Nigeria.* Harlow: Longman, 1972.

Alpers, E.A. *The East African Slave Trade.* Nairobi: Historical Association of Tanzania, Paper No.3, 1967.

Ambler, C.H. *Kenyan Communities in the Age of Imperialism.* New Haven & London: Yale University Press, 1988.

Anderson, B. *Imagined Communities: Reflections on the Origins and Spread of Nationalism.* London: Verso, 1991, 1983.

Arnold, G. *Africa: a modern history.* London: Atlantic Books, 2005.

Austen, R. *African Economic History: internal development and external dependency*. London: James Currey, 1987.

Austin, G. 'Resources, Techniques and Strategies South of the Sahara: revising the factor endowments perspective on African economic development, 1500–2000', *Economic History Review*, 61:3 (2008).

Bates, R. *Markets and States in Tropical Africa: the political basis of agricultural policies*. Berkeley, CA: University of California Press, 1981.

Bayly, C. *The Birth of the Modern World, 1780–1914*. Oxford: Blackwell, 2004.

Becker, F., J. Cabrita *et al.* (eds.), 'Special Feature: Africa and the Indian Ocean', *Journal of African History*, 55:2 (2014).

Bennett, G. 'Tribalism in Politics', in P.H. Gulliver (ed.), *Tradition and Transition in East Africa: studies of the tribal element in the modern era*. London: Routledge & Kegan Paul, 1969.

Bennett, N.R. *Arab versus European: diplomacy and war in nineteenth-century East Central Africa*. New York & London: Holmes & Meier, 1986.

Black, J. *Contesting History: narratives of public history*. London: Bloomsbury, 2014.

Bovill, E.W. *The Golden Trade of the Moors*. London: Oxford University Press, 1958.

Branch, D. *Kenya: between hope and despair, 1963–2011*. New Haven: Yale University Press, 2011.

Brantlinger, P. 'Victorians and Africans: the Genealogy of the Myth of the Dark Continent', *Critical Enquiry*, 12:1 (1985).

Braudel, F. *The Mediterranean and the Mediterranean World in the Age of Philip II*. Berkeley & Los Angeles: University of California Press, 1994 (1st pub., 1949).

Brennan, J. 'Communications and Media in African History', in J. Parker & R. Reid (eds.), *The Oxford Handbook of Modern African History*. Oxford: Oxford University Press, 2013.

Burton, A. (ed.), *The Urban Experience in Eastern Africa, c. 1750–2000*. Nairobi: British Institute in Eastern Africa, 2002.

Cameron, R. & L. Neal, *A Concise Economic History of the World*. Oxford: Oxford University Press, 1989.

* Cannadine, D. *Ornamentalism: how the British saw their empire*. London: Penguin, 2001.

Chabal, P. and J.-P. Daloz. *Africa Works: Disorder as Political Instrument*. Oxford: James Currey, 1999.

Chrétien, J-P. & G. Prunier (eds.) *Les ethnies ont une histoire*. Paris: Karthala, 1989.

Clapham, C. 'Introduction: analysing African insurgencies', in C. Clapham (ed.), *African Guerrillas*. Oxford: James Currey, 1998.

Clarke, P.B. *Black Paradise: the Rastafarian movement*. Wellingborough: Aquarian Press, 1986.

Coleman, J.S. *Nationalism and Development in Africa: selected essays*. Berkeley, CA: University of California Press, 1994.

Colls, R. *Identity of England*. Oxford: Oxford University Press, 2002.

Conrad, S. *German Colonialism: a short history*. Cambridge: Cambridge University Press, 2012.

Constantine, S. 'Migrants and Settlers', in Judith Brown & Wm. Roger Louis (eds.), *The Oxford History of the British Empire, Vol IV: the twentieth century*. Oxford: Oxford University Press, 1999.

Cooper, F. *Africa since 1940: the past of the present*. Cambridge: Cambridge University Press, 2002.

'Possibility and Constraint: African independence in historical perspective', *Journal of African History*, 49:2 (2008).

Africa in the World: capitalism, empire, nation-state. Cambridge, MA: Harvard University Press, 2014.

Citizenship between Empire and Nation: remaking France and French Africa, 1945–1960. Princeton, NJ: Princeton University Press, 2014.

Curtin, Philip D. *The Image of Africa: British ideas and action, 1780–1850*. Madison, WI: University of Wisconsin Press, 1964.

Davidson, B. *Which Way Africa? The search for a new society*. Harmondsworth: Penguin, 1964.

The Black Man's Burden: Africa and the curse of the nation-state. London: James Currey, 1992.

Decalo, Samuel. *Coups and Army Rule in Africa: motivations and constraints*. New Haven & London: Yale University Press, 1990.

Denoon, D. & A. Kuper, 'Nationalist Historians in Search of a Nation: the "new historiography" in Dar es Salaam', *African Affairs*, 69/227 (1970).

Donham, D. & W. James (eds.), *The Southern Marches of Imperial Ethiopia: essays in history and social anthropology*. Cambridge: Cambridge University Press, 1986.

Dorman, S., D. Hammett & P. Nugent (eds.) *Making Nations, Creating Strangers: states and citizenship in Africa*. Leiden: Brill, 2007.

Duggan, C. *The Force of Destiny: a history of Italy since 1796*. London: Penguin, 2007.

Ehret, C. *Ethiopians and East Africans: the problem of contacts*. Nairobi: East African Publishing House, 1974.

Ellis, S. & G. Ter Haar. *Worlds of Power: religious thought and political practice in Africa*. London: Hurst, 2004.

Falola, T. & M. Heaton, *A History of Nigeria*. Cambridge: Cambridge University Press, 2008.

Ford, J. & R. de Z. Hall, 'The History of Karagwe (Bukoba District)', *Tanganyika Notes and Records*, 24 (1947).

Freund, B. *The Making of Contemporary Africa: the development of African society since 1800*. Basingstoke: Palgrave, 1998 [1st ed., 1984].

Fuglie, K. '"Vent-for-Surplus" as a Source of Agricultural Growth in Northeast Thailand, 1950–1986', *Economic Development Center*, University of Minnesota, *Bulletin 89–3* (March 1989).

Fukuyama, F. *The End of History and the Last Man*. London: Penguin, 1992.

Gavshon, A. *Crisis in Africa: battleground of East and West*. Harmondsworth: Penguin, 1981.

Gellner, E. *Nations and Nationalism*. Oxford: Blackwell, 1983.

Geschiere, P. *The Perils of Belonging: autochthony, citizenship and exclusion in Africa and Europe*. Chicago: University of Chicago Press, 2009.

Gewald, J.-B., M. Hinfelaar, & G. Macola (eds.), *One Zambia, Many Histories: towards a history of postcolonial Zambia*. Leiden: Brill, 2008.

Gillon, W. *A Short History of African Art*. London: Penguin, 1991.

Guibernau, M. & J. Hutchinson (eds.) *History and National Destiny: ethnosymbolism and its critics*. Oxford: Blackwell, 2004.

Gutteridge, W.F. *Military Regimes in Africa*. London: Methuen, 1975.

Hammond, J. *Fire from the Ashes: a chronicle of the revolution in Tigray, Ethiopia, 1975–1991*. Lawrenceville NJ: Red Sea Press, 1999.

Hastings, A. *The Construction of Nationhood: ethnicity, religion and nationalism*. Cambridge: Cambridge University Press, 1997.

Henige, D. *The Chronology of Oral Tradition: quest for a chimera*. Oxford: Clarendon Press, 1974.

Hodgkin, T. *Nationalism in Colonial Africa*. London: Frederick Muller, 1956.

Holt, P.M. & M.W. Daly, *A History of the Sudan: from the coming of Islam to the present day*. Harlow: Longman, 2000.

Hopkins, A.G. *An Economic History of West Africa*. London: Longman, 1973.

    'Rethinking Decolonisation', *Past and Present*, 200:1 (2008).

    'The New Economic History of Africa', *Journal of African History*, 50:2 (2009).

Howard, M. *War in European History*. Oxford: Oxford University Press, 2009.

Iliffe, J. *A Modern History of Tanganyika*. Cambridge: Cambridge University Press, 1979.

Africans: the history of a continent. Cambridge: Cambridge University Press, 1995, 2007.

James, W., D. Donham, E. Kurimoto & A. Triulzi (eds.), *Remapping Ethiopia: socialism and after*. Oxford: James Currey, 2002.

Johnston, A. *South Africa: inventing the nation*. London: Bloomsbury, 2014.

Kasfir, S.L. 'Visual Cultures', in J. Parker & R. Reid (eds.), *The Oxford Handbook of Modern African History*. Oxford: Oxford University Press, 2013.

Kimambo, I.N. & A.J. Temu (eds.) *A History of Tanzania*. Nairobi: East African Publishing House, 1969.

Kopytoff, I. 'The Internal African Frontier: the making of African political culture', in I. Kopytoff (ed.), *The African Frontier: the reproduction of traditional African societies*. Bloomington & Indianapolis: Indiana University Press, 1987.

Law, R.C.C. *The Slave Coast of West Africa 1550–1750*. Oxford: Clarendon Press, 1991.

Laye, C. *L'Enfant noir*. Paris: Librarie Plon, 1954.

Lee, J.M. *African Armies and Civil Order*. London: Chatto & Windus, 1969.

Lentz, C. *et al.* (eds.) Themed Section: 'Celebrating independence jubilees and the millennium: national days in Africa'. *Nations and Nationalism*, 19:2 (2013).

Levtzion, N. *Ancient Ghana and Mali*. London: Methuen, 1973.

Lewis, I.M. *The Modern History of Somaliland*. London: Weidenfeld & Nicolson, 1965.

A Modern History of the Somali. Oxford: James Currey, 2002.

Livingstone, D. 'Dr Livingstone's Cambridge Lectures [December 1857]', in B. Harlow & M. Carter (eds.), *Archives of Empire, II: The Scramble for Africa*. Durham NC & London: Duke University Press, 2003.

Lonsdale, J. 'The Emergence of African Nations', in T.O. Ranger (ed.), *Emerging Themes of African History*. Nairobi: Heinemann, 1968.

'Town Life in Colonial Kenya', in A. Burton (ed.), *The Urban Experience in Eastern Africa, c. 1750–2000*. Nairobi: British Institute in Eastern Africa, 2002.

Lovejoy, P. *Transformations in Slavery*. Cambridge: Cambridge University Press, 1983.

Lugard, F.D. *The Dual Mandate in British Tropical Africa*. Edinburgh & London: William Blackwood & Sons, 1923.

Mair, L. *African Societies*. Cambridge: Cambridge University Press, 1974.

Mamdani, M. *Citizen and Subject: contemporary Africa and the legacy of late colonialism*. Princeton: Princeton University Press, 1996.

Maxwell, D. 'Christianity', in John Parker & Richard Reid (eds.), *The Oxford Handbook of Modern African History*. Oxford: Oxford University Press, 2013.

McCaskie, T.C. 'Cultural Encounters: Britain and Africa in the nineteenth century', in A. Porter (ed.), *The Oxford History of the British Empire, Vol. III: the nineteenth century*. Oxford & New York: Oxford University Press, 1999.

McCorristine, S. *Spectres of the Self: thinking about ghosts and ghost-seeing in England, 1750–1920*. Cambridge: Cambridge University Press, 2010.

McCracken, J. *A History of Malawi 1855–1966*. Woodbridge: James Currey, 2012.

Myint, H. 'The Classical Theory of International Trade and the Underdeveloped Countries', *Economic Journal*, 68 (June 1958).

Thiong'o, N.W. 'On the Abolition of the English Department', in Ngugi wa Thiong'o, *Homecoming: essays on African and Caribbean literature, culture and politics*. London: Heinemann, 1972.

Ochefu, Y.A. & C.B.N. Ogbogbo, 'The Role of Historical Societies in Nigeria's Development', *Afrika Zamani*, 13 & 14 (2005–6).

Ogot, B.A. (ed.) *Kenya Before 1900*. Nairobi: East African Publishing House, 1976.

Oliver, R. & A. Atmore. *Medieval Africa, 1250–1800*. Cambridge: Cambridge University Press, 2001.

Pakenham, T. *The Scramble for Africa, 1876–1912*. London: Weidenfeld & Nicolson, 1991.

Parkin, D. (ed.), *Town and Country in Central and Eastern Africa*. London: Oxford University Press, 1975.

Phillips, T. (ed.) *Africa: the art of a continent*. London: Royal Academy of Arts, 1996.

Plumb, J.H. *The Death of the Past*. London: Pelican, 1973; 1st ed. 1969.

Ranger, T.O. 'The Invention of Tradition in Colonial Africa', in T.O. Ranger & E. Hobsbawm (eds.), *The Invention of Tradition*. Cambridge: Cambridge University Press, 1983.

  'The Invention of Tradition Revisited: the case of Africa', in T.O. Ranger & O. Vaughan (eds.), *Legitimacy and the State in Twentieth-Century Africa*. Basingstoke: Macmillan, 1993.

Reid, R.J. *Frontiers of Violence in Northeast Africa: genealogies of conflict since c. 1800*. Oxford: Oxford University Press, 2011.

  'Past and Presentism: the "precolonial" and the foreshortening of African history', *Journal of African History*, 52:2 (2011).

  Warfare in African History. New York: Cambridge University Press, 2012.

'The Fragile Revolution: rethinking war and development in Africa's violent nineteenth century', in E. Akyeampong, R.H. Bates, N. Nunn, & J.A. Robinson (eds.), *Africa's Development in Historical Perspective*. New York: Cambridge University Press, 2014.

'States of Anxiety: history and nation in modern Africa', *Past and Present*, 229:1 (2015).

Reno, W. *Warfare in Independent Africa*. New York: Cambridge University Press, 2011.

Richards, D. *Masks of Difference: cultural representations in literature, anthropology and art*. Cambridge: Cambridge University Press, 1994.

Roberts, A.D. (ed.) *Tanzania Before 1900*. Nairobi: East African Publishing House, 1968.

'Nyamwezi trade', in R. Gray & D. Birmingham (eds.), *Pre-Colonial African Trade: essays on trade in central and eastern Africa before 1900*. London: Oxford University Press, 1970.

A History of Zambia. New York: Africana Publishing Company, 1976.

Robinson, R. & J. Gallagher, with A. Denny. *Africa and the Victorians: the official mind of imperialism*. London: Macmillan, 2nd edition, 1961.

Sheriff, A. *Slaves, Spices and Ivory in Zanzibar: integration of an East African commercial empire into the world economy, 1770–1873*. London: James Currey, 1987.

Smith, A.D. *The Ethnic Origins of Nations*. Malden MA & Oxford: Blackwell, 1986.

'Gastronomy or Geology? The role of nationalism in the reconstruction of nations', *Nations and Nationalism*, 1:1 (1995).

Myths and Memories of the Nation. Oxford: Oxford University Press, 1999.

Spear, T. 'Neo-traditionalism and the Limits of Invention in British Colonial Africa', *Journal of African History*, 44:1 (2003).

Streets, H. M. *Races: the military, race and masculinity in British imperial culture, 1857–1914*. Manchester: Manchester University Press, 2004.

Thomas, E. *South Sudan: a slow liberation*. London: Zed Books, 2015.

Thompson, E.P. *The Making of the English Working Class*. London: Penguin, 1991.

Tilly, C. *Coercion, Capital and European States, AD 990–1992*. Oxford: Blackwell, 1992.

Uzoigwe, G.N. 'Precolonial Military Studies in Africa', *Journal of Modern African Studies*, 13:3 (1975).

'The Warrior and the State in Precolonial Africa', in A.A. Mazrui (ed.), *The Warrior Tradition in Modern Africa*. Leiden: Brill, 1977.

Vansina, J. *Paths in the Rainforests: toward a history of political tradition in Equatorial Africa*. London: James Currey, 1990.

Wilks, I. *Asante in the Nineteenth Century*. Cambridge: Cambridge University Press, 1975.

Williams, P.D. *War and Conflict in Africa*. Cambridge: Polity, 2011.

Wilson, A. *The Challenge Road: women and the Eritrean revolution*. Trenton NJ: Red Sea Press, 1991.

Woets, R. 'The Recreation of Modern and African Art at Achimoto School in the Gold Coast (1927–52)', *Journal of African History*, 55:3 (2014).

Woolf, D. *A Global History of History*. Cambridge: Cambridge University Press, 2011.

Young, C. *The African Colonial State in Comparative Perspective*. New Haven & London: Yale University Press, 1994.

Zewde, B. *A History of Modern Ethiopia 1855–1991*. Oxford: James Currey, revised 2nd ed., 2001.

Zimmerman, A. 'Africa in Imperial and Transnational History: multi-sited historiography and the necessity of theory', *Journal of African History*, 54:3 (2013).

Index

CPSIA information can be obtained
at www.ICGtesting.com
Printed in the USA
LVHW080920300121
677898LV00015B/60